Aesthetics of Music

Volume 8

Books by David Whitwell

Philosophic Foundations of Education
Foundations of Music Education
Music Education of the Future
The Sousa Oral History Project
The Art of Musical Conducting
The Longy Club: 1900–1917
A Concise History of the Wind Band
Wagner on Bands
Berlioz on Bands
Chopin: A Self-Portrait
Schumann: A Self-Portrait In His Own Words
Mendelssohn: A Self-Portrait In His Own Words
Liszt: A Self-Portrait In His Own Words
La Téléphonie and the Universal Musical Language
Extraordinary Women
Essays on the Modern Wind Band
Essays on Performance Practice

Aesthetics of Music Series

Aesthetics of Music in Ancient Civilizations
Aesthetics of Music in the Middle Ages
Aesthetics of Music in the Early Renaissance
Aesthetics of Music in Sixteenth-Century Italy, France and Spain
Aesthetics of Music in Sixteenth-Century Germany, the Low Countries and England
Aesthetics of Baroque Music in Italy, Spain, the German-Speaking Countries and the Low Countries
Aesthetics of Baroque Music in France
Aesthteics of Baroque Music in England

The History and Literature of the Wind Band and Wind Ensemble Series

Volume 1 The Wind Band and Wind Ensemble Before 1500
Volume 2 The Renaissance Wind Band and Wind Ensemble
Volume 3 The Baroque Wind Band and Wind Ensemble
Volume 4 The Classical Period Wind Band and Wind Ensemble
Volume 5 The Nineteenth-Century Wind Band and Wind Ensemble
Volume 6 A Catalog of Multi-Part Repertoire for Wind Instruments or for Undesignated Instrumentation before 1600
Volume 7 Baroque Wind Band and Wind Ensemble Repertoire
Volume 8 Classic Period Wind Band and Wind Ensemble Repertoire
Volume 9 Nineteenth-Century Wind Band and Wind Ensemble Repertoire
Volume 10 A Supplementary Catalog of Wind Band and Wind Ensemble Repertoire
Volume 11 A Catalog of Wind Repertoire before the Twentieth Century for One to Five Players
Volume 12 A Second Supplementary Catalog of Early Wind Band and Wind Ensemble Repertoire
Volume 13 Name Index, Volumes 1–12, The History and Literature of the Wind Band and Wind Ensemble

www.whitwellbooks.com

David Whitwell

Aesthetics of Music

VOLUME 8
AESTHETICS OF BAROQUE MUSIC IN ENGLAND

Edited by Craig Dabelstein

Whitwell Publishing • Austin, Texas, USA

Whitwell Publishing, Austin 78701
www.whitwellbooks.com

© 1996, 2013 by David Whitwell
All rights reserved. First edition 1996.
Second edition 2013

Printed in the United States of America

Paperback
ISBN-13: 978-1-936512-66-9
ISBN-10: 1936512661

Composed in Minion Pro

CONTENTS

	Foreword	vii
	Acknowledgements	xi
1	The Musical Scene in England	1
2	Aesthetics Views of English Musicians	21
3	Roger North	41
4	Jacobean Philosophy	57
5	Francis Bacon	77
6	Jacobean Poetry	93
7	Milton	129
8	Jacobean Theatre	155
9	Jacobean Prose	209
10	Restoration Philosophers	223
11	Restoration Philosophers of Aesthetics	263
12	Restoration Theatre	303
13	Dryden	321
14	Restoration Poetry	347
15	Restoration Non-Fiction	377
16	Restoration Fiction	391
17	Restoration Manners	407
18	Pepys	431
19	Restoration Journals	445
	Bibliography	467
	Index	473
	About the Author	479
	About the Editor	481

FOREWORD

WE DEFINE MUSIC to be that form of music performed live before listeners. We define Aesthetics in Music to be a study of the nature of the perception of music by the listener.

We believe the performance of music in actual practice falls naturally into four classes. These are Art Music, Educational Music, Functional Music and Entertainment Music.

I. ART MUSIC

Art Music we believe is defined by four conditions, *all* of which *must always be present*. These are:

1. *Art music is inspired.* Art music is music in which it seems evident that the composer has made an honest attempt to communicate genuine feelings. Feelings, which may range from lofty and noble to superficial and vulgar, must be presumed to be generally recognizable in music, as they are in any other art form, including painting, sculpture, dance, and architecture. In Art Music, lofty and noble feelings are paramount.

    Due to the common genetically understood nature of emotions, it must also be understood that in music emotions or feelings cannot be 'faked.' They will always be recognized as such by any contemplative listener.

2. *Art Music has no purpose other than the communication of its own aesthetic content.* Art Music is free of any purpose or function, save the spiritual communication of pure beauty.

3. *Art Music is that which enjoys a performance faithful to the intent of the composer.*

4. *Art Music must have a listener capable of contemplation.*

If any of these conditions are missing, the performance must result in a lesser aesthetic experience. For example, the *Ninth Symphony* of Beethoven played in a stadium, during the half-time of a professional football game, would fail for the lack of the presence of Condition Number Four. The same Symphony heard in a concert hall, but in a poor performance, not faithful to the intent of the composer, would fail for the lack of the presence of Condition Number Three.

II. Educational Music

Educational Music may or may not have the same conditions as Art Music, excepting Condition Number Two; it may or may not occur within an educational institution. Educational Music is didactic music, music which has the specific and *additional* aim to educate. In the strictest sense, if the *primary purpose* of Music is to educate, it cannot be Art Music—for Art Music has no purpose.

III. Functional Music

Functional Music is music put at the service of something else. We include here, for example, all kinds of religious music, music for weddings, music for the military, and occupational music. Functional Music may share the same conditions as Art Music, excepting Condition Number Two.

One may ask, How can a Mozart Mass be called Functional Music, and not Art Music? If the observer were not contemplatively listening to the music, but were rather contemplating religious thoughts, then the Mozart Mass becomes merely a very high level of Functional Music. If, on the other hand, the observer is a contemplative listener of music, forgetting about religion, then the Mozart Mass is Art Music, but has failed in its purpose as church music.

Military and wedding music are examples of music in which the contemplative listener is missing entirely. How about airport, supermarket and elevator music where there is no listener at all? According to the definition we have given above, recorded music without listeners is not to be considered music at all.

IV. Entertainment Music

Entertainment Music is music with no object other than to please. It will always be missing Condition Four, the contemplative listener. For this reason, Entertainment Music may be inspired music, but the composer is unlikely to be inspired by lofty and noble emotions, knowing there will be no contemplative listener. Entertainment Music and Art Music can never be the same thing because of Condition Number Two: Art Music has no purpose other than the communication of its own aesthetic content. It is inconsistent with the nature of great art to have any extrinsic purpose, including the purpose to entertain.

The first philosopher to address the impact which Art has on an observer was Aristotle, in his *Poetics*, as part of a discussion of Tragedy, which like music has both a material, written form and a live performance form. In this treatise, Aristotle first considers the nature and contribution of each of the specific components of the written form of the Tragedy in his typically methodical style. His great contribution, however, comes when he has completed this discussion, for he then goes beyond the material form of the play itself to discuss the observer. He makes it clear that not only is the end purpose of the elements of the play to produce a specific experience in the observer, but that the nature of this experience is what distinguishes Tragedy from other dramatic forms, such as Spectacle. It was in this moment that he created a new branch of Philosophy which we call 'Aesthetics.'

Our purpose is to provide a source book of representative descriptions of actual performances, observations by philosophers, poets and other commentators which contribute insights to our understanding of what music meant to listeners during the early Renaissance. It is for this reason that when discussing contemporary treatises on music that we concentrate on those passages which offer insights relative to the aesthetics of music and musical performance rather than the usual technical subjects such as scales, modes and counterpoint which fill most books on Renaissance music.

Since traditional musicology has focused almost exclusively on sacred and secular vocal music of the Renaissance, we have also included numerous references which we hope will reveal a much wider world of music during this period.

We are also interested in contemporary views on the physiology of knowing, especially with regard to the relationship of the senses and Reason, and related psychological ideas, such as Pleasure and Pain and the Emotions, which might offer a frame of reference for their perspective on the perception of music.

This is the final volume in a series of eight, ranging from the music of the ancient civilizations through the Baroque Period.

David Whitwell
Austin, Texas

ACKNOWLEDGMENTS

This new edition would not have been possible without the encouragement and help of Craig Dabelstein of Brisbane, Australia. His experience as a musician and educator himself has contributed greatly to his expertise as editor of this volume.

> David Whitwell
> Austin, 2013

1   THE MUSICAL SCENE IN ENGLAND

MUSIC OF THE COURT

One is inclined to feel sympathy for James I (1603–1625),[1] the first of the Stuarts, for not only was it his unhappy destiny to follow the great Elizabeth, but he was a poor physical specimen.[2] Among his many failings was a distinctly divine self-image which contributed to the civil unrest and regicide which followed. His persecution of Puritans and Catholics led to the famous departure of the American colonists. This and his sponsorship of a famous bible made it impossible for history to forget him.

Although he maintained a significant musical establishment,[3] nothing about his court could inspire further aesthetic growth. His tastes extended little beyond entertainment, as is perhaps best symbolized by the accounts centering on the visit of the King of Denmark in 1606.[4] In the principal entertainment, an allegorical arrival of the Queen of Sheba at the court of Solomon, the 'Queen of Sheba' was drunk and spilled a tray of goodies in the lap of the Danish king. Three other actresses, Faith, Hope and Charity were also drunk and,

> Hope did assay to speak, but wine rendered her endeavours so feeble that she withdrew ... Faith was then all alone, for I am certain she was not joined with good works, and left the court in a staggering condition; Charity came to the king's feet, and seemed to cover the multitude of sins her sisters had committed ... She then returned to Hope and Faith, who were both sick and spewing in the lower hall.[5]

---

[1]   Our purpose here is not an attempt to summarize the development of Baroque music itself in England, and its composers, but rather to present a brief overview of the environment in which the music was performed and its general aesthetic nature. At the same time, we take the opportunity to include important material not found in general music history texts.

[2]   Christopher Hibbert, *Charles I* (New York: Harper, 1968), 17ff., quotes a contemporary description of a large body over weak, thin legs; eyes watery and too large; and,

> with a large tongue, over a small jaw, which caused him to make a distasteful splashing noise when drinking and to dribble gravy into his beard and wine down the side of his cup.

[3]   Centering on consorts of flutes, oboes and trombones, some of whom doubled on cornett, in addition to the usual trumpets and drums. See Thurston Dart, 'The Repertory of the Royal Wind Music,' *The Galpin Society Journal* 11 (May, 1958): 75, and Walter Woodfill, *Musicians in English Society* (Princeton: Princeton University Press, 1953), 179, 296ff.

[4]   John Nichols, *The Progresses of Queen Elizabeth* (London, 1805), III, quotes an eyewitness, Henry Robart, who was especially taken by the appearance of the Danish king with his timpani players riding horses while playing. It was, he said, 'a thing verie admirable to the common sort, and much admired.'

[5]   Robert Ashton, *James I* (London: Hutchinson, 1969), 242ff.

Sir John Harington, who was present for these celebrations, confirms the general climate.

> We had women, and indeed wine too, of such plenty, as would have astonished each sober beholder ... Those, whom I never could get to taste good liquor, now follow the fashion, and wallow in beastly delights. The ladies abandon their sobriety, and are seen to roll about in intoxication.

The highest form of Jacobean musical entertainment was the masque, allegorical theater pieces whose nature might be characterized by the titles of three of Ben Johnson's masques, 'Masque of Beauty' (1607), 'Pan's Anniversary' (1624) and 'The Fortunate Isles' (1624). A typical masque usually began with a prologue in verse, with songs and changes of scenery, followed by a dance, actors, and then a main dance in which the maskers invited the royal spectators to dance with them. Instrumental music for the overture or for changes of scenery were often played by one of the wind consorts, but sometimes by string consorts as well.

One of the most interesting eyewitness accounts we have of one of these performances is by the Venetian ambassador in London, Horatio Busino, describing a performance of Ben Johnson's 'Pleasure Reconciled to Virtue,' performed 6 January 1618.[6] He describes the hall and the ladies present in the audience, regarding whose clothes he found had 'no folds so that any deformity, however monstrous, remains hidden.' More interesting is his description of the king's entrance.

> On entering the house, the cornets and trumpets to the number of fifteen or twenty began to play very well a sort of recitative.

No one knows what kind of music this was, which substituted for the usual fanfares. Although Jonson also uses the term 'Stylo recitativo' in his 'Of Lovers made Men' (1617), there is little extant information on English musical practice this early in the century to allow the obvious association with the new Italian movement we call opera.[7]

This masque, according to Busino, began with a 'very chubby Bacchus' who sang in an undertone before the king, followed by another stout, drunken figure, 'Bacchus's cupbearer.' The first principal dance was by twelve figures dressed in barrels and wicker-baskets with an accompaniment of cornetts and trumpets. Next came a gigantic man representing Hercules and twelve boys in the 'guise of frogs,' who danced and were then driven off by Hercules. A scene change brought dawn at Mount Atlas, where high priests and goddesses 'sang some jigs.' Busino was not impressed.

> It is true that, spoiled as we are by the graceful and harmonious music of Italy, the composition did not strike us as very fine.

---

6   *Calendar of State Papers and Manuscripts existing in the Archives of Venice*, 1617–1619, 110ff.

7   See Gustave Reese, *Music in the Renaissance* (New York: Norton, 1959), 883.

After a final dance by twelve masked cavaliers, our ambassador, 'half disgusted and weary,' left for home at half-past two o'clock in the morning, after having been at court for eleven hours!

We may assume the lesser lords imitated the practice of the court of James. If they did not maintain a musical establishment, they could always hire musicians for special occasions—as when the Earl of Cumberland hired the York civic wind band to perform for a masque he gave in 1636.[8] Richard Brathwaite, in his *Some Rules and Orders for the Government of the House of an Earle* (1621) details the music required for special banquets.

> At great feasts, or in time of great strangers, when it is time for the Ewer to cover the table for the Earle; [the Trumpeter] ... is to sounde to give warning, and the drumme to play till the Ewer is readie to goe up with the service, and then to give place to the Musitians, who are to play ... upon Shagbutte, Cornetts, Shalmes, and other instruments going with winde. In meale times to play upon Violls, Violins, or other broken musicke.[9]

Braithwaite also gives us a glimpse of the highly organized use of music for travel.

> When the Earle is to ride a journey, [the trumpet] is early every morning to sound, to give warning, that the Officers may have time to make all things ready for breakfast, and the grooms of the stable to dress and feed the horses. When it is breakfast time, he is to make his second sounding: breakfast ended, and things in a readiness, he is to sound the third time, to call to horse. He is to ride foremost, both out and into any town, sounding his trumpet. Upon the way he may sound for pleasure. But if he see the day so spent that they are like to bring late to their lodging, he is to sound the 'Tantara,' to move them to hasten their pace.[10]

But since there was some danger that all this trumpet playing might frighten the horses, the trumpeter had an even earlier duty. In what was surely the lowest moment for the proud trumpeter, he had,

> to goe often into the Stable, to acquainte the horses with the sound of the trumpet, and the noise of the drumme.[11]

Walls, in a book on Baroque music,[12] leaves the impression that the noble class in England in the seventeenth century modeled themselves after Castiglione, *The Courtier*, and were therefore practicing musicians. He points to William Cavendish, Duke of Newcastle, as one who indulged in poetry and music 'the greater part of his time.' We believe it is incorrect

---

8 Woodfill, *Musicians in English Society*, 260.

9 Quoted in Paul Jones, *The Household of a Tudor Nobleman* (Urbana: University of Illinois, 1918), 175. This is one of the earliest references to violins in art music in England. *The Diary of Anthony Wood* maintains in 1658, in describing a violin virtuoso, that 'nor any in England saw the like before.' See Robert Donnington, *The Interpretation of Early Music* (New York: Faber, 1964), 535.

10 Ibid., 229.

11 Ibid.

12 Peter Walls, 'London, 1603-49,' in *The Early Baroque Era* (Englewood Cliffs: Prentice Hall, 1994), 285.

to leave the impression that Cavendish was typical of his class. As we have pointed out in a previous volume, there is considerable evidence that in the latter part of the sixteenth century manners were changing and the English noble no longer considered the ability to actually perform music as appropriate to his status. The performance of music was being relegated to the servant class and this is stated again quite directly in James Cleland's *The Institution of a Young Nobleman* (1607).

> Delight not also to be in your own person a player upon instruments, especially upon such as commonly men get their living with.[13]

A contributing reason for this was an attitude that the noble should never be expected to exert himself to the degree required to achieve an expert level at any skill. This would certainly be required to be proficient as a performer of music, as Robert Dowland, in his *Varietie of Lute-lessons* of 1610 points out.

> Perfection in any skill cannot be attained unto without the waste of many years, much cost, and excessive labor and industry.[14]

This attitude in no way prevented the noble from enjoying music as a listener. Roger North, in his various essays, frequently wrote of the tradition of private music in the great households during the early part of the seventeenth century. In one passage, in particular, he recalls the music in the home of his grandfather, Lord North.

> He kept an organist in the house, which was seldom without a professional music master. And the servants of parade, such as gentlemen ushers, and the steward, and clerk of the kitchen also played; which with the young ladies my sisters singing, made a society of music, such as was well esteemed in those times. And the course of the family was to have solemn music three days in the week, and often every day, as masters supplied novelties for the entertainment of the old lord.[15]

Charles I was also weak in physique, and suffered from a speech impediment, but he was a much stronger personality than his father. Had he chosen as a model Elizabeth I he might have been a great king. But he followed the model of his father and lost the monarchy and was beheaded. After becoming king in 1625, after only four years he found so many of his subjects in opposition that he dissolved Parliament and ruled alone for eleven years. During this period when political lines were drawn between his followers (Cavaliers) and the Puritans (Roundheads), war broke out with the Scotch Presbyterians. Charles reconvened Parliament to raise funds, it refused and he dismissed it again. The next Parliament, called the Long Parliament, supported the Scottish position. Civil War followed and the new Parliament, entirely Puritan, beheaded Charles.

---

13   James Cleland, *The Institution of a Young Nobleman* (Oxford, 1607), V, xxv.
14   Quoted in Donnington, *The Interpretation of Early Music*, 118.
15   Quoted in John Wilson, *Roger North on Music* (London: Novello, 1959), 10.

Charles combined his musical establishment with that of his father to create a body of some sixty-five musicians.[16] A surviving contract for one of them in 1640 reveals that they were exempt from some taxes, were free from arrest and another document records they were provided with both printed music and manuscript paper ('Italian musique cards').[17]

According to John Playford, writing in 1674, Charles was particularly interested in his private church music, 'which with much zeal he would hear reverently performed, and often appointed the Service and anthems himself, being by his knowledge in music a competent judge therein.'[18] While there were some masques and other larger entertainments under Charles I, the accounts center mostly on the provision of musicians for meals.[19] Fortunately, the musicians were able to work out a rotation system so the same men did not have to play for every meal.[20]

Roger North recalls that during the period of the Civil War, during the reign of Charles I, music making flourished on a private basis, even though public productions were of necessity curtailed.

> Among other arts, music flourished, and exceedingly improved, for the King, being a virtuous prince, loved an entertainment so commendable as that was, and the Fantasia manner held through his reign, and during the troubles; and when most other good arts languished music held up her head, not at Court nor in profane Theaters, but in private society, for many chose rather to fiddle at home, than to go out and be knocked on the head abroad; and the entertainment was very much courted and made use of, not only in country but city families, in which many of the ladies were good consortiers; and in this state was music daily improving more or less till the time of the happy Restoration.[21]

The trumpeters seem to have been paid more than most musicians, not only because of their constant use for giving signals but because they had to serve as ambassadors when the nobles traveled. The trumpeter was considered the equivalent of a passport, or a 'white flag,' and was supposed to be allowed to cross enemy lines unharmed. Thus, the diary of one who accompanied the Earl of Arundel on a journey through Germany in 1636 mentions,

> whilst our trumpeter was allowed to visit … the castle in order to ask French permission for our further passage.[22]

---

16 For the funeral of James I, payments were made to 21 trumpets, 21 'Musicians for the windy Instruments,' and 13 'Musitions for Violins.'

17 London, Lord Chamberlains Accounts, vol. 738, p. 75, for January 10, 1629.

18 John Playford, *An Introduction to the Skill of Music* [1674] (Ridgewood: Gregg Press, 1966), preface.

19 The meals themselves must have been rather amazing. Every year, at Whitehall Palace alone, Charles and his company consumed 3,000 carcasses of beef, 14,000 sheep and lambs, 24,000 birds, together with vast quantities of pigs, fish, boars and bacon. See Hibbert, *Charles I*, 112.

20 Henry Lafontaine, *The King's Music* (New York: Da Capo Press, 1973), 72ff.

21 Quoted in Wilson, *Roger North on Music*, 294.

22 Francis Springell, *Connoisseur & Diplomat* (London: Maggs Bros., 1936), 89.

Sad to say, this particular trumpeter was murdered when the party was near Nürnberg.[23]

> His Excellency's Gentleman of the Horse and his Trumpeter, together with the corpse of their guide, the Postmaster, were found ... It appeared that each must have witnessed the death agonies of his companions. The head of the Gentleman of the Horse had been shattered by a pistol shot, the Trumpeter's head had been cut off and the guide's head had been split open.[24]

After the death of Charles I, the Puritan extremists tried to create a democratic government, but it soon developed into a Protectorate under Cromwell. Religious toleration was established and Jews were readmitted after having been banished for centuries. After Cromwell's death anarchy returned and now even the Puritans were in disarray. After much dissension the public finally was willing for a return of the Stuarts.

The Restoration Period in England begins with the return of Charles II in 1660. Some called him the 'happy king,' and well he might have been, having spent fourteen years enjoying France with no cares of government. An Italian diplomat said of him,

> His fiercest enemies are diligence and business. He worships comforts, pleasures, and practical jokes, hates implacably all sort of work, and loves with the greatest enthusiasm every kind of play and diversion.[25]

As a collector of mistresses he was without equal for his generation, thus setting the example for both his court and Restoration theater. One of the most memorable lines of the seventeenth century was spoken by one of his ladies when the crowd mistook her for a newly arrived French (and Catholic) mistress. From her coach window she exclaimed, 'Be silent, good people, I am the *Protestant* whore!'[26] This young lady was Nell Gwynn (1650–1687), who was born in a coalyard garret in Drury Lane and developed her singing and acting ability in the lowest barrooms. She was fortunate to live at the time when female parts on the stage were first allowed to be played by women and her success on the stage first brought her to the attention of the king. She collected considerable funds from the king's purse, but it must be noted that she gave much of this money to private charities, including Chelsea Hospital. A letter by Mme de Sévigné in Paris records the character of this girl, and also mentions a child who is usually overlooked in the literature on Charles II.

> The actress is as haughty as the Duchess of Portsmouth [another mistress of the king]; she insults her, makes faces at her, attacks her, frequently steals the King from her, and boasts of his prefer-

---

23 When another royal trumpeter was killed while on a diplomatic mission to Poland, the court documents seem more concerned with the loss of the king's silver trumpet. See Richard McGrady, 'The Court Trumpeters of Charles I and Charles II,' *The Music Review* 35 (1974), 227.

24 Ibid., 80.

25 Lorenzo Magalotti, *Relazione d'Inghilterra* [1668] (Waterloo, Ont.: Wilfrid Laurier University Press, 1980).

26 Sir Arthur Bryant, *King Charles II* (London: Collins, 1955), 238.

ence for her. She is young, indiscreet, confident, meretricious, and pleasant; she sings, dances, and acts her part well. She has a son by the king, and wishes to have him acknowledged.[27]

There was of course a great celebration surrounding the coronation of Charles II. One eyewitness mentions the participation of wind bands representing the various trade guilds[28] and pay records document the presence of the king's wind band.[29] It appears that some of the compositions in Matthew Locke's 'ffor his Majesty's Sagbutts & Cornetts' were used for the coronation.[30]

Roger North recalled the musical preferences of Charles II.

> He had lived some considerable time abroad, where the French music was in request, which consisted of an Entry and then Brawles, as they were called, that is motive aires, and dances. And it was, and is yet a mode among the *Monseurs*, always to act the music, which habit the King had got, and never in his life could endure any music that he could not act by keeping the time; which made the common *andante* or else the step-tripla the only musical styles at Court in his time. And after the manner of France, he set up a band of 24 violins to play at his dinners, which disbanded all the old English music at once. He was a lover of slight songs, and endured the accompaniment very well, provided he could keep the time.[31]

As North indicated, Charles II developed an even larger musical establishment, with twenty-four violins (modeled after the '24 Violons du Roi' of France),[32] a wind band which grew to sixteen players by 1663, and an assortment of lutes, voices, trumpets and drummers. The overall responsibility for performance fell to Nicholas Lanier and one document refers to his authority over rehearsals.

---

27 Quoted in Françoise Marguerite Sévigné, *Letters of Madame de Sévigné*, ed. Richard Aldington (London: Routledge, 1937), I, 170.

28 *The Diary of John Evelyn* (Oxford: Clarendon Press, 1955), for April 22, 1661.

29 London, Lord Chamberlain Accounts, vol. 741, page 118.

30 George Grove, *The New Grove Dictionary of Music and Musicians*, ed. Stanley Sadie (London: Macmillan, 1980), XI, 109.

31 Quoted in Wilson, *Roger North on Music*, 299ff.

32 Peter Holman, in 'London: Commonwealth and Restoration,' in *The Early Baroque Era*, 312, points out that the violin, at the beginning of the seventeenth century, was used only by players of dance music. Then he suggests it began to be used in the string fantasias of Coprario, Lupo, et. al. All English scholars make this assumption, even though most of the actual manuscripts bear no designation of instruments. The appearance of the 'French violin clef' is no proof, for this same clef was also used for the oboe in the *Le Grands Hautbois* in Paris. Holman states that the violin 'became acceptable in serious musical circles … in the late 1650s.' Curiously, as proof he offers a quotation by an eyewitness who actually says the contrary.

> [Gentlemen in private meetings] play'd three, four, and five parts all with *viols*, as treble-viol, tenor, counter-tenor and bass, with either an organ or virginals or harpsicon joy'nd with them: and they esteemed a *violin* to be an instrument only belonging to a common fidler, and could not indure that it should come among them for feare of making their meetings seem to be vain and fidling.

Roger North [see Wilson, *Roger North on Music*, 222] made the interesting observation that it was the superiority of the new violin which helped change the multi-part style into the melody-bass character of the new *galant* style. In a viol consort, he says, everyone felt comfortable playing any part, but after the appearance of the violin 'few or none cared to play under it, as supposing all the spirit of the consort lay in that.'

> Nicholas Lanier … hath power to order and convocate [his Majesty's musick] at fitt time of practize and service … If any of them refuse to wayte at such convenient tymes of practize and service … I shall punish them either in their persons or their wages.[33]

A document of 18 June 1669, however, announced the 'retrenchment of his Majesty's musick.'[34] From this time on the numbers of players are dramatically reduced. The wind band, for example, falls to ten and by 1679 to five. An engraving of the coronation of James II shows a fife player and four drummers, eight royal trumpeters and the wind band, which is now only three players.[35] Roger North, in his autobiography, comments on the influence of various national styles heard in the court music at this time.

> The court about this time entertained only the theatrical music and French air in song, but that somewhat softened and variegated; so also was the instrumental more vague and with a mixture of caprice … But we found most satisfaction in the Italian, for their measures were just and quick, set off with wonderful solemn *Grave's*, and full of variety. The old English Fancys were in imitation of an elder Italian sort of sonata … At length the time came off the French way and fell in with the Italian, and now that holds the ear. But still the English singularity will come in and have a share.[36]

During the reign of William and Mary (1689–1694) an order was given to the Dean of the Chapel Royal, on 23 February 1689, that there was to be no further instrumental music in the Chapel, except for the organ.[37] On the other hand, a new ensemble appears at this time, an Hautboisten band modeled after the famous one in Paris. It was this ensemble which performed the funeral music for Queen Mary by Henry Purcell. We share, even today, the reaction of one who heard the original performance of this music.

> I appeal to all that were present, as well such as understand Music, as those that did not, whither they ever heard any thing so rapturously fine and solemn & so Heavenly in the Operation, which drew tears from all; & yet a plain, Naturall Composition; which shows the power of Music, when 'tis rightly fitted & Adapted to devotional purposes.

---

33   Lord Chamberlain Accounts, vol. 741, page 316.

34   Holman, 'London: Commonwealth and Restoration,' 314, incorrectly says 'the Wind Music effectively ceased to exist' at this time.

35   Contained in Francis Standford, *The History of the Coronation of … James II* (London, 1687). Curiously the wind band is identified as 'Two Sackbuts and a double Courtal,' whereas in fact there is pictured two slide trumpets and a cornett.

36   Quoted in Wilson, *Roger North on Music*, 25.

37   Donald Burrows, 'London: Commercial Wealth and Cultural Expansion,' in *The Late Baroque Era* (Englewood Cliffs: Prentice Hall, 1994), 355.

This ensemble appears to remain the basic royal wind band until 1750 and its repertoire included a dozen or so works by Handel.[38]

With the accession of Anne in 1702 the musical establishment in the court began to expand again and Burrows points to the regular employment of more than sixty musicians at this time.[39] The patronage of opera under George I during the next decade continued this growth in activity and during the 1730s it expanded further as various members of the royal family pursued their own support of music.

CIVIC MUSIC

Public concerts in England, in the modern sense of the word, began after the Restoration as privately sponsored events. However humble the occasion, there was nevertheless the crucial distinction that it was music to be listened to. An interesting definition in this regard is given by Hawkins.

> But a concert, properly so called, was a sober recreation; persons were drawn to it, not by an affectation of admiring what they could not taste, but by a genuine pleasure which they took in the entertainment.[40]

The best known of these privately sponsored concerts is first mentioned in a 30 December 1672 issue of the London *Gazette*.

> This is to give notice, that at Mr. John Banister's house (now called the Musick-school) over against the George tavern in White Fryers, this present Monday, will be musick performed by excellent masters, beginning precisely at 4 of the clock in the afternoon, and every afternoon for the future, precisely at the same hour.

Future issues of the paper advertise a great variety of vocal and instrumental performances, such as a 'rare concert of four Trumpets Marine, never heard of before in England.'

One of the most curious hosts of these privately held concerts was a poor coal supplier in Clerkenwell, named Thomas Britton. Aside from the concerts he began in 1678, this self-educated music lover acquired an extensive library of books and music.[41] Britton organized his concerts in a room above that in which he stored his coal, entered by stairs outside the

---

38 Handel's 'Fireworks Music,' originally, *Grand Overture of Warlike Instruments*, was composed for nine-part Hautboisten with the addition of the trumpets and drums referred to in the title. Because its first performance was given with some sixty players doubling the parts, it is always thought of today as a composition for a large ensemble. Handel was also familiar with a wind band piece played in Naples during Christmas by the civic wind band [*pifferari*]. This became the 'Pastoral Symphony' of the *Messiah* and Handel has conscientiously acknowledged this by writing the abbreviation *pifa* at the beginning of this music in his autograph score.

39 Burrows, 'London: Commercial Wealth and Cultural Expansion,' 364.

40 John Hawkins, *A General History of the Science and Practice of Music* (1776) (New York: Dover Reprint, 1963), II, 762.

41 A catalog of these hundreds of books and scores is quoted in Ibid., II, 792ff.

building. In spite of the despicable house, in a poor area of London, these concerts drew even members of the aristocracy. A prior wrote the following lines in honor of this poor coal dealer.

> Tho' doom'd to small-coal, yet to arts ally'd,
> Rich without wealth, and famous without pride;
> Musick's best patron, judge of books and man,
> Belov'd and honour'd by Apollo's train;
> In Greece or Rome sure never did appear
> So bright a genius in so dark a sphere.[42]

By the end of the century newspaper advertisements suggest a wider public concert activity, now often held in the York Buildings and Stationers' Hall. Many concerts lasted up to two hours and seem to have been characterized by great variety. In 1697 the concept of a continuing series of concerts appears for the first time.

In 1656 one William Davenant persuaded the Protectorate government to allow him to reopen a theater, under the promise that he would produce not a play but an opera. While his first effort, *First Dayes Entertainment*, was an opera in name only, and while further obstacles remained, nevertheless opera, and opera for the public, was firmly established in England by the early years of the eighteenth century.

But it was Italian opera which swept up the public, not English opera, and we can see in an advertisement of 1705, by Thomas Clayton (1673-1725), some sense of concern that this new medium would be understood by the English public.

> The Design of this Entertainment being to introduce the *Italian* manner of Musick on the *English* stage, which has not been before attempted: I was oblig'd to have an *Italian* Opera translated ... The Musick being Recitative, may not, at first, meet with that general Acceptation as is to be hop'd for, from the Audience's being better acquainted with it: but if this Attempt shall be a means of bringing this manner of Musick to be us'd in my Native country, I shall think all my Study and Pains very well employ'd.[43]

But soon it was genuine Italian opera, sung in Italian, which won over the public. Addison, for one, was confused.

> Our great-grandchildren will be very curious to know the reason why their forefathers used to sit together like an audience of foreigners in their own country, to hear whole plays acted before them in a tongue which they did not understand.[44]

---

42 Quoted in Ibid, II, 790. Britton's death was as curious as his life. A locally famous ventriloquist, making his voice appear from far away, informed Britton that he would die in a few hours. Britton returned to his house, where he took to his bed and died with in a few days.

43 Quoted in Ibid., 358.

44 *The Spectator*, Nr. 18.

During the 1730s a genuine English medium became popular in the broadest sense of the word. This was, of course, the Oratorio, and it brought concerts with great numbers of performers as well as listeners.

Perhaps we should acknowledge at this point that the contribution made to English musical life by large numbers of foreign musicians, who had begun coming to England for political reasons during the sixteenth century, continued. Among them were numerous talented Germans, foremost of which was Handel. The question which no English-speaking person wants to face is, What would eighteenth-century English music be without the foreign-born composers? The greatest English-born composer who ever lived, Purcell, saw this clearly in 1690. 'English music,' he said, 'is yet but in its nonage, a forward child, which gives hope of what it may be hereafter … when the masters of it shall find more encouragement.'[45]

At the end of the seventeenth century, as mentioned above, the Hautboisten band arrived in England—from France, in spite of its Germanized name. The preference for the Hautboisten band instrumentation during the early eighteenth century, apparently led to an expansion of oboe and bassoon players in London. This seems to be inferred by several accounts of concerts which included works for bassoon ensembles. One of these was a concert given at Stationers' Hall, in 1713, which included 'an uncommon piece of Musick by Bassoons only.'[46] Even more extraordinary is an advertisement for a concert at Lincoln's Inn Theater in 1744, which promised a,

> new concerto grosso of 24 bassoons, accompanied by Signor Caporale on the violoncello, intermixed with Duettos by 4 doublebassoons, accompanied by a German flute, the whole blended with numbers of violins, hautboys, fifes, tombany's, French horns, trumpets, drums and kettle-drums.[47]

During the seventeenth century a great wave of involvement in music performance swept the middle class in England. One wonders if it were a private retreat from the grim public face of the civil war and the Puritans. Pepys, in his famous diary, observed every third boat on the Thames contained virginals and he gives the impression that everyone he knew performs music and sings.[48] Indeed, a great explosion of popular song ensued and credit must be given to Charles II who brought back from Paris a lighter mood in music. The great public response confirmed what the music theorists had failed to see for a thousand years: music is not mathematics.

This broad interest by the middle class in actually performing music can be documented by a profusion of publications which began to appear in the first decade of the seventeenth

---

45   Quoted in Charles Burney, *General History of Music* (New York: Dover, 1957), II, 399.
46   John Ashton, *Social Life in the Reign of Queen Anne* (London: Chatto & Windus, 1911), 277.
47   London, *General Advertiser* (October 21, 1744).
48   Pepys, *Diary*, for September 2, 1666 and January 16, 1660.

century. Soon great quantities of music, including songs and works for lute, viol and virginal were in circulation, both in print and in manuscript.[49]

More difficult to document, but nevertheless evident, was an equally broad participation in music making by the lower classes. One form of music which does survive are the so-called 'broadside ballads,' popular songs printed for this facet of society. One source of music which was apparently frequently heard by members of the lower class was the local barber shop. Barbershops were often equipped with instruments, upon which the waiting customer could perform. The barbers as well are often mentioned in literature as engaging in performance as an outside source of income. While there is little extant documentation about the actual music making of these barber musicians, we do find some interesting details in a poem written in honor of John Est, who apparently had a certain reputation for his performance in London. We also read here the titles of seven popular songs as presumably representative of the repertoire of the barbers.

> In former time 't hath been upbrayded thus,
> That barber's musick was most barbarous,
> For that the cittern was confin'd unto
> The Ladies Fall, or John come kiss me now,
> Green Sleeves, and Puddng Pyes, with Nell's delight,
> Winning of Bolloigne, Essex' last good night.
> But, since reduc'd to this conformity,
> And company became society,
> Each barber writes himself, in strictest rules,
> Master, or bachelor i' th' musick schools,
> How they the mere musitians do out-go,
> These one, but they have two strings to their bow.
> Barber musitians who are excellent,
> As well at chest, as the case instrument,
> Henceforth each steward shall invite his guest
> Unto the barber's and musitian's feast,
> Where sit ye merry, whilst we joy to see
> Art thus embrac'd by ingenuity.

THE WAIT BANDS

As we have pointed out in our discussion in a previous volume, by the end of the sixteenth century the civic wind band tradition in England had begun to decline. Pepys, after hearing the Cambridge Waits in 1667 observed, 'But Lord! what sad music they made.'[50]

---

49   Walls, 'London, 1603–49,' 288ff, provides a fine summary of this activity.
50   Quoted in Woodfill, *Musicians in English Society*, 174.

One reason for the decline lay in the fact that the wind instrument was no longer the exclusive instrument of the professional musician. The demands for wider choices of musical expression forced the civic musicians to obtain wider skills, which must have tended to lower their abilities on all, as is clear in a description of the Norwich Waits in 1600.

> Passing the gate … where … stood the City Waits … such Waits few Cities in our Realm have the like, none better; who beside their excellency in wind instruments, their rare cunning on the Viol and Violin, their voices be admirable, every one of them able to serve in any Cathedral Church in Christendom.[51]

Perhaps this demand for more diverse skills was partly to blame, but in any case the professional discipline of this institution had also begun to break down by the end of the sixteenth century. During the seventeenth century entire civic wind bands were being disbanded, including Leicester (1602), Manchester (1620), Coventry (1635), Canterbury (1640, for 'disorders and misbehaviour'[52]) and Durham (1684, for 'indecent expression' toward the mayor[53]). In 1612, curiously, the entire civic wind band of Chester disappeared without a trace.

> George Musitian exhibiteth his petician desiring that he and his fellow musitians may be admitted Waytes of this Cittie instead of the waytes now absent, finding instruments of his own charge to perform the service; which is deferred to be graunted untill it may be understode what are become of the ould waytes.[54]

Even the distinguished London Waits appear to have suffered this demise, as a 1625 edict by the civic government suggests.

> Through the contentions and ill dispositions of some particular persons of this society [of waits] the whole company suffereth often in their credits and reputations by uncivil and retorting of bitter and unsavory jests and calumnious aspersions upon one or other of them; which only nourish the discord and confusion amongst them with continual quarreling and heartburning yea especially in the times of their service to his honorable city.[55]

By the eighteenth century the proud London Waits had declined sufficiently as to become the object of cruel humor in contemporary literature.

> We blundered on in pursuit of our felicity, but scarce had walked the length of a horse's tether, ere we heard a noise so dreadful and surprising, that we thought the devil was riding on hunt-

---

51 Quoted in Joseph Bridge, 'Town Waits and their Tunes,' in *Proceedings of the Musical Association* (London, 1927–1928), 85.
52 Ibid., 73.
53 Ibid., 72.
54 Ibid., 73.
55 Woodfill, *Musicians in English Society*, 43ff.

ing through the City, with a pack of deep-mouthed hell-hounds, to catch a brace of tallymen for breakfast ...

One was armed, as I thought, with a faggot-bat, and the rest with strange wooden weapons in their hands in the shape of clyster pipes, but as long, almost, as speaking-trumpets. Of a sudden they raised them to their mouths, and made such a frightful yelling, that I thought the world had been dissolving and the terrible sounds of the last trumpet to be within an inch of my ears.

Under these amazing apprehensions I asked my friend what was the meaning of this infernal outcry? 'Prithee,' says he, 'what's the matter with thee? Why these are the City Waits, who play every winter's night through the streets.'

'Lord bless me!' said I, 'I am very glad it's no worse. Prithee let us make haste out of the hearing of them.'

At this my friend laughed at me. 'Why, what,' says he, 'don't you love music? These are the topping tooters of the town, and have gowns, silver chains, and salaries, for playing *Lillabolaro* to my Lord Mayor's Horse through the City.'

'Marry,' said I, 'if his horse liked their music no better than I do, he would soon fling his rider for hiring such bugbears to affront his ambleship.'[56]

For those wait bands who managed to continue on, there are numerous records of their activity as watch musicians, performing for a variety of civic and university celebrations (including the laying of the cornerstone of the Bodleian Library), processions and for private weddings. Among the more artistic appearances by these civic bands was their employment in the theater. It was no doubt one of these bands which was honored by the testimonial of Samuel Pepys to the power of their music. After he had attended a play, *The Virgin Martyr*, in 1668, he wrote in his famous diary,

> But that which did please me beyond any thing in the whole world was the wind-musique when the angel comes down, which is so sweet that it ravished me, and indeed, in a word, did wrap up my soul so that it made me really sick, just as I have formerly been when in love with my wife; that neither then, nor all the evening going home, and at home, I was able to think of any thing, but remained all night transported, so as I could not believe that ever any musick hath that real command over the soul of a man as this did upon me: and makes me resolve to practice wind-musique, and to make my wife do the like.[57]

It is also important to remind the reader that these civic wind bands continued to perform concerts before the public. In London these were given every Sunday evening, between seven and eight o'clock, from a turret of the Royal Exchange. Woodfill is one of the very few scholars who has recognized the role of these civic wind bands in the development of concerts as we know them today.

---

56 Ned Ward, *The London Spy*, ed. Arthur Hayward (New York: Doran, 1927), 29ff.
57 Pepys, *The Diary of Samuel Pepys* (London, 1924), VII, 319ff, for February 25–27, 1668.

It places the earliest public concerts in England a century before the concerts begun by John Banister in 1672, the accepted date for the first public concerts in England. Banister's concerts stand as the first commercial venture of the kind in London, but take second place to the waits' concerts for antiquity and continuity of existence.[58]

The Minstrels

In a previous volume we have discussed the formation of the unique independent minstrels guild in London, which was an attempt to preserve casual performance rights for resident musicians of London against the remaining wandering musicians. This guild, ever attempting to strengthen its authority, acquired a new charter from the city in 1604, now changing its name to 'Master Wardens and Commonality of the Art or Science of the Musicians of London.'[59] Among the usual regulations concerning weddings, etc., two attract the attention of the modern reader. One reflects the rapidly changing preference for strings by stating that any consort of Violins must include at least four wind players. Another regulation forbids members from walking through the city with 'an instrument uncased or uncovered,' which must have been aimed at identifying the resident musician from those poorer vagrants who did not own cases.

Unfortunately the renewed zeal of this guild alarmed the royal musicians, who set out in 1634 to deliberately destroy the independent guild—and they succeeded. The true wandering minstrel continued to be the object of various civic and national government edicts. During a debate in Parliament in 1656 on the topic of rouges, vagabonds and beggars, one member asked that,

> fiddlers and minstrels be included, as they did corrupt the manners of the people and inflame their debauchery by lewd and obscene songs.[60]

Another member hasted to plea that the London Waits not be included.

We may assume such edicts had little effect, as indeed is reflected in yet another of 1677, which worried that,

> foreign musicians, Swiss fiddlers, pipers, waits and others do frequently play up and down in all parts of this City, expressly contrary to divers good orders of the Common Council. On this the Court ordered and strictly enjoined that no manner of person or persons not being free of this city do use or exercise singing or playing upon any instrument in any common Hall, Tavern, Inn, Alehouse, or any other like place within this City.[61]

---

58 Woodfill, *Musicians in English Society*, 50.
59 See H. A. F. Crewdson, *The Worshipful Company of Musicians* (London: Charles Knight, 1971), 40.
60 Bridge, 'Town Waits and their Tunes,' 67ff.
61 Crewdson, *The Worshipful Company of Musicians*, 168.

CHURCH MUSIC

During the Jacobean and Cromwell Periods large scale church performances were accompanied by wind instruments, as we read in an account of King James' visit to St. Paul's Cathedral in 1620.

> ... they began to celebrate Divine Service, which was solemnly performed with organs, cornets, and sagbots.[62]

In the King's Chapel, such performances appear to have been a regular occurrence, as suggested by an order of 1633.

> Order to be observed throughout the year by his Majesty's musitions for the wind instruments for waiting in the Chappell ...[63]

The major cathedrals of England, including York, Norwich, Exeter, Winchester, Worchester, Salisbury, Durham and Lincoln, followed this practice[64] and some churches, such as the Chapel Royal in Scotland, actually imported wind players from London for this purpose.[65] Parrott found only one reference for this entire period which even mentions string instruments in the church.[66] Aside from the fact that it was the wind instrumentalists who had for so long been regarded as the *professional* musicians, at least one observer concluded that strings simply could not play in tune as well as winds. String instruments, he noted,

> ar often out of tun; (Which soomtime happeneth in the mids of the Musik, when it is neither good to continue, nor to correct the fault) therefore, to avoid all offence (where the least shoolde not bee givn) in our Chyrch-solemnities onely the Winde-instruments (whose Notes ar constant) bee in use.[67]

The great crisis in English church music came with the civil war and the Cromwell Period, brought about by the views of the Puritans. The Puritans wanted a return to the simple, unaccompanied psalms of the early Christians and in the prefaces of their song books we can see their belief in the moral value of such music.

---

62 Quoted in John Nichols, *The Progresses of King James the First* (London, 1828), 601.

63 Quoted in Lafontaine, *The King's Music*, 87. One observer suggests that the winds were located in performance 'in the middle of the Choristers.' See Elias Ashmole, *The Autobiographical Notes of Elias Ashmole*, ed. C. H. Josten (Oxford: Clarendon Press, 1966), IV, 1380.

64 Andrew Parrott, 'Grett and Solompne Singing,' *Early Music* 6, no. 2 (April, 1978): 184, doi: 10.1093/earlyj/6.2.182; and Woodfill, *Musicians in English Society*, 149.

65 William Dauney, *Ancient Scottish Melodies* (Edinburgh, 1838), 365.

66 Parrott, 'Grett and Solompne Singing,' 186.

67 Charles Butler, *Principles of Musick* (1636), quoted in Parrott, Ibid.

> Set forth and allowed to be sung in all churches, of all the people before and after sermons: and moreover in private houses, for their godly solace and comfort, laying apart all ungodly songs and ballads, which tend only to the nourishing of vice, and the corrupting of youth.[68]

The stream of opinion which allowed the Puritans to prevail had actually begun much earlier, particularly with respect to the organ. The organ had come under attack during the reign of Edward VI[69] and during the reign of Elizabeth survived a motion for abolition by a single vote.[70] As an aftermath of the civil war, during the 1640s many cathedral organs were damaged. An account from Exeter, for example, records that soldiers,

> brake down the organs, and taking two or three hundred pipes with them in a most scorneful and contemptuous manner, went up and down the streets piping with them; and meeting with some of the Choristers of the Church, whose surplices they had stolne before, and imployed them to base servile offices, scoffingly told them, 'Boyes, we have spoyled your trade, you most goe and sing hot pudding pyes.'[71]

The Puritan attacks against instrumental music of all kinds was that it obscured the important thing—the *words* the singers were singing. A typical complaint was made by Peter Smart in 1630.

> Our Durhamers have been so eager upon piping and singing, that instead of the Morning Prayer at 6 of the clock, which was wont to be read distinctly and plainly, for Schoolers, and Artificers before they began their work, they brought in a solemne Service, with singing and Organs, Sackbuts and Cornets, little whereof could be understood of the people, neither would they suffer the Sacrament to be administered without a continuall noise of Musick, both instrumentall and vocal, to the great disturbance of these holy actions.[72]

In addition, as this same preacher observed, the Puritans wished to remove from the service all the elaborate trappings of the Catholic tradition. The view was that these, including music, distracted the worshiper.

> This makes me call to remembrance, a strange speech little better than blasphemy, uttered lately by a young man, in the presence of his Lord, and many learned men: 'I had rather goe forty miles to a good service, then two miles to a Sermon.' And what meant he by a good service? His meaning was manifest; where goodly Babylonish robes were worn, imbroydered with images. Where he might heare a delicate noise of singers, with Shakebuts, and Cornets, and Organs, and if it were possible, all kinde of Musicke, used at the dedication of Nabuchodonosors golden Image …

---

68 Sternhold and Hopkins, *Whole Book of Psalms*, quoted in Walls, 'London, 1603–49,' 295.
69 H. Davey, *History of English Music* (London, 1921), 107. A Church document of this period lists the organ as one of '84 Faults and Abuses of Religion.'
70 G. Ornsby, ed., 'The Correspondence of John Cosin, D.D.,' in *Surtee Society* (London, 1869), LII, 166.
71 Holman, 'London: Commonwealth and Restoration,' 307.
72 Peter Smart, *A Catalogue of Superstitious Innovations* (London, 1642), 9.

> For if religion consist in Alter-ducking, Cope-wearing, Organ-playing, piping and singing … If I say religion consist in these and such like superstitious vanities, ceremoniall fooleries, apish toyes, and popish trinckets, we had never more Religion then now.[73]

One result of the abandonment of instrumental music in the church at this time was a consequent loss of both church musicians and the teachers of the next generation. It was out of this concern that a petition was made to the government by a group of composers in 1657.

> By reason of the late dissolution of the Choirs in the Cathedrals where the study and practice of the Science of Music was especially cherished, Many of the skillful Professors of the said Science have during the late Wars and troubles died in want, and there being now no preferment or Encouragement in the way of Music, no man will breed his child in it, so that it must needs be, that the Science itself, must die in this Nation, with those few Professors of it now living, or at least it will degenerate much from that perfection lately attained unto.[74]

With his Restoration, Charles II introduced in his court the string orchestra tradition he had observed in Paris and thus it was at this time, in 1662, that strings made their entrance in the English church, as is precisely documented by John Evelyn.

> [One] of his Majesties Chaplains preached: after which, instead of the ancient grave and solemn wind musique accompanying the Organ was introduced a Consort of 24 Violins between every pause, after the French fantastical light way, better suited for a Tavern or Play-house than a Church: The was the first time of change, & now we no more heard the Cornet, which gave life to the organ, that instrument quite left off in which the English were so skillful.[75]

According to Roger North, the regional cathedrals of Durham and York continued to depend on wind instruments, even to substitute for missing voices.

> They have ordinary wind instruments in the choirs, as the cornett, sackbut, double curtal and others, which supply the want of voices, very notorious there; and nothing can so well reconcile the upper parts in a choir, since we can have none but boys and those none of the best, as the cornett (being well sounded) doth; one might mistake it for a choice eunuch.[76]

---

[73] Peter Smart, *A Sermon Preached in the Cathedrall Church of Durham, July 7, 1628* (London, 1640), 22ff.

[74] Quoted in Holman, 'London: Commonwealth and Restoration,' 307ff.

[75] *The Diary of John Evelyn*, III, 347ff, for December 21, 1662.

[76] Quoted in Wilson, *Roger North on Music*, 40.

MILITARY MUSIC

Military music in England at the dawn of the seventeenth century consisted only of the use of signals by the trumpet, fife and drum and military treatises of the period provide the names of many signals specific to each of these instruments. This required a level of musical appreciation on the part of the ordinary soldier far beyond that required today.

> Every soldier shall diligently observe and learn the distinct and different sounds of Drums, Fifes, and Trumpets, that he may know to answer and obey each of them in time of service.[77]

The drummer, because of this responsibility and because he was a noncombatant, led a contemporary writer to observe that he should be considered,

> rather a man of peace than of the sword, and it is most dishonorable in any man wittingly and out of knowledge to strike him or wound him.[78]

Further responsibilities led to the establishment of the position of 'Drum-major.' Among these responsibilities, other than being a man 'of great perfection in his science,'[79] were seeing to the provisions of the drums and fifes,[80] the discipline of these players ('with his staff correct the drums which fail in their duty'[81]) and 'likewise be well skilled in several languages and tongues.'[82]

The trumpeter was also carefully chosen and, according to Elton, must be 'a politic, discreet and cunning person.'[83] Sir James Turner adds,

> The trumpeter should be witty and discreet, and must drink little, so that he may be rather apt to circumvent others, rather than be circumvented; he should be cunning, and wherever his is sent, he should … observe warily the works, guards, and sentinels of an enemy, and give an account of them.[84]

A publication of 1635 says the trumpeter was given a sword, but with a broken point—to demonstrate that he was a noncombatant.[85]

---

77 *Lawes and Ordinances of Warre*, quoted in Grove, *Dictionary*, XII, 316.
78 Markham, quoted in Henry Farmer, *Military Music* (London: William Reeves, 1912), 40.
79 Thomas Digges, *An Arithmetical Warlike Treatise* (London, 1590).
80 Gerat Barry, *A Discourse of Military Discipline* (Brussels, 1634).
81 Du Praissac, *The Art of Warre* (Cambridge, 1639).
82 Richard Elton, *The Compleat Body of the Art Military* (London, 1650).
83 Ibid.
84 Sir James Turner, *Pallas Armata* (1683).
85 *Souldier's Accidence*, quoted in Farmer, *Military Music*, 40.

During the seventeenth century the timpani was introduced into the English military, but restricted to the higher ranking officers. In the early years of the eighteenth century the artillery units were allowed to have timpani and rather than carry them on horses they constructed special wagons for the purpose. A curious order during the Flanders Campaign of 1747 required the timpani players to 'mount the kettledrum carriage' and play all night long—presumably to make the enemy think the artillery was still firing.[86]

The military version of the Hautboisten band appears in 1678, together with the creation of the new Horse Grenadiers, and consisted of four oboes and two bassoons.[87] These bands, of course, played music and not mere signals. Therefore some officials considered them a luxury, as we can see in an order of 1731 which informed the Grenadier Company of the Honorable Artillery Company of London that they might have 'one curtail three hautboys and no more!'[88]

These players had to be recruited from the civilian world, rather than within the military, and it appears the Drum-major and Sergeant-trumpeter had the authority to 'impress,' which is to say kidnap, musicians for this purpose. It stands to reason that such players probably presented discipline problems for the career military leaders. Undoubtedly this explains a newspaper notice of 1724, which read,

> We hear that the Musick belonging to the 2d Regiment of Guards have been this Week at Richmond to beg their Royal Highnesses Pardon for their ill Conduct on the Thames some Days ago at Richmond.[89]

---

86 One of the few extant letters by Handel is one of February 24, 1750, requesting the loan of the 'Artillery Kettle Drums for use in the Oratorio's in this season.'

87 Peter Panoff, *Militärmusik* (Berlin: K. Siegismund, 1944), 130.

88 Henry Farmer, *Handel's Kettledrums* (London: Hinrichsen, 1965), 43.

89 Edward Croft-Murray, 'The Wind-Band in England,' in *Music & Civilisation* (London, 1980), 142.

2 AESTHETIC VIEWS OF ENGLISH MUSICIANS

ON THE PHILOSOPHY OF AESTHETICS

One finds, among these musicians, virtually no discussion of aesthetics beyond the subject of music. An exception is an interesting discussion by Charles Avison on the analogies between music and painting. Avison assumes that most of his public will be familiar with the basic aesthetic principles of the latter, but not the former, therefore he writes of the analogies between painting and music as a means of explaining musical composition to the general reader.[1] Both arts, he finds, are based on geometry and a sense of proportion in their subject. Whereas painting depends on design, coloring and expression, music depends on melody, harmony and expression. As Avison considers melody the most important element of music, he describes the relationship of the other elements as follows.

> Melody, or air, is the work of invention, and therefore the foundation of the other two [harmony and expression], and directly analogous to design in painting. Harmony gives beauty and strength to the established melodies, in the same manner as coloring adds life to a just design. And, in both cases, expression arises from a combination of the other two, and is no more than a strong and proper application of them to the intended subject.

He considers the mixture of light and shade in painting to be analogous to consonance and dissonance in music. Likewise, the elements of fore-ground, the effect of distance, etc., in painting corresponds in music to the ranges of the various parts, treble, tenor and bass. A charming analogy concerns the viewer and listener. Just as a viewer must stand at a certain distance to appreciate perspective in a painting, so the listener must be removed somewhat from the sound source to properly hear the correct balances.

> To stand close by a bassoon, or double-bass, when you hear a concert, is just as if you should plant your eye close to the fore-ground when you view a picture; or, as if in surveying a spacious edifice, you should place yourself at the foot of a pillar that supports it.

---

[1] Charles Avison, *An Essay on Musical Expression* [London, 1753] (New York: Broude Reprint, 1967), 20ff. Avison (1709–1770) was an organist and composer. We remind the reader that in music treatises we are interested only in comments which reflect on aesthetics, leaving out all technical discussion of the grammar of music.

Curiously, when Avison discusses the styles of painting, which he calls 'the grand, the terrible, the graceful, the tender, the passionate, the joyous,' he associates these qualities not with the emotions of music, but rather with the musical instruments.

ON THE AESTHETICS OF MUSIC

Regarding general definitions of music, we continue to find among the seventeenth-century musicians strong traces of the views of the Scholastic teachings of the medieval universities. Charles Butler, writing in 1636, clearly reflects the old distinction between theoretical and practical music when he defines music as consisting of what he calls 'Precepts and Uses or Ends.'[2] Precepts are taught through singing and composition; the Ends are two: Ecclesiastical, for the service of God, and Civil, for the solace of men. Butler's discussion of musical instruments reflects the final period in which the consort principle is a dominant aesthetic principle and he mentions in particular the popularity of the 'Set of Viols and Set of Waits,' the latter being a reference to the civic wind bands.

We see a specific remnant of Scholasticism in Christopher Simpson who, as late as 1667, still refers to music as a member of the family of mathematics.

> In this divine use and application, music may challenge a preeminence above all the other mathematical sciences as being immediately employed in the highest and noblest office that can be performed by men or angels.[3]

He then divides music into three categories, the first of which is the 'theory or mathematical part.' Next is the practical part, 'which designs, contrives and disposes those sounds into so many strange and stupendous varieties.' The third is the performer, after which he adds, 'any one of which three parts of music considered in itself is a most excellent art or science.'

Simpson follows this definition of music with a comment that vocal music is made 'for the solace and civil delight of man.' Among the vocal forms he first mentions the madrigal, followed by the interesting observation (for 1667!) that 'Dramatic or Recitative Music is yet something of a stranger to us here in England.'

He ranks the fantasia [*fancy*] as the highest kind of instrumental music, which he says unfortunately few people understand, 'their ears being better acquainted and more delighted with light and airy music.' Following this, 'in dignity,' is the pavan, which he notes was once ordained for grave and stately dancing, but now has 'grown up to a height of composition made only to delight the ear.'

---

2   Charles Butler, *The Principles of Musik in Singing and Setting* [1636] (New York: Da Capo Press, 1970), 93. Butler (d. 1647) was a music theorist attached to Oxford whose interests extended to agriculture and grammar.

3   Christopher Simpson, *A Compendium of Practical Music*, Second Edition of 1667 (Oxford: Blackwell, 1970), 76. Simpson (d. 1669) was a composer of string music, especially for the viola da gamba.

By the second half of the seventeenth century, however, most definitions of music had left mathematics behind and had begun to focus on music's relationship to the emotions. John Playford, for example, writing in 1674, found,

> Music is an Art unsearchable, Divine and Excellent, by which a true concordance of sounds or harmony is produced, that rejoiceth and cheereth the hearts of men.[4]

An important new influence on aesthetics was the rise of public concerts, which made the element of popularity, or fashion, a topic of concern which we will see below in several contexts. Thomas Mace, with his rather serious religious perspective, was at a loss to understand how mere public taste could take precedence over principles of art.

> But I cannot understand, how Arts and Sciences should be subject unto any such Fantastical, giddy or inconsiderate toyish conceits, as ever to be said to be in Fashion, or out of Fashion.[5]

In this regard he specifically objected to the current fashion of significantly doubling the upper voice in ensembles, thereby emphasizing melody over harmony and disrupting the equality of parts found in former styles.

By the end of the Baroque, we see in Avison a complete break with Scholastic dogma. It must have been much more dramatic at the time, than it seems to us, for him to state that musical communication is *not* of the realm of Reason.

> After all that has been, or can be said, the energy and grace of musical expression is of too delicate a nature to be fixed by words: it is a matter of taste, rather than of reasoning, and is, therefore, much better understood by example than by precept.[6]

For some musicians, the contemplation of the nature of music led to an almost Platonic view of music as a representative of a larger, divine harmonic order of the universe. This seems to have been in mind, for example, when the composer and organist, Martin Peerson (1572–1650) wrote in the dedication for his *Mottets or Grave Chamber Music* (1630),

> that heaven upon earth, which it found here, in Musicke and Harmonicall proportions, the being whereof is beyond Mortalitie and regulates the whole frame of nature in her being and Motions.[7]

---

4 John Playford, *An Introduction to the Skill of Music* [1674] (Ridgewood: Gregg Press, 1966), preface. Playford (1623–1686) was a publisher and amateur composer and theorist.

5 Thomas Mace, *Musick's Monument* [1676] (Paris: Éditions du Centre National de la Recherche Scientifique, 1966), 232ff. Mace (1613–1709) was a 'clerk' at Trinity College, Cambridge.

6 Avison, *An Essay on Musical Expression*, 81.

7 Quoted in Walls, 'London, 1603–49,' 283.

Some Englishmen searched for more concrete connections between the mystery of music and the physical laws of Nature. One of these was Robert Flud (1574–1637), a philosopher and physician whose extensive writings were largely ignored in the generations following him because he was a known member of the Rosicrucians.[8] Flud imagined the Earth and planets organized in a cosmic musical instrument, which he called a Mundane Monochord. The following, taken from his book, *De Musica Mundana* (1617), will give the reader some indication of the nature of his speculation.

> But it is to be considered that in this mundane monochord the consonances, and likewise the proper intervals, measuring them, cannot be otherwise delineated than as we divide the instrumental monochord into proportional parts; for the frigidity, and also the matter itself, of the earth, as to the thickness and weight thereof, naturally bears the same proportion to the frigidity as the matter of the lowest region, in which there is only one fourth part of the natural light and heat, as 4 to 3, which is the sesquitertia proportion; in which proportion a diatessaron consists, composed of three intervals, namely, water, air, and fire; for the earth in mundane music is the same thing as the fundamental in music, unity in arithmetic, or a point in geometry; it being as it were the term and sound from which the ratio of proportional matter is to be calculated. Water therefore occupies the place of one tone, and the air that of another interval more remote; and the sphere of fire, as it is only the summit of the region of the air, kindled or lighted up, possesses the place of a lesser semitone. But in as much as two portions of this matter are extended upwards as far as to the middle heaven to resist the action of the supernatural heat; and the same number of parts of light, act downwards against these two portions of matter, these make up the composition of the sphere of the sun, and naturally give it the attribute of equality, and by that means the sesquialtera proportion is produced, in which three parts of the lower spirit or matter of the middle heaven are opposed to the two parts of the solar sphere, producing the consonant diapente: for such is the difference between the moon and the sun, as there are four intervals between the convexity of this heaven and the middle of the solar sphere, namely, those of the entire spheres of the moon, Mercury, and Venus, compared to full tones, and the half part of the solar sphere, which we have compared to the semitone.

Christopher Simpson was moved by what he regarded as apparent, if mysterious, relationships between music and the rest of creation.

> I cannot but wonder, even to amazement, that from no more than three concords (with some intervening discords) there should arise such an infinite variety, as all the music that ever has been or ever shall be composed. And my wonder is increased by a consideration of the seven gradual sounds or tones, from whose various positions and intermixtures those concords and discords do arise. These gradual sounds are distinguished in the scale of music by the same seven letters which in the calendar distinguish the seven days of the week; to either of which, the adding of more is but a repetition of the former over again.

---

8   Flud was educated in the arts at Oxford, but his interests turned to physics. He traveled widely before resuming his studies in chemistry and physics. He eventually took a degree in medicine and became a member of the college of physicians in London.

> The mysterious number of seven, leads me into a contemplation of the universe, whose creation is delivered unto our capacity (not without some mystery) as begun and finished in seven days, which is thought to be figured long since by Orpheus his seven stringed lyre. Within the circumference of this great universe, be seven globes or spherical bodies in continual motion, producing still new and various figures, according to their diverse positions one to another. When with these I compare my seven gradual sounds, I cannot but admire the resemblance of their harmonies, the concords of the one so exactly answering to the aspects of the other; as an unison to conjunction, an octave to an opposition; the middle consonants to a diapason, to the middle aspects of an orb; as a third, fifth, sixth, in music, to a trine, quartile, sextile in the Zodiac. And as these by moving into such and such aspects bodies; so those, by passing into such and such concords, transmit into the ear an influence of sound, which doth not only strike the sense, but even affect the very soul, stirring it up to a devout contemplation of that divine principle from whence all harmony proceeds; and therefore very fitly applied to sing and sound forth his glory and praise.[9]

The View of Music in Society

Following the chaos of the civil war and the disruption of traditional life during the Cromwell Period, it should be no surprise to find reflections of a very difficult period for the arts. We see this clearly in the preface of John Playford's *Introduction to the Skill of Music* of 1674.

> But music in this age (like other arts and sciences) is in low esteem with the generality of people, our late and Solemn Music, both vocal and instrumental, is now jostled out of esteem by the new Courants and jigs of foreigners, to the grief of all sober and judicious understanders of that formerly solid and good music: nor must we expect harmony in peoples' minds, so long as Pride, Vanity, Faction, and Discords are so predominant in their lives.[10]

Playford mentions the low current state of the arts once again, following a plea for the use of English in art song.

> This author having set most of his examples and graces to the Italian words, it cannot be denied but the Italian language is more smooth and better vowelled than the English, by which it has the advantage in music, yet of late our language is much refined, and so is our music, to a more smooth and delightful way and manner of singing after this new method ... Therefore such as desire to be taught to sing after this way, need not seek after Italian or French masters, for our own nation was never better furnished with able and skillful artists in music than it is at this time, though few of them have the encouragement they deserve, nor must music expect it as yet, when all other arts and sciences are at so low an ebb.[11]

---

9   Christopher Simpson, *Division-Violist* (1654), here (London: Curwen, 1965, facsimile of 1665 edition), 23ff.
10 Playford, *An Introduction to the Skill of Music*, preface.
11 Ibid., 56.

One finds many references to a loss of seriousness in English music. Mace, writing of the pavane in 1676, describes them as grave, sober, full of art and profundity, 'but seldom used, in these our *Light Days*.'[12] Similarly, in the preface to a publication of sonatas by Purcell, we find,

> The author has faithfully endeavored a just imitation of the most famed Italian Masters; principally, to bring the seriousness and gravity of that sort of music into vogue, and reputation among our countrymen, whose humor, 'tis time now, should begin to loath the levity, and balladry of our neighbors ... The author has no more to add, but his hearty wishes that his Book may fall into no other hands but theirs who carry Musical Souls about them.[13]

For many writers, the lighter style was inevitably linked to the new fashion of the virtuoso, which seemed to follow the violin from Italy. Avison saw seventeenth-century music as a general transformation from music as a composer's medium to music as a performer's medium.

> Thus the old music was often contrived to discover the composer's art, as the modern is general calculated to display the performer's dexterity.[14]

In particular he laments the decay of the old style represented by the fantasias of the early seventeenth century. Today, he says, there is only 'that deluge of unbounded *Extravaganzi*, which the unskillful call invention, and which are merely calculated to show an execution, without either propriety or grace.'[15]

> Thus they strive, rather to surprise than to please the hearer: and, as it is easier to discern what is excellent in the *Performance*, than *Composition* of music; so we may account, why many have been more industrious to improve and distinguish themselves in the *Practice*, than the *Study* of this science.

What caused this transformation? Avison suggests first the lack of taste in the public had often caused 'the Masters to sacrifice their art to the gross judgment of an indelicate audience.' Second, he points to the use of 'trifling and unfruitful' melodies, unsuitable for development, compounded by composers who simply no longer take the time revise or rewrite.[16]

---

12 Quoted in Donnington, *The Interpretation of Early Music*, 401.

13 Henry Purcell (1658–1695), *Sonatas of III Parts* (1683), quoted in Sam Morgenstern, *Composers on Music* (New York: Pantheon, 1956), 32. The editor indicates this preface was actually written by John Playford.

14 Avison, *An Essay on Musical Expression*, 44.

15 Ibid., 31ff.

16 It is quite interesting to read of Avison's judgment of contemporary composers in this regard. He begins with the lowest group, those defective in harmony and invention, 'a fit amusement for children.' Here he includes Vivaldi, Alberti and Locatelli. In the next higher category, 'rising above the former in dignity,' he points to Hasse, Porpora, Terradellas and Lampugniani. The composers of the highest regard, in his opinion, are composers unknown today: Vinci, Bononcini and Astorgo. In another place [Ibid., 52ff], however, when speaking of contemporary composers who emphasized harmony in their compositions, he praises 'the chaste and faultless' Corelli, the 'bold and inventive' Scarlatti, the 'sublime' Caldara, 'the graceful and spirited' Rameau and, of course, Handel.

On the Purposes of Music

Following the movement begun by the humanists during the late Renaissance, English writers during the seventeenth century began to focus on the emotions as a fundamental component of aesthetics. It was in the context of this background of the earlier humanists, that Charles Butler (1636) spoke of emotions in terms of the 'divine frenzy' mentioned by the ancient Greek philosophers.

> [Good composing is impossible] unless the Author, at the time of Composing, be transported as it were with some Musical fury; so that himself scarce knoweth what he doth, nor can presently give a reason for his doing.[17]

The most interesting commentary on this question, in a general sense, is by Charles Avison, who began his book on aesthetics in music with this sentence:

> If we view this art in its foundations, we shall find, that by the constitution of man it is of mighty efficacy in working both on his imagination and his passions.[18]

While Avison recognized that music enters our awareness through the external senses, he found it was rather the internal senses which understand and profit.

> The capacity of receiving pleasure from these musical sounds, is, in fact, a peculiar and internal sense; but of a much more refined nature than the external senses: for in the pleasures arising from our internal sense of harmony, there is no prior uneasiness necessary, in order to our tasting them in their full perfection ... It is their peculiar and essential property, to divest the soul of every unquiet passion, to pour in upon the mind, a silent and serene joy, beyond the power of words to express, and to fix the heart in a rational, benevolent, and happy tranquility.

Avison gives great emphasis to his belief that music creates only 'sociable and happy passions' and tends to subdue those which are contrary to this. He recognizes that it is generally believed that the power of music can affect every emotion, however,

> I would offer to the consideration of the public, whether this is not a general and fundamental error. I would appeal to any man, whether ever he found himself urged to acts of selfishness, cruelty, treachery, revenge, or malevolence by the power of musical sounds? Or if he ever found jealousy, suspicion, or ingratitude engendered in his breast, either from harmony or discord? I believe no instance of this nature can be alleged with truth. It must be owned, indeed, that the force of music may urge the passions to an excess, or it may fix them on false and improper objects, and may thus be pernicious in its effects: But still the passions which it raises, though they may be misled or excessive, are of the benevolent and social kind, and in their intent at least are disinterested and noble.

---

17 Butler, *The Principles of Musik*, 92.

18 Avison, *An Essay on Musical Expression*, 2ff.

He immediately recognizes that some readers might consider the emotions of terror and grief to be an exception to what he has just written. But, no,

> terror raised by musical expression is always of that grateful kind, which arises from an impression of something terrible to the imagination, but which is immediately dissipated, by a subsequent conviction, that the danger is entirely imaginary … As to grief, it will be sufficient to observe that as it always has something of the social kind for its foundation, so it is often attended with a kind of sensation, which may with truth be called pleasing.

He admits it is difficult to give a reason for his theory, but ventures the explanation that since music immediately places the mind in a pleasurable state, the mind tends to associate with those emotions most agreeable to it.

> From this view of things therefore it necessarily follows, that every species of musical sound must tend to dispel the malevolent passions, because they are *painful*; and nourish those which are benevolent, because they are *pleasing*.

From the perspective of the seventeenth-century composer, the question of the emotions often began with the relationship with the words in sung poetry. For William Byrd, writing in his *Gradualia* (1605), the words were indeed the point of origin for his inspiration.

> There is a certain hidden power, as I learned by experience, in the thoughts underlying the words themselves; so that, as one meditates upon the sacred words and constantly and seriously considers them, the right notes, in some inexplicable manner, suggest themselves quite spontaneously.[19]

John Playford, quoting, in 1647, an unnamed 'English gentleman who had lived long in Italy,' reflects the growing influence of Italian music.

> To which manner I have framed my last Ayres for one voice to the Theorbo, not following that old way of composition, whose music not suffering the words to be understood by the hearers, for the multitude of divisions made upon short and long syllables, though by the vulgar such singers are cried up for famous. But I have endeavored in those my late compositions, to bring in a kind of music, by which men might as it were talk in harmony, using in that kind of singing a certain noble neglect of the song (as I have often heard at Florence by the actors in their singing operas) in which I endeavored the imitation of the conceit of the words, seeking out the chords more or less passionate … But, as I said before, those long windings and turnings of the voice are ill used, for I have observed that divisions have been invented, not because they are necessary unto a good fashion of singing, but rather for a certain tickling of the ears of those who do not well understand what it is to sing passionately; for if they did, undoubtedly divisions would have been abhorred, there being nothing more contrary to passion than they are … Whereas those that well understand the conceit and the meaning of the words … and can distinguish

---

19 Quoted in Donnington, *The Interpretation of Early Music*, 112.

where the passion is more or less required. Which sort of people we should endeavor to please with all diligence, and more to esteem their praise, than the applause of the ignorant vulgar.[20]

Similarly, in 1667 Christopher Simpson wrote,

> When you compose music to words, your chief endeavor must be that your notes do aptly express the sense and affections [*humour*] of them. If they be grave and serious, let your music be such also; if light, pleasant or lively, your music likewise must be suitable to them. Any passion of love, sorrow, anguish and the like is aptly expressed by chromatic notes and bindings. Anger, courage, revenge, etc., require a more strenuous and stirring movement. Cruel, bitter, harsh, may be expressed with a discord which, nevertheless, must be brought off according to the rules of composition.[21]

The most important English writer on this subject was Charles Avison, who wrote with great insight. In beginning a chapter called 'On Musical Expression, as it relates to the Composer,' Avison first dismisses text-painting as a proper source of communicating feeling in music. He makes the very important point that such devices only cause the listener to focus on secondary effects and not on the genuine feelings.

> Now all these I should choose to style imitation, rather than expression; because, it seems to me, that their tendency is rather to fix the hearers attention on the similitude between the sounds and the things which they describe, and thereby to excite a reflex act of the understanding, than to affect the heart and raise the passions of the soul.[22]

Likewise, music composed for poetry can only assist the emotion of the words and cannot literally be synonymous with the words. In fact, he suggests, the composer who strives to 'catch each particular epithet or metaphor' of the poetry will always, in the end, 'hurt the true aim of his composition.' His aim, according to Avison, must be rather to reflect the emotions in a more general sense.

> What then is the composer, who would aim at true musical expression, to perform? I answer, he is to blend such an happy mixture of melody and harmony, as will affect us most strongly with the passions or affections which the poet intends to raise: and that, on this account, he is not principally to dwell on particular words in the way of imitation, but to comprehend the poet's general drift or intention … If he attempts to raise the passions by imitation, it must be such a temperate and chastised imitation, as rather brings the object before the hearer, than such a one as induces him to form a comparison between the object and the sound. For, in this last case, [the listener's] attention will be turned entirely on the composer's art, which must effectually

---

20 Playford, *An Introduction to the Skill of Music*, 38ff.
21 Simpson, *A Compendium of Practical Music*, 77.
22 Avison, *An Essay on Musical Expression*, 57ff.

check the passion. The power of music is, in this respect, parallel to the power of eloquence: if it works at all, it must work in a secret and unsuspected manner.[23]

Modern clinical research indicates that musical perception in the brain depends greatly on a genetic repertoire of melodic patterns. It is most likely that these melodic patterns carry the basic emotional keys to which we, as listeners, respond. Therefore, as Avison correctly observes, a strophic song, which has a variety of verses to the same melody, is based on an impossible aesthetic premise. Avison calls this new style a 'remarkably ridiculous' one of the English of his day.

> I mean our manner of setting a single trifling melody, repeated to many verses, and all of them, perhaps, expressive of very different sentiments or affections, than which, a greater absurdity cannot possibly be imagined, in the construction of any musical composition whatsoever.[24]

In his search for melody, Avison cautions the composer to 'shun all the means of catching the common [popular] melody, which so strangely infects and possesses too many composers.' Better if he banish himself from 'almost every place of public resort and fly, perhaps, to monasteries, where the genuine charms of harmony may often be found.'[25]

Avison makes some interesting comments relative to the character of individual instruments and the expression of emotions. The oboe, he says, should be associated with gay and cheerful music and, interestingly enough, the transverse flute with 'languishing or melancholy style.'[26] The role of the trumpet is to animate and inspire courage, whereas the horn is to enliven and clear the spirits.

Some of Avison's most interesting and valuable comments deal with the nature of the familiar Italian words which today we associate primarily with tempo. It is the character of such words as 'Allegro' or 'Adagio,' not the 'time or measure,' he says, which distinguished their particular expression and he ties this idea with what he calls the three 'species of music: Church, Theater and Chamber.' Therefore,

> the same terms which denote Lively and Gay, in the Opera, or Concert Style, may be understood in the practice of Church Music as Cheerful and Serene ... Wherefore, Allegro [in church music] should always be performed somewhat slower than is usual in concerti and opera.[27]

Turning to the perspective of the performer, we begin by quoting an anonymous Jacobean song which reminds us that the performer has no doubt always, to some degree, performed to please himself.

---

23 Ibid., 69ff. In a footnote, Avison reflects that the 'wonderful effects' attributed to the ancient Greek composers must have been to 'the pure simplicity of melody.'
24 Ibid., 83ff.
25 Ibid., 87.
26 Ibid., 112ff.
27 Ibid., 123ff.

> My mistress is in musicke passinge skillful
> and singes & plaies her part at the first sight
> But in her play she is exceeding wilfull
> & will no plaie but for her owne delight.
> Nor touche a stringe nor plaie a pleasinge straine
> unless you catch her in a merie vaine.[28]

The most interesting comments relative to the performer at this time reflect the considerable freedom, by modern standards, permitted in expressing emotions. John Playford reflects an unusual degree of rubato.

> We see how necessary a certain judgment is for a musician, which sometimes useth to prevail above art
>
> ......
>
> I call that the noble manner of singing, which is used without tying a man's self to the ordinary measure of time, making many times the value of the notes less by half, and sometimes more according to the conceit of the words; whence proceeds that excellent kind of singing with a graceful neglect.[29]

Mace, in making similar comments in 1676, seems to suggest that the freedom in time extended even to form. If, he says, the music falls into sections, these may be played,

> according as they best please your own fancy, some very briskly, and courageously, and some again gently, lovingly, tenderly and smoothly.
>
> ......
>
> Beginners must learn strict time; but when we come to be masters, so that we can command all manner of time, at our own pleasures; we then take liberty ... to break time; sometimes faster and sometimes slower, as we perceive, the nature of the thing requires.[30]

Avison's discussion of the role of the performer, with respect to the communication of emotions in music, takes a surprising turn. Avison had an unusually accurate perception of the importance of communicating emotion in music and he wrote at a time when the performer had much more freedom than the performer today. It appears surprising, therefore, to find him recommending adherence to the score. Actually, we must view his comment in the context of his concern that Baroque music had become a performer's art and his desire to restore the center of aesthetic attention on the composer. In any case, he must have been one of the first to argue for a performance aesthetic which would become so characteristic of our own time.

---

28   Quoted in Walls, 'London, 1603–49,' 286.
29   Playford, *An Introduction to the Skill of Music*, 46, 52.
30   Mace, *Musick's Monument*, 429, 432.

> For, as musical expression in the composer, is succeeding in the attempt to express some particular passion; so in the performer, it is to do a composition justice, by playing it in a taste and style so exactly corresponding with the intention of the composer, as to preserve and illustrate *all* the beauties of his work.[31]

Since, as Aristotle established, aesthetics in the performing arts only has real meaning in the observer, we find particularly interesting comments on the seventeenth-century listener. First, there is William Byrd's plea for a contemplative listener, in the preface to his *Psalmes, Songs and Sonnets* of 1611.

> Only this I desire; that you will be but as careful to hear them well expressed, as I have been both in the composing and correcting of them. Otherwise the best song that ever was made will seem harsh and unpleasant, for that the well expressing of them, either by voices or instruments is the life of our labors, which is seldom or never well performed at the first singing or playing. Besides a song that is well and artificially made cannot be well perceived nor understood at the first hearing, but the oftener you shall hear it, the better cause of liking you will discover: and commonly that song is best esteemed with which our ears are most acquainted.[32]

One vivid portrait of an attentive audience is found in a description of a performance of Handel.

> The audience was so enchanted with this performance, that a stranger who should have seen the manner in which they were affected, would have imagined they had all been distracted.[33]

This suggestion of the distracted minds of the listeners was also mentioned by James Talbot, writing of the Sarabande in 1690. He describes it as soft and passionate in character, 'apt to move the Passions and to disturb the tranquility of the Mind.'[34]

On 'Ethos'

By Ethos, or the Doctrine of Affections, we go beyond merely communicating emotions to the listener to the idea that music can specifically affect the character of the listener. Charles Butler, in 1636, expresses this idea in language similar to that used by nearly all early writers.

> Music ... having a great power over the affections of the mind, by its various Modes produces in the hearers various affects.[35]

---

31 Avison, *An Essay on Musical Expression*, 107ff.
32 Quoted in Donnington, *The Interpretation of Early Music*, 117.
33 J. Mainwaring, *Memoirs of Handel* (1760), quoted in Donnington, Ibid., 96.
34 Quoted in Ibid., 402.
35 Butler, *The Principles of Musik*, 112.

John Playford, in 1674, is much more specific.

> Nor doth music [not] only delight the mind of man, and beast, and birds, but also conduceth much to bodily health by the exercise of the voice in song, which doth clear and strengthen the lungs, and if to be also joined the exercise the limbs, none need fear asthma or consumption; the want of which exercise is often the death of many students: Also much benefit hath been found thereby, by such as have been troubled with defects in speech, as stammering and bad utterance. It gently breathes and vents the Mourners grief, and heightens the joy of them that are cheerful: it abates spleen and hatred, the valiant soldier in fight is animated when he hears the sound of the trumpet, the fife and drum: All mechanical artists do find it cheers them in their weary labors. Scaliger (Exercet. 302) gives a reason of these effects, because the spirits about the heart taking in that trembling and dancing air into the body, are moved together, and stirred up with it; or that the mind, harmonically composed, is roused up at the tunes of music. And farther, we see even young babes are charmed asleep by their singing nurses, nay the poor laboring beasts at plow and cart are cheered by the sound of music, though it be but their master's whistle.[36]

Thomas Mace made fervent testimonials to the power of music. He begins in a passage where he is lamenting the music of former times, specifically the consort music of the early seventeenth century.

> We had for our grave music, Fancies of 2, 3, 5, and 6 parts to the organ; interposed (now and then) with some pavans, allmaines, solemn, and sweet delightful ayres; all of which (as it were) so many Pathetical Stories, Rhetorical and sublime discourses; subtle, and acute argumentations, so suitable, and agreeing to the inward, secret, and intellectual faculties of the soul and mind; that so set them forth according to their true praise, there are no words sufficient in language; yet what I can best speak of them, shall be only to say, that they have been to myself (and many others), as divine raptures, powerfully captivating all our unruly faculties, and affections (for the time) and disposing us to Solidity, Gravity, and Good Temper, making us capable of Heavenly, and Divine influences.
>
> It is a great pity few believe thus much; but far greater, that so few know it.[37]

The fashion today, he laments, has replaced these things with an emphasis on the virtuoso performer, 'the Great Idol,' and music,

> which is rather fit to make a man's ears glow, and fill his brains full of frisks, etc., than to season, and sober his mind, or elevate his affection to Goodness.

---

36 Playford, *An Introduction to the Skill of Music*, preface. Playford also relates,

> Myself, as I traveled some years since near Royston, met a herd of stags, about twenty, upon the road following a bagpipe and a violin, which while the music played they went forward, when it ceased they all stood still.

37 Mace, *Musick's Monument*, 234. One of the interesting things Mace presents in his book is his design for the ideal performance hall.

During his discussion of country church music, Mace's heartfelt testimonial to the moral virtues of music becomes more personal.

> For if [children] be once truly principled in the grounds of piety and music when they are young, they will be like well-seasoned vessels, fit to receive all other good things to be put into them. And I am not only subject to believe, but am very confident, that the vast jarrings, the dischording-untunableness, over-spreading the face of the whole earth, might be much rectified, and put into tune sooner this way, than by any other way that can be thought upon.
>
> This I speak from an experience in my own soul, who am a man subject to the passions and imperfections of the worst of men. Yet by this virtue, this sublime elixir of musical and harmonical divinity, have found as much (in a comparative way) as this comes to, upon my own soul and violent passions.
>
> It cannot be too often repeated, how the evil spirit departed from Saul, when David played upon his harp. True music being a certain Divine-Magical-Spell, against all diabolical operations in the souls of men. But how little this is taken notice of, believed, or regarded by most, is grievous and lamentable to be thought upon.[38]

Performance Practice

When Orlando Gibbons wrote in the preface to his *Madrigals and Mottets* of 1612,

> Experience tells us that songs of this nature are usually esteemed as they are well or ill performed,[39]

he was reflecting in part a transformation taking place during the seventeenth century in which the spotlight was moving from the composer to the performer. Perhaps this also prompted John Playford's observation, 'Art admitteth no Mediocrity.'[40]

This attention to performance was extended to the smallest details, even to a single note, as Christopher Simpson observed, 'Loud and soft sometimes occur in one and the same note.' This is apparently what Roger North had in mind when he wrote,

> Learn to fill, and soften a sound, as shades in needlework, in sensation, so as to be like also a gust of wind, which begins from a soft air, and fills by degrees to a strength as makes all bend, and then softens away again into a temper, and so vanish.[41]

With the movement toward a more homophonic style of music, there followed a new interest in the quality of ensemble sound. In particular, one frequently reads of the necessity for

---

38 Ibid., 12.
39 Quoted in Donnington, *The Interpretation of Early Music*, 117.
40 Playford, *An Introduction to the Skill of Music*, 41.
41 Both quoted in Donnington, *The Interpretation of Early Music*, 487.

hearing the lower voices, to balance the ear's natural tendency to focus on the highest part. A typical comment is found in the writings of Thomas Mace.

> You may add to your press a pair of violins, to be in readiness for any extraordinary jolly or jocund consort occasion; but never use them but with this proviso, viz., be sure you make an equal provision for them, by the addition and strength of basses, so that they may not out-cry the rest of the musick, the basses especially; to which end it will be requisite you store your press with a pair of lusty, full-sized Theorboes, always to strike in with your consorts or vocal musick, to which that instrument is most naturally proper.[42]

As part of the new attention to performance, the seventeenth-century treatises discuss improvisation, or ornamentation, in great detail. Our interest lies only in those comments which reflect on the aesthetic nature of ornamentation and these seem to fall into two areas of concern. First, several writers stress that ornamentation must not obscure the words, as Charles Butler points out in 1636.

> Too much quaint Division, too much shaking and quavering of the Notes, all harsh straining of the Voices beyond their natural pitch, as they are odious and offensive to the ear; so do they drown the right sound of the words.[43]

Second, there seemed to be a concern that ornamentation must sound natural. This point is charmingly made by Anthony Aston, who writes in 1748 of a boy whose singing was interrupted by a suggestion that he add improvisation [run a Division] in a certain place.

> O let him alone, said Mr. Purcell; he will grace it more naturally than you, or I, can teach him.[44]

Relative to this second concern was an often expressed suggestion that something important was lost if the composer attempted to actually write out the ornamentation. Charles Burney recalled Henry Purcell complaining that writing everything out robs music of its special quality of being performed in the present tense ['modernized by a judicious performer']. When one plays written music, it is automatically music of the past ['obsolete and old fashioned'].

> Purcell, who composed for ignorant and clumsy performers was obliged to write down all the fashionable graces and embellishments of the times, on which accounts, his Music soon became obsolete and old fashioned; whereas the plainness and simplicity of Corelli have given longevity to his works, which can always be modernized by a judicious performer, with very few changes or embellishments.[45]

---

42 Quoted in Hawkins, *A General History of the Science and Practice of Music* (1776), II, 732.
43 Butler, *Principles of Musik* (London, 1636), quoted in Donnington, *The Interpretation of Early Music*, 153.
44 Anthony Aston, *Brief Supplement to Colley Cibber, Esq.* (1748), quoted in Ibid., 155.
45 Burney, *A General History of Music* [1776], II, 443.

Avison joins many others in observing that ornamentation was 'impossible to be expressed' in notation. His chief concern was that since every performer viewed this practice individually, the result was that the student became 'discouraged in the progress of his study.'[46]

EDUCATIONAL MUSIC

Mace also emphasizes the importance of training children in music. Not only does he have in mind the improvement of church music, but he reminds the reader of the social advantages associated with music education.

> It will adorn your children much more than ten times the cost can be worth, which you shall bestow upon them in the gaining of it.
> Besides, it will make them acceptable to all ingenious people, and valued amongst the best. They will be more capable of preferment in the world, in case of any necessity.[47]

He recommends that all children in grammar school should have one hour of music taught them every day. The cost of finding a music teacher would be minimal, or as he calls it a 'little-poor-trifle' or 'pitiful inconsiderable.'

Handel as a teacher, was remembered by Charles Burney, who was nineteen at the time (1745) he describes.

> He was a blunt and peremptory disciplinarian on these occasions, but had a humor and wit in delivering his instructions, and even in chiding and finding fault, that was peculiar to himself, and extremely diverting to all but those on whom his lash was laid.[48]

Judging by an extant letter of Handel to Johann Mattheson, however strict the former may have been in his discipline, he was at least not a teacher who blindly followed former dogma. When Mattheson had questioned the value of continuing to study the old Scholastic, math-based rules of composing in the style of earlier polyphony, Handel indicates he generally agrees with this viewpoint, adding,

> The question seems to me to reduce itself to this: whether one should prefer an easy & most perfect Method to another that is accompanied by great difficulties capable not only of disgusting pupils with Music, but also making them waste much precious time that could better be employed in plunging deeper into this art & in the cultivation of one's genius?[49]

---

46 Avison, *An Essay on Musical Expression*, 126.
47 Mace, *Musick's Monument*, 14ff.
48 Charles Burney, *A General History of the Science and Practice of Music* (London, 1789), IV, 666.
49 George Friedrich Handel, letter to Johann Mattheson, February 24, 1719, quoted in Piero Weiss, *Letters of Composers Through Six Centuries* (Philadelphia: Chilton, 1967), 63.

Avison, in his concern for the direction of English music, makes a number of suggestions for educating would be composers. He recommends it would be helpful if someone would publish a history of important composers, explaining their 'characteristic taste and manner.'[50] He seemed to feel support and direction was necessary to prevent young talents from turning their attention 'to instant profit, rather than to future fame.'

FUNCTIONAL MUSIC

Especially because of the intrusion of the Puritans, there was considerable discussion of church music by seventeenth-century musicians. In view of subsequent history, we find particularly interesting John Playford's observation, in 1674, that music is the only science allowed in the doors of the church.[51]

With regard to aesthetics, the most interesting writer is Thomas Mace, who writes on the emotions of the music, performer and congregation in a way which would never have been allowed by the Church fathers in former centuries. Mace, to make a modern paraphrase, said let's appeal to *both* brains, the rational and the emotional.

> All things in the church, and in its service, would be contrived and ordered, that the common-poor-ignorant-people might be so much capable as it is possible of apprehending, discerning or understanding; so, as they might unite their voices, hearts and affections together with the congregation and the service.[52]

Mace mentions the affections of the congregation in the above, and indeed he places considerable emphasis on the importance of the church composer reflecting emotions, especially with regard to the words of the Psalms, in his music. This entire relationship, of music and words, and of their impact on man, was regarded by Mace as little studied.

> There being a very great affinity, nearness, naturalness or sameness between language and music, although not known to many. And it is a bemoanable pity to consider how few there are who know, but fewer who consider, what wonderful-powerful-efficacious virtues and operations of music has upon the souls and spirits of men divinely-bent.[53]

In this regard, Mace concluded his book with the thought that music might be the form of communication used in heaven.

---

50 Avison, *An Essay on Musical Expression*, 98.
51 Playford, *An Introduction to the Skill of Music*, preface.
52 Mace, *Musick's Monument*, 1.
53 Ibid., 3.

> And I am subject to believe (if in Eternity we shall make use of any languages, or shall not understand one another, by some more spiritual conveyances, or infusions of perceptions, than by verbal language) that music itself may be that eternal and celestial language.[54]

When Mace turns his attention to country churches, he finds the Psalms tortured and tormented, the Service dishonored, coarse and made ridiculous by the quality of the music. He was particularly exercised by the quality of the singing and declared it better not to sing at all than sing out of tune. This, because of the close relationship he perceived between music and the divine.

> For as I often used to say, that as conchording unity in music is a lively and very significant simile of God, and Heavenly joys, and felicities, so on the contrary, jarring discords are as apt a simile of the Devil, or Hellish tortures.[55]

Considering that if even one with an absolute voice is 'uncertain of singing in tune,' he wonders what can one expect from 'the unskilfull-inharmonious-coarse-grained-harsh-voice?' Certainly God takes no pleasure from such 'halt, lame and blind sacrifices.' Mace's solution for helping the country congregation is the organ and he writes at length explaining the kind of instrument needed, how the funds can be raised and how to find an organist.

The cathedral churches Mace also found wanting, with insufficient numbers of singers. The small numbers were further decimated by frequent absences,

> by reason of sickness, indispositions, hoarseness, colds, business, and many other accidents, and necessary occasions, men must be absent, disabled, or impeded from doing their duties; so that at such times, the Service must suffer: and such like accidents happen too often.[56]

And, of those present, 'few of them are (or can possibly be) masters in the art of song, or singing; much less in the art of music in general.'

The reason for this state of affairs was the poor pay given cathedral singers, which Mace found 'very low, inconsiderable, insufficient, unbecoming and uncomfortable.' As a consequence, the singers often were forced to take other jobs. Why should we be surprised, Mace asks, that when they sing in church they 'make sour faces, and cry, or roar out aloud.' He concludes,

> Now I say, these things considered how certainly true they are, first in reference to the [singers] pitiful-poor-wages, and likewise to the general dead-heartedness, or zeal-benumbed-frozen-affections in these our time, toward the encouragement of such things; how can it be imagined that such [singers] should be fit and able performers in that duty, which necessarily depends

---

54 Ibid., 272.
55 Ibid., 3.
56 Ibid., 23ff.

upon education, breeding and skill in that quality of music, which is both a costly, careful and a laborious-attainment, not at all acquirable (in its excellency) by an inferior-low-capacitated men.

Avison, whose entire discussion of musical expression was based on the communication of emotions, even stressed that the church organist must feel the appropriate emotions while he plays if he is to succeed.

> If our organist is a lover of poetry, without which, we may dispute his love for music; or indeed, if he has any well-directed passions at all, he cannot but feel some elevation of mind, when he hears the psalm preceding his voluntary, pronounced in an awful and pathetic strain: It is then he must join *his* part, and with some solemn air, relieve, with religious cheerfulness, the calm and well-disposed heart. Yet, if he feels not this divine energy in his own breast, it will prove but a fruitless attempt to raise it in that of others.[57]

He also finds the congregation does not sing with enough emotion and makes the interesting observation that he wishes they sang as they do when they visit a foreign church, without reading line by line.

---

57 Avison, *An Essay on Musical Expression*, 88.

3 ROGER NORTH

ROGER NORTH (1653–1734), an amateur musician born to a well-to-do family and educated in law, brought to his writing a breadth of knowledge not enjoyed by his contemporaries who wrote on music and who were primarily working musicians. Of all the English Baroque writers on music before Avison, North is the only one whom might be also called a philosopher.

ON THE PHYSIOLOGY OF AESTHETICS

Roger North seemed to understand through deduction and observation that the mind of man is clearly divided into rational and experiential forms of understanding, or what we refer to today as the left and right hemispheres of the brain. In the following passage he attempts to explain the distinction between rational learning, such as language, and music. After so many centuries during which higher education in music emphasized so-called 'speculative,' or as we would say today, theoretical, music, it is of the utmost significance that North attempts here to separate real musical learning from conceptual studies. In the final sentence he hints at the lesson we still have not learned, that conceptual teaching is foreign to what children instinctively love in music.

> The teaching of music and languages are very different, although the masters of the former affect the methods used by them of the other; that is, a sort of grammar to be [learned] by heart, whether it be or be not understood. The difference lies in this, that languages are mere memory, and come from the arbitrary use of nations, and may be as well one way or another; and this use grammarians endeavor to reduce to rule, which must be learnt and remembered. But music is taken from nature itself, and depends on body in a physical sense, even as the mathematical sciences do, and takes place finally in our imagination and fancy; and therefore should be taught by explaining it to the understanding as well as by giving the rules to which the practice of it is reduced. And for this reason it is that in the musical science the rules are very few, and those but introductory as it were to show what the subject matter is, that the learner might not have the trouble of being an original inventor of the whole science ... And yet the real knowledge that belongs to music is dilated enough, and it is through that, that a man must learn the skill of a musician, whether he be showed it, or gathers it of himself by observation, as generally is done ... As for children, I think easier ways might be found than the soured and mysterious Gamut, which they must rehearse *antrorsum & retrorsum*, without the least proffer to them of an explanation of it.[1]

---
1   Quoted in Wilson, *Roger North on Music*, 59.

He touches on the distinction between language and music again in his attempt to explain what makes a good melody [*Ayre*], admitting he cannot express this in words.

> The design here is not to frame rules for composition, which is of another nature, and must extend much wider to comprehend the many items of that art in which learners will need to be informed; but only to frame some Idea or Notion of Ayre, which cannot fully be expressed in words.[2]

North is the first English writer of the Baroque to attempt to speculate on the nature of the perception of music. Like Aristotle he has observed that people tend to like best the music they already know. But this suggests that mere familiarity, and not intrinsic values, makes music so powerful in its communication. North seems to know this cannot be correct, but he is unable to explain it. It is interesting that we find here the earliest written rationale for the *ritornello* principle.

> I am of opinion that use goes a great way in the acceptance of music, and that be it really in true judgment better, if folks are not used to the manner they will not like it … as if music had not the virtue intrinsically to please, but doth it by accident or custom, after some acquaintance with it. It is certain that the air of music is improved by repetition, and is always better the second time than the first, and so on, till some novelty suppresseth it. For this reason it is that we have so many repeats and *ritornellos*.[3]

In another place he adds an additional explanation for the *ritornello* principle, which also reflects the ancient philosophers' concern for the transitory nature of music.

> And the reason is, the sense is always better satisfied in a foreknowledge of what is to come, than to be surprised with anything entirely new, which comes, and is gone before it is enough reflected upon.[4]

North is also the first English musician to address the important aesthetic principle of universality in music.

> I am of opinion that if a musical entertainment doth not please all tastes, it is not as it should be, and there is fault in the design, composition, or performance … It seems better, and much more heroic, to calculate music by the measures of universal knowledge, and experience of Humane Nature, with all the passions and affections indifferently incident to all men; and this, done by a lofty instructed genius, and rightly understood, will assuredly pass for good music [Air].[5]

---

[2] Ibid., 84.
[3] Ibid., 69.
[4] Ibid., 177ff.
[5] Ibid., 70ff.

North had obviously given much thought to the element of time in music and concluded that there is also something universal about the perception of time, perhaps even something genetic in character ('planted … in our vital faculties').

> As for the arm in swinging, I shall appeal to it as governed by pendulum law. Nothing unequal timed is pleasing, as if equality had planted its capital residence in our vital faculties.[6]
>
> ……
>
> Nothing of failure is less excused than missing time; for the audience being once possessed of a current measure, esteems it an injury to be interrupted by any fracture, and are apt to continue it in their minds in its due course as it should have been till turned adrift by the miscarriage, and until they can get a new hold to conduct them.[7]

ON THE AESTHETICS OF MUSIC

Before considering North's formal attempts to define and classify music, we should like to note a remarkable passage in which he surveys the obstacles and limitations which are always conspiring to make great music making difficult.

> It is a greater undertaking to set forth a piece of music, than a poem, for that requires only the poet's wit and pains. But music demands not only utmost spirit and decorum in the composition, but little less than perfection in the performance, which is not always found; and the nicety in that quarter is such, that any miscarriage spoils the design. And diverse other mishaps poor music is liable to, as bad instruments, missing tune or time, and what is worst of all, the taste of the audience is commonly prejudicate and bizarre. Some affect one kind and will not bear another, and few allow any to be good that jumps not with their caprice.[8]

The core of North's definition of music, with respect to performance, is his classification of four types of music: solitary, social, ecclesiastical and theatrical. By solitary music he means the music one makes for oneself, either for amusement or for solace.

> With respect to amusement, and relief of an active mind distressed either with too much, or too little employment, nothing under the sun hath that virtue, as a solitary application to music. It is a medicine without any nausea or bitter, and is taken both for pleasure and cure.[9]

---

6   Ibid., 95.

7   Ibid., 96.

8   Ibid., 70.

9   Ibid., 257ff.

His most interesting comments on 'social music' are relative to goals which the composer should attempt to achieve.

> People are apt to censure the whole according to the first and last relish.
>
> ......
>
> Whether the subject be merry or sad, the beginning of a work ought to be serious, and as much as may be majestic.
>
> ......
>
> There should be a continual regard to Humanity; for if there be in Nature any means to move the passions and affections, which were never denied to music, those ought to be pursued, as the best or rather the only means to please.

Church music, more than any kind of music, satisfied two of North's preferences—it was completely solemn ('all levities are excluded') and it was composed of a large sound, with an accompanied full chorus. Here, he says, 'is a body of melody and harmony to fulfill the sharpest appetite to music.' It is interesting that he also mentions the aesthetic advantage given the music by the architecture of the building in which it is performed.

North laments a serious shortage of singers available for church choirs and for this reason he recommends that perhaps the time has come to admit female singers into the choir.

> One might without a desperate solescisme maintain that if females were taken into the choirs instead of boys, it would be a vast improvement of choral music, because women come to a judgment as well as voice, which the boys's do not arrive at before their voices perish ... But both text[10] and morality are against it; and the Roman usage of castration is utterly unlawful, and a scandalous practice where it is used.

Regarding music for the theater, North objected to a tendency for melody to be common in style, vulgar he says, and because of the emphasis on melody the inner parts tended to have little purpose. This music, he says, should be left to its proper owners, the ordinary musicians. Such popular music 'is most apt for driving away thinking, and letting in dancing.'

North concludes his definition of music by adding that the two primary purposes of music are to please and to communicate emotions.

> Therefore in order to find the criteria of Good Music we must look into Nature itself, and the truth of things. Music hath two ends. First to please the sense, and that is done by the pure Dulcor of harmony, which is found chiefly in older music ... Secondly, to move the emotions, or excite the passion; and that is done by measures of time joined with the former [the emotions]. And it must be granted that pure impulse, artificially acted and continued, hath great power to excite men to act, but not to think.[11]

---

10 I Corinthians 14:34:

>   As in all the churches of the saints, the women should keep silence in the churches.

11 Quoted in Wilson, *Roger North on Music*, 291ff.

He now expands on these ideas, beginning by returning to the point he wishes to stress about time and rhythm.

> I must sever the virtue of time in music, from the music itself, as having another scope and effect; and may be said to stir up comfortable actions, but not to excite thinking or please the sense.
>
> And as to all of music, besides the bare pleasing the sense, it must be referred to a power, by similar sounds, of bringing to our minds or memory the state of joy or grief, or of less important affections, as may be conform to what we hear. As for instance, who can hear the miserable clamor of one in affliction, without compassion? And whence that, but from a sensible reflection or memory of the same or like circumstances? And music by its sounds doth the same, and through the same operation of mind; for a savage, or brute, that hath no reflex thoughts, is not at all moved by compassionate sounds … I have instanced grief, but the case is the same in all the various states of humanity; for by hearing certain sounds that are like what men commonly use by way of expressing their then present condition, our minds are affected accordingly …
>
> But as to the point of better or worse intrinsically, reason may determine, but feeling [*humour*] must govern and pronounce. For the states of Humanity are infinitely various, and admit of all degrees of good and evil, important or frivolous, sane or distracted. And it must be granted that music which excites the best, most important and sane thinking and acting is, in true judgment, the best music; and this will fall upon the ecclesiastical style.

Views of Music in Society

English literature of the late sixteenth century was strongly critical of young men who, upon completion of the university, went to Italy to 'complete' their education. It is interesting therefore, that North not only approved such travel to Italy, once referring to her as 'Italy, where music is queen,'[12] but attributed to this exposure an important influence on English music.

> The other circumstance I hinted was the numerous train of young travelers of the best quality & estates, that about this time went over into Italy & resided at Rome & Venice, where they heard the best music and learned from the best masters … and they came home confirmed in the love of the Italian manner, & some contracted no little skill & proved exquisite performers; then came over Corelli's first consort that cleared the ground of all other sorts of music whatsoever; by degrees the rest of his consorts & at last the concerti came, all of which are to the musicians like the bread of life.[13]

---

12   Ibid., 9.

13   Roger North, *The Musicall Gramarian* (Oxford: Oxford University Press, 1925), 37.

But on the other hand, North did not consider all foreign styles equally good and in thinking along these lines he adopts one of his more pessimistic tones.

> As Rome was destroyed by the Asiatic luxury, so the musical republic will sink to nothing under the weight of these numerous curiosities lately brought over it. The flourishing of an art or science, is the number and value of the professors, and those obtaining their end, which in music is pleasure, and an innocuous employ of spare time, with a recreation, in the intervals of business, the gain and credit is egregious; all which fell out when the art was plain and practicable and most sober families in England affected it. Now it is come to that pass, that few but professors can handle it, and the value is derived upon high flights & numbers of capital performers, which may have brought an audience but the promiscuous and diffused practice of music in remote parts about England is utterly confounded. And an ostentatious pride hath taken Apollos' chair and almost subverted his monarchy.[14]

ON THE PURPOSES OF MUSIC

For North, the central purpose and meaning of music, and consequently the core of his understanding of aesthetics in music, is its ability to communicate feeling. We understand today that it *is* the most important virtue of music, but, before the humanists began to think in these terms during the sixteenth century, this had been a concept opposed for a thousand years by the Church, and therefore for the entire early history of modern university study in music. While North is indebted to the earlier humanists, none of them expressed so clearly the dimension of this role of music.

> My thoughts are first in general that music is a true pantomime or resemblance of Humanity in all its states, actions, passions and emotions. And in every musical attempt reasonably designed, Humane Nature is the subject ... so that a hearer shall put himself into the same condition, as if the state represented were his own ... So the melody should be referred to [man's] thoughts and emotions. And an artist is to consider what manner of expression men would use on certain occasions, and let his melody, as near as may be, resemble that.[15]

In vocal music North considers the matter of expressing emotions rather obvious, as they are contained in the words the singer sings—thus the singer is much to blame if he fails to express the proper emotions.[16] In objecting to 'ridiculous absurdities' which result in some singers 'humoring the words,' North makes an important observation.

---

14 Ibid., 41.

15 Quoted in Wilson, *Roger North on Music*, 110ff.

16 Ibid., 112.

For the sounds are not to represent the things commonly signified by words, but the thoughts of the person that uses them.[17]

He discounts most of what we call 'text-painting' as something which corrupts music and as not reflecting what he means by expressing emotions.[18] Neither does merely the use of high or low pitches accomplish this. Because he finds some cantatas have lines more instrumental in character, he concludes that only singers should compose vocal music.[19]

The communication of specific emotions in instrumental music, because there are no words, North finds it more difficult, indeed 'we are much more at a loss than before.'[20] In this case, he finds the composer has primarily two resources. The first is harmony, 'which runs through the whole work and like the soul animates the mass ... therefore it is a chief care.'

> The other is Humanity. I do not recollect any action of inanimates, and scarce of brutes, that can be brought under imitation in music, without relation to Humanity ...
>
> And here I must once for all observe that a fool can never be a good composer, nor a good painter. We do no mean of certain felicities that some derive from Nature, such as buffoonery and the like, but of reasonable invention; and who should ever be capable to represent anything, whereof he hath in his own mind no manner of Idea? Works of art in perfection do not come by accident but by design, though many times an happy conjuncture of the work and the spirits shall instill what may be called the sublime, at another time perhaps not to be reached; yet even that must fall under the correction of a good judgment, else it may prove *ignis fatuus* and good for nothing. Therefore a composer if he would not be counted a trifler, should understand the affairs of the world, and men; in a word, Humane Nature, with all its passions and affections, whereof in his compositions there must be found some sort of resemblance, as well as Harmony; as if he aimed to instruct, as well as to please ...
>
> And so music consists of harmony, and measure, which is called time. And in effect harmony works upon the thoughts, and the time upon the actions, of humane kind ... And it may be a rule, that no music can be well timed, that may not be danced, or with which men's actions may not conform.

Next, North attempts to deal more specifically with emotions.[21]

> As for the passion of grief, it must be considered that every man living hath been sensible of it in himself, or in others, and acquainted with, or felt, the [mortal] occasions, and heard or made those dolorous cries that proceed from it.

---

17 Ibid., 112ff.

18 In another place [Ibid., 266], North makes this point again and states that text-painting does not communicate emotions, because,

> ... having no relation to any state of humanity, such sounds lay hold of no passion ...

19 Ibid., 113ff.

20 Ibid., 115ff.

21 Ibid., 119ff.

For such emotions, which he categorizes as 'sedate griefs,' one ordinarily uses the flat keys. However,

> the utterances of extreme pain, torture, or fright in any creature can never be represented in music, for they are always the worst of discord. But the extremes of joy and happiness are commonly expressed in the sharp keys, imitating trumpets and merry sings usual on such occasion; and all the dancing, theatrical, and festive music is chiefly of that kind.

He follows this with a very rare view of the familiar Italian words which refer only to tempo today, but originally carried more subjective meanings.

> But the hardest task is to square with a state either of business or of common conversation, unless the *Allemand* and *Fugue* do it. The *Adagios* are designed for pure and simple harmony, for which reason measure of time is so little regarded in them. The *Grave* comes nearer a sober conversation, and the *Allegro* light and chirping. The *Tremolo* is fear and suspicion, the *Andante* is a walking about full of concern, the *Ricercata* is a searching about for somewhat out of the way; the *Affectuoso* is expostulating, or *amour*; and so every other manner, as masters are pleased to title them, are but so many states of humane life, as they have a fancy to represent or imitate.

It is particularly interesting to find North assigning some responsibility to listener for the perception of the feelings expressed in the music.

> If the listeners did not extend only their long ears to the entertainment in music, but a regulated understanding also, they would please themselves with exercising their critical talents upon it, which scarcely any do now, but say only, This is very better, that worse. And they are very free of their tokens of rapture—very fine, great, stately, full, ayery, and such like indefinites—but not a wise word why or wherefore; all which a cat may pretend to as well as a man … The study of this art hath enough to recommend it, being assisting to the composer and instructing to the hearers of music, and indeed adds a pleasure to life; for by all experience it is found, that no art gives equal pleasure to the ignorant and intelligent in it, but much the greatest share redounds to the latter.[22]

On this subject, in another place North suggests that the listener needs to be a certain distance from the music, although unfortunately he does not elaborate on this idea. It occurs to him as he is objecting to the difficulty the listener has in hearing fast, multi-part instrumental works such as fugues, or fugal allegros.

> Perhaps an ear placed in the middle of the performers may distinguish somewhat, but at a decent position, the sum is a musical din, and no better; and music, like pictures, ought to have a just distance, or else the parts it consists of, which in all entertainments ought to be perceptible, will blend as in a mist.[23]

---

22 Ibid., 124.
23 Ibid., 189.

North now offers some observations on the communication of emotions in various forms. Church music he has observed can have such effect that the listeners find 'they could not conceive any one nerve or vein in their whole body to be at rest.'[24] Church music 'being maintained in such a rigorous chastity, and ever serious ... [is] universally esteemed the best of music.' Of operas, he observes,

> There is certainly magnificence enough in them, and they may exhibit all the powers of Art, to move the audience ... There is nothing of music heretofore known among us, that ever matched the valuable part of our operas.

'Soft music,' presumably some forms of chamber music, North has found does not move the listener as the larger church and opera forms.

> Soft music is also useful in a private application, as to dispose great persons to rest, and thereby laudable beyond imagination; so also chamber entertainments, and decoration of a song, or at a levee, are all very good, and may please, but not ravish.

Indeed, anything which centers on entertainment, fails, in North's view, to achieve the higher purpose of music.

> Lord! how at the wagging of an elbow the whole theater claps, though no single note is heard: just like a circle of fools laughing at the wagging of a feather, such power hath ignorance and partiality. I would go to such music and pay my scott as I do to the posture man, or a rope dancer, to see somewhat done which I scarce thought possible. But if I went for the sake of the music in earnest, it should be to feel my spirits moved, and together with the delightful sounds, enjoy the gentle enlivenings of passions, which ... may justly be accounted the best of human life.[25]

Going beyond the communication of emotions, North seemed to believe with the ancient Greeks that music had the ability to affect character, something no doubt he arrived at primarily from his own amateur music making in the home. Unfortunately he does not elaborate on this, taking an easier path by making observations on the secondary effect of music. North reflects on the early days of the seventeenth century when amateur music making in the country homes of the upper class flourished. He saw a link between the rising professional level of performance, and the consequent centering of performance in London, with the decline of the earlier amateur tradition. Taking music out of the home, in his view, created the opportunity for a decline in morals.

> And this is done by observing that vice will start up to fill the vacancy. When we know not how to pass the time, we fall to drink. If company is not at home, we go out to markets and meetings to find such as will join in debauchery. There can scarce be a full family kept, because this

---
24 Ibid., 125ff.
25 Ibid., 129.

humor of drunkening let in all manner of lewdness. Even fathers and daughters, with servants and children male and female, go into promiscuousness. And it is scarce reasonable to expect better unless you can provide diversion, to fill the time of the less employed part of a gentile family … By this you may judge what profit the public hath from the improvement of music. I am almost of Plato's opinion, that the state ought to govern the use of it.[26]

On Performance

North discusses performance problems in some detail, but we remind the reader that our interest lies primarily in those comments which reflect on questions of aesthetics. First, he was clearly concerned that the impression which the performance of music makes on the listener depended to some degree on simple precision. As he observes in some manuscript notes,

> Music demands not only utmost spirit, and decorum in the composition, but little less than perfection in the performance, which is not always found.[27]

He found this was most often achieved by the presence of the composer, reminding us that before our century virtually every composition was composed for one performance. This is especially important to remember with regard to Baroque music, which was usually written with the specific talents of the particular performers in mind.

> In solemn consorts, it would scarce be possible to proceed without some one director of the time; who is commonly the composer.[28]

In another place, North makes an extraordinary recommendation regarding ensemble precision.

> To my very great hazard of reputation, I have affirmed that with 2 violins set to play the same part, if perfectly in tune to each other, it is better music is one goes a little before or behind the other, than when they play (as they zealously affect) together. For in that, nothing is achieved by the doubling, but a little loudness; but in the other way, by the frequent dissonances there is a pleasant seasoning obtained.[29]

---

26 Ibid., 11ff.
27 Quoted in Donnington, *The Interpretation of Early Music*, 118.
28 Quoted in Wilson, *Roger North on Music*, 105.
29 Ibid., 172.

This irregularity 'gives an excellence few have observed or will allow' and 'must be done with great moderation.' In his view, however, it produces a,

> sparkle in the accord, as air and light doth to the eye in a landscape, and is an elegance which painters in their art cannot describe … for in all arts the sovereign beauty, as of women, are a *je ne scay quoy*.

North especially appreciated dynamic variation in performance, in particular a controlled *crescendo* and *diminuendo*. He thought the voice was most adapt at this, followed by wind instruments and then strings, including the new violin which he calls 'the nightingale of instruments.'[30] He thought it a nice idea if phrases began loud and ended soft. Ties and dissonance should 'pressed hard,' which creates attention in the listener.

> Then when you come off into a sweeter calmer air, as to a cadence, which often follows such passages, then be soft and easy, as much as to say, Be content all is well.

North, in his autobiography, points to his study of the music for decisions such as the above.

> I was very much assisted as a performer by my knowledge of and acquaintance with the music. It gave me courage as well as skill to fill and swell where the harmony required an emphasis.[31]

He also observes that it might help performances if the soft passages were notated in red ink and the loud in black ink.

On Singing

In North's discussion of singing in general,[32] we find that, as with instrumental music, his preference was for full, if not loud, sound.

> They say the English have no good voices, because few sing well … The English have generally voices good enough, though not up to the pitch of warmer countries; witness the cries and ballad singers—some women singing in the streets with a loudness and drowns all other noise, and yet firm and steady. Now what a sound would that be in a theater, cultivated and practiced to harmony! … But come into the theater or music-meeting, and you shall have a woman sing like a mouse in a cheese, scarce to be heard, and for the most part her teeth shut.

Among North's objections to singers was that their training has been in the fundamentals of vocal training, but not in the essentials of ear-training and musicianship.

---

30 Ibid., 218ff.
31 Quoted in Donnington, *The Interpretation of Early Music*, 489.
32 Quoted in Wilson, *Roger North on Music*, 215ff.

> They do not understand the art of music that sing in public, but are scholars and taught [by those] not able to do anything themselves, and consequently cannot well distinguish when they do well and when ill. For this reason they will be horribly out of tune; and all this by a little understanding would correct itself in others as also in themselves. If it be said, some have no ears and cannot; I answer, send them to shops and trades, and let not the public be molested with their want of ears.

He also finds among singers, that 'women are fearful of the distortion of the face, which is their *sanctum sanctorum*, and therefore the sound is checked.'

On Programming

In the first public concerts in London which were known to North, he was bothered by what he perceived to be a lack of aesthetic order. Whether it be a fireworks display, or comedy or tragedy, he attributed the success with the audience with a plan in which the event began slowly and gradually increased in intensity. But in concerts he found only disorganized variety.

> A song, fugue, a solo or any single piece may be very good in their several kinds, but for want of a due coherence of the whole, the company will not be pleased. And thus it is with the music exhibited in London publicly for a half crown. A combination of masters agree to make a consort as they call it, but do not submit to the government of any one, as should be done, to accomplish their design. And in the performance, each take his parts according as his opinion is of his own excellence. The master violin must have its solo, then joined with a lute, then a fugue, or sonata, then a song, then the trumpet and oboe, and so other variety, as it happens ... And the company knows not whether all is ended, or anything is more to come, and what.[33]

An even worse idea for programming, in the view of North, was competition. While he admits the importance of aristocratic money in supporting music, he is much opposed to a current trend in London whereby nobles contribute money to a 'pot' to be given to the performer who pleases them best in a concert. Competition in music, he says, has largely negative results.

> Instead of encouraging the endeavors of all, the happy victor only was pleased, and all the rest were discontented and some who thought they deserved better, were almost ready to [give up music] ... So much a mistake it is to force artists upon a competition, for all but one are sure to be malcontents.[34]

---

33 Ibid., 13ff.

34 Roger North, *Memoirs of Music*, ed. Edward Rimbault (London: Bell, 1846), 118ff. An advertisement in the London Gazette for March 21, 1699, reads,

> Several persons of quality having, for the encouragement of musick advanced 200 guineas, to be distributed in 4 prizes, the first of 100, the second of 50, the third of 30 and the four of 20 guineas shall be adjudged to compose the best.

After concluding, from his own experience, that no concert should last more than one hour, North writes of some additional objections to the new emphasis on professional concerts. First, he observes that since performance is itself a pleasurable activity, the players enjoy a pleasure 'which the audience cannot pretend to.' Second, because the performers play so well, the members of the audience who may be amateur performers become discouraged, wishing to achieve such a level of performance themselves but knowing they cannot.

Another source of puzzlement for the aristocratic audience may have been related to their deportment. North points to an Italian violinist, Nicolai Matteis, whose popularity in London was hampered by his artistic demands when he played at court, for he,

> behaved himself *fastously*; no person must whisper while he played, which sort of attention had not been the fashion at Court.[35]

Improvisation

On the subject of ornamentation, we are again concerned with comments which reflect on some aspect of aesthetics, and not the usual recitation of rules. North begins by attempting to explain the contribution of ornamentation to the beauty of the composition.

> Gracing is like lace on a garment, which doth not give a beauty without an handsome contour of the whole. And such effect is there from the true, though the plainest, music; which may be wholly spoiled by the offering at graces, which loose the sound without giving any compensation for it, but is not much mended by even the best gracing, because the delicacy lies in true harmony of sound, which is the substance; the rest is pretty, but trifling, and of little weight ... But in common cadences, and passages, it is left to the performer.[36]
>
> ......
>
> And a plain sound not thus set off, is like a dull plain color, or as a bad copy of a good picture, that wants the spirit and life, which a sparkling touch gives it. Thus a life and warmth in the coloring of a picture is well resembled to graces in music, that are not the body but the soul that enlivens it, or as the animal spirits that cannot be seen or felt, but yet make that grand difference between a living and a dead corpse.[37]

North is one of many musicians during the Baroque who, influenced by the long tradition of improvisation in music, question whether it is even possible to write on paper 'all' of the music. In a discussion of 'The Art of Gracing,'[38] North finds,

---

35 Ibid., 123.
36 Quoted in Wilson, *Roger North on Music*, 27.
37 Ibid., 28.
38 Ibid., 149ff.

> It is the hardest task that can be, to pen the manner of artificial Gracing of an upper part. It hath been attempted, and in print, but with woeful effect. One that hears, with a direct intent to learn, may be shown the way by a notation, but no man ever taught himself that way. The spirit of that art is incommunicable by writing, therefore it is almost inexcusable to attempt it.

He observes the growing tendency for composers to attempt to write everything out and reflects the objections by the performers to this new practice. His final comment here is very interesting. One often finds quoted an early critic who maintained that Italian composers of this period wrote what they wanted played and therefore there should be no further improvisation. We believe North's understanding is probably the more accurate, at least for music before the very end of the Baroque.

> But to set them down in the music book is such pains, and for the continual use and smallness of them, so intricate, puzzling and unintelligible, that with the best musicians they are altogether omitted. But of late some masters, to encourage their scholars by ease, have in their printed songs done it. But if it be for the ease of scholars who have been taught, in remembering their lesson, it is very disadvantageous to the better performers … for it is not easy to know which is the true note, and where the emphasis falls, so the beauty is lost. The Italians who I think may be our masters, never express ornamentation, but write the true note which governs the harmony, and leave the ornamentation to the skill and capacity of the performer.

And again,

> The most skillful of the elder Italians leave all those matters [ornamentation] to the performers, and write their music plain … But they had the soul of music in their compositions, which the moderns, with their many motive and slurring ornaments, have corrupted.[39]

EDUCATIONAL MUSIC

North writes in several places on the subject of music education, a subject which he seems to have given more thought to than most of his contemporaries.[40] His first recommendation is that the teacher should be older, rather than a young man. The older man has more experience and is more likely to have reasons for what he teaches, as opposed to mere intuition. Also the younger teacher is much more likely to seduce the children, especially the daughters, whereas the older man who has a family of his own will be more prudent.

One should teach music the way one teaches the beginner in manufacture, he suggests, beginning with the fundamentals and proceeding step by step. North stresses that the beginning point in music is tone, the development of a clear plain sound with no ornaments. Next

---
39 Ibid., 263.
40 Ibid., 16ff.

he recommends the development of a crescendo of this tone, 'the louder and harsher the better.' This is how one learns to develop body in the sound, 'which else will be faint and weak.'

> Then next I would have them learn to fill, and soften a sound, as shades in needlework, by imperceptible steps, so as to be alike a gust of wind which begins with a soft air, and fills by degrees to a strength as makes all bend, and then softens away again … and so vanish.

North recommends careful teaching of ornaments, especially trills, which disturb the basic pitch. He also advises the introduction of lessons in harmony at an early stage in teaching. This is all so complicated and difficult that the child is unlikely to want to pursue music for pleasure. Therefore the parent must insist.

> But parents have authority, and do exert it in these cases, to oblige their children to endure the fatigue of learning many things, which they would altogether decline if left to themselves. Therefore if there be not either compulsion, or an extraordinary inclination and perseverance, it is in vain for a master to pursue teaching; and the one supposed, the other must be granted.

Since the study of fundamentals is so tedious, North recommends getting the student into an ensemble, 'which is the greatest perfection and pleasure music can afford to performers.'

North returns to the tedious nature of the study of fundamentals with some advice which might well be considered by modern music education. There is, North reminds us, more to music than meets the eye.

> It were to be wished that a talent of unfolding secrets in music, so making them familiar to the understanding of beginners, went always along with the profession of teaching.[41]

He concludes by lamenting the opportunities for music education then available in England.

> And as to the learning of music in general, I must out of my experience say, that of those persons who are so happy to acquire it, more teach themselves, than are taught. And all that advantage is from society: for all arts are more effectually learned under a social than under a solitary discipline, and none more eminently so than music … It is an unhappiness in England that there are not music schools for young people to be taught, [as there are] reading and writing schools.[42]

---

41 Ibid., 60.
42 Ibid., 238.

FUNCTIONAL MUSIC

On the subject of church music, we find only one comment by North which is out of the ordinary. Speaking of chant, he observes,

> Now to give a censure of this kind of music, I must own myself far from approving it, because there is no scheme or design in it; for beginning middle and ending are all alike, and it is rather a murmur of accords, than music.[43]

---

[43] North, *The Musicall Gramarian*, 9.

4 JACOBEAN PHILOSOPHY

AS WE HAVE MENTIONED ABOVE, the first half of the seventeenth century in England, with its civil wars and the agitation by the Puritans, offered a poor climate for prose in general. For these reasons, in philosophy one finds a curious mixture of some remarkably objective thought juxtaposed with Puritan dogma. These Protestant preachers were capable of twisting any passage of scripture, or any reference from ancient literature, in order to amplify their severe demands of religious discipline. A typical example of the latter is John Bunyan's extension of the famous Greek temple inscription, to read, 'Know thyself, what a vile, horrible, abominable sinner thou art.'[1]

ON THE PHYSIOLOGY OF AESTHETICS

Robert Burton, in his classic *The Anatomy of Melancholy* (1621), offers little beyond 'weird science' in his discussion of brain function.[2] Being limited to the observation of brains in cadavers, he curiously sees a 'fore and hinder' division of the brain, instead of a right and left hemisphere. Like Descartes, he makes the incorrect deduction that the significant action occurs in the spaces between the folds of the brain, rather than in the brain itself. It is into these spaces that 'animal spirits' travel from the heart.

Much of what we associate with the brain, Burton locates in the 'soul,' which in turn he subdivides into the faculties of vegital, sensitive and rational.[3]

> This *sensible soul* is divided into two parts, *apprehending* or *moving*. By the *apprehensive* power we perceive the species of sensible things, present or absent, and retain them as wax doth the print of a seal. By the *moving* the body is outwardly carried from one place to another, or inwardly

---

1 'The Saints' Knowledge of Christ's Love,' in *The Works of John Bunyan*, ed. George Offor (London: Blackie and Son, 1853), II, 28. John Bunyan (1628–1688) is considered the greatest prose writer among the Puritans of the seventeenth century. Only the Bible was so widely read in English homes for the subsequent three centuries. Bunyan was also the epitome of the 'hell and brimstone' preacher.

2 Robert Burton, *The Anatomy of Melancholy*, ed. Floyd Dell (New York: Tudor Publishing Company, 1938), 134ff. Robert Burton (1577–1640) was educated at Oxford and became vicar of St. Thomas Church in that town. Although this book has little validity in view of modern knowledge, it had a long history of influence, including Charles Lamb, Milton, Keats and Thackeray.

3 Ibid., 135ff.

moved by spirits & pulse. The apprehensive faculty is subdivided into two parts, inward or outward; outward, as the five senses, of touching, hearing, seeing, smelling, tasting …

In the 'rational soul' Burton places all aspects of what we understand as Reason today.[4] The soul itself, he locates in the brain.

The emotions, on the other hand, Burton does not locate in the brain, but in the heart (as did many earlier philosophers). The heart, he says,

is the seat and fountain of life, of heat, of spirits, of pulse, and respiration: the Sun of our body, the King and sole commander of it: the seat and organ of all passions and affections … by whose motion it is dilated or contracted, to stir and command the humors in the body: as in sorrow, melancholy; in anger, choler; in joy, to send the blood outwardly; in sorrow, to call it in; moving the humors, as horses do a chariot.[5]

These 'humors,' which are mentioned extensively in seventeenth-century literature, especially in Germany, are given the following definition by Burton.[6]

A humor is a liquid or fluent part of the body, comprehended in it, for the preservation of it; and is either innate or born with us, or adventitious and acquisite …

Blood is a hot, sweet, temperate, red humor, prepared in the *meseraick* veins, and made of the most temperate parts of the *chylus* in the liver, whose office is to nourish the whole body, to give it strength and color, being dispersed by the veins through every part of it. And from it *spirits* are first begotten in the heart, which afterwards by the *arteries* are communicated to the other parts.

Pituita, or phlegm, is a cold and moist humor, begotten of the colder parts of the *chylus* (or white juice coming out of the meat digested in the stomach) in the liver; his office is to nourish and moisten the members of the body, which, as the tongue, are moved, that they be not over dry.

Choler is hot and dry, bitter, begotten of the hotter parts of the *chylus*, and gathered to the gall: it helps the natural heat and senses, and serves to the expelling of excrements.

Melancholy, cold and dry, thick, black, and sour, begotten of the more faeculent part of nourishment, and purged from the spleen, is a bridle to the other two hot humors, *blood* and *choler*, preserving them in the blood, and nourishing the bones. These four humors have some analogy with the four elements, and to the four ages in man.

We might mention here, a clever syllogism by John Donne, in his 'Paradoxes and Problems,' by which he demonstrates the superiority of intelligence in women.

They that have the most reason are the most alterable in their designs, and the darkest and most ignorant, do seldom change; therefore Women changing more than Men, have also more Reason.[7]

---

4 Ibid., 144ff.

5 Ibid., 133.

6 Ibid., 128ff.

7 John Donne, 'Paradoxes and Problems,' in *Selected Prose*, ed. Helen Gardner (Oxford: Clarendon Press, 1967), 5. John Donne (1573-1631) studied at both Oxford and Cambridge, but as a born Catholic was not permitted to receive a degree. After various attempts at professions brought him to poverty, he converted to the official Church, became famous for his sermons and eventually became Dean of St. Paul's.

In William Harvey, in his *Lectures on the Whole of Anatomy* (1616), we see one of the great thinkers in the early field of medicine commenting on current medical theories, before his brilliance as an original thinker suddenly emerged. In this early work we find largely weird science.[8] He divides the trunk of the body into three sections, and it is in the middle portion where he locates the vital spirits and the emotions.[9]

Harvey published his classic study on the circulation of the blood in 1628, after ideas he had worked out by 1615, a work which must be regarded as the first legitimate study of its kind in modern medicine. Of most importance to our topic is a passage in which he discusses the 'spirits' which are mentioned in many seventeenth-century discussions dealing with the emotions and music. He begins with a review of current beliefs.

> Medical Schools admit three kinds of spirits; the natural spirits flowing through the veins, the vital spirits through the arteries, and the animal spirits through the nerves; whence physicians say, based on Galen, that sometimes the parts of the brain are oppressed by sympathy, because the faculty with the essence, i.e., the spirit, is overwhelmed; and sometimes this happens independently of the essence.[10]

But Harvey is the first among philosophers to clearly acknowledge that,

> we have found none of all these spirits by dissection, neither in the veins, nerves, arteries, nor other parts of living animals.

Harvey notes that professors speak of other kinds of spirits, the spirit of fortitude, of prudence, of patience and 'the holy spirit of wisdom.' But of these he remarks, 'there is nothing more uncertain and questionable.' Still, for all his inability to recognize any physical form of 'spirit,' Harvey nevertheless recognizes an existence of something more than metaphor.

> Blood and these spirits signify one and the same thing, though different,—like generous wine and its spirit; for as wine, when it has lost all its spirit, is no longer wine, but a vapid liquor or vinegar; so blood without spirit is not blood, but something else—clot or cruor.[11]

The great preacher, John Bunyan, was not interested in such clinical insights relative to anatomy. It is to the soul that he attributes understanding, judgment, the emotions and the senses.[12] Regarding the latter, he categorically states that it is not the body which hears, but the soul—a conclusion he somehow based on Job 4:12–13.

---

8   He declared, for example, that a long neck in men was a sign of timidity. William Harvey, *Lectures on the Whole of Anatomy*, trans. C. D. O'Malley (Berkeley: University of California Press, 1961), 156. William Harvey was physician to the king and a professor of the College of Physicians in London.

9   Ibid., 35.

10 *The Works of William Harvey*, ed. Robert Willis (Reprinted New York: Johnson Reprint Corp., 1965), 116ff.

11 Ibid., 117.

12 'The Greatness of the Soul,' in *The Works of John Bunyan*, I, 110ff.

> Now a word was brought to me stealthily,
> my ear received the whisper of it.
> Amid thoughts from visions of the night.

In another place, Bunyan gives an example of the 'truth' of the senses being corrupted by Reason. This is the sense of height, as in the distance to heaven which he says 'is obvious to our senses [except] when it is dealt with by our corrupted reason.'[13]

Today, in view of the recent discoveries in clinical research of brain function, we understand by the separate natures of the left and right hemispheres much of what earlier philosophers pondered in the competition between Reason and the emotions. We now know, for example, that it is the right hemisphere which supplies emotional color to the left hemisphere's vocabulary, thus rendering precise meaning. It is interesting that Bunyan arrived at the essence of this purely by intuition.

> The best prayers have often more groans than words: and those words that it has are but a lean and shallow representation of the heart, life and spirit of the prayer.[14]

John Donne also arrived by intuition at the (incorrect) idea that it is the heart which rules man. In a treatise known as 'Meditation II,' he calls the heart, and not the brain, the 'Principalitie, and in the Throne, as King, the rest as Subjects.'[15] In another place, he suggests that if Nature explains how we differ in our 'essence,' we would all be alike, whether idiot or 'Wizard,' as we all have the same *kind* of Reason.[16] This is a conclusion easily arrived at before the modern understanding of brain hemispheres. Donne is essentially correct with respect to the left hemisphere, where all men are identical in knowledge (all agree two plus two is four, etc.), but it is in the right hemisphere where we are unique, its understanding being experiential and therefore differing with each man.

For most philosophers, however, it was still a battle between Reason and the emotions. Joseph Hall, like nearly all clerics before him, warns that the affections can overwhelm Reason. The affections he calls the 'secret factors of sin and Satan,' which must be controlled by Reason and religion.

> If there be any exercise of Christian wisdom, it is in the managing of these unruly emotions ... Reason has always been busy in undertaking this so necessary a moderation; wherein, although she has prevailed with some of colder temper; yet those which have been of more stubborn metal,

---

13 'The Saints' Knowledge of Christ's Love,' in Ibid., II, 8ff.

14 'On Praying in the Spirit,' in Ibid., I, 631.

15 John Donne, *Devotions Upon Emergent Occasion*, ed. Anthony Raspa (Montreal: McGill-Queen's University Press, 1975, 56.

16 John Donne, 'Paradoxes and Problems,' in *Selected Prose*, 13.

like unto grown scholars, which scorn the ferule and ruled their minority, have still despised her weak endeavors ... Christianity gives not rules, but power, to avoid this short madness.[17]

Burton also acknowledges the great power, and danger, of the emotions in their capability to overwhelm Reason.

> Good discipline, education, philosophy, divinity, may mitigate and restrain these passions in some few men at some times, but for the most part they domineer, and are so violent, that as a torrent, bears down all before, and overflows his banks, lays bare the fields, lays waste the crops, they overwhelm reason, judgment & pervert the temperature of the body. The charioteer is run away with, nor does the chariot obey the reins.[18]

The physiological process by which the emotions overcome Reason, according to Burton, begins as follows:

> Thus in brief, to our imagination comes, by the outward sense or memory, some object to be known (residing in the foremost part of the brain) which he, misconceiving or amplifying, presently communicates to the heart, the seat of all emotions. The pure spirits forthwith flock from the brain to the heart by certain secret channels, and signify what good or bad object was presented; which immediately bends itself to prosecute or avoid it, and, withal, draws with it other humors to help it. So in pleasure, concur great store of purer spirits; in sadness, much melancholy blood; in ire, choler.[19]

James Harrington's utopian *Oceana* (1656) presents a rather simplistic view of man as being torn between his reason and his emotions. In his view, the entire purpose of laws is to prevent man from following his emotions. The reader should perhaps be reminded that this book was written during the Commonwealth Period, when Puritan values were so strongly emphasized.

> The soul of man (whose life or motion is perpetual contemplation or thought) is the mistress of two potent rivals, the one reason, the other passion, that are in continual suit; and, according as she gives up her will to these or either of them, is the felicity or misery which man partakes in this mortal life.
>
> For, as whatever was passion in the contemplation of a man, being brought forth by his will into action, is vice and the bondage of sin; so whatever was reason in the contemplation of a man, being brought forth by his will into action, is virtue and the freedom of soul ...

---

17 'Heaven upon earth,' in *The Works of Joseph Hall, D. D.*, ed. Philip Wynter (New York: AMS Press, 1969), VII, 14ff. Joseph Hall (1574–1656) was a bishop in the Church of England.
18 Robert Burton, *Anatomy of Melancholy*, 218.
19 Ibid., 219.

> If the liberty of a man consists in the empire of his reason, the absence whereof would betray him to the bondage of his passions, then the liberty of a commonwealth consists in the empire of her laws.[20]

We have mentioned in these volumes another manifestation of the separate functions of the twin hemispheres of the brain, and that is the strong preference which the speaking and writing left hemisphere assigns to the right hand. Among the examples of this prejudice in this literature, we find John Donne praying,

> with thy left hand lay his body in the grave ... and with thy right hand receive his soul into thy Kingdom ...,[21]

and Bunyan promising those saved will sit at the right hand of God.[22] It is 'on the right hand,' that Christiana and Prudence hear 'a most curious melodious note, with words,' made by birds in Bunyan's *Pilgrim's Progress*.[23]

As Harvey was the first to take courageous steps away from the myths concerning various 'spirits' flowing through the body, he was also the first to break away from the thousand-year-old Church dogma which held that the senses could not be trusted. Harvey was a rare philosopher who gave full credit to information derived from the senses, with the understanding that the role of Reason is to make judgments on that information. He illustrates his understanding of the association of Reason and the senses by making a comparison with geometry.

> Were nothing to be acknowledged by the senses without evidence derived from reason, or occasionally even contrary to the previously received conclusions of reason, there would now be no problem left for discussion. Had we not our most perfect assurances by the senses, and were not their perceptions confirmed by reasoning, in the same way as geometricians proceed with their figures, we should admit no science of any kind; for it is the business of geometry, from things sensible, to make rational demonstration of things that are not sensible.[24]

Thus, because he gives the senses legitimacy, and the personal experience which results, he can observe,

> How difficult is it to teach those who have no experience, the things of which they have not any knowledge by their senses!

---

20 Henry Morley, *Ideal Commonwealths* (Port Washington: Kennikat Press, 1968), 192ff.
21 John Donne, 'Seventeenth Prayer,' in *Devotions Upon Emergent Occasion*, 90.
22 'Saved by Grace,' in *The Works of John Bunyan*, I, 362.
23 'Pilgrim's Progress,' in Ibid., III, 205.
24 *The Works of William Harvey*, 131.

In his *The Generation of Animals*, Harvey demonstrates a very modern understanding that it is the brain into which all the senses directly feed and where their information is examined.[25]

A line in Romans 10:17, 'So faith comes from what is heard, and what is heard comes by the preaching of Christ,' inspires the Puritan preacher, Joseph Hall, to offer this discussion of two of our senses, sight and hearing.

> These two are the senses of instruction: there is no other way for intelligence to be conveyed to the soul, whether in secular or spiritual affairs: the eye is the window, the ear is the door by which all knowledge enters: in matters of observation, by the eye; in matters of faith, by the ear.[26]

On Education

Joseph Hall draws on the metaphor of a cracked bell to begin an attack on teachers.

> What a harsh sound does [a cracked] bell make in every ear! The metal is good enough; it is the rift that makes it so unpleasingly jarring.
>
> How too like is this bell to a scandalous and ill-lived teacher. His calling is honorable; his noise is heard far enough; but the flaw, which is noted in his life, mars his doctrine, and offends those ears which else would take pleasure in his teaching. It is possible that such a one even by that discordous noise, may ring in others into the triumphant church of heaven; but there is no remedy for himself but the fire.[27]

He was also concerned with the dangers of sending children to school in the cities, especially foreign ones.

> The concourse of a populous city affords many brokers of villainy, which live upon the spoils of young hopes, whose very acquaintance is destruction. How can these novices, that are turned loose into the main ere they know either coast or compass avoid these rocks and shelves, upon which both their estates and souls are miserably wrecked? ... Do we send our sons to learn to be chaste in the midst of Sodom?[28]

Burton observes that universities can give degrees, but for all the world they cannot 'give learning, make philosophers, artists, orators or poets.'[29] After expressing this qualification on the end of education, he calls attention to the pitfalls facing the student. If they are of

---

25 Ibid., 432.
26 'The Baolm of Gilead,' in *The Works of Joseph Hall*, VII, 78.
27 'Occasional Meditations,' in Ibid., X, 146.
28 'A just Censure of Travel,' in Ibid., IX, 531ff.
29 Robert Burton, *Anatomy of Melancholy*, 263ff.

a docile personality, 'they are either seduced by bad companions, they come to grief with wine and women.' If they be 'studious, industrious, of ripe wits and good capacities,' then,

> how many diseases of body and mind must they encounter! No labor in the world like unto study! It may be, their temperature will not endure it, but, striving to be excellent, to know all, they lose health, wealth, wit, life, and all.

And after all of this, after his education is completed, what does he look forward to?—perhaps a position as a chaplain in a gentleman's house, or secretary to a nobleman or be assigned a small rectory. But these positions are all insecure, and 'to say truth, it is the common fortune of most scholars to be servile and poor, to complain pitifully, and lay open their wants to their respectless patrons.'

> Now for poets, rhetoricians, historians, philosophers, mathematicians, sophisters, etc., they are like grasshoppers, sing they must in Summer, and pine in the Winter, for there is no preferment for them.

In view of these prospects, Burton was not surprised that most students were attracted only to those professions which held out the promise of large financial rewards.

> Our ordinary students, right well perceiving in the universities how unprofitable these poetical, mathematical, and philosophical studies are, how little respected, how few patrons, apply themselves in all haste to those three commodious professions of law, medicine and divinity, sharing themselves between them, rejecting these arts in the mean time, history, philosophy, philology, or lightly passing over them, as pleasant toys fitting only table talk, and to furnish them with discourse.

Burton is quick to add that he does not intend a general condemnation of the two great universities of England, Oxford and Cambridge, but their reputation is tarnished by the fact that a few 'idiots & mountebanks' have slipped through and some now hold important theological positions.[30]

> Meantime learned men, endowed with the graces of a holy life, and bearing the burden and heat of the day, by some unfair destiny serve these men, perhaps contented with a very small salary, called by plain names, humble, obscure, and needy, though far more worthy, and unhonored lead a private life, buried in some scanty country Living, or imprisoned all their lives in their college, and languish in obscurity.

Abraham Cowley divided all knowledge into that which comes from God, divine, and that which comes from Nature, natural philosophy. He was particularly insistent that men should not just depend on the philosophy of the ancients, but should always turn to the 'fountains of nature.' In particular he blames the universities for only training men to learn

---
30 Ibid., 280ff.

to comment on Aristotle, rather than to go beyond him. Consequently, in the past thousand years, Cowley finds the only 'ornament or advantage added to the uses of Humane Society' to be guns and printing.³¹

In his 'Advancement of Experimental Philosophy,' Cowley outlines a utopian college. In addition to twenty professors, his list of staff includes sixteen young scholars to serve as servants to the professors; a librarian, who also serves as 'Apothecary, Druggist, and Keeper of Instruments, Engines, etc.'; and 'four old Women' who keep the house clean.³² It is particularly interesting that he would have only sixteen of the twenty professors in residence at any one time, with the remaining four 'always traveling beyond the Seas,' presumably to build the experiential side of their education. For those present and teaching, in order to preserve their time for that purpose, none may be married, or be a lawyer or clergyman on the side. The students, whom he would not charge, he would limit to about two hundred.

Cowley does not mention music as part of his curriculum. Music appears in an article called 'Of Solitude.' Although he seems to place very little value on Solitude itself, not to mention entertainment, he recommends one can,

> stop up all those gaps in our time, either Musick, or Painting, or Designing, or Chemistry, or History, or Gardening, or twenty other things will do it usefully and pleasantly; and if he happen to set his affections upon poetry (which I do not advise him too immoderately) that will over do it.³³

Bunyan often uses the word 'professor' to mean simply one who professes to believe in the teachings of the church. In a few places, however, he seems to have in mind professors in an academic sense. In one of these passages he speaks of those professors clinging to their 'methods' and not only declares they shall never enter heaven, but groups them together with 'dogs, sorcerers, whoremongers, murderers and idolaters.'³⁴

ON THE PSYCHOLOGY OF AESTHETICS

Regarding the emotions in general, the Rev. Joseph Hall concludes the heart of man is wholly designed for fraud,

> the affections mocking us in the object, measure, manner; and in all of them the heart of man is deceitful.³⁵

---

31 Preface to 'Experimental Philosophy,' in *The Complete Works of Abraham Cowley,* ed. Alexander Grosart (New York: AMS Press, 1967), II, 285ff. Abraham Cowley (1618–1667) attracted great attention as a young poet, but little later in his life.

32 The professor would receive an annual salary of 120 Pounds, the librarian 30 and the cleaning women, 10.

33 'Of Solitude,' in *The Complete Works of Abraham Cowley,* Ibid., II, 317. In another article, 'Of Agriculture,' he departs from his topic to make a typical Puritan objection to dance.

34 'The Strait Gate,' in *The Works of John Bunyan,* I, 372.

35 'The Great Impostor,' in *The Works of Joseph Hall,* V, 163.

In discussing his contention that there is no difference between the emotion of anger and madness, he offers a rather extraordinary portrait of anger.

> Raging madness is a short madness; what else argues the shaking of the hands and lips; paleness or redness or swelling of the face; glaring of the eyes; stammering of the tongue; stamping with the feet; unsteady motions of the whole body; rash actions ... distracted and wild speeches? And madness is nothing but continued rage.[36]

Later in this treatise he concludes 'he is a rare man that has not some kind of madness reigning in him.' The kinds of madness he had in mind were melancholy, pride, false devotion, ambition or covetousness, anger, laughing madness of extreme mirth, drunken madness, outrageous lust, curiosity and profaneness and atheism.[37]

For most English writers at this time, discussion on the emotions centered on melancholy. Harvey, in 1616, appeared interested in melancholy, but offered little discussion. He mentions that 'physicians differ regarding the melancholy juice' and suggests melancholics lack pleasant disposition and talent and wonders if its origin were related to the 'splen-stone.'[38]

Burton associates a transitory form of melancholy with mortality itself, for every man experiences it on some occasion. This form comes and goes with,

> every small occasion of sorrow, need, sickness, trouble, fear, grief, passion, or perturbation of the mind, any manner of care, discontent, or thought, which causes anguish, dullness, heaviness and vexation of spirit, any ways opposite to pleasure, mirth, joy, delight, causing forwardness in us, or a dislike. In which equivocal and improper sense, we call him melancholy, that is dull, sad, sour, lumpish, ill-disposed, solitary, any way moved, or displeased. And from these melancholy dispositions no man living is free, no Stoic, none so wise, none so happy, none so patient, so generous, so Godly, so divine, that can vindicate himself; so well-composed, but more or less, some time or other he feels the smart of it. Melancholy in this sense is the character of Mortality.[39]

Finally, John Donne makes a rare association between color and the 'affections.'

> For we, when we are melancholy, wear black; when lusty, green; when forsaken, tawny; pleasing our own inward affections.[40]

---

36 'Holy Observations,' in Ibid., VII, 541.
37 Ibid., 542.
38 Harvey, *Lectures on the Whole of Anatomy*, 93ff.
39 Burton, *Anatomy of Melancholy*, 125.
40 Donne, 'Paradoxes and Problems,' in *Selected Prose*, 12.

The only one of these philosophers who concerned himself much with Pleasure and Pain was the Puritan preacher, Joseph Hall. He seemed intent on making the point that man can never find happiness in this life.

> The nature of man is extremely querulous. We know not what we would have, and when we have it, we know not how to like it. We would be happy; yet we would not die. We would live long; yet we would not be old … We are loath to work; yet are weary of doing nothing. We have no desire to stir; yet find long sitting painful.[41]

Curiously, in another place he seems to blame God for this condition.

> Now, we are never so bare as not to have some benefits; never so full as not to want something, yea as not to be full of wants. God hath much ado with us; either we lack health, or quietness, or children, or wealth, or company, or ourselves in all these.[42]

In another work, 'The Fourth Decade,' Hall writes extensively on the importance of moderating pleasure.[43] Typical of his thoughts here, are:

> Pleasure is like a snake: admit the head and the rest follows.
> A little honey is sweet; much, fulsome.
> What are the goodly sumptuous buildings we admire, but a little burnt and hardened earth?

In another place he says the pleasures of the Christian should be 'masculine and temperate.'[44] In this same treatise he also comments on the brevity of pleasure.

> Who ever enjoyed full delight for a day? or if he could, what is he the better for it tomorrow? He may be worse, but who ever is the better for his yesterday's feast?[45]

Another topic which Hall turns to under the discussion of Moderation is the 'avoidance of curiosity,' by which he means 'the search or determination of immaterial and superfluous truth.'[46] He returns to this idea in another work, where he announces there are three kinds of Truth: the necessary, the profitable and the impertinent.[47] It is only the second of these which 'are worthy of our studious and careful disquisition.'

---

41 'The Remedy of Discontentment,' in *The Works of Joseph Hall*, VI, 554.
42 'The waters of Marah,' in Ibid., I, 101.
43 'The Fourth Decade,' in Ibid., VII, 216ff.
44 'Christian Moderation,' in Ibid., VII, 404.
45 Ibid., 412.
46 Ibid., 451.
47 'The Peacemaker,' in Ibid., VII, 628.

ON THE PHILOSOPHY OF AESTHETICS

Harvey, as we have seen above, bestowed a new respectability to the senses. He returns to this topic in his book, *The Generation of Animals*, where he contrasts the artist with the scientist.

> [Those things which] have become firmly fixed in the mind of the artist, do, in fact, constitute art and the artistic faculty; art, indeed, is the reason of the work in the mind of the artist. On the same terms, therefore, as art is attained to, is all knowledge and science acquired; for as art is a habit with reference to things to be done, so is science a habit in respect of things to be known: as that proceeds from the imitation of types or forms, so this proceeds from the knowledge of natural things. Each has its origin in sense and experience, and it is impossible that there can rightly be either art or science without visible instance or example. In both, that which we perceive in sensible objects differs from the image itself which we retain in our imagination or memory ... That in the artist and man of science is a sensible thing, clearer, more perfect; this is a matter of reason and more obscure: for things perceived by sense are more assured and manifest than matters inferred by reason, inasmuch as the latter proceed from and are illustrated by the former. Finally, sensible things are of themselves and antecedent; things of intellect, however, are consequent, and arise from the former, and, indeed, we can in no way attain to them without the help of the others.[48]

In his book of advice to his son, King James I comments 'that Art is better learned by practice than speculation.'[49] Later he recommends to his son the study of all the arts and sciences, because of their mutual relationships.

> But since all arts & sciences are linked every one with the other, their greatest principles agreeing in one (which moved the poets to [consider] the nine Muses to be all sisters) study them, that out of their harmony ye may suck the knowledge of all faculties, & consequently, be on the counsel of all crafts, that ye may be able to contain them all in order; knowledge & learning is a light burden, the weight whereof will never press your shoulders.[50]

There is little discussion by these philosophers on any specific art form. Perhaps they were all considered as being too light in character. Bunyan, in any case, includes dramatic theaters in a list, including 'an alehouse, a whorehouse, sports, pleasures and sleep,' of those things which block the ear from the word of God.[51] In his *Pilgrim's Progress*, he includes dramatic plays in a list with juggling, cheats, games, fools, apes, knaves and rogues.[52]

---

48 *The Works of William Harvey*, 157.

49 James I, *Basilicon Doron* (1599) (Menston: Scolar Press, 1969), 67.

50 Ibid., 106ff. Among the activities which the king does not recommend to his son is all 'violente exercises, such as foote-ball.' [Ibid., 143]

51 'Saved by Grace,' in *The Works of John Bunyan*, I, 352.

52 'Pilgrim's Progress,' in Ibid., III,127.

ON THE AESTHETICS OF MUSIC

Bunyan, in his *Pilgrim's Progress*, includes a passage with several metaphors based on music. We find most interesting here the characterization of the music of the trombone consort as 'doleful,' a description found in other literature of the sixteenth and seventeenth centuries in England, and the entire discussion of the bass part. Here Bunyan speaks through the character, Great-heart.

> The wise God will have it so; some must pipe, and some must weep. Now Mr. Fearing was one that played upon his bass; he and his fellows sound the sackbut, whose notes are more doleful than the notes of other music are; though, indeed, some say the bass is the ground of music. And, for my part, I care not at all for that profession that begins not in heaviness of mind. The first string that the musician usually touches is the bass, when he intends to put all in tune. God also plays upon this string first, when he sets the soul in tune for himself. Only here was the imperfection of Mr. Fearing, he could play upon no other music but this, till towards his latter end.
>
> I make bold to talk thus metaphorically, for the ripening of the wits of young readers; and because, in the book of Revelations, the saved are compared to a company of musicians that play upon their trumpets and harps, and sing their songs before the throne.[53]

In another figure of speech, Bunyan describes the cry of the beggar as a 'shrill trumpet.'[54]

On the Purpose of Music

The Puritan preacher, Joseph Hall, recognizes pleasure to be a purpose of music, but that does not mean he condones it for that purpose. He mentions the 'lyre and harp, timbrel and flute' played at banquets referred to in Isaiah 5:12, but he can see only 'profane and careless souls who spend their time in jollity and pleasure!'[55]

> I am sure I have a thousand times more cause of joy and cheerfulness than the merriest of all those wild and jovial spirits: they have a world to play withal; but I have a God to rejoice in: their sports are trivial and momentary; my joy is serious and everlasting.

The most familiar purpose for music given in early literature is to soothe either the performer or the listener. In one of his sermons, John Donne explains that God gave man music to settle his emotions.

---

53 Ibid., 215. For the 'pipe' reference, see Matthew 11:16. For the Revelations passages, see 8:2 and 14:2.
54 'Upon the Beggar,' in *A Book for Boys and Girls*, in Ibid., III, 758.
55 'The Breathings of the Devout Soul,' in *The Works of Joseph Hall*, VIII, 8ff.

> And, to tune us, to compose and give us a harmonie and concord of affections, in all perturbations and passions, and discords in the passages of this life.[56]

The Reverend Joseph Hall writes in several places of the special solace on hearing music at night.

> How sweetly doth this music sound in this dead season! In the daytime it would not, it could not so much affect the ear. All harmonious sounds are advanced by a silent darkness.

Hall finds a parallel in the glad tidings of salvation in the 'night of persecution of our private affliction.'[57] He expands on this idea in another work called 'Songs in the Night.'

> There is no time wherein [songs of praise] can be unseasonable: yea, rather, as all our artificial melody is wont to sound sweetest in the dark, so those songs are most pleasing to thee which we sing in the saddest night of our affliction …
> The night is a dismal season, attended with solitude and horror, and an aggravation of those pains and cares whereof the day is in any sort guilty … Songs in the night, are not, cannot be of nature's making, but are the sole gift of the heavenly Comforter.
> And if we, out of the strength of our moral powers, shall be setting songs to ourselves in the night of our utmost disconsolation, woe is me, how miserably out of tune they are! how harsh, how misaccented, how discordous even to the sense of our own souls, much more in the ears of the Almighty, in whom dwells nothing beneath an infinite perfection!
> But the songs that thou, O God, puttest into the mouths of thy servants in the night of their tribulation are so exquisitely harmonious, as that thine angels rejoice to hear them, and disdain not to match them with their hallelujahs in heaven.[58]

In still another treatise, Hall recommends for those who 'howl in the night of their affliction,' singing at night.[59] He mentions here again his contention that music sounds best in the night.
Gervase Markham, in his *Countrey Contentments* (1615), places this purpose on almost a functional level.

> A gentleman should not be unskillful in Music, that whensoever either melancholy, heaviness of his thoughts, or the perturbations of his own fancies, stirreth up sadness in him, he may remove the same with some godly Hymn or Anthem, of which David gives him ample examples.[60]

The purpose of music to soothe, stated in this way, seems almost music therapy. But there are also in this literature some remarkable illustrations of actual music therapy. Burton, in

---

56 John Donne, 'A Sermon preached at Pauls Crosse,' in *Five Sermons* (Menston: Scolar Press, 1970), 3.
57 'Occasional Meditations,' in *The Works of Joseph Hall*, X, 142.
58 'Souls in the Night,' in Ibid., VII, 326.
59 'The Breathings of the Devout Soul,' in Ibid., VIII, , 18ff.
60 Quoted in Donnington, *The Interpretation of Early Music*, 117.

his study of melancholy, lists what he considers the basic 'diseases of the mind.' Among 'Dotage, Phrenzy, Madness, Hydrophobia, and Llycanthropia,' we are surprised to find 'St. Vitus' Dance.' His discussion of this condition is rather interesting.

> S. Vitus' Dance; the lascivious dance, Paracelsus calls it, because they that are taken with it, can do nothing but dance till they be dead, or cured. It is so called, for that the parties so troubled were wont to go to S. Vitus for help, & after they had danced there a while, they were certainly freed. It is strange to hear how long they will dance, & in what manner, over stools, forms, tables; even great-bellied women sometimes (and yet never hurt their children) will dance so long that they can stir neither hand nor foot, but seem to be quite dead. Only in red clothes they cannot abide. Musick above all things they love, & therefore Magistrates in Germany will hire Musicians to play to them, and some lusty sturdy companions to dance with them. This disease hath been very common in Germany, as appears by those relations of Sckenkius, and Paracelsus in his book of Madness, who brags how many several persons he hath cured of it. Felix Platerus reports of a woman in Basle whom he saw, that danced a whole month together.[61]

In his discussion of the remedies for melancholy, Burton devotes a brief chapter to music. There have been many means by which philosophers and physicians have attempted to 'exhilarate a sorrowful heart,' he notes, but for him there is nothing so powerful as 'a cup of strong drink, mirth, musick, and merry company.'[62] After citing some high recommendations of music by ancient writers, Burton observes,

> Musick is a tonic to the saddened soul, a [powerful cannon] against melancholy, to rear and revive the languishing soul, affecting not only the ears, but the very arteries, the vital and animal spirits; it erects the mind, and makes it nimble. This it will effect in the most dull, severe, and sorrowful souls, expel grief with mirth, and if there be any clouds, dust, or dregs of cares yet lurking in our thoughts, most powerfully it wipes them all away, and that which is more, it will perform all this in an instant: cheer up the countenance, expel austerity, bring in hilarity, inform our manners, mitigate anger ... Our divine Musick, not only to expel the greatest griefs, but it doth extenuate fears and furies, appeases cruelty, abates heaviness, and to such as are watchful it causes quiet rest; it takes away spleen and hatred, be it instrumental, vocal, with strings, or wind; it leads us by the spirit, it cures all irksomeness and heaviness of the soul. Laboring men, that sing to their work, can tell as much, and so can soldiers when they go to fight, whom terror of death cannot so much affright, as the sound of trumpet, drum, fife, and such like musick, animates; the fear of death, as Censorinus informs us, musick drives away. It makes a child quiet, the nurse's song; and many times the sound of a trumpet on a sudden, bells ringing, a carman's whistle, a boy singing some ballad tune early in the street, alters, revives, recreates, a restless patient that cannot sleep in the night. In a word, it is so powerful a thing that it ravishes the soul, the Queen of the senses, by sweet pleasure (which is a happy cure) and corporal tunes, pacifies our incorporeal soul, and rules it without words, and carries it beyond itself, helps, elevates, extends it.

---

61 Burton, *Anatomy of Melancholy*, 124.

62 Ibid., 478ff.

Burton continues with a number of illustrations and testimonials to the effectiveness of music therapy taken from early literature. In the last of these he quotes Scaliger, who, being always pleased with music and musicians, makes the interesting comment, 'I am well pleased to be idle amongst them.' Burton then concludes by commenting on some possible dangers of music.

> And what young man is not [pleased with music]? As it is acceptable and conducing to most, so especially to a melancholy man; provided always, his disease proceed not originally from it, that he be not some light Inamorato, some idle phantastick, who capers in conceit all the day long, and thinks of nothing else but how to make Jigs, Sonnets, Madrigals, in commendation of his mistress. In such cases Musick is most pernicious, as a spur to a free horse will make him run himself blind, or break his wind; for Musick enchants, as Menander holds, it will make such melancholy persons mad, and the sound of those Jigs and Horn-pipes will not be removed out of the ears a week after … Many men are melancholy by hearing Musick, but it is a pleasing melancholy that it causes, and therefore to such as are discontent, in woe, fear, sorrow, or dejected, it is a most present remedy; it expels cares, alters their grieved minds, and eases in an instant.

Another ancient purpose of music is to play a role in courtship. John Donne recognizes music as one of three necessary tools for the conquest of women.

> They have found where was the easiest, and most accessible way, to solicit the chastity of a woman, whether *Discourse*, *Musicke*, or *Presents*.[63]

On the other hand, Burton suggests that,

> To hear a fair young gentlewoman play upon the virginals, lute, viol, and sing to it … are the chief delight of lovers.[64]

Finally, John Donne gives one purpose of music as being a rather functional tool for memory. Much of the instructions in the bible were given in the form of music, he maintains, for God then 'was sure they would remember.'[65]

There is very little discussion of performance techniques by these philosophers, but one comment on the prevalence of improvisation is very enlightening indeed. John Donne, in a letter of ca. 1600, is speaking of the importance of not depending on books for one's education, but on personal observation and experience. Then, in analogy, he adds his observation that everyone would rather hear improvised music than that which was notated.

> For both listeners and players are more delighted with voluntary than with sett musicke.[66]

---

63 Donne, 'A Sermon Preached at Saint Pauls upon Christmasse day. 1621,' in *Selected Prose*, 209.

64 Burton, *Anatomy of Melancholy*, 699.

65 Donne, 'A Lent Sermon Preached at White-hall, February 12, 1619,' in *Selected Prose*, 183.

66 John Donne, Letter [ca. 1600], quoted in Ibid., 109. In a Sermon [Ibid., 278] Donne again criticizes the fact that education has limited us to seeing Nature through Aristotle's spectacles, medicine through Galen's and the universe through Ptolemy's.

ART MUSIC

John Bunyan includes two scenes in his *Pilgrim's Progress* which record Art Music. First there are the 'excellent virginals' in the dining room of Prudence, which she played before singing an 'excellent' song about Jacob's ladder.[67] Later Christiana plays the viol, and her daughter, Mercy, the lute for their guests. Although the music is described as 'merry disposed,' it had no effect on Mr. Despondency.[68]

In these volumes we have emphasized the importance of the contemplative listener as part of the definition of art music. Bunyan includes a poem, 'Upon a Skillful Player on an Instrument,' in his *A Book for Boys and Girls*, which goes further in its emphasis of the importance of the *educated* listener as a link in the communication of music.

> He that can play well on an instrument,
> Will take the ear, and captivate the mind
> With mirth or sadness; for that it is bent
> Thereto, as music in it place doth find.
> But if one hears that has therein no skill,
> (As often music lights of such a chance)
> Of its brave notes they soon be weary will:
> And there are some can neither sing nor dance.[69]

FUNCTIONAL MUSIC

In his 'Solomon's Temple Spiritualized,' Bunyan reviews at length the descriptions of church singing mentioned in both the Old and New Testaments. The only comments which Bunyan makes regarding church music of his own time are that the music should be contemporary in its themes and that it should be sung in the proper spirit and with understanding.

> And answerable to this, is the church to sing now new songs, with new hearts for new mercies. New songs, I say, are grounded on new matter, new occasions, new mercies, new deliverances, new discoveries of God to the soul, or for new frames of heart; and are such as are most taking, most pleasing, and most refreshing to the soul …
>
> I pray God it be done by all those that now-a-days get into churches, in spirit and with understanding.[70]

---

67 'Pilgrim's Progress,' in *The Works of John Bunyan*, III, 204.
68 Ibid., III, 229.
69 'Upon a Skillful Player on an Instrument,' in *A Book for Boys and Girls*, in *The Works of John Bunyan*, III, 761.
70 'Solomon's Temple Spiritualized,' in Ibid., III, 496.

John Donne contrasts the use of musical instruments in the Jewish and Christian religions.

> In the first institution of thy Church, in this world, in the foundation of thy Militant Church, among the Jews, thou didst appoint the calling of the assembly in, to be by Trumpet, and when they were in, then thou gave them the sound of bells, in the garment of the priest. In the Triumphant Church, thou employs both too, but in an inverted order; we enter into the Triumphant Church by the sound of bells ... and then we receive our further edification, or consummation, by the sound of Trumpets, at the Resurrection. The sound of thy Trumpets thou didst impart to secular and civil uses too, but the sound of bells only to sacred.[71]

In his autobiography, there is a passage which hints that Bunyan had a familiarity with dance music such as we might not have expected. He quotes 1 Corinthians 13:1, 'If I speak in the tongues of men and of angels, but have not love, I am a noisy gong or a clanging cymbal,' as a metaphor for the men of the church. But then, his explanation of this verse includes the following,

> A clanging cymbal is an instrument of music, with which a skillful player can make such melodious and heart-inflaming music, that all who hear him play can scarcely hold from dancing.[72]

Bunyan provides an illustration of welcoming music, in his *Pilgrim's Progress*, where he gives an extended description of the music he foresees will meet those who arrive in heaven.

> There came out also at this time to meet them, several of the king's trumpeters, clothed in white and shining raiment, who, with melodious noises, and loud, made even the heavens to echo with their sound ...
>
> This done, they compassed them round on every side; some went before, some behind, and some on the right hand, some on the left ..., continually sounding as they went, with melodious noise, in notes on high ... Thus, they walked on together; and as they walked, ever and anon these trumpeters, even with joyful sound, would, by mixing their music with looks and gestures, still signify to Christian and his brother, how welcome they were into their company.[73]

Later in the Celestial City, 'the trumpets continually sound so melodiously,' that people could not sleep yet they woke as refreshed as if they had.[74] And, in his poem, 'One Thing is Needful,' Bunyan also finds string instruments in heaven,

> The strings of music here are tuned
> For heavenly harmony.[75]

---

71 Donne, *Devotions Upon Emergent Occasion*, 83.
72 *The Works of John Bunyan*, I, 44ff. Having a more primitive translation, Bunyan gives 'tinkling' for 'clanging' and 'charity' for 'love.'
73 'Pilgrim's Progress,' in Ibid., III, 165.
74 Ibid., 240. A similar musical welcome is described in 'The Holy War,' in Ibid., III, 359.
75 'One Thing is Needful,' in Ibid., III, 733.

Bunyan, also provides an unusual reference to signal music in his 'The Holy War,' where he describes a drummer who served under Lord Lucifer and the Diabolonians.

> This, to speak truth, was amazingly hideous to hear; it frightened all men seven miles round, if they were but awake and heard it.[76]

Later the drummer gives various signals and again the observation is made, 'no noise was ever heard upon earth more terrible.'

James Harrington's *Oceana*, which is clearly a utopian play for a future England, was widely read and attacked. The book is largely a very detailed outline of government, down to specific instructions to the trumpeters and drummers who accompany those who make public announcements.[77]

In the important medieval music guilds, the leader was often called a 'king,' reflecting the only kind of societal organization anyone knew of. By the sixteenth century the music guilds in England had greatly deteriorated in quality and so in this work there is some attention paid to the control of these 'kings' in organizing events to which the public would contribute money, such as exhibiting trained bears.[78]

ENTERTAINMENT MUSIC

A rare example of entertainment music with a purpose is mentioned by John Donne in a sermon when he speaks of 'that good custom in these cities, [where] you hear cheerful street musick in the winter mornings.'[79]

---

76 'The Holy War,' in Ibid., III, 342, 347.

77 Morley, *Ideal Commonwealths*, 249ff. The trumpeters are to be paid about half the pay of an ordinary soldier; the drummers even less.

78 Ibid., 335ff.

79 Donne, 'A Sermon Preached at White-hall, February 29, 1628,' in *Selected Prose*, 328.

5   FRANCIS BACON

FRANCIS BACON (1561–1626) was referred to by Will Durant as 'the greatest and proudest intellect of the age' and Durant places him at the head of the Age of Reason.[1] If he was not the inventor of inductive reasoning (the study of nature through experience and experiment) as he is often credited, he may at least be credited with being one of those who popularized the scientific method. His quest for knowledge through experimentation caused his death when his attempt to forestall putrefaction in a fowl with ice led to a fever.

Bacon, son of a high government official, served in Parliament, was a successful lawyer and eventually held important government posts himself. Unfortunately he was prone to bribes, participated in corruption and was eventually sent to prison in the Tower.

ON THE PHYSIOLOGY OF AESTHETICS

Bacon's basic ideas on the nature of the organization of man and his mind are expressed in his *The Advancement of Learning*. Man's understanding, he says, is the seat of learning and has three divisions: Memory, taught through history; Imagination, taught through poetry; and Reason, taught through philosophy.[2] The study of History he divides into Natural, Civil and Ecclesiastical. Of these three we are most interested in the history of Nature, for this he further subdivides into the three divisions of Creatures, Marvels and the Arts.[3]

As for the study of human knowledge itself, Bacon states that it consists of two fields: the study of the substance of the soul or mind itself and the study of the functions of its faculties.[4] As for the first of these, Bacon finds that all previous attempts to explain the soul leave one 'in a maze.' Since the soul is a divine gift, therefore, he concludes, it can only be understood by divine inspiration and is not a subject for philosophy.

Turning to that which can be studied, Bacon comes tantalizingly close to deducing the basic operation of the brain by finding it divided into Understanding and Reason on one hand,

---

[1] Will Durant, *The Age of Reason Begins* (New York: Simon and Schuster, 1961), 169, 183.
[2] *The Advancement of Learning*, in *The Works of Francis Bacon*, ed. James Spedding (Cambridge: Cambridge University Press, 1869), VI, 182,
[3] Ibid., VI, 184.
[4] Ibid., VI, 254ff.

and Appetite and Affection on the other.[5] He then adds a faculty of Imagination, independent of either and through which both Reason and the Affections operate.

Bacon finds the knowledge gained from personal experience to be that of 'false appearances,' as compared to reality.[6] In other words, he fails to perceive the understanding gained by personal experience is valid and important, for it is this which distinguishes the individual. In another place, however, he gives quite a contrary assessment of experiential knowledge.

> The knowledge of man is as the waters, some descending from above, and some springing from beneath; the one informed by the light of nature, the other inspired by divine revelation. The light of nature consists in the notions of the mind and the reports of the senses; for as for knowledge which man receives by teaching, it is cumulative and not original.[7]

Bacon also writes of the danger which emotion represent to Reason and in fact suggests that man is only able to function rationally because imagination forms a 'confederacy' with Reason against the affections.[8] He admits that emotion, like Reason, is capable of good, but finds this distinction,

> The affection beholds merely the present; reason beholds the future and sum of time.[9]

It fails to occur to him that this is one of the great virtues of music, that it communicates with the listener in the present tense, whereas all of the world of the intellect is past tense by its very definition.

In another place he speaks of the danger by which emotion threatens Reason by using the analogy of the afflictions of the body and again with the analogy of the wind which stirs up the calm waters of the ocean.[10] Finally, he concludes,

> The poets and writers of histories are the best doctors of this knowledge; where we may find painted forth with great life, how affections are kindled and incited; and how pacified and reframed ... how they work, how they vary, how they gather and fortify, how they are enwrapped one within another, and how they do fight and encounter one with another.

Later he makes a statement which reminds one of the tendency of the academic world.

> In the mind whatsoever knowledge reason cannot at all work upon and convert, is mere intoxication, and endangers a dissolution of the mind and understanding.[11]

---

5   Ibid., 258ff. He finds Reason has four separate faculties, those to invent, to seek, to judge and to communicate.
6   Ibid., 278.
7   Ibid., 207.
8   Ibid., 299.
9   Ibid.
10 Ibid., 336.
11 Ibid., 404.

On the Senses

Although Bacon correctly associated the senses with the brain, we can see vividly how he, and other philosophers before him, had to grope in total darkness for rational explanations, lacking as they did the discoveries of modern medical research.

> The senses are alike strong both on the right side and on the left; but the limbs on the right side are stronger. The cause may be, for that the brain, which is the instrument of sense, is alike on both sides; but motion and abilities of moving are somewhat helped from the liver, which lies on the right side. It may be also, for that the senses are put in exercise indifferently on both sides from the time of our birth; but the limbs are used most on the right side, whereby custom helps; for we see that some are left-handed; which are such as have used the left hand most.[12]

For Bacon, the greatest form of pleasure was that of the left hemisphere of the brain, far surpassing any pleasures of the senses.

> For the pleasure and delight of knowledge and learning, it far surpasses all others in nature: for shall the pleasures of the affections so exceed the senses, as much as the obtaining of desire or victory exceeds a song or a dinner; and must not of consequence the pleasures of the intellect or understanding exceed the pleasures of the emotions? We see in all other pleasures there is satiety...which shows well they be but deceits of pleasure, and not pleasures; and that it was the novelty which pleased, and not the quality ... But of knowledge there is no satiety, but satisfaction and appetite are perpetually interchangeable; and therefore appears to be good in itself simply, without fallacy or accident.[13]

On Education

In his *The Advancement of Learning*, Bacon suggests that much of the 'looseness or negligence' of society was due to the lack of regard in the selection of teachers and adds a timeless observation:

> The ancient wisdom of the best times did always make a just complaint that states were too busy with their laws and too negligent in point of education.[14]

Bacon, in this regard, calls upon the ancient Orpheus myth, in which the music of Orpheus calmed the savage beasts, which he presents as a metaphor for education. If education, laws, religion, books, sermons, etc., are not heard by the youth, then 'all things dissolve into anar-

---

12 *Natural History*, Century IX, Section 876, in Ibid., V, 105.
13 *The Advancement of Learning*, in Ibid., VI, 167.
14 Ibid., VI, 108ff.

chy and confusion.'¹⁵ Later Bacon returns to this idea in contending that proficiency in the liberal arts 'softens and humanizes the manners. It takes away the wildness and barbarism and fierceness of men's minds.'¹⁶

Bacon contends that the universities do not appreciate that the liberal arts are the true foundation for the professions.

> Among so many great foundations of colleges in Europe, I find it strange that they are all dedicated to professions, and none left free to arts and sciences at large ... If any man think philosophy and universality to be idle studies, he does not consider that all professions are from them served and supplied.¹⁷

Curiously, he appears to have even been somewhat ambivalent with regard to study itself, as he notes in an essay, 'Of Studies.'

> To spend too much time in studies is sloth; to use them too much for ornament, is affectation; to make judgment wholly by their rules, is the humor of a scholar. They perfect nature, and are perfected by experience: for natural abilities are like natural plants, that need pruning.¹⁸

On the Psychology of Aesthetics

In Book Eight of his *Natural History*, Bacon discusses the physical effects of the passions on the body. Here he includes fear, joy, anger, light displeasure, shame, wonder, laughing, lust, grief and pain:

> Grief and pain cause sighing, sobbing, groaning, screaming and roaring, tears, distorting of the face, grinding of the teeth, sweating. Sighing is caused by the drawing in of a greater quantity of breath to refresh the heart that labors; like a great draught when one is thirsty. Sobbing is the same thing stronger ... Tears are caused by a contraction of the spirits of the brain; which contraction by consequence astringeth the moisture of the brain, and thereby sends tears into the eyes.¹⁹

In Bacon's *History of Life and Death*, he discusses the emotions from the perspective of their physical influence on the body. Among his more interesting contentions, we find,

---

15 Ibid., VI, 145ff. In *De Sapientia Veterum* [Ibid., XIII, 111] Bacon uses the myth as a metaphor for natural, moral and civic philosophy. Earlier writers had also often interpreted this myth for their various purposes. Erasmus, for example, used it in commenting on divorce. The real meaning of the myth was that music calms the savage beast within man.

16 Ibid., 163.

17 *The Advancement of Learning*, in Ibid., VI, 174ff.

18 'Of Studies,' in Ibid., XII, 252.

19 *Natural History*, Century VIII, Section 714, in Ibid.

> Great joys attenuate and diffuse the spirits, and shorten life; ordinary cheerfulness strengthens the spirits …
> Sensual impressions of joys are bad …
> Joy suppressed and sparingly communicated comforts the spirits more than joy indulged and published.[20]
> Grief and sadness, if devoid of fear, and not too keen, rather prolong life …[21]
> Great fears shorten life.
> Suppressed anger is a kind of vexation, and makes the spirit to prey upon the juices of the body.
> Envy is the worst of passions, and preys on the spirits …
> A light shame hurts not, because it slightly contracts the spirits and then diffuses them …
> Love, if not unfortunate, and too deeply wounding, is a kind of joy …
> Hope is of all the emotions the most useful, and contributes most to prolong life.[22]

Bacon correctly observes that the motions of the face 'disclose the present humor and state of the mind and will.'[23] For this reason, in another place he recommends that one maintain a 'steadfast countenance, not wavering, etc., in conversation.'[24]

ON THE PHILOSOPHY OF AESTHETICS

In his *The Advancement of Learning*, Bacon seems to define for the creative arts a rather low station.

> For Arts of Pleasure Sensual, the chief deficiency in them is of laws to repress them. For as it has been well observed that the arts which flourish in times while virtue is in growth, are military; and while virtue is in state, are liberal; and while virtue is in declination, are voluptuary … With arts *voluptuary* I couple practices *joculary*; for the deceiving of the senses is one of the pleasures of the senses.[25]

In a later translation of this same work, however, Bacon appears to have concluded that he cast his net too widely. Now he assigns a higher appreciation for the arts associated with sight and hearing, but retains his lower estimate for those associated with the other senses.

---

20 Later [*History of Life and Death*, in Ibid., X, 144], he states that sudden grief or fear can produce sudden death. In addition, 'Many have died from great and sudden joys.'

21 In his 'Medical Remains' [Ibid., VII, 424], Bacon offers the recipe for making a 'wine against adverse melancholy, preserving the senses and the reason.' This involves roots of bugloss, misted with wine containing three ounces of refined gold, etc.

22 *History of Life and Death*, in Ibid., X, 98ff.

23 *The Advancement of Learning*, in Ibid., VI, 238.

24 'Civil Conversation,' in Ibid., XIII, 309.

25 *The Advancement of Learning*, in Ibid., VI, 253.

> To the eye belongs Painting, with innumerable other arts of magnificence in matter of Buildings, Gardens, Dresses, Vases, Gems, etc.; to the ear Music, with its various apparatus of voices, wind, and strings; and of all the sensual arts those which relate to Sight and Hearing are accounted the most liberal; for as these two senses are the purest and most chaste, so the sciences which belong to them are the most learned; both being waited upon by the Mathematics, and one [painting] having some relation to memory and demonstrations, the other [music] to manners and emotions of the mind. The rest of the sensual pleasures, with the arts appertaining to them, are held in less honor, as being nearer akin to luxury and magnificence. Unguents, perfumes, delicacies of the table, and especially stimulants of lust, stand more in need of a censor to repress than a master to teach them.[26]

On Beauty

Bacon's observations on Beauty are limited to physical beauty, such as his comment, 'Virtue is nothing but inward beauty; beauty nothing but outward virtue.'[27] In his essay, 'on Beauty,' he does digress once to the subject of painters. Painters, he observes, could paint a face on the basis of geometrical proportions, or by taking the best parts of many models, but it would always be the case that no one but the painter would like them.

> Not but I think a painter may make a better face than ever was; but he must do it by a kind of felicity (as a musician makes an excellent melody in music) and not by rule. A man shall see faces, that if you examine them part by part, you shall find never a good; and yet altogether do well.[28]

On Art versus Nature

Bacon makes the classic definition, 'Nature is the mirror of art,'[29] although in another place he cautions, 'It is not art, but abuse of art, when instead of perfecting nature it perverts her.'[30] Noting that the artist can create a rainbow faster than Nature, he writes, 'For Art, if nothing stand in the way, is far swifter than Nature and is the better runner and comes sooner to the goal.'[31]

---

26 Ibid., fn. 1.
27 Ibid., IX, 156.
28 'Of Beauty,' in Ibid., XII, 226.
29 *The Advancement of Learning*, Book V, in Ibid., IX, 77.
30 Ibid., IX, 115.
31 *De Sapientia Veterum*, in Ibid., XIII, 143.

His most interesting observation on this topic comes as he is reflecting on the organization of written history.

> I am rather induced to set down the history of arts as a species of natural history, because it is the fashion to talk as if art were something different from nature, so that things artificial should be separated from things natural, as differing totally in kind … looking upon art merely as a kind of supplement to nature; which has power enough to finish what nature has begun or correct her when going aside, but no power to make radical changes, and shake her in the foundations; an opinion which has brought a great deal of despair into human concerns.[32]

He disputes such a conviction, believing that an artist painting a scene of nature is still the work of nature, as the man is also inseparable from nature.

On Poetry

Bacon defines poetry as 'a part of learning in measure of words,' but he takes care to distinguish it from 'real' learning because poetry is a 'feigned history,' addressed to the imagination. It is for this reason that 'painters and poets have always been allowed to take what liberties they would.'[33] But Bacon does not intend this as criticism, but rather as the heart of the very virtue of poetry. The purpose of poetry, therefore, is to raise the mind of men, through the employment of their imagination, to ideas higher than those which would be stimulated by their observations of the real world.

> Therefore, because the acts or events of true history have not that magnitude which satisfies the mind of man, poetry feigns acts and events greater and more heroic.

It was because of this ability to draw thoughts above those of the real world, that poets were always said to be divinely inspired. Bacon discusses this and points, as well, to the capacity of music to affect manners.

> Therefore it was ever thought to have some participation of divineness, because it does raise and erect the mind, by submitting the shews of things to the desires of the mind; whereas reason buckles and bows the mind into the nature of things. And we see that by these insinuations and congruities with man's nature and pleasure, joined also with the agreement and consort it has with music, it has had access and estimation in rude times and barbarous regions, where other learning stood excluded.

Bacon concludes this discussion of poetry with a remarkable tribute, although since poetry was still associated with the dramatic arts, Bacon makes a quick retreat.

---

32 *A Description of the Intellectual Globe*, in Ibid., X, 407ff.
33 *The Advancement of Learning*, in Ibid., VI, 202ff.

> For being as a plant that comes of the lust of the earth, without a formal seed, poetry has sprung up and spread abroad more than any other kind. But to ascribe unto it that which is due; for the expression of emotions, passions, corruptions, and customs, we are beholding to poets more than to the philosophers' works; and for wit and eloquence not much less than to orators' harangues. But it is not good to stay too long in the theater.[34]

For all this, in his history of Henry VII, Bacon observes in passing that men who are too conversant with poets become conceited.[35]

On Drama

Bacon's only important reflection on drama seems to suggest that he saw its primary purpose as one of education.

> Dramatic Poetry, which has the theater for its world, would be of excellent use if well directed. For the stage is capable of no small influence both of discipline and of corruption. Now of corruptions in this kind we have enough; but the discipline has in our times been plainly neglected. And though in modern states play-acting is esteemed but as a toy, except when it is too satirical and biting; yet among the ancients it was used as a means of educating men's minds to virtue. Nay, it has been regarded by learned men and great philosophers as a kind of musician's bow by which men's minds may be played upon. And certainly it is most true, and one of the great secrets of nature, that the minds of men are more open to impressions and emotions when many are gathered together than when they are alone.[36]

ON THE AESTHETICS OF MUSIC

While Bacon was obviously much interested in music, he rarely writes of its fundamental definition. In his *The Advancement of Learning*, he seems to reflect the old Scholastic definition that music is one of a series of studies dependent on mathematics.[37] Perhaps his most interesting remarks on this subject are found in his *Sapientia Veterum*.

> For it seems there are two kinds of harmony and music; one of divine providence, the other of human reason; and to the human judgment, and the ears as it were of mortals, the government of the world and nature, and the more secret judgments of God, sound somewhat harsh and untunable; and though this be ignorance, such as deserves to be distinguished with the ears

---
34 Ibid., 206.
35 *History of the Reign of Henry VII*, Preface, in Ibid., XI, 34.
36 *The Advancement of Learning*, Book II, in Ibid., VIII, 441ff.
37 *The Advancement of Learning*, in Ibid., VI, 227.

of an ass, yet those ears are worn secretly and not in the face of the world—for it is not a thing observed or noted as a deformity by the vulgar.[38]

Finally, Bacon concludes his discussion of music in his *Natural History* by presenting, without discussion, the categories under which music might be discussed. We particularly wish he might have elaborated on Number five.

1. Musical, unmusical
2. Treble, bass
3. Flat, sharp
4. Soft, loud
5. Exterior, interior
6. Clean, harsh or purling
7. Articulate, inarticulate.

ON THE PERCEPTION OF MUSIC

Bacon devotes Book Two of his *Natural History* to considerations on the nature of music and sound. His inspiration seems to have been his thought that the quality of the intellectual discussion of the theories behind music did not equal the quality of the performance with which he was familiar.

> Music, in the practice, hath been well pursued and in good variety; but in the theory, and especially in the yielding of the causes of the practice, very weakly; begin reduced into certain mystical subtilities, of no use and not much truth.[39]

Unfortunately, much of Bacon's speculation on the nature of sound and music is based on a faulty understanding of the physics of sound, as, indeed, the conclusions of most early writers were. The most fundamental misunderstanding was with regard to the nature of sound itself. Simply put, early writers did not understand that the sounds we hear are vibrations created by a string or an instrument, etc. Indeed, Bacon states 'The sound is not created between the bow and the string; but between the string and the air.' He believed the musical instrument set in motion something he called 'local motion,' and it was here the sound was created. His clearest explanation reads,

> It would be extreme grossness to think that the sound in strings is made or produced between the hand and the strings, or the quill and the string, or the bow and the string, for those are but *vehicula motus*, passages to the creation of the sound; the sound being produced between the

---

38 *De Sapientia Veterum*, in Ibid., XIII, 100.
39 *Natural History*, Op. cit., Section 101, in Ibid.

string and the air; and that not by any impulsion of the air from the first motion of the string, by the return or result of the string, which was strained by the touch, to his former place; which motion of result is quick and sharp; whereas the first motion is soft and dull. So the bow tortures the string continually, and therefore holds it in a continual trepidation.[40]

Failing to perceive the true nature of vibrations, Bacon is led to a number of curious conclusions. Since he regarded that the sound is created in the air immediately surrounding the instrument, it seemed to him that particular force was necessary to set this air in motion, as one could clearly see in wind players.

For as for other wind instruments, they require a forcible breath; as trumpets, cornets, hunters' horns, etc., which appeareth by the blown cheeks of him that windeth them.[41]

He also misunderstood, in this regard, the physical action of the wind player and the resultant sound. All pipes, he says, have 'a blast, as well as a sound.' Even speech, he concluded, results from the 'expulsion of a little breath.'[42] This explosion of air which he associates with tone production leads him to observe,

It hath been anciently reported, and is still received, that extreme applause and shouting of people assembled in great multitudes, have so rarefied and broken the air, that birds flying over have fallen down, the air being not able to support them.[43]

Since Bacon understood music to be created in the air, and not in the vibrations, he was at a loss to explain why vibrating tongs set in water seem to produce sounds under water where there is no air present.[44] He also appears to have been somewhat mystified by the existence of echoes. If it were a real [corporeal] sound, then the echo would have to have been produced in a similar fashion as the original sound, that is by a violin string, a trumpet tone, etc. Since this is obviously not the case, Bacon took the echo to be 'a great argument for the spiritual essence of sounds.'[45]

Failing to understand the nature of vibrations led to a number of other curious conclusions. To his ear, the bass was generally stronger than the treble. From this perception he makes this conclusion.

In harmony, if there be not a discord to the bass, it doth not disturb the harmony though there be a discord to the higher parts ... And the cause is, for that the bass striking more air, doth

---

40 Ibid., Section 137.
41 Ibid., Section 116.
42 Ibid., Section 125.
43 Ibid., Section 127.
44 Ibid., Section 133.
45 Ibid., Section 287.

overcome and drown the treble (unless the discord be very odious); and so hideth a small imperfection.[46]

Similarly, he adds, but cannot explain, that stopping high on a string not only produces a high pitch, but a dull sound.[47] His failure to understand vibrations leads him to strange explanations for dynamics.

The loudness and softness of sounds is a thing distinct from the magnitude and exility of sounds; for a bass string, though softly struck, gives the greater sound; but a treble string, if hard struck, will be heard much further off. And the cause is, for that the bass string strikes more air; and the treble less air, but with a sharper percussion.[48]

On the subject of acoustics, Bacon finds the explanation in everything except the materials of the instruments themselves.

All instruments that have either returns, as trumpets; or flexions, as cornets; or are drawn up and put from, as sackbuts; have a purling sound: but the recorder or flute, that have none of these inequalities, give a clear sound. Nevertheless, the recorder itself, or pipe, moistened a little in the inside, sounds more solemnly, and with a little purling or hissing.[49]

Bacon touches on acoustics again in his fictional, *New Atlantis*. Among his descriptions of various civic buildings in this utopian town there is a kind of experimental acoustic studio.

We have also sound-houses, where we practice and demonstrate all sounds and their generation. We have harmony which you have not, of quarter-sounds and lesser slides of sounds. Diverse instruments of music likewise to you unknown, some sweeter than any you have; with bells and rings that are dainty and sweet. We represent small sounds as great and deep, likewise great sounds extenuate and sharp; we make diverse tremblings and warblings of sounds, which in their original are entire. We represent and imitate all articulate sounds and letters, and the voices and notes of beasts and birds. We have certain helps which, set to the ear, do further the hearing greatly; we have also diverse strange and artificial echoes, reflecting the voice many times, and, as it were, tossing it; and some that give back the voice louder than it came, some shriller and some deeper, yea some rendering the voice, differing in the letters or articulate sound from that they receive. We have all means to convey sounds in trunks and pipes, in strange lines and distances.[50]

In an attempt to explain what aesthetic principles result in the 'pleasing' quality in music, Bacon looked for correspondence with the sense of sight. In his *Natural History*, the element

---

46 Ibid., Section 109.
47 Ibid., Section 156.
48 Ibid., Section 163.
49 Ibid., Section 170.
50 *New Atlantis*, in Ibid., V, 407.

of 'pleasing' in sight, he found, is in that which has equality, good proportion or correspondence and these he considered identical with music. In addition,

> The division and quavering, which please so much in music, have an agreement with the glittering of light; as the moon-beams playing upon a wave.[51]

He also briefly points to the correspondence between music and oratory, suggesting that imitation and fugal writing can be equated to repetition and traduction in rhetoric.

Returning to his comparison of sight and hearing, Bacon notes that the eye sees a vast panorama of objects, keeping them all separate, whereas this is not pleasing with respect to sound.

> The sweetest and best harmony is, when every part or instrument is not heard by itself, but a conflation of them all; which requires one to stand some distance off.[52]

Bacon also observes that 'some consorts of instruments are sweeter than others,' but this is, he says, 'a thing not sufficiently yet observed.'[53]

Next Bacon offers a variety of observations regarding the most pleasing sounds obtainable from various instruments. A pipe, he maintains, if moist inside, but without actual drops of water, sounds 'a more solemn sweet' than if dry.[54] Music sounds better indoors during frosty weather. If one sings into the hole of a drum, it makes the singing sweeter.

> And so I conceive it would, if it were a song in parts, sung into several drums; and for the handsomeness and strangeness sake, it would not be amiss to have a curtain between the place where the drums are and the listeners.

Bacon observes that sounds are better if one's mind is concentrated on only one sense, hearing. Therefore he suggests that music sounds better at night than during the day.[55]

Bacon makes only two brief references to the 'Music of the Spheres,' a topic still much discussed by philosophers and astronomers, in particular by Kepler.

> The heavens turn about in a most rapid motion, without noise to us perceived; though in some dreams they have been said to make an excellent music.[56]

---

51 *Natural History,* Section 111, 113, in Ibid.

52 Ibid., Section 224ff.

53 Ibid., Section 278.

54 Ibid., Section 230ff. In his 'Physiological Remains,' however, Bacon says of bells,

> It is probable that it is the dryness of the metal that helps the clearness of the sound, and the moistness that dulls it. [Ibid., VII, 389]

55 Bacon also mentions in passing [Ibid., Section 241] the subject of 'counterfeiting the distance of voices.' But he sees no purpose for this, other than for 'imposture, in counterfeiting ghosts or spirits.'

56 Ibid., Section 115.

In a catalog of projected histories, Bacon includes a 'History of Sounds in the upper region (if there be any).'[57]

Finally, we might mention that in his *History of Dense and Rare*, Bacon, while discussing 'motion of dilatation and contraction in the air by heat,' mentions without further identification a musical instrument 'played by the rays of the sun.'[58]

On the Purpose of Music

Bacon passes by the usual discussion on the purposes of music for pleasure and to solace the listener in preference to concentrating on its direct physical affect. We have mentioned above one of his observations on the influence of music on manners, but his most extensive discussion is found in his *Natural History*.

> It has been anciently held and observed, that the sense of hearing and the kinds of music most in operation upon manners; as to encourage men and make them warlike; to make them soft and effeminate; to make them grave; to make them light; to make them gentle and inclined to pity; etc. The cause is, for that the sense of hearing strikes the spirits more immediately than the other senses, and more incorporeally than the smelling. For the sight, taste, and feeling, have their organs not of so present and immediate access to the spirits, as the hearing has. And as for the smelling (which indeed works also immediately upon the spirits, and is forcible while the object remains), it is with a communication of the breath or vapor of the object odorate; but harmony, entering easily, and mingling not at all, and coming with a manifest motion, doth by custom of often affecting the spirits and putting them into one kind of posture, alter not a little the nature of the spirits, even when the object is removed. And therefore we see that tunes and airs, even in their own nature, have in themselves some affinity with the affections: as there be merry tunes, doleful tunes, solemn tunes; tunes inclining men's minds to pity; warlike tunes, etc. So as it is no marvel if they alter the spirits, considering that tunes have a predisposition to the motion of the spirits in themselves. But yet it hath been noted, that though this variety of tunes disposes the spirits to variety of passions conform unto them, yet generally music feeds that disposition of the spirits which it finds. We see also that several airs and tunes do please several nations and persons, according to the sympathy they have with their spirits.[59]

---

57 'Catalog of Particular Histories,' in Ibid., VIII, 374.

58 *History of Dense and Rare*, in Ibid., X, 265.

59 *Natural History*, Section 114, in Ibid.

On this general subject, Bacon also makes a very interesting comment touching on music therapy.

> This variable composition of man's body has made it as an instrument easy to distemper; and therefore the poets did well to conjoin Music and Medicine in Apollo: because the office of medicine is but to tune this curious harp of Man's body and to reduce it to harmony.[60]

On Performance Practice

Bacon discounts quarter tones as being incapable of harmony, but makes the following exception.

> Nevertheless we have some slides or relishes of the voice or strings, as it were continued without notes from one tone to another, rising or falling, which are delightful.[61]

In his *The Advancement of Learning*, Bacon, in speaking of a Latin proverb, 'all things change, but nothing is lost,'[62] comments on the pleasures which come from hearing such minor points of improvisation.

> Is not the precept of a musician, to fall from a discord or harsh accord upon a concord or sweet accord, alike true in emotion? Is not the improvisation [*trope*] of music, to avoid or slide from the close or cadence, common with the trope of rhetoric of deceiving expectation? Is not the delight of the quavering upon a stop in music the same with the playing of light upon the water?[63]

Bacon wrote an essay, 'Of Masques and Triumphs,' but in apologizing for including this subject among his other essays, he adds that masques and triumphs 'are but toys, to come amongst serious observations.' Nevertheless, he cannot hide his enjoyment of them.

> Dancing to song is a thing of great state and pleasure. I understand it, that the song be in choir, placed aloft, and accompanied with some broken music; and the verse be fitted to the device. Acting in song, especially in dialogues, has an extreme good grace; I say acting, not dancing (for that is a mean and vulgar thing); and the voices of the dialogue would be strong and manly (a bass and a tenor; no treble); and the verse high and tragical; not nice or dainty. Several choirs, placed one over against another, and taking the voice by catches, anthem-wise, give great pleasure.[64]

---

60 *The Advancement of Learning*, in Ibid., VI, 242.
61 *Natural History*, Section 110, in Ibid.
62 *Omnia mutantur, nil interit.*
63 *The Advancement of Learning*, in Ibid., VI, 210.
64 'Of Masques and Triumphs,' in Ibid., XII, 209ff.

Among the specific recommendations for the music of masques, Bacon suggests,

> Let the songs be loud and cheerful, and not chirpings or purlings. Let the music likewise be sharp and loud, and well placed …
>
> Let anti-masques not be long; they have been commonly of fools, satyrs, baboons, wildmen, antics, beasts, sprites, witches … Let the music of them be recreative, and with some strange changes.

6 JACOBEAN POETRY

THE PURITAN MOVEMENT IN ENGLAND, which had been increasing in strength since the sixteenth century, had a significant influence on the climate for the arts. Not only did they cause the complete closing of the theaters, but music, especially that which was associated with dance, came under specific criticism. Poetry as well was attacked and even John Donne, whom many consider to be, excepting Milton, the greatest poet of the Jacobean period, seems to admit that some poetry was a 'sin.' He also mentions in particular some types of poets beneath his respect, including actors, some preachers, composers of love poetry and those who address requests to the aristocracy.

> Though Poetry indeed be such a sin
> As I think that brings dearths, and Spaniards in,
> Though like the Pestilence and old fashioned love,
> Ridingly it catch men; and doth remove
> Never, till it be [destroyed]; yet their state
> Is poor, disarmed, like Papists, not worth hate:
> One ... gives idiot actors means
> (Starving himself) to live by his labored scenes.
> As in some organ, puppets dance above
> And bellows pant below, which do move.
> One would move Love by rhythms ...
> And they who write to Lords, rewards to get,
> Are they not like singers at doors for meat?[1]

The strict Puritan, George Wither, in a dedication 'to the meeke ingenuous Reader,' admits the state in which poetry was viewed, but points out that some poetry is commendable.

> Though much contempt is cast on poetry,
> The Meek, and men of Ingenuity,
> Still, entertain her with respective ears
> When, on her proper errand she appears.
> For, sacred things, and things most pertinent

---

[1] 'Satyre II,' *The Complete Poetry of John Donne,* ed. John T. Shawcross (New York: New York University Press, 1968), 18. John Donne (1573–1631) studied at both Oxford and Cambridge, but as a born Catholic was not permitted to receive a degree. After various attempts at professions brought him to poverty, he converted to the official Church, became famous for his sermons and eventually became Dean of St. Paul's.

> To man's well being, by that instrument,
> Have been conveyed, even in every nation.²

In perhaps a further insight into the climate then current for poetry, Wither follows the above with a second dedication to the critics, 'To the scornfully Censorious.'

> What have we here? says pride-puft-ignorance,
> More Poetry? yes fool; more, too, perchance,
> Then thou wilt like; and, more, for thee to jeer,
> Till foaming at thy mouth, thy brains appear
> Through witless Choler, when thy soul shall dread,
> What, thou with scornful disrespect, have read.³

Finally, in a 'Hymn for a Poet,' written for those poets who were not yet 'past grace,' Wither suggests they begin to base their poems on Old Testament models. The poetry of the ancient Greeks, being inspired by heathen gods, he discounts as the results of 'lust and wine.'⁴

Until the latter part of the Renaissance, virtually all poetry was intended to be sung. While in the seventeenth century it was usually now to be spoken or read, nevertheless the long association with music had not been forgotten. For example, Abraham Cowley, in his 'Davideis,' observes,

> Though no man heard it, though no man rehearse,
> Yet will there still be musick in my verse.⁵

An occasional poem still implies it should be sung, as we see in an 'Ode' to Venus by Ben Jonson.

> For thy soft ears sake
> Shall Verse be set to harp and lute,
> And Phrygian oboe, not without the flute.⁶

---

2   *Works of George Wither* (New York: Franklin, 1967), Spenser Society, Nr. 26-27, 'Halelviah,' Hymn LX. George Wither (1588–1667), one of the so-called Cavalier Poets was an officer in the Puritan army and most of his poetry is political in nature.

3   Ibid. In his 'The Schollers Purgatory,' Wither makes a scathing attack on book publishers and book sellers. [See Spenser Society, Nr. 12]

4   Ibid., Spenser Society, Nr. 26-27, 'Halelviah,' Hymn LX.

5   'Davideis,' in *The Complete Works of Abraham Cowley*, ed. Alexander Grosart (New York: AMS Press, 1967), I, 49. Abraham Cowley (1618–1667) attracted great attention as a young poet, but little later in his life.

6   *The Complete Poetry of Ben Jonson*, ed. William Hunter (New York: Norton, 1963), 267.

In other poems such references seem only rhetorical, as for example in one by Edmund Waller.

> This last complaint that indulgent ears did pierce
> Of just Apollo, President of Verse,
> Highly concerned, that the Muse should bring
> Damage to one whom he had taught to sing.[7]

One also notices that most of the Jacobean poets wrote poetry which carries the title, 'A Song,' among them the famous poem by John Donne, 'Go, and catch a falling star.' Some of these poems carry an indication of the composers who actually set the work to music. An early publication of the poetry of Richard Lovelace, for example, identifies those composers who set his 'songs' to music, including Henry and William Lawes, John Laniere, Thomas Charles, 'Mr. Curtes' and John Wilson.[8] Among the poetry of Edward, Lord Herbert of Cherbery (d. 1648), the association with a specific composer is included in the title. One is entitled, 'Ditty to the tune of A che del Quantomio of Pesarino,' and another 'A Ditty to the tune of Coseferite, made by Lorenzo Allegre to one sleeping to be sung.'[9] Finally, Phineas Fletcher wrote a number of original poems 'which may be sung,' to traditional psalm tunes.[10] Perhaps in these cases the poets still thought of their poems as music. In fact, Swinburne once called the poet, Herrick, 'the greatest song-writer ever born of English race.'[11]

The influence of the ancient lyric poets of Greece is still much in evidence among the seventeenth-century English poets. Even surrounded by the Puritan threats, one still finds the poet appealing to the Muses for inspiration, as for example Herrick in his 'To Apollo. A short Hymn':

> Phoebus! when that I a Verse,
> Or some numbers more rehearse;
> Tune my words, that they may fall,
> Each way smoothly Musical.[12]

---

7   'At Pens-hurst,' in *Edmund Waller, Poems* (Menston: Scolar Press, 1971), 22. Edmund Waller (1606–1687) came from a royalist family, but took the side of the Puritans. He became very popular during the Restoration.

8   *The Poems of Richard Lovelace*, ed. C. H. Wilkinson (Oxford: Clarendon Press, 1930). Richard Lovelace (1618–1657), one of the Cavalier Poets, was devoted to the king and imprisoned by the Puritans.

9   Edward Herbert, *Occasional Verses* (Menston: The Scholar Press, 1969), 26, 29.

10 Phineas Fletcher (1582–1650), 'The Purple Island,' in Frederick Boas, *Giles and Phineas Fletcher Poetical Works* (Cambridge: University Press, 1909), II, 250ff.

11 Quoted in *The Poetical Works of Robert Herrick*, ed. L. C. Martin (Oxford: Clarendon Press, 1963), xx. Herrick (1591–1674) is considered one of the most gifted of the so-called Cavalier Poets. He was a graduate of Cambridge and became a prior in Devonshire.

12 *The Poetical Works of Robert Herrick*, 122.

Another Herrick poem pleas for Apollo to 're-inspire my fingers.'[13] Ben Jonson points to the difficulty in the loss of such inspiration, in 'An Elegie on my Muse.'

> Thou hast no more blows, Fate, to drive at one:
> What's left a Poet, when his Music is gone?
> Sure, I am dead, and know it not! I feel
> Nothing I do; but, like a heavy wheel,
> Am turned with an others powers.[14]

Abraham Cowley comments on the impact on the poet himself of the 'divine fury,' or creative frenzy, mentioned by the ancient Greek poets.

> More poetry! You'll cry, dost thou return,
> Fond man, to the disease thou has forsworn?
> It has reached thy marrow, seized they inmost sense,
> And force or reason cannot draw it thence.[15]

As for himself,

> I can be serious too when business calls,
> My frenzy still has lucid intervals.

One still finds many pastoral works which, as they had been for centuries, followed the models of the ancient Greek lyric poets. Since these works describe mostly the music of ancient rural myths, and not of contemporary performance practice, we will not dwell on these references. However, one poet whom we especially associate with this kind of poetry, William Browne (1591–1643), wrote an extremely long pastoral work called 'Britannia's Pastorals,' in which two passages caught our eye. One is a reference to a shepherd who selects his instrument to match the emotion to be expressed, 'Couple his bass Pipe with their baser Tone.'[16] The second is a reference to Pythagoras's supposed discovery of the proportions of the lower overtones while observing a blacksmith.

> Fondly have some been led to think, that Man
> Musiques invention first of all began
> From the dull Hammers stroke; since well we know
> From sure tradition that hath taught us so.[17]

---

13 Ibid., 280.

14 *The Complete Poetry of Ben Jonson*, 258.

15 Preface to 'de Plantarum,' in *The Complete Works of Abraham Cowley*, I, 239.

16 William Browne, 'Britannia's Pastorals,' Book I, Song 5.

17 Ibid., Book II, Song 4. The story of Pythagoras' discovery, as it has been handed down, is impossible.

Another passage which attracted our attention is found in Phineas Fletcher's 'Brittain's Ida' and is interesting for its reference to the organizing of hunting dogs into consorts, something mentioned in sixteenth-century literature, including Shakespeare.

> His joy was not in musiques sweete delight,
> (Though well his hand had learnt that cunning arte)
> Or dainty songs to daintier ears indite;
> But through the plains to chase the nimble Hart,
> With well tuned hounds …[18]

These poets do not elaborate much on the purpose of poetry. Only Wither specifically lists among the purposes of poetry, prophesy and 'to stir the affections.'[19] For Robert Herrick, it seems to have sufficed that poetry serve as entertainment.

> In sober mornings, do not thou rehearse
> The holy incantation of a verse;
> But when that men have both well drunk, and fed,
> Let my enchantments then be sung, or read.[20]

ON THE PHYSIOLOGY OF AESTHETICS

The most interesting comments on the organization of man's faculties, with respect to insights relative to aesthetics, center on the separateness of Reason and the emotions. In Phineas Fletcher's poem, 'The Purple Island,' largely a description of a city as a metaphor for a map of anatomy, we have an early description of the twin hemispheres of the brain surrounded by the skull. It is here that he identifies the location of the senses, arts and Beauty.

> Here all the senses dwell, and all the arts;
> Here learned Muses by their silver spring:
> The Citie severed in two diverse parts,
> Within the walls, and Suburbs neighboring;
> The Suburbs girt but with the common fence,
> Founded with wondrous skill, and great expense;
> And therefore beautie here keeps her chief residence.[21]

---

18 'Brittain's Ida,' in *Giles and Phineas Fletcher Poetical Works*, II, 348.
19 *Works of George Wither*, Spenser Society, Nr. 18, 'Prosopopoeia Britannica,' dedication.
20 *The Poetical Works of Robert Herrick*, 7.
21 Fletcher, 'The Purple Island,' in *Giles and Phineas Fletcher Poetical Works*, II, 54.

Ben Jonson distinguishes both the intellect and the emotions in a sonnet to Mary Wroth on the subject of becoming a better poet.

> Nor is my Muse, or I ashamed to owe it
> To those true numerous Graces; whereof some,
> But charm the Senses, others over-come
> Both brains and hearts.[22]

Herrick seems aware of the same distinction when he writes, 'The Eyes by tears speak, while the Tongue is mute,'[23] and,

> In prayer the lips never act the winning part,
> Without the sweet concurrence of the heart.[24]

The severe Puritan, George Wither, reverts to the old Catholic Church position in stressing that in this competition between Reason and the emotions, Reason must control man.

> Expelling those whom Virtues presence grace,
> And in their steads these hurtful Monsters placed;
> Fond Love, and Lust, Ambition, Enmitie,
> Foolish Compassion, Joy and Jealousy,
> Fear, Hope, Despair, and Sadness, with the Vice
> Called Hate; Revenge, and greedy Avarice,
> Choler, and Cruelty: which I perceived
> To be the only causes Man's bereaved
> Of quietness and rest. Yea, these I found
> To be the principal and only ground
> Of all pernicious mischiefs that now rage,
> Or have disturbed him in any age.
> These losing Reason, their true Prince, began
> To breed disturbance in the heart of Man.[25]

We know today that it is the right hemisphere of the brain which adds emotional color, or meaning, to the vocabulary of the left hemisphere and emotional meaning to the notated form of music. A poem by Edward Herbert, 'To a Lady who did sing excellently,' is a remarkable testimonial to this process. He says the words have no sense until sung by the lady.

---

22 *The Complete Poetry of Ben Jonson*, 166.
23 *The Poetical Works of Robert Herrick*, 58.
24 Ibid., 346.
25 Wither, Spenser Society, Nr. 9, 'Of Man,' 26.

When our rude & unfashioned words, that long
A being in their elements enjoyed,
Senseless and void,
Come at last to be formed by thy tongue,
And from thy breath receive that life and place,
And perfect grace,
That now thy power diffused through all their parts
Are able to remove
All the obstructions of the hardest hearts,
And teach the most unwilling how to love.

When they again, exalted by thy voice,
Tuned by the soul, dismissed into the air,
To us repair,
A living, moving, and harmonious noise,
Able to give the love they do create
A second state,
And charm not only all his griefs away,
And his defects restore,
But make him perfect, who, the Poets say,
Made all was ever yet made heretofore.[26]

In these volumes we have traced throughout the literature of all centuries passages which contain an evident preference for the right hand, as an unconscious reflection of the speaking and writing left hemisphere of the brain. This same prejudice is much in evidence in the poetry of seventeenth-century England. This is very striking in a poem by Ben Jonson called 'On my First Son,' where we find, 'Farewell, thou child of my right hand.'[27] In this case, the child's name was Benjamin, which in Hebrew means, 'child of the right hand.'

Additional examples of right hand preference can be seen in Richard Crashaw's poem inspired by Matthew 2:11 (the visit of the three kings after the birth of Jesus),

Whether by your eye or by your right hand you honor them.[28]

and in Abraham Cowley's discussion of Hazel in his book on plants, where he observes,

In search of golden mines a Hazle wand
The wise Diviner takes in his Right-hand.[29]

---

26 Herbert, *Occasional Verses*, 44ff.

27 *The Complete Poetry of Ben Jonson*, 20.

28 'The Gifts of the Persian Sages,' in *The Complete Poetry of Richard Crashaw*, ed. George Williams (New York: New York University Press, 1972), 280.

29 *Of Plants*, in *The Complete Works of Abraham Cowley*, I, 276.

George Wither, in his book of emblems, entitles one picture, 'The Right-hand way is Virtue's path.' The essence of the poem which follows is that virtue's path is the more difficult. He concludes,

> And, though the Left-hand-way, more smoothness hath,
> Let us go forward, in the Right-hand-path.[30]

John Donne also emphasizes the importance of the right hand, as a symbol of Faith, over the left hand which he incorrectly associates with Reason.

> Reason is our soul's left hand, Faith her right,
> By these we reach divinity, that's you;
> Their loves, who have the blessings of your light,
> Grew from their reason, mine from faire faith grew,
> But as, although a squint lefthandedness
> Be ungracious, yet we cannot want that hand,
> So would I, not to increase, but to express
> My faith, as I believe, so understand.[31]

There are also examples in this literature of obvious prejudice against the left hand, as for example in Thomas Dekker.

> All the Skies
> Danced to the sounds of several Harmonies;
> Both Angels and Arch-angels loudly sung,
> All Heaven was but One Instrument well strung.
> But They, who on the Left-hand were set by,
> (As Out-casts) shooke and trembled fearefully.[32]

A similar prejudice is expressed by Herrick.

> God has a Right Hand, but is quite bereft
> Of that, which we do nominate the Left.[33]

Finally, a curious poem in praise of Christmas by Thomas Traherne pleads with music to enliven the senses. Few Christmas poems must begin, 'Shall Dumpish Melancholy spoil my Joys …'

---

30 Wither, *A Collection of Emblemes* (1635), in Rosemary Freeman, *English Emblem Books* (Menston, Yorkshire: Scolar Press, 1968), 160.

31 'To the Countesse of Bedford,' *The Complete Poetry of John Donne*, 220ff.

32 Thomas Dekker, 'Dekker his Dreame,' in *The Non-Dramatic Works of Thomas Dekker*, ed. Alexander Grosart (New York, Russell & Russell, 1963), III, 29.

33 *The Poetical Works of Robert Herrick*, 394.

Shake off thy Sloth, my drowsy Soul, awake;
With Angels sing
Unto thy King,
And pleasant Musick make;
Thy Lute, thy Harp, or else thy Heart-strings take,
And with thy Musick let thy Sense awake.[34]

ON THE PSYCHOLOGY OF AESTHETICS

A proverb by George Herbert accurately reflects the universal, and genetic, nature of the emotions, although as was the case with most early writers he misunderstood the communication of feelings to be in the eyes, rather than the face.

The eyes have one language everywhere.[35]

Like poets of all centuries, these poets focus on the emotion of Love above all others. As representative of them all, we single out one passage by George Wither, from his book of emblems, in which he uses music as a metaphor for Love. 'For, Love's a good Musician' he says,

Each word he speaks, will presently appear
To be melodious raptures in your ear:
Each gesture of his body, when he moves,
Will seem to play, or sing, a Song of Loves:
The very looks, and motions of his eyes,
Will touch your heart-strings, with sweet harmonies …
Nay, even those discords, which occasioned are,
Will make your Music, much the sweeter, far.[36]

On the traditional aesthetic topic of Pleasure and Pain, the poet, George Herbert, as a rector, finds pleasure only in the future.

Yet if we rightly measure,
Man's joy and pleasure
Rather hereafter than in present is.[37]

---

34 'On Christmas-Day,' in *Thomas Traherne, Centuries, Poems and Thanksgivings* (Oxford: Clarendon Press, 1958), 110. Thomas Traherne (1634–1674) published no poetry during his life and his name was not known until the discovery of a manuscript in 1910.

35 'Jacula Prudentum,' in *The Poems of George Herbert*, ed. Ernest Rhys (London: Walter Scott, 1885), 249. George Herbert (1593–1633) devoted most of his poetry to the Church of England, which he served as a rector near Salisbury. None of his poetry was published during his lifetime. Some publications refer to him as a 'late orator of the University of Cambridge.'

36 Wither, *A Collection of Emblemes*, 82.

37 'Man's Medley,' in *The Poems of George Herbert*, 133.

Andrew Marvell has written a poem called, 'A Dialogue between the Resolved Soul and Created Pleasure,' in which Pleasure offers various enticements in an attempt to win over the soul. Among these is Music, toward which Soul first indicates it would be nice if she had time.

> PLEASURE. Hark how musick then prepares
> For thy stay these charming aires,
> Which the posting winds recall,
> And suspend the river's fall.
> SOUL. Had I but any time to lose,
> On this I would it all dispose.
> Cease tempter! None can chain a mind,
> Whom this sweet chordage cannot bind.[38]

All readers of the literature of the sixteenthth century and Baroque period will notice a curious, almost masochistic, absorption with melancholy and other emotions of a dark nature. It is from this perspective that we find several poets who concentrate on the positive nature of grief. For example, George Wither observes in his 'Vaticinia Poetica,' that 'Our pains do show what Ease and Pleasures are.'[39] In another place he seems to prefer suffering.

> By suffering, I have more contentment had,
> Than ever I acquired by slothful ease;
> And, I by Grief, so joyful have been made,
> That I will bear my cross, while God shall please.[40]

John Donne seems of the same persuasion when he observes, 'For, all our joys are but fantastical,' but 'pain is true.'[41]

Robert Herrick assigns the direct responsibility for both Pleasure and Pain to God.

> God suffers not His Saints, and servants dear,
> To have continual pain, or pleasure here:
> But look how night succeeds the day, so He
> Gives them by turns their grief and jollitie.[42]

---

38 'A Dialogue between the Resolved Soul and Created Pleasure,' in *The Complete Works of Andrew Marvell* (New York: AMS Press, 1966), I, 96. Andrew Marvell (1621–1678) was popular under both the Cromwell and early Restoration periods. He also served as a secretary to Milton after the the famous poet became blind.

39 *Wither*, Spenser Society, Nr. 18, 'Vaticinia Poetica,' 27.

40 Wither, *A Collection of Emblemes*, 23.

41 'Satyre II,' *The Complete Poetry of John Donne*, 92.

42 *The Poetical Works of Robert Herrick*, 394.

ON THE PHILOSOPHY OF AESTHETICS

There is very little discussion of their aesthetic principles by any of these poets, although we believe one proverb by George Herbert refers to the arts.

> Honor and profit lie not in one sack.[43]

Even the nature of Beauty, other than on the subject of women, is little discussed by these poets. Herrick offers a curious definition,

> Beauty, no other thing is, than a Beam
> Flashed out between the Middle and the Extreme.[44]

Sir John Suckling reminds the reader that Beauty is in the eye of the beholder.

> There's no such thing as that we beauty call,
> It is mere cosenage all;
> For though some long ago
> Liked certain colors mingled so and so,
> That doth not tie me now from choosing new:
> If I a fancy take
> To black and blue,
> That fancy doth it beauty make.[45]

Regarding the ancient aesthetic topic of whether Art should imitate Nature, and to what degree, we have an interesting poem in honor of Shakespeare by Ben Jonson, in which the poet observes that 'though the matter of poets be Nature,' it is the art of the poet which must shape it. In a reflection on Shakespeare's own labor, Jonson notes,

> For a good poet's made, as well as born.
> And such wert thou.[46]

A similar reflection is made by Herrick.

> Man is composed here of a two-fold part;
> The first of Nature, and the next of Art:
> Art presupposes Nature.[47]

---

43 'Jacula Prudentum,' in *The Poems of George Herbert*, 246.

44 *The Poetical Works of Robert Herrick*, 33.

45 'Sonnet II,' in *The Works of Sir John Suckling*, ed. Hamilton Thompson (New York: Russell & Russell, 1964), 15. Sir John Suckling (1609–1642), associated with the 'Cavalier Poets,' was a notorious gambler and courtier of Charles, he was forced to flee to France where he took his own life. One of his poems, 'A Session of the Poets' [Ibid., 9ff], characterizes many of the Jacobean poets.

46 *The Complete Poetry of Ben Jonson*, 373ff.

47 *The Poetical Works of Robert Herrick*, 153.

An unusual reflection on this subject, in an Ode by Richard Lovelace, contends that not only can Art not surpass Nature, but *should* not.

> For since thy birth gave thee no beauty, know
> No poets pencil must or can do so.[48]

ON THE AESTHETICS OF MUSIC

We find in this literature no specific attempt to offer a definition of music as a general topic. The closest discussion we find is a poem by Andrew Marvell which is a virtual history of music called 'Musick's Empire.'

> First was the world as one great cymbal made,
> Where jarring winds to infant Nature played;
> All musick was a solitary sound,
> To hollow rocks and murmuring fountains bound.
>
> Jubal first made the wilder notes agree,
> And Jubal tuned Musick's jubilee;
> He called the echoes from their sullen cell,
> And built the organ's city, where they dwell.
>
> Each sought a consort in that lovely place,
> And virgin trebles wed the manly bass,
> From whence the progeny of numbers new
> Into harmonious colonies withdrew;
>
> Some to the lute, some to the viol went,
> And others chose the cornet eloquent;
> These practicing the wind, and those the wire,
> To sing man's triumphs, or in heaven's choir.
>
> Then Musick, the mosaic of the air,
> Did of all these a solemn noise prepare,
> With which she gained the empire of the ear,
> Including all between the earth and sphere.[49]

---

48 'Ode,' in *The Poems of Richard Lovelace*, 151.
49 'Music's Empire,' in *The Complete Works of Andrew Marvell*, I, 131ff.

On the Perception of Music

The only subject which falls under the topic of the perception of music which seemed to interest these poets was the old myth of the 'Music of the Spheres.' Some poets seem to suggest this music could actually be heard, among them Ben Jonson whose 'Pastoral Dialog' begins,

> Come with our voices, let us warre,
> And challenge all the Spheres,
> Till each of us be made a Star,
> And all the world turn Ears.[50]

Robert Herrick makes a similar suggestion in his poem 'To Musick. A Song.'

> Musick, thou *Queen of Heaven*, care-charming-spel,
> That strikes a stillness in hell:
> Thou that tames Tigers, and fierce storms that rise
> With thy soul-melting Lullabies:
> Fall down, down, down, from those thy chiming spheres,
> To charm our souls, as thou enchant our ears.[51]

George Wither, on the other hand, says no. In his 'Vaticinia Poetica,' in a poem called 'Song,' we find,

> Sound out, ye everlasting Spheres,
> That Musick, which no mortal hears …[52]

Two poets suggest that the 'Music of the Spheres' cannot be heard, but can be felt. John Donne seeks to make this point in his reference to three kinds of choirs.

> Make all this All, three Choirs, heaven, earth, and spheres,
> The first, Heaven, hath a song, but no man hears,
> The Spheres have Musick, but they have no tongue,
> Their harmony is rather danced than sung;
> But our third Choir, to which the first gives ear,
> (For, Angels learn by what the Church does here)
> This Choir hath all.[53]

---

50 *The Complete Poetry of Ben Jonson*, 131.

51 *The Poetical Works of Robert Herrick*, 103.

52 *Wither*, Spenser Society, Nr. 18, 'Vaticinia Poetica,' 'Song.'

53 'Upon the translation of the Psalmes by Sir Philip Sydney,' *The Complete Poetry of John Donne*, 389. Donne also mentions the 'Spheares Musick' in 'Valediction of the booke,' [Ibid., 117] and in his 'Obsequies to the Lord Harrington' [Ibid., 260].

Richard Crashaw makes the same assertion in his Hymn, 'The Name of Jesus,' in which he mentions the Music of the Spheres 'which dull mortality more feels than hears.'[54]

On Music as Part of the Culture

In seventeenth-century England, Odes with music became a familiar accompaniment to the celebrations of the aristocracy. To cite only one of these, an 'Ode for Her Majesties Birthday, 1630,' mentions music throughout its subject of the nine Muses. One of the muses sings,

> THALIA. Let our trumpets sound;
>   And cleave both air and ground,
>   With beating of our Drum's:
>   Let every lyre be strung,
>   Harp, lute, theorbo sprung,
>   With touch of dainty thumb's![55]

A poem by George Withers, a strong Puritan, complains that the musicians who so eagerly wrote 'their lyrics, heroic poems and odes' for Cromwell, now after his fall immediately changed their colors and returned to composing for the new king.

> Yea, all her Songs unto this present day,
> Are but the same, new set another way:
> And, their composers do deserve no more
> Than *begging Fiddlers* begging at the door.
> Who if it might their servile ends advance,
> Would, to the same tune play the devil a dance.[56]

The celebration of New Year's Day was another inspiration for many Odes and poems. One of these by Ben Jonson attracted our attention.

> New yeares, expect *new* gifts: Sister, your harp,
> Lute, lyre, theorbo, all are called today.
> Your change of Notes, the *flat*, the *meane*, the *sharpe*,
> To show the rites, and to usher forth the way.[57]

---

54 'The Name of Jesus,' in *The Complete Poetry of Richard Crashaw*, 32. Crashaw mentions the Music of the Spheres again in his 'Upon the Kings Coronation,' lines 21ff; 'Hymn in the Glorious Epiphanie,' lines 131ff and in 'The Teare' [Ibid., 51]. Henry Vaughan refers to the Music of the Spheres in his 'The Tempest,' in *The Works of Henry Vaughan*, 461. Lovelace mentions the Music of the Spheres in *The Poems of Richard Lovelace*, ed. C. H. Wilkinson (Oxford: Clarendon Press, 1930), 26, 92, 114, 160, 187.

55 *The Complete Poetry of Ben Jonson*, 220ff.

56 Wither, Spenser Society, Nr. 22, 'Speculum Speculativum,' 71.

57 *The Complete Poetry of Ben Jonson*, 241.

Another testimony to the familiarity of music, as a part of the culture, is found in its use as a figure of speech. George Wither uses the ancient Greek metaphor of harmony to represent an ordered government.

> Musique may teach of difference in degree,
> The best tuned Common-Weales will framed be.[58]

A similar sentiment is made by John Suckling, in his New Year's poem to the king in 1640,

> May all the discords in your state
> (Like those in music we create)
> Be governed at so wise a rate,
> That what would of itself sound harsh, or fright,
> May be so tempered that it may delight.[59]

Thomas Carew uses the metaphor of harmony to represent the sum of the features of the face of a lady recently deceased.

> The harmony of colors, features, grace,
> Resulting Aires (the magicke of a face)
> Of musical sweet tunes, all which combined
> To this dark Vault.[60]

One particularly touching figure of speech is found in George Herbert's prayer to be put to use in God's employment.

> Lord, place me in Thy concert; give one strain
> To my poor reed![61]

The trumpet as a metaphor for an important communication was used a number of times by these poets. Perhaps there are no better representatives than those found in the poetry of King James I himself. One reads,

> So Homer was a sounding trumpet fine
> Amongst the Greeks into his learned days.[62]

---

58 Wither, Spenser Society, Nr. 10, 'Epithalamia,' 465.

59 *The Works of Sir John Suckling*, 7.

60 Thomas Carew, 'Epitaph on the Lady S.,' in *The Poems of Thomas Carew*, ed. Rhodes Dunlap (Oxford: Clarendon Press, 1964), 55. Thomas Carew (1594–1639), one of the 'Cavalier' poets, was trained in law but gained his reputation as a poet among the upper class.

61 'Employment,' in *The Poems of George Herbert*, 51.

62 'A Sonnet,' in *New Poems of James I*, ed. Allan Westcott (New York: AMS Press, 1966), 29.

The king used this same metaphor in another work, the fragment of a wedding poem.

> Which by the trumpet of my verse I made for to resound
> From pole to pole through every where of this immobile round.[63]

Of course, the most familiar figure of speech involving the trumpet is its use as a metaphor for the Day of Judgment. In Richard Crashaw we also get some description of its sound on that august day.

> that trump! whose blast shall run
> An even round with the circling Sun.[64]

The use of this figure of speech by George Herbert, in a poem called 'Doomsday,' concludes with a strange twist. 'Dust,' here, refers to the dead.

> Come away,
> Make this the day.
> Dust, alas, no music feels,
> But Thy trumpet; then it kneels,
> As peculiar notes and strains
> Cure tarantula's raging pains.[65]

On the Purpose of Music

An important purpose of music, of course, is simply for pleasure. In this regard we notice George Wither's comments on the loss of music during the civil wars in England.

> And where sweet musique hath refresht the ear,
> Sad groans of ghosts departing, now we hear.[66]

The most frequently mentioned purpose of music in earlier literature was its capacity to soothe the feelings of the listener. Among the many poems in this literature which mention this, there is an Epigram by Ben Jonson written for the publication of a book of music by Alphonso Ferrabosco.

---

63 'An Epithalamion,' in Ibid., 47.
64 'In Meditation of the Day of Judgment,' in *The Complete Poetry of Richard Crashaw*, 189. A similar use of this metaphor is found in 'An Elegie on my Muse,' in *The Complete Poetry of Ben Jonson*, 258.
65 'Doomsday,' in *The Poems of George Herbert*, 195.
66 Wither, Spenser Society, Nr. 12, 'Campo-Musae,' 16.

> Which Musick had; or speake her knowne effects,
> That she removeth cares, sadness ejects,
> Declineth anger, persuades clemencie,
> Doth sweeten mirth, and heighten pietie.[67]

Another reference to this purpose which we like, is by Thomas Carew, in a poem inspired by the illness of a friend.

> Then let the God of Musick, with still charms,
> Her restless eyes in peaceful slumbers close,
> And with soft strains sweeten her calm repose.[68]

After George Wither mentions this purpose,

> But, though that all the world's delight forsake me,
> I have a Muse, and she shall Musicke make me:
> Whose airy notes, in spite of closest cages,
> Shall give content to me, and after ages …,[69]

a shepherd questions if only those who sing are happy? His companion does not answer the question, but, like the old troubadours, points to the association of music and Spring.

> WILLY. Those that sing not, must be sad?
>   Did'st thou ever that Bird hear
>   Sing well; that sings all the year?
>   Tom the Piper does not play
>   Till he wears his pipe away:
>   There's a time to slack the string,
>   And a time to leave to sing.
> PHILARETE. Yea; but no man now is still,
>   That can sing, or tune a quill.
>   Now to chant it, were but reason;
>   Song and Musicke are in season.[70]

At the end of the poem, Wither again returns to the ability of music to soothe.

> The Muses teach us Songs to put off cares,
> Graced with as rare and sweet conceits as theirs.[71]

---

67 *The Complete Poetry of Ben Jonson*, 65.
68 'Upon the sickness of …,' in *The Poems of Thomas Carew*, 31.
69 *Wither*, Spenser Society, Nr. 10, a Sonnet, in 'the Shepheards Hunting,' 529.
70 Ibid., 534ff.
71 Ibid., 558.

The poet, George Herbert, a rector in the Church of England, emphasized the solace to be found in church music. In a poem entitled, 'Church Music,' he writes,

> Sweetest of sweets, I thank you! when displeasure
> Did through my body wound my mind,
> You took me hence, and in your house of pleasure
> A dainty lodging me assigned.[72]

Herbert appears to have been a poet with considerable background in music. In his biography, by Izaak Walton, we find,

> During which time all, or the greatest diversion from his study, was the practice of music, in which he became a great master, and of which he would say, 'That it did relieve his drooping spirits, compose his distracted thoughts, and raised his weary soul so far above the earth, that it gave him an earnest of the joys of heaven before he possessed them.'[73]
>
> ……
>
> His chief recreation was music, in which heavenly art he was a most excellent master, and did himself compose many divine hymns and anthems, which he set and sung to his lute or viol; and through he was a lover of retiredness, yet his love to music was such, that he went usually twice every week on certain appointed days to the cathedral church in Salisbury; and at his return would say, that his time spent in prayer and cathedral music elevated his soul, and was his heaven upon earth. But before his return thence to Bemerton, he would usually sing and play his part at an appointed private music meeting; and, to justify this practice, he would often say, religion does not banish mirth, but only moderates and sets rules to it.

Walking once to such a chamber music rehearsal with his friends, Herbert apparently encountered a man with a horse in distress, whom he stopped to help. When his clergy friends suggested that he had 'disparaged himself by so dirty an employment,' he responded that,

> the thought of what he had done would prove music to him at midnight, and that the omission of it would have upbraided and made discord in his conscience … 'And now let us tune our instruments.'

Walton tells us that days before Herbert's death,

> he rose suddenly from his bed and couch, called for one of his instruments, took it into his hand, and said,
>   My God, my God!
>   My music shall find Thee,
>   And every string
>   Shall have his attribute to sing.

---

72 'Church Music,' in *The Poems of George Herbert*, 59.

73 Ibid., 260ff.

Finally, for Abraham Cowley, even the birds sing to soothe themselves.

> And when no Art affords me help or ease,
> I seek with verse my griefs to appease.
> Just as a bird that flies about
> And beats itself against the cage,
> Finding at last no passage out,
> It sits and sings, and so overcomes its rage.[74]

The most important purpose of music is, of course, to express emotions and in this literature one finds reference to the communication of rather strong emotions. Consider, for example, Richard Lovelace's poem called 'Dialogue for Lute and Voice.'

> What sacred charm may this then be in harmonie,
> That thus can make the angels wild, the devils mild,
> And teach low Hell to Heaven to swell,
> And the high Heaven to stoop to Hell.[75]

A poem by Robert Herrick entitled 'To Musick' also points to the expression of strong emotions by music.

> Begin to charm, and as thou strike mine ears
> With thy enchantment, melt me into tears.
> Then let thy active hand scu'd over thy Lyre:
> And make my spirits frantic with the fire.
> That done, sink down into a silvery strain;
> And make me smooth as balm, and oil again.[76]

Quite different, is another poem by Herrick.

> The mellow touch of musick most doth wound
> The soul, when it doth rather sigh, then sound.[77]

Several poems in this literature concentrate on the expression of grief through music, as for example one by Edmund Waller.

> GALATEA. You that can tune your sounding strings so well
>   Of ladies beauties, and of love to tell;
>   Once change your note, and let your lute report

---

[74] 'Friendship in Absence,' in *The Complete Works of Abraham Cowley*, II, 139.

[75] 'A Dialogue. Lute and Voice,' in *The Poems of Richard Lovelace*, 161.

[76] *The Poetical Works of Robert Herrick*, 67.

[77] Ibid., 12.

> The justest grief that ever touched the court.
> THIRSIS. Fair Nymph, I have in your delights no share,
>   Nor ought to be concerned in your care,
>   Yet would I sing if I your sorrows knew,
>   And to my aid invoke no Muse but you.
> GALATEA. Hear then, and let your song augment our grief
>   Which is so great, as not to wish relief.[78]

Similarly, Ben Jonson, in lyrics for a song by Henry Youll published in 1608, reads,

> Slow, slow, fresh fount, keep time with my salt tears,
> Yet slower, yet, o faintly gentle springs:
> Listen to the heavy part the musique bears,
> 'Woe weeps out her division, when she sings.'[79]

John Donne finds such strong emotions can be described by poetry, but need music to be fully expressed and to provide a sense of catharsis.

> But when I have done so,
> Some man, his art and voice to show,
> Doth set [to music] and sing my pain,
> And, by delighting many, frees again
> Grief, which verse did restrain.
> To Love, and Grief tribute of verse belongs,
> But not of such as pleases when 'tis read,
> Both are increased by such song.[80]

In the poetry of George Wither, we find two interesting references to the ancient Greek concept that music could change manners. In one poem, which he disseminated by passing it out a loophole in the Tower of London where he was imprisoned, he decided it 'would better stir up the hearts of some, by being sung, than read.' In this complaint on the manners of London, the stern Puritan poet implores London to turn to music to help improve the behavior of the citizens.

> Thou, London, whofoe're doth weep,
>   Do, on thy viol, play and sing;
> Thy children, daily revel keep …[81]

---

78 'Thirsis, Galateat,' in *Edmund Waller, Poems*, 49ff.
79 *The Complete Poetry of Ben Jonson*, 328.
80 'The triple Foole,' *The Complete Poetry of John Donne*, 99.
81 *Wither*, Spenser Society, Nr. 18, 'A Warning-Piece to London,' 34.

Before his 'Hymn for a Musician,' Wither writes a comment suggesting that some musicians have manners which might be improved by changing their repertoire.

> Many musicians are more out of order than their instruments: such as are so, may by singing this Ode, become reprovers of their own untunable affections. They who are better tempered, are hereby [reminded] what music is most acceptable to God, and most profitable to themselves.[82]

There are considerably more poems which refer to music therapy. While the ancient Greeks used harmony as a metaphor to represent the well-ordered person, Henry Vaughan begins at an earlier point in suggesting that God designed man of music. Curiously, the latest research in physics in England and Switzerland have confirm that man indeed consists of specific vibrating tones.

> Thus doth God *Key* disordered man
> (Which none else can,)
> Tuning his breast to rise, or fall;
> And by a sacred, needful art
> Like strings, stretch every part
> Making the whole most Musical.[83]

George Wither also was thinking of some remote time, writing of 'He that first taught his Musicke such a strain,'

> He in his troubles eased the body's pains,
> By measures raised to the souls ravishing.[84]

In another poem he makes a specific plea for music therapy.

> Teach me the skill,
> Of him, whose Harp assuaged
> Those passions ill,
> Which oft afflicted Saul.
> Teach me the strain
> Which calms mind's enraged;
> And, which from vain
> Affections, doth recall.[85]

---

82 Ibid., Nr. 26–27, 'Halelviah,' Hymn XXXVIII.
83 'Affliction,' in *The Works of Henry Vaughan*, ed. L. C. Martin (Oxford: At the Clarendon Press, 1957), 460.
84 *Wither*, Spenser Society, Nr. 10, 'The Shepheards Hunting,' 506.
85 Ibid., Nr. 26–27, 'Halelviah,' Hymn XXXVIII.

A similar plea is found in Robert Herrick's poem called 'To Musick, to becalm a sweet-sick-youth.'

> Charms, that call down the moon from out her sphere,
> On this sick youth work your enchantments here:
> Bind up his senses with your numbers, so,
> As to entrance his pain, or cure his woe.
> Fall gently, gently, and a while him keep
> Lost in the civil Wilderness of sleep:
> That done, then let him, dispossessed of pain,
> Like to a slumbering Bride, awake again.[86]

Richard Crashaw, in a tribute to the Dutch philosopher, Leonard Lessius (1554–1623), and his book on 'Life and Health,' states that a healthy man has no need of medicine [physick], especially if he has money and music.

> That which makes us have no need
> Of physick, that's Physick indeed.
> Hark hither, Reader! wilt thou see
> Nature her own physician be?
> Wilt' see a man, all his own wealth,
> His own musick, his own health;
> A man whose sober soul can tell
> How to wear her garments well.[87]

The most extended discussion of music therapy is found in the work of Abraham Cowley. In his poem on the troubles of David, 'Davideis,' he mentions the passage in the Old Testament in which David and his harp cure the rage of Saul. He then pauses in his story of David to wonder how it is that music has this great power and concludes that the answer must lie in the relationship of physics to the body.

> And true it was, soft Musick did appease
> The obscure fantastic Rage of Saul's disease.
> Tell me, oh Muse (for thou, or none canst tell
> The mystic powers that in blessed verse [*Numbers*] dwell,
> Thou their great Nature knows, not is it fit
> This noblest gem of thine own crown to omit)
> Tell me from whence these heavenly charms arise;
> Teach the dull world to admire what they despise.
> As first a various unformed hint we find
> Rise in some god-like poet's fertile mind,

---

86 *The Poetical Works of Robert Herrick*, 99.

87 'To the Reader,' in *The Complete Poetry of Richard Crashaw*, 511.

Until all the parts and words their places take,
And with just marches Verse and Musick make;
Such was God's poem, this world's new essay;
So wild and rude in its first draught it lay;
The ungoverned parts no correspondence knew,
An artless war from thwarting motions grew;
Until they to number and fixed rules were brought
By the eternal mind's poetic thought.
Water and air be for the tenor chose.
Earth made the bass, the treble flame arose;
To the active moon a quick brisk stroke he gave,
To Saturn's string a touch more soft and grave.
The motions straight, and round, and swift, and slow,
And short, and long, were mixed and woven so,
Did in such artful figures smoothly fall,
As made this decent measured Dance of All.
And this is Musick; sounds that charm our ears,
Are but one dressing that rich science wears.
Though no man heard it, though no man rehearse,
Yet will there still be musick in my verse.
In this great world so much of it we see;
The lesser, man, is all over harmony.
Storehouse of all proportions! single Choir!
Which first God's breath did tunefully inspire![88]
From hence blessed musick's heavenly charms arise,
From sympathy which them and to man allies.
Thus they our souls, thus they our bodies win.
Not by their force, but party that's within.
Thus the strange cure on our split blood applied,
Sympathy to the distant wound does guide.
Thus when two brethren strings are set alike,
To move them both, but one of them we strike.
Thus David's lyre did Saul's wild rage control,
And tuned the harsh disorders of his soul.[89]

In his own notes for this passage, Cowley clearly desired to go into more detail on this question. He began by reviewing several of the more familiar anecdotes in ancient literature in which music affected behavior. But music therapy is more than this.

---

88 'Inspire,' at this time in England was a synonym for 'to blow,' as to inspire a flute.

89 'Davideis,' in *The Complete Works of Abraham Cowley*, I, 49.

> Neither should we wonder, that passions should be raised or suppressed … But that it should cure settled diseases in the body, we should hardly believe, if we had not both human and divine testimony for it.[90]

Cowley then adds, in addition to the testimony in the Old Testament, the well-known and documented instances in which music had cured the poison left by the bite of the Tarantula spider. But how does one explain it? He now turns to speculation which had occurred in more modern times.

> For the explication of the reason of these cures, the Magicians fly to their *Colcodea*; the Platonicks to their *Anima Mundi*; the Rabbis to Fables and Prodigies not worth the repeating. Baptista Porta in his *Natural Magick*, seems to attribute it to the *Magical Power of the Instrument*, rather than of the *Musick*; for he says, that Madness is to be cured by the Harmony of a Pipe made of Hellobore, because the juice of that plant is held good for that purpose; and the Sciatique by a musical instrument made of Poplar, because of the virtue of the Oil of that tree to mitigate those kind of pains. But these, and many sympathetical experiments are so false, that I wonder at the negligence or impudence of their Relators. Picus. Mirand. says, That Musick moves the spirits to act upon the soul, as medicines do to operate upon the body, and that it cures the body by the soul, as medicine does the soul by the body.

At this point, Cowley offers his own explanation for the power of music to heal the body, which appears to have been based on the writings of the German philosopher, Athanasius Kircher (1601–1680).

> I conceive the true natural Reason to be, that in the same manner as musical sounds move the outward air, so that does the inward, and that the spirits, and they the Humors (which are the seat of diseases) by Condensation, Rarefaction, Dissipation, or Expulsion of Vapors, and by virtue of that sympathy of proportion, which I express afterwards in verse. For the producing of the effect desires, Athan. Kercherus requires four conditions: 1. Harmony. 2. Number and Proportion. 3. Efficacious and pathetical words joined with the harmony (which—by the way—were fully and distinctly understood in the musick of the ancients) And 4. an adapting of all these to the constitution, disposition, and inclinations of the patient. Of which, and all things on this subject, he is well worth the diligent reading, [in his] *Liber de Arte magnâ Consoni et Dissoni*.

On Performance Practice

In the poetry of Robert Herrick there are several references to the quality of singers and singing. In one poem he suggests the voice is more appreciated if accompanied.

> Rare is the voice itself; but when we sing
> To the lute or viol, then 'tis ravishing.[91]

---

90 Ibid., 67.
91 *The Poetical Works of Robert Herrick*, 331.

So ravishing, he writes in another poem, that singing turns man into an angel.

> So long as you did not sing, or touch your Lute,
> We knew it was flesh and blood, that there sat mute.
> But when your playing, and your voice came in,
> 'Twas no more you then, but a *Cherubin*.[92]

And again,

> Let but thy voice engender with the string,
> And angels will be borne, while thou dost sing.[93]

Herrick also mentions the less successful singer, in a poem called, 'Upon a hoarse singer.'

> Sing me to death; for till thy voice be clear,
> 'Twill never please the palate of my ear.[94]

Among the many pastoral poems of seventeenth-century England, Richard Crashaw has written one called 'Musicks Duell,'[95] which presents a contest in music, a familiar element in the pastoral poems of the lyric poets of ancient Greece. The present poem includes an unusually vivid description of the technique of the lute player. While artistic liberty is evident here, we quote some of these passages for the reader who might find insights into actual seventeenth-century technique, for other sources of this period describe an extraordinarily wide range of emotions in lute performance. The poem begins as the lute player is playing only to soothe himself.

> Under production of an Oak; there sat
> A sweet Lute-master: in whose gentle airs
> He lost the day's heat, and his own hot cares.

A nightingale flies to a nearby tree and sings in such a way that the lute player decides to challenge the bird to a musical duel. He,

> Awakes his Lute, and against the fight to come
> Informs it, in a sweet *Praeludium*
> Of closer strains, and ere the war begin,
> He lightly skirmishes on every string
> Charged with a flying touch.

---

92 Ibid., 95.
93 Ibid., 102.
94 Ibid., 152.
95 'Musicks Duell,' in *The Complete Poetry of Richard Crashaw*, 535ff.

The bird counters with 'a thousand sweet distinguished tones and reckons up in soft divisions.' Then the player of the lute resumes,

> His nimble hands instinct then taught each string
> A capering cheerfulness; and made them sing
> To their own dance; now negligently rash
> He throws his arm, and with a long drawn dash
> Blends all together; then distinctly trips
> From this to that; then quick returning skips
> And snatches this again, and pauses there.

The bird begins again, 'meets art with art' and 'with tender accents' amazes the lute player. Now the lute player tries harder.

> Strains higher yet; that tickled with rare art
> The tattling strings (each breathing in his part)
> Most kindly do fall out; the grumbling bass
> In surly groans disdains the treble's grace.
> The high perched treble chirps at this, and chides,
> Until his finger (Moderator) hides
> And closes the sweet quarrel, rouses all
> Hoarce, shrill, at once; as when the trumpets call
> Hot Mars to the Harvest of Death's field, and woo
> Mens' hearts into their hands.

When the bird sings again, our poet makes a reference to the importance of melody, one of the significant departures of the Baroque from the earlier polyphonic era.

> … the sugared nest
> Of her delicious soul, that there does lie
> Bathing in streams of liquid melody;
> Music's best seed-plot …

Now the lute player plays for the last time.

> Every smooth turn, every delicious stroke
> Gives life to some new grace; thus doth he invoke
> Sweetness by all her names; thus, bravely thus
> (Fraught with a fury so harmonious)
> The lute's light *Genius* now does proudly rise,
> Heav'd on the surges of swollen Rhapsodies.
> Whose flourish (Meteor-like) doth curl the air
> With flash of high-born fancies: here and there

Dancing in lofty measures, and anon
Creeps on the soft touch of a tender tone:
Whose trembling murmurs melting in wild aires
Runs to and fro, complaining his sweet cares
Because those precious mysteries that dwell,
In musick's ravished soul he dare not tell,
But whisper to the world: thus do they vary
Each string his note, as if they meant to carry
Their Masters blest soul (snatcht out at his ears
By a strong ecstasy) through all the spheres
Of Musicks heaven; and seat it there on high
In the *Empyraeum* of pure Harmony.
At length (after so long, so loud a strife
Of all the strings, still breathing the best life
Of blest variety attending on
His fingers fairest revolution
In many a sweet rise, many as sweet a fall)
A full-mouthed *Diapason* swallows all.

Exhausted and unable to take another turn, the bird dies.
    Finally, there is a reference to performance practice in a proverb by George Herbert,

Great strokes make not sweet music.[96]

ART MUSIC

In a Hymn which George Wither called, 'A Hymn after a Feast,' we find a reference to the ancient custom of a brief concert after a banquet, after the tables have been cleared.

When is it fitter to begin
The Song intended, now,
Then when our Table spread hath bin
And Cups, did overflow?[97]

There are in this literature some interesting humorous descriptions of performers of art music. Andrew Marvel presents a poem in satire of an English priest and amateur musician.

Now as two instruments to the same key
Being tuned by art, if the one touched be,

---
96 'Jacula Prudentum,' in *The Poems of George Herbert*, 243.
97 *Wither*, Spenser Society, Nr. 26–27, 'Halelviah,' Hymn XXXIII.

> The other opposite as soon replies,
> Moved by the air and hidden sympathies;
> So while he with his gouty fingers crawls
> Over the lute, his murmuring belly calls,
> Whose hungry guts, to the same straightness twined,
> In echo to the trembling strings repined.[98]

Richard Lovelace composed a humorous poem in response to a woman who wished to sing a duet with him.

> This is the prettiest motion:
> Madam, the Alarms of a Drum
> That calls your Lord, set to your cries,
> To mine are sacred *Symphonies*.
>
> What, though 'tis said I have a voice;
> I know 'tis but that hollow noise
> Which (as it through my pipe doth speed)
> Bitterns do Carol through a Reed;
> In the same key with Monkeys Jiggs,
> Or Dirges of Proscribed Pigs,
> Or the soft Serenades above
> In calm of night, when cats make love …
>
> Yet can I Musick too; but such,
> As is beyond all voice or touch;
> My mind can in fair order chime,
> Whilst my true heart still beats the time:
> My soul so full of Harmonie,
> That it with all parts can agree:
> If you winde up to the highest fret
> It shall descend an [octave] from it,
> And when you shall vouchsafe to fall
> Sixteen above you it shall call,
> And yet so dis-affenting one,
> They both shall meet an unison.
>
> Come then bright Cherubin begin!
> My loudest Musick is within:
> Take all notes with your skillful eyes,
> Hark if mine do not sympathize!
> Sound all my thoughts, and see expressed
> The *Tablature* of my large breast,
> Then you'll admit that I too can

---

98 'Fleckno, an English Priest at Home,' in *The Complete Works of Andrew Marvell*, I, 229ff.

Musick above dead sounds of man;
Such as alone doth bless the spheres,
Not to be reached with human ears.[99]

Finally, a curious reference to what we suppose must qualify as art song, as opposed to functional music, is mentioned in the preface to Wither's Hymn LIX.

It is usual for prisoners brought to suffer for death, to sing at the place of their execution, that they may testify their hope of a joyful Resurrection.[100]

The Hymn in question was intended to be sung on such an occasion.

We have, in these volumes, argued that the presence of a contemplative listener is a requirement for true art music. The poet, Robert Herrick, describes the listener in two poems based on ancient subjects. In his 'A Canticle to Apollo,' we read,

Play Phoebus on thy Lute;
And we will all sit mute:
By listening to thy Lyre,
That sets all ears on fire.[101]

And, in a song to Sapho,

When thou do'st play, and sweetly sing,
Whether it be the voice or string,
Or both of them, that do agree
Thus to entrance and ravish me:
This, this I know, I'm oft struck mute;
And die away upon thy Lute.[102]

In yet another poem, Herrick mentions the listeners in Hell!

So smooth, so sweet, so silvery is thy voice,
As, could they hear, the Damned would make no noise,
But listen to thee, (walking in thy chamber)
Melting melodious words, to Lutes of Amber.[103]

George Wither observes that one can see the impact of the music on a listener simply by observing his face.

---

99 'To a Lady that desired me I would beare my part with her in a Song,' in *The Poems of Richard Lovelace*, 90ff.
100 *Wither*, Spenser Society, Nr. 26–27, 'Halelviah,' Hymn LIX.
101 *The Poetical Works of Robert Herrick*, 151.
102 Ibid., 142.
103 Ibid., 22.

> And, by the same it may appear
> What music most affects your ear.
> Deny it not; for (by your leave)
> We by your looks, your heart perceive.[104]

Edmond Waller has a character announce that he will impact the listener in the tradition of Orpheus.

> There while I sing, if gentle love be by
> That tunes my lute, and winds the strings so high;
> With the sweet sound of *Sacharissa's* name,
> I'll make the listening savages grow tame.[105]

His own reaction to hearing his lady sing is equally dramatic.

> Such moving sounds, from such a careless touch,
> So unconcerned herself, and we so much.
> What Art is this, that with so little pains,
> Transports us thus, and over the spirit reigns?
> The trembling strings above her fingers proud,
> And tell their joy for every kiss aloud.
> Small force there needs to make these tremble so,
> Touched by that hand; who would not tremble through?
> Here Love takes stand, and while she charms the ear
> Empties his quiver on the listening Deer.
> Musick so softens and disarms the mind,
> That not an arrow does resistance find.[106]

We find a similar reaction by Andrew Marvell, who is completely conquered by a lovely singer.

> To make a final conquest of all me,
> Love did compose so sweet an enemy,
> In whom both beauties to my death agree,
> Joining themselves in fatal harmony;
> That, while she with her eyes my heart does bind,
> She with her voice might captivate my mind.
>
> I could have fled from one but singly fair;
> My disentangled soul itself might save,
> Breaking the curled trammels of her hair;

---

104 Wither, *A Collection of Emblemes*, 117.
105 'The Battel of the Summer Islands,' in *Edmund Waller, Poems*, 54.
106 'On my Lady Isabella playing on the Lute,' in *Edmund Waller, Poems*, 78.

> But how should I avoid to be her slave,
> Whose subtile art invisibly can wreath
> My fetters of the very air I breathe?[107]

Finally, we should mention that some of the poems of this literature are written in honor of composers famous to their day. Robert Herrick has written poems in honor of Henry Lawes,[108] and William Lawes.[109] Phineas Fletcher has left a poem which is a tribute to Thomas Tomkins.

> For thee the Muses leave their silver well,
> And marvel where thou all their art hast found.[110]

Richard Crashaw has written a poem, 'Upon the death of a friend,' in honor of a musician whose identity is unknown.

> He, that once bore the best part, is gone.
> Whose whole life Musick was; wherein
> Each virtue for a part came in.
> And though that Musick of his life be still
> The Musick of his name yet soundeth shrill.[111]

FUNCTIONAL MUSIC

Among the poets who were Puritans, we find, of course, many poems which focus on the praise of God. One which calls upon a number of musical instruments for this purpose is by George Wither.

> Come, oh come in pious Laies [songs],
> Should we God-Almighty's praise.
> Hither bring in one consent,
> Heart, and voice, and instrument.
> Musick-add of every kind;
> Sound the Trumpet, the Cornet winde.
> Strike the Viol, touch the Lute.
> Let nor Tongue, nor String be mute.[112]

---

107 'The Fair Singer,' in *The Complete Works of Andrew Marvell*, I, 110.

108 *The Poetical Works of Robert Herrick*, 276.

109 Ibid., 288.

110 Fletcher, in *Giles and Phineas Fletcher Poetical Works*, II, 233.

111 'Upon the Death of a Friend,' in *The Complete Poetry of Richard Crashaw*, 477ff.

112 Wither, Spenser Society, Nr. 26–27, 'Halelviah,' Hymn I.

Richard Creshaw's Hymn, 'The Name of Jesus,' also calls upon a number of instruments to praise Jesus.

> Wake Lute and Harp
> And every sweet-lipped thing
> That talks with tuneful string;
> Start into life, and leap with me
> Into a hasty Fitt-tuned Harmony
> ......
>
> Complaining Pipes, and prattling Strings,
> Bring all the store
> Of Sweets you have; And murmur that you have no more.
> Come, near to part,
> Nature and Art!
> ......
>
> Bring all your Lutes and Harps of Heaven and Earth;
> What ever cooperates to the common mirth
> Vessels of vocal Joys,
> Or you, more noble architects of Intellectual Noise,
> Cymbals of Heaven, or Human spheres,
> Solicitors of Souls or Ears.[113]

In another poem, Crashaw makes a rare reference to string instruments in Heaven.

> When some new bright Guest
> Takes up among the stars a room,
> And Heaven will make a feast,
> Angels with crystal viols come ...[114]

The strict Puritan, George Wither, in his book of emblems, under the title, 'Though Music be of some abhorred, She, is the Handmaid of the Lord,' seems to reserve music's purpose primarily for the church.

> To Music, and the Muses, many bear
> Much hatred; and, to whatsoever ends
> Their soul-delighting-raptures tuned are,
> Such peevish dispositions, it offends.
> Some others, in a moral way, affect
> Their pleasing strains (or, for a sensual use)
> But, in God's Worship, they the same suspect;

---

113 'The Name of Jesus,' in *The Complete Poetry of Richard Crashaw*, 32ff.

114 'The Weeper,' in Ibid., 129.

(Or, tax it rather) as a great abuse.
The first of these, are full of Melancholy;
And, Pity need, or Comfort, more than blame;
And, soon, may fall into some dangerous folly,
Unless they labor, to prevent the same.
The last, are giddy things, that have befooled
Their judgments, with beguiling *fantasies,*
Which (if they be not, by discretion, schooled)
Will plunge them into greater vanities.

For, Music, is the Handmaid of the Lord,
And, for his Worship, was at first ordained:
Yea, therewithall she fitly doth accord;
And, where devotion thrives, is retained.
She, by a natural power, helps to raise,
The mind of God, when joyful Notes are sounded:
And, passions fierce distemperatures, allays;
When, by grave tones, the melody is bounded.
It, also may in mystic-sense, imply
What music, in ourselves, ought still to be;
And, that our jarring-lives to certify,
We should in voice, in hand, and heart, agree:
And, sing out, faith's new songs, with full consent,
Unto the Laws, ten-stringed instrument.[115]

This same poet, in a Hymn composed in 1650, comments on the importance of sincerity of spirit in church music.

There is no musick in our Songs,
That's worthy to be heard of thee;
Because, our hearts, eyes, ears, and tongues,
Profaned, and untuned be.[116]

A similar observation is made by George Herbert, who contends that church music is not effective unless the heart of the listener is in the right place.

The fineness which a hymn or psalm affords
Is, when the soul unto the lines accord.[117]

---

[115] Wither, *A Collection of Emblemes*, 65. In a 'Hymn for a Musician [Spenser Society, Vols 26–27], Wither appears to use the 'ten string law' as a metaphor for the Ten Commandments.

[116] *Wither,* Spenser Society, Nr. 22, 'Hymne 1.'

[117] 'A True Hymn,' in *The Poems of George Herbert*, 175.

A poem by George Herrick on the subject of Christmas is especially interesting for its reference to improvisation.

> What sweeter musick can we bring,
> Than a Carol, for to sing
> The Birth of this our heavenly King?
> Awake the voice! Awake the string!
> Heart, ear, and eye, and everything
> Awake! the while the active finger
> Runs divisions with the singer.[118]

In another poem which comments on performance practice in church music, Herrick writes,

> Comely acts well; and when he speaks his part,
> He doth it with the sweetest notes of Art:
> But when he sings a *Psalm*, there's none can be
> More cursed for singing out of tune than he.[119]

A wedding hymn by Richard Crashaw makes music a metaphor for married love.

> May their whole life a sweet song prove
> Set to two well composed parts,
> By musickes noblest master, Love,
> Played on the strings of both their hearts.[120]

The only interesting references to military music in this literature are by George Wither. In one poem he offers advice to the public on getting ready for war.

> Away with idle Cithers, Lutes, and Tabers,
> Let knocks requite the Fiddlers for their labors.
> Bring in the war-like Drum; 'twill musicke make ye,
> That from your drowsy pleasures will awake ye:
> Or else the heartening Trumpet, that from far
> May sound unto you all the points of War.
> Let Dances turn to Marches.[121]

---

118 *The Poetical Works of Robert Herrick*, 364.

119 Ibid., 266.

120 'Epithalamium,' in *The Complete Poetry of Richard Crashaw*, 489.

121 *Wither*, Spenser Society, Nr. 9, 'On Presumption,' 288.

Another poem was written during the civil wars.

> Hark! how the Drums beat! how the Trumpets are
> Sounding Alarms to a second-war,
> Before the first is done![122]

ENTERTAINMENT MUSIC

Wither also makes a passing reference to genuine popular music.

> I might have brought some other things to pass,
> Made Fiddlers Songs, or Ballads, like an Ass.[123]

---

122 Ibid., Nr. 12, 'Carmen Expostulatorium,' 3.
123 Ibid., Nr. 10, 'A Satyre,' 439.

7 MILTON

JOHN MILTON (1608–1674) is considered by the English to be their greatest poet after Shakespeare. His cultural development began in childhood due to unusually active parents, his father being a legal writer and musician and his mother an activist in charitable causes. He tells us that his early studies included music.

> I gave myself up entirely to reading the Greek and Latin writers; exchanging, however, sometimes, the country for the town, either for the purchase of books, or to learn something new in mathematics, or in music, which at the time furnished the sources of my amusement.[1]

A later comment suggests that this early experience in music may have helped determine that his path was to be poetry and literature.

> Amid the rugged difficulties of the Arts, that having lost all hope of obtaining quiet, I began to think sorrowfully … that it would be better to forget the Arts completely.[2]

His formal studies in England included extensive readings in the literature of the major European countries, in addition to expanding the religious studies which had begun in his strongly Puritan home. His studies completed, his generous father enabled Milton to tour France and Italy. He was particularly taken by Italy, which he called 'the retreat of civility and of all polite learning,'[3] and while there met a number of literati, including the aged Galileo.

ON THE PHYSIOLOGY OF AESTHETICS

Although a Puritan, Milton fully shared the old Catholic view that Reason must rule man's activities.

> But know that in the Soul
> Are many lesser Faculties that serve

---

1 'A Second Defence of the English People,' in *The Works of John Milton,* ed. Frank Patterson (New York: Columbia University Press, 1931–1938), VIII, 121.
2 'Prolusions,' in Ibid., XII, 251.
3 'A Second Defence of the English People,' in Ibid., VIII, 115.

> Reason as chief; among these Fancy next
> Her office holds; of all external things,
> Which the five watchful Senses represent,
> She forms Imaginations, Aerie shapes,
> Which Reason joining or disjoining, frames
> All what we affirm or what deny.[4]

And he agreed with the old Church that the support of Reason was a primary church concern. 'The Church,' he maintained, 'hath in her immediate care those inner parts and affections of the mind where the seat of reason is.'[5] This was, of course, due to constant competition between Reason and the emotions for the possession of man. 'Take heed,' warns Milton, 'least Passion sway thy Judgment.'[6] In his famous 'Paradise Lost' he writes,

> Sensual Appetite, who from beneath
> Usurping over sovereign Reason claimed
> Superior sway.[7]

Milton did not seem to recognize the emotions as an entirely separate faculty apart from Reason. As he points out in one place, man is made in the image of God, 'not so much in body, as in unity of mind and heart.'[8] It is curious that he even associates laughter primarily with Reason, 'every man is able to laugh because he is rational.'[9] Neither did Milton speculate on the origin of the fundamental vehicle of Reason, language. He was content to assume that both the language of Adam, as well as those supplied the builders of the tower of Babel, was divinely provided.[10]

Even though there is little to suggest that Milton recognized the separateness of intellect and the emotions, and he certainly did not deduce the separate functions of the twin hemispheres of the brain, he does acknowledge the separate characters of the hands. Like so many philosophers of the past, he clearly associates dominance with the right hand (left hemisphere).

---

4 'Paradise Lost,' V, 100ff, in Ibid., II, 147.
5 'Church-Government,' in Ibid., III, 182.
6 'Paradise Lost,' VIII, 635, in Ibid., II, 258.
7 'Paradise Lost,' IX, 1129ff, in Ibid., II, 300.
8 'Tetrachordon,' in Ibid., IV, 93.
9 'The Art of Logic,' I, iii, in Ibid., XI, 31. In another place, he says both anger and laughter are 'rational' faculties. ['Animadversions,' in Ibid., III, 108]
10 'The Art of Logic,' I, xxiv, in Ibid., XI, 221. In his treatise, 'On Education' [Ibid., IV, 281], Milton remarks that he admires the distinct and clear pronunciation of Italian and suggests the poor pronunciation of Englishmen evolved because they were hesitant to open their mouths for fear of letting in cold air!

... where I shall Reign at thy right hand ...[11]

......

Should intermitted vengeance arm again
His red right hand to plague us?[12]

......

Our own right hand
Shall teach us highest deeds.[13]

......

... the first assay
Of this right hand provoked ...[14]

......

Come therefore O thou that hast the seven stars in thy right hand, appoint thy chosen priests according to their Orders.[15]

Two passages which include reference to the left hand are curious. First, on the basis of modern clinical brain research we know the left hemisphere of the brain often appears to deny the existence of the (mute) right hemisphere. This, in an autobiographical comment, we are tempted to think that Milton here was suggesting that by writing with his left hand (right hemisphere) he was revealing 'myself' as being 'inferior to myself,' or the (speaking and writing) left hemisphere. He had the right idea but it works the other way around, as it is the right hemisphere which is the real self.

Lastly, I should not choose this manner of writing wherein knowing myself inferior to myself, led by the genial power of nature to another task, I have the use, as I may account it, but of my left hand.[16]

Another passage appears factually wrong, for in the great majority of the species it is the right hand, and not the left, which is associated with Reason (left hemisphere). The point Milton probably wished to make was that kings value power over Reason.

Kings most commonly, though strong in Legions, are but weak at Arguments; as they who ever have accustomed from the Cradle to use their will only as their right hand, their reason always as their left.[17]

---

11 'Paradise Lost,' II, 868, in Ibid., II, 68.

12 'Paradise Lost,' II, 173, in Ibid., II, 44.

13 'Paradise Lost,' V, 865, in Ibid., II, 174.

14 'Paradise Lost,' VI, 153, in Ibid., II, 183.

15 'Animadversions,' in Ibid., III, 147. Milton appears to have had in mind Revelations 1:16:

   In his right hand he held seven stars, from his mouth issued a sharp two-edged sword ...

16 'Church-Government,' in Ibid., III, 235.

17 'Eikonoklastes,' Preface, in Ibid., V, 63.

Finally, those who are confused, says Milton, do not know their right from their left. Writing of tyrants, who, by cunning and dexterity, 'winde themselves by shifting ground into places of more advantage,' Milton concludes 'with them there is no certain hand right or left.'[18]

Regarding education, after a passing reflection of Puritan philosophy in noting that the end of education is to 'repair the ruines of our first Parents' (original sin) and to know God correctly,[19] Milton elsewhere defines the scope of early education.

> They should have here also schools and academies at their own choice, wherein their children may be bred up in their own sight to all learning and noble education not in grammar only, but in all liberal arts.[20]

The educational topic which Milton seemed to never tire of bring up was the inadequacy of the old church-supported universities. Universities, he says, were intended to be the 'seed plots of piety and the Liberal Arts,' but became 'nurseries of superstition, and empty speculation.'[21] By this he meant the 'Scholastic' tradition, which in his view,

> has introduced perpetual discord into the schools, which indeed has hindered to an extraordinary degree the happy progress of those who are learning.[22]

He considered it a particular error of the English universities that they have 'not yet well recovered from the Scholastic grossness of barbarous ages.'[23] The universities, he says, produce 'scholastical trash.'[24] In another place he speaks of the 'delusions and trifling inconsistencies with which [the Scholastic philosophy] books everywhere abound.'[25]

ON THE PSYCHOLOGY OF AESTHETICS

We find little in Milton which touches on the psychological aspects of aesthetics. His most direct definition of the emotions in general is merely a restatement of views of older writers.

> The affections are love, hatred; joy, sorrow; hope, fear; and anger.
> Love is to be so regulated, that our highest affections may be placed on the objects most worthy of them.[26]

---

18 'The Tenure of Kings,' in Ibid., V, 56.
19 'On Education,' in Ibid., IV, 277.
20 'Readie and Easie Way to establish a free Commonwealth,' in Ibid., VI, 145.
21 'An Apology,' in Ibid., III, 336.
22 'Prolusions,' III, in Ibid., XII, 167.
23 'On Education,' in Ibid., IV, 278.
24 'Means to Remove Hirelings,' III, in Ibid., VI, 95.
25 'Prolusions,' III, in Ibid., XII, 163.
26 'The Christian Doctrine,' in Ibid., XVII, 203.

Regarding Pleasure and Pain, in one treatise Milton seems to find Pleasure associated with the natural condition of man.

> For surely to every good and peaceable man it must in nature needs be a hateful thing to be the displeaser ...; much better would it like him doubtless to be the messenger of gladness and contentment, which is his chief intended business.[27]

In his 'Paradise Lost,' however, he argues for a higher end.

> Judge not what is best
> By pleasure, though to Nature seeming meet,
> Created, as thou art, to nobler end.[28]

In a letter to Carolo Dato, a noble of Florence, Milton mentions another theme often found in early literature, 'such pain as is almost the invariable accompaniment of any great delight yielded to men.'[29]

ON THE PHILOSOPHY OF AESTHETICS

We begin our exploration of Milton's views on Art with his remarkable tribute to the contribution of the Arts to society.

> Where no arts flourish, where all knowledge is banished, where indeed there is no trace of a good man, there savageness and frightful barbarism rage about ... Europe, from the whole of which during several early centuries all good arts had perished; for a long time the presiding Muses had abandoned all the universities of that age: blind Ignorance had pervaded and taken possession of everything; nothing was heard in the schools except the absurd dogmas of most stupid monks.[30]

Milton's most interesting comments relative to Art in general are centered in the perception of Art and in related educational aspects. We are not surprised, in view of his comments on the association of the emotions with the intellect, to find him writing, 'The perception of all art and of all science concerns only the intellect.'[31] On the other hand, in another place he

---

27 'Church-Government,' in Ibid., III, 231.
28 'Paradise Lost,' XI, 604, in Ibid., II, 367.
29 Letter of April 21, 1647, in Ibid., XII, 47.
30 'Prolusions,' in Ibid., XII, 259. Milton's only derogatory remark on artists is found in his 'Means to Remove Hirelings' [Ibid., VI, 71], where he mentions in passing that to charge a man who comes of his own accord to be baptized is 'a piece of paltry craft, befitting none but beggarly artists.'
31 'Prolusions,' in Ibid., XII, 261.

refers to the old Scholastic distinction between the 'speculative' and the practice of art and here he leans more toward the practical rather than the conceptual.

> For as none can judge of a painter, or a sculpturer but he who is an artist, that is, either in the *Practice* or the *Theory*, which is often separated from practice, and judges learnedly without it.[32]

The most extensive discussion on the general nature of Art by Milton is found in the preface to his 'The Art of Logic.' He begins with a reference to Art and Nature,

> For art is used for the purpose of aiding nature, not of hindering it; when it is employed too anxiously and too subtly, and especially where it is unnecessary, it blunts rather than sharpens capacities which are already of themselves acute enough, just as surely as in medicine the use of excessive and unnecessary remedies weakens the health rather than builds it up.

Art, he says, consists of 'doctrine,' the orderly study of its precepts, and 'science,' which is the art absorbed in the mind and now practiced. He considered the real essence of an art to be a kind of model to teach man. His understanding was that the Greeks considered 'anything unworthy of the name of art which does not make its aim good or useful for human life and honorable to the precepts of art.'

This was based on his premise 'that the primal mover of every art is God,' from which it follows,

> The assisting causes were the men divinely taught and eminent for ability who in the past discovered the individual arts. The method of discovering these was much like the method of painting; for as there are in a picture two things—the subject and the art of painting—so in the discovery of an art, nature or practice and the example of skillful men corresponds to the archetype, and logic to the art of the painter—natural logic at least, which is the very faculty of reason in the mind of man, according to that common saying: Art imitates nature.

He seems to deduce from Aristotle that Reason is formed through the help of sense, observation, induction and experience. But since the precepts of the arts are only stated in general terms, they can only be studied in the observation of specific examples. Therefore, all depends on the senses. Skill in an Art, he says, depends in practice alone.

Finally, in his 'Prolusions,' Milton writes,

> What, on the other hand, has Ignorance to say? I feel, my hearers, she is veiled in darkness, is benumbed, is afar off, looks around for means of escape, complains that life is short, art is long. By all means in truth let us remove the two great stumbling blocks to our studies: the one of knowledge poorly taught, the other of our own slothfulness. With the permission of Galen, or whoever else it was, quite the contrary will it be: life will be long, art short. Nothing is more

---

32 'An Apology,' in Ibid., III, 346.

excellent than art, and nothing also requiring more labor: nothing more sluggish than we, nothing more negligent.[33]

Milton does not discuss in detail any of the traditional topics associated with the philosophy of aesthetics in the arts. He discusses Beauty only with respect to women, although he does create two memorable phrases, 'Beauty is nature's coin' and 'Beauty is Nature's brag.'[34]

Apart from one paragraph given above, on the ancient question of whether Art should imitate Nature, Milton offers only one additional phrase without further discussion, 'Nature taught Art.'[35] In fact, in his treatise on 'Church-Government' Milton mentions in passing that he does not have time to elaborate on,

> whether the rules of Aristotle herein are strictly to be kept, or nature to be followed, which in them that know art, and use judgment is no transgressions, but an enriching of art.[36]

For so great a poet, one is surprised to find few references to his craft. Certainly he does not hesitate to reveal his love for the art.

> Now poets who are truly so called, I love and reverence; and it is one of the most frequent and delightful of my pleasures to listen to their song.[37]

In frequent pastoral settings in his poems, Milton often mentions the poets of older times, especially the epic poets. A typical example is found in 'Paradise Lost.'

> Others more mild,
> Retreated in a silent valley, sing
> With notes Angelical to many a Harp
> Their own Heroic deeds.[38]

The purpose of poetry, Milton says, is 'rousing to high flight the mind.'[39] He apparently also wanted the poet to have a *clear* mind, contending that a poet must be 'free of crime, pure and chaste, and a character unyielding, and a name without taint,' and drink only water.[40]

Milton's reflections on dramatic poetry begin with his disagreement with the views of the early Church fathers.

---

33 'Prolusions,' in Ibid., XII, 273.
34 'A Mask,' in Ibid., I, 112ff.
35 'Paradise Regained,' in Ibid., II, 434.
36 'Church-Government,' in Ibid., III, 237.
37 'A Second Defense of the English People,' in Ibid., VIII, 79.
38 'Paradise Lost,' II, 546ff, in Ibid., II, 57.
39 'Prolusions,' in Ibid., XII, 163.
40 'Elegia Sexta,' in Ibid., I, 212.

> It does not follow that it is necessary to abolish altogether the performance of plays. This on the contrary would be quite senseless; for what in the whole of philosophy is more impressive, purer, or more uplifting than a noble tragedy, what more helpful to a survey at a single glance of the hazards and changes of human life?[41]

He elaborates on the virtues of the theater in the introduction to his 'Samson Agonistes,' which he calls a 'dramatic poem.'

> Tragedy, as it was anciently composed, hath been ever held the gravest, moralest, and most profitable of all other Poems; therefore said by Aristotle to be of power, by raising pity and fear, or terror, to purge the mind of those and such-like passions—that is, to temper and reduce them to just measure with a kind of delight, stirred up by reading or seeing those passions well imitated. Nor is Nature wanting in her own effects to make good his assertion; for so, in Medicine, things of melancholic hue and quality are used against melancholy, sour against sour, salt to remove salt humors.

In his introduction to 'Samson,' Milton also reflects on the decline of contemporary English theater. His words of praise above, he notes, were to,

> vindicate Tragedy from the small esteem, or rather infamy, which in the account of many it undergoes at this day, with other common Interludes; happening through the poet's error of intermixing comic stuff with tragic sadness and gravity, or introducing trivial and vulgar persons ... to gratify the people.

In the preface to 'Paradise Lost,' Milton again disparages contemporary English theater.

> Not without cause therefore some both Italian and Spanish poets of prime note have rejected rhyme both in longer and shorter works, as have also our best English Tragedies, as a thing of itself, to all judicious ears, trivial and of no true musical delight.[42]

Perhaps these passages offer some insight to explain Milton's comment that 'the frequenting of Theaters against her husbands mind' is sufficient cause for divorce.[43]

In the end, in his treatise 'On Education' Milton recommends for the curriculum of students the study of the famous commentaries on playwrighting by Aristotle, Horace and Castelvetro.

---

41 On 'Spectacles,' in 'Commonplace Book,' in Ibid., XVIII, 207. He also adds here that the early writer, Lactantius, argued that all of music should be abolished from society.
42 'Paradise Lost,' in Ibid., II, 6.
43 'Divorce,' in Ibid., III, 487.

This would make [the students] soon perceive what despicable creatures our common Rhymers and Playwriters be, and show them, what religious, what glorious and magnificent use might be made of Poetry both in divine and humane things.[44]

Curiously, however, in his treatise, 'On Education,' Milton recommends the ancient Greek and Latin plays themselves only as an antidote for weariness.[45] Nevertheless, in an outline for a projected tragedy on the subject of the fall of Adam, Milton planned for a Greek-style chorus to sing of the battle and victory, a hymn of creation and a song to bewail Adam's fall.[46]

ON THE AESTHETICS OF MUSIC

As we have noted above Milton was born into a musical family and enjoyed some study of music during his youth. If he did not continue as an active performer, his appreciation of music remained and his poetry is full of reference to it. Consider this remarkable tribute:

> Do not look down on song divine, creation of the bard, for naught graces more finely than does song his heavenly source, his heavenly seed, his mind mortal in origin, for song still keeps holy traces of Prometheus's fire. The gods above love song, and song has power to rouse the quaking depths of Tartarus, to bind fast the gods of the deeps below; song restrains with triple adamant the unfeeling [men]. By song the secrets of the far-distant future are revealed by the daughters of Phoebus, and by quivering Sibyls, pale of lips. The sacrificer composes songs at the holy alters … I too shall go, wearing a golden crown, through the realms of the skies, wedding sweet strains to the soft-sounding plectrum.[47]

We know some of his tastes, as for example this comment which follows a reference to the loud trumpet in one poem.

> Me softer airs befit, and softer strings
> Of Lute, or Viol still, more apt for mournful things.[48]

And we know some of his preferences among composers, as we see in a sonnet in praise of the songs of the English composer, Henry Lawes.

> Harry whose tuneful and well measured Song
> First taught our English Musick how to span
> Words with just note and accent.[49]

---

44 'On Education,' in Ibid., IV, 286.
45 'On Education,' in Ibid., IV, 285.
46 'Outlines for Tragedies,' in Ibid., XVIII, 231.
47 'Ad Patrem,' in Ibid., I, 271.
48 'The Passion,' in Ibid., I, 24.
49 'To Mr. H. Lawes, on his Aires,' in Ibid., I, 63.

We can also see the extent of Milton's familiarity with music in his frequent use of various aspects of music in his figures of speech. He uses 'harmony' to represent aspects of social order, a metaphor which had been popular with the ancient Greeks. In his treatise on church government, for example, it stands for the discipline needed in social organization.

> Nor is there any sociable perfection in this life civil or sacred that can be above discipline, but she is that which with her musical chords preserves and holds all the parts thereof together.[50]

He even uses this metaphor when writing on the subject of divorce.

> Nature, from whence are derived the issues of love and hatred distinctly flowing through the whole mass of created things, and that God's doing ever is to bring the due likenesses and harmonies of his works together, except when out of two contraries meet to their own destruction.[51]

Similarly, harmony is a metaphor for the relationship between two persons.

> For I no sooner in my Heart divined,
> My Heart, which by a secret harmonie
> Still moves with thine, joined in connection sweet.[52]

He uses the organ to represent one who stimulates others to action.

> As in an Organ from one blast of wind
> To many a row of Pipes the sound-board breathes.[53]

Music is, of course, the most satisfactory symbol for feeling and is one often used by Milton. A poignant example is his use of a musical metaphor to express his sadness in thinking of the death of Jesus.

> For now to sorrow must I tune my song,
> And set my Harp to notes of saddest woe.[54]

In his 'Second Defence of the English Peoples,' after a discussion of King Charles, Milton uses the loud trumpeter as a metaphor for a critic.

> Having thus dispatched Charles, he is now preparing, with no little blustering, his attack upon me: 'After these preludes, the wonderful Salmasius will blow the terrible trumpet.' You prognosticate health, and give us notice of a new king of musical harmony: for when that terrible trumpet

---

50 'Church-Government,' in Ibid., III, 185.
51 'Divorce,' in Ibid., III, 418.
52 'Paradise Lost,' X, 357ff, in Ibid., VIII, 53.
53 'Paradise Lost,' I, 708, in Ibid., II, 33.
54 'The Passion,' in Ibid., I, 23.

shall be blown, we can think of no fitter accompaniment for it than a reiterated crepitation. But I would advise Salmasius not to inflate his cheek overmuch: for you may take my word for it, that the more it is swollen out, the fairer will he present it for slaps, in musical response, while both his cheeks ring again, to this modulated tone of the wonderful Salmasius.[55]

Milton also made numerous historical references to music, beginning with the Greek myths where he finds the gods 'contended only for beauty, or in music.'[56] Milton was wrong in fact, but perhaps current in Puritan thought, when he described ancient man as having no music of any kind, 'when suddenly Arts and Sciences divinely inspired the rude hearts of men.'[57]

In a letter, he mentioned the public musical entertainments of 'truly Roman magnificence' given by Cardinal Barberini,[58] and in his 'Commonplace Book,' Milton makes an interesting comment on even earlier Roman musical history. Ignatius, the third bishop of Antioch after Peter, he reports, was the first to devise antiphonal singing in the church. The organ he says was first introduced to France by ambassadors of the Byzantine Emperor, Constantine V, who brought organs to King Pepin.[59]

With respect to the early music history of his own country, Milton mentions Begabredus, who 'is recorded to have excelled all before him in the Art of Music,'[60] and contends that it was the Saxons under whom the liberal arts, including music, first flourished.[61] We wish for more detail, when he mentions that King Alfred disguised himself as a musician and, by playing his lute and singing, functioned as a spy.[62]

On the Perception of Music

Milton's only emphatic comment on the perception of music is that variety is crucial.

> Variety (as both Musick and Rhethorick teacheth us) erects and rouses an Auditory, like the masterful running over many chords and divisions; whereas if men should ever be thumming the drone of one plain song, it would be a dull opiate to the most wakeful attention.[63]

---

55 'A Second Defence,' in Ibid., VIII, 53.
56 'A Second Defence of the English People,' in Ibid., VIII, 193.
57 'Prolusions,' VII, in Ibid., XII, 273.
58 'Familiar Letters,' in Ibid., XII, 41.
59 'To Leonora, as She Sings at Rome,' in Ibid., I, 229.
60 'De Musica,' in Ibid., XVIII, 140.
61 Ibid., 169.
62 'History of Britain,' in Ibid., X, 234.
63 'Animadversions,' in Ibid., III, 133.

We feel we must include here the obvious attention which Milton devoted to the question of the Music of the Spheres. He mentions this frequently in his poetry, beginning with the music of creation.

> Up he rode
> Followed with acclamation and the sound
> Symphonious of ten thousand Harps that tuned
> Angelic harmonies: the Earth, the Air
> Resounded, (thou remember'st, for thou heardst)
> The Heavens and all the Constellations rung,
> The Planets in their station listening stood.[64]

Several poems speak of the music of the spheres being in nine-parts, representing the seven known planets, the sun and our moon. In the poem, 'The Hymn,' we find,

> Ring out ye Crystal spheres,
> Once bless our humane ears,
> (If ye have power to touch our senses so)
> And let your silver chime
> Move in melodious time;
> And let the Base of Heavens deep Organ blow,
> And with your ninefold harmony
> Make up full consort to the Angelike symphony.[65]

And again in 'Arcades,'

> But else in deep of night when drowsiness
> Hath locked up mortal sense, then listen I
> To the celestial Sirens harmony,
> That sit upon the nine enfolded Spheres.[66]

Why, even God listens to the music of the spheres.

> And in their motions harmonie Divine
> So smooths her charming tones, that Gods own ear
> Listens delighted.[67]

---

64 'Paradise Lost,' VII, 557, in Ibid., II, 231. In the same poem [V, 178] there is a reference to stars that move 'in mystic Dance not without Song.'
65 'The Hymn,' in Ibid., I, 6.
66 'Arcades,' in Ibid., I, 74.
67 'Paradise Lost,' in V, 625ff, Ibid., II, 166.

In several places, such as in his masque composed for a performance at Ludlow Castle in 1634, Milton refers to the music of the spheres as 'the Starry Quire.'[68] One of these 'starry choir' references provides the only attempt by Milton to describe the actual music, 'a never-dying melody, a song beyond all describing.'[69]

Eventually, Milton contributes a lengthy discussion, 'On the Music of the Spheres,' which appears to be intended to be used in a lecture called 'In the Public Schools.' Milton is suspicious, but he seems to leave open the possibility of the Music of the Spheres. He wonders, how can we be expected to hear this music of the heavens, since our concerns are so earth-bound.

> If there is any place for a man of my poor powers, fellow students, after so many speakers of consequence have been heard today, I shall attempt even at this moment to express, in accordance with my small ability, how well I wish the established exercise of the present occasion; and I shall follow, albeit far outdistanced, in the course of this day's demonstration of eloquence. Accordingly, while I avoid and shun entirely those common and ordinary topics of discourse, the purpose of this day and likewise of those who, I suspected, would speak appropriately concerning matters fitted to the time, kindles and straightaway rouses my mind to attempt with ardor some new theme. These two reasons are able to furnish incentives or keenness to one somewhat sluggish and for the most part possessed of a dull wit. Wherefore, a few words at least suggest themselves to be pronounced, as they say, with open hand and with rhetorical embellishment, about that famous heavenly harmony, concerning which very shortly there is to be a disputation with the closed fist; consideration of the time being observed, which now presses me on and restrains me. I would prefer, however that you, my hearers, should regard these things as said in jest.
>
> For what sane man would have thought that Pythagoras, that god of the philosophers, at whose name all mortals of his age stood up in very sacred veneration;—who, I say, would have thought that he would ever have expressed in public an opinion so uncertainly founded? Surely, if indeed he taught the harmony of the spheres and that the heavens revolved with melodious charm, he wished to signify by it, in his wise way, the very loving and affectionate relations of the orbs and their eternally uniform revolutions according to the fixed laws of necessity. Certainly, in this he imitated either the poets or, what is almost the same thing, the divine oracles, by whom no secret and hidden mystery is exhibited in public, unless clad in some covering or garment. That most skillful interpreter of Mother Nature, Plato, has followed him, since he affirms that certain sirens sit one upon each of the circles of the heavens and hold spell-bound gods and men by their most honey-sweet song. And finally, this agreement of things universal and this loving concord, which Pythagoras secretly introduced in poetic fashion by the term Harmony, Homer likewise suggested significantly and appropriately by means of that famous golden chain of Jove hanging down from heaven.
>
> Aristotle, the envious and perpetual calumniator of Pythagoras and Plato, desiring to pave a way to renown on the shattered opinions of these great men, imputed to Pythagoras the unheard symphony of the heavens and tunes of the spheres. But if either fate or necessity had decreed that your soul, O Father Pythagoras, should have been translated into me, there would not have

---

68 'A Masque,' in Ibid., I, 89. A song in this masque also mentions 'all Heaven's Harmonies.' [Ibid., I, 94].
69 'Ad Patrem,' line 35.

been lacking one who would easily have come to your rescue, however great the infamy under which you were laboring at the moment. Indeed, why should not the celestial bodies during their everlasting courses evolve musical sounds? Does it not seem fair to you, O Aristotle? Truly, I hardly believe your intelligences would be able to endure with patience that sedentary toil of the rolling heavens for so many ages, unless that ineffable song of the stars had prevented your departure and by the charm of its melody had persuaded a delay. It would be as if you were to take away from heaven those beautiful little goddesses and should deliver the ministering gods to mere drudgery and to condemn them to the treadmill. Nay indeed, Atlas himself long ago would have withdrawn his shoulders from a heaven that was about to fall, had not that sweet song soothed, with its most delightful charm, him, gasping and sweating under his great burden. In addition to these things the Dolphin, wearied of his constellation, would long ago have preferred his own seas to heaven, if he had not rightly been burning with the thought that the singing orbs of the sky excelled by far the sweetness of Arion's lyre. Why, credible it is that the lark itself should fly right up to the clouds at early dawn, and that the nightingale should spend the whole lonely night in song, in order that they may adjust their strains to the harmonic mode of the sky, to which they listen attentively. Thus also from the very beginning of things the story has prevailed about the Muses dancing day and night around the altar of Jove; hence from remote antiquity skill with the lyre has been attributed to Phoebus; for this reason the ancients believed Harmonia ought to be regarded as the daughter of Jove and Electra, whom the whole choir of heaven is said to have lauded in song when she had been given Cadmus in marriage.

But supposing no one on earth had ever heard this symphony of the stars, does it therefore follow that all has been silent beyond the circle of the moon, and lulled to sleep by the benumbing silence? Nay rather, let us blame our feeble ears which are not able, or are not worthy, to overhear the songs and such sweet tones. But this melody of the sky is not really unheard; for who, O Aristotle, would have conceived of your meteors as dancing in the mid-region of the air, except that, when they hear the singing heavens clearly on account of their nearness, they cannot restrain themselves from performing a choral dance?

But Pythagoras alone of mortals is said to have heard this song; unless that good man was both some deity and native of the sky, who perchance by direction of the gods had descended for the purpose of instructing the minds of men with holy knowledge and of calling upon them to improve. Certainly he was a man who combined in himself the whole gamut of virtues and who was worthy to converse with the very gods like unto himself and to enjoy the company of the celestials. Therefore, I do not wonder that the gods, loving him very much, permitted him to take part in the most secret mysteries of Nature.

Moreover, the boldness of the thieving Prometheus seems to be the reason why we hear so little this harmony, a deed which brought upon humanity so many ills and likewise took away this happiness from us, which we shall never be permitted to enjoy so long as we remain brutish and overwhelmed by wicked animal desires[70]; for how can those be susceptible of that heavenly sound whose souls, as Persius says, are bent toward the earth and absolutely devoid of celestial matters? But if we possessed hearts so pure, so spotless, so snowy, as once upon a time Pythagoras had, then indeed would our ears be made to resound and to be completely filled with that most delicious music of the revolving stars; and then all things would return immediately as it were to that golden age; then, at length, freed from miseries we should spend our time in peace, blessed and envied even by the gods.[71]

---

[70] In 'An Apology,' in Ibid., III, 306, Milton also states that 'celestial music is inaudible to the unchaste.'
[71] 'On the Music of the Spheres,' in Ibid., XII, 149ff.

On the Purpose of Music

In a sonnet Milton seems to argue for an inherent value in music, when he suggests that for those who understand music, hearing it often is not unwise.

> Whence we may rise
> To hear the Lute well touched, or artful voice
> Warble immortal Notes and Tuscan Ayre?
> He who of those delights can judge, And spare
> To interpose them oft, is not unwise.[72]

Milton often, especially in the pastoral settings, has his characters listen to music purely for pleasure, for example the reference 'with jocond Music charm his ear' in 'Paradise Lost,'[73] or in the pastoral figure in 'Il Penseroso' who awakes to sweet music.

> And as I wake, sweet musick breath
> Above, about, or underneath,
> Sent by some spirit to mortals good,
> Or the unseen Genius of the Wood.[74]

A more extended example is found in another poem, 'The Hymn'

> When such musick sweet
> Their hearts and ears did greet,
> As never was by mortal finger struck,
> Divinely-warbled voice
> Answering the stringed noise,
> As all their souls in blissfull rapture took ...
> Such Musick (as 'tis said)
> Before was never made ...
>
> She knew such harmony alone
> Could hold all Heaven and Earth in happier union.[75]

The most traditional purpose for music given in early literature is to soothe the listener, as we find in a lovely pastoral scene in Milton's 'Mask.'

> I sat me down to watch upon a bank
> With Ivy canopied, and interwove

---

72 'Sonnet XX,' in Ibid., I, 67.
73 'Paradise Lost,' in I, 787, Ibid., II, 36.
74 'Il Penseroso,' in Ibid., I, 45.
75 'The Hymn,' in Ibid., I, 5.

> With flaunting Honeysuckle, and began
> Wrapt in a pleasing fit of melancholy
> To mediate upon my rural minstrelsie,
> Till fancy had her fill …[76]
>
> Ever against eating Cares,
> Lap me in soft *Lydian* Aires …
> Untwisting all the chains that tie
> The hidden soul of harmony.[77]

In the poem, 'Mansus,' Milton describes Apollo: 'to the strains of the lute, he soothed with his voice the hard labors of his exile.'[78] A rather specific instance is found in 'Paradise Regained,' when Jesus says to Satan that 'I would delight my private hours with music or with poem' for the purpose of solace, provided it is in the Hebrew language.[79]

The most important purpose of music is to express feeling and the emotionally expressive nature of music is vividly discussed by Milton in a poem dedicated to his father. The portion below begins with reference to the ancient Rhapsodists who sang epic poetry and concludes with a very interesting tribute to the close relationship of music and oratory, skills which Milton apparently admired in his father. One can indeed find a close relationship between music and oratory in the sense that it is the right hemisphere of the brain which provides the emotional coloring which determines meaning for both. Milton, unaware of modern discoveries in brain function, instinctively uses 'music' as a metaphor for this right hemisphere emotional input.

> Songs, were wont, in olden days, to adorn the rich feasts of kings, when luxury, and the limitless abyss of the bottomless gullet were yet unknown, and the banquet tables foamed only with modest wines. In those days, the bard, seated in accord with custom at the holiday feast, his unshorn locks bound with leaves form the oak-tree, used to sing of the achievements of heroes, exploits worthy of imitation, and the foundations, laid broad and wide, of the world, and of gods creeping, and of acorns that formed food for gods, and of the lightning-bolt not yet sought from Aetna's grot. In brief, what pleasure will there be in music well attuned if it is empty of voice, empty of words and of their meanings, and of numbers that talk? Such strains befit the woodland choirs, not Orpheus, who by his songs, not by his lyre, and by his singing compelled to tears the shades that were done with life: it is from his *song* that he has these praises.
>
> Persist not, I pray you, to hold cheap the holy Muses, nor think them idle, poor, for through their bounty you yourself skillfully compose a thousand strains to measures fit, and, since you have been trained to vary your tuneful voice by a thousand modulations, you would of right be heir of Arion's fame. Wherein is it strange if it has fallen to your lot to sire me, a poet, if we, knit so closely together by dear ties of blood, should pursue arts of one blood, and kindred studies?[80]

---

76 'A Mask,' in Ibid., I, 105.

77 'L'Allegro,' in Ibid., I, 39.

78 'Mansus,' in Ibid., I, 293.

79 'Paradise Regained,' IV, 331, in Ibid., II, 471.

80 'Ad Patrem,' in Ibid., I, 274ff.

Another tribute to the expressive power of music is found in a sonnet,

> When, beautiful, thou speakest, or, in mood of happiness, sing in such guise that the hardest and wildest oak is moved to feeling, one must guard the gateways to ear and eye.[81]

We also find in Milton's work references to the ancient Greek assertion that music can change one's character or manners. In the poem 'Arcades,' he attributes to music the ability to raise man above disturbing influences.

> Such sweet compulsion doth in musick lie,
> To lull the daughters of Necessity,
> And keep unsteady Nature to her law,
> And the low world in measured motion draw
> After the heavenly tune, which none can hear
> Of human mold with gross unpurged ear.[82]

In the poem, 'To Leonora, as She Sings at Rome,' music is referred to as a 'Third Intelligence' which comes from Heaven which enters the throat of the singer and 'graciously teaches mortal hearts the power to grow accustomed insensibly to sounds immortal.'[83]

Finally, one poem contains a brief reference to music used for prophesy, 'Then sing of secret things that came to pass.'[84]

On Performance Practice

Milton, in a publication known as 'An Apology,' mentions in passing that he must be careful in abruptly breaking off his text,

> unless I can provide against offending the ear, as some Musicians are wont skillfully to fall out of one key into another without breach of harmony.[85]

In another place Milton observed that he regarded the performer's art to lie equally in the performer and in the instrument.

> I am luckier by far in my body of judges than either Orpheus or Amphion; for they merely applied their fingers cunningly and skillfully to little strings, attuned with pleasing harmony;

---

81 'Sonnet II,' in Ibid., I, 49.
82 'Arcades,' in Ibid., I, 74.
83 'To Leonora, as She Sings at Rome,' in Ibid., I, 229.
84 'At a Vacation Exercise,' in Ibid., I, 20.
85 'An Apology Against a Pamphlet called A Modest Confutation of the Animadversion.' (1642), in Ibid., III, 341.

and an equal portion of the charm of both lay in the strings themselves and in the proper and correct movement of the hands.[86]

Finally, there is this analogy based on a singer, 'as a good song is spoiled by a lewd singer.'[87]

ART MUSIC

Milton frequently mentions art songs in a pastoral setting, in particular in his Masque[88] and in his poem, 'Arcades.' Another pastoral poem, 'Elegia Sexta,' includes instrumental art music: 'Now the Thracian lyre, too, with its fretted gold, sounds for you, touched softly by an artist hand.'[89]

The presence of the contemplative listener also identifies true art music, as in this example:

> Such as the wise *Demodocus* once told
> In solemn Songs at King *Alcinous* feast,
> While sad *Ulisses* soul and all the rest
> Are held with his melodious harmony
> In willing chains and sweet captivity.[90]

And also in 'Paradise Lost,'

> Their Song was partial, but the harmony
> (What could it less when Spirits immortal sing?)
> Suspended Hell, and took with ravishment
> The thronging audience.[91]

EDUCATIONAL MUSIC

In Milton's treatise, 'On Education,' he recommends music for the student's periods of rest, for education in manners and to temper the passions.

> The interim of unsweating themselves regularly, and convenient rest before meat may both with profit and delight be taken up in recreating and composing their travailed spirits with the solemn

---

86 'Oration,' in Ibid., XII, 211.
87 'Animadversions,' in Ibid., III, 176.
88 'A Mask,' in Ibid., I, 105, lines 546ff.
89 Lines 43ff.
90 'At a Vacation Exercise,' in Ibid., I, 20.
91 'Paradise Lost,' II, 552, in Ibid., II, 57.

and divine harmonies of Musick heard or learned; either while the skillful organist plies his grave and fancied descant, in lofty fugues, or the whole Symphony with artful and unimaginable touches adorn and grace the well studied chords of some choice Composer; sometimes the Lute, or soft Organ stop waiting on elegant Voices either to Religious, martial, or civil verses; which if wise men and Prophets be not extremely out, have a great power over the dispositions and manners, to smooth and make them gentle from rustic harshness and distempered passions. The like also would not be unexpedient after Meat to assist and cherish Nature in her first concoction, and send their minds back to study in good tune and satisfaction.[92]

In another place, perhaps a hint of Milton's views of the music appropriate for education can be found in a passage in which he questions the advisability of civic censorship.

If we think to regulate Printing, thereby to rectify manners, we must regulate all recreations and pastimes, all that is delightful to man. No musick must be heard, no song be set or sung, but what is grave and *Dorick*. There must be licensing dancers, that no gesture, motion, or deportment be taught our youth but what by their allowance shall be thought honest ... It will ask more than the work of twenty licensers to examine all the lutes, the violins, and the guitars in every house; they must not be suffered to prattle as they do, but must be licensed what they may say. And who shall silence all the airs and madrigals, that whisper softness in chambers? ... The villages also must have their visitors to enquire what lectures the bagpipe and the rebec reads even to the ballatry, and the gammuth of ever municipal fiddler, for these are the Countryman's Arcadia's and his Monte Mayors.[93]

FUNCTIONAL MUSIC

Given the strong Puritan roots of Milton, we are not surprised to find numerous references to music in a religious context. In his treatise on 'Church-Government,' Milton, after pointing to the numerous instances of songs and lyric poetry in the Old Testament, defines the purpose of church music. Music, he says, should be a,

power beside the office of a pulpit, to inbreed and cherish in a great people the seeds of virtue, and public civility, to allay the perturbations of the mind, and set the affections in right tune, to celebrate in glorious and lofty Hymns the throne and equipage of Gods Almightinesse, and what he works, and what he suffers to be wrought with high providence in his Church, to sing the victorious agonies of Martyrs and Saints, the deeds and triumphs of just and pious Nations.[94]

---

92 'On Education,' in Ibid., IV, 288ff.
93 'Areopagitica,' in Ibid., IV, 317.
94 'Church-Government,' in Ibid., III, 238.

Like all early Christian writers, Milton is disrespectful toward the music of the 'pagans,' which is to say the ancient Greeks.

> While they loudest sing
> The vices of their Deities, and their own
> In Fable, Hymn, or Song, so personating
> Their Gods ridiculous, and themselves past shame.
> Remove their swelling Epithets thick laid
> As varnish on a Harlots cheek, the rest,
> Thin sown with aught of profit or delight,
> Will far be found unworthy to compare
> With *Sion's* songs, to all true tastes excelling,
> Where God is praised aright.[95]

On more contemporary religious themes, Milton devotes one entire poem, 'At a solemn Musick,' to the use of music as a metaphorical expression of the joy of religious life.

> Blest pair of Sirens, pledges of Heaven's joy,
> Sphere-born harmonious Sisters, Voice, and Verse,
> Wed your divine sounds, and mixed power employ
> Dead things with inbreathed sense able to pierce,
> And to our high-raised phantasie present,
> That undisturbed Song of pure concent,
> Ay sung before the saphire-colored throne
> To him that sits thereon
> With Saintly shout, and solemn Jubily,
> Where the bright Seraphim in burning row
> Their loud up-lifted Angel trumpets blow,
> And the Cherubick host in thousand choirs
> Touch their immortal Harps of golden wires,
> With those just Spirits that wear victorious Palms,
> Hymns devout and holy Psalms
> Singing everlastingly;
> That we on Earth with undiscording voice
> May rightly answer that melodious noise;
> As once we did, till disproportioned sin
> Jarred against natures chime, and with harsh din
> Broke the fair musick that all creatures made
> To their great Lord, whose love their motion swayed
> In perfect Diapason, whilst they stood
> In first obedience, and their state of good.
> O may we soon again renew that Song,

---

95 'Paradise Regained,' IV, 339, in Ibid., II, 471.

And keep in tune with Heaven, till God ere long
To his celestial consort us unite,
To live with him, and sing in endless morn of light.⁹⁶

There are two interesting passages which are concerned with the actual music of the service, first from the poem, 'Il Penseroso,'

But let my due feet never fail,
To walk the studious Cloisters pale,
And love the high embowed Roof,
With antique Pillars massy proof,
And storied Windows richly dight,
Casting a dim religious light.
There let the pealing Organ blow,
To the full voiced Choir below,
In Service high, and Anthems clear,
As may with sweetness, through mine ear,
Dissolve me into extasies,
And bring all Heaven before mine eyes.⁹⁷

In his 'Eikonoklastes,' Milton reflects on the joy and gladness 'between the Singing men and the organs' of the king's chapel. He cannot help but wonder, however, in a reference to Latin texts, 'how they should join their hearts in unity to songs not understood.'⁹⁸

Another religious theme, under which Milton discusses music at length, is the creation of the world. In his 'Paradise Lost,' on the seventh day God rested, but, says Milton, he did not rest in silence.

But not in silence holy kept; the Harp
Had work and rested not, the solemn Pipe,
And Dulcimer, all Organs of sweet stop,
All sounds on Fret by String or Golden Wire
Tempered soft Tunings, intermixt with Voice
Choral or Unison ...
Creation and the six Days acts they sung.⁹⁹

After God tells Adam he must leave Eden, the angel, Michael, leads Adam to the top of a high hill where he can see visions of the future. Among the things predicted for the future, Adam hears music.

---

96 'At a solemn Musick,' in Ibid., I, 27ff.
97 'Il Penseroso,' in Ibid., I, 45.
98 'Eikonoklastes,' in Ibid., V, 263.
99 Ibid., VII, 594ff.

> Whence the sound
> Of Instruments that made melodious chime
> Was heard, of Harp and Organ; and who moved
> Their stops and chords was seen: his volant touch
> Instinct through all proportions low and high
> Fled and pursued transverse the resonant fugue.[100]

Adam, in these same visions, also hears the 'Carol' which the angels sing, announcing the birth of Jesus.[101]

In the continuation of his story of man, in 'Paradise Regained,' God announces he will create a son 'of female Seed' to 'earn Salvation for the Sons of men.' Upon this announcement, celestial music is heard.

> So spake the Eternal Father, and all Heaven
> Admiring stood a space, then into Hymns
> Burst forth, and in Celestial measures moved,
> Circling the Throne and Singing, while the hand
> Sung with the voice, and this the argument.
> Victory and Triumph to the Son of God
> Now entering his great duel, not of arms,
> But to vanquish by wisdom hellish wiles.[102]

Now Satan takes Jesus up on a mountain to show him the kingdoms he may posses if he follows Satan. Among the visions shown Jesus we find,

> And all the while Harmonious Airs were heard
> Of chiming strings, or charming pipes and winds …[103]

In reference to the schools of ancient Greece, Satan promises Jesus he shall learn the secret power of music.

> There thou shalt hear and learn the secret power
> Of harmony in tones and numbers hit
> By voice or hand, and various-measured verse,
> *Aeolian* charms and *Dorian Lyric* Odes.[104]

---

[100] 'Paradise Lost,' XI, 558ff, in Ibid., II, 365.

[101] Ibid., XII, 365.

[102] 'Paradise Regained,' I, 168ff, in Ibid., II, 411.

[103] Ibid., II, 362.

[104] Ibid., IV, 254.

Milton delighted in describing the music of angels. In a poem, 'Upon the Circumcision,' Milton portrays the singing of the angels who announced the birth of Jesus.

> Ye flaming Powers, and winged Warriours bright,
> That erst with Musick, and triumphant song
> First heard by happy watchful Shepherds ear,
> So sweetly sung your Joy the Clouds along
> Through the soft silence of the listening night.[105]

His 'Paradise Lost,' has several descriptions of the heavenly music of angels, for example,

> Then Crowned again their golden Harps they took,
> Harps ever tuned, that glittering by their side
> Like Quivers hung, and with Preamble sweet
> Of charming symphonie they introduce
> Their sacred Song, and waken raptures high;
> No voice exempt, no vice but well could join
> Melodious part, such concord is in Heaven.[106]

Angels, whom Milton describes as 'millions of spiritual Creatures' who 'walk the Earth Unseen, both when we wake, and when we sleep,' perform both vocal and instrumental music.

> Celestial voices to the midnight air,
> Sole, or responsive each to others note
> Singing their great Creator: oft in bands
> While they keep watch, or nightly rounding walk
> With Heavenly touch of instrumental sounds
> In full harmonic number joined, their songs
> Divide the night, and lift our thoughts to Heaven.[107]

One of the fallen angels in 'Paradise Lost' contemplates being reinstated and having to celebrate God 'with warbled hymns, and to his Godhead sing forced Hallelujahs.'[108]

> Speak ye who best can tell, ye Sons of light,
> Angels, for ye behold him, and with songs
> And choral symphonies, Day without Night,
> Circle his Throne rejoicing.[109]

---

[105] 'Upon the Circumcision,' in Ibid., I, 26.
[106] 'Paradise Lost,' in III, 365ff, Ibid., II, 90.
[107] 'Paradise Lost,' in IV, 682ff, Ibid., II, 130ff. Celestial Choirs are mentioned again in Book VII, 254.
[108] 'Paradise Lost,' II, 240ff, in Ibid., II, 46.
[109] 'Paradise Lost,' V, 160ff, in Ibid., II, 149.

A final religious theme involving music is that of ritual sacrifice. Milton, in his classic 'Paradise Lost,' finds an ancient tradition for the more recent continental experience of the music which accompanied the burning of the Huguenots.

> First Moloch, horrid King besmeared with blood
> Of human sacrifice, and parents tears,
> Though for the noyse of Drums and Timbrels loud
> Their childrens cries unheard, that past through fire
> To his grim Idol.[110]

Other kinds of Entertainment Music are rarely mentioned by Milton. The most interesting reference to dinner music is found in a stage direction in Milton's masque,

> The Scene changes to a stately Palace, set out with all manner of deliciousness: soft Musick, Tables spread with all dainties.[111]

There is but one mention to wedding music, but it is a curious reference to 'the unexpressive nuptial Song'[112]

Military music is mentioned in 'Paradise Lost,' where Milton describes 'Trumpets loud and Clarions upreared' and 'Sonorous metal blowing Martial sounds.'[113] Shortly after these lines Milton follows the mistake of early English writers who mistakenly translated the Greek aulos as a member of the flute family, or 'pipes.' Here he credits music with the power to clear the troubled minds of the soldiers.

> With solemn touches, troubled thoughts, and chase
> Anguish and doubt and fear and sorrow and pain
> From mortal or immortal minds. Thus they
> Breathing united force with fixed thought
> Moved on in silence to soft Pipes that charmed
> Their painful steps over the burnt soil.

In 'Paradise Lost' as well, the description of the angels Michael and Gabriel at war against Satan begins with martial music.

> Nor with less dread the loud
> Ethereal Trumpet from on high began to blow …

---

110 'Paradise Lost,' I, 394, in Ibid., II, 22.

111 'Masque,' lines 657ff, in Ibid., I, 109.

112 'Lycidas,' in Ibid., I, 83.

113 'Paradise Lost,' I, 532ff, in Ibid., II, 27. Another description of the sound of the trumpet is found at the beginning of 'Paradise Regained,'

> Now had the great Proclaimer with a voice
> More awful than the sound of Trumpet …

In silence their bright Legions, to the sound
Of instrumental Harmonie that breathed
Heroic Ardor to adventurous deeds.[114]

Finally, there is only one reference to an actual trumpet signal, 'to Arms the matin Trumpet Sung.'[115] and one reference to hunting horns.

Oft listening how the Hounds and Horn
Cheerily rouse the slumbering morn.[116]

ENTERTAINMENT MUSIC

In a pastoral elegy, Milton describes the spirit of the Muses as it enters the performers of Entertainment Music.

It is no wonder, then, that through you three gods, their powers divine coordinated, brought to birth songs so sweet. Now the Thracian lyre, too, with its fretted gold, sounds for you, touched softly by an artist hand. Amid the hanging tapestries is heard the lyre that with its skillful dancing measures guides the feet of the maidens. Let sights so glorious detain *your* Muse at least, and let them call back whatever inspiration enervating indulgence in wine drives away. Believe me, while the ivory shall send forth its strains, and the holiday-making throng of dancers, keeping time to the *plectrum*, shall fill the vaulted, perfumed chambers, you will know full well that Phoebus is making his way, voicelessly, through your heart, even as some sudden glow of warmth makes its way through your very marrow; and through the maidens' eyes, and through their fingers as they sound forth their strains, Thalia will glide swiftly into your bosom, and master it utterly.[117]

---

114 'Paradise Lost,' in VI, 60ff, Ibid., II, 180.

115 'Paradise Lost,' VI, 525, in Ibid., II, 196.

116 'L'Allegro,' in Ibid., I, 36.

117 'Elegia Sextat,' in Ibid., I, 211.

8   JACOBEAN THEATRE

JACOBEAN THEATER IS REPRESENTED by the generation of playwrights after the great period of Elizabethan theater at the end of the sixteenth century. If this repertoire contains no poet of the stature of Marlowe or Shakespeare, nevertheless this literature offers many insights into music values at the beginning of the seventeenth century in England. While the artistic value of this literature does not equal that of the Elizabethan, it was more popular. The Globe Theater, after it was rebuilt in 1613, held two thousand spectators and by 1631 there were seventeen theaters in or near London. The increased number of spectators was due in large part to the fact that the plays were mostly now comedies, as is mentioned in the Prologue of Thomas Dekker's *The Roaring Girle*.

> Shall fill with laughter our vast Theater,
> That's all which I dare promise: Tragick passion,
> And such grave stuffe, is this day out of fashion.[1]

This literature, especially the comedies centering on the pursuit of love, was increasingly the object of attack by the Puritans, who eventually forced the closure of all theaters. The playwrights made some attempt to respond to these attacks, such as the satirical moment in Thomas Middleton's *The Family of Love* (IV, i), where an elderly court lady advises two young courtiers on the recreation she approves.[2]

> MISS PURGE. For your better instructions, therefore, you must never hereafter frequent taverns nor tap-houses, no masques nor mummeries, no pastimes nor playhouses.
> GUDGEON. Must we have no recreation?
> MISS PURGE. Yes, on the days which profane lips call holydays, you may take your spaniel and spend some hours at the duck-pond.

---

1 Thomas Dekker (b. 1570) was a very fluent writer, producing plays of his own and in collaboration with others, in addition to 'entertainments' and pamphlets on a variety of subjects. It has been said that no writer gave a more vivid picture of London at this time. He, however, failed to earn a living and was often in prison—once for three years. Nothing is known of him after the 1630s.

2 Thomas Middleton (1570–1627) became a lawyer in Gray's Inn in 1593, thus many of his plays center on the law.

In 1612, in response to this growing conservative criticism of the theater, Thomas Heywood published in London a small treatise called *An Apology for Actors*.[3] He admits some members of his profession are less than honorable.

> I also could wish, that such as are condemned for their licentiousnesse, might by a general consent bee quite excluded our society; for, as we are men that stand in the broad eye of the world, so should our manners, gestures, and behaviours, savour of such government and modesty, to deserve the good thoughts and reports of all men … Let me entreat you not to censure hardly of all for the misdeed of some.

Heywood also offers some positive arguments on behalf of theater. First, it is an ornament to the city, something which foreign visitors can report on when they return home. Second, theater contributes to the improvement of the language.

> Secondly, our English tongue, which hath been the most harsh, uneven, and broken language of the world, part Dutch, part Irish, Saxon, Scotch, Welsh, and indeed a gallimaffry of many, but perfect in none, is now by this secondary meanes of playing continually refined, every writer striving in himselfe to adde a new florish unto it; so that in processe, from the most rude and unpolisht tongue, it is growne to a most perfect and composed language, and many excellent workes and elaborate poems writ in the same, that many nations grow inamored of our tongue (before despised).

The third argument offered in defense of the theater is also interesting. Recognizing that general public education was not yet known, Heywood credits plays for contributing to the education of the public, not only with respect to history but also in the field of behavior.

> We present men with the ugliness of their vices to make them the more to abhorre them; as the Persians use, who, above all sinnes loathing drunkennesse, accustomed in their solemne feasts to make their servants and captives extremely overcome with wine, and then call their children to view their nasty and lothsome behaviour, making them hate that sinne in themselves, which shewed so grosse and abhominable in others.

Ben Jonson, in the dedication to his comedy, *Volpone*, concurs with the first point which Haywood makes above.[4] He also finds that in this age 'poetry, and the professors of it hear so ill on all sides.' He contributes his opinion that one cannot be a good poet unless he is first a good man.

---

3 Little is known of the life of Thomas Heywood (1575–1648). Much of his work may be lost, for he once wrote that he had written, or helped write, some 220 plays!

4 Ben Jonson (1573–1637) served as a soldier in Flanders and in 1598 killed a fellow actor in a duel. In his first success in writing plays, *Every Man in his Humor*, one of the actors was Shakespeare. After another period in prison, he became a popular figure in court life.

The playwright, John Webster,[5] wrote a brief prose work entitled 'New Characters Drawne to the life of Severall Persons, in Severall Qualities' (1615), which includes a paragraph on 'An excellent Actor.' The most interesting observation here reads,

> He is much affected to painting, and tis a question whether that make him an excellent Player, or his playing an exquisite painter. He adds grace to the Poets labours: for what in the Poet is but verse [*ditty*], in him is both verse and musicke.

Perhaps John Marston[6] had in mind an actor with less concern for aesthetics, when he has Antonio, in *Antonio and Mellida*, Part II (II, ii), observe,

> Madam, I will not swell, like a tragedian,
> In forced passion of affected strains.

It is important to remember that drama, like music, has both a written and a performance form. And like music, Marston points out that it is the performance form which is important.

> If any shall wonder why I print a comedy, whose life rests much in the actor's voice …[7]

And again later,

> Comedies are writ to be spoken, not read; remember the life of these things consists in action.[8]

Also, as the musician of the Baroque was invited to improvise on the page before him, so we must assume that a similar tradition on the theater stage remained from earlier times. Thomas Middleton seemed to find a strength in this tradition—at least on the French and Italian stage. In his *The Spanish Gipsy* (IV, ii), Fernando responds regarding a proposed play,

> So, so; a merry tragedy! There is a way
> Which the Italians and the Frenchmen use,
> That is, once a word given, or some slight plot,
> The actors will extempore fashion out
> Scenes neat and witty.

Some playwrights, however, were not amused. In the prologue to his *The Whore of Babylon*, Dekker uses music as a metaphor for the pain of the author who is forced to accept the

---

[5] John Webster (1580–1625) besides writing his own plays, collaborated with seven other writers. Little is known of his personal life, other than his being a son of a member of the Merchant Taylors' Company.

[6] John Marston (1575–1634) was apparently trained in law. His first efforts in poetry were ordered burned by the archbishop of Canterbury for licentiousness. He collaborated with Chapman and Jonson in *Eastward Ho*, which resulted in their all going to prison. In 1607 Marston gave up the theater and became a minister.

[7] Marston, *The Fawn*, 'To the Equal Reader.'

[8] Ibid., 'To the Reader.'

extemporaneous lines of the actors. He is not certain how often the players have changed his lines, since he has not heard all their performances,

> But of this my knowledge cannot fail, that in such Consorts, many of the Instruments are for the most part out of tune, And no marvel; for let the Poet set the note of his Numbers, even to Apollo's own Lyre, the Player will have his own Crochets, and sing false notes, in despite of all the rules of Musick.

In this environment there remained some playwrights with clear aesthetic goals. Jonson, in the dedication to his comedy, *Volpone*, admits that theater in his time [*stage-poetry*] is 'nothing but ribaldry, profanation, blasphemy, all license of offense to God and man.'[9] The principal end of the theater [*poesy*] as he saw it was 'to inform men in the best reason of living.' It is clear from the Prologue of his *Every Man in his Humour*, that Jonson did not respect those playwrights who pandered to public taste.

> Though need make many Poets, and some such
> As art and nature have not bettered much;
> Yet ours, for want, hath not so loved the stage,
> As he dare serve the ill customs of the age:
> Or purchase your delight at such a rate,
> As, for it, he himself must justly hate.

Jonson mentions the value of the theater to teach again in his *Timber; or Discoveries made upon Men and Matter* (published in 1641), but now adds the purpose of aesthetic delight. Here he writes that the purpose of both tragedy and comedy is to 'delight and teach.' We find a similar purpose in the Prologue of Beaumont and Fletcher's *The Knight of the Burning Pestle*.

> Our intent was at this time to move inward delight, not outward lightness.[10]

John Ford,[11] in the Epilogue of his *The Broken Heart*, reveals his purpose was aimed specifically at the upper level, the best, of society.

> Our writer's aim was in the whole addressed
> Well to deserve of all, but please the best.

---

9   In Jonson's comedy *The Silent Woman* (IV, iv), Morose says, 'I would sit out a play that were nothing but fights at sea, drum, trumpet, and target!'

10 Francis Beaumont (1584–1616), son of a judge, was educated in Oxford and eventually practiced law. His collaboration with Fletcher began in about 1605. John Fletcher (1579–1625), reared in a family long distinguished in literature, was educated at Cambridge. He was one of countless persons who died of the plague.

11 Of John Ford (1586-after 1639) little is known, other than he was also a lawyer.

Thomas Dekker, in the prologue to *The Whore of Babylon*, was one of several playwrights who hoped the audience would understand that poetic truth is not the same as historical truth.

Know that I write as a Poet, not as an Historian, and that these two do not live under one law.[12]

The Jacobean playwrights, unlike the Renaissance humanists, were no longer dreaming of recreating ancient drama. Staples of the old Greek plays, such as the chorus, are rarely found. In his 'To the Readers' before his tragedy *Sejanus*, Jonson apologizes that the reader will not find this work corresponding to the form of ancient Roman tragedies. Among other things he admits this work lacks 'a proper chorus.'[13] We must take this to mean a chorus which comments on the action, for two acts do end with the stage direction, 'Chorus—*of musicians*.'

The three trumpet fanfares which always began the first dramas of the modern European tradition were, in the beginning, probably for the purpose of gathering an audience. In the Jacobean productions, with a noisy audience of two thousand persons of all classes, these trumpet calls may have continued for the purpose of signaling the beginning of the play. We see, for example, in Marston's *Antonio and Mellida*, Part II (III, i), the stage direction,

The cornet sounding for the Act[14]

The stage direction, 'After the second sounding,' found incorporated into the prologue in several plays, such as in Jonson's *Every Man Out of his Humour*, is also a remnant of this old tradition.

The English plays of this period are filled with other kinds of incidental music. At the beginning of the seventeenth century these musicians must have been provided by the civic wind bands, known as Waits, as was the case in the Elizabethan theater. Indeed, several plays mention the Waits by name, as for example Beaumont and Fletcher's *The Knight of the Burning Pestle* (Prologue).

> CITIZEN. What stately Musick have you?
>   You have Shawms.
> PROLOGUE. Shawms? no.
> CITIZEN. No?
>   I'm a thief if my mind did not give me so.
>   Ralph plaies a stately part,
>   And he must needs have Shawms:
>   I'll be at the charge of them myself,
>   Rather than we'll be without them.

---

12 In George Chapman's *The Revenge of Bussy D'Ambois*, the author's letter of dedication contains a similar statement.

13 In his tragedy *Catiline* he does use a 'proper chorus,' which comments at length on the action. For additional examples of a chorus in the ancient style, see: Beaumont and Fletcher's *The Prophetess*; Thomas Dekker's *Old Fortunatus*; Thomas Heywood's *The Faire Maid of the West* and *If you know not me, you know no body*.

14 Also Marston's *Antonio and Mellida*, Part II, V.

PROLOGUE. So you are like to be.
CITIZEN. Why and so I will be,
  There's two shillings,
  Let's have the Waits of Southwark,
  They are as rare fellows as any are in England;
  And that will fetch them all o'r the water, with a vengeance,
  As if they were mad.
PROLOGUE. You shall have them.

Later, in II, iii,

WIFE. The Fidlers go again Husband.
CITIZEN. I Nell, but this is scurvy Musick: I gave the whore-son gallows money, and I think he has not got me the Waits of Southwark, if I hear him not anon, I'll twinge him by the ears.

Additional references to the Wait bands can be seen in Jonson's *A Tale of a Tub* (V, x), where the music for an internal masque is provided by the 'Hilts waits' and in Thomas Heywood's *A Woman Kilde with Kindnesse*,[15] where we find, 'while the Towne Musitians finger their frets within.'

But even if these civic institutions are not always mentioned by name, it is difficult to imagine where else the playwrights would have found musicians capable of supplying the wide variety of instruments mentioned in some plays. Consider, for example, the numerous instruments mentioned in the stage directions of Beaumont and Fletcher's *The Little French Lawyer*. In Act III, 'Musick' is introduced to add 'mirth to our Wine.' The recipient of this honor, Cleremont, is not appreciative. 'A hogs pox stop your pipes,' and 'Plague dam your Whistles,' he cries. It is only here that the stage direction identifies the 'music' as a recorder consort. In Act IV the stage directions call for 'Cornet. Musick within,' which Vertaigne calls 'choice Musick.' Soon 'Still Musick'[16] is called for and then 'Musick for the Dance.'

In Act V the stage directions are most unusual, beginning with,

A Horrid noise of Musique within

followed almost immediately by a reference to a trombone consort and a military band.

A strange Musick. Sackbut & Troop Musick

Of the sound of this music,

---

15 *The Dramatic Works of Thomas Heywood* (New York: Russell & Russell, 1964), II, 95. This edition is a reprint of an 1874 one which, in a misguided attempt to ease the reading, omitted all references to scenes and most Acts. Therefore we cite page numbers.

16 In Beaumont and Fletcher's *The Two Noble Kinsmen* (V, i) the stage directions call for 'Still Musick of Recorders.'

ANABEL. What's that? how sad and hollow,
  The sound comes to us.
LAMIRA. Groaning? or singing is it?
ANABEL. The wind I think, murmuring amongst old rooms.

Until the second half of the sixteenth century 'Musician' meant the wind player, who was the professional musician. It is from this perspective that we understand a comment in Dekker's *The Sun's-Darling* (IV, i), when Folly comments, 'Now have I more air than ten Musicians.'

For plays with less complicated musical demands, such as those requiring only music for dancing, we must suppose the less expensive street musicians were used. Such musicians are identified in Jonson's *A Tale of a Tub*.

Old Father Rosin, the chief minstrel here:
Chief minstrel too of Highgate: she has hired him
And all, his two boys for a day and a half.[17]

Later (II, i), Father Rosin is described as leading a 'consort of fiddling boys,' thus confirming his name as a pun.

In Beaumont and Fletcher's *Wit at Several Weapons* (V, i), there is a scene dealing with the payment of casual musicians. After most of the details are arranged for an internal masque, an Old Knight asks what else is needed.

OLD KNIGHT. Why what wants then?
WITTY. Nothing but charge of Musick,
  That must be paid, you know.
OLD KNIGHT. That shall be my charges, I'll pay the Musick.
  What ever it cost.

After the masque, the Old Knight wants to back out of of paying for the music.

RUINOUS. You must pay for your Musick first, Sir.
OLD KNIGHT. Now? Must? are there musty Fidlers? are Beggars choosers ...

Unable to avoid paying, the Old Knight now attempts to negotiate a better price.

OLD KNIGHT. How? bate ten pound? what's the whole sum then?
WITTY. Faith Sir, a hundred pound, with much adoe,
  I got fifty bated, and faith Father, to say truth,
  'Tis reasonable for men of their fashion.

---

17 I, iv. The titles of some of their popular songs are given, 'Tom Tiler,' 'Jolly Joiner,' and 'Jovial Tinker.' Another popular tune, 'Paggington's Pound' is mentioned in Jonson's *Bartholomew Fair* (III, v). In Beaumont and Fletcher's *The Chances* (III, iii), the popular song 'John Dorrie' is mentioned.

> OLD KNIGHT. La, la, la down, a hunder'd pound? La, la, la,
>   You are a consort of Thieves, are you not?
> WITTY. No Musicians, Sir, I told you before.
> OLD KNIGHT. Fiddle faddle, is it not a robbery? a plain robbery.
> WITTY. No, no, no, by no means Father, you have received
>   For your money, nay and that you cannot give back,
>   'Tis somewhat dear I confess, but who can help it?
>   If they had been agreed with before-hand,
>   'Twas ill forgotten.
> OLD KNIGHT. Case up your instruments, I yield, here, as robb'd and
>   Taken from me, I deliver it.
> WITTY. No Sir, you have performed your promise now,
>   Which was, to pay the charge of Musick, that's all.
> OLD KNIGHT. I have heard no Musick, I have received none, Sir,
>   There's none to be found in me, nor about me.
> WITTY. Why Sir, here's witness against you, you have danced,
>   And he that dances, acknowledges a receipt of Musick.
> OLD KNIGHT. I deny that, Sir, look you, I can dance without Musick, do you see, Sir? And I can
>   sing without it too; you are a Consort of Thieves, do you hear what I do?
> WITTY. Pray you take heed, Sir, if you do move the Musick again, it may cost you as much more …
> OLD KNIGHT. Musick's too damnable dear.

Such musicians, then and now, are more concerned with money than art. Marston, in *The Malcontent* (I, iii), complains that once he is paid, he is gone!

> MALEVOLE. I am in haste, be brief.
> PASSARELLO. As your fiddler when he is paid.

ON THE PHYSIOLOGY OF AESTHETICS

This light-hearted Jacobean literature was little concerned with philosophy. Very rare are comments such as that in George Chapman's *Bussy D'Ambois*, where the first line reads, 'Fortune, not Reason, rules the state of things.' We were struck by one comment which almost seems to refer to the twin functions, one rational and one experiential, of the hemispheres of the brain. In the introduction to his comedy, *The Staple of News*, Jonson bemoans the fate of the author of a play and the abuse he receives from actors. The poet, he says,

> doth sit like an unbraced drum with one of his heads beaten out: for, that you must note, a poet hath two heads as a drum has, one for making, the other repeating.

We have cited in the previous volumes of this series numerous instances in the literature of every era in which references are made to the prejudice in the favor of the right hand, which is a manifestation of the fact that only the left hemisphere of the brain can speak, and the fact that it tends to deny the existence of the right hemisphere. We note two examples of this in the plays of Dekker, the first being *If This be not a Good Play* (III, ii), where there is a discussion of the right eye being favored over the left. A more conventional example is his *The Wonder of a Kingdom* (IV, iv). A stage direction indicates 'Musicke within,' which is followed by,

> *Alphonsina*. What's the matter sir?
> *Nicoletto*. I hear a lute, and sure it comes this way.
> *Alphonsina*. My most loved Lord, step you aside, I would not have you seen for the saving of my right hand.

When the 'Musicke' comes in view, Nicoletto says, 'Pox on your Catts guts.'

There is also virtually no discussion in these plays of the relationship of the senses and Reason, another familiar Scholastic topic. As nearly all early philosophers argued the primacy of the eye, it is unusual to find in Beaumont and Fletcher's *The Little Thief* (IV, i), in a passage centered on hearing church bells, a rare reference to the value of the ear being higher than the eye.

> Boy. To intreat a knowledge of you, whether it be
>   By the Ear you ring thus cunningly, or by the Eye;
>   For to be plain, he has laid ten pounds upon it.
> Wildbrain. But which way has he laid?
> Boy. That your Ear guides you,
>   And not the Eye.
> Toby. Has won, has won, the Ear's our only instrument:
> Boy. But how shall we be sure on it.
> Toby. Put all the lights out, to what end serve our eyes then?

ON THE PHILOSOPHY OF AESTHETICS

The most interesting comment on the aesthetics of art in general is Jonson's comment that art must be based on Reason. In his comedy *The Alchemist* (I, ii) we find,

> Face. Speak you this from art?
> Subtle. Aye, sir, and reason too: the ground of art.

There are several comments dealing with the traditional aesthetic question of the relationship of Art and Nature. In Beaumont and Fletcher's *The Martial Maid* (III, iii), Vitelli observes, 'Art cannot counterfeit what Nature could make but once.' The question is placed in the context of the acting profession in George Chapman's *The Gentleman Usher* (I, i), when Medice says,

> My lord, away with these scholastique wits,
> Lay the invention of your speech on me,
> And the performance too; I'll play my part,
> That you shall say, Nature yields more than Art.[18]

Jonson, again complaining that theater has decayed to the point of becoming mere entertainment, mentions this topic in the 'To the Reader' of his comedy *The Alchemist*.

> The concupiscence of dances and antics so reigneth, as to run away from Nature and be afraid of her, is the only point of art that tickles the spectators.

One result of writing to please the lowest instincts of the audience was, of course, that the playwrights developed an audience that aspired no higher. A rare regret is expressed in the prologue of Beaumont and Fletcher's *The Fair Maid of the Inn*.

> A Jigg shall be clapt at, and every rhyme
> Praised and applauded by a clamorous chime.
> Let ignorance and laughter dwell together,
> They are beneath the Muses pity.

ON THE AESTHETICS OF MUSIC

In spite of all the comedy in these plays, and the constant satire of the lifestyles of every level of society, one often finds a clear recognition of quality music. The most frequent adjective for quality music was the word 'choice,' as we find in Middleton's *Blurt, Master-Constable*, where the duke requests,

> Let this bright morning merrily be crowned
> With dances, banquets, and choice music's sound.

One metaphor for the highest quality of music was the ancient Greek notion of the 'Music of the Spheres.' Thus we find in Marston's *The Insatiate Countess* (III, iv),

> Let sphere-like music breathe delicious tones.

---

18 George Chapman (1559–1634) possessed a university education and was known for his translations of Homer, which were widely printed during his life. He went to prison, with Jonson and Marston, for his participation in writing the play, *Eastward Ho!*

And in Dekker's *Old Fortunatus* (I, i), Fortune says,

> No more: curse on: your cries to me are Musicke,
> And fill the sacred roundure of mine ears,
> With tunes more sweet then moving of the Spheres.[19]

On Music and Society

The actual dialog of these plays contains numerous clues which offer insight to the general familiarity with music by society. First, the playwrights express concern at the decline of music and the arts. We see this in Jonson's tragedy, *Sejanus* (I, i), where Sabinus observes,

> We [lack] the fine arts and their thriving use,
> Should make us graced, or favored of the times,

and with regard to music in particular in the 'To the Readers of this Comedy' in Beaumont and Fletcher's *The Knight of the Burning Pestle*.

> Gentlemen, the World is so nice in these our times, that for Apparel, there is no fashion, For Musick, which is a rare Art, (though now slighted) No Instrument.

In another place, Beaumont and Fletcher's *The Noble Gentleman*, (Prologue), these playwrights seem to lament that wit is now dedicated only to seeking applause—but, they hold out the hope this may change.

> Wit is become an Antick, and puts on
> As many shapes of variation,
> To court the times applause, as the times dare,
> Change several fashions, nothing is thought rare
> Which is not new, and followed, yet we know
> That what was worn some twenty years ago,
> Comes into grace again.[20]

---

19 For additional references to the 'Music of the Spheres' see: John Webster's *The Dutchesse of Malfy* (I, i); Thomas Dekker's *The Virgin Martyr* (V, ii) and *The Noble Spanish Soldier* (II, i); George Chapman's *The Blind Beggar* (Scene viii), a reference to the music of the spheres as a metaphor for a couple's feelings, 'To echo sweetly to our celestial tunes'; Beaumont and Fletcher's *The Prophetess* (II, i), Delphia, a prophetess, gives a speech which includes 'The Musick of the Spheres attending on us'; and Marston's *Antonio and Mellida*, Part II (III, i).

20 A similar thought is found in Thomas Middleton's *Mayor of Queenborough* (I, i),

> Fashions, that are now called new,
> Have been worn by more than you.

One clear indication of the familiarity of music by at least the educated class can be found in the frequent instances of humor, metaphors and other figures of speech which required some knowledge of music to be understood. The significance of this is perhaps best seen in the fact that virtually nothing of this nature is routinely found in the theater today.

Regarding the use of music in a humorous context, we mention only two examples. First, humor based on the confusion of the senses is found in Marston's *Antonio and Mellida*, Part II (III, ii), when Balurdo enters with a bass viol and says, 'I have the most respective fiddle; did you ever smell a more sweet sound?' The second example involves a play on the word 'noise,' which the early seventeenth-century audience understood to be a synonym for instrumental music. In Jonson's comedy, *The Silent Woman*, Act III, scene vii begins,

> CLERIMONT. By your leave, ladies. Do you want any music? I have brought you variety of noises. Play, sirs, all of you.
>
> [*Music of all sorts*]
>
> MOROSE. Oh, a plot, a plot, a plot, a plot upon me! This day I shall be their anvil to work on, they will grate me asunder. 'Tis worse than the noise of a saw.
>
> CLERIMONT. No, they are hair, rosin, and guts. I can give you the receipt.
>
> TRUEWIT. Peace, boys.
>
> CLERIMONT. Play, I say.

Nothing makes the point more than the use of music as a metaphor, for without an understanding of music the entire meaning is lost. Among the numerous examples of the use of music as a metaphor, found in the Jacobean plays, we might begin with the famous metaphor coined by Plato, by which 'harmony' was used to represent the healthy, well-adjusted body. Two examples in this literature which are used in the Platonic sense are found in Middleton's *Michaelmas Term* (I, i),

> STALEWOOD. Faith, like a lute that has all the strings broke; nobody will meddle with her.
>
> REARAGE. Fie, there are doctors now in town will string her again, and make her sound as sweet as ever she did.[21]

and in Chapman's *The Blind Beggar* (Scene iii), when Leon observes,

> Love decks the countenance, spiriteth the eye,
> And tunes the soul in sweetest harmony.

An example of a metaphor in which music represents 'out of tune' health can be found in *Every Man out of his Humour* (III, ix). Here, Jonson presents a scene in a room at court and Fastidius sings to Saviolina, accompanying himself on a viol.

---

21 Perhaps another example of this kind is found in Thomas Middleton's *The Phoenix*, which ends with, 'In my blood peace's music ...'

FASTIDIUS. By the soul of music, lady (*hum, hum*).
SAVIOLINA. Would we might hear it once.
FASTIDIUS. I do more adore and admire your (*hum, hum*) predominant perfections than (*hum, hum*) ever I shall have power and faculty to express (*hum*).
SAVIOLINA. Upon the viol de gambo, you mean?
FASTIDIUS. It's miserably out of tune, by this hand.
SAVIOLINA. Nay, rather by the fingers.
MACILENTE. [*Aside*] It makes good harmony with her wit.

A frequent figure of speech is the use of music as a metaphor for the state of being pleased. This is the meaning of an expression in Dekker's *The Roaring Girl* (V, ii) when Alexander says, 'I finde it in the musicke of my heart.' In Cyril Tourneur's, *The Atheist's Tragedy*, we find an unusual example of this kind of metaphor[22] in Act V, which begins with the stage direction 'music.' D'Amville doesn't appreciate the music, saying 'Cease that harsh music,' but when he picks up some gold, he uses music as a metaphor for his pleasure.

> Here sounds a music whose melodious touch
> Like angels' voices ravishes the sense.

In Dekker's *The Honest Whore*, Part II (V, ii), we find the earliest version that we know of a now familiar figure of speech. Bellafront says,

> Let mercy touch your heart-strings gracious Lord
> That it may sound like musike in the eare
> Of a man desperate.

Aside from its metaphorical usage, it is an odd expression. Is the alternative 'music for the eye?' We wonder if in some way this expression had its roots in the Scholastic university distinction of 'speculative' and 'practical' music, which, as in universities today, meant one kind of music for the eye and another for the ear. We should also point out that Dekker corrects this medieval misunderstanding in his *The Witch of Edmonton* (III, iii), when Old Carter makes the observation, 'There's no musick but in sound, sound it must be.'

Music is also used as a metaphor for various aspects of speech. Two usages which are familiar today are found in Heywood's *The Golden Age*,[23] when Jupiter observes 'Womens tongues and hearts have different tunes,' and in Chapman's *All Fools* (V, ii), where 'sing your old song no more,' is used for an often repeated phrase. In Chapman's *Bussy D'Ambois* (I, ii), there is a similar metaphor for one who speaks well. Bussy says to Pyra, a court lady, 'your descants do marvelous well fit this ground.' We might also mention two lines which appear later (IV, i), when Tamyra observes,

---

22 Cyril Tourneur surfaces as a writer in 1613, before which little is known. He accompanied Sir Edward Cecil on several sea voyages and died in Ireland in 1626 of an unknown disease acquired at sea.

23 *The Dramatic Works of Thomas Heywood*, III, 68.

> You could all this time be at concord with him,
> That still hath played such discords on your honor.

We also find music used as a metaphor for various aspects of time. In Beaumont and Fletcher's *The Little Thief* (Act III), music is used as a metaphor for 'time to get organized.'

> And tune our Instruments till the Consort come
> To make up the full noise.

In Middleton's *A Fair Quarrel* (I, i) we find music used as a metaphor by Russell to express to two gentleman that it is the wrong time to duel. Put your swords away, he says,

> Hide 'em, for shame! I had thought soldiers
> Had been musical, would not strike out of time,
> But to the consort of drum, trumps, and fife:
> 'Tis madmen-like to dance without music,
> And most unpleasing shows to the beholders,
> A Lydian verse to a Doric note.

Finally, we mention a line which would have been humorous to a university student of music. In a humorous scene in Middleton's *Your Five Gallants* (II, i) a 'music house' is used as a metaphor for a house of prostitution. Among the dialog of three young 'gallants,' we find,

> PRIMERO. La, I tell you;—you'll bear me witness, gentlemen,
>   If their complaints come to their parents' ears,
>   They're words of art I teach 'em, nought but art.
> GOLDSTONE. Why, 'tis most certain.
> BUNGLER. For all [students] know that *musica est ars*.

During much of the fifteenth and sixteenth centuries the ability to sing and perform on a musical instrument was considered a necessary accomplishment of a gentleman. In England at the end of the sixteenth century this begins to change, although we find a few references in the early seventeenth century plays which still refer to the gentleman as an amateur musician. In Beaumont and Fletcher's *The Loyal Subject* (II, i) a character called Ancient, who identifies himself as a soldier and a gentleman, sings a song and then observes,

> 'Tis a singing age Sir,
> A merry moon here now: I'le follow it:
> Fidling, and fooling now, gains more than fighting.

In another play by these authors, *The Coronation* (I, i), the Queen agrees that the qualities of the Gentleman include dancing, singing and playing the lute. On the other hand, these qualities may not be appropriate for a guard, for

> How can he stand
> Upon his guard, who hath Fidlers in his head,
> To which, his feet must ever be a dancing?

Passarello, an entertainer attached to Bilioso, an old marshal, in Marston's *The Malcontent* (I, iii), suggests the gentleman did not sing well.

> Yes, I can sing, fool, if you'll bear the burden; and I can play upon instruments, scurvily, as gentlemen do.

In Jonson we find two references of the gentleman which are related to university life. In the literature of the late sixteenth century in England there was much criticism of the universities for allowing young men to indulge in poetry, rather than in more important subjects. It is in this perspective that we find in *Every Man in his Humour* (I, i), an old gentleman, Knowell (a pun, of course), who observes,

> Myself was once a student; and, indeed,
> Fed with the selfsame humour he is now,
> Dreaming on naught but idle poetry,
> That fruitless and unprofitable art,
> Good unto none, but least to the professors,
> Which then, I thought the mistress of all knowledge:
> But since, time, and the truth have waked my judgment,
> And reason taught me better to distinguish
> The vain from the useful learnings.

In his *The Staple of News* (I, v), Jonson is more indulgent when a young man is described,

> A pretty scholar, and a Master of Arts,
> Was made or went out Master of Arts in a throng,
> At the university; as before, one Christmas,
> He got into a masque at court, by his wit,
> And the good means of his cithern, holding up thus
> For one o'the music. He's a nimble fellow!

The plays also give witness to the fact that music was included in the skills of the well-educated young lady at this time. Middleton refers to this in three separate plays,[24] first in *Women Beware Women* (III, ii), where Fabricio observes,

> She has the full qualities of a gentlewoman;
> I've brought her up to music, dancing, what not,
> That may commend her sex, and stir her husband.

---

24 Thomas Middleton's *A Chaste Maid in Cheapside* begins with Maudlin asking her daughter, Moll, if she has played her virginal lessons and practiced her dancing.

In *No Wit, no Help Like a Woman's* (IV, i), Sir Twilight commends his daughter as a 'proper gentlewoman' who,

> Sings, dances, plays,
> Touches an instrument with a motherly grace.

And in *A Trick to Catch the Old One* (I, ii) a young lady is described as having been sent to London,

> to learn fashions, practice music; the voice between her lips, and the viol between her legs, she'll be fit for a consort very speedily.

In Heywood's *A Woman Kilde with Kindnesse*,[25] Charles says of a bride to be,

> First her Birth
> Is Noble, and her education such
> As might become the Daughter of a Prince,
> Her owne tongue speakes all tongues, and her owne hand
> Can teach all strings to speake in their best grace
> From the shrill treble, to the hoarsest base.

In Beaumont and Fletcher's *The Womans Prize* (III, i), we find music used as a metaphor for four important characteristics of a young woman.

> TRANIO. Tell me but this; what dost thou think of women?
> ROWLAND. Why, as I think of Fiddles, they delight me,
>   Till their strings break.
> TRANIO. What strings?
> ROWLAND. Their Modesties,
>   Faiths, Vows, and Maidenheads, for they are like Kits
>   The have but four strings to 'em.

In another play, *The Loyal Subject* (III, vi), these authors address this topic in a humorous vein. Alinda, son of a Russian general, is coaching a young lady, Honora, on the skills she will need.

> ALINDA. Play with your Bracelets, sing: you must learn to rhyme too,
>   And riddle neatly; studie the hardest language,
>   And 'tis no matter whether it be sense, or no,
>   So it go seemlie off ...
> HONORA. Have ye schools for all these mysteries?
> ALINCA. O yes.

---

25 *The Dramatic Works of Thomas Heywood*, II, 93.

As in the sixteenth century, the Jacobean playwrights somewhat ridicule that special class of gentleman known as the courtier. This being the case, references to music and the arts are also often presented in humorous contexts when associated with the court and the courtier.

In Dekker's *The Wonder of a Kingdom* (III, i) a courtier places 'the rarest musicians' in a category with cooks and the 'fairest girles, that will sell sinne for gold.' In another play by Dekker, *The Roaring Girl* (IV, i), we find,

ALEXANDER. What is he there?
SEBASTIAN. A Gentleman, a musitian sir, one of excellent fingering.
ALEXANDER. *[Aside]* Aye, I think so, I wonder how they scapt her.
SEBASTIAN. Has the most delicate stroke sir.
ALEXANDER. *[Aside]* A stroke indeed, I feel it at my heart.
SEBASTIAN. Puts down all your famous musitians.
ALEXANDER. *[Aside]* Aye, a whore may put down a hundred of them.

We have mentioned above, the Scholastic division of music into the 'speculative' and the 'practical.' Jonson satirizes this idea in a pedagogy for the courtier's practice of facial expressions in his comedy, *Cynthia's Revels* (II, iii).

But now, to come to your face of faces, or courtier's face, 'tis of three sorts, according to our subdivision of a courtier, elementary, practic, and theoric. Your courtier theoric is he that hath arrived to his farthest, and doth now know the court rather by speculation than practice; and this is his face: a fastidious and oblique face, that looks as it went with a vice, and were screwed thus. Your courtier practic is he that is yet in his path, his course, his way, and hath not touched the punctilio, or point of his hopes; his face is here: a most promising, open, smooth, and overflowing face, that seems as it would run and pour itself into you. Somewhat a northerly face. Your courtier elementary is one but newly entered, or as it were in the alphabet, or *ut-re-mi-fa-sol-la* of courtship. Note well this face, for it is this you must practice.[26]

We are fond of a passage in Beaumont and Fletcher's *The Elder Brother* (I, ii), where a young lady, Angellina, is explaining her rather modern requirements in a husband.

ANGELLINA. Troth as of the Courtier, all his Songs and Sonnets, his Anagrams, Acrosticks, Epigrams, his deep and Philosophical Discourse of Nature's hidden Secrets, makes not up a perfect Husband ... No, no, Father, though I could be well pleased to have my Husband a Courtier, and a Scholar, young, and valiant; these are but gawdy nothings, if there be not something to make a substance.
LEWIS. And what is that?
ANGELLINA. A full Estate, and that said, I've said all; and get me such a one with these Additions, farewell Virginity.

---

26 In Jonson's comedy *The Silent Woman* (V, ii) Centaur observes of a court lady, 'she is a perfect courtier, and loves nobody, but for her uses: and for her uses, she loves all.'

In Chapman's *Bussy D'Ambois* (I, ii), we find a specific reference to the courtier's ability to play a string instrument.

> TAMYRA. The man's a courtier at first sight.
> BUSSY. I can sing prick-song, lady, at first sight; and why not be a courtier as suddenly?

In Chapman's *All Fools* (II, i), there is a very interesting, and unusually lengthy, discussion of the cultural training of the young courtier, in this case Valerio, son to a knight. Cornelio, a gentleman aspiring to be more active in the court, begins by commenting on how much he admires Valerio for his self-education, which includes music.

> He has stolen languages, Italian, Spanish
> And some spice of the French, besides his dancing,
> Singing, playing on choice instruments …

Valerio modestly responds,

>   Toys, toys, a pox; and yet they be such toys,
>   As every Gentleman would not be without.

He is asked to demonstrate his musical skills, but pleas he is out of shape.

> CORNELIO. Prythee Val,
>   Take thy Theorbo for my sake a little.
> VALERIO. By heaven, this month I touched not a Theorbo.
> CORNELIO. Touched a Theorbo? marke the very word.
>   Sirra, go fetch.
>   *Exit Page.*
> VALERIO. If you will have it, I must needs confess,
>   I am no husband of my qualities.

While the page goes to get a Theorbo, Valerio dances and is complimented, but he is still requested to play.

> CORNELIO. Come sweet Val, touch and sing.
> DARIOTTO. Foote, will you hear
>   The worst voice in Italy?
> CORNELIO. O God, sir.
>   *[Valerio] sings.*
>   Courtiers, how like you this?
> DARIOTTO. Believe it excellent.
> CORNELIO. Is it not natural?
> VALERIO. If my father heard me,

>   Foot, he'd renounce me for his natural son.
> DARIOTTO. By heaven, Valerio, and I were thy father,
>   And loved good qualities as I do my life,
>   I'd disinherit thee: for I never heard
>   Dog howl with worse grace.
> CORNELIO. Go to, Courtier,
>   You deal not courtly now to be so plain,
>   Nor nobly, to discourage a young Gentleman,
>   In virtuous qualities, that has but stolen them.

Later (III, i) the Page offers the courtiers advice on the proper treatment of women, which is basically to keep them in the home, busy with 'sowing, singing, playing [instruments], childing, dancing, or so on.'

ON THE PURPOSE OF MUSIC

In Tourneur's, *The Atheist's Tragedy* (III, iii), we find the observation that music *must* have a purpose. Sebastian, in the course of using music as metaphor for Charlemont's emotional state, says, 'But trebles and basses make poor music without purpose [*means*].'

The most frequently mentioned purpose of music in all early literature is to soothe the feelings of the listener, and we continue to find many such references in the Jacobean plays. In Marston's *Antonio and Mellida* (III, ii), Andrugio, Duke of Genoa, says, 'My soul grows heavy: boy, let's have a song.' After the stage direction, 'a song,' Andrugio responds,

> 'Tis a good boy, and by my troth, well sung.
> O, and thou felt'st my grief, I warrant thee.

In another Marston play, *What You Will* (II, i), Quadratus sings of music being one of the things which ward off sorrow,

> *Music, tobacco, sack, and sleep,*
> *The tide of sorrow backward keep.*

In Beaumont and Fletcher's *The Lovers Progress* (III, i) A Friar offers to have one of his novices sing to solace Clarange, who responds,

> And it will come timely,
> For I am full of melancholy thoughts,
> Against which I have heard with reason Musick
> To be the speediest cure, 'pray you apply it.'

The novice's song begins,

> *A Dieu fond love, farewel you wanton powers,*
> *I am free again.*

Following the song,

> FRIAR. How do ye approve it?
> CLARANGE. It is a Heavenly Hymn, no ditty Father,
>   It passes through my ears unto my soul,
>   And works divinely on it.

In Beaumont and Fletcher's *The Spanish Curate* (III, ii), we find,

> We have brought Musick to appease his spirit,
> And the best Song we'll give him.[27]

And in these author's *Thierry and Theodoret* (III, i), after the stage direction calls for 'Soft Musick,' Thierry observes, 'Musick drowns all sadness.'

In Heywood's *A Woman Kilde with Kindnesse*,[28] a character is impatient and threatens,

> quickly, if the Musicke overcome not my mellancholly, I shall quarrell.

There are also, in these plays, a few instances where music fails in its purpose to soothe. In Middleton's *A Chaste Maid in Cheapside* (V, ii), a mother asks her daughter to sing a song to relieve her sorrow, but the daughter sings such a tragic song that the mother can only respond, 'O, I could die with music!'

Similarly, in Heywood's *The Iron Age*, Part II,[29] a stage direction reads,

> *Musicke and healthing within.*

after which, Orestes laments,

> Oh Cethus what's this musicke unto me,
> That am composed of discords? What are healths
> To him that is struck heart-sick?

While such references to music which fails to soothe may be found in earlier literature, one almost never finds a circumstances where the music goes beyond failing to actually

---

27 In Beaumont and Fletcher's *The Loyal Subject* (I, ii), Alinda observes she has too much grief to sing.
28 *The Dramatic Works of Thomas Heywood*, II, 97.
29 Ibid., III, 409.

create an adverse effect in the listener. We find such a case in Beaumont and Fletcher's *The Coronation* (III, i), when the Queen complains,

> This is not Musick
> Sprightly enough, it feeds the soul with melancholy.

Similarly, in these author's *The Queen of Corinth* (III, ii), after the stage direction, 'A sad Song,'

> *Weep no more, nor sigh nor groan*
> *Sorrow calls no time that's gone …*
>
> AGENOR. These heavy Ayres feed sorrow in her Lady,
>   And nourish it too strongly; like a Mother
>   That spoiles her Child with giving on't the will.

In Dekker's *Old Fortunatus* (III, i) a boy serenades Orleans with a lute, but the latter begs him to leave, saying, 'This musicke makes me but more out of tune.'

Another purpose of music is to delight, or for pleasure. In the 'Induction' to Marston's *What You Will*, we find,

> Music and poetry were first approved
> By common sense; and that which pleased most,
> Held most allowed pass: know, rules of art
> Were shaped to pleasure, not pleasure to your rules.

In Beaumont and Fletcher's *Wit at Several Weapons* (II, i), Cunningam reflects,

> With purpose that my harmony shall reach
> And please the Ladies ear …

In the plays of Dekker there are also several interesting references to the purpose of music being to please. In *Westward Ho* (IV, ii), we find mention of one of the characteristics which so fascinated the ancient Greek philosophers, the fact that music is the only art which cannot be seen. Here, the Earle philosophizes,

> Go, let musicke
> Charme with her excellent voice an awfull silence
> Through all this building, that her sphaery soule
> May (on the wings of Ayre) in thousand formes
> Invisibly flie, yet be enjoyed.

In Dekker's *Old Fortunatus* (II, ii), Fortunatus observes he has been ravished with divine raptures of 'Dorick, Lidian and Phrigian harmonies' and in *Lust's Dominion* (I, i) the Queen Mother says,

> Chime out your softest strains of harmony,
> And on delicious Musicks silken wings
> Send ravishing delight to my loves ears,
> That he may be enamored of your tunes.

The most important purpose of music is to express feelings. Among the passages in this literature which interest us in this regard, we first notice a reference in Dekker's *The Honest Whore*, Part I (I, ii) where the very term 'Musician' is synonymous with an emotional person. Here a wife describes her placid husband as one who never gets upset with servants, has no more sting than an ant, etc., thus she concludes a 'Musitian will he never be.' Perhaps this was also intended in Middleton's *The Witch* (II, i) when Isabella comments, 'I will not grumble, sir, like some musician.'

Regarding the expression of feeling through music, we especially notice some lines in Beaumont and Fletcher's *The Faithful Shepherdess* (V, i) where a Priest observes he is willing to hear a shepherd's song *only* if it is sung with feeling.

> 'Tis good to hear ye, Shepherd, if the heart
> In this well sounding Musick bear his part.

In another Beaumont and Fletcher play, *The Tragedy of Valentinian* (II, iv), just before the lyrics for songs of love, Licinius calls for music,

> She is coming up the stairs; Now the Musick;
> And as that stirs her, let's set on.

We have an insight into the deep expressions of emotion expressed in song at this time in Marston's *Antonio and Mellida* (IV, i), in the instructions of Antonio to a Page before the latter sings.

> I prithee sing, but mark my words
> Let each note breathe the heart of passion,
> The sad extracture of extremest grief.
> Make me a strain speak groaning like a bell
> That tolls departing souls;
> Breathe me a point that may enforce me weep,
> To wring my hands, to break my cursed breast,
> Rave, and exclaim, lie grovelling on the earth,
> Straight start up frantic, crying, Mellida!
> Sing but, 'Antonio hath lost Mellida,'

And thou shalt see me like a man possess'd
Howl out such passion, that even this brinish marsh
Will squeeze out tears from out his spongy cheeks:
The rocks even groan, and—prithee, prithee sing.

Another Marston play reminds us that the feelings expressed in music must be genuine. In *Antonio and Mellida*, Part II (IV, ii) Antonio, Pandulfo and Alberto enter the stage with daggers and we read,

> ANTONIO. Wilt sing a dirge, boy?
> PANDULFO. No, no song; 'twill be vile out of tune.
> ALBERTO. Indeed, he's hoarse; the poor boy's voice is cracked.
> PANDULFO. Why, coz! why should it not be hoarse and cracked,
>   When all the strings of nature's symphony
>   Are cracked and jar? Why should his voice keep tune,
>   When there's no music in the breast of man?

In Marston we also find references to the communication of feelings of love through music, as in *Antonio and Mellida* (III, ii), where Castillo makes plans, before a song.

> I will warble to the delicious conclave of my mistress' ear: and strike her thoughts with the pleasing touch of my voice.

In another play, Marston speaks of music's power to inspire physical love.[30] In Marston's *The Insatiate Countess* (III, iv) Isabella calls upon the power of music.

> Harmonious music, breathe thy silver airs
> To stir up appetite to Venus' banquet,
> That breath of pleasure that entrances souls …

In the plays of Beaumont and Fletcher we find three references to another purpose of music, music therapy. In *The Mad Lover* (IV, i), Stremon observes,

> He shall not this day perish, if his passions
> May be fed with Musick; are they ready?

And in Beaumont and Fletcher's *The Captain* (III, iv), we read,

> JULIO. What, has she musick?
> WOMAN. Yes, for Heavens sake stay,
>   'Tis all she feeds upon.

---

30 In Marston's *Antonio and Mellida*, Part II (I, ii), Nutriche has a dream in which he hears three fiddlers playing a hornpipe during his seduction of a lady.

In the most famous play by these same authors, *The Knight of the Burning Pestle* (II, i), an old merchant predicts that one who laughs and sings will be protected from a wide variety of illness.

> Let each man keep his heart at ease
> No man dies of that disease,
> He that would his body keep
> From diseases, must not weep,
> But whoever laughs and sings,
> Never his body brings
> Into Fevers, Gouts, or Rhumes,
> Or lingeringly his Lungs consumes:
> Or meets with aches in the bone,
> Or Catarrhs, or griping Stone.

We have a rather unusual instance in Dekker's *The Wonder of a Kingdom* (III, ii), where a nurse rejects the idea of music therapy.

> THE DUKE OF FLORENCE. Call for the Musicke.
> ANGELO. Makea no noise, but bring in de Fidlers, and play sweet—
> NURSE. Oh out upon this Doctor; hang him, does he think to cure dejected Ladies with Fidlers —

An interesting example of music being used for the purpose of social protest can be found in Beaumont and Fletcher's *The Humourous Lieutenant* (II, ii). Contemplating the results of a loss in a battle, the lieutenant fears he will be the object of songs of satire.

> Now shall we have damnable Ballads out against us,
> Most wicked madrigals: and ten to one, Colonel,
> Sung to such lowsie, lamentable tunes.

Among the more functional purposes of music, we find music used to awaken a character, as the use of a cornett to awaken the sleeping Mellida in Marston's *Antonio and Mellida*, Part II (I, ii).

> ANTONIO. Boy, wind thy cornet: force the leaden gates
>   Of lazy sleep fly open with thy breath …
>   [*One winds a cornet within*]
>   Hark, madam, how yon cornet jerketh up
>   His strain'd shrill accents in the capering air,
>   As proud to summon up my bright-cheek'd love!

In Dekker's *Old Fortunatus* (III, i) the stage direction calls for 'Musicke still' and Shaddow prepares to wake Andelocia.

Musicke? O delicate warble: O these Courtiers are most sweete triumphant creatures. Seignior, Sir: Monsieur: sweete Seignior; this is the language of the accomplishment: O delicious strings: these heavenly wire-drawers have stretched my master even out of length: yet at length he must wake: master?

Reference to music used for a coronation is found in Dekker's *Sir Thomas Wyatt* (I, i), when Northumberland says,

> Trumpets and Drums, with your notes resound,
> Her royal name, that must in state be crowned.

Later (II, ii), regarding the coronation procession, we read,

> The streets are full, the town is populous,
> The people gape for noveltie. Trumpets speak to them,
> That they may answer with an echoing crie,
> God save Queene Jane, God save her Majestie.

Finally, we read of a trumpet giving the signal for dinner in Dekker's *The Wonder of a Kingdom* (IV, ii).

On the Incidental Music in the Plays

This practice was still sufficiently common that in a rare play which did not use incidental music,[31] Heywood's *The English Traveller*, the playwright felt compelled to make an explanation in the Prologue.

> A Strange Play you are like to have, for know,
> We use no Drum, nor Trumpet, nor Dumbe show;
> No Combat, Marriage, not so much today,
> As song, Dance, Masque to bumbaste out a Play;
> Yet these all good, and still in frequent use
> With our best Poets; nor is this excuse
> Made by our Author, as if want of skill
> Caused this defect; it's rather his selfe will.

Nevertheless, in the dialog, when the situation involves a banquet, a character is quick to *refer* to music, commenting that there will be the 'best consort in the Citie, for six parts.'

---

31 Thomas Heywood, in his *An Apology for Actors*, tells of an incident in 1600 when invading Spaniards, landing and hearing the trumpets and drums participating in a play given in a coastal town, believed they have been discovered and fled.

The incidental music in the Jacobean plays serves many purposes. Often the music is required when time is needed for the entrance of characters. Thus when Cupid descends from the ceiling, the stage directions call for cornetts to play in Beaumont and Fletcher's *Cupid's Revenge* (Act II) and for recorders in Heywood's *Loves Mistris*.[32] Similarly, stage directions call for music in Middleton's *A Game of Chess*, while the various pieces enter the stage, while in Chapman's *The Widow's Tears* (III, ii),

Musique: Hymen descends; and six Sylvanes enter beneath.

Music is called for frequently to open a scene.[33] One of the more unusual instances is found in Marston's *The Malcontent*, which begins with a stage direction,

The vilest out-of-tune music being heard …

The following dialog includes,

PIETRO. Where breathes that music?
BILIOSO. The discord rather than the music is heard from the malcontent Malevole's chamber.

Similarly, music is called for to end a scene.[34] Some of these stage directions are rather interesting in terms of the instruments used. In Marston's *The Tragedy of Sophonisba*, for example, Act I ends with the stage direction:

The cornets and organs playing loud full music

While one does not ordinarily think of the cornett as 'loud music,' we find this again in Marston's *Antonio and Mellida*, Part II (IV, ii), when Piero Sforza says,

Come, despite of fate,
Sound loudest music, let's pace out in state!
            The cornets sound—Exeunt

This same play ends with a stage direction which reads simply 'A song.' However, just before, Antonio gives us an insight into the kind of song intended by the playwright.

Sound doleful tunes, a solemn hymn advance,
To close the last act of my vengeance.

---

32 *The Dramatic Works of Thomas Heywood*, V, 129.

33 See also Marston's *Antonio and Mellida* (I, i), 'The cornets sound a battle within,' and *The Tragedy of Sophonisba*, which begns, 'Cornets sound a march.'

34 See also Beaumont and Fletcher's *The Prophetess*, with flourishes and Alarms to end scenes in IV, iv and v, and 'Loud Music' which ends Marston's *Antonio and Mellida*, Part II (II, ii).

As with the Elizabethan plays, the stage directions very frequently call for music to introduce important personages to the stage. In both bodies of repertoire one comes to expect a trumpet fanfare to announce the entrance of a king. In one such instance, in Dekker's *Satiromastix* (II, i), the dialog which follows is unusually interesting.

ALL. The King's at hand.
TERRILL. Father the King's at hand.
 Musicke talke louder, that thy silver voice,
 May reach my Soveraignes eares.
SIR VAUGHAN. I pray do so, Musitions bestir your fingers, that you may have us all by the eares.
SIR QUINTILIAN. His grace comes, a Hall varlets, where by my men? blow, blow your colde
 Trumpets till they sweate; tickle them till the sound again.

One presumes, in the case of a king, that trumpets are intended even if the stage direction is not specific, as in Beaumont and Fletcher's *A King, and No King* (I, i), when the king enters,[35] the stage direction reads,

Enter Etc. Senet Flourish.

It is an interesting exception, therefore, in James Shirley's *The Cardinal* (III, ii),[36] when a stage direction says simply 'Hautbois,' after which Antonio says, 'This music speaks the king upon entrance.' In Dekker's *The Welsh Embassador* (V, iii) the brother to the king is introduced by 'Hoboyes.'[37]

Queens are also entitled to trumpets and in Heywood's *If you know not me, you know no body*,[38] after the stage direction reads 'Trumpets afar off,' Sir Thomas Ramsie says,

The Queene hath dined: the trumpets sound already,
And give note of her coming.—Bid the Waits
And Hoboyes to be ready at an instant.

---

35 In Act II, when the king again enters, the stage direction calls for a Flourish only. Similar uses in *The Mad Lover* (I, i); in *The Double Marriage* (III, i), 'Flourish Cornets' for the entrance of Ferrand, Tyrant of Naples; in *Women Pleased* (V, i) a trumpet introduces a Knight.

36 James Shirley (1596–1666), sometimes called 'the last of the Elizabethans,' was educated at the Merchant Taylors' School and at Oxford. Both he and his wife died as a result of the London fire of 1666.

37 See also Thomas Dekker's *The Noble Spanish Soldier* (I, i), 'Enter in Magnificent state, to the sound of lowd musick, the King and Queene'; in *The Wonder of a Kingdom* (III, i); in George Chapman's *Alphonsus Emperor of Germany* (II, ii), 'A train of ladies following with music,' his *The Tragedy of Caesar and Pompey* (III, i), where the stage direction indicates not only that a trumpet announces the entrance of nobles, but also walks before them as they enter, and *The Blind Beggar* (Scene iv) when nobles enter there is an unusual reference to music in the stage direction, simply 'with sound;' and Thomas Heywood's *King Edward the Fourth, Part I*, [*The Dramatic Works of Thomas Heywood*, I, 58] 'The Trumpets sound, and enters King Edward.'
 Somewhat more rare, there is no stage direction, but the equivalent in the dialog. See: 'Sound drums, and trumpets for my Lord,' in Thomas Dekker's *The Wonder of a Kingdom* (IV, i and V, ii); in Cyril Tourneur's, *The Revenger's Tragedy* (III, v), Hippolito says, 'Music's at our ear; they come.'

38 *The Dramatic Works of Thomas Heywood*, I, 316.

In Chapman's *The Blind Beggar* (Scene ii), the queen Aegiale is brought onto the stage 'with a sound of Horns,' in a very rare reference to horns outside the domain of hunting. In Marston's *What You Will* (V, i) the advice is given,

> When you hear one wind a cornet, she is coming down Saint Mark's Street.

A wide variety of other important persons are introduced with music in the Jacobean plays. These include a general in Beaumont and Fletcher's *The Double Marriage* (II, i), 'Flourish. Trumpets, Cornets'; the captain of a ship in Heywood's *Fortune by Land and Sea*[39]; and recorders to introduce Venus in his *Loves Mistris*.[40]

Often the stage directions refer to a specific musical form. The most frequent of these is the Flourish, which we see contrasted with another form, the Senet, in Dekker's *Satiromastix* (III, ii).[41]

> *Trumpets sound a florish, and then a sennate: Enter King*

But there must have been a variety of kinds of Flourish, for at the conclusion of Marston's *The Tragedy of Sophonisba* we read of the cornetts playing 'a short flourish,' whereas his *The Tragedy of Sophonisba* Act III concludes with a stage direction for a 'full' flourish.

> *With a full flourish of cornets, they depart.*

And presumably a Flourish of a different character was required in Webster's *Appius and Virginia*, when, after the final line of dialog, the stage direction calls for a Flourish as a character is taken in a procession to her tomb.

George Chapman's *Revenge for Honor* (V, ii), ends with a very unusual stage direction calling for a Flourish, one intended to be played by recorders.

Another musical form, which is also frequently found in the Elizabethan plays, is the Senet. We see this form in Marston's *Antonio and Mellida*, Part II (V, ii), where a stage direction reads,

> *A song. The song ended the cornets sound a senet.*

In this scene a dance (the 'measure,' a stately dance) takes place, accompanied by the following stage direction which refers to the special alcoves for music, situated above and below the stage.

---

39 Ibid., VI, 413.

40 Ibid., V, 96.

41 See also many cornet flourishes in Marston's *Antonio and Mellida* and in his *The Malcontent* (IV, i), where a flourish by cornetts is associated with the announcement of the arrival of a military guard. In Act V of Jonson's comedy *Cynthia's Revels* in internal masque contains the numerous sounding of 'flourish' and 'charge,' although no specific instruments are mentioned.

While the measure is dancing, Andrugio's *ghost is placed betwixt the music-houses.*

It is generally presumed that the Senet and Flourish were both of a fanfare character, but there is never specific information to reveal the distinction. They are only distinguished in the terms themselves, as in Marston's *Antonio and Mellida* (I, i) where the stage direction calls for 'the cornets to sound a senet' when three ladies enter the stage, but when the duke embraces them 'the cornets sound a flourish.'[42]

Another fanfare-type form which is frequently found in Elizabethan plays is the Tucket. In the Jacobean plays we find only a single instance when the stage direction reads 'Sound a tucket,' as characters process across the stage in Jonson's *The Case is Altered* (I, ix).

Yet another form which is used only once in this literature is the Rouse. In Jonson's comedy *The Silent Woman* (III, vii), Otter announces he has trumpeters and a drum offstage and calls for a 'rouse for bold Britons.'

A musical form which suggests trumpets or cornetts is the March, a form which appears in only one Jacobean play—apart from the 'dead march,' which was for drums. In this one play, Marston's *The Tragedy of Sophonisba*, however, the March is used in a variety of circumstances. Early in the play (I, ii), the stage direction calls for the cornets to play a march as preparations are made for a tournament. Later in this play (III, ii) the cornetts play a march for the entrance of Roman generals. In this same play (V, ii) there is a battle scene with numerous cornett marches, as well as 'a march far off,' a 'flourish' and 'a charge.' After the battle the stage direction calls for 'soft music,' while Massinissa says to this music,

sounds soft as Leda's breast
Slide through all ears.

Still later in this play (V, iv) the cornetts play a march for a triumphal procession.

One finds an occasional Parley in these plays,[43] presumably performed by trumpets. In Beaumont and Fletcher's *The Double Marriage* (V, i) the stage directions call for 'Sound a parley,' and then after the discussion,

Alarum Flourish. Trumpets. Retreat.

There are only a few clues to the actual musical styles of these fanfare-type performances. In Marston's *Antonio and Mellida* (I, i) a duke refers to a Flourish as 'fresh' and 'triumphal' and in Beaumont and Fletcher's *Four Moral Representations* such a performance is called 'cheerful.' Usually, however, for the trumpets the emphasis is on power. In fact, in two plays this power is equated to an earthquake! We find the actual word 'earthquake' used with

---

42 See also many cornett senets in Marston's *Antonio and Mellida* and a senet to open a scene in his *Antonio and Mellida*, Part II (II, i).

43 See also Beaumont and Fletcher's *The Humourous Lieutenant* (III, vi) and Thomas Heywood's *The foure Prentises of London*.

respect to the trumpet in Beaumont and Fletcher's *The False One* (III, ii) and again in Jonson's comedy, *The Silent Woman* (IV, ii) where the stage directions call for 'trumpets sounding' to wake Morose. A few lines later Morose refers to their sound as follows:

> They have rent my roof, walls, and all my windows asunder with their brazen throats.

We also find two interesting descriptions of the trumpeter himself. In Dekker's *Old Fortunatus* (I, ii), a character named Shaddow suggests that trumpeters had a way of being among the survivors.

> Nay by my troth, master, none flourish in these withering times, but Ancient bearers and trumpeters.

Another interesting description of a trumpeter is found in Dekker's *Westward Ho*, (I, ii), where we find what appears to be a description of a court trumpeter, as seen by one somewhat jealous of his lifestyle, 'he wears good clothes, and is ranked in good company, but he does nothing.'

> He came lately from the university, and loves City dames only for their victuals, he hath an excellent trick to keep Lobsters and Crabs sweet in summer ... for which I do suspect he hath been Clarke to some Noblemans kitchen. I have heard he never loves any Wench.

Horns are usually mentioned in the context of hunting, as in Beaumont and Fletcher's *The Sea-Voyage* (II, i) where, after the stage direction 'Horns within,'[44] a character refers to the music as 'free hunters Musick.' One may presume that the hunting horns played recognizable signals, which no doubt explains an occasional reference to cornetts playing *like* horns. In Beaumont and Fletcher's *The Two Noble Kinsmen* (III, i) after 'Wind horns' several times, one finds 'Wind horns of Cornets' and in Marston's *The Malcontent* (III, ii), in a scene set in a forest, a stage direction reads,

> *Cornets like horns within.*

The same was undoubtedly true of trumpet signals, for in Beaumont and Fletcher's *The Prophetess* (IV, iv), the stage direction calls for 'A Trumpet,' Aurelia recognizes it as 'A *Roman* Trumpet.'

Trombones rarely appear in the Jacobean plays by name, although there are additional occasions in which 'solemn music,' a common synonym for trombones, is used. The trombone consort was a standard component in official civic music of the sixteenth century and

---

[44] Similar instances of 'wind horns' in Beaumont and Fletcher's *Thierry and Theodoret* (II, i) and *The Two Noble Kinsmen* (III, v) and in Thomas Dekker's *Patient Grissil* (I, i) and *The Shoemakers' Holiday* (II, ii); and Thomas Heywood's *A Maden-head well lost*.

we see them in this role in Middleton's *Mayor of Queenborough* (III, iii), in a dialog between a Barber and Simon, the mayor.

> BARBER. Joy bless you, sir!
>   We'll drink your health with trumpets.
> SIMON. I with sackbuts,
>   That's the more solemn drinking for my state.

Another reference, in Beaumont and Fletcher's *The Mad Lover* (III, i), indicates drums and trombones playing together.

> *A Dead March within of Drum and Sagbutts*

After this performance, Calis asks,

> What mournfull noise is this comes creeping forward?

In both Elizabethan and Jacobean plays the oboes appear in indoor scenes, often in association with banquets as we see in Beaumont and Fletcher's *The Bloody Brother* (II, iii), where the stage direction reads,

> *Hoboys, a banquet.*

One might assume that the oboe players doubled on the flutes. In Beaumont and Fletcher's *The Maids Tragedy* (I, i), for example, we notice the stage directions call for off-stage oboes, which are soon followed by the indication of recorders.

In Dekker's *The Whore of Babylon* (Act II) there is a 'dumb show,' for which the stage direction reads 'The Hault-boyes sound.' The noble listeners are unamused.

> EMPRESS OF BABYLON. Who sets those tunes to mock us? Stay them …
> FIRST CARDINAL. No more: your musick must be dumb.

There are numerous references to incidental music in these plays for which we read only 'still music.' Sometimes this seems a matter of style, as in Marston's *The Fawn* (IV, i) where the stage direction 'soft music playing' is characterized in the following dialog as 'music of sweetly agreeing perfection.' On other occasions it seems primarily a matter of dynamics, as in Marston's *Antonio and Mellida*, Part II, (I, ii).

> PANDULFO. Entreat the music strain their instruments
>   With a slight touch …
>   [*Music sounds softly*]

One case which speaks of softer dynamics is quite curious, especially as it involves a rare mention of string instruments by name.[45] In Marston's *The Tragedy of Sophonisba* (IV, i) a witch appears while a stage direction specifies,

Infernal music plays softly whilst Ericho enters ...

Soon this music is heard again and now the stage direction identifies the instruments as 'a treble viol, a bass lute, etc. play softly.' Upon hearing this 'infernal' music, Syphax observes,

Hark! Hark! now softer melody strikes mute
Disquiet Nature. O thou power of sound,
How thou dost melt me! Hark! now even heaven
Gives up his soul amongst us.

Flutes are found in association with funerals.[46] In Marston's *Antonio and Mellida* (V, i) a stage direction reads,

The still flutes sound a mournful senet.
Enter a funeral procession.

An interesting example, musically, is found at the conclusion of Marston's *The Tragedy of Sophonisba*, when Sophonisba's body is carried in with 'mournful solemnity.' For this procession the stage directions call for,

Organ and recorders play to a single voice.

The appearance of drums on both the Elizabethan and Jacobean stage was fairly common.[47] Rather unusual, however, is a stage direction in Beaumont and Fletcher's *The Loyal Subject* (I, iii) which calls for 'Drums in cases.'

The one form which seems to have been associated with the drums was the 'dead march.'[48] A typical example is found at the beginning of Act V of Beaumont and Fletcher's *Bonduca*,

A soft dead march within.

---

45 In Beaumont and Fletcher's *The Chances* (II, ii), another string instrument is mentioned, 'Lute sounds within.'

46 In Marston's *Antonio and Mellida*, Part II (IV, i), before a discussion of death, 'The still flutes sound softly.'

47 Also see: Beaumont and Fletcher's *The Mad Lover* (I, i), [Drums within], and *The Pilgrim* (III, iv); Thomas Dekker: the beginning of *The Whore of Babylon* (V, iii); the end of *The Shoemakers' Holiday* (I, i); *Lust's Dominion* (IV, i and iii); *If This be not a Good Play* (IV, iii); in George Chapman's *The Blind Beggar* (Scene vii); Thomas Heywood's *The Rape of Lucrece*; *The Golden Age*; *The Iron Age*, Part II; *The foure Prentises of London*; *If you know not me, you know no body*; and a rare speaking part for a drummer in Beaumont and Fletcher's *The Two Noble Kinsmen* (III, v). The ancient pipe and tabor is mentioned in Thomas Dekker's *The Shoemakers' Holiday* (III, iii).

48 See also Thomas Dekker's *Sir Thomas Wyatt* (I, ii); in Cyril Tourneur's, *The Atheist's Tragedy* (III, i), for the funeral of Charlemont; Thomas Heywood's *The foure Prentises of London* [*The Dramatic Works of Thomas Heywood*, II, 178] and *If you know not me, you know no body* [Ibid., I, 238].

Sometimes the stage directions call for soft drums, as in Beaumont and Fletcher's *Bonduca* (II, i), 'Drum softly within,' and perhaps in another work by these authors, *The Maid in the Mill* (II, v),

Drums afar off. A low March.

An interesting example of soft drum playing is found in Heywood's *The foure Prentises of London*,[49] where after a stage direction reads simply 'soft march,' Godfrey commands,

But soft, that Drumme should speak the Pagans tongue.

The character of drum players is sometimes questioned in early literature. An example is found in Beaumont and Fletcher's *The Burning Pestle* (V, i) a cannon is not in working order and the reason given for the missing flint is 'The Drummer took it out to light Tobacco.'

Bagpipes appear only in Beaumont and Fletcher's *The Prophetess* (V, iii), for dancing.

There is also a single reference to a singing choir. In Beaumont and Fletcher's *Monsieur Thomas* (V, iii), after the Abbess says 'to the Quire then,' the stage directions read 'Musick singing.'

There are also instances of stage directions which call for music but do not identify the actual instruments the playwright had in mind. A typical example is Marston's *Antonio and Mellida*, Part II (I, ii), where we find,

Music sounds a short strain

Often we encounter the familiar 'Loud music' or 'Soft music' without further identification. In one case, in Heywood's *Loves Mistris*,[50] they seem to play at the same time. Pfiche calls 'Let me hear some musicke—Loud—And Still,' which is indeed followed by a stage direction reading,

Loude Musicke, and still Musicke.

A more philosophic example, in this regard, if found in Middleton's *The Spanish Gipsy* (III, ii). Following an off-stage flourish, Soto enters in disguise and carrying a cornett. Francisco says, 'but, fellow, bring your music along with you too?' Soto responds,

Yes, my lord, both loud music and still music; the loud is that which you have heard, and the still is that which no man can hear.

We also find some interesting examples of unidentified music which represents various aspects of the spirit world. In Beaumont and Fletcher's *The Pilgrim* (V, iv), 'Musick and Birds'

---

49 *The Dramatic Works of Thomas Heywood*, II, 223.

50 Ibid., V, 108.

in the stage direction refers to music of Fairies and in Thomas Dekker's *The Virgin Martyr* (V, i) one of two references to music of the spirit world reads, 'tis in the Ayre, or from some better place, a power divine.'

In Heywood's *The Witches of Lancashire*[51] there is a curious and interesting scene in which the musicians who are to play for dances are apparently put under a spell and are unable to perform their duty. First, no sooner do they begin then mysteriously each player begins to play a separate, and different, tune! The stage direction reads,

Musicke. Every one a severall tune.

After the guests register their dismay, the musicians are revealed in person in the 'music room' above the stage. This is expressed in the program direction,

Musitians shew themselves above.

The musicians now complain that though they play their string instruments, no sound comes out. The guests begin to suspect witchcraft, leading one person to observe,

I have heard my Aunt say twenty times, that no Witchcraft can take hold of a *Lancashire* Bagpipe, for it selfe is able to charme the Devil.

In Dekker's *If This be not a Good Play* (I, i) begins with the stage direction,

Enter (at the sound of hellish musick), Pluto and Charon

In Beaumont and Fletcher's *The Double Marriage* (II, i), strange music is heard from the sea.

[Strange Musick within, Hoboys.]
Ascanio. Hark what noise is this?
   What horrid noise is the Sea pleased to sing.
   A hideous Dirge to our deliverance?
Virolet. Stand fast now.
[Within strange cries, horrid noise, Trumpets.]

In another play by these authors, *The Sea-Voyage* (V, i), a phantom ship is seen, after which we find the stage direction,

[Horid Musick]
Raymond. What dreadful sounds are these?
Aminta. Infernal Musick,
   Fit for a bloody Feast.
Albert. It seems prepared

---

51 Ibid., IV, 215ff.

To kill our courages e'er they divorce
Our souls and bodies.

ART MUSIC

The stage plays of this period are filled with songs, usually with the lyrics provided.[52] In the plays of Marston there are frequently stage directions which simply indicate 'A song within,' without any clues to the character of the song. One case in which we would have liked a clue to the nature of the music is found in *The Malcontent* (II, iii) where Mendoza stands outside the room from which the music is heard, waiting to murder Ferneze. What kind of music is heard while a character waits to kill?

To continue with this morbid line of thought, in Beaumont and Fletcher's *The Bloody Brother* (III, ii) a song is sung by a group of men about to be hung.

Come, Boys, sing cheerfully, we shall ne'r sing younger.
We have chosen a loud tune too, because it should like well.

And in Webster's *The Dutchesse of Malfy* (IV, ii), a stage direction reads,

Here (by a Mad-man) this song is sung, to a dismall kind of Musique.

Finally, a stage direction calls for 'Soft sad music' in Ford's *The Broken Heart* (IV, iii). The lyrics for a despondent off-stage song are given, following which Orgilus observes,

A horrid stillness
Succeeds this deathful air.

As was the case with the Elizabethan theater, the subjects of the Greek myths and the ancient lyric poets are often repeated in these plays. Beaumont and Fletcher's *The Faithful Shepherdess* (I, i), a pastoral play after the models of the ancient lyric poets, includes a song in praise of Pan.

Sing his praises that doth keep
Our flocks from harm,
Pan the Father of our Sheep,
And arm in arm

---

52 See also Dekker's *The Shoemakers' Holiday* (I, iv) and Heywood's *The Rape of Lucrece*, for songs sung in Dutch; Dekker's *Old Fortunatus* (I, i), for a song with chorus; Dekker's *Patient Grissil* (V, ii), for a wedding song; Dekker's *The Noble Spanish Soldier* (I, ii) a song in dialog between 'Question' and 'Answer'; and Middleton's *The Spanish Gipsy*, for several songs with chorus; *More Dissemblers Besides Women* (IV, i), for a Gypsy song; and *The Witch* (V, ii), for a witch's song.

> *Tread we softly in a round,*
> *Whilest the hollow neighbouring ground*
> *Fills the Musick with her sound.*

In Heywood's *Loves Mistris*[53] there is a scene which recreates the ancient Greek myth of the musical contest between Apollo and Pan. Although in ancient literature this was an instrumental contest, here it is played out in singing, the lyrics of which are given by Heywood. At the end of this contest, Apollo passes a condemnation on Pan,

> Henceforth be all your rural musicke such,
> Made out of Tinkers, Pans, and Kettle-drummes;
> And never henceforth may your fields be graced
> With the sweet musick of Apollo's lyre.

We find a song based on the Old Testament in a text Dekker wrote for a pageant given for the inauguration of the Mayor of London in 1629. Included is a song about the invention of music by 'Tuballcayne.'[54]

> *Brave Iron! Brave Hammer! from your sound,*
> *The Art of Musicke has her Ground,*
> *On the Anvil, Thou keep'st Time.*

Some songs are accompanied by the singer, as in Marston's *The Dutch Courtezan* (I, ii), when Franceschina sings an art song while accompanying herself on the lute.

There are also a number of genuine ensemble songs, an example of which is found in Jonson's comedy, *Poetaster*, at the end of Act IV, scene v. The reader will also note Crispinus's reference to vocal improvisation.

> HERMOGENES. *Then, in a free and lofty strain,*
>   *Our broken tunes we thus repair;*
> CRISPINUS. *And we answer them again,*
>   *Running division on the panting air:*
> ALBIUS. *To celebrate this feast of sense,*
>   *As free from scandal as offense.*
> HERMOGENES. *Here is beauty, for the eye;*
> CRISPINUS. *For the ear, sweet melody;*
> HERMOGENES. *Ambrosiac odors, for the smell;*
> CRISPINUS. *Delicious nectar, for the taste;*
> ALBIUS. *For the touch, a lady's waist;*
>   *Which doth all the rest excel!*

---

53 *The Dramatic Works of Thomas Heywood*, V, 123ff. Marston's *Antonio and Mellida* (V, i) has a singing contest, with the duke servng as the judge.

54 Genesis 4:22.

The most frequent songs, in this literature which tends toward comedy, are love songs. In Marston's *The Dutch Courtezan* (V, ii), Freevil sings a song of contemplation of love. One notices his reference to a frequent complaint among early philosophers that Reason cannot explain love.

O Love, how strangely sweet
Are thy weak passions!
That love and joy should meet
In self-same fashions!
O who can tell
The cause why this should move?
But only this,—
No reason ask of Love!

In Shirley's *The Cardinal* (V, iii) off-stage music and a love song play an unusually prominent role in establishing the background of the action to come. The characters are Placentia, a servant to a duchess, and the colonel, Hernando.

> HERNANDO. What do they talk of, prithee?
> PLACENTIA. His grace is very pleasant
> *A lute is heard.*
>   And kind to her; but her replies are after
>   The sad condition of her sense, sometimes
>   Unjointed.
> HERNANDO. They have music.
> PLACENTIA. A lute only.
>   His grace prepared; they say, the best of Italy,
>   That waits upon my lord.
> HERNANDO. He thinks the duchess
>   Is stung with a tarantula.
> PLACENTIA. Your pardon;
>   My duty is expected.
> *Exit.*
> HERNANDO. Gentle lady!—
>   A voice too!
> *Song within.*

After an off-stage song, for which the lyrics are given, Hernando continues,

> If at this distance I distinguish, 'tis not
> Church music; and the air's wanton, and no anthem
> Sung to 't, but some strange ode of love and kisses.
> What should this mean?

A few songs provide some information on the aesthetics of song writing. First, in Jonson's comedy, *Cynthia's Revels* (IV, iii), Hedon sings a song of love,

> *Oh, that joy so soon should waste!*
> *Or so sweet a bliss*
> *As a kiss*
> *Might not for ever last! …*
> *Oh, rather than I would it smother,*
> *Were I to taste such another,*
> *It should be my wishing*
> *That I might die, kissing.*

Hedon says he made both the verses and the music and asks Amorphus how he likes it. Amorphus answers,

> A pretty air! In general, I like it well: but in particular your long note on 'die' did arride me most, but it was somewhat too long.

Amorphus offers to sing a better song, one written in honor of the lady Annabel, sister to the King of Aragon, who was thinking of him when she lay dying. According to Amorphus, as a gracious gift she left him her glove, 'which golden legacy the Emperor himself took care to send after me, in six coaches, covered all in black velvet, attended by the state of his empire.' In appreciation, Amorphus relates, he took up his lyra and sang this song.

> *Thou more than most sweet glove*
> *Unto my more sweet love,*
> *Suffer me to store with kisses*
> *This empty lodging …*

When he had finished singing,

> AMORPHUS. How like you it, sir?
> HEDON. Very well in troth.
> AMORPHUS. But very well? Oh, you are a mere mammothrept in judgment, then. Why, do you not observe how excellently the [verse] is affected in every place? That I do not marry a word of short quantity to a long note? Nor an ascending syllable to a descending tone? Besides, upon the word 'best' there, you see how I do enter with an odd minim, and drive it thorough the breve, which no intelligent musician, I know, but will affirm to be very rare, extraordinary, and pleasing.

Another reference to a song which perhaps carries information on aesthetics is found in Beaumont and Fletcher's *The Elder Brother* (IV, iv).[55] Here a song is offered for entertainment, with the promise it will not be an 'Anthem, nor one with borrowed Rhymes out of the School of Vertue.' After a stage direction which reads only 'A song,' the listener refers to its style.

This was never penned at Geneva, the Note's too sprightly.

Finally, in the comedy, *Poetaster*, there is a scene (II, ii) where Jonson recalls a comment frequently repeated in ancient literature, to the effect that singers never want to sing when asked, but once begun, never want to stop. Here, Hermogenes is several times begged to sing, but invariably answers only 'Cannot sing.' Eventually he sings and pleads to sing another song, but the company is not interested. Julia observes,

> It is the common disease of all your musicians that they know no mean, to be entreated, either to begin or end.

Later (IV, v), Hermogenes scores a nice point of his own. After making an uninvited observation, he is rebuked somewhat for speaking out of place, and answers, 'Oh, 'tis our fashion to be silent when there is a better fool in place.'

On Serenades

One continues to find interesting accounts of the serenades which were mentioned so frequently in Renaissance literature.[56] In Marston's *What You Will* (I, i) Jacomo brings his servant, Philus, to sing a serenade for him at the window of his beloved. As he hands the poem he has written to Philus to sing, Jacomo apologizes for its general lack of style, wit and for the corrections here and there.

> JACOMO. Boy, could not Orpheus make the stones to dance?
> PHILUS. Yes, sir.
> JACOMO. By our Lady, a sweet touch. Did he not bring Eurydice out of hell with his lute?
> PHILUS. So they say, sir.
> JACOMO. And thou canst bring Celia's head out of the window with thy lute. Well, hazard thy breath. Look sir, here's a ditty.
> 'Tis foully writ, slight wit, crossed here and there,
> But where thou find'st a blot, there falls a tear.

---

55 See also in Beaumont and Fletcher: *The Spanish Curate* (II, iv), sung with lute; *The Tragedy of Valentinian*, 'Musick and Song' (V, ii), and a solo song, with chorus (V, viii); *The Chances*; *The Bloody Brother*, including a drinking song; *The Lovers Progress* (III, i), a song sung by a ghost; *The Knight of Malta* (III, i), a strophic song with four verses, sung by soldiers.

56 Additional serenades can be found in Jonson's comedy *The Devil is an Ass* (II, vi); Marston's *The Dutch Courtezan* (II, i) for a serenade with '*Pages with torches and Gentlemen with music*' and Beaumont and Fletcher's *The Little French Lawyer* (I, i), for a passing reference to a serenade as 'morning musique.'

Philus sings, although Marston does not give the actual song. Jacomo complains that it is not effective because it was not sung with enough passion.

> Fie! peace, peace, peace! it hath no passion in it.
> O melt thy breath in fluent softer tunes,
> That every note may seem to trickle down
> Like sad distilling tears, and make—O God!
> That I were but a poet, now to express my thoughts,
> Or a musician but to sing my thoughts,
> Or anything but what I am.—Sing it over once more,
> My grief's a boundless sea that hath no shore.

There are two interesting descriptions of serenades in Beaumont and Fletcher. First, in *The Spanish Curate* (II, i), Leandro explains he would rather court his love by dancing and fiddling indoors, than stand in the cold and serenade her.

> Or fiddle out whole frosty nights (my friends)
> Under the window, while my teeth keep tune,
> I hold no handsomeness. Let me get in,
> There trot and fiddle where I may have fair play.

In *Wit at Several Weapons* (III, i) a page and a string player are hired to sing a serenade.

> SIR GREGORY. What, are they come?
> PAGE. And placed directly, Sir,
>   Under the window.
> SIR GREGORY. What may I call you, Gentleman?
> BOY. A poor servant to the Viol, I'm the Voice, Sir.
> SIR GREGORY. In good time Master Voice?
> BOY. Indeed good time does get the mastery.

The serenade itself begins,

> *Fain would I wake you, Sweet, but fear*
> *I should invite you to worse cheer;*
> *In your dreams you cannot fare*
> *Meaner than Musick.*

When the lady responds, the text suggests the musician was being paid by the hour.

> SIR GREGORY. I hear her up, here Master Voice,
>   Pay you the Instruments, save what you can.

On Instrumental Performances

One finds a few examples of genuine instrumental performances which are descriptions of art music in this literature. In Dekker's *Satiromastix* (V, ii), after the stage direction calls for 'Soft Musicke,' the king reflects,

> Sound Musicke, thou sweet suiter to the air,
> Now woo the air again, this is the hour,
> Writ in the Calender of time, this hour,
> Musicke shall spend.

In Middleton's *A Mad World, my Masters* (II, i), we find a description of instrumental music of a 'concert' nature, including a rare account in the play repertoire of a secular organ performance.

> SIR BOUNTEOUS. My music! give my lord a taste of his welcome.
> *[A strain played by the consort; Sir Bounteous makes a courtly honor to Follywit, and seems to foot the tune.]*
> So—How like you our airs, my lord? are they choice?
> FOLLYWIT. They're seldom matched, believe it …
> SIR BOUNTEOUS. The musicians are in ordinary, yet no ordinary musicians. Your lordship shall hear my organs now.
> FOLLYWIT. I beseech you, sir Bounteous!
> SIR BOUNTEOUS. My organist!
> *[The organs play]*
> Come, my lord, how does your honor relish my organs?
> FOLLYWIT. A very proud air, i'faith, sir.
> SIR BOUNTEOUS. O, how can't choose? A Walloon plays upon 'em, and a Welchman blows wind in their breech.
> *[A song by the organs]*

In Beaumont and Fletcher's *The Captain* (II, ii) we find another reference to a private performance.

> FABRICIO. When is this musique?
> FREDERICK. From my Sisters chamber.
> FABRICIO. The touch is excellent, let's be attentive.
> JACOMO. Hark, are the Waits abroad?
> FABRICIO. Be softer prethee,
>   'Tis private musick.

In Marston's *The Dutch Courtezan* (III, iii) there is a possible reference to an instrumental concert, when Mulligrub says,

> Come, let's go hear some music … Let's go hear some doleful music.

In these volumes we have pointed to the presence of a contemplative listener as a hallmark of art music. In Marston's *Antonio and Mellida*, Part II (II, ii), a character, Piero, actually stands and listens to off-stage music

> *A song within.—Exit Piero at the end of the song.*

In Heywood's *The Rape of Lucrece*[57] a tragic song moves one listener to tears.

> *Lucretius.* To these lamenting dames what canst thou sing?
>   Whose griefe through all the Romane Temples ring.

Valerius then sings a song which begins,

> *Lament Ladies lament*
> *Lament the Roman land …*
> HORATIUS. This musicke mads me, I all mirth despise.
> LUCRETIUS. To heare him sing drawes rivers from mine eyes.

Thomas Middleton's *More Dissemblers Besides Women* begins with an off-stage song, of which Lactantio reflects,

> Welcome, soul's music! I've been listening here
> To melancholy strains from the duchess' lodgings.

Act I, of this play, ends with another song, of which the listener, Dondolo, observes, 'O rich, ravishing, rare, and enticing!' Quite different are some lines in Middleton's *Blurt, Master-Constable* (II, ii), where Imperia, a courtesan, requests happy music.

> Sing, sing, sing; some old and fantastical thing, for I cannot abide these dull and lumpish tunes; the musician stands longer a-pricking them than I would do to hear them. No, no, no, give me your light ones, that go nimbly and quick, and are full of changes, and carry sweet divisions.

We are particularly drawn to a song which concludes Jonson's comedy, *Cynthia's Revels*, and appears to refer to an Aristotelian catharsis.

> *Now each one dry his weeping eyes,*
> *And to the well of knowledge haste;*
> *Where purged of your maladies,*
> *You may of sweeter waters taste.*

---

57 *The Dramatic Works of Thomas Heywood*, V, 181.

EDUCATIONAL MUSIC

In Dekker's *The Roaring Girl* (IV, i), we find a reflection of the small value placed on music education by the upper class at this time. Here we have Moll, disguised in the dress of a man.

>ALEXANDER. Now sir I understand you professe musique.
>MOLL. I am a poore servant to that liberal science sir.
>ALEXANDER. Where is it you teach?
>MOLL. Right against Cliffords Inne.
>ALEXANDER. Hum that's a fit place for it: you have many schollers.
>MOLL. And some of worth, whom I may call my masters.
>ALEXANDER. Aye true, a company of whoremasters; you teach to sing too?
>MOLL. Marry do I sir.
>ALEXANDER. I think you'll find an apt scholler of my son, especially for pricke-song.
>MOLL. I have much hope of him.
>ALEXANDER. I am sorry for it, I have the less for that.

In Middleton's *More Dissemblers Besides Women* there is a character, Crotchet, who is a singing teacher. Act V begins with an extended attempt by Crotchet to give a singing lesson to a Page, who is one of the principal female characters in disguise. The Page is an unwilling student who begins by observing that she has 'a great longing to bite a piece of the musician's nose off.' As the lesson begins,

>CROTCHET. Rehearse your gamut, boy.
>PAGE. Who'd be thus toiled for love, and want the joy?
>CROTCHET. Why, when! begin, sir: I must stay your leisure?
>PAGE. Gamut *[sings] a, re, b, me*, etc.
>CROTCHET. *[sings] Ee la*: aloft! above the clouds, my boy!
>PAGE. It must be a better note than *ela*, sir,
>   That brings musicians thither; they're too hasty,
>   The most part of 'em, to take such a journey,
>   And must needs fall by the way.
>CROTCHET. How many clefs are there?
>PAGE. One clef, sir.
>CROTCHET. O intolerable heretic
>   To voice and music! do you know but one clef?
>PAGE. No more, indeed, I, sir;—and at this time I know too much of that.
>CROTCHET. How many notes be there?
>PAGE. Eight, sir.—I fear me I shall find nine shortly,
>   To my great shame and sorrow. O my stomach!
>CROTCHET. Will you repeat your notes then? I must *sol fa* you;
>   Why, when, sir?
>PAGE. A large, a long, a breve, a semibreve,
>   A minim, a crotchet, a quaver, a semiquaver …

Now Crotchet and the Page sing a 'prick-song,' after which Crotchet asks the waiting-lady,

> How like you this, modonna?
> CELIA. Pretty;
> He will do well in time, being kept under.
> CROTCHET. I'll make his ears sore and his knuckles ache else.
> CELIA. And that's the way to bring a boy to goodness, sir.

We find another brief, actual lute lesson—all as a double-entendre of another activity—in Cyril Tourneur's, *The Atheist's Tragedy* (IV, i).

> CATAPLASMA. Lirie, your lute and book.
> SEBASTIAN. Well said. A lesson o'the'lute to entertain the time with till she comes.
> CATAPLASMA. Sol, fa, mi, la ... mi, mi, mi ... Precious! Dost not see 'mi' between the two crotchets? Strike me full there ... So ... forward ... This is a sweet strain and thou finger'st it beastly. 'Mi' is a large there and the prick that stands before 'mi' a long; always halve your note ... ♩ Now ... Run your division pleasingly with those quavers. Observe all your graces i'the touch ... Here's a sweet close ... strike it full—it setts off your music delicately.

FUNCTIONAL MUSIC

In the Jacobean plays one finds a number of references to incidental music used in cult religious services.[58] In Jonson's tragedy *Sejanus* (V, lines 170ff), written in the style of ancient Roman plays, includes a simulated ancient religious sacrifice, in which the stage direction calls for the ancient *Tubicines* (trumpets) and *Tibicines* (aulai) to sound as the priest prepares for the ceremony.

There are two cult ceremonies with music mentioned in the plays of Beaumont and Fletcher. First, in *The Knight of Malta* (II, v) the stage directions call for a Flourish, to announce the beginning of a cult religious rite.

> And so let's march to the Temple, sound those Instruments,
> That were the signal to a day of blood;
> Evil beginning hours may end in good.

Later in this same play (V, ii) the stage direction describes music for another service.

> *Musick.*
> *An Alter discovered, with Tapers, and a Book on it.*
> *The two Bishops stand on each side of it; Mountferrat,*
> *as the Song is singing, ascends up the Altar.*

---

58 See also Beaumont and Fletcher's *Bonduca* (III, i), for music for a Druid sacrifice, and Dekker's *The Virgin Martyr* (III, ii), for music for a pagan service in worship of an 'Image of great Jupiter,' and *The Sun's-Darling* begins with a song at the altar to the worship of the Sun.

In *The Two Noble Kinsmen* (V, i) a rather detailed religious service begins with Thesius,

> Now let 'em enter, and before the gods
> Tender their holy Prayers.

This is immediately followed by a 'Flourish of Cornets.' Later 'Musick' is heard while doves are released. After the ritual of bowing to the goddess, the stage direction calls for 'Still Musick of Recorders.' At the end of the service, a mechanical tree appears, bearing a single rose. The stage direction now reads,

> *Here is heard a sodain twang of Instruments,*
> *and the Rose falls from the Tree.*

A reference to music in a traditional religious service can be seen in Jonson's comedy *The Alchemist* (III, ii), where Subtle is criticizing a pastor from Amsterdam, Tribulation Wholesome, and makes this reference to church music.[59]

> SUBTLE. And get a tune, to call the flock together:
>   For (to say sooth) a tune does much with women,
>   And other phlegmatic people; it is your bell.
> ANANIAS. Bells are profane: a tune may be religious.

In Webster's *The Dutchesse of Malfy* (III, iv), there is a ceremony for the installation of Cardinals, for which the stage direction reads,

> *During all which Ceremony, this Verse is sung*
> *(to very sollemne Musique) by divers Church-men.*

And in Beaumont and Fletcher's *The Pilgrim* (V, vi) an extended service at an altar with stage directions also calling for 'Solemn Musick' throughout. There is also an interesting reference to a funeral service at the conclusion of Beaumont and Fletcher's *Cupid's Revenge* (V, i), where Age commands,

> Go, and let the Trumpets sound
> Some mournful thing, whilst we convey the body
> Of this unhappy Prince unto the Court.

---

59 See also Beaumont and Fletcher's *The Pilgrim* (V, vi), for an extended service at an altar with stage directions calling for 'Solemn Musick' throughout, and a service accompanied by recorders in John Ford's, *The Broken Heart* (V, iii).

Most references to wedding music in the Jacobean plays deal with dancing and it is usually the lowly fiddler who plays.[60] In Dekker's *Satiromastix* (I, i) we find a humorous lack of appreciation for this musician.

> … and last of all in cursing the poore nodding fidlers, for keeping Mistress Bride so long up from sweeter Revels.

There are also occasional references to actual wedding songs.[61] In Marston's *The Tragedy of Sophonisba* (I, ii) the stage direction calls for four boys, dressed as cupid and dancing 'a fantastic measure' to the music of cornetts. Soon a larger ensemble sings a wedding song.

> *Chorus, with cornets, organ and voices. Io to Hymen!*

There are many references of incidental music for dancing in this literature and often specific dances are mentioned. In Middleton's *Women Beware Women* (III, ii) we find a humorous review of the dances associated with various levels of society.

> Plain men dance the measures, the sinquapace [galliard] the gay;
> Cuckolds dance the hornpipe, and farmers dance the hay;
> Your soldiers dance the round, and maidens that grow big;
> Your drunkards, the canaries; your whore and bawd, the jig.
> Here's your eight kind of dancers; he that finds
> The ninth let him pay the minstrels.

In another Middleton play, *Mayor of Queenborough* (II, ii), the stage directions call for the cornetts to 'sound a lavolta,' for dancing. In Marston's *The Malcontent* (IV, i) a call goes out for music for dancing the branle, but the characters indicate they have forgotten the steps. Guerrino reviews the dance as follows,

> Why, it is but two singles on the left, two on the right, three doubles forward, a traverse of six round: do this twice, three singles side, galliard trick-of-twenty, coranto-pace; a figure of eight, three singles broken down, come up, meet, two doubles, fall back, and then honor.

As for the music, Aurelia calls out,

> Music, sound high, as in our heart! sound high!

Finally, in Dekker's *Old Fortunatus* (III, i), on observing the music is playing but no one is dancing, Athelstane says 'Here's Musicke spent in vaine, Lords, fall to dancing.'

---

60 See Beaumont and Fletcher's *The Maid in the Mill* (V, ii) for a reference to hiring 'Fidlers' for dance music for a wedding. In Marston's *The Dutch Courtezan* (II, iii) there is a reference to dance music being performed by an ensemble of six flutes.

61 For the lyrics for a wedding song, see John Ford's *The Broken Heart* (III, v).

We have seen the frequent use of incidental music to introduce noble personages to the stage. Such circumstances are also found in the dialog, as in Beaumont and Fletcher's *The Martial Maid* (I, iii), when the virtuous lady, Eugenia, calls for music to welcome Alvarez.

> Let [us have] choice Musick
> In the best voice that ever touched human ear,
> For joy hath tied my tongue up, speak your welcome.

In another Beaumont and Fletcher play, *Wit at Several Weapons* (V, i), Lady Ruinous calls,

> Let's have Musick, let that sweet breath at least
> Give us her airy welcome.

Finally, we have a reference to an inadequate musical welcome in Beaumont and Fletcher's *The Coxcomb* (I, i), when Uberto observes,

> We must have Musick too, or else you give us,
> But half a welcome.

Military music is frequently mentioned in both the Elizabethan and Jacobean play repertoire. In Beaumont and Fletcher's *The Two Noble Kinsmen* (V, iii) there is a lengthy battle scene in which there are repeated stage directions for cornetts, although in one instance 'Trumpets sound as to a Charge.' The grim reality for which military music functions is recognized in Beaumont and Fletcher's *The Martial Maid* (V, iii) when, after the stage direction calls for 'Drums within,' Sayavedra observes,

> Hark their Drums speak their insatiate thirst
> Of blood, and stop their ears against pious peace.

Thus, sometimes we find military music is not appreciated. In Beaumont and Fletcher's *The Humourous Lieutenant* (I, ii), a stage direction reads 'Drums a March,' but Celia is not impressed.

> Pox on these bawling Drums.

Later (II, iv) the lieutenant also exhibits no love of the military drums.

> I hate all noises too,
> Especially the noise of Drums.

Usually, however, military music was romantically praised, as in Chapman's *Revenge for Honor* (I, i), when Osman says of the soldier and his music.

> Want of exercise
> Renders all men of actions dull as doormice;
> Your soldier only can dance to the drum,
> And sing a hymn of joy to the sweet trumpet:
> There's no music like it.

In Heywood's *King Edward the fourth, Part I*,[62] lord Howard says,

> And that the drumme and trumpet both beganne
> To sound warres cheerfull harmony.

ENTERTAINMENT MUSIC

We get a small hint of the long, dull hours of the upper class for which constant entertainment was needed in Chapman's *All Fools* (V, ii). Here, young courtiers are sitting around and in the mood for entertainment. Valerio suggests,

> Come on, lets varie our sweet time
> With sundry exercises. Boy. Tobacco.
> And Drawer, you must get us musique too,
> Call us in a cleanly noyse.

The most artistic form of entertainment which used music in Jacobean England was the masque. For the early seventeenth century period we have extant rather lengthy accounts of the masques written by Ben Jonson.[63] In his masques the wind band functions prominently, usually identified by the contemporary synonym 'loud music.' This music often is used for the purpose of allowing time for stage movement, as we can see in a stage direction in 'The Masque of Queens,'

> At which the loud music sounded as before,
> to give the masquers time of descending.

Later there is a dance in which 'the first was to the cornets, the second to the violins.' At the end of this masque, Jonson credits the music to 'my excellent friend Alfonso Ferrabosco.'

In Jonson's 'Pleasure Reconciled to Virtue,' there is evidence of a wider use of instruments, beginning with 'wild music of cymbals, flutes and tabors.' There also appears to have been a wider use of voices, as a later stage direction suggests.

---

62 *The Dramatic Works of Thomas Heywood*, I, 102.

63 The texts for 'The Masque of Queens,' 'Oberon,' 'Mercury Vindicated from the Alchemists at Court,' and 'Pleasure Reconciled to Virtue,' are given in Robert Adams, *Ben Jonson's Plays and Masques* (New York: Norton, 1979).

> *Mercury called to Daedalus in this following speech, which was after*
> *repeated in song by two trebles, two tenors, a bass, and the whole chorus.*

Marston wrote the text for the 'Montebank's Masque,' given at court on 16 February 1618. In the course of this masque the characters provide lists of brief tidbits of wisdom. Masculine reminds us that it was still not generally believed, Galileo and Copernicus notwithstanding, that the earth revolved around the sun, when he observes 'A Drunkard is a good philosopher; for he thinks that the world goes round.' Feminine offers an observation which is not quite clear at a distance of nearly four hundred years.

> An English virgin sings sweeter here than at Brussels;
> For a voluntary is sweeter than a forced note.

The most interesting of these are given by the character, Neuter.

> Musicians cannot be but healthful;
> For they live by good air.

> Playhouses are more necessary in a well-governed Commonwealth than public schools;
> For men are better taught by example than precept.

> A Kennel of hounds is the best Consort;
> For they need no tuning from morning to night.[64]

> The Court makes better Scholars than the University;
> For where a King vouchsafes to be a teacher, every man blushes to be a non-proficient.

Among the numerous songs, we are attracted to one which is entitled 'The Song and Dance Together.'

> *Lightly rise, and lightly fall you*
> *In the motion of your feet:*
> *Move not till our notes do call you;*
> *Music makes the action sweet.*
> *Music breathing blows the fire*
> *Which Cupid's feeds with fuel.*

Another masque for which the full text and lyrics survive is Chapman's 'The Maske of the Gentlemen of the two combin'd houses, or Inns of Court, the Middle-Temple, and Lincolns Inne.'[65] This work seems to have been performed by six instrumentalists, who first appear not as musicians at all, but disguised as priests. Later we read of music for six lutes, then six lutes and six voices. They changed to some unnamed instruments, for we next read 'Other

---

64 Several passages in sixteenth-century literature, including one by Shakespeare, suggest some nobles organized their hunting dogs as a consort, by the pitch of their bark.

65 See Allan Holaday, *The Plays of George Chapman; the Comedies* (Urbana: University of Illinois Press, 1970), 565ff.

Musique, and voices.' Still later, for a torch-light procession, the six musicians apparently played wind instruments, for they are described as 'Loude Musick.'

There were also internal masques with in the Jacobean plays themselves.[66] One such example is found in Middleton's *Your Five Gallants* (V, ii). In this masque there is music played by cornetts, as well as a song which begins,

> *Sound lute, bandora gittern,*
> *Viol, virginals, and cittern;*
> *Voices spring, and lift aloud*
> *Her name that makes the music proud!*

In Marston's *The Malcontent* (V, iii) a masque is given, which is introduced by the appearance of Mercury 'with loud music.' The nobles who play the roles in this masque enter to music of cornetts, as expressed in the stage direction,

> *The song to the cornets, which playing, the mask enters ...*

The dancing is also done to cornetts,

> *... then the cornets sound the measure, one change, and rest.*

At the conclusion of the masque the stage direction reads,

> *Cornets sound the measure over again; which danced, they unmask.*

When the duke is discovered, having removed his mask, the cornetts play a flourish.[67]

A few of the great Renaissance style allegorical entertainments continued into the Baroque and although in nearly every case the music is lost, some of the descriptions, however, are enlightening. Thomas Dekker was also involved in writing 'The Magnificent Entertainment Given to King James,' a major allegorical work associated with the arrival of James I for his

---

66 Internal masques are also found in Beaumont and Fletcher's *The Maids Tragedy* (I, i); *The Mad Lover* (IV, i); *A Wife for a Moneth* (II, i); *The Coronation* (IV, I); *The Coxcomb* (I, i); *Women Pleased* (V, iii), an internal masque introduced by a stage direction reading, 'Musick in divers places'; *The Queen of Corinth* (II, ii), an internal masque, for which the the stage directions specify 'singing and dancing to a horrid Musick;' *The Passionate Mad-man* (II, i). The 'Masque of the Gentlemen' by Francis Beamont is printed in Beaumont and Fletcher, *Complete Plays* (Cambridge: University Press, 1912), X, 281; In Thomas Dekker's *Satiromastix* (V, ii); In George Chapman's *Byron's Tragedy* (II, i). See also Beaumont and Fletcher's *The False One* (III, iv), with Isis singing of 'Songs, dances, Timbrels, drums' used in the worship of Nilus and laborers singing 'To delight his streams let's sing.'

67 The written text for masques by Thomas Middleton are given in *The Works of Thomas Middleton* (New York: AMS Press, 1964), VII: 'The World tost at Tennis' (1620), which includes stage directions for 'Music striking up a light fantastic air' and 'Loud music sounding,' for Jupiter; 'The Inner-Temple Masque' (1619); the masque 'The Triumphs of Truth' with 'The Entertainment at the Opening of the New River' (1613).

coronation in 1603.[68] Among the interesting references to music, there was a banquet with music by 'The Wayts and Haultboyes of London.'

In English literature from the time of the Middle Ages the word 'noise' was almost always associated with wind instruments. Dekker, however, seems to use the word to encompass instrumental music in general, including strings,[69] as in this descriptions of an ensemble accompanying a boy singer.

> His Majestie, being ready to go one, did most graciously feed the eyes of beholders with his presence, till a Song was spent: which to a loude and excellent Musicke (composed of Violins and other rare Artificiall Instruments) …

Strings are also mentioned relative to a pageant involving the nine Muses.

> And being come near to the Arbor, they gave a sign with a short flourish from all their Cornets, that his Majestie was at hand: whose princely eye whilest it was delighting itself with the quaint object before it, a sweet pleasure likewise courted his ear in the shape of Musicke, sent from the voices of nine Boys (all of them Queristers of St. Paul's) who in that place presenting the nine *Muses* sang the verse following to their Viols and other Instruments.

At this point the text describes the Summer banqueting house, a building nearly forty-five feet square.

> We might (that day) have called it, *The Musicke roome*, by reason of the change of tunes, that danced round about it; for in one place [time] we heard a noyse of cornets, in a second, a consort, the third (which sat in sight) a set of Viols, to which the *Muses* sang.

Soon the nine Muses were joined by the seven Liberal Arts and the text makes reference to the near disappearance of the liberal arts during the Middle Ages and gives credit to the monarchy for their present prosperity.

> Arts that were threatened to be trod under foot by Barbarisme, now (even at sight of his Majestie, who is the *Delian* Patron both of the *Muses* and *Arts*) being likewise advanced to most high preferment …

Marston was involved in the creation of the 'Entertainment of Alice, Dowager-countess of Derby,' given for her arrival at Ashby.[70] When her Ladyship approached the park around

---

68 The entire text is quoted in *The Dramatic Works of Thomas Dekker,* ed. Fredson Bowers (Cambridge: University Press, 1955), II, 253. A contemporary notes that not everything written was actually used on the occasion. In Ibid., III, 227ff, the text, with lyrics for songs, is given for a 'Triumph' as part of the Lord Mayor Procession of 1612; in Ibid., IV, 812ff is the text for a Pageant given in 1628 for the inauguration of Richard Deane as Mayor of London, the music of which features primarily cornett consorts.

69 See also Dekker, *Westward Ho* (V, ii) where a stage direction reads, 'Enter a noyse of Fidlers.'

70 Most of the text for the speakers and songs are quoted in *The Works of John Marston,* ed. A. H. Bullen (London: Nimmo, 1887), III, 387ff.

the house 'a full noise of cornets winded' and as she entered the park 'treble cornets reported one to another, as giving warning of her Honor's nearer approach.' As she entered the house 'a consort softly played,' while a speaker greeted her with poetry.

Within the house a masque was given, its songs alternating with consorts of oboes and cornets. In a typical song, we hear the allegorical character, Ariadne, sing,

> *Music and gentle night,*
> *Beauty, youth's chief delight,*
> *Pleasures all full invite*
> *Your due attendance to this glorious room;*
> *Then, if you have or wit or virtue, come,*
> *Oh, come! oh, come!*

The first mention of string instruments is when the 'violins played a new measure,' to which the masquers danced. After some more songs, there were additional dances, 'measures, galliards, corantos, and levaltos.'[71]

Music was a requirement for banquets,[72] for as as we see in Jonson's *The Staple of News* (III, ii), not a drop of wine could be poured without it.

> Your meat should be served in with curious dances,
> And set upon the board with virgin hands,
> Tuned to their voices; not a dish removed,
> But to the music, nor a drop of wine
> Mixed with his water without harmony.

We see the same sense of urgency in Middleton's *Blurt, Master-Constable* (II, ii), when Imperia, a courtesan, commands,

> So, so, so, so; here is a banquet; sit, sit, sit. Signior Curvetto, thrust in among them. Soft music, there! do, do, do.

In the plays it is usually the oboes who are mentioned relative to the music for banquets. Thus in Beaumont and Fletcher's *The Tragedy of Valentinian* (V, viii), as Maximus and Eudoxia enter in state, the stage direction reads,

---

71 The written text for Entertainments by Thomas Middleton are given in *The Works of Thomas Middleton* (New York: AMS Press, 1964), VII: 'The Magnificent Entertainment for King James' (1603); 'The Cities Love. An entertainment by water, at Chelsey and White-hall' (1616); 'The Tryumphs of Honor and Industry' (1617); 'The Triumphs of Love and Antiquity' (1619); 'The Sun in Aries' (1621); 'The Triumphs of Honor and Virtue' (1622); 'The Triumphs of Integrity' (1623); 'The Triumphs of Health and Prosperity' (1626). Also see *The Dramatic Works of Thomas Heywood*, IV, 'Londons Ius Honorarium,' 'Londons Sinus Salutis,' and 'Londini Speculum'; V, 'The Port of Piety' and 'Londons Peaceable Estate.'

72 See also Beaumont and Fletcher's *Thierry and Theodoret* (II, i), 'Loud musick, A Banquet set out'; Cyril Tourneur's, *The Atheist's Tragedy* (II, i), where a stage direction reads, 'Music, a banquet, in the night' and Thomas Heywood's *The Iron Age*, where a program direction reads, 'Lowd Musicke. A long table, and a banquet in state.'

> *A Synnet with Trumpets.*
> *With a Banket prepared, with Hoboies, Musick, Song*

And again in Beaumont and Fletcher's *The Maids Tragedy* (IV) a stage direction reads,

> *Banquet. Enter King, Calianax. Hoboyes play within.*

When there were royal guests the trumpets often performed their memorized works before the banquet table. It was perhaps with this in mind, in Beaumont and Fletcher's *Wit Without Money* (V, i), in preparation for a banquet, that Valentine cries out, 'let me have forty Trumpets.'

Members of the rising middle-class also aspired to have music for their dinner guests, but often the host's daughter had to suffice. In Beaumont and Fletcher's *The Humourous Lieutenant* (I, i) a common citizen inviting gentlemen and ladies to his home for a meal promises music and a performance by his daughter.

> Some Musick I'le assure you too,
> My toy, Sir, can play o'th' Virginals.

Finally, there are numerous references in these plays of the poor street musicians and these references are nearly always expressions of contempt. In Jonson's comedy, *Poetaster* (III, iv), a comment made in passing gives us what must be a description of one of the last of the true minstrels, the now poor vagrant musician. Tucca observes,

> We must have you turn fiddler again, slave, get a bass violin at your back, and march in a tawny coat, with one sleeve, to Goose fair.

And in Jonson's comedy, *The Silent Woman* (III, iii), Clerimont observes,

> The smell of the venison, going through the street, will invite one noise of fiddlers or other.

In Beaumont and Fletcher's *The Honest Man's Fortune* (V, i), Mountage says to a man,

> Ye have travell'd like a Fidler to make faces,
> And brought home nothing but a case of tooth-picks.

In Beaumont and Fletcher play, *The Chances* (V, iii), a 'Fidler' is hung for robbing a mill.

The Jacobean playwright who seemed most interested in these street musicians was Thomas Dekker, although he too treats them with contempt, as we see in his *The Whore of Babylon* (II, ii), when Campeius observes,

> Like common Fidlers, drawing down others meate
> With lickorish tunes, whilst they on scraps do eate.

A more extended dialogue is found in his *Westward Ho* (V, i), where Frank Monopoly, a nephew to the Earle, complains that the fiddlers have not begun to play, especially since the ladies have arrived.

> MONOPOLY. Why Chamberlin? will not these Fidlers be drawn forth? are they not in tune yet? Or are the Rogues afraideth Statute, and dare not travel so far without a passport? ...
> *[Enter Chamberlin]*
> CHAMBERLIN. Anon sir, here sir, at hand sir.
> MONOPOLY. Where's this noise? what a lowsie Townes this? Has *Brainford* no musick in it.
> CHAMBERLIN. The are but rozining sir, and they will scrape themselves into your company presently.
> MONOPOLY. Plague on their Cats guts, and their scraping: dost not see women here, and can we thinkst thou be without a noise then?
> CHAMBERLIN. The truth is sir, one of the poor instrument caught a sore mischance last night: his most base bridge fell down, and belike they are making a gathering for the reparations of that.
> WHIRLEPOOLE. When they come, lets have em with a pox.

In *If This be not a Good Play* (II, i) we find a description of no less than 140 street musicians.

> BRISCO. Without now waits
>   Musicke in some ten languages: each one sweares
>   (By *Orpheus* fiddle-case) they will tickle your eares
>   If they can't do it with scraping.
> NARCISSO. Theres seven score Noise at least of English fidlers.
> IOUINELLI. Seven score! they are able to eate up a city in very scraps.
> BRISCO. Very base-viol men most of them: besides whole swarmes of Welsh harpes, Irish bagpipes, Jewes trompes, and French kitts.
>   All these made I together play:
>   But their damned catter-wralling,
>   Frightened me away.

Finally, in *The Witch of Edmonton* (III, iv), a poor fiddler, known as 'Sawgut' finds his instrument makes no sound and he laments,

> I'll lay mine Ear to my Instrument, that my poor Fiddle is bewitch'd. I play'd 'The Flowers in May,' even now, as sweet as a Violet; now 'twill not go against the hair: you see I can make no more Musick than a Beetle of a Cow-turd.

9   JACOBEAN PROSE

THE FIRST HALF OF THE SEVENTEENTH CENTURY in England, with its civil wars and the aggressive influence of the Puritans, offered a poor climate for fine fiction. This is not to say great numbers of works were not published, but prose by fine writers was not abundant. Although the writers we quote here make philosophical comments, they are not real philosophers, and thus are not found in the earlier chapter on philosophy. Here are rather reflections on contemporary Jacobean life, made by doctors, preachers, playwrights and writers of prose.

ON THE PHYSIOLOGY OF AESTHETICS

For the reasons given above, it was also a period in which there was little interest in the philosophical contemplation of the working of the mind. What discussion there was was centered, as with much of Europe, on the emotions. Sir Thomas Browne, a physician as well as a writer of prose, comments in his 'Religio Medici' on the nature of Reason and the emotions.

> As reason is a rebel to faith, so passion is to reason. As the propositions of faith seem absurd to reason, so the theorems of reason do to passion, and both to reason; yea, a moderate and peaceable discretion may so state and order the matter, that they may be all kings, and yet make but one monarchy.[1]

Whatever this monarchy included for Browne, it did not include the wisdom of the public.

> If there be any among those common objects of hatred I do condemn and laugh at, it is that great enemy of reason, virtue, and religion, the multitude; that numerous piece of monstrosity, which, taken asunder, seem men, and the reasonable creatures of God, but, confused together, make but one great beast, and a monstrosity more prodigious than Hydra.[2]

---

[1] *Sir Thomas Browne's Works*, ed. Simon Wilkin (London: Pickering, 1836), II, 27. A few pages later [Ibid., 32] Browne gives as an example of the conflict between faith and reason, the theological problem represented that no horses were discovered in America, in view of the fact that all animals covering the Earth were supposed to have come from the Ark. Sir Thomas Browne (1605–1682), one of the best prose writers of the period, was educated at Oxford and became a provincial doctor in Norwich.

[2] Ibid., II, 86.

Thomas Fuller, in an article 'Of Phancie,' describes fantasy in a definition which clearly reflects the restraints of Puritanism.

> An inward sense of the soul, for awhile retaining and examining things brought in thither by the common sense. It is the most boundless and restless faculty of the soul ... The chief diseases of the Phancie are, either that they are too wild and high-soaring, or else too low and groveling, or else too desultory and overvoluble.[3]

We have noted, in these volumes, that throughout history literature reflects a conspicuous preference for the right hand, or negative references to the left hand—as in Thomas Dekker's mention of 'some left-handed Priest.'[4] We understand this today as a manifestation, demonstrated in clinical research, of the left brain's curious refusal to admit the existence of the right hemisphere. In seventeenth-century England this right hand preference became associated with moral values. Sir Thomas Browne, for example, in his *Enquiries into Vulgar and Common Errors*, takes a passage in the Old Testament,

> A wise man's heart inclines him toward the right, but a fool's heart toward the left

and interprets it to mean one's choice of traveling the right way in the path of virtue or the left road, one of vice.[5] Later in this same book, Browne, who was also a physician, devotes an entire chapter, 'Of the Right and Left Hand,' to the question of the curious priority given the right hand. He begins by representing himself as suspicious of any basis for this prejudice, although he acknowledges several passages in the Old Testament which clearly emphasize the right hand.[6]

He advances several arguments why no basis can be found in Nature for this prejudice, including the fact that no similar preference can be found in other animals, nor is a preference clear in very young children. Most important, he points out that none of the senses honor such a prejudice, nor can he find any meaningful evidence among the internal organs. In the end he finds even the fact that more persons are right-handed to be a matter of custom, and not of nature.

---

3 Thomas Fuller, *The Holy State and the Profance State* [1642], ed. Maximilian Walten (New York: AMS Press, 1966), II, 177. Thomas Fuller (1608–1661) was a chaplain to Charles II.

4 Thomas Dekker, 'The Seven Deadly Sinnes of London' (1606), in *The Non-Dramatic Works of Thomas Dekker*, II, 109. Thomas Dekker (b. 1570) was a very fluent writer, producing plays of his own and in collaboration with others, in addition to 'entertainments' and pamphlets on a variety of subjects. It has been said that no writer gave a more vivid picture of London at this time. He, however, failed to earn a living and was often in prison—once for three years. Nothing is known of him after the 1630s.

5 'Enquiries into Vulgar and Common Errors,' *Sir Thomas Browne's Works*, III, 6. The passage in question is Ecclesiastes 10:2.

6 Ibid., III, 13ff. He also mentions several curious myths, among them that the Amazon women amputated their right breast, for freer use of the bow, and that 'a woman upon a masculine conception advances her right leg.'

On Education

Several reflections on education in this literature, colored by Puritanism, paint a dim view of education. Fuller, in his description called 'The General Artist,' describes rather negatively the man who attempts to become expert in all the Liberal Arts, for 'he that sips of many arts, drinks of none.'[7] As a metaphor for the study of languages, as an adjunct to the Liberal Arts, Fuller offers the following,

> His mother-tongue was like the dull musick of a monochord, which by study he turns into the harmony of several instruments.

The scholar studies Rhetoric, 'the mother of lies,'

> Nor is he a stranger to poetry, which is musick in words; nor to music, which is poetry in sound: both excellent sauce, but they have lived and died poor, who made them their meat.

Thomas Overbury has left a character study of the 'mere scholar,' which is somewhat lacking in respect.

> A mere scholar is an intelligible Ass. Or a silly fellow in black, that speaks sentences more familiarly than sense. The antiquity of his university is his creed, and the excellency of his college (though but for a match at Foot-ball) an article of his faith. He speaks Latin better than his mother-tongue, and is a stranger to no part of the world but his own country ... In a word, he is the Index of a man, and the Title-page of a scholar, or a Puritan in morality, much in profession, nothing in practice.[8]

We might also point out that Izaak Walton, in his *The Compleat Angler*, mentions an author, a Mr. Hales, who was ridiculed for writing a book on fencing. This was, Walton points out, because 'that art was not to be taught by words, but practice.'[9]

ON THE PHILOSOPHY OF AESTHETICS

There are also very few passages in this literature which concern themselves with the traditional questions of aesthetics in art. We do find one interesting observation by Sir Thomas Browne, in his 'Religio Medici,' which briefly touches on the ancient question regarding the relationship of Art to Nature.

---

7 Fuller, *The Holy State and the Profance State*, II, 72ff.

8 *The 'Conceited Newes' of Sir Thomas Overbury and His Friends*, ed. James Savage (Gainesville: Scholars' Facsimiles, 1968), 120ff. Sir Thomas Overbury (1581–1613) was also a poet.

9 Izaak Walton, *The Compleat Angler* (London: Oxford University Press, 1935), 6. Izaak Walton (1593–1683) is best known for his biographies of contemporary English writers.

Now, nature is not at variance with art, nor art with nature; they being both the servants of his providence. Art is the perfection of nature. Were the world now as it was the sixth day, there were yet a chaos. Nature has made one world, and art another. In brief, all things are artificial; for nature is the art of God.[10]

In general, the most interesting comments touching on aesthetics are concerned with practice rather than with theory. Several writers supply us with a rather dim perspective of the poet at this time. The view of Thomas Dekker is clear when he offers advice on how to act like a poet.

If you be a Poet, and come into the Ordinary (though it can be no great glory to be an ordinary Poet) order yourself thus. Observe no man, doff not cap to that Gentleman today at dinner, to whom, not two nights since, you were beholden for a supper; but, after a turn or two in the room, take occasion (pulling out your gloves) to have some Epigram, or Satyre, or Sonnet fastened in one of them, that may (as it were vomittingly to you) offer itself to the Gentlemen: they will presently desire it: but, without much conjuration from them, and a pretty kind of counterfeit loathness in yourself, do not read it; and though it be none of your own, swear you made it.[11]

According to Dekker, poets will not even be welcome in Hell.

Very fewe Poets can be suffered to live there, the Colonel of Conjurers drives them out of his Circle, because he fears they will write libels against him: yet some pittifull fellows (that have faces like fire-drakes, but wits colde as Whetstones, and more blunt) not Poets indeed, but ballad-makers, rub out there, and write Infernals.[12]

John Earle has left a description of the poet who composes for hire, whom he calls a 'pot-poet.' He is always ready, in case of house fire or the death of a great man, to pour out verses which Earle finds 'not altogether as hobbling as an Almanac.'

A poet-poet is the dregs of wit; yet mingled with good drink may have some relish. His inspiration are more real than others'; for they do but feign a God, but he has his by him. His verses run like the tap, and his invention as the barrel ebbs and flows at the mercy of the spigot. In thin drink he aspires not above a ballad, but a cup of sack inflames him and sets his muse and nose afire together.[13]

---

10 *Sir Thomas Browne's Works*, II, 23.

11 Thomas Dekker, 'The Guls Horn-Booke' (1609), II, 240.

12 Thomas Dekker, 'The Seven Deadly Sinnes of London' (1606), II, 99.

13 John Earle, *Microcosmography* [1628] (St. Clair Shores: Scholarly Press, 1971), 65. John Earle (1600–1665) was a chaplain to Charles II, during the king's exile, and a dean of Westminster during the Restoration.

But Thomas Overbury allows even less respect for this kind of poet.

> A Rymer is a fellow whose face is hatcht all over with impudence, and should he be hanged or pilloried it is armed for it. He is a Juggler with words, yet practices the Art of most uncleanly conveyance. He doth boggle very often; and because himself winks at it, thinks it is not perceived: the main thing that ever he did, was the tune he sang to. There is nothing in the earth so pitiful, no not even an Ape-carrier, he is not worth thinking of, and therefore I must leave him as nature left him; a Dunghill not well laid together.[14]

As playwrights were also still poets, we find similarly uncomplimentary characterizations of the world of the theater. Thomas Dekker offers humorous advice to the courtier on how to act at the theater, in his 'How a Gallant should behave in a play-house.' Among much other advice, Dekker suggests that it is good to call attention to yourself in the audience.

> It shall crown you with rich commendation, to laugh aloud in the midst of the most serious and saddest scene of the terriblest Tragedy.

Among the advantages gained, you identify yourself as a gentleman, since you obviously have nothing better to do than be in the theater. Also, you 'publish your temperance to the world,' for you could also be drinking in a tavern.

Before the play begins, he recommends organizing a card game. Then on the third trumpet sound (announcing the play is to begin),

> to gal the Ragga-muffins that stand aloofe gaping at you, throw the cards round about the Stage, just upon the third sound, as though you had lost.

If the playwright has embarrassed you with an epigram, or shown interest in your mistress, then in the middle of the play,

> you rise with a screwed and discontented face from your stool to be gone: no matter whether the Scenes be good or no; the better they are the worse do you distract them: and, being on your feet, sneake not away like a coward, but salute all your gentle acquaintances.

For this behavior, the poet may 'cry a pox on you,' but don't worry, says Dekker, 'there's no musick without frets.' And if you elect not to actually leave, you can still disturb things by making others laugh, 'mew at passionate speeches, blare at merrie, finde fault with the musicke ... whistle at the songs.'[15]

In Thomas Fuller, whose views are always centered in moral values, we find a more serious reflection of drama.

---

14 *The 'Conceited Newes' of Sir Thomas Overbury and His Friends*, 214ff. John Webster (1580–1625) apparently stole this passage word for word, using it in his 'New Characters Drawne to the life of Severall Persons, in Severall qualities' of 1615.

15 Thomas Dekker, 'The Guls Horn-Booke' (1609), II, 246ff.

> Two things are set forth to us in stage plays: some grave sentences, prudent counsels, and punishment of vicious examples: and with these desperate oaths, lustful talk, and riotous acts are so personated to the life, that wantons are tickled with delight, and feed their palates upon them. It seems the goodness is not portrayed out with equal accents of liveliness as the wicked things are: otherwise men would be deterred from vicious courses, with seeing the woeful success which follows them. But the main is, wanton speeches on stages are the devils ordinance to beget badness.[16]

Only in the writings of Thomas Overbury, in his *Characters*, do we find a more positive consideration of the theater.

> Play-houses are more necessary in a well-governed Common-wealth, than schools.[17]

In another place, where Overbury is discussing the characteristics of the 'excellent actor,' we find,

> He is much affected to painting, and it is a question whether that makes him an excellent player, or his playing an exquisite painter. He adds grace to the poet's labors: for what in the poet is but a verse, in him is both verse and musick.[18]

ON THE AESTHETICS OF MUSIC

Sir Thomas Browne, in his 'Religio Medici,' offers a personal perspective on the universal relationship of music and man.

> For there is a music wherever there is a harmony, order, or proportion; and thus far we may maintain 'the music of spheres' for those well-ordered motions, and regular paces, though they give no sound unto the ear, yet to the understanding they strike a note most full of harmony. Whatsoever is harmonically composed delights in harmony, which makes me much distrust the symmetry of those heads which declaim against all church music. For myself, not only from my obedience but my particular genius I do embrace it: for even that vulgar and tavern music, which makes one man merry, another mad, strikes in me a deep fit of devotion, and a profound contemplation of the first composer. There is something in it of divinity more than the ear discovers: it is an hieroglyphical and shadowed lesson of the whole world, and creatures of God,—such a melody to the ear, as the whole world, well understood, would afford the understanding. In brief, it is a sensible fit of that harmony which intellectually sounds in the ears of God. I will not say, with Plato, the soul is an harmony, but harmonic, and has its nearest sympathy with music.[19]

---

16 Thomas Fuller, *The Holy State and the Profane State*, II, 185ff.
17 *The 'Conceited Newes' of Sir Thomas Overbury and His Friends*, 299.
18 Ibid., 210.
19 *Sir Thomas Browne's Works*, II, 106ff.

Izaak Walton makes a comment in passing intended to reflect his view that what man hears is conditioned by his perspective as a listener.

> What musick doth a pack of dogs then make to any man, whose heart and ears are so happy as to be set to the tune of such instruments?[20]

In another place he offers an explanation for how the early knowledge of music survived the Flood. 'Others say,' he reports, that Seth, one of the sons of Adam engraved the knowledge of mathematics and music, and the rest of previous knowledge, on pillars.[21]

Modern philologists believe that vocal music, as a form of communicating feeling, must have preceded even the most primitive of languages. It is from this perspective that our eye was drawn to Thomas Dekker's essay on lowlife in London, in which he discusses a slang speech of the underworld called 'canting.'

> This word *canting* seems to be derived from the Latin verbe (*canto*) which signifies in English, to sing, or to make a sound with words, that is to say to speake. And very aptly may *canting* take his *derivatio a cantando*, from singing, because amongst these beggarly consorts that can play upon no better instruments, the language of *canting* is a kinde of musicke, and he that in such assemblies can *cant* best, is counted the best Musician.[22]

The familiarity of the general English society with music was such that one finds in ordinary discussion an extraordinary range of musical metaphors. Consider, for example, the broad variety of uses by Thomas Dekker:

To represent the well-together person,

> What monsters they please to set [on] all the world and all the people in it out of tune, and the worse Musicke they make, the more sport it is for him.[23]

As a metaphor for the four winds,

> East, West, North, and South, the foure Trumpetters of the Worlde, that never blow themselves out of breath …[24]

To describe a papal representative who tries to be all things to all people,

> He's like an Instrument of sundry strings,
> Not one in tune, yet any note he sings.[25]

---

20 Walton, *The Compleat Angler*, 31.
21 Ibid., 38.
22 Thomas Dekker, 'Lanthorne and Candle-Light' (1609), III, 194.
23 Thomas Dekker, 'The Divels Last Will and Testament' (1609), III, 357.
24 Thomas Dekker, 'The Seven Deadly Sinnes of London' (1606), II, 97
25 Thomas Dekker, 'A Papist in Armes' (1606), II,174.

To describe 'cooperation' between two people,

> As strings of an instrument, though we render several sounds, yet let both our sounds cadence [*close up*] in sweet concordant Musicke.[26]

For reading,

> ... nor the slumbers of a conscience that hath no sting to keep it waking more delicate than the musicke which I found in reading ...[27]

To represent the Spanish and French conspiring against the English.

> To be short, such strange mad musick doe they play upon their Sacke-buttes.[28]

On the reader's sympathy with his writing.

> If the Notes please thee, my paines are well bestowed. If to thine ear they found untuneable, much are they not to be blamed, in regard they are the Aires of a Sleeping Man.[29]

Other writers were equally creative in their use of music in figures of speech. Thomas Fuller, in warning the reader to beware of 'boisterous and over-violent exercise,' writes,

> Ringing oftentimes has made good musick on the bells, and puts mens bodies out of tune.[30]

Thomas Overbury uses music as a metaphor to characterize the duties of the lawyer.

> He knows so much in Musique, that he affects only the most and cunningest discords; rarely a perfect concord, especially sung, except in *fine*.[31]

Finally, we don't know what else it could be than a nice pun, when John Earle describes a Puritan mother who would not allow her daughters to study the virginals, 'because of their affinity with organs.'[32]

---

[26] Thomas Dekker, 'The Dead Tearme' (1608), IV, 71.
[27] Thomas Dekker, 'Warres' (1609), IV, 102.
[28] Thomas Dekker, 'The Seven Deadly Sinnes of London' (1606), II, 44.
[29] Thomas Dekker, 'Dekker his Dream,' (1620), III, 12.
[30] Thomas Fuller, *The Holy State and the Profane State*, II, 184.
[31] *The 'Conceited Newes' of Sir Thomas Overbury and His Friends*, 119,
[32] 'A She Precise Hypocrite,' in John Earle, *Microcosmography*, 73.

On the Purpose of Music

Thomas Browne offers, as an example of the frequently mentioned capacity of music to soothe, a unique interpretation of the myth of Orpheus.

> There were a crew of mad women retired unto a mountain, from whence, being pacified by his music, they descended with boughs in their hands; which, unto the fabulosity of those times, proved a sufficient ground to celebrate unto all posterity the magic of Orpheus's harp.[33]

Thomas Dekker also mentions this purpose of music in one passage where he writes of 'Musicke charming thine ear,'[34] but in another place he refers to the absence of music to soothe those in prison.

> What musicke hath he to cheer up his Spirits in this sadness? none but this, he hears wretches (equally miserable) breaking their heart-strings every night with groans, every day with sighs, every hour with cares.[35]

Thomas Browne is perplexed by the strange nature of dreams and points to music as soothing means of preparing for trouble-free sleep.

> Half our days we pass in the shadow of the earth; and the brother of death exacts a third part of our lives. A good part of our sleep is peered out with visions and fantastical objects, wherein we are confessedly deceived. The day supplies us with truths; the night with fictions and falsehoods, which uncomfortably divide the natural account of our beings. And, therefore, having passed the day in sober labors and rational enquiries of truth, we are fain to betake ourselves into such a state of being, wherein the soberest heads have acted all the monstrosities of melancholy, and which unto open eyes are no better than folly and madness.
>
> Happy are they that go to bed with grand music, like Pythagoras, or have ways to compose the fantastical spirit, whose unruly wanderings take off inward sleep.[36]

Another traditional purpose of music is to attract the ladies, as we see in Thomas Overbury, in a character sketch of a Lover, where he suggests the lover must be proficient in music.

> His fingers are his Orators, and he expresses much of himself upon some instrument.[37]

---

33 *Sir Thomas Browne's Works*, II, 220.
34 Thomas Dekker, 'The Seven Deadly Sinnes of London' (1606), II,128.
35 Thomas Dekker, 'Jests to Make you Merrie' (1607), II, 341.
36 *Sir Thomas Browne's Works*, IV, 355.
37 *The 'Conceited Newes' of Sir Thomas Overbury and His Friends*, 78.

We find one interesting reference to music therapy, where Sir Thomas Browne, a physician as well a writer of prose, could find no reason to question the folk legends of the use of music to cure the bite of the Tarantula.

> Some doubt many have of the *tarantula*, or poisonous spider of Calabria, and that magical cure of the bit thereof by music. But since we observe that many attest it from experience; since the learned Kircherus has positively averred it, and set down the songs and tunes solemnly used for it; since some also affirm the *tarantula* itself will dance upon certain strokes, whereby they set their instruments against its poison, we shall not at all question it.[38]

FUNCTIONAL MUSIC

There is an interesting and humorous reference to church music in which Thomas Dekker describes the manners of the courtier in church.

> Never be seen to mount the steps into the choir, but upon a high Festival day, to prefer the fashion of your doublet, and especially if the singing-boys seem to take note of you: for they are able to buzz your praises above their Anthems, if their voices have not lost their maidenheads: but be sure your silver spurs dog your heels, and then the Boyes will swarm about you like so many white butter-flyes, when you in the open Choir shall draw forth a perfumed embroidered purse (the glorious sight of which will entice many Country-men from their devotion to wondering) and quoyt silver into the Boyes hands, that it may be heard above the first lessons, although it be read in a voice as big as one of the great Organs.
>
> This noble and notable Act being performed, you are to vanish presently out of the Choir, and to appear again in the walk.[39]

Another rather unusual view of church music is found in John Earle's characterization of 'The Common Singing-men in Cathedral Churches.' They are, he says,

> a bad society, and yet a company of good fellows, that roar deep in the choir, deeper in the tavern. They are the eight parts of speech, which go to the Syntaxis of Service, and are distinguished by their noises much like bells, for they make not a consort but a peal. Their pastime or recreation is prayers, their exercise drinking, yet herein so religiously addicted that they serve God oftenest when they are drunk … Though they never expound the scripture they handle it much, and pollute the Gospel with two things, their conversation and their thumbs. Upon work-days they behave themselves at prayers as at their pots, for they swallow them down in an instant. Their gowns are laced commonly with streamings of ale, the superfluities of a cup or throat above measure. Their skill in melody makes them the better companions abroad, and their anthems abler to sing catches. Long-lived for the most part they are not, especially the

---

38 'Enquiries into Vulgar and Common Errors,' in *Sir Thomas Browne's Works*, II, 536.
39 Thomas Dekker, 'The Guls Horn-Booke' (1609), II, 233ff.

bass, they overflow their bank so oft to drown the organs. Briefly, if they escape arresting, they die constantly in God's service; and to take their death with more patience, they have wine and cakes at their funeral: and now they keep the Church a great deal better, and help to fill it with their bones as before with their noise.[40]

There are also a number of interesting references to music occurring in civic life. One of these, by Dekker, is relative to the plague of 1603.

I was amazed to remember what dead Marches were made of three thousand trooping together; husbands, wives & children being led as ordinarily to one grave, as if they had gone to one bed.[41]

In another place he mentions the Lord Mayor's Parade.

… demanded of his Waterman why there was such drumming, and piping, and trumpetting, and wherefore all those Barges (like so many Water-pageants) …[42]

John Earle presents a portrait of a musician frequently seen in both civic and court duties, the trumpeter.

A trumpeter is the elephant with the great trunk, for he eats nothing but what comes through this way. His profession is not so worthy as to occasion insolence, and yet no man so much puffed up. His face is as brazen as his trumpet, and (which is worse) as a fiddler's, from whom he differs only in this, that his impudence costs you more. The sea of drink and much wind make a storm perpetually in his cheeks, and his look is like his noise, blustering and tempestuous … He is the common attendant of glittering folks, whether in the court or stage, where he is always the prologue's prologue.[43] He is somewhat in the nature of a hogshead, shrillest when he is empty; when his belly is full he is quiet enough.[44]

Thomas Overbury, in his description of the professional 'tinker,' which appears to have included the blacksmith craft, mentions the old myth about Pythagoras and the blacksmith.

From his Art was Musicke first invented, and therefore is he always furnished with a song: to which his hammer keeping tune, proves that he was the first founder of the Kettle-drumme. Note that where the best Ale is, there stands his musick most upon crotchets.[45]

---

40 John Earle, *Microcosmography*, 94.
41 Thomas Dekker, 'The Wonderfull Yeare of 1603,' I, 112.
42 Thomas Dekker, 'Jests to Make you Merrie' (1607), II, 287.
43 Since the fifteenth century, at least, three trumpet signals indicated the play was about to begin.
44 John Earle, *Microcosmography*, 79ff.
45 The 'Conceited Newes' of Sir Thomas Overbury and His Friends, 124. In *Sir Thomas Browne's Works*, IV, 191, one will find a treatise called 'Of Cymbals, etc.,' which reviews references to this instrument in early literature.

We might also mention here two reports of music in other countries. Edward Browne, writing to his father Sir Thomas Browne in 1668, reports during a visit to Vienna,

> In the emperor's chappell is very good musick, vocall and instrumentall, performed by Italians, whereof some are eunuchs.[46]

In a visit to Köln, in 1673, he reports to his father,

> We have with us here one Mr. Christmas, the best trumpet in England ... and a little boy who exceeds all upon the violin, and Mr. Hadly upon the flagelet, which instrument he has so improved as to invent large ones, and outgoes in sweetness all the basses whatsoever upon any other instrument.[47]

Finally, one interesting reference to dance music is found in Dekker. While discussing the theater of ancient Rome (some of which he claims seated 80,000 audience members!), he makes a reference in passing regarding upper class dance of his own time.

> In these [theaters] they sometimes saw plays tragicall, or comicall, with all sorts of musicke, *Doricke*, *Chromaticke*, soft and delicate, *Lidian*, *Nypolydian* mournfull, fit for Tragedies: and to these sorts of musicke they had all sorts of Dancing; and *Hyporchema* (in time of a pestilence) a dance to *Apollo* in the Campe; the *Pyrichian*, which was a dance in Armour. In the Chamber (as we now have) dances, with wanton gesticulation. All which, as well *Musicke* as *Daunces*, they borrowed from the *Greekes*.[48]

ENTERTAINMENT MUSIC

We find several interesting descriptions of entertainment music worthy of mention, particularly in the works of Thomas Dekker. One of his fictional works creates a satire of an aristocratic masque, danced by devils in Hell. Of particular interest is his description of the masquers drum,

> They had a *Drum*, after which they marched (two & two) & that was made of an old *Cauldron*, the head of it being covered with the skins of two flailed *Spanish Inquisitors*, and a hole (for vent)

---

46   *Sir Thomas Browne's Works*, I, 159. Browne himself advised his son, in a letter of 1667 [Ibid., I, 152],

> You are mightily improved in your violin, but I would by no means have you practice upon the trumpet, for many reasons.

Perhaps this was because his son served on a naval ship and the trumpet sounds may have been confused as signals.

47   Ibid., I, 206.
48   Thomas Dekker, 'A Strange Horse-Race' (1609), III, 319ff.

beaten out at the very bottom: the Drum-stickes were the shinbones of two *Dutch-Free-booters*: So that it sounded like a *Switzers Kettle-drum*.[49]

In the literature of the latter Middle Ages and Renaissance one begins to find increasingly frequent reference to the 'beer fiddler,' a representative of the last of the old minstrel tradition. His reputation delayed the acceptance of the strings into court and church life (they are rarely mentioned before 1550) and kept the wind instrument players in place as the 'professional' musicians. Although this fiddler is often mentioned in passing, rarely do we get so lengthy a description as we do in John Earle's, 'A Poor Fiddler.'

> A poor fiddler is a man and a fiddle out of case: and he in worse case than his fiddle. One that rubs two sticks together (as the Indians strike fire), and rubs a poor living out of it; partly from this, and partly from your charity, which is more in the hearing than giving him, for he sells nothing dearer than to be gone. He is just so many strings above a beggar, though he have but two: and yet he begs too, only not in the downright 'for God's sake,' but with a shrugging 'God bless you,' and his face is more pained than the blind man's. Hunger is the greatest pain he takes, except a broken head sometimes, and the laboring *John Dory*. Otherwise his life is so many fits of mirth, and it is some mirth to see him. A good feast shall draw him five miles by the nose, and you shall track him again by the scent. His other pilgrimages are fairs and good houses, where his devotion is great to the Christmas; and no man loves good times better. He is in league with the tapsters for the worshipful of the inn, whom he torments next morning with his art, and has their names more perfect than their men. A new song is better to him than a new jacket, especially if bawdy, which he calls merry, and hates naturally the Puritan, as an enemy to this mirth. A country wedding and Whitsun ale are the two main places he domineers in, where he goes for a musician, and overlooks the bagpipe. The rest of him is drunk, and in the stocks.[50]

Dekker is especially brutal in his treatment of the vagrant fiddler. In one place he refers to 'Common Juglers, Fidlers, and Players' called 'Beasts,'[51] and in another place he describes a man as 'his acquaintance is more cheape, than a common Fidlers.'[52] In his 'The Ravens Almanacke,' we find,

> O you common Fidlers likewise that scrape out a poore living out of dryed Cats guts: I prophesie that many of you shall this yeare be troubled with abominable noises and singing in your heads: insomuch that a great part of you shall die beggars, and those that survive shall feed upon melody for want of meat, playing by two of the clock in a frostie morning under a Window, and then be mocked with a shilling tied (through a hole) to a string, which shall be thrown to make it jingle in your ears, but presently be drawn up again, while you rake in the durst for a largesse.[53]

---

49 Thomas Dekker, 'The Catch-Pols Masque' (1609), III, 365.
50 John Earle, *Microcosmography*, 38ff.
51 Thomas Dekker, 'The Dead Tearme' (1608), IV, 55.
52 Thomas Dekker, 'The Seven Deadly Sinnes of London' (1606), II, 96.
53 Thomas Dekker, 'The Ravens Almanacke' (1609), IV, 192ff.

This poor musician was often found in the tavern, as, for all reports, was Dekker. In one of his stories he mentions 'Harlots and Fidlers, in a Tavern,'[54] and in another,

> May it therefore please thee (O thou pay-mistress to all the fidlers that should haunt our houses, if thou wouldest put them in tune) to send (at least) some of thy Harpers to sound their nine-penie musicke in our eares.[55]

---

54 Thomas Dekker, 'Lanthorne and Candle-Light' (1609), III, 296.
55 Thomas Dekker, 'The Peace is Broken' (1609), IV, 160. Walton, *The Compleat Angler*, 80ff, contains a number of of lyrics for popular songs as sung in an inn, including the actual music for a two-part song by Henry Lawes.

10 RESTORATION PHILOSOPHERS

THE RESTORATION PERIOD IN ENGLAND can be viewed as an environment which somewhat limited the development of philosophy. First, the court, which in a monarchal society usually leads the culture and establishes the 'Mode,' when it returned from its exile in Paris brought an atmosphere to London which was hardly conducive to higher intellectual pursuits. This climate was described by Andrew Marvell, a poet in favor during both the Cromwell and Charles II periods.

> A colony of French possess the Court;
> Pimps, priests, buffoons, in privy-chamber sport.
> Such slimy monsters never approached a throne,
> Since Pharaoh's days, nor so defiled a crown.[1]

This life of the court, together with the influence of the strong Puritan movement throughout the seventeenth century, had the effect of strengthening all kinds of religious fundamentalism.[2] As this took center stage, philosophy was left in many cases in the hands of the theologians. Neither their interests nor those of the court were conducive to much discussion of the fine arts. Consequently, some of the great minds of England, men such as David Hume, came to see the battle for the Enlightenment as a battle to be fought only in the territory of the left hemisphere of the brain, and to this day it is often called 'the age of Reason.'

THOMAS HOBBES (1588–1679)

Thomas Hobbes was born to an Anglican clergyman of strong personality, but who left his family to be reared by his brother. After a stay at Oxford, two gifts of fate fell in the lap of Hobbes. He was hired as a secretary to Francis Bacon, which must have pointed him toward philosophy, and he was employed by the wealthy Cavendish family, who would support and protect him most of his life.

---

[1] 'Britannia and Raleigh,' in *The Complete Works of Andrew Marvell*, I, 326. Andrew Marvell (1621–1678) served as a secretary to Milton after the the famous poet became blind.

[2] It was this period, especially in the philosophy of the Scottish Presbyterians and the Quakers, which played so great a role in the development of religious philosophy in America.

The philosophy of Hobbes is centered in mathematics, materialism and in social organization and when writing outside of those fields his comments tend to be rather superficial. According to one biographer, Hobbes was addicted to music and was a performer on the bass viol, and 'at night, when he was abed, and the doors made fast, and was sure nobody heard him, he sang aloud.'[3] When living in Paris for a number of years he was a friend of Mersenne, who was unusually interested in all aspects of the philosophy of music. The fact, therefore, that music is hardly mentioned in the writings of Hobbes only affirms once again that, unlike the other major countries, music had ceased to be a topic in English philosophy.

On the Physiology of Aesthetics

Hobbes follows a general line of thought at this time, although he is somewhat more dogmatic, in contending that all thoughts of man have their origin in the senses.

> There is no conception in a man's mind, which has not at first, totally, or by parts, been begotten upon the organs of sense. The rest are derived from that original.[4]

In one respect he was more perceptive than most of his contemporaries. By deduction, or by intuition, he seems to have clearly understood that the mind has two distinctly different processes for dealing with information. Whereas today we would simply say left and right brain, or rational versus experiential, Hobbes comes rather close in one place when he observes, 'Of the powers of the mind there be two sorts, cognitive and imaginative.'[5] In another place he writes that there are two kinds of knowledge, one based on the senses and the other, called science, is based on 'the truth of propositions.'[6] Hobbes is very much on track for the character of the left hemisphere of the brain, when he writes that Reason is analogous to mathematics, for it consists of,

> reckoning, that is adding and subtracting, of the consequences of general names agreed upon for the marking and signifying of our thoughts.[7]

The purpose of Reason is to find Truth, but 'as in arithmetic, unpracticed men must, and professors themselves may often, err.' He also contends, in several places, that 'Experience is only memory.'[8]

---

3 John Aubrey, *Brief Lives*, ed. O. Dick (Ann Arbor, 1957), 150ff.
4 *Leviathan*, I, i.
5 'Human Nature,' I, vii.
6 Ibid., VI, i.
7 *Leviathan*, I, v.
8 Ibid., I, ii.

Hobbes is more interesting reading when he writes of the functions of the right hemisphere of the brain. First, the definition with which he begins the following is remarkably accurate.

> From the principal parts of Nature, Reason and Passion, have proceeded two kinds of learning, mathematical and dogmatical. The former is free from controversy and dispute, because it consists in comparing figure and motion only, in which things truth and the interest of men do not oppose each other. But in the other there is nothing undisputable, because it compares men, and meddles with their right and profit, in which, as often as reason is against a man, so often will a man be against reason.[9]

Whereas most early philosophers deal with the tendency of the passions to interfere with Reason as a moral problem, Hobbes focuses on another very accurate observation, that it is the emotional coloring provided by the right hemisphere, the general location of the emotions, which gives meaning to the vocabulary of the left hemisphere. His perspective on this is political eloquence and he discusses in several places the necessity for the orator to use passion to make his language effective. In one place he states that Instigation is to raise passion from opinion; Persuasion is to beget opinion from passion. Remarkably, he continues by observing that passion is what convinces. Truth does not matter.

> In raising an opinion from passion, any premises are good enough to enforce the desired conclusion; so, in raising passion from opinion, it is no matter whether the opinion be true or false, or the narration historical or fabulous; for, not the truth, but the image, makes passion. A tragedy well acted, affects no less than a murder.[10]

In another rather remarkable discussion of eloquence, Hobbes says the purpose of eloquence is to makes things other than as they are, according to the desires of the speaker.

> Speakers do not endeavor so much to fit their speech to the nature of things, as to the passions of the minds to whom they speak; whence it happens, that opinions are delivered not by right reason, but by a certain violence of mind. Nor is this fault in the man, but in the nature itself of eloquence, whose end, as all the masters of rhetoric teach us, is not truth (except by chance), but victory; and whose property is not to inform, but to allure.[11]

He no doubt saw the goal of this as reaching consensus, or as we would say in the arts, universality.

> For the faculty of speaking powerfully, consists in a habit acquired of putting together passionate words, and applying them to the present passions of the hearer.[12]

---

9 'Human Nature,' Dedication.
10 Ibid., XIII, vii.
11 *Philosophical Rudiments Concerning Government and Society*, X, xi. See also *Leviathan*, II, xxv.
12 *De Corpore Politico*, II, viii, §14.

On the Senses

Hobbes was one of the last philosophers who contended that much of the senses and emotions were centered in the heart. Therefore his physical explanation is rather complicated.

> The organs of sense … are found to be certain spirits and membranes, which, proceeding from the *pia mater*, involve the brain and all the nerves; also the brain itself, and the arteries which are in the brain; and such other parts, as being stirred, the heart also, which is the fountain of all sense, is stirred together with them. For whensoever the action of the object reaches the body of the sentient, that action is by some nerve propagated to the brain; and if the nerve leading thither be hurt or obstructed, that the motion can be propagated no further, no sense follows. Also if the motion be intercepted between the brain and the heart by the defect of the organ by which the action is propagated, there will be no perception.[13]

In another place his explanation is somewhat easier to read,

> Sense proceeds from the action of external objects upon the brain, or some internal substance of the head; and the passions proceed from the alteration there made, and continued to the heart.[14]

He contends that the senses work best one at a time. Study is 'a possession of the mind' by one of the senses, hence when we read we see the letters 'successively one by one.' Imagination is what is left after the object producing the sensory impression is no longer present.

Hearing, he says, is received in the tympanum of the ear, which has its own nerve leading directly to the heart.[15]

On the Psychology of Aesthetics

In Hobbes, the emotions and the concepts of Pleasure and Pain are all mixed in together with the senses and he makes little effort to separate them. He fails to deduce that the basic emotions are genetically universal, contending, 'They err, that say the idea of anything is universal.'[16] His distrust of the emotions is almost like that of one of the early Church fathers.

> All passions that produce strange and unusual behavior are called by the general name of madness.[17]

---

13 *Leviathan*, IV, xxv, §4. See also, *Elements of Philosophy*, IV, xxv, §2ff.
14 'Human Nature,' X, i.
15 *Elements of Philosophy*, IV, xxv, §10.
16 Ibid., v, §7.
17 *Leviathan*, I, viii.

Hobbes contends that all voluntary motions are caused by the emotions.[18] He thinks of these in terms of motion, those approaching called *appetite* and those retiring called *aversions*. It is under these labels that he organizes the emotions, those associated with appetite, such as love, are good; those associated with aversion are bad. When these emotions are caused by the senses, they may take on the additional labels of delight, or trouble of mind. Pleasure may therefore be called 'pleasure of sense.' Thus he concludes,

> Pleasures of the mind ... are generally called Joy.[19] In the like manner, displeasures are some in the sense, and called Pain.

For Hobbes the physical nature of pleasure and pain, which he regarded as also a sense, are closely related to the process by which he believed the senses worked.

> The sense of pleasure and pain, proceeds not from the reaction of the heart outwards, but from continual action from the outermost part of the organ towards the heart. For the origin of life being in the heart, that motion in the sentient, which is propagated to the heart, must necessarily make some alternation or diversion of vital motion, namely, by quickening or slackening, helping or hindering the same. Now when it helps, it is pleasure; and when it hinders, it is pain, trouble, grief, etc.[20]

In another discussion he writes,

> Conceptions are ideas which are really nothing but motion in some internal substance of the head. This motion, not stopping there, proceeds to the heart, [where] of necessity there must either help or hinder the motion which is called vital. When it helps it is called delight, contentment, or pleasure, which is nothing but the motion about the heart, as conception is nothing but motion in the head ... But when such motion weakens or hinders the vital motion, then it is called pain.[21]

Later he writes that 'motion and agitation of the brain we call conception' but when this is 'continued to the heart' it is called passion.[22]

---

18 Ibid., I, vi.

19 In another place ['Human Nature,' IX, xiii] he adds,

> There is a passion that has no name; but the sign of it is that distortion of the face which we call laughter, which is always joy.

20 *Elements of Philosophy*, IV, xxv, §12.

21 'Human Nature,' VII, i.

22 'Human Nature,' VIII, i.

On the Philosophy of Aesthetics

The only art form of which Hobbes engages in a discussion of aesthetics is poetry.[23] He begins by defining the purpose of poetry in general to be both for delight and for education.

> The poets, whose work it is, by imitating human life, in delightful and measured lines, to avert men from vice, and incline them to virtuous and honorable actions.

Next, Hobbes considers the basic types of poetry.

> There is neither more or less than six sorts of poesy. For the heroic poem narrative is called an *epic poem*; the heroic poem dramatic, is *tragedy*. The scommatic narrative is *satire*; dramatic is *comedy*. The pastoral narrative, is called simply *pastoral*, anciently *bucolic*; the same dramatic, *pastoral comedy* …
>
> They that take for poesy whatsoever is written in verse, will think this division imperfect, and call in sonnets, epigrams, eclogues, and the like pieces, which are but essays, and parts of an entire poem.

Hobbes briefly mentions the origin of poetry as being associated with the religion of the ancient Greeks. When they employed poetry for the praise of their gods, this was done,

> in holy songs called hymns; and the composers of them were called prophets and priests, before the name of poet was known.

The reason these early priests wrote in verse, he reminds the reader, was because their poetry was intended to be sung. This, he notes, is no longer the custom, although it has begun to be revived in recent years in Italy. Hobbes observes that some poets still continue the ancient tradition of dedicating their poems to one of the Muses, a practice to which he objects.

> But why a Christian should think it an ornament to his poem, either to profane the true God, or invoke a false one, I can imagine no cause, but a reasonless imitation of custom; of a foolish custom, by which a man enabled to speak wisely from the principles of nature, and his own meditation, loves rather to be thought to speak by inspiration,[24] like a bagpipe.

One of the great characteristics of poetry is what Hobbes calls *fancy*, or imagination, and this faculty of mind he finds responsible for the very progress of man.

> All that is beautiful or defensible in building; or marvelous in engines and instruments of motion; whatsoever commodity men receive from the observations of the heavens, from the description

---

[23] 'The Answer of Mr. Hobbes to Sir William Davenant's Preface before *Gondibert*,' in *The English Works of Thomas Hobbes*, ed. William Molesworth (London: Bohn, 1839), IV, 443ff.

[24] At this time in England, 'to inspire' was a synonym for 'to blow,' as in a musical instrument.

of the earth, from the account of time, from walking on the seas; and whatsoever distinguishes the civility of Europe, from the barbarity of the American savages; is the workmanship of fancy.

He also discusses the ancient aesthetic question on the relationship between Art and Nature.

For as truth is the boundary of the historical, so the resemblance of truth is the utmost limit of of poetical liberty. In old times amongst the heathen [the Greek poets], such strange fictions and metamorphoses were not so remote from the articles of their faith, as they are now from ours, and therefore were not so unpleasant. Beyond the actual works of nature a poet may now go; but beyond the conceived possibility of nature, never ...
  In him that professes the imitation of nature, as all poets do, what greater fault can there be, than to betray an ignorance of nature in his poem?

Hobbes discusses several aesthetic criteria for epic, or heroic, poems. The dialect should be that of the court, not 'of the inferior sort of people.' One must avoid such metaphors as would not occur to a gentleman and one must not represent great persons in 'cruelty, or the sordid vices of lust and drunkenness.' Finally, the poet must not write anything in an epic poem which produces too much laughter.

The delight of an epic poem consists not in mirth, but admiration. Mirth and laughter are proper to comedy and satire. Great persons, that have their minds employed on great designs, have not leisure enough to laugh.

On the Aesthetics of Music

In his classic work of philosophy, *The Leviathan*, Hobbes includes a chapter in which he attempts to organize all 'subjects of knowledge.'[25] In this organization there are implicit value judgments. It is no surprise he finds the subject of the study of sounds to be Music. It is unexpected and revealing, however, that he regards the subject of the study of passions to be Ethics!
  In another place he suggests that the listener does not find new appreciation, but rather a loss of interest in music when he hears it repeated. This may very well be, since he refers to its loss of 'force,' another hint that the art of improvisation was more interesting to the listener at this time than 'set,' or notated, music, a point we have seen expressed by other English writers.

The phrases of poesy, as the melodies of music, with often hearing become insipid; the reader having no more sense of their force, than our flesh is sensible of the bones that sustain it.[26]

---

25 *Leviathan*, I, ix.
26 'The Answer of Mr. Hobbes to Sir William Davenant's Preface before *Gondibert*,' in *The English Works of Thomas Hobbes*, IV, 455.

On the Perception of Music

Hobbes regarded sound as being in the mind, not in the instrument. For him, the proof of this was in the echo. He believed that if the sound we hear is in the instrument which produces it, it would not be possible to 'disconnect' the sound from its original source, as happens in an echo.

> Neither is sound in the thing we hear, but in ourselves. One manifest sign thereof is, that as a man may see, so he may hear double or treble, by multiplication of echoes, which echoes are sounds as well as the original; and not being in one and the same place, cannot be inherent in the body that makes them. Nothing can make anything which is not in itself; the clapper has no sound in it, but motion, and makes motion in the internal parts of the bell; so the bell has motion, and not sound, that imparts motion to the air; and the air has motion, but not sound; the air imparts motion by the ear and nerve unto the brain; and the brain has motion but not sound; from the brain, it rebounds back into the nerves outward, and thence it becomes an apparition [idea] without, which we call sound.[27]

When Hobbes discusses musical sounds, it is only at a rather primitive level, such as distinguishing strong and weak, high and low and clear and 'hoarse.'[28] Hoarse, he calls a 'whispering and hissing' he regards as being caused by an interruption in the air column, as in singing when the air 'in going out rakes the superficies of the lips.'

In his only real discussion of music, the reader is struck by the disinterest Hobbes has for a subject in which he was said to be 'addicted.'

> Concerning the delight of hearing, it is diverse, and the organ itself not affected thereby: simple sounds please by equality, as the sound of a bell or lute: insomuch as it seems, an equality continued by the percussion of the object upon the ear, is pleasure; the contrary is called harshness, such as is grating, and some other sounds, which do not always affect the body, but only sometime, and that with a kind of horror beginning at the teeth. Harmony, or many sounds together agreeing, please by the same reason as the unison, which is the sound of equal strings, equally stretched. Sounds that differ in any height, please by inequality and equality alternate, that is to say, the higher note strikes twice, for one stroke of the other, whereby they strike together every second time; as is well proved by Galileo, in his first dialogue concerning local motion: where he also shows, that two sounds differing a fifth, delight the ear by an equality of striking after two inequalities; for the higher note strikes the ear thrice, while the other strikes but twice. In like manner he shows wherein consists the pleasure of concord, and the displeasure of discord, in each difference of notes. There is yet another pleasure and displeasure of sounds, which consists in consequence of one note after another, diversified both by accent and measure; whereof that which pleases is called a melody; but for what reason one succession in tone and measure is a more pleasing tune than another, I confess I know not; but I conjecture the reason to be, for

---

27 'Human Nature,' II, ix.
28 *Elements of Philosophy*, IV, xxix, §1ff.

that some of them imitate and revive some passion which otherwise we take no notice of, and the other not; for no tune pleases but for a time, as neither does imitation.[29]

This last 'conjecture' is actually another brilliant intuitive insight by Hobbes. Modern clinical research suggests man is born with a genetically universal repertoire of melodic fragments, which in turn appear to have emotional meaning.

JOHN LOCKE (1632–1704)

John Locke studied ancient languages, rhetoric, logic and ethics at Oxford and eventually earned a degree in medicine. He held various government positions of largely clerical nature. This experience produced a philosopher who seemed only aware of the faculties of the left hemisphere of the brain. He wrote very little on the emotions, the individual senses or any of the arts. When discussing time, for example, unlike previous philosophers, music is never mentioned.

On the Physiology of Aesthetics

Locke goes to some length to contend that man is born with no innate ideas.[30] For him it was sufficient proof that there is no such thing as universal, genetic knowledge in the example one found no such things in children and idiots.[31] All knowledge, therefore, has its origin outside the mind.

> The senses at first let in particular ideas, and furnish the yet empty cabinet; and the mind by degrees growing familiar with some of them, they are lodged in the memory, and the names given to them: afterwards, the mind, proceeding farther, abstracts them, and by degrees learns the use of general names.[32]

Later he expands on this by maintaining that all ideas enter the mind either by the observation of the senses of external objects or by the reflection of the mind on previously gained sensory information.[33] He goes so far as to conclude,

---

29 'Human Nature,' VIII, 2.

30 'Essay on Human Understanding,' in *The Works of John Locke* (London, 1823; reprinted in Aalen: Scientia Verlag, 1963), I, ii, §1ff.

31 Ibid., I, ii, §5.

32 Ibid., I, ii, §15.

33 Ibid., II, i, §2ff. Again, he seems to have derived his conclusions largely from the learning process in children.

> The whole extent of our knowledge or imagination reaches not beyond our own ideas limited to our ways of perception.[34]

Since Locke has maintained that all knowledge arrives in the mind by way of the senses, he asks, 'What need is there for Reason?'[35]

> Very much; both for the enlargement of our knowledge, and regulating our assent: for it has to do both in knowledge and opinion, and is necessary and assisting to all our other intellectual faculties.

He finds Reason consists of four parts: discovery of truths, placing them in order and connection, perceiving their connection and making a correct conclusion. The errors in Reason he finds caused primarily by a lack of ideas or in the employment of wrong principles or doubtful terms, etc.

Nothing demonstrates so clearly the left-brain perspective of Locke as his discussion of language.[36] He defines the end of language as consisting of three things: to communicate to another person, to do so quickly and with ease and to convey knowledge of things. He seems completely unaware of the input of emotional tone by the right hemisphere of the brain, which in fact is largely responsible for meaning in spoken language. As the old observation goes, 'It is not what we say, but how we say it!'

When Locke considers perception, it pertains to the information of one of the senses and it is inseparable from the mind's concentration on that sense. While Locke not only knew nothing of the specific functions of the separate hemispheres of the brain, and was in addition the epitome of the left-brain man, it is interesting that he had observed that when one is 'intently employed' on some idea and there is music playing, one does not hear it.

> A sufficient impulse there may be on the organ; but if not reaching the observation of the mind, there follows no perception; and though the motion that uses to produce the idea of sound be made in the ear, yet no sound is heard.[37]

In his discussion of the senses, Locke contends that God purposely gave man limited ability in his senses.[38] By way of illustration he proposes that if our sense of hearing were a thousand times stronger we would be distracted by perpetual noise.

> We should in the quietest retirement be less able to sleep or meditate, than in the middle of a sea-fight.

---

34 Ibid., III, xi, §23.
35 Ibid., IV, xvii, §1ff.
36 Ibid., III, x, §23.
37 Ibid., II, ix, §4.
38 Ibid., II, xxiii, §12.

He was, however, one of the first philosophers who understood correctly the physics of sound.

> That which is conveyed into the brain by the ear is called sound; though, in truth, till it come to reach and affect the perceptive part, it be nothing by motion.
>
> The motion, which produces in us the perception of sound, is a vibration of the air, caused by an exceeding short, but quick, tremulous motion of the body from which it is propagated; and therefore we consider and denominate them as bodies sounding.
>
> That sound is the effect of such a short, brisk, vibrating motion of bodies form which it is propagated, may be known from what is observed and felt in the strings of instruments ... as long as we perceive any sound come from them; for as soon as that vibration is stopped, or ceases in them, the perception ceases also.[39]

On Education

Locke's treatise on education begins with a very lengthy discussion of manners in children. His basic philosophy was quite Spartan, to develop sufficient toughness to withstand the challenges of life. Children should not be allowed to wear hats, even in winter, their feet should be washed in cold water, etc. Indeed, he finds tenderness by the parents greatest danger to children.[40] Even crying he says 'is a fault that should not be tolerated in children.' If it can't be stopped by 'a look, or a positive command ... blows must.'[41]

Among the disciplines which Locke recommends for children is dancing, in fact, as soon as they are capable of learning it. The purpose of this has nothing to do with the art of dance, but only to develop 'manly thoughts and carriage.'[42] The only creativity he emphasizes is in recreation, which he contends should not be organized but left to the children to plan.

When Locke finally arrives at his recommendation for the actual course of study for children he begins with reading, which he says should begin as soon as the child can speak.[43] He does not endorse, however, having children read the Bible.

> For what pleasure or encouragement can it be to a child, to exercise himself in reading those parts of a book where he understands nothing?

---

39 'Elements of Natural Philosophy,' in *The Works of John Locke*, III, 325ff.

40 'Thoughts Concerning Education,' in Ibid., IX, 7ff.

41 Ibid., 102ff.

42 Ibid., 50. George Savile, Marquis of Halifax (1633–1695), a contemporary of Locke, in 'Advice to a Daughter,' warns ladies to remember the reason why they learned to dance in the first place, which was to acquire grace in movement. Reason beyond this will lead to rebuke.

> It is better for a woman never to dance, because she has no skill in it, than to do it too often, because she does it well. [See *The Complete Works of George Savile*, ed. Walter Raleigh (Oxford: Clarendon, 1912), 36]

43 Ibid., 142ff.

Next he recommends learning writing and, that which he seems to regard as closely related, drawing. Drawing is, of course, a right hemisphere function and unrelated to writing. Without his understanding this, it is interesting that Locke has nevertheless observed that in drawing a simple picture one can express more than in 'a whole sheet of paper in writing.'[44] He quickly adds that only a little instruction in drawing is enough.

> I do not mean that I would have your son a perfect painter; to be that to any tolerable degree, will require more time than a young gentleman can spare from his other improvements of greater moment.[45]

As soon as the child can speak English, Locke recommends languages, especially French and Latin. Here he also adds that the parent should not think of encouraging the child to become a poet, indeed for the parent to do so he says 'is to me the strangest thing in the world.'[46] Neither should the parent encourage wit in the child, for he may become a successful rhymer and then imagine 'what company and places he is likely to spend his time in, nay, and estate too.' Poetry, he concludes,

> is a pleasant air, but a barren soil; and there are very few instances of those who have added to their patrimony by anything they have reaped from thence. Poetry and gaming, which usually go together, are alike in this too, that they seldom bring any advantage, but to those who have nothing else to live on.

On the Psychology of Aesthetics

Locke associates Pleasure and Pain, generic names he gives to virtually all the emotions, with the ideas of the mind which are received by sensation or reflection.

> Delight or uneasiness, one or the other of them, join themselves to almost all our ideas, both of sensation and reflection: and there is scarce any affection of our senses from without, any retired

---

44 Ibid., 151.

45 In a letter to Edward Clarke (January 27, 1688), Locke writes that he himself would have liked to have been a painter, were it not for the same objections, and the fact that 'all the time, pains, and money shall be ... thrown away to no purpose.'

George Savile also makes some curious judgments on education, among them we find:

> Many aspire to learn what they can never comprehend, as others pretend to teach what they themselves do not know.
>
> The vanity of teaching often tempts a man to forget he is a blockhead.
>
> A little learning misleads, and a great deal often stupefies the understanding.

[See 'Moral Thoughts and Reflections,' in *The Complete Works of George Savile*, 240, 242]

46 Ibid., 167.

thought of our mind within, which is not able to produce in us pleasure or pain. By pleasure and pain I would be understood to signify whatsoever delights or molests us most; whether it arises from the thoughts of our minds, or anything operating on our bodies.[47]

Locke seemed to correctly understand that the pleasure or pain we associate with the body is in fact 'the thought or perception of the mind.'[48] In a significant departure from old church dogma, he refuses to accept that they are good or evil in themselves.

> Things then are good or evil only in reference to pleasure or pain. That we call good, [is that] which is apt to cause or increase pleasure or diminish pain in us.

It is in this context that he introduces the emotions.

> Pleasure and pain, and that which causes them, good and evil, are the hinges on which our passions turn: and if we reflect on ourselves, and observe how these, under various considerations, operate in us, what modifications or tempers of mind, what internal sensations they produce in us, we may thence form to ourselves the ideas of our passions.

Thus, for example, he defines Joy as 'a delight of the mind from the consideration of the present or assured approaching possession of a good.'

On the Aesthetics of Music

Rarely has there been a philosopher who so completely failed to appreciate music. His most extensive explanation of his disinterest is found in his treatise on education.[49]

> Music is thought to have some affinity with dancing, and a good hand, upon some instruments, is by many people mightily valued. But it wastes so much of a young man's time, to gain but a moderate skill in it, and engages often in such odd company, that many think it much better spared: and I have, amongst men of parts and business, so seldom heard any one commended or esteemed for having an excellency in music, that amongst all those things, that ever came into the list of accomplishments, I think I may give it the last place.

He makes an identical assessment in a letter to Edward Clarke in 1686.

> Musique—I find by some mightily valued but it wastes so much of one's time to gain but a moderate skill in it and engages in such odd company that I think it much better spared. And

---

47 'Essay on Human Understanding,' II, vii, §1ff.
48 Ibid., II, xx, §1ff.
49 'Thoughts Concerning Education,' in *The Works of John Locke*, IX, 191.

amongst all those things that ever come into the list of accomplishments I give it next to Poetry the last place.⁵⁰

Locke makes only one observation touching with the perception of music and again the emphasis is on the external, sound, which becomes an impression in the mind.

> Sounds also ... are modified by diversity of notes of different length put together, which make that complex idea called a tune, which a musician may have in his mind when he hears or makes no sound at all, by reflecting on the ideas of those sounds so put together silently in his own fancy.⁵¹

The only reference Locke makes to the purpose of music comes in his correspondence. In a letter to Lady Calverley, in 1689, Locke, in describing local activities which might be of interest to the Lady, mentions concerts [*Musick meetings*] which he associates with those entertainments of 'pleasure and delight.'⁵² The only other reference to the purpose of music is found in a letter to an unknown correspondent, where Locke says of a lady friend that she 'pleases herself with her own harmony and sings away her anger.'⁵³

The only reports of actual performances recalled by Locke were of church music. In a letter to John Strachey, written in December 1665, Locke describes church music he heard while traveling in Germany.

> I went to the Lutheran church, I found them all merrily singing with their hats on. So that by the posture they were in and the fashion of the building, not altogether unlike a theater, I was ready to fear that I had mistook the place. I thought they had met only to exercise their voices, for after a long stay they still continued on their melody, and I verily believe they sung the 119th psalm, nothing else could be so long, that [which] made it a little tolerable was that they sing better than we do in our churches and are assisted by an organ.⁵⁴

In another letter to the same correspondent during this trip, Locke describes the music of a Christmas service in a Catholic church in Germany, the Stiftskirche in Cleves. He begins the letter describing a pageant given in the church.

> This was the show: the Musick to it was all vocal in the choir adjoining: but such as I never heard. They had strong voices, but so ill-tuned, so ill-managed, that it was their misfortune as well as ours, that they could be heard. He that could not, though he had a cold, make better Musick with *Chevy Chase* over a pot of smooth ale deserved well to pay the reckoning and go away [with] a thirst. However I think they were the most honest singing men, I ever have

---

50 Quoted in *The Correspondence of John Locke*, ed. E. S. De Beer (Oxford: Clarendon, 1976), II, 782.
51 'Essay on Human Understanding,' II, xviii, §3.
52 *The Correspondence of John Locke*, III, 615.
53 Ibid., I, 21.
54 Ibid., I, 236.

seen, for they endeavored to deserve their money, and earned it certainly with pains enough: for what they lacked in skill, they made up in loudness, and variety, everyone had his own tune, and the result of all was much like the noise at Parliament, where everyone endeavors to cry loudest. Besides the men there were a company of little choristers. I thought when I saw them at first, they had danced to the others Musick ... for they were jumping up and down about a good charcoal fire, that was in the middle of the Choir ... But it was not dancing, but singing they served for; when it came to their turns, away they ran to their places, and there they made as good harmony as a consort of little pigs.[55]

ISAAC NEWTON (1642–1727)

Isaac Newton was, without any doubt, the greatest mind ever born to England. He was truly a natural scientist, interested in everything which passed his eye. While all the world knows of his immense contributions to optics and gravitation, one is staggered at the thought of the time he spent on less productive efforts. The rough estimate based on one sale catalog, the Portsmouth Collection, Cambridge, indicates a million and a half words on theology and chronology; half a million on alchemy and one hundred and fifty thousand words on problems of coinage and the Mint. And he also wrote on mathematics, chemistry, astronomy and of course philosophy. It is comforting to read he was a poor student in school.

On Education

No doubt due in part to his own unsatisfactory experience in school, Newton wrote a brief treatise, 'Of Educating Youth in the Universities,' although the work was left unpublished during his lifetime. It is of interest to read here what an ideal university curriculum was to Newton, and also to discover him still listing music as a subject to be taught by the mathematics professor!

> Undergraduate students are to be instructed by tutors in Humanities, Greek, Philosophy, Mathematics and a tutor to read Logic, Ethics, the Globes, principles of Geography and Chronology in order to understand History.
> The humanities and Greek lecturers are to set tasks in Latin and Greek writers once a day for the first-year students, and once a week for the rest, and to examine diligently, instruct briefly and punish by further exercises such faults as concern the lecturers.
> The philosophy lecturer is to read first those introductory principles of natural philosophy, time, space, body, place, motion and its laws, force, mechanical powers, gravity and its laws, hydrostatics, projectiles solid and fluid, circular motions and the forces relating to them. This is followed by natural philosophy beginning with the general system of the world and then

---

55   Ibid., I, 244ff.

> proceeding to the particular constitution of this earth and the things therein, meteors, elements, minerals, vegetables, animals, and ending with anatomy, if he has skills therein. He is also to examine in Logic and Ethics.
>
> The mathematics lecturer is to first read easy and useful practical things, then Euclid, spheres, projections of the sphere, the construction of maps, trigonometry, astronomy, optics, music, algebra, etc.[56]

Newton cautions the professors to assign major reading assignments during the vacation breaks and examine the students upon their return. He also recommends that the lecturers be given only three-year appointments and that they, in turn, elect their administrators. 'No regard to Seniority or anything but merit.'

Regarding student life, Newton recommends that religious periods of fasting should, in so far as the students are concerned, 'have a shadow of religion without any substance.' Otherwise the students are forced to seek their meals outside the campus, where they will be tempted to get in trouble.

> This does great mischief by sending young students to find suppers abroad where they get into company and grow debauched.

Finally, in Newton's view, the influence of the campus should extend even to the alumni!

> All Graduates without exception found by the Proctors in Taverns or other drinking houses, unless with travelers at their Inns, shall at least have their names given in to the Vice-Chancellor who shall summon them to answer for it before the next Consistory.

On the Aesthetics of Music

Newton's earliest scientific interest in music lay in the mathematical division of the octave, a subject which first appears in a notebook from his college days. The reader must remember that the modern system of tuning became only generally known during Newton's lifetime, replacing several tuning systems which all differed in their calculation of the whole and half-steps, as these intervals are not consistent in the overtone series. Thus in this early notebook, dating ca. 1665, one finds a study of the modes, as well as a logarithmic comparison of a scale divided into twelve equal parts with an equally tempered one.

Newton mentions in a letter to John Collins in February 1670, that he had been working on a system using logarithms to express the relationships between the tones of the scale.

---

56 Quoted in *Unpublished Scientific Papers of Isaac Newton*, ed. A. Rupert Hall (Cambridge: University Press, 1962), 369ff. Newton's manuscript is largely in the form of notes and incomplete sentences, which, for ease in reading, we have edited.

> In finding the aggregate of the terms of a musical progression there is one way by logarithms very obvious (by subducting the logarithm of each denominator from that of the numerator, etc.) which I supposed to be the ordinary way in practice.[57]

Less than two weeks later, he writes the same correspondent announcing that he sees yet another system of applying logarithms to the scale, 'but the calculations for finding out those rules would be still more troublesome.'[58]

Collins was also working in this direction and during the Spring had sent his system to Newton. Newton writes a diplomatic rejection in July, reading,

> Something I have yet to say and that's about your paper concerning the aggregate of the terms of a musical progression: Namely your way deduced from Mercators squaring of the Hyperbola is the same with the last of those two I had sent you together before. Only I had taken a great deal of pains to bring it to such a form as might be most convenient for practice and so had made it so intricate as to other respects that it is no wonder if you did not discern its fountain or by what method I had composed it. I beg your pardon therefore for that obscurity.[59]

Collins perhaps still failed to understand, for the following December, he writes to another colleague complaining of Newton,

> After I had sent him what I had to say about the musical progression he sent me word he had completed that problem, but neither promised nor has as yet communicated how.[60]

One of Newton's great contributions to science, and to optics in particular, was his paper of 1672, 'New Theory about Light and Colors.' Always hesitant to publish, this paper formulated his discovery in 1666 that sunlight is not a simple white, but a compound of red, orange, yellow, green, blue, indigo and violet, which emerge when light is passed through a prism. Always, by his own nature, looking for fundamental laws, Newton was at the same time obsessed with finding a correspondence between the rays of light and the vibrations of sound. His earliest extant, and most complete, discussion of this is found in a letter of 7 December 1675, to Henry Oldenburg, secretary of the Royal Society.[61]

> Thus much of refraction, reflection, transparency & opacity. And now to explain colors; I suppose, that as bodies of various sizes, densities, or tensions, do by percussion or other action excite sounds of various tones & consequently vibrations in the Air of various bigness so when the rays of light, by impinging on the stiff refracting superficies excite vibrations in the aether, those rays, whatever they be, as they happen to differ in magnitude, strength or vigor, excite

---

57 *The Correspondence of Isaac Newton,* ed. H. W. Turnbull (Cambridge: University Press, 1959), I, 24.
58 Ibid., I, 27.
59 Ibid., I, 31.
60 Ibid., I, 55.
61 Ibid., I, 376ff.

vibrations of various bigness; the biggest, strongest or most potent rays, the largest vibrations & others shorter, according to their bigness strength or power.

After an explanation of the physical process of the eye, Newton continues,

and there I suppose, affect the sense with various colors, reds & yellows; the least with the weakest, blues & violets; the middle with green, and a confusion of all, with white, much after the manner, that in the sense of hearing Nature makes use of aërial vibrations of several bignesses to generate sounds of diverse tones, for the analogy of Nature is to be observed. And further, as the harmony & discord of sounds proceed from the proportions of the aereall vibrations; so may the harmony of some colors, as of a golden & blue, & the discord of others, as of red & blue proceed from the proportions of the aethereall. And possible color may be distinguished into its principal degrees, red, orange, yellow, green, blue, indigo, and deep violet, on the same ground, that sound within an eighth is graduated into tones.

With this letter, Newton enclosed a graph,[62] showing the correlation of the basic colors with relative notes of music. Regrettably, although he discusses in detail the relationships of the colors relative to this graph, he does not offer here a precise description of their correspondence to music. Nevertheless, Newton remained interested in this topic and he discusses it again in the publication of his *Opticks* in 1704.[63] Whatever was Newton's private understanding on this subject we are left in some doubt. To his correspondents who wanted more information, he would sometimes apologize that with regard to music, 'I have not so much skill in that science as to understand it well.'[64]

From his studies of optics, Newton had made important discoveries relative to light waves, establishing their speed and that they moved in straight lines. We may assume that he was at least casually thinking of the correspondence of these laws with musical sound waves as well, or so a letter to John North in 1677 suggests.[65] North had sent Newton a new treatise on music by his elder brother, Francis, for review and Newton makes extensive corrections regarding the nature and direction of sound waves, as well as on the relationships between vibrating strings. At length, Newton evidently tired and signed off.

The discourse also about breaking of tones into higher notes seems very ingenious and judicious, but I lack experience to discern whether altogether solid, & much follows about Tunes, the scale of Music, & consorts; this requiring a combination of musical & mathematical skill, & therefore I shall content myself with having thus far animadverted upon the author.

---

62 Reproduced in Ibid., I, 377.

63 See *Opticks*, Book I, Part ii, Prop. 3 and in Book II, Part i, Ops. 14, and in Part iii, Prop. 16. Newton refers to the correspondence between music and light waves again in a letter to Dr. William Briggs in April 1685. [Ibid., II, 418].

64 Letter, February 1676, to Oldenburg regarding a 'Mr. Berchhenshaw's scale of Musick,' in Ibid., I, 420.

65 Ibid., II, 205ff. John and Francis were brothers to Roger North, whom we have treated separately.

A letter to Oldenburg in June 1672 is concerned with Newton's answering objections by Robert Hooke to some of his theories. One sentence is of particular interest, as it demonstrates that Newton correctly understood that music is in the vibrations, not in the instrument or the ear—a topic still much under discussion by some writers.

> But when Mr. Hooke would insinuate a difficulty in these things by alluding to sounds in the *string* of a musical instrument before percussion, or in the *Air* of an *Organ bellows* before its arrival at the pipes, I must confess I understand it as little as if he had spoken of light in a piece of wood before it be set on fire.[66]

Newton's correspondence reveals his interest in other topics related to music and sound. An early letter of 1669 informs an unknown friend,

> Another useful instrument lately invented here, is Sir Samuel Morelands loud speaking Trumpett, of which he has written a book or history with the title *Tuba Stentorophonica*, value one shilling, by which persons may discourse at about a mile and a half distance, if not more.[67]

And in yet another letter, Newton reveals he has received a request for information about an ear-trumpet for the deaf.[68] Newton mentions such a device made 'after the form of Mr. Mace's Otocoustion,' draws a picture of it, reports it comes in several sizes and that he has heard, 'the biggest do ye best.'

WILLIAM PENN (1633–1718)

William Penn, the son of the admiral who had captured Jamaica for England, attended Oxford but was expelled for refusing to attend Anglican services in 1661. Returning home, his father whipped him and threw him out of the house for good. All this contributed to his becoming one of the most strict and fervent of the Quaker preachers. His preaching led to a famous trial in 1669 in which the jury acquitted him and the judge imprisoned the jury for doing so! In 1677 he traveled to America to help bring Quakerism to the new continent and one of the states still carries his name.

---

66 Ibid., I, 177.
67 Ibid., I, 5. Such a megaphone was used in the French navy until well into the nineteenth century.
68 Ibid., I, 359.

On the Physiology of Aesthetics

Nearly all the writings of Penn are those of a 'hell and brimstone' preacher, indeed, reading him is to read the history of the Protestant movement in America. Needless to say, the topics we have been following in these volumes are not germane to his. Only in a comment in passing, or in his maxims, are we able to gain some hint of his thoughts on subjects which are not immediately related to religion. On a topic such as Reason, he is naturally similar to the ancient Church fathers, as two maxims illustrate.

> A reasonable opinion must ever be in danger, where reason is not the judge.
> ......
>
> Reason, like the sun, is common to all: and it is for want of examining all by the same light and measure, that we are not all of the same mind.[69]

His only reflection on the senses is closely related.

> The satisfaction of our senses is low, short, and transient: but the mind gives a more raised and extended pleasure, and is capable of an happiness founded upon reason; and bounded and limited by the circumstances that bodies are confined to.[70]

On Education

Penn is somewhat more expansive on the subject of education, although again like an old Church philosopher, he first questions the need for too much knowledge. In his sermon, 'No Cross, no Crown,' Penn lists four things 'the consequences of which have brought an equal misery to its evil.' The first of these which he gives is, 'an inordinate pursuit of knowledge.'[71]

In his autobiography, Penn briefly discusses education, recommending only the most functional subjects.

> I recommend the useful parts of mathematics, as building houses or ships, measuring, surveying, dialing, navigation, etc., but agriculture is especially in my eye: let my children be husbandmen and housewives; it is industrious, healthy, honest, and of good example ... and diverts the mind from being taken up with the vain arts and inventions of a luxurious world.[72]

---

69 'Maxims,' in *The Select Works of William Penn* (London: William Phillips, 1825), III, 405.
70 Ibid., III, 363.
71 'No Cross, no Crown,' in Ibid., I, 388.
72 Ibid., I, 56ff.

These same values in education he repeats in his maxims, emphasizing the practical, the natural, and even the creative, all before the academic.

> The first thing obvious to children, is what is sensible; and that we make no part of their rudiments.
>
> ......
>
> We press their memory too soon, and puzzle, strain and load them with words and rules; to know grammar and rhetoric, and a strange tongue or two, that it is ten to one may never be useful to them.
>
> ......
>
> Children had rather be making of tools, and instruments of play; shaping, drawing, framing, and building, than getting some rules of propriety of speech by heart.
>
> ......
>
> It were happy if we studied nature more in natural things; and acted according to nature; whose rules are few, plain, and most reasonable.[73]

On the Psychology of Aesthetics

Penn's only reference to the emotions, outside of the negative associations with religious beliefs, is found in another maxim dealing with the rearing of children.

> We are too apt to awaken and tune up their passions by the example of our own; and to teach them to be pleased, not with what is best, but with what pleases best.[74]

On the Philosophy of Aesthetics

Penn's only reference to art, in the sense of the fine arts, is also centered in the practical, in practice rather than the 'speculative.'

> Art is good, where it is beneficial. Socrates wisely bounded his knowledge and instruction by practice.[75]

Curiously, Penn devotes more space to applause, which we must assume is due to religious concerns with pride and humility.

---

73 'Maxims,' in Ibid., III, 354.
74 Ibid., III, 370.
75 Ibid., III, 371.

> As there is no passion in us sooner moved, or more deceivable, so for that reason there is none over which we ought to be more watchful, whether we give or receive it: for if we give it, we must be sure to mean it, and measure it too.
>
> ......
>
> It is much easier for him to merit applause, than hear of it: and he never doubts himself more, or the person that gives it, than when he hears so much of it.[76]

One reads among the more severe philosophers of seventeenth-century England that the only good purpose of dance is to instruct one in proper carriage. Penn cannot see even this value. He speaks of the 'fantastic dancing-masters' and criticizes parents who pay money for their children to learn to dance, and then wonders,

> And what is this behavior, but fantastic, cramp postures, and cringings, unnatural to their shape, and if it were not fashionable, ridiculous to the view of all people.[77]

On the Aesthetics of Music

In the few references to music in his sermons, Penn's view is invariably negative. He avoids entirely the innumerable instances of praise for music in the Old Testament. In a typical passage, which he based on Amos 6:4–5, Penn warns,

> Woe unto you Protestants ... that chant to the sound of music of the viol, and invent to yourselves instruments of music.[78]

He includes music again in a list of luxuries not appropriate to a Christian, and he considers all of them 'an excessive indulgence of self in ease and pleasure ... A disease as epidemical as killing: it creeps into all stations and ranks of men.'[79]

> Sumptuous apparel, rich unguents, delicate washes, stately furniture, costly cookery, and such diversions as balls, masques, concerts [*music-meetings*], plays, romances, etc., which are the delight and entertainment of the times, belong not to the holy path that Jesus and his true disciples and followers trod to glory.

---

76 Ibid., III, 401.

77 'No Cross, no Crown,' in Ibid., I, 409.

78 'Truth Exalted,' in Ibid., I, 122. He makes the same point in 'No Cross, no Crown,' Ibid., I, 456. Amos 6: 4, 5 reads,
>   Woe to those who lie upon beds of ivory ...
>   who sing idle songs to the sound of the harp,
>   and like David invent for themselves instruments of music.

79 'No Cross, no Crown,' in Ibid., I, 454ff.

Later in this sermon, Penn promises condemnation for those who attend such diversions.

> There is but little need to drive away that, by foolish divertissements, which flies away so swiftly of itself; and when once gone, is never to be recalled. Plays,[80] parks, balls, treats, romances, musics, love sonnets, and the like, will be a very invalid plea for any other purpose than their condemnation, who are taken and delighted with them.[81]

Needless to say, Penn never described in his publications any specific musical performance he may have heard in England. In fact, the only such description is found in a publication describing his impressions of the new world. Penn includes a brief description of the music of the Indians, as part of what he calls their worship service.

> The other part is their cantico, performed by round dances, sometimes words, sometimes songs, then shouts, two being in the middle that begin, and by singing and drumming on a board, direct the chorus: their postures in the dance are very antic, and differing, but all keep measure. This is done with equal earnestness and labor, but great appearance of joy.[82]

DAVID HUME (1711–1776)

David Hume, born into a Scottish Presbyterian family, studied at the University of Edinburgh, but left before graduation to pursue philosophy and indeed wrote his great *Treatise on Human Nature* at age twenty-six. He tried law briefly, but found it 'nauseous.' He traveled and worked at various jobs, never quite having a career although he became one of the great representatives of the Enlightenment in philosophy. He knocked the foundation out from under Christianity, not to mention traditional metaphysics, of which he said 'commit it to the flames, for it is nothing but sophistry and illusion.'[83]

---

80 In this same sermon, in Ibid., 482ff, Penn attacks plays for their 'profane babblings and fabulous stories,' rejects the argument that anything can be learned from plays and pronounces them fit only for Heathens.

81 Ibid., 469.

82 'A General Description of Pennsilvania,' in Ibid., III, 230.

83 Josiah Royce, *The Spirit of Modern Philosophy* (Boston, 1892), 98. He also breaks with all previous philosophy by declaring that animals are endowed with thought and reason. Earlier philosophy had considered this the primary distinction between man and animals.

On the Physiology of Aesthetics

Hume begins much like Locke, but what Locke thought of as the sensory observation of external objects, Hume expands to include 'all our sensations, passions and emotions.'[84] Like Locke, the remaining part of understanding involved the mind's reflection on these products of the senses. In summary, Hume inadvertently touches on the true essence of our understanding, a brain hemisphere for thinking and another for feeling.

> I believe it will not be very necessary to employ many words in explaining this distinction. Everyone of himself will readily perceive the difference between feeling and thinking.

The terms Hume prefers for the above distinction are Sensation and Reflection.

How exactly sensory information is recorded in the soul, he is unsure.[85] But once there, a 'copy' of this impression is made and this he calls an 'idea.' If one would vary this idea, it can be done only through increasing or diminishing its force and vivacity. Any other kind of change must necessitate a different impression.[86]

Whereas earlier philosophers had always treated the senses as a kind of tool of Reason, Hume, while assigning them importance in gathering the materials for 'ideas,' nevertheless, makes a remarkable departure.

> As to those impressions, which arise from the senses, their ultimate cause is, in my opinion, perfectly inexplicable by human reason, and it will always be impossible to decide with certainty, whether they arise immediately from the object, or are produced by the creative power of the mind, or are derived from [God].[87]

With respect to his study of human nature, he says, this question is not in any way material to it. No sensory impression by itself ever implies the existence of any other impression or object. This, he says, happens only through experience.[88]

---

84 *A Treatise of Human Nature*, I, i, §1.

85 Ibid., I, i, §2. We find it curious that the English were still speaking of the 'soul' as a physical entity. Richard Bentley (1662–1742) was more specific, believing all sensation was experienced not in the brain, nor in the body, but in the 'soul.' [See *The Works of Richard Bentley, D. D.*, ed. Alexander Dyce (London: MacPherson, 1838), III, 39ff, 46] How could Bentley, master of Trinity College, personal friend of Newton and Locke, and author of a dissertation on the *Epistles of Phalaris*, which is certainly one of the most extraordinary, scholarly books ever written, believe, 'It cannot be the brain which imagines those qualities to be in itself.' And how could such a brilliant intellectual admit 'we cannot conceive the manner of the soul's action and passion,' and therefore offer only a weak negative proof for his contention?

> ... at least of such as are proved from the impossibility or absurdity of the contrary, a way of proof that is allowed for infallible demonstration.

86 Ibid., I, iii, §7.

87 Ibid., I, iii, §4.

88 Ibid., I, iii, §6.

Hume, like all earlier philosophers, speculated from the perspective that man had, as we might say today, only a left hemisphere of the brain. Early philosophy, therefore is impressive in so far as it deals with the province of the left hemisphere. But, when early philosophers tried to explain the qualities of the right hemisphere in terms of left hemisphere function, they are often simply wrong. Hume, for example, was very taken by an idea he credited to Berkeley that general ideas are only a series of individual ideas.[89] Hume concludes therefore that we cannot understand general concepts other than by first understanding the individual constituent parts. But this is not true for the right hemisphere, whose holistic skill permits us to see, and understand, a large painting without any attention, initially, to individual detail. And most listeners listen to and 'understand' music with no awareness of the grammar of music at all!

A similar error involves the perception of music. Hume contends that when you hear five successive notes played by a flute, you receive five impressions—they do not 'add up' to a sixth perception.[90] But we know today the there are certain genetic and universal emotional qualities which accompany the succession of pitches. It is more probable that every succession of five pitches carries one or more impressions beyond those of the individual notes. Hume appears to fear he may be on thin ice here for he qualifies his contention by saying there are no additional impressions, 'unless nature has so framed its faculties that it feels some new original impression arise from such a contemplation.'

But there are other problems in Hume's reasoning, based on contemporary lack of understanding of the function of the two hemispheres of the brain. One has to do with the nature of self-identity. We know today that the information in the left hemisphere is primarily spectator information, something we have read or been told. The information we hold in this hemisphere we share with everyone—two plus two is four to all men. It is in the experiential right hemisphere of the brain that we have identity as individuals, if we mean by self-identity that we differ from other people. Writing as if we consisted only of a left brain, Hume had a problem with self-identity, for he wanted to describe it in left brain language. Indeed, he concluded,

> The identity, which we ascribe to the mind of man, is only a fictitious one, and of a like kind with that which we ascribe to vegetables.[91]

Given the separate specialities of the two hemispheres, and their general preference to attack problems separately rather than as an equal partnership, man is often torn between thinking and feeling. Although, of course, Hume knew nothing of the medical facts, it is remarkable that he so clearly understood this separateness from purely an intuitive basis. The following is quite extraordinary for his time.

---

89 Ibid., I, i, §6 and I, iv, §2..
90 Ibid., I, ii, §3.
91 Ibid., I, iv, §6.

> All our reasonings concerning causes and effects are derived from nothing but custom; and that belief is more properly an act of the sensitive, than of the cogitative part of our natures.[92]

In another place he writes,

> Reason alone can never be a motive to any action of the will; and secondly, it can never oppose passion in the direction of the will ...
> Nothing can oppose or retard the impulse of passion, but a contrary impulse.[93]

He is also quite correct, in this section, when he concludes 'Reason exerts itself without producing any sensible emotion.' The principal role he assigns Reason is one primarily of identification, thus he finds seven forms of its activity: resemblance, identity, relations of time and place, proportion in quantity or number, degrees in any quality, contrariety and causation.[94]

The mind of Hume was racing far ahead of contemporary thought in the universities and it is no wonder he doubted their currency, as he mentions in a discussion of education in ancient Greece.

> Education had then a mighty influence over the minds of men, and was almost equal in force to those suggestions of the senses and common understanding, by which the most determined skeptic must allow himself to be governed. But at present, when the influence of education is much diminished ...[95]

On the Psychology of Aesthetics

Hume raises the entire subject of the emotions to a higher level than any former philosopher, even going so far as to make feeling dominant over ideas. No one had ever before written anything so extraordinary as the following.

> All probable reasoning is nothing but a species of sensation. It is not solely in poetry and music, we must follow our taste and sentiment, but likewise in philosophy. When I am convinced of any principle, it is only an idea, which strikes more strongly upon me. When I give the preference to one set of arguments above another, I do nothing but decide from my feeling concerning the superiority of their influence.[96]

---

92 Ibid., I, iv, §1.
93 Ibid., II, iii, §3.
94 Ibid., I, iii, §1.
95 'Dialogues Concerning Natural Religion,' Part I.
96 *A Treatise of Human Nature*, I, iii, §8.

By deciding from his feelings, Hume means the awareness of experience, by which he also means 'belief.' This, he says, is 'almost absolutely requisite to the exciting of our passions.'[97] Thus, he says, the coward is always afraid of everything and,

> a person of a sorrowful and melancholy disposition is very credulous of everything, that nourishes his prevailing passion.

Hume seemed to also be aware of the universality of the basic emotions.

> The minds of all men are similar in their feelings and operations; nor can any one be actuated by an affection, of which all others are not, in some degree, susceptible.[98]

In attempting to analyze the operation of the emotions, Hume begins with his division of human understanding into impressions (or sensation) and ideas (or reflections). Impressions he subdivides into original, which are the senses, and secondary, which are the passions.[99] The latter Hume further subdivides into calm and violent. But every emotion or passion has its own range of intensity.

> Of the first kind is the sense of beauty and deformity in action, composition, and external objects. Of the second are the passions of love and hatred, grief and joy, pride and humility. This division is far from being exact. The raptures of poetry and music frequently rise to the greatest height; while those other impressions, properly called passions, may decay into so soft an emotion, as to become, in a manner, imperceptible. But as in general the passions are more violent than the emotions arising from beauty and deformity.

Hume finds some passions occur as a single idea in the mind, but most are associated with additional emotions. For example, he says disappointment can give rise to anger, anger to envy and envy to malice. This suggests that man experiences a flood of near-simultaneous emotions, which Hume accounts for as follows.

> It is difficult for the mind, when actuated by any passion, to confine itself to that passion alone, without any change or variation. Human nature is too inconstant to admit of any such regularity. Changeableness is essential to it. And to what can it so naturally change as to affections or emotions, which are suitable to the temper, and agree with that set of passions, which then prevail?[100]

---

97 Ibid., I, iii, §10.
98 Ibid., III, iii, §1.
99 Ibid., II, i, §1. Like most early philosophers, Hume did not realize that pains in the body are not actually felt there, but rather in the brain.
100 Ibid., II, i, §5.

Curiously, Hume himself is sometimes inconstant. In another place, for example, he writes, 'every cause of that passion must be in some measure *constant*, and hold some proportion to the duration of ourself, which is its object.'[101]

Hume has observed, through studies in anatomy, that nerves from the nose and palate 'are so disposed ... to convey such peculiar sensation to the mind.'[102] It is clear to him, therefore, the emotions are experienced in the brain. But, knowing the mind only in its left hemisphere nature, as we would say today, his subsequent discussion becomes rather convoluted, as he attempts to discuss emotions in left brain terms, such as cause and effect, etc.

With regard to Pleasure and Pain, Hume also recognizes a genetic universality at work.

> There is implanted in the human mind a perception of pain and pleasure, as the chief spring and moving principle of all its actions.[103]

He goes on to distinguish between pleasure or pain caused from direct feeling and that contained in memory or an idea. The former, he notes, is always the stronger.[104] In another place, he contends pleasure is heightened if the memory is fresh, or if it is a pleasure which is suitable to our way of life.[105]

Above all, Hume found the concept of Pleasure and Pain, the emotions and basic moral definitions all interrelated. 'Everything related to us,' he writes, 'which produces pleasure or pain, produces likewise pride or humility.'[106] Later he contends that pleasure and pain are the 'primary causes' of vice and virtue, which also produce pride and humility as 'unavoidable attendants.'[107]

> It is easy to observe, that the passions, both direct and indirect, are founded on pain and pleasure, and that in order to produce an affection of any kind, it is only requisite to present some good or evil. Upon the removal of pain and pleasure, there immediately follows a removal of love and hatred, pride and humility, desire and aversion, and of most of our reflective or secondary impressions ...
>
> The mind by an *original* instinct tends to unite itself with the good, and to avoid the evil.[108]

---

101 Ibid., II, i, §9.

102 Ibid., II, I, §5.

103 Ibid., I, iii, §10.

104 Ibid., I, iii, §10.

105 Ibid., II, iii, §7.

106 Ibid., II, i, §6.

107 Ibid., II, i, §7.

108 Ibid., II, iii, §9.

On the Philosophy of Aesthetics

On Beauty

Hume states that beauty is not found in the object, but rather in the pleasure in viewing it, 'merely a passion or impression in the soul.'[109] In another place, Hume contends that beauty is enhanced if the art object is also useful.[110] In his essay, 'Of the Standard of Taste,' Hume argues that even if an art work is specifically intended to produce pleasure through beauty, it often will not happen because the viewer lacks 'that delicacy of imagination.'[111] In this discussion he also offers his recommendations for developing this delicacy of imagination. The first is that one will improve one's ability to judge an art form if one actually practices that art.

> But allow him to acquire experience in those objects, his feeling becomes more exact and nice. He not only perceives the beauties and defects of each part, but marks the distinguishing species of each quality, and assigns it suitable praise or blame.

Secondly, one can improve one's judgment by not one, but repeated, viewing of the particular art work. The first time we view it the relationship of the parts is not clear, the characteristics of the style are barely distinguished, etc. And finally, one learns by comparison with similar art works.

> The coarsest daubing contains a certain luster of colors and exactness of imitation, which are so far beauties, and would affect the mind of a peasant or Indian with the highest admiration. The most vulgar ballads are not entirely destitute of harmony or nature; and none but a person familiarized to superior beauties, would pronounce their numbers harsh, or narration uninteresting.

Finally, he observes,

> Many men, when left to themselves, have but a faint and dubious perception of beauty, who yet are capable of relishing any fine stroke, which is pointed out to them.

---

109 Ibid., II, i, §8.
110 Ibid., III, iii, §1.
111 'On the Standard of Taste,' in *David Hume, The Philosophical Works* (Aalen: Scientia Verlag, 1964 reprint), III, 272ff.

On Universality

Because he has found both the emotions and pleasure and pain to be of a universal nature, Hume seems to conclude that the greater the art, the greater will be its universality.

> The principles of every passion, and of every sentiment, is in every man; and when touched properly, they rise to life, and warm the heart, and convey that satisfaction, by which a work of genius is distinguished from the adulterate beauties of a capricious wit and fancy.[112]

Hume expands on universality in an essay, 'Of the Rise and Progress of the Arts and Sciences,' which begins with an interesting discussion of the element of chance in the creation of high art.[113] In the end, he seems to conclude that what he has called chance may not actually be chance, due to the universality of emotions.

> But there is a reason, which induces me not to ascribe the matter altogether to chance. Though the persons, who cultivate the sciences with such astonishing success, as to attract the admiration of posterity, be always few, in all nations and all ages; it is impossible but a share of the same spirit and genius must be antecedently diffused throughout the people among whom they arise, in order to produce, form, and cultivate, from their earliest infancy, the taste and judgment of those eminent writers. The mass cannot be altogether insipid, from which such refined spirits are extracted. 'There is a God within us,' says Ovid, 'who breathes that divine fire, by which we are animated.' Poets, in all ages, have advanced this claim to inspiration. There is not, however, anything supernatural in the case. Their fire is not kindled from heaven. It only runs along the earth; is caught from one breast to another; and burns brightest, where the materials are best prepared, and most happily disposed. The question, therefore, concerning the rise and progress of the arts and sciences, is not altogether a question concerning the taste, genius, and spirit of a few, but concerning those of a whole people; and may, therefore, be accounted for, in some measure, by general causes and principles.

It is this universality, Hume finds, which in turn gives some validity to the public's judgment.

> Popular fame may be agreeable even to a man, who despises the vulgar; but it is because their multitude gives them additional weight and authority.[114]

---

112 'On Eloquence,' in Ibid., III, 172.

113 'Of the Rise and Progress of the Arts and Sciences,' in Ibid., III, 174ff.

114 *A Treatise of Human Nature*, II, i, §11. In III, ii, §10 , Hume broadens this idea to say, 'The general opinion of mankind has some authority in all cases; but in … morals it is perfectly infallible.'

On Taste

In an essay on 'The Delicacy of Taste and Passion,' Hume contrasts the relative virtues of developing sensitive passions and tastes.[115]

> Some people are subject to a certain *delicacy of passion*, which makes them extremely sensible to all the accidents of life, and gives them a lively joy upon every prosperous event, as well as a piercing grief, when they meet with misfortunes and adversity ... People of this character have, no doubt, more lively enjoyments, as well as more pungent sorrows, than men of cool and sedate tempers. But, I believe, when everything is balanced, there is no one, who would not rather be of the latter character, were he entirely master of his own disposition ...
>
> There is a *delicacy of taste* observable in some men, which very much resembles this delicacy of passion, and produces the same sensibility to beauty and deformity of every kind, as that does to prosperity and adversity, obligations and injuries. When you present a poem or a picture to a man possessed of this talent, the delicacy of this feeling makes him be sensibly touched with every part of it ... A polite and judicious conversation affords him the highest entertainment; rudeness or impertinence is as great a punishment to him. In short, delicacy of taste has the same effect as delicacy of passion. It enlarges the sphere both of our happiness and misery, and makes us sensible to pains as well as pleasures, which escape the rest of mankind.
>
> I believe, however, everyone will agree with me, that, notwithstanding this resemblance, delicacy of taste is as much to be desired and cultivated as delicacy of passions is to be lamented, and to be remedied, if possible.

Having distinguished these two tastes, Hume now concentrates on how the development of higher taste can help control the emotions. We must point out that this assumption that one must 'conquer' the emotions is only another manifestation of the dominance of the left hemisphere of the brain and its particular tendency to deny the existence of the right hemisphere where the emotions lie.

> Whatever connection there may be originally between these two species of delicacy, I am persuaded, that nothing is so proper to cure us of this delicacy of passion, as the cultivating of that higher and more refined taste, which enables us to judge of the characters of men, of compositions of genius, and of the productions of the nobler arts. A greater or less relish for those obvious beauties, which strike the senses, depends entirely upon the greater or less sensibility of the temper. But with regard to the sciences and liberal arts, a fine taste is, in some measure, the same with strong sense, or at least depends so much upon it, that they are inseparable. In order to judge aright of a composition of genius, there are so many views to be taken in, so many circumstances to be compared, and such a knowledge of human nature requisite, that no man, who is not possessed of the soundest judgment, will ever make a tolerable critic in such performances. And this is a new reason for cultivating a relish in the liberal arts ...
>
> But perhaps I have gone too far in saying, that a cultivated taste for the polite arts extinguishes the passions, and renders us indifferent to those objects, which are so fondly pursued by the rest

---
115 'On the Delicacy of Taste and Passion,' in *David Hume, The Philosophical Works*, III, 91ff.

of mankind. On farther reflection, I find, that it rather improves our sensibility for all the tender and agreeable passions; at the same time that it renders the mind incapable of the rougher and more boisterous emotions.

Curiously, in another essay Hume argues that in the case of oratory the English need to develop more prominent emotions.

> Perhaps it may be acknowledged, that our modern customs, or our superior good sense, if you will, should make our orators more cautious and reserved than the ancient, in attempting to inflame the passions, or elevate the imagination of their audience. But, I see no reason, why it should make them despair absolutely of succeeding in that attempt. It should make them redouble their art, not abandon it entirely. The ancient orators seems also to have been on their guard against this jealousy of their audience; but they took a different way of eluding it. They hurried away with such a torrent of sublime and pathetic, that they left their hearers no leisure to perceive the artifice, by which they were deceived. Nay, to consider the matter aright, they were not deceived by any artifice. The orator, by force of his own genius and eloquence, first inflamed himself with anger, indignation, pity, sorrow; and then communicated those impetuous movements to this audience.[116]

In another essay, 'Of the Standard of Taste,' Hume concentrates on the problem of identifying taste, when it is conspicuous that everyone has an individual taste. We must acknowledge here excellent support for the argument that the aesthetics of music must be found in the individual listener, and not in the music itself. Also notable here is the distinction he draws between the possibility of universality in perception by the left and right brain's response, which he identifies as the perception of 'opinion' versus 'sentiment.'

> Among a thousand different opinions which different men may entertain of the same subject, there is one, and but one, that is just and true; and the only difficulty is to fix and ascertain it. On the contrary, a thousand different sentiments, excited by the same object, are all right: Because no sentiment represents what is really in the object. It only marks a certain conformity or relation between the object and the organs or faculties of the mind; and if that conformity did not really exist, the sentiment could never possibly have being. Beauty is no quality in things themselves. It exists merely in the mind which contemplates them; and each mind perceives a different beauty. One person may even perceive deformity, where another is sensible of beauty; and every individual ought to acquiesce in his own sentiment, without pretending to regulate those of others. To seek the real beauty, or real deformity, is as fruitless an inquiry, as to pretend to ascertain the real sweet or real bitter. According to the disposition of the organs, the same object may be both sweet and bitter; and the proverb has justly determined it to be fruitless to dispute concerning tastes.[117]

---

116 'On Eloquence,' in *David Hume, The Philosophical Works*, in Ibid., III, 169.
117 'On the Standard of Taste,' in Ibid., III, 268ff.

Later he discovers further obstacles to determining a standard of taste. One of these is the age of the viewer.

> A young man, whose passions are warm, will be more sensibly touched with amorous and tender images, than a man more advanced in years, who takes pleasure in wise philosophical reflections concerning the conduct of life and moderation of the passions.

On Tragedy

Hume's fascination with the emotions is documented by his lengthy study of the passions in Book Two of his *Treatise of Human Nature*. With all his attempts to rationalize the workings of the emotions in that study, he was clearly intrigued by the reactions of the observers of Tragedy, who seemed to *enjoy* the tragic events seen on the stage.

> It seems an unaccountable pleasure, which the spectators of a well-written tragedy receive from sorrow, terror, anxiety, and other passions, that are in themselves disagreeable and uneasy. The more they are touched and affected, the more are they delighted with the spectacle; and as soon as the uneasy passions cease to operate, the piece is at an end … The whole heart of the poet is employed, in rousing and supporting the compassion and indignation, the anxiety and resentment of his audience. They are pleased in proportion as they are afflicted, and never so happy as when they employ tears, sobs, and cries to give vent to their sorrow, and relieve their heart, swollen with the tenderest sympathy and compassion.[118]

In his attempt to explain this apparent paradox, Hume first concludes that,

> the heart likes naturally to be moved and affected. Melancholy objects suit it, and even disastrous and sorrowful, provided they are softened by some circumstance.

The circumstance which softens these emotions in the theater, he finds, is the fact that the viewer understands the events on the stage are not real, they are a fable. Further, Hume believed that the tragic emotions on the stage are also seen surrounded by art and in the end the artistic nature of the production overcomes the impact of the tragic emotions.

> The impulse or vehemence, arising from sorrow, compassion, indignation, receives a new direction from the sentiments of beauty. The latter, being the predominant emotion, seize the whole mind, and convert the former into themselves, at least tincture them so strongly as totally to alter their nature. And the soul, being, at the same time, roused by passion, and charmed by eloquence, feels on the whole a strong movement, which is altogether delightful.

---
118 'Of Tragedy,' in Ibid., III, 258ff.

On Painting

In his essay on 'The Rise of Arts and Sciences,' Hume contends that it is the case of all artists, that when they are young they do not recognize their own genius. Only experience and repeated successful reactions help develop confidence.[119] While the 'applause of the world' is vital to his development, Hume wonders if the importation of the finest art of other countries as models is a productive idea.

> Perhaps, it may not be for the advantage of any nation to have the arts imported from their neighbors in too great perfection. This extinguishes emulation, and sinks the ardor of the generous youth. So many models of Italian painting brought into England, instead of exciting our artists, is the cause of their small progress in that noble art.

The Catholic Counter Reformation of the late Renaissance had included a strong emphasis on a return to realism in painting. Hume makes an interesting observation on the impact of this movement on artists.

> Most painters appear in this light to have been very unhappy in their subjects. As they wrought much for churches and convents, they have chiefly represented such horrible subjects as crucifixions and martyrdoms, where nothing appears but tortures, wounds, executions, and passive suffering, without any action or emotion.[120]

If he finds the demand for Truth in painting unproductive, Hume makes a rather different case for poetry.

> Poets themselves, although liars by profession, always endeavor to give an air of truth to their fictions; and where that is totally neglected, their performances, however ingenious, will never be able to afford much pleasure.[121]

He qualifies this by contending that the feelings which arise from poetry are very different from the genuine ones.

On the Aesthetics of Music

Hume, like other philosophers of this period in England, wrote little on the subject of music, a fact which can only be taken as a measure of how much ground music had lost, in a very brief period of time, as a relevant branch of philosophy. This is to be regretted, for there are hints in Hume's correspondence that he had an interest as a listener, at least for opera. In a

---

[119] 'Of the Rise of Arts and Sciences,' in Ibid., III, 195ff.
[120] Ibid., 265.
[121] *A Treatise of Human Nature*, I, iii, §10.

letter of 1748, while visiting The Hague, he complains that he finds no opera there.[122] On a boat ride down the Danube, he finds the changing scenery reminds him of the rapid scene changes in opera.[123] And in another place, Hume makes this curious passing reference to the exaggerated emotional display of opera.

> Were a stranger to drop, on a sudden, into this world, I would show him, as a specimen of its ills, an hospital full of diseases, a prison crowded with malefactors and debtors, a field of battle strewed with carcasses, a fleet floundering in the ocean, a nation languishing under tyranny, famine, or pestilence. To turn the gay side of life to him, and give him a notion of its pleasures; whither should I conduct him? to a ball, to an opera, to court? He might justly think, that I was only showing him a diversity of distress and sorrow.[124]

Hume makes only one reference, in his philosophical writings, to the perception of music. He has contended that the mind is capable of achieving correctness even though it has only an 'obscure' notion of that aim, and by way of illustration he uses the musician.

> A musician finding his ear becoming every day more delicate, and correcting himself by reflection and attention, proceeds with the same act of the mind, even when the subject fails him, and entertains a notion of a complete third or octave, without being able to tell whence he derives his standard.[125]

In only two places does Hume refer to the purposes of music. The first is a rather unenthusiastic reference to the purpose of delight.

> Our sense of music, harmony, and indeed beauty of all kinds gives satisfaction, without being absolutely necessary to the preservation and propagation of the species.[126]

In the other, music is included with other arts whose purpose includes a positive effect on the emotions of the observer.

> Nothing is so improving to the temper as the study of the beauties, either of poetry, eloquence, music, or painting. They give a certain elegance of sentiment to which the rest of mankind are strangers. The emotions which they excite are soft and tender. They draw off the mind from the hurry of business and interest; cherish reflection; dispose to tranquility; and produce an agreeable melancholy, which, of all dispositions of the mind is the best suited to love and friendship.[127]

---

122 Letter to John Home (March 3, 1748), quoted in *The Letters of David Hume*, ed. J. Greig (Oxford: Clarendon, 1932), I, 115.
123 Ibid., 125.
124 'Dialogues Concerning Natural Religion,' Part X.
125 *A Treatise of Human Nature*, I, ii, §4.
126 'Dialogues Concerning Natural Religion,' Part X.
127 'On the Delicacy of Taste and Passion,' in *David Hume, The Philosophical Works*, III, 93.

In all the writings of Hume, there is only one description of an actual performance, his impressions of hearing the singing of psalms by Catholic Church singers. This is found in a strange report of his visit to Knittelfeld, in lower Austria.

> But as much as the country is agreeable in its wildness; as much are the inhabitants savage & deformed & monstrous in their appearance. Very many of them have ugly swelled throats: idiots & deaf people swarm in every village; and the general aspect of the people is the most shocking I ever saw. One would think, that this was the great road, through which all the barbarous nations made their irruptions into the Roman Empire, they always left here the refuse of their armies before they entered into the enemy's country; and that from thence the present inhabitants are descended. Their dress is scarce European as their figure is scarce human. There happened, however a thing today, which surprised us all. The Empress Queen, regarding this country as a little barbarous, has sent some Missionaries of the Jesuits to instruct them. They had sermons today in the street under our windows, attended with Psalms. And believe me, nothing could be more harmonious, better tuned, or more agreeable than the voices of these savages, and the chorus of a French Opera does not sing in better time.[128]

GEORGE BERKELEY (1685–1753)

George Berkeley, Ireland's contribution to philosophy of this period, became absorbed with the writings of Locke at an early age. He appears to us to have become obsessed with the growing emphasis on materialism, which as a facet of the Enlightenment distracted man's thoughts from God. His answer was *Of the Principles of Human Knowledge* which argued that no matter exists apart from its perception in the mind. Contemporaries found this concept difficult to challenge, although in a famous anecdote Samuel Johnson, discussing this with Boswell, kicked a large stone and said, 'I refute it thus!'

On the Physiology of Aesthetics

Berkeley begins his famous *Of the Principles of Human Knowledge* with a definition assumed by all philosophers of his time. Its only significance, chronologically, was that it specifically omitted any form of genetic, or God-given knowledge, as had been assumed by some earlier philosophers.

---

128 Letter to John Home (April 28, 1748), in *The Letters of David Hume*, 130.

> It is evident to any one who takes a survey of the objects of human knowledge, that they are either ideas actually imprinted on the senses, or else such as are perceived by attending to the passions and operations of the mind, or lastly ideas formed by help of memory and imagination.[129]

What comes next, however, is his original thesis which generated so much discussion among his contemporaries. He does not bother to argue here whether mind is different from spirit, soul, or oneself; however one regards the essence of mind, what exists there is *all* that exists.

> Neither our thoughts, nor passions, nor ideas formed by the imagination, exist without the mind, is what everybody will admit. And it seems no less evident that the various sensations or ideas imprinted on the sense, however blended or combined together (that is, whatever objects they compose) cannot exist otherwise than in a mind perceiving them.[130]

His real point can be made clear by considering what he writes in another place about sound.[131] Sound, he maintains, is simply vibrations in the air.[132] When we call it 'sound,' we are really referring to our sense of hearing. In other words, to use an old riddle, Berkeley would say a tree falling in the woods where there was no one to hear, it would produce vibrations in the air, but no sound.

> PHILONOUS. Can any sensation exist without the mind?
> HYLAS. No certainly.
> PHILONOUS. How then can sound, being a sensation exist in the air, if by the *air* you mean a senseless substance existing without the mind?
> HYLAS. You must distinguish, Philonous, between sound as it is perceived by us, and as it is in itself; or (which is the same thing) between the sound we immediately perceive, and that which exists without us. The former indeed is a particular kind of sensation, but the latter is merely a vibrative or undulatory motion in the air.

In another place, Berkeley summarizes the process of mental activity as a chain leading from man to God.

> Sense supplies images to memory. These become subjects for fancy to work upon. Reason considers and judges of the imaginations. And these acts of reason become new objects to the understanding. In this scale, each lower faculty is a step that leads to one above it. And the uppermost naturally leads to the Deity.[133]

---

129 *Of the Principles of Human Knowledge*, in *The Works of George Berkeley, Bishop of Cloyne*, ed. A. Luce (London: Nelson, 1964), II, 4.

130 Ibid., II, 42.

131 'First Dialogue between Hylas and Philonous,' in Ibid., II, 181ff.

132 Berkeley can be careless, for in another place [*Of the Principles of Human Knowledge*, Ibid., II, 41] he uses 'sound' to mean the vibrations produced by the instrument.
   Hearing conveys sounds to the mind in all their variety of tone and composition.

133 'Siris,' in Ibid., V, 140.

Berkeley does not discuss education, apart from another dialogue, where he has Alciphron complain that universities are 'nurseries of prejudice, corruption, barbarism, and pedantry.' Lysicles answers that he had a great time at the university, but since he never looked at books he can't comment on the value of the education.[134] In another place, Berkeley warns philosophers of,

> sliding back into the obscure subtlety of the schoolmen, which for so many ages like some dread plague, has corrupted philosophy.[135]

On the Psychology of Aesthetics

Berkeley does not discuss the emotions, but does make one reference to Pleasure and Pain. He admits that 'happiness is the end to which created beings naturally tend,' and that this happiness is principally a pleasure of sense.[136] He contends that it is the nature of Pleasure that our 'appetites must always be craving, to preserve pleasure.' Berkeley finds three basic kinds of pleasure, that of reason, of imagination and of the senses. Of these, the philosopher concludes,

> Reason, therefore, being the principal part of our nature, whatever is most reasonable should seem most natural to man. Must we not therefore think rational pleasures more agreeable to humans than those of sense?

On the Philosophy of Aesthetics

A letter of 1727,[137] in which Berkeley mentions the current taste and price in Italian paintings, suggests that he had some familiarity with the arts. His only discussion of aesthetics in the arts, however, is his consideration of the nature of Beauty.[138] His primary purpose was to use this subject as yet another illustration that things can exist only in the mind. He refutes several traditional definitions, such as Beauty consists of symmetrical proportions ('the proportions of an ox would not be beautiful to a horse,' etc). He finally concludes that Beauty is that which has some useful purpose and whose end is to please.[139]

---

134 'Fifth Dialogue of Alciphron,' in Ibid., III, 197.
135 'De Motu,' in Ibid., IV, 41ff.
136 'Second Dialogue of Allciphron,' in Ibid., III, 83ff.
137 Quoted in Ibid., VIII, 177.
138 'Third Dialogue of Alciphron,' in Ibid., III, 123ff.
139 Ibid., 128.

Virtually the only other comments Berkeley makes on the arts in general is in his 'The Querist,' where his main concern seems to be for society to find a way to support the arts without the need of contributions from foreign countries.[140]

We have quoted in several places in these volumes reports of the very informal atmosphere which accompanied performances in the theater. In a letter of 1713,[141] Berkeley mentions attending the premiere of *Cato*, a play by Addison, and sitting with the playwright 'in a side box, where he had a table and two or three flasks of burgundy and champagne.'

ON THE AESTHETICS OF MUSIC

As with all the important philosophers of the Baroque in England, we must point out again how absent is the topic of music from their consideration. This is particularly striking in the case of those who appear to have been active in attending concerts and opera. Berkeley, as a case in point, not only describes concerts in detail in his correspondence,[142] but was apparently an avid collector of instruments.

> Your care in providing the Italian psalms set to music, the four-stringed bass violin, and the antique bass viol, require our repeated thanks. We have already a bass viol made in Southwark, AD 1730, and reputed the best in England. And through your means we are possessed of the best in France. So we have a fair chance for having the two best in Europe.[143]

The nearest Berkeley comes to a philosophical definition of music is one which again refers to his basic hypothesis that everything exists only in the mind.

> Though harmony and proportion are not objects of sense, yet the eye and the ear are organs which offer to the mind such materials by means whereof she may apprehend both the one and the other.[144]

In only one place does Berkeley refer to the purpose of music and it is the important observation that art music has no functional purpose. In an unpublished notebook, Berkeley observes that there are two kinds of Pleasure, one which incites you to something else

---

140 'The Querist,' in Ibid., VI, 115–121.

141 Quoted in Ibid., VIII, 65. In another letter [Ibid., 152], Berkeley thanks a correspondent for sending a poem called, 'America, or the Muse's Refuge.'

> The muse, offended at this age, these climes
> Where nought she found fit to rehearse,
> Waits now in distant lands for better times,
> Producing subjects worthy verse ...

142 Quoted in Ibid., VIII, 69.

143 Quoted in Ibid., VIII, 261.

144 'Siris,' in Ibid., V, 140.

while the other is self-sufficient. 'Thus the pleasure of eating is of the former sort, of Musick is the later sort.'[145]

Finally, we might mention one use of music as a metaphor by Berkeley. Wishing to suggest that what is good for the mind is good for the body, Berkeley notes in passing, 'For if the lute be not well tuned, the musician fails in his harmony.'[146]

---

[145] 'Notebook A,' in Ibid., I, 101.
[146] 'Siris,' in Ibid., V, 31.

11 RESTORATION PHILOSOPHERS OF AESTHETICS

IN AN EARLIER VOLUME we have discussed at length the fact that in the latter years of the sixteenth century English gentlemen began to disassociate themselves with music, in so far as being active performers. This was due in part to an expanding wealth, which, as in ancient Rome, had the effect of turning music over to the slaves—a philosophy still largely in place in the English-speaking world today. Another strong influence was, of course, the rapidly growing Puritan movement, whose preachers spoke out with great contempt against the arts and even pulled down the church organs.

Francis Hutcheson, in an essay on the foundations of morality sent to the *London Journal* in 1725, looks back on these influences and considers their impact on English society. He complains that the preachers, the 'moralists,' are always talking about Reason ruling the human emotions, but Hutcheson finds this unrealistic in ordinary life.

> A man in deep sorrow will not be immediately easy, upon your demonstrating that his sorrow can be of no advantage to him.[1]

Hutcheson is equally critical of the limited vision of the academic world, which seems interested only in seeking the highest good, the *Summum Bonum*, and in the process 'fly so high' that 'one must be well advanced in a visionary temper to be profited by them.' These 'school-men,' he says 'seldom mention the delights of humanity.' The more recent philosophers, Hutcheson maintains,

> observing the trifling of the school-men, have very much left out of their systems, all enquiries into happiness, and speak only of the external advantages of peace and wealth in the societies where we live.

What he had in mind is illustrated in a statement by Thomas Hobbes on the values of the English upper class.

> Riches are honorable; as signs of the power that acquired them: and gifts, cost, and magnificence of houses, apparel, and the like, are honorable, as signs of riches. And nobility is honorable

---

[1] 'An Essay upon the Foundations of Morality, according to the Principles of the Ancients,' in *Francis Hutcheson On Human Nature*, ed. Thomas Mautner (Cambridge: University Press, 1993), 104ff.

by reflection, as a sign of power in the ancestors: and authority, because a sign of the strength, wisdom, favor and riches by which it is attained.[2]

In spite of this environment, there were some who wrote on aesthetics in the arts. Indeed, some of them, men such as Shaftesbury and Hutcheson, while little known today, left significant philosophical treatises on the arts.

WILLIAM TEMPLE (1628–1699)

For the modern reader, one finds in William Temple a style of writing so vivid, and a philosophy so perceptive, that it seems as if written in our own time. His best known work is his essay, 'On Ancient and Modern Learning,' which propelled his young friend Jonathan Swift into a literary career. However, with respect to aesthetics we find most interesting his essay, 'Of Poetry.' His remarks are of particular interest to us because he associates so closely the natures of music and poetry.

Temple begins by confronting directly the aesthetic view of his peers, one by which the arts had come to be regarded merely something for the *idle*.

> The two common shrines to which most men offer up the application of their thoughts and their lives are profit and pleasure; and, by their devotions to either of these, they are vulgarly distinguished into two sects, and called either busy or idle men. Whether these terms differ in meaning or only in sound, I know very well may be disputed, and with appearance enough, since the covetous man takes perhaps as much pleasure in his gains as the voluptuous does in his luxury, and would not pursue his business, unless he were pleased with it, upon the last account of what he most wishes and desires, nor would care for the increase of his fortunes, unless he thereby proposed that of his pleasures too, in one kind or other; so that pleasure may be said to be his end, whether he will allow to find it in his pursuit or not.[3]

He returns to his peers again at the very end of this essay.

> I know very well that many who pretend to be wise by the forms of being grave are apt to despise both poetry and music as toys and trifles too light for the use or entertainment of serious men: but whoever find themselves wholly insensible to these charms would, I think, do well to keep their own counsel, for fear of reproaching their own temper and bringing the goodness of their natures, if not of their understandings, into question: it may be thought at least an ill sign, if not an ill constitution, since some of the Fathers went so far as to esteem the love of music as a sign of predestination, as a thing divine and reserved for the felicities of heaven itself.[4]

---

2   Thomas Hobbes, 'Human Nature,' VIII, 5.

3   'Of Poetry,' in *Five Miscellaneous Essays by Sir William Temple*, ed. Samuel Monk (Ann Arbor: University of Michigan Press, 1963), 173.

4   Ibid., 202.

In considering the definition, or essence, of poetry, Temple takes note of the fact that poetry had often been associated, in some way or other, with the divine. He cannot take this literally and offers his own interpretation.

> The more true and natural source of poetry may be discovered by observing to what god this inspiration was ascribed by the ancients, which was Apollo, or the sun, esteemed among them the god of learning in general, but more particularly of music and of poetry. The mystery of this fable means, I suppose, that a certain noble and vital heat of temper, but especially of the brain, is the true spring of those two arts or sciences: this was that celestial fire which gave such a pleasing motion and agitation to the minds of those men that have been so much admired in the world, that raises such infinite images of things so agreeable and delightful to mankind; by the influence of this sun are produced those golden and unexhausted mines of invention which has furnished the world with treasures so highly esteemed and so universally known and used in all the regions that have yet been discovered. From this arises that elevation of genius which can never be produced by any art or study, by pains or by industry, which cannot be taught by precepts or examples; and therefore is agreed by all to be the pure and free gift of heaven or of nature, and to be a fire kindled out of some hidden spark of the very first conception.[5]

To create fine poetry, Temple finds there must be a necessary balance between creative inspiration and the 'coldness of good sense and soundness of judgment.' Since, as the reader will find below, Temple so closely associated the emotions with everything meant by inspiration, we cannot help but regard this as another intuitive recognition of the separate hemispheres of the brain, which also specialize in the rational and the emotional.

> There must be a great agitation of mind to invent, a great calm to judge and correct; there must be, upon the same tree, and at the same time, both flower and fruit. To work up this metal into exquisite figure, there must be employed the fire, the hammer, the chisel, and the file. There must be a general knowledge both of nature and of arts, and, to go the lowest that can be, there are required genius, judgment, and application; for, without this last, all the rest will not serve turn, and none ever was a great poet that applied himself much to anything else.[6]

With regard to the purpose of poetry in general, it is clear that for Temple it was to involve the emotions of the listener, or reader.

> For there is no question but true poetry may have the force to raise passions and to allay them, to change and to extinguish them, to temper joy and grief, to raise love and fear, nay, to turn fear into boldness, and love into indifference and into hatred itself: and I easily believe that the disheartened Spartans were new animated and recovered their lost courage by the songs of Tyrtaeus.[7]

---

5   Ibid., 179.

6   Ibid., 180.

7   Ibid., 176.

Another reference to this purpose also alludes to the universality of the emotions.

> Whoever does not affect and move the same present passions in you that he represents in others, and at other times raise images about you, as a conjurer is said to do spirits, transport you to the places and to the persons he describes, cannot be judged to be a poet, though his measures are never so just, his feet never so smooth, or his sounds never so sweet.[8]

He associates additional purposes with individual forms of poetry, as story with the epic poem, love with the lyric poem, grief with elegy and reproach with satire. Dramatic poetry, he finds, consists of all of these plus instruction,

> to show the beauties and the rewards of virtue, the deformities and misfortunes or punishment of vice; by examples of both to encourage one, and deter men from the other; to reform ill customs, correct ill manners, and moderate all violent passions.[9]

In his consideration of contemporary poetry in England, we find it interesting that Temple first elects to avoid the subject of criticism, to discuss the 'official' rules of poetry. He notes that too much has already been written, especially by the French. He concludes little insight has been added over what one could have found in Aristotle and Horace.

> The truth is, there is something in the genius of poetry too libertine to be confined to so many rules: and whoever goes about to subject it to such constraints loses both its spirit and grace, which are ever native, and never learned, even of the best masters.[10]

In reviewing contemporary English poetry, Temple finds the great forms, especially the epic poem, have disappeared. Poets now are content with 'the scraps,' by which he means sonnets, odes, elegies, satires and panegyrics. He regards the principal addition to the art in his time has been humor and he finds nowhere else but in England such 'sharpness of wit and pleasantness of humor.'[11] He continues with an interesting observation on the influence of climate on the English character.

> But, with all this, our country must be confessed to be what a great foreign physician called it, the region of spleen, which may arise a good deal from the great uncertainty and many sudden changes of our weather in all seasons of the year. And how much these affect the heads and hearts, especially of the finest tempers, is hard to be believed by men whose thoughts are not turned to such speculations. This makes us unequal in our humors, inconstant in our passions, uncertain in our ends, and even in our desires.

---

8   Ibid., 183
9   Ibid., 187.
10 Ibid., 181ff.
11 Ibid., 200.

On the Aesthetics of Music

Temple finds the great power of poetry in its unique combination of portrait, music and eloquence. Here, in addition to acknowledging the genetic universality of music, he considers the natural power of music, which is to move the emotions.

> The powers of music are either felt or known by all men, and are allowed to work strangely upon the mind and the body, the passions and the blood; to raise joy and grief, to give pleasure and pain, to cure diseases and the mortal sting of the tarantula; to give motions to the feet as well as the heart, to compose disturbed thoughts, to assist and heighten devotion itself. We need no recourse to the fables of Orpheus or Amphion, or the force of their music upon fishes and beasts; it is enough that we find the charming of serpents, and the cure or allay of an evil spirit or possession attributed to it in [the Bible].[12]

THOMAS RYMER (1641–1713)

Thomas Rymer was born to a well to do family in the north of England and studied at Cambridge. He was not one of the great minds of seventeenth-century England, but we must mention him in passing because his *The Tragedies of the Last Age* (1677) and *A Short View of Tragedy* (1692) were widely read and therefore must have touched a chord with a number of people. Both of these books are, in effect, histories of the theater and each contains lengthy descriptions of individual plays. We will limit our consideration to his original thoughts which are relevant to subjects we have been following in these volumes.

In his survey of the writings of the ancient writers on drama, Rymer mentions that after some study of philosophy and manners, he had determined that,

> our Philosophers agreed well enough with theirs, in the main; however, that our playwrights have forced another way to the wood; a by-road, that runs directly cross to that of Nature, Manners and Philosophy which gained the Ancients so great veneration.[13]

Although Rymer agreed with Aristotle that one purpose of drama was to purge, and not pamper, the emotions, nevertheless he contended that, as in man, Reason must rule. 'Fancy,' or creative imagination, in a play, he contends, is like faith in religion, making 'far discoveries' and 'soaring above Reason.' However, he warns,

> Fancy leaps, and frisks, and away she's gone; whilst Reason rattles the chains, and follows after. Reason must consent and ratify whatever by fancy is attempted in its absence; or else it is all null

---

12 Ibid., 177.

13 *The Tragedies of the Last Age*, in *The Critical Works of Thomas Rymer*, ed. Curt Zimansky (New Haven: Yale University Press, 1956), 18.

and void in law. However, in the contrivance and economy of a play, reason is always principally to be consulted. Those who object against reason, are the Fanaticks in Poetry, and are never to be saved by their good works.[14]

Rymer has been discounted by contemporary critics, primarily due to his criticism of Shakespeare. But we must remember that for much of the seventeenth century in England, the degree to which Shakespeare towered over his contemporary playwrights was not fully recognized. Rymer, for one, found much to criticize. To cite only one example, he suggests that Shakespeare's genius rested with comedy and not tragedy.

> In Tragedy he appears quite out of his element; his brains are turned, he raves and rambles, without any coherence, any spark of reason, or any rule to control him, or set bounds to his frenzy.[15]

A few lines later Rymer calls *Othello* a 'senseless trifling tale.'

On the Philosophy of Aesthetics

Rymer's only original comment, which we find unusual, is relative to the purpose of drama. In his view of the theater, the central feature is action and action is what the audience wants to see. Sight, he finds, is so central to the theater that even language is secondary.

> *Action* is speaking to the eyes; and all Europe over plays have been represented with great applause, in a tongue unknown, and sometimes without any language at all.[16]

Further, it is the action which is the agent for emotion.

> This thing of *Action* finds the blindside of human kind an hundred ways. We laugh and weep with those that laugh or weep; we gape, stretch, and are very *dotterels* by example.

On the Aesthetics of Music

The only discussion of substance on the subject of music by Rymer is given to opera, a topic he includes, no doubt, because many writers during the seventeenth century had believed that the great popularity of opera had greatly diminished the fortunes of the theater. Rymer himself is quite a harsh critic of opera.

---

14 Ibid., 19ff.
15 *A Short View of Tragedy*, VIII.
16 *A Short View of Tragedy*, I.

What would Horace have said to the *French Opera* of late so much in vogue? There it is for you to bewitch your eyes, and to charm your ears. There is a Cup of Enchantment, there is Musick and Machine: *Circe* and *Calipso* in conspiracy against Nature and good Sense. It is a Debauch the most insinuating, and the most pernicious; none would think an Opera and Civil Reason, should be the growth of one and the same Climate ...

Away with your Opera from the Theater, better had they become the Heathen Temples ...

In the French, not many years before was observed the like vicious appetite, and immoderate Passion for *vers Burlesque*.

They were currant in Italy an hundred years, ere they passed to this side the Alps; but when once they had their turn in France, so right to their humor, they over ran all; nothing wise or sober might stand in their way. All were possessed with the Spirit of *Burlesk*.[17]

So prevailing was the style of burlesque, claims Rymer, that in 1649 there was published in Paris a 'serious treatise' on Jesus with the title, *La Passion de Nostre Seigneur, En vers Burlesques*.

WILLIAM WOTTON (1666–1727)

William Wotton, chaplain to the earl of Nottingham, published his *Reflections upon Ancient and Modern Learning* (1694) as a rebuttal to William Temple's essay, 'Of Ancient and Modern Learning,' which had suggested that little insight had been added to those of the ancient writers. Wotton first comments that it is easy to admire the ancients, 'for the distance of time takes off envy.'[18] Nature, he says, has nothing to do with the prominence of either the ancient or modern writers. If it has to do with Nature, he wonders,

Why have we heard of no orators[19] among the inhabitants of the Bay of Soldania, or eminent poets in Peru?

Two advantages he concedes to the ancient orators were, first, that the Greek language has 'a vast advantage above any other language that has ever yet been cultivated by learned men,' and, second, that the nature of the present age is such that the listener is always suspecting 'a Trick in everything that is said to move the passions.'

---

17 *A Short View of Tragedy*, I.
18 *Reflections upon Ancient and Modern Learning*, III.
19 Wotton defines orators as 'all those writers in prose who took pains to beautify and adorn their style.'

On the Physiology of Aesthetics

We have noted that during the seventeenth century there seems to have been an increasing awareness, by deduction or intuition, of the twin natures of man which have their origin in the separate functions of the left and right hemispheres of the brain. The aspect of this which is fundamental to Wotton's discussion is that all men essentially agree with the data held in the left hemisphere (no one disputes two plus two is four), but because the right hemisphere is largely experiential, and everyone has memory banks of unique experiences, we differ in our right hemisphere observations. This, in a phrase, is why 'Art is in the eye of the beholder.'

Wotton begins his discussion on ancient and modern 'eloquence and poesie,' with an interesting comment relative to the above. He notes, first, that it would be reasonable to assume that those who had studied a topic the most, should be the accepted judges of it. However, he has observed that even people with no study of oratory never hesitate to accept their own opinion as valid. That which we would identify as reactions based on individual experience, Wotton attributes rather to the universality of common sense.

> The foundations of eloquence of all sorts lying in common sense, of which every man is in some degree a master, most ingenious men have, without any study, a little insight into these things. This little insight betrays them immediately to declare their opinions, because they are afraid, if they should not, their reputation would be in danger.[20]

How different is the left hemisphere!

> Talk with such men about a law case, or a problem in geometry, if they never studied those things, they will frankly tell you so, and decline to give their opinion.

Wotton finds it curious, also, that in the case of a play or poem out of twenty men you will find twenty different opinions, right or wrong. On superficial contemplation this should be a contradiction, for plays and poetry consist of language, which is left hemisphere and the idea of language would not exist if people could not agree on definitions. But, in fact, it is the contribution of the emotional color by the right hemisphere which renders much of meaning to communication in language—*how* we say something means everything. Wotton, unwittingly, recognizes this when he adds,

> In most of these things our Passions are some way or other concerned; at least, being accustomed to have them moved, we expect it, and think ourselves disappointed when our expectation is deceived.

---

20 *Reflections upon Ancient and Modern Learning*, III.

On the Philosophy of Aesthetics

Wotton's discussion of the various art forms are largely focused on those of the ancient literature, with little original thought on aesthetics. We do find one interesting exception when he writes of epic poetry, which he finds tends to be *too* complete, leaving nothing to the imagination of the listener/reader.

> It is a fault in Heroick Poetry, to fetch things from their first originals; and to carry the thread of the narrative down to the last event, is altogether as dull ... Men should rise from the table with some appetite remaining and a poem should leave some view of something to follow, and not quite shut the scenes.[21]

On the Aesthetics of Music

It is the twenty-fourth chapter of Wotton's book, which he calls, 'Of Ancient and Modern Musick,' which is of particular interest. He begins by referring to William Temple's (nearly correct) assertion that all knowledge of ancient Greek music is lost and that (incorrect) all modern music is based on the rules of church music of the Middle Ages.

> Sir William Temple having assured us that it is agreed by the learned, that the science of Musick, so admired by the ancients, is wholly lost in the world. And that what we have now is made up of certain notes that fell into the fancy of a poor Friar, in chanting his Matins.

Wotton concludes, therefore, that 'it may seem improper to speak of Musick here, which ought rather to have been ranked among those sciences wherein the Moderns have ... been found to have been out-done by the Ancients.' However, he adds, he is impelled to make several observations about ancient and modern music.

Like a medieval philosopher, Wotton is still thinking of music as a branch of mathematics. Therefore, he first finds it curious that while mathematicians are conversant with earlier writers, musicians are not.

> Whereas all modern mathematicians have paid a mighty deference to the ancients; and have not only used the names of *Archimedes*, *Apolonius* and *Diophantus*, and the other ancient mathematicians with great respect; but have also acknowledged, that what further advancements have since been made, are, in a manner, wholly owing to the first rudiments, formerly taught. Modern musicians have rarely made use of the writings of *Aristoxenus*, *Ptolemee*, and the rest of the ancient musicians; and, of those that have studied them, very few, unless their editors have confessed that they could understand them. Others have laid them so far aside, as useless for their purpose; that it is very probable, that many excellent composers have scarce ever heard of their names.

---
21 Ibid., IV.

Nevertheless, he proposes that the essence of ancient music, insofar as its purpose, has not been entirely lost.

> Musick has still, and always will have very lasting charms. Wherefore, since the moderns have used their utmost diligence to improve whatever was improved in the writings of all sorts of ancient authors, upon other equally difficult and very often not so delightful subjects, one can hardly imagine but that the world would, long ere now, have heard something more demonstrably proved of the comparative perfection of ancient Musick, with large harangues in the commendation of the respective inventors, if their memory had been preserved, than barely an account of the fabulous stories of *Orpheus* or *Amhion*, which either have no foundation at all, or, as Horace understood them, are allegorically to be interpreted of their reducing a wild and savage people to order and regularity. But this is not urged against Sir William Temple, who is not convinced of the extent of modern industry, sagacity and curiosity; but to other admirers of ancient Musick, who, upon hearsay, believe it to be more perfect than the modern.

The reason for this he gives in a brief, but interesting, suggestion that there are physical laws underlying music itself, which must create similarities between ancient and modern music.

> Musick is a Physico-Mathematical Science, built upon fixed rules, and stated proportions; which, one would think, might have been as well improved upon the old foundations, as upon new ones, since the grounds of Musick have always been the same. And Guido's scale, as Dr. Wallis assures us, is the same for substance with the *Diagramma Veterum*.

One argument in favor of modern music which Wotton advances is that it is assumed it has the potential for more variety.

> The ancients had not, in the opinion of several who are judges of the matter, so many gradations of half-notes and quarter-notes between the whole ones as are now used; which must of necessity introduce an unspeakable variety into modern Musick, more than could formerly be had. Because it is in notes, as in numbers, the more there are of them, the more variously they may be combined together.

Wotton's next topic is by far the most interesting with respect to aesthetics. Rarely addressed at such length, is the general nature of the impressions of the listener. He begins by observing that on one level, all listeners appreciate certain basic qualities in music. These things he considers universal, regardless of the education of the listener.

> It is very probably that the ancient Musick had all that which still most affects common hearers. Most men are moved with an excellent voice, are pleased when time is exactly kept, and love to hear an instrument played true to a fine voice, when the one does not so far drown the other, but that they can readily understand what is sung, and can, without previous skill, perceive that the one exactly answers the other throughout; and their passions will be effectually moved with sprightly or lamentable compositions. In all which things the ancients, probably, were very perfect.

He continues by distinguishing between the 'skilled' listener of music and the 'common' listener.[22] The skilled listener, according to Wotton, listens to the details, as left brain conceptual ideas, rather than on a more holistic level. Leaving no doubt, he uses the analogy of looking at a painting. The expert, he says, looks at the detail, the technique and, for all we can tell, never sees the entire painting!

> To the [ancient] men, many of our modern compositions, where several parts are sung or played at the same time, would seem confused, intricate, and unpleasant: though in such compositions, the greater this seeming confusion, the more pleasure does the skillful hearer take in unraveling every several part, and in observing how artfully those seemingly disagreeing tones join, like true-cut Tallies, one within another, to make up that united concord, which very often gives little satisfaction to common ears; and yet it is in such sort of compositions, that the Excellency of Modern Musick chiefly consists. For, in making a judgment of Musick, it is much the same thing as it is of pictures. A great judge in Painting does not gaze upon an exquisite piece so much to raise his passions, as to inform his judgment, as to approve, or to find fault. His eye runs over every part, to find out every excellency; and his pleasure lies in the reflex act of his mind, when he knows that he can judiciously tell where every beauty lies, or where the defects are discernible: which an ordinary spectator would never find out.

The 'common' man, however, is interested in the theme or story of the painting and the emotions seen in it. Likewise in music, says Wotton, the common man has his 'passions raised,' without any contribution to his 'understanding.'

> The chief thing which the [common] man wants, is the story; and if that is lively represented, if the figures do not laugh when they should weep, or weep when they should appear pleased, he is satisfied. And this, perhaps, equally well, if the piece be drawn by Raphael, as by an ordinary master, who is just able to make things look like life.
>
> So likewise in Musick; He that hears a *numerous* Song, set to a very moving tune, exquisitely sung to a sweet instrument, will find this passions raised, while his understanding, possibly, may have little or no share in the business. He scarce knows, perhaps, the names of the notes, and so can be affected only with an Harmony, of which he can render no account. To this man, what is intricate, appears confused; and therefore he can make no judgment of the true excellency of those things, which seem *fiddling* to him only, for want of skill in *Musick*.

---

22 After the break-through in the medical understanding of left and right brain hemisphere function, in the 1960s, this became a big topic in the field of music. 'Common' listeners, and musicians who do not concentrate on conceptual data, listen to music primarily with the left ear (right hemisphere). Musicians listening for conceptual parts of music, listen with the right ear (left hemisphere). From this follows the obvious conclusion that one of the chief effects of music schools is to ruin persons as listeners.

Again, for the 'skilled' listener of music, the satisfaction comes not simply from the emotions of the music, but from the combination of the emotions with intellectual understanding.

> The skill or ignorance of the composer serve rather to entertain the understanding, rather than to gratify the passions of a skillful master; whose passions are then the most thoroughly raised, when his understanding received the greatest satisfaction.

Never did a writer so miss the point of music; never did a writer offer so vivid an insight into the origin of the philosophy of modern music schools.

Wotton's concluding thoughts are also remarkable. He concedes that ancient music better achieved than modern, the 'great End of Musick, which is to please the audience.' Ancient music better moved the emotions, and even changed the very nature of the listener, than modern music. And yet, he says modern music is more perfect!—to everyone except the general audience.

> Indeed, the great End of Musick, which is to please the audience, was anciently, perhaps, better answered than now; though a modern master would then have been dissatisfied, because such consorts as the ancient Symphonies properly were, in which several instruments, and perhaps voices, played and sung the same part together, cannot discover the extent and perfection of the art, which here only is to be considered, so much as the compositions of our modern Operas.
>
> From all this it may, perhaps, be not unreasonable to conclude, that though those charms of Musick, by which men and beasts, fishes, fowls and serpents, were so frequently enchanted, and their very natures changed, be really and irrecoverably lost; yet the art of Musick, that is to say, of singing, and playing upon harmonious instruments, is, in itself, much a more perfect thing, though, perhaps, not much more pleasant to an unskillful audience, than it ever was among the ancient Greeks and Romans.

CHARLES GILDON

Charles Gildon, who flourished during the late sixteenth century, used his *The Life of Mr. Thomas Betterton, the Late Eminent Tragedian* as a vehicle for a discussion of the art of gesture, intended for actors, lawyers and preachers.

ON THE PHYSIOLOGY OF AESTHETICS

We have provided numerous illustrations, in these volumes, of the strong prejudice for the right hand expressed in early literature. We understand today that this is in part explained by the curious inclination of the left hemisphere of the brain, the speaking and writing hemisphere, to deny the existence of the right hemisphere. In Gildon's discussion of the actor's gestures we can see how vividly this idea was felt.

He recommends the practice of observing one's own gestures in a mirror, but quickly points out that this practice includes a great disadvantage in the fact that everything is seen backwards. He finds this particularly serious with respect to the hands.

> When you make a motion with your right hand, the reflection makes it seem as done by the left, which confounds the gesture, and gives it an awkward appearance.[23]

Later, we see how extraordinarily important the right–left hand question was to Gildon.

> If an action comes to be used by only one hand, that must be the right, it being indecent to make a gesture with the left alone … When you speak of your self, the right and not the left hand must be applied to the bosom, declaring your own faculties, and passions; your heart, your soul, or your conscience, but this action generally speaking, should be only applied or expressed by laying the hand gently on the breast.[24]

On the Psychology of Aesthetics

Most early philosophers had made the mistaken conclusion that the emotions could be read in the eyes, whereas actually it is in the face itself. It was from this mistaken perspective that Gildon provides the aspiring actor with an extraordinary survey of the expression of emotions he finds communicated by the eyes.

> To express Nature justly, one must be master of Nature in all its appearances, which can only be drawn from observation, which will tell us, that the passions and habits of the mind discover themselves in our looks, actions and gestures.
>
> Thus we find a rolling eye that is quick and inconstant in its motion, argues a quick but light wit; a hot and choleric complexion, with an inconstant and impatient mind; and in a woman it gives a strong proof of wantonness and immodesty. Heavy dull eyes a dull mind, and difficulty of conception. For this reason we observe, that all or most people in years, sick men, and persons of a phlegmatic constitution are slow in the turning of their eyes.
>
> That extreme propensity to winking in some eyes, proceed from a soul very subject to fear, arguing a weakness of spirit, and a feeble disposition of the eye-lids.
>
> A bold staring eye, that fixes on a man, proceeds either from a blockish stupidity, as in rustics; impudence, as in malicious persons; prudence, as in those in authority, or incontinence as in lewd women.

---

23 Charles Gildon, *The Life of Mr. Thomas Betterton, the Late Eminent Tragedian* [1710] (London: Frank Cass Reprint, 1970), 54ff.

24 Ibid., 74ff.

> Eyes inflamed and fiery are the genuine effect of choler and anger; eyes quiet, and calm with a secret kind of grace and pleasantness are the offspring of love and friendship …
>
> Eyes lifted on high show arrogance and pride, but cast down express humbleness of mind. Yet we lift up our eyes when we address ourselves in prayer to God, and ask anything of him.[25]

On the Aesthetics of Music

Gildon digresses from his discussion of the means of communication by the actor to comment on the nature of music. Among several interesting observations here, we find him one of few critics to understand that music is specifically of the province of the right hemisphere of the brain, and not of the world of Reason. On the other hand, his view that music is enhanced by the addition of poetry is curiously the reverse of the contention of most writers of this period. As the reader will see below, Gildon was rather hostile toward opera. He agreed with other drama critics of this period that the popularity of opera had greatly diminished the importance of English theater. Thus, he writes here: return music to the theater and don't make it a separate 'entertainment.'

> It must, however, be allowed, that Music discovers a wonderful power, a power not to be resisted; but I am afraid, that power acts more on the body, than the mind, or by the body on the mind; the ear has a pleasing sensation at melodious sounds, and that gratifies the mind, which cannot naturally be uneasy when the body is delighted with agreeable sensations. But this proves Music as transporting, as it is to be but a sensual pleasure, and deriving no part from Reason, nor directing any part to the gratification of the rational soul. But then this power and force of Music is heightened by the addition of poetry, which among the ancients even in dancing was very seldom left out; for passionate words give a double vigor to harmony, and make for it a surer way to the heart, than when the soul is unconcerned in the bare and solitary notes. And vocal music is agreed by all to be the most noble, and most touching, that tone being esteemed the most excellent, which comes nearest to vocal sounds.
>
> Music therefore ought still, as originally it was, to be mingled with the drama, where it is subservient to poetry, and comes into the relief of the mind, when that has been long intense on some noble scene of passion, but ought never to be a separate entertainment of any length.[26]

---

25 Ibid., 41ff. Gildon also provides a lengthy discussion on the use of the voice for emotional expression [Ibid., 85–144] and some interesting speculation on the nature of gesture in Greek dance [Ibid., 144–155].

26 Ibid., 157ff.

On Opera

Earlier, Gildon had written at length on the negative influence on English drama by French ballet and Italian opera.

> And while our own poets were neglected, the French dancers got estates; and this by the influence of those, who at the same expense might have made their own names and their country famous for the encouragement of the polite arts and sciences, now neglected to a degree of barbarity, greater, than most nations on this side of Lapland.
>
> I must admit, that the excuse of our leaders seems greater and more reasonable in the indulgence they show to music, in their subscriptions for Italian singers …[27]

While Gildon believed that vocal music represented music in its highest potential, this alone did not justify opera for him.

> But although we allow the vocal the preeminence of all other sorts of music, yet we cannot without the greatest absurdities receive even that on subjects improper for it, or in a manner unnatural, that is, as it is offered to us in our Opera's with which of late the Town (I mean the leading part of the audience) has been perfectly intoxicated, and in that drunken fit has thrown away more thousands of Pounds for their support, than would have furnished us with the best poetry, and the best music in the world, without declaring against common sense. Operas have been said to be the invention of modern Italy, e'er the Return of Learning, and in the midst of that barbarous ignorance, with which the inundations of Vandals, Goths, Huns and Lombards had over-whelmed it; but I think it is pretty plain, that the Romans were, before that, sunk as far from their ancient learning and sense.

Gildon next turns to the debate regarding the aesthetic priority of French versus Italian opera, and mentions several books on this topic, although he does not name their authors. He proceeds, after mentioning one of the French books, to make his case for the excellence of the operas of Purcell.

> Although if I had any thing to do with this controversy, I should very much doubt the judgment of the Frenchman from one instance of many, where he admires the Italians for singing out of tune, that they may give the better relish to the fine harmony, that succeeds; as if a man should admire it as a perfection in another to speak nonsense first, to give the better taste to sense afterwards.
>
> I confess, I was a little surprised, to hear of and see this book with notes [music?] by Signor H…. or some creature of his; for I thought they would never have ventured so far out of their depth, as to launch from mere sound into sense, from pricking musical notes, to writing; since that was the only effectual way they could take to convince the world, that we were imposed on by those, who were not content to bubble us of our money for airs and recitatives unless they told us to our faces, that we know nothing of the matter, and music, therefore, receive whatever stuff they would be graciously pleased to bestow upon us.

---
27 Ibid., 155ff.

> But this author puts a great stress on the taking of his compositions, and the miscarriage of those of others, when he had before denied, that we knew anything of the matter. But if he allow that, as a test of the excellence of his opera, that will be much stronger for Mr. Henry Purcell, whose music supported a company of young raw actors, against the best and most favored of that time, and transported the town for several years together, as they do yet all true lovers of music. Let any master compare *twice ten hundred deities*, the music in the *Frost Scene*, several parts of the *Indian Queen*, and twenty more pieces of Henry Purcell, with all the *Arrieto's*, *Dacapo's*, *Recitativo's* of *Camilla*, *Pyrrbus*, *Clotilda*, etc. and then judge which excels. Purcell penetrates the heart, makes the blood dance through your veins, and thrill with the agreeable violence offered by his Heavenly Harmony; the *Arietto's* are pretty light Airs, which tickle the ear, but reach no further; Purcell moves the passions as he pleases, nay, *Paints* in Sounds …

Gildon mentions that this same anonymous book has indicated that English taste has improved since the time of Purcell and that the public should no longer 'relish any of these things.' In answer, he suggests,

> I would therefore fain know how our taste is mended? Do the promiscuous audience know more of the art of harmony and music? No—not one in a thousand understands one single note. How shall these therefore give the preference to this new music, to that of Henry Purcell's?

Gildon now addresses himself to the purpose of opera, in particular the question, should the purpose of opera be merely to please?

> But to return from this digression, in vindication of our English music, to the absurdities of operas; I think the degeneracy of the age is but too apparent, in the setting up and encouraging so paltry a diversion, that has nothing in it either manly or noble.
> But, says a certain gentleman, the business of the stage is to *please*, and if this pleasure be found in operas, what signifies all the objected absurdities? Although this be a very ridiculous defense, and will hold of the most scandalous and dullest things in Nature; yet I have heard it urged by men of allowed wit, and indeed, who had more of that, than of Reason, and judgment, which is founded on that. But if this be really a good argument, *Clince of Barnet, Bartholomew-Fair* drolls, nay a *Jack-pudding* entertainment in *Moor-Fields* are noble entertainments, for all these please, and have as good a title to the stage, as operas, nay, from Reason as better, as not subject to so many absurdities …
> Would therefore a man of sense be for a diversion, which levels his understanding with that of the refuse of the Mob? Yet the following of operas does this, and insisting in their vindication, that whatever pleases deserves encouragement, since it is a scandal to be pleased with some things, as proving but a weak capacity, or a very unpolished taste.
> There are some pleasures, which none but men of fine sense, and a Gust for the art, can distinguish, as in painting, engraving, etc., while the vulgar look with an equal eye on the best and the worst. A certain country squire of my acquaintance was drinking in a country alehouse, in which seeing several notable cuts, as of the *Prodigal, Robin Hood* and *Little John*, and some other scurvy prints, worse than ever Overton sold, he turned to the gentleman, who sat next him, and

said, 'Well! this painting is a noble Art.' And indeed an engraving of old Vanhove's, or worse, if any worse can be, would please the vulgar, as well as one of Edlinch, Audrand, or any of the Italian cuts; and a piece of mere sign-dauber is as valuable in the eyes of a gross and common understanding, as one of Raphael's or Thornbill's. And so in music, a Taber and Pipe, a Cymbal or Horn-pipe, will ravish the mob, more than the admirable Mr. Shoar with his incomparable lute; and the Ballad Tune *Lilly Bullero* more, than a fine Sonata of Corelli. And thus in poetry, the millions will prefer Bunyan and Quarles to Milton and Dryden; and sure no gentleman of fine taste and genius in all these things, but would be ashamed to urge such an argument as pleasing, since all these, which are scandalous, please the most in number.

ANTHONY COOPER, EARL OF SHAFTESBURY (1671–1713)

Anthony Cooper, known simply as Shaftesbury, was a student of Locke, but as a wealthy and cultured gentleman, he was comfortable in discussing the arts, which was a subject rarely mentioned by Locke. While Durant perhaps exaggerates in finding that Shaftesbury 'almost founded aesthetics in modern philosophy,'[28] his voice was certainly one of the few heard on this subject at this time among the upper class in England. His famous essays were published in 1711.

ON THE PHYSIOLOGY OF AESTHETICS

Although philosophers of this period knew nothing of the medical facts of the separate hemispheres of the brain, many were beginning to sense that there was more to man than Reason. Shaftesbury could not have been more accurate than when he speaks of both heart and brain.

> We are returned to our old article of advice: that main preliminary of self-study and inward converse which we have found so much wanting in the authors of our time. They should add the wisdom of the heart to the task and exercise of the brain, in order to bring proportion and beauty into their works.[29]

But, in the end, like the philosophers of old, he believed that Reason must rule.

> Thus we find how far worth and virtue depend on a knowledge of right and wrong, and on a use of reason, sufficient to secure a right application of the affections.[30]

---

28 Will Durant, *The Age of Louis XIV* (New York: Simon and Schuster, 1963), 590.
29 Shaftesbury, *Characteristics of Men, Manners, Opinions, Times*, 'Advice to an Author,' II, iii.
30 Ibid., 'Concerning Virtue or Merit,' II, iii.

In another place he seems to contrast creativity with Reason and one cannot help but observe here that art has fallen so low in esteem that creativity is equated with madness.

> Every man indeed who is not absolutely beside himself, must of necessity hold his fancies under some kind of discipline and management. The stricter this discipline is, the more the man is rational and in his wits. The looser it is, the more fantastical he must be, and the nearer to the madman's state. This is a business which can never stand still. I must always be a winner or loser at the game. Either I work upon my fancies, or they on me. If I give quarter, they will not. There can be no truce, no suspension of arms between us. The one or the other must be superior and have the command. For if the fancies are left to themselves, the government must of course be theirs. And then, what difference between such a state and madness?[31]

The only remarks Shaftesbury makes on education clearly reflect the prejudices of a wealthy gentleman looking down on traditional studies. By 'virtuoso,' he means a gentleman who affects great knowledge on the arts, especially poetry.

> I am persuaded that to be a virtuoso (so far as befits a gentleman) is a higher step towards the becoming a man of virtue and good sense than the being which in this age we call a scholar. For even rude Nature itself, in its primitive simplicity, is a better guide to judgment than improved sophistry and pedantic learning … The mere amusements of a gentlemen are found more improving than the profound researches of pedants; and in the management of our youth we are forced to have recourse to the former, as an antidote against the genius peculiar to the latter.[32]

In a footnote to this passage, Shaftesbury complains that Letters have been banished from the universities to distant cloisters. He continues,

> The sprightly arts and sciences are severed from philosophy, which consequently must grow dronish, insipid, pedantic, useless, and directly opposite to the real knowledge and practice of the world and mankind. Our youth accordingly seem to have their only chance between two widely different roads: either that of pedantry and school-learning, which lies amidst the dregs and most corrupt part of ancient literature, or that of the fashionable illiterate world, which aims merely at the character of the fine gentleman.

---

31 Ibid., 'Advice to an Author,' III, ii.
32 Ibid., III, iii.

On the Psychology of Aesthetics

All philosophers of the seventeenth century attempted to define the nature of the various emotions, but in Shaftesbury we almost feel we are reading of the beginning of modern psychology.

> The study of human emotion cannot fail of leading me towards the knowledge of human nature and of myself.
> This is the philosophy which by Nature has the preeminence above all other science or knowledge.[33]

In a footnote in his 'Miscellaneous Reflections,' Shaftesbury indicates he believes the emotions are genetic. Referring to an anonymous philosopher, whose anecdote he has quoted, Shaftesbury adds,

> Perhaps if the philosopher would accordingly examine himself and consider his natural passions, he would find there were such belonged to him as Nature had premeditated in his behalf, and for which she had furnished him with ideas long before any particular practice or experience of his own.[34]

But if the emotions are in some sense genetic, Shaftesbury still recognized an inequality in their strength among individual men. It is interesting that he uses music, which is the very expression of emotions, as a metaphor to describe his views on this subject.

> Upon the whole, it may be said properly to be the same with the affections or passions in an animal constitution as with the strings of a musical instrument. If these, though in ever so just proportion one to another, are strained beyond a certain degree, it is more than the instrument will bear: the lute or lyre is abused, and its effect lost. On the other hand, if while some of the strings are duly strained, others are not wound up to their due proportion, then is the instrument still in disorder, and its part ill performed. The several species of creatures are like different sorts of instruments; and even in the same species of creatures (as in the same sort of instrument) one is not entirely like the other, nor will the same strings fit each. The same degree of strength which winds up one, and fits the several strings to a just harmony and consort, may in another burst both the strings and instrument itself. Thus men who have the liveliest sense, and are the easiest affected with pain or pleasure, have need of the strongest influence or force of other affections, such as tenderness, love, sociableness, compassion, in order to preserve a right balance within, and to maintain them in their duty, and in the just performance of their part, whilst others, who are of a cooler blood, or lower key, need not the same allay or counterpart, nor are made by Nature to feel those tender and endearing affections in so exquisite a degree.[35]

---

33 Ibid., III, i.
34 Ibid., 'Miscellaneous Reflections,' IV, ii, fn.
35 Ibid., 'Concerning Virtue or Merit,' II, iii.

Regarding the traditional aesthetic subject of Pleasure and Pain, Shaftesbury observes that it is common knowledge that Pleasure can be of either the body or the mind. Of these, the pleasures of the mind are the greatest.[36] He even contends that the study of mathematics produces a higher pleasure than that of sense.[37] Yet, it was also evident to him that all Pleasure and Pain are based on the emotions.

> Now the mental enjoyments are either actually the very natural affections themselves in their immediate operation, or they wholly in a manner proceed from them, and are no other than their effects.
>
> If so, it follows that, the natural affections duly established in a rational creature being the only means which can procure him a constant series or succession of the mental enjoyments, they are the only means which can procure him a certain and solid happiness.[38]

On the Philosophy of Aesthetics

Shaftesbury writes extensively on his philosophy of aesthetics in the arts. We find particularly interesting his observations on the character of the artist himself. He begins by suggesting that the artist has the ability to connect with humanity in all its breadth.

> The mind, which is spectator or auditor of other minds, cannot be without its eye and ear, so as to discern proportion, distinguish sound, and scan each sentiment or thought which comes before it. It can let nothing escape its censure. It feels the soft and harsh, the agreeable and disagreeable in the affections; and finds a foul and fair, a harmonious and a dissonant, as really and truly here as in any musical numbers or in the outward forms or representations of sensible things. Nor can it withhold its admiration and ecstasy, its aversion and scorn, any more in what relates to one than to the other of these subjects. So that to deny the common and natural sense of a sublime and beautiful in things, will appear an affectation merely, to any one who considers duly of this affair.[39]

Another characteristic of the artist which Shaftesbury evidently admired was the conviction to stand by his artistic beliefs.

> There is nothing more certain than that a real genius and thorough artist of whatever kind can never, without the greatest unwillingness and shame, be induced to act below his character, and for mere interest be prevailed with to prostitute his art or science by performing contrary to its known rules … Be they ever so idle, dissolute, or debauched, how regardless soever of other

---

36 Ibid., II, i.
37 Ibid., II, i.
38 Ibid., II, i.
39 Ibid., II, iii.

rules, they abhor any transgression in their art, and would choose to lose customers and starve rather than a base compliance with the world to act contrary to what they call the justness and truth of work.

'Sir,' says a poor fellow of this kind to his rich customer, 'you are mistaken in coming to me for such a piece of workmanship. Let who will make it for you as you fancy, I know it to be wrong. Whatever I have made hitherto has been true work. And neither for you sake or anybody's else shall I put my hand to any other.'

This is virtue! real virtue and love of truth; independent of opinion and above the world …

Our modern authors, on the contrary, are turned and modeled (as themselves confess) by the public relish and current humor of the times. They regulate themselves by the irregular fancy of the world, and frankly admit they are preposterous and absurd, in order to accommodate themselves to the genius of the age. In our days the audience makes the poet, and the bookseller the author, with what profit to the public, or what prospect of lasting fame and honor to the writer, let any one who has judgment imagine.[40]

Shaftesbury also noticed that the finest artists aimed for an ideal definition of perfection.

However difficult or desperate it may appear in any artist to endeavor to bring perfection into his work, if he has not at least the idea of perfection to give him aim he will be found very defective and mean in his performance. Though his intention be to please the world, he must nevertheless be, in a manner, above it, and fix his eye upon that consummate grace, that beauty of Nature, and that perfection of numbers which the rest of mankind, feeling only by the effect whilst ignorant of the cause, term the *je ne scay quoy*, the unintelligible or the 'I know not what,' and suppose to be a kind of charm or enchantment of which the artist himself can give no account.[41]

Shaftesbury also devotes much attention to the impact of art on the individual. In the following, in addition to defining some elements of taste, he suggests the arts help define the standard of humanity.

By gentlemen of fashion, I understand those to whom a natural good genius, or the force of good education, has given a sense of what is naturally graceful and becoming. Some by mere nature, others by art and practice, are masters of an ear in music, an eye in painting, a fancy in the ordinary things of ornament and grace, a judgment in proportions of all kinds and a general good taste in most of those subjects which make the amusement and delight of the ingenious people of the world. Let such gentlemen as these be as extravagant as they please, or as irregular in their morals, they must at the same time discover their inconsistency, live at variance with themselves, and in contradiction to that principle on which they ground their highest pleasure and entertainment.[42]

---

40 Ibid., 'Advice to an Author,' II, iii.
41 Ibid., III, iii.
42 Ibid., 'Freedom of Wit and Humor,' IV, ii.

Even those gentlemen who pretend to be disinterested in the arts are nevertheless affected. We also see here the hallmark of the aristocratic view of the arts among the upper class in England since the beginning of the seventeenth century, which was admiration of art, but not the artist.

> The men of pleasure, who seem the greatest condemners of this philosophical beauty, are forced often to confess her charms. They can as heartily as others commend honesty; and are as much struck with the beauty of a generous part. They admire the thing itself, though not the means.[43]

Shaftesbury contends that even the character of the artist himself experiences positive impact from his art. Included here are additional characteristics of high art.

> For those artists who copy from another life, who study the graces and perfections of minds, and are real masters of those rules which constitute this latter science, it is impossible they should fail of being themselves improved, and amended in their better part …
>
> He notes the boundaries of the passions, and knows their exact tones and measures; by which he justly represents them, marks the sublime of sentiments and action, and distinguishes the beautiful from the deformed, the amiable from the odious. The moral artist who can thus imitate the Creator, and is thus knowing in the inward form and structure of his fellow creatures, will hardly, I presume, be found unknowing in himself, or at a loss in those numbers which make the harmony of a mind.[44]

On the subject of the definition of Beauty, nearly all of Shaftesbury's comments center on Truth. In this passage he also digresses to the question of the relationship of Art and Nature.

> And thus, after all, the most natural beauty in the world is honesty and moral truth. For all beauty is truth. True features make the beauty of a face; and true proportions the beauty of architecture; as true measures that of harmony and music. In poetry, which is all fable, truth still is the perfection …
>
> A painter, if he has any genius, understands the truth and unity of design; and knows he is even then unnatural when he follows Nature too close, and strictly copies Life. For his art allows him not to bring all nature into his piece, but a part only. However, his piece, if it be beautiful, and carries truth, must be of a whole, by itself, complete, independent, and withal as great and comprehensive as he can make it …
>
> The mere face-painter, indeed, has little in common with the poet; but, like the mere historian, copies what he sees, and minutely traces every feature and odd mark. It is otherwise with the men of invention and design. It is from the many objects of nature, and not from a particular one, that those geniuses form the idea of their work. Thus the best artists are said to have been indefatigable in studying the best statues: as esteeming them a better rule than the most perfect human bodies could afford. And thus some considerable wits have recommended the best poems as preferable to the best of histories; and better teaching the truth of characters and nature of mankind.[45]

---

43 Ibid., IV, ii.

44 Ibid., 'Advice to an Author,' I, iii.

45 Ibid., 'Freedom of Wit and Humor,' IV, iii.

In a dialogue which follows, Shaftesbury establishes his conviction that it is not the art object which is beautiful, but the skill of the artist.[46]

In addition to Shaftesbury's comments on nature and art above, as he continues his discussion of this topic he concentrates on one's *own* nature, the passions. We also note here one of the earliest references to the concept of an artist writing or composing for posterity, as well as the present.

> Of all other beauties which virtuosos pursue, poets celebrate, musicians sing, and architects or artists, of whatever kind, describe or form, the most delightful, the most engaging and pathetic, is that which is drawn from real life, and from the passions. Nothing affects the heart like that which is purely from itself, and of its own nature …
>
> Let poets, or the men of harmony, deny, if they can, this force of Nature, or withstand this moral magic. They, for their parts, carry a double portion of this charm about them. For in the first place, the very passions which inspires them is itself the love of numbers, decency and proportion; and this too, not in a narrow sense, or after a selfish way (for who of them composes for himself?), but in a friendly social view, for the pleasure and good of others, even down to posterity and future ages. And in the next place, it is evident in these performers that their chief theme and subject, that which raises their genius the most, and by which they so effectually move others, is purely manners and the moral part. For this is the effect, and this the beauty of their art: 'in vocal measures of syllables and sounds to express the harmony and numbers of an inward kind, and represent the beauties of a human soul by proper foils and contrarieties, which serve as graces in this limning, and render this music of the passions more powerful and enchanting.'[47]

Another topic upon which Shaftesbury wrote at length, was on the development of taste.

> How long ere a true taste is gained! How many things shocking, how many offensive at first, which afterwards are known and acknowledged the highest beauties! For it is not instantly we acquire the sense by which these beauties are discoverable. Labor and pains are required, and time to cultivate a natural genius over so apt or forward … Which way should we come to understand better? which way be knowing in these beauties? Is study, science or learning necessary to understand all beauties? And for the sovereign beauty, is there no skill or science required? In painting there are shades and masterly strokes which the vulgar understand not, but find fault with; in architecture there is the rustic; in music the chromatic kind, and skillful mixture of dissonances.[48]

Later Shaftesbury considers whether it is opinion, the judgment of the many, which determines taste. He concludes on the contrary,

> It is we ourselves create and form our taste. If we resolve to have it just, it is in our power. We may esteem and resolve, approve and disapprove, as we would wish. For who, would not rejoice

---

46   Ibid., 'Miscellaneous Reflections,' II.

47   Ibid., 'Freedom of Wit and Humor,' IV, ii.

48   Ibid., 'The Moralists,' III, ii.

to be always equal and consonant to himself, and have constantly that opinion of things which is natural and proportionable?[49]

Among Shaftesbury's comments on poetry, we find his comments on the development of this art in England the most interesting.

> The British Muses may well lie abject and obscure, especially being as yet in their mere infant state. They have hitherto scarce arrived to anything of shapeliness or person. They lisp in their cradles; and their stammering tongues, have nothing besides their youth and rawness can excuse, have hitherto spoken in wretched pun and quibble. Our dramatic Shakespeare, our Fletcher, Jonson, and our epic Milton preserve this style. And even a latter race, scarce free of this infirmity, and aiming at a false sublime, with crowded simile and mixed metaphor, entertain our raw fancy and unpracticed ear, which has not as yet had leisure to form itself and become truly musical.
>
> But those reverend bards, rude as they were, according to their time and age, have provided us however with the richest ore. To their eternal honor they have withal been the first of Europeans who, since the Gothic model of poetry, attempted to throw off the horrid discord of jingling rhyme.[50]

In discussing the drama, Shaftesbury documents most of the prevailing complaints one reads elsewhere and, indeed, his own personal enthusiasm is conspicuously missing. It is interesting that he focuses on the influence on theater by the women in attendance.

> It is alleged indeed by our stage poets, in excuse for vile ribaldry and other gross irregularities, both in the fable and language of their pieces, that their success, which depends chiefly on the ladies, is never so fortunate as when this havoc is made on virtue and good sense, and their pieces are exhibited publicly in this monstrous form. I know not how they can answer it to the fair sex to speak (as they pretend) experimentally, and with such nice distinction of their audience. How far this excuse may serve them in relation to common amours and love adventures I will not take upon me to pronounce; but I must own, I have often wondered to see our fighting plays become so much the entertainment of that tender sex.[51]

......

> We find, indeed, our theater become of late the subject of a growing criticism. We hear it openly complained 'that in our newer plays as well as in our older, in comedy as well as tragedy, the stage presents a proper scene of uproar,—duels fought, swords drawn, many of a side, wounds given and sometimes dressed too, the surgeon called and the patient probed and attended upon the spot. That in our tragedy nothing is so common as wheels, racks, and gibbets properly adorned, executions decently performed, headless bodies and bodiless heads exposed to view, battles fought, murders committed, and the dead carried off in great numbers.' Such is our politeness!'

---

49 Ibid., 'Miscellaneous Reflections,' II.
50 Ibid., 'Advice to an Author,' II, i.
51 Ibid., II,iii.

Nor are these plays, on this account, the less frequented by either of the sexes, which inclines me to favor the conceit [we] have suggested concerning the mutual correspondence and relation between our royal theater and popular circus or bear garden …

But then I must add too, that the excessive indulgence and favor shown to our playwrights, on account of what their mere genius and flowing vein afford, has rendered them intolerably supine, conceited, and admirers of themselves. The public having once suffered them to take the ascendant, they become, like flattered princes, impatient of contradiction or advice. They think it a disgrace to be criticized, even by a friend … He thinks it necessary, indeed (lest his learning should be called in question), to show the world that he errs knowingly against the rules of art. And for this reason, whatever piece he publishes at any time, he seldom fails, in some prefixed apology, to speak in such a manner of criticism and art as may confound the ordinary reader, and prevent him from taking up a part which, should he once assume, would prove fatal to the impotent and mean performance.[52]

On the subject of the critic, Shaftesbury is rather unique in the fact that he finds only praise. The following is one of several similar passages.

I take upon me absolutely to condemn the fashionable and prevailing custom of inveighing against critics as the common enemies, the pests and incendiaries of the commonwealth of Wit and Letters. I assert, on the contrary, that they are the props and pillars of this building; and that without the encouragement and propagation of such a race, we should remain as Gothic architects as ever.[53]

On the Aesthetics of Music

There are only a few comments by Shaftesbury which touch on the definition of the nature of music. In one he seems to imply that the laws of music are found in nature itself.

Should a writer upon music, addressing himself to the students and lovers of the art, declare to them 'that the measure or rule of harmony was caprice or will, humor or fashion,' it is not very likely he should be heard with great attention or treated with real gravity. For harmony is harmony by nature, let men judge ever so ridiculously of music.[54]

In another place, Shaftesbury curiously includes music with architecture (and beautiful stones, woods, rivers, mountains, etc.) as belonging to the inanimate classification.[55] This strikes us

---

52 Ibid., 'Miscellaneous Reflections,' V, i.
53 Ibid., 'Advice to an Author,' II, ii.
54 Ibid., III, iii.
55 Ibid., 'Miscellaneous Reflections,' III, ii, fn.

as quite odd, for one of the most conspicuous characteristics of music in the seventeenth century was that it was invariably *live*.

On the general topic of the universality of music, Shaftesbury is not entirely consistent. In the following, he appears to argue for a genetic understanding of some elements of the musical experience.

> Nothing surely is more strongly imprinted on our minds, or more closely interwoven with our souls, than the idea or sense of order and proportion. Hence all the force of numbers, and those powerful arts founded on their management and use. What a difference there is between harmony and discord! cadency and convulsion! What a difference between composed and orderly motion, and that which is ungoverned and accidental! …
>
> Now as this difference is immediately perceived by a plain internal sensation, so there is withal in reason this account of it, that whatever things have order, the same have unity of design, and concur in one; are parts constituent of one whole or are, in themselves, entire systems … What else is even a tune or symphony, or any excellent piece of music, than a certain system of proportioned sounds?[56]

The following, however, appears to argue against universality.

> If a musician were cried up to the skies by a certain set of people who had no ear in music, he would surely be put to the blush, and could hardly, with a good countenance, accept the benevolence of his auditors, till they had acquired a more competent apprehension of him, and could by their own senses find out something really good in his performance. Till this were brought about, there would be little glory in the case, and the musician, though ever so vain, would have little reason to be contented.[57]

In another place, after asking some rhetorical questions, he suggests sufficient universality that everyone can judge.

> If a musician performs his part well in the hardest symphonies he must necessarily know the notes and understand the rules of harmony and music. But must a man, therefore, who has an ear, and has studied the rules of music, of necessity have a voice or hand? Can not he possibly judge a fiddle but who is himself a fiddler?[58]

In only one place does Shaftesbury touch on the subject of purpose in music, which in this case is musical therapy. He begins this discussion with a brief reference to the beginning of the arts in the ancient period.

> It may be easily perceived from hence that the goddess Persuasion must have been in a manner the mother of poetry, rhetoric, music, and the other kindred arts. For it is apparent that where

---

56 Ibid., 'The Moralists,' II, iii.
57 Ibid., 'Enthusiasm,' V.
58 Ibid., 'Miscellaneous Reflections,' V, ii.

chief men and leaders had the strongest interest to persuade, they used the highest endeavors to please. So that in such a state or polity as has been described, not only the best order of thought and turn of fancy, but the most soft and inviting numbers, must have been employed to charm the public ear, and to incline the heart by the agreeableness of expression.

Almost all the ancient masters of this sort were said to have been musicians. And tradition, which soon grew fabulous, could not better represent the first founders or establishers of these larger societies than as real songsters, who, by the power of their voice and lyre, could charm the wildest beasts, and draw the rude forests and rocks into the form of fairest cities. Nor can it be doubted that the same artists, who so industriously applied themselves to study the numbers of speech, must have made proportionable improvements in the study of mere sounds and natural harmony, which of itself must have considerably contributed towards the softening the rude manners and harsh temper of their new people.[59]

Finally, as we have contended in these volumes that one important hallmark of art music is the presence of the contemplative listener, we were interested to read Shaftesbury also emphasizing this point.

When the persuasive arts were grown thus into repute, and the power of moving the affections became the study and emulation of the forward wits and aspiring geniuses of the times, it would necessarily happen that many geniuses of equal size and strength, though less covetous of public applause, of power, or of influence over mankind, would content themselves with the contemplation merely of these enchanting arts. These they would the better enjoy the more they refined their taste and cultivated their ear. For to all music there must be an ear proportionable. There must be an art of hearing found ere the performing arts can have their due effect, or anything exquisite in the kind be felt or comprehended.[60]

In another place, Shaftesbury suggests that the listener's perception of music is to some degree limited by the perspective from his own culture.

The best music of barbarians is hideous and astonishing sounds.[61]

---

59 Ibid., 'Advice to an Author,' II, ii.
60 Ibid.
61 Ibid., 'Advice to an Author,' II, ii.

FRANCIS HUTCHESON (1694–1746)

Francis Hutcheson was born in Ireland, the son of a Presbyterian minister. He attended the university at Glasgow, where he studied the classics, philosophy and theology and from 1729 he held the chair of moral philosophy. In the field of aesthetics, he frankly acknowledged his debt to Shaftesbury. Hutcheson, in our opinion, is greatly under-recognized today. His was a far better mind than many of his more famous English Restoration philosophers.

On the Psychology of Aesthetics

Hutcheson's principal study of the emotions is a publication he called *An Essay on the Nature and Conduct of the Passions and Affections* (1742). He begins his essay on the passions with a sentence which we regard as a watershed in English psychology, representing a point at which England had at long last caught up with European thinking. Never again would the world regard the emotions as inherently evil, nor that they were located in the heart.

> The Nature of human actions cannot be sufficiently understood without considering the emotions and passions; or those modifications or actions of the mind consequent upon the apprehension of certain objects or events, in which the mind generally conceives good or evil.[62]

Hutcheson begins with a series of basic contentions: that our senses give the power to perceive things, that our mind can contemplate those perceptions and that pleasure or pain can result either as a direct consequence of the observation or of contemplation. But now he adds another dimension: there is also a subsequent moral conclusion of this process.

> In like manner, emotions, tempers, sentiments, or actions, reflected upon in ourselves, or observed in others, are the constant occasions of agreeable or disagreeable perceptions, which we call Approbation, or Dislike. These Moral Perceptions arise in us as necessarily as any other sensations; nor can we alter, or stop them, while our previous opinion or apprehension of the emotion, temper, or intention of the agent continues the same; any more than we can make the taste of Wormwood sweet, or that of Honey bitter.[63]

Hutcheson then proposes a classification system for discussing the senses. The first class refers to the External Senses, seeing, hearing, etc. The second class refers to our mental perceptions which result, our Internal Sense. He calls the third class the Public Sense, an innate empathy which he recognizes as 'our determination to be pleased with the happiness of others, and to be uneasy at their misery.' He pauses to note that it is this sense which can become confused in the theater.

---

[62] *An Essay on the Nature and Conduct of the Passions*, I, i.
[63] Ibid.

That which is presented to the eye by the most exact painting, or the action of an actor, gives no pain to those who remember that there is no misery felt. When man by imagination conceives real pain felt by an actor, without recollecting that it is merely feigned, or when they think of the real story represented, then, as there is a confused opinion of real misery, there is also pain in compassion.

The fourth class he calls Moral Sense, by which 'we perceive Virtue or Vice in ourselves or others.' The fifth class is Sense of Honor,

> which makes the approbation or gratitude of others, for any good actions we have done, the necessary occasion of pleasure; and their dislike, condemnation, or resentment ... the occasion of that uneasy sensation called Shame.

Hutcheson, believing that Pleasure and Pain are based in these five classes of senses, now turns to the willful response to the impressions of the senses, which he calls Desires and Aversions. Here he also finds five classes, beginning with the Desire of Sensual Pleasure, dealing with the external senses. The second class is the Desires of the Pleasures of Imagination, or the internal sense. The third class is the Desires of the Pleasures arising from Public Happiness, or the aversion to the pains arising from the misery of others. Fourth, is Desires of Virtue and Aversion to Vice and fifth, of course, is the Desire of Honor and Aversion to Shame.

In some concluding thoughts to this first chapter, one can see how small a step it is from Hutcheson to the birth of modern Psychology. In illustrating the complexity of the emotions, he observes,

> Let it be premised, that there is a certain Pain or Uneasiness accompanying most of our violent desires. Though the object pursued be good, or the means of pleasure, yet the desire of it generally is attended with an uneasy sensation.

And conversely,

> There is also a peculiar pleasant sensation of joy, attending the gratification of any desire, beside the sensation received from the object itself, which we directly intended.

Whereas Hutcheson had intended the previous chapter to focus on sensation, in Chapter Two he now considers Affections and Passions. Earlier philosophers had sometimes used these terms rather loosely, even as synonyms, but Hutcheson is careful to define them. Affection is what we would call the basic emotions, such as joy and sorrow, and they arise generally from sensation. Passion he considers a more outward, willful and much stronger form of emotion.

> When the word Passion is imagined to denote anything different from the Affections, it includes a strong Brutal Impulse of the Will, sometimes without any distinct notions of good, public or

private ... and prolongs and strengthens the affection sometimes to such a degree, as to prevent all deliberate reasoning about our conduct.[64]

The great question for all earlier philosophers was, how does one control such passions? For more than a thousand years it was considered sufficient to simply propose that Reason must control the passions.[65] Hutcheson, reflecting perhaps the fundamentalist atmosphere of the Restoration period, turns to moral philosophy, rather than some abstract concept of 'Reason,' to be the policeman of our passions. From this point on in his treatise, this idea is a constant presence.

Our moral sense, though it approves all particular kind of affection or passion, as well as *calm particular Benevolence* abstractedly considered; yet it also approves the restraint or limitation of all particular affections or passions, by the *calm universal Benevolence*. To make this desire prevalent above all particular affections, is the only sure way to obtain constant self-approbation.

Hutcheson now gives a long list of simple definitions for various forms of Good and Evil. The most interesting aspect of this discussion is his evident belief that much of this is genetic, 'implanted in our Nature.'[66] This leads him to wonder why these ideas are innate. Some, for example, say their purpose is to incite us to action, an idea he dismisses. At length he admits this answer may be beyond us.

It must be very difficult for beings of such imperfect knowledge as we are, to answer such questions: we know very little of the constitution of Nature, or what may be necessary for the perfection of the whole.[67]

He concludes this chapter with a plea for the goal of balancing our affections and passions. This is very difficult due to a topic he has thus far avoided, yet one frequently mentioned in earlier literature, the Temperament. Earlier philosophers had contended that a man is constituted with a tendency toward a specific Temper, caused by a prevalence or absence of various fluids in the body. For Hutcheson, the point was that if this be true, then one is by nature unbalanced, rendering the goal of balance in emotions the more difficult.

The sensations of anger in some Tempers are violent above their proportion; those of ambition, avarice, desire of sensual pleasure, and even of natural affection, in several dispositions, possess the mind too much, and make it incapable of attending to anything else. Scarce any one Temper is always constant and uniform in its passions ... Custom, Education, Habits and Company may often contribute much to this disorder.

---

64 Ibid., II, i.

65 It is worthy of reflection how much of Western society has been shaped by this philosophy. It may well be at the heart, for example, of our educational system which is designed only for the left hemisphere of the brain.

66 Ibid., II, v. Hutcheson also discussed the innate emotions in an 'Inaugural Lecture on the Social Nature of Man' (1730). See *Francis Hutcheson on Human Nature*, ed. Thomas Mautner (Cambridge: University Press, 1993), 136ff.

67 Ibid., II, vi.

Hutcheson now devotes a long exposition to the nature of individual emotions. Let us merely quote his definition of Love, which is clearly that of a fundamentalist preacher and not a lover.

> Love denotes desire of the happiness of another, generally attended with some approbation of him as innocent at least, or being of a mixed character, where Good is generally prevalent.'[68]

He now begins to delve into the complexities of the emotions. Joy, for example, he considers a natural internal sensation. However, there is nothing natural which leads one to the public interest. His purpose in the rest of the treatise was to teach the reader how to control his emotions, but he recognizes we may not be designed by nature to do this easily.

> [It is as if God] had given us the strongest dispositions toward what he had in his Laws prohibited; and directed us, by the frame of our Nature, to the meanest and most contemptible pursuits.[69]

He proposes to address this by considering, under five classifications, what else excites our emotions other than self-interest. First, he contends, our emotions can arise from Moral Sense and Sense of Honor. Among other things, we learn of this from poetry.

> When we form the idea of a morally good action, or see it represented in the Drama, or read it in the Epics or Romance, we feel a desire arising of doing the like. This leads most Tempers into an imagined series of adventures, in which they are still acting the generous and virtuous part, like to the Idea they have received.[70]

Under this classification he also defines Ambition as 'a violent desire of honor, but generally in a bad sense.'

The second source of emotions, apart from self-interest, is that they may 'tend towards the state of others, abstractly from any consideration of their Moral Qualities.'

> These affections or passions extend to all perceptive natures, when there is no real or imagined opposition of interest ...
> Since our Moral Sense represents Virtue as the greatest happiness to the person possessed of it, our public affections will naturally make us desire the Virtue of others.[71]

The emotions of the third class he calls, 'public affections, jointly with moral perceptions of the Virtue or Vice of the Agents.'

---

68 Ibid., III, i.
69 Ibid., III, ii.
70 Ibid., III, iii.
71 Ibid., III, iv.

> When Good appears attainable by a person of Moral Dignity, our desire of his happiness, founded upon esteem or approbation, is much stronger than that supposed in the former class.[72]

The fourth classification we hesitate to paraphrase.

> The passions of the fourth class arise from the same moral sense and public affections, upon observing the actions of Agents some way attached to each other, by prior ties of Nature or good Offices, or disengaged by prior Injuries.

Epic poetry and drama, he says, are 'calculated to raise these complicated passions; and in Oratory we study to do the same.'[73] His final classification is 'any of the former kinds, complicated with selfish passions.'

In Chapter Four, Hutcheson begins to focus on the control of the emotions. The first consideration is to understand that what we must control is not the emotion itself, but our opinions formed from it.

> We are so constituted by Nature, that, as soon as we form the idea of certain objects or events, our desire or aversion will arise toward them; and consequently our affections must very much depend upon the Opinions we form, concerning anything which occurs to our mind, its qualities, tendencies, or effects.[74]

One illustration he provides for this includes a reference to music.

> No man is distressed for lack of fine smells, harmonious sounds, beautiful objects, wealth, power or grandeur, previously to some opinion formed of these things as good.

The point Hutcheson hopes to make is that man must control his opinion as related to emotion. For example, he points out that it is by controlling opinion that we can remember simple and nourishing food suffices over 'the rarest and most expensive.' Under this long discussion of Opinion, or perception, and the emotions, we should mention two places in which he speaks of music and the arts, for it throws light on his estimation of them as well as on the manners of the time. First, regarding the Desire of Beauty, he stresses one must separate this emotion from the concept of possession or property. Regarding the 'more curious Works of Art,' he observes,

> If this sense or desire of Beauty itself be accompanied with the desire of possession or property; if we let it be guided by Custom, and receive associations of foreign ideas in our fancy of dress, equipage, furniture, retinue; if we relish only the Modes of the Great, or the marks of distinction as beautiful; if we let such desires grow strong, we must be very Great indeed, before we can

---

72 Ibid., III, v.
73 Ibid., III, vi.
74 Ibid., IV, i.

secure constant pleasure by this sense: and every disappointment or change of fortune must make us miserable. The like Fate may attend the pursuit of speculative sciences, poetry, Musick or painting; to excel in these things is granted but to few. A violent desire of distinction and eminence may bring on vexation and sorrow for the longest life.[75]

In another place, Hutcheson considers the opinions of others, the 'Judgment of Spectators,' and rhetorically offers them two models.

> Let them see one entirely employed in Solitude with the most exquisite Tastes, Odors, Prospects, Painting, Musick; but without any Society, Love or Friendship, or any opportunity of doing a kind or generous action.

In contrast, let them see,

> A man employed in protecting the poor and fatherless, receiving the blessings of those who were ready to perish, and making the widow to sing for joy; a father to the needy, an avenger of oppression … Which of the two would a Spectator choose? Which would he admire, or count the happier, and most suitable to human Nature?[76]

This treatise becomes progressively a sermon on moral philosophy rather than a study of the emotions, therefore we will not tarry. He does eventually recommend a series of conclusions relative to the control of the emotions. It requires, he contends, constant discipline, resignation of sensual pleasures and in general not allowing the mundane to obscure the moral. In this last instance, he mentions the universities for the only time.

> The pursuits of the Learned have often as much folly in them as any others, when studies are not valued according to their Use in Life, or the real pleasures they contain, but for the Difficulty and Obscurity, and consequently the Rarity and Distinction … If these studies be only matters of amusement and speculation, instead of leading us into a constant discipline over ourselves, to correct our hearts, and to guide our actions, we are not much better employed, than if we had been studying some useless Relations of Numbers, or Calculations of Chance.
>   There is not indeed any part of knowledge which can be called entirely useless. The most abstracted parts of Mathematics, and the knowledge of mythological History, or ancient allegories, have their own pleasures not inferior to the more gay Entertainments of Painting, Musick or Architecture; and it is for the advantage of Mankind that some are found, who have a taste for these studies. The only fault lies in letting any of those *inferior Tastes* engross the whole man to the exclusion of the nobler pursuits of *Virtue* and *Humanity*.[77]

---

75 Ibid., IV, iii.

76 Ibid., V, iv.

77 Ibid., VI, ii.

On the Philosophy of Aesthetics

Hutcheson's book, *An Inquiry into the Original of our Ideas of Beauty and Virtue* (1729), consists of two separate treatises, one on Beauty and one on Morals, of which we shall only be concerned with the first. Hutcheson begins by defining some terms as they had become generally accepted. 'Sensations' refers merely to our being aware of an object through one of the senses. Any idea which the mind forms regarding any sensation is called an 'Abstraction.' He pauses at this point to observe that Pleasure and Pain may arise either from the sensation or from the mind's consideration of it. There are also 'complex' abstractions based on sensory perception, as for example a face versus a simple color.

> So in Musick, the pleasure of a fine composition is incomparably greater than that of any one note, how sweet, full, or swelling soever.[78]

Next, Hutcheson defines the 'Sense of Beauty' to be an *internal* sense, distinguished from the simple perceptions of a beautiful object, such as a color.[79] By way of illustration, he points out that any man can distinguish between two notes if one is 'higher, lower, sharper, or flatter when separately sounded,' and yet they may find no pleasure in a composition.

> This greater capacity of receiving such pleasant ideas we commonly call a *fine Genius* or *Taste*. In Musick we seem universally to acknowledge something like a distinct sense from the external one of hearing, and call it a *good ear*.[80]

In this regard he mentions a term one finds at this time in English philosophy, the Virtuoso. This is the gentleman who affects great knowledge in details of poetry, or anything else, yet has no demonstrable good taste. Here Hutcheson mentions an important truth regarding music, that one can enjoy a musical performance without any actual knowledge of music itself. We explain this today by saying we perceive music as listeners in the right hemisphere of the brain, whereas the 'knowledge' is the grammar of music in the left hemisphere.[81] Hutcheson's explanation is that the enjoyment of music, by the person who knows nothing of music, is simply due to the concept of internal sense of beauty.

The pleasure which one feels from the internal sense of beauty is, according to Hutcheson, not dependent on any knowledge, principles or causes of any kind. Further, an internal sense of beauty must exist *before* an art can be put to a utilitarian purpose. Hence, he says, a sense of beauty must be present before one can lay out a formal garden, or do successful work in architecture.

---

78 *An Inquiry into the Original of our Ideas of Beauty and Virtue*, Treatise I, I, viii.

79 Hutcheson also observes that one may have an internal perception of beauty, with no external sensation being present. An example would be *thinking* of a performance of music.

80 Ibid., I, x.

81 Perhaps a similar, but more vivid, example is love. Who has not had a very distinct concept of love, yet found great difficulty in writing a love letter (the love is on one side; the words in the other).

Hutcheson now makes a fundamental distinction between Beauty which is 'Original' or 'Comparative.' Original beauty refers to the beauty found directly in an object, but Hutcheson quickly adds that this perception of beauty is nevertheless in the mind, not in the object. He now offers the definition that Original Beauty exists in a 'compound ratio of Uniformity and Variety.' He provides a number of illustrations. A cube is more beautiful than a pyramid, because it has greater variety with equal uniformity. 'Greater uniformity increases beauty amidst equal variety,' thus a square is more beautiful than a trapezoid. The Beauty of Nature, he contends, is explained by the 'surprising uniformity amidst an almost infinite variety.' He concludes by noting that there is a natural beauty in time, pointing to the fixed, regular rhythms of music, 'which is observed in dancing.'[82] Hutcheson also associates with 'Uniformity' the concept of proportion, a frequently offered definition of beauty.

Hutcheson now brings music into his discussion. He considers it an Original form of beauty, rather than a Comparative one, because 'Harmony is not usually conceived as an imitation of anything else.'[83] To his concept of 'Uniformity' he associates the fact that 'harmony often raises pleasure in those who know not what is the occasion of it,' the concept of concord as well as order in time and tonality. Any artificial change in this 'Uniformity' would result in some form of dissonance.

> This will appear, by observing the dissonance which would arise from tacking parts of different tunes together as one, although both were separately agreeable. A like Uniformity is also observable among the basses, tenors, trebles of the same tune.

But, Hutcheson was also aware that beautiful music is often filled with dissonant chords or tones. He finds the explanation for this, in part, in his other essential of beauty, 'Variety.'

> There is indeed observable, in the best compositions, a mysterious effect of discords. They often give as great pleasure as continued harmony; whether by refreshing the ear with Variety, or by awaking the attention, and enlivening the relish for the succeeding harmony of concords, as shades enliven and beautify pictures, or by some other means not yet known. Certain it is however that they have their place, and some good effect in our best compositions.

After this discussion of Original Beauty, Hutcheson now turns to 'Comparative Beauty,' which is the *imitation* of some Original Beauty. Hutcheson contends that it is possible to have a sense of Comparative Beauty in the mind, even though the original object was not beautiful. He believed this was most effectively used in descriptive poetry. In this regard he offers an interesting observation.

> Perhaps very good reasons may be suggested from the nature of our passions, to prove that a poet should not draw his characters perfectly virtuous; these characters indeed abstractly considered might give more pleasure, and have more beauty than the imperfect ones which occur

---
82 This is undoubtedly a reference to a very unique aspect of music: it is the only art which cannot be *seen*.
83 *An Inquiry into the Original of our Ideas of Beauty*, I, II, xiii.

in life with a mixture of good and evil. But it may suffice at present to suggest against this choice that we have more lively ideas of imperfect men with all their passions, than of morally perfect heroes, such as really never occur to our observation; and of which consequently we cannot judge exactly as to their agreement with the copy.[84]

Finally, the idea of Comparative Beauty with respect to the efforts of any artist carries with it the implication of what Hutcheson calls design, meaning that the artist has a clear idea of what he is about to do. As obvious as this may seem today, Hutcheson felt compelled to devote an entire chapter to proving chance has no role in art.[85]

Hutcheson next considers the very important question of universality relative to the sense of beauty. He begins with the rhetorical question, 'if there is such a thing as a sense of beauty, is there such a thing as a sense of the disagreeable?' Before giving his answer, he first defines 'deformity' as 'only the absence of beauty, or deficiency in the beauty expected.'

> Thus *bad Musick* pleases *Rusticks* who never heard better, and the finest ear is not offended with tuning of instruments if it be not too tedious, where no harmony is expected; and yet much smaller dissonances shall offend amidst the performance, where harmony is expected.[86]

Thus he concludes, 'Our sense of beauty seems designed to give us positive pleasure, but not positive pain or disgust, any farther than what arises from disappointment.'

In returning to universality, Hutcheson concludes that his principle of beauty, 'Uniformity' is universal. What man, he asks, would choose an irregular curve or a trapezoid for the plan of his house?

But, if there is such a concept as universality, he asks, how does one account for the 'very different judgments concerning the internal and external senses' among various men?

> The reason of this different judgment can be no other than this, that we have got distinct names for the external senses, and none, or very few, for the internal; and by this are led, as in many other cases, to look upon the former as some way more fixed and real and natural, than the latter.[87]

By way of example he points out that this is how the internal sense of harmony got its name, 'a good *ear*.' In addition to his argument, we would remind the reader that the names are in the left hemisphere of the brain, but the experience is in the right and differs with each person.

It seems clear that the universality which Hutcheson accepts, as in the case of the house plan above, is the result of experience and observation of nature. He specifically denies any

---

84 Ibid., IV, iii.
85 Ibid., V.
86 Ibid., VI, i.
87 Ibid., VI, ix.

form of innate knowledge. While on this general subject, since the emotions are universal, Hutcheson pauses to pay tribute to their role in music.

> There is also another charm in Musick to various persons, which is distinct from the harmony, and is occasioned by its raising agreeable passions. The human voice is obviously varied by all the stronger passions; now when our ear discerns any resemblance between the melody of the composition, whether sung or played upon an instrument, either in its time, or modulation, or any other circumstance, to the sound of the human voice in any passion, we shall be touched by it in a very sensible manner, and have Melancholy, Joy, Gravity, Thoughtfulness excited in us by a sort of *Sympathy* or *Contagion*. This same connection is observable between the very Air of a Tune, and the Words expressing any passion which we have heard it fitted to, so that they shall both recur to us together, though but one of them affects our senses.
>
> Now in such a diversity of pleasing or displeasing ideas which may be joined with forms of bodies, or tunes, when men are of such different dispositions, and prone to such a variety of passions, it is no wonder 'that they should often disagree in their fancys of objects, even although their sense of beauty and harmony were perfectly uniform'; because many other ideas may either please or displease, according to persons tempers and past circumstances … And this may help us in many cases to account for the diversity of fancy, without denying the Uniformity of our internal sense of beauty.[88]

Hutcheson now considers the possible influence of several external aspects on our internal sense of beauty. The first he discusses he calls 'custom,' by which he means experience. First he contends that experience does not create a *new* sense. However it can expand our awareness, such as preparing us for receiving 'more complex ideas of beauty in bodies, or harmony in sounds, by increasing our attention and quickness of perception.'[89] Experience can 'make us quicker in apprehending the Truth' and make us 'more capable of retaining and comparing complex ideas,' but all this, he contends, 'presupposes a natural sense of Beauty in Uniformity.'

Another recognized external influence is education, which he generally discounts of having much effect. First of all, we already have our own internal sense of beauty, based on experience, and, second,

> The effect of education is this, that thereby we receive many speculative opinions, which are sometimes true and sometimes false; and are often led to believe that objects may be naturally apt to give Pleasure and Pain to our external senses, which in reality have no such qualities. And further, by Education there are some strong associations of ideas without any Reason, by mere accident sometimes, as well as by design, which it is very hard for us ever after to break asunder.[90]

---

88 Ibid., VI, xii.
89 Ibid., VII, ii.
90 Ibid., VII, iii.

JAMES HARRIS (1709–1780)

James Harris was a gentleman sufficiently wealthy that he had no need to work. He studied law and held a seat in parliament as well as some minor posts in government. His *Three Treatises* on music, painting and poetry were published as a single volume in London in 1744.

On the Aesthetics of Music

The most interesting observations by Harris are all related to the role of the emotions in music, and especially in their role when music and poetry are combined. In the passage we find most valuable, Harris begins with a simple acknowledgement to the power of music to excite the emotions.

> There are various emotions which may be raised by the power of music. These are sounds to make us cheerful, or sad; martial or tender; and so of almost every other emotion which we feel.[91]

Harris seems to be yet another seventeenth-century philosopher who has intuitively understood the twin sides of our personality, the rational versus experiential/emotional, or the left versus the right hemisphere of the brain. Although he generally underestimates the affect of the emotions on man, he is quite correct, in the following, that different listeners can have different experiences listening to the same compositions, according to the circumstances under which they listen. Thus, one listening to Mozart in a cathedral, but thinking of religion, will experience functional music. Another, thinking not of God but Mozart, will hear art music. Harris is in error, however, in imagining that all depends on a reciprocal partnership between the two hemispheres of the brain, 'emotions and ideas,' as it might more accurately be described as a choice between one or the other.

> It is also further observable that there is a reciprocal operation between our emotions and our ideas, so that by a sort of natural sympathy certain ideas necessarily tend to raise in us certain emotions, and those emotions, by a sort of counter operation, to raise the same ideas. Thus ideas derived from funerals, tortures, murders and the like, naturally generate the emotion of melancholy. And when by any physical causes that emotion happens to prevail, it as naturally generates the same doleful ideas.
>
> And hence it is that ideas derived from external causes have, at different times, upon the same person so different an effect. If they happen to suit the emotions which prevail within, then is their impression most sensible and their effect most lasting. If the contrary be true, then is the effect contrary. Thus for instance, a funeral will much more affect the same man if he sees it when melancholy than if he sees it when cheerful.[92]

---

91 *Three Treatises*, VI, 1ff.
92 Ibid.

Although Harris's pretense is an objective study of the principal arts, in reading him it is immediately evident that his real passion is poetry. Thus when he discusses poetry set to music, he is an old-fashioned sixteenth-century humanist who believes the whole point must be the poetry.

> It is evident that [poetry and music] can never be so powerful singly as when they are properly united. For poetry, when alone, must be necessarily forced to waste many of its richest ideas in the mere raising of affections, when to have been properly relished, it should have found those affections in their highest energy. And music, when alone, can only raise affections, which soon languish and decay if not maintained and fed by the nutritive images of poetry. Yet must it be remembered in this union, that poetry ever have the precedence, its utility as well as dignity being by far the more considerable.[93]

He does, interestingly enough, concede music one advantage.

> A poet, thus assisted, finds not an audience in a temper, averse to the genius of his poem, or perhaps at best under a cool indifference, but by the preludes, the symphonies and concurrent operation of the music in all its parts, roused into those very affections which [the poet] would desire …
>
> And hence the genuine charm of music, and the wonders which it works, through its great composers: a power which consists not in imitations and the raising idea, but in the raising emotions to which ideas may correspond. There are few to be found so insensible, I may even say so inhumane, as when good poetry is justly set to music, not in some degree to feel the force of so amiable a union. But to the muses' friends it is a force irresistible, and penetrates into the deepest recesses of the soul.[94]

Finally, Harris acknowledges the special problem of opera and its popularity, in spite of the objections by so many critics of the theater. For the modern audience it is the music which moves, not the plot—no one would go to *Don Giovanni* for the story. But, for Harris it was the words, the poetry, which gave meaning to opera. In response to those who say the singing of poetry in opera lacks 'probability and resemblance to nature,' Harris suggests,

> To one indeed who has no musical ear this objection may have weight. It may even perplex a lover of music if it happen to surprise him in his hours of indifference. But when he is feeling the charm of poetry so accompanied, let him be angry (if he can) with that which serves only to interest him more feelingly in the subject and support him in a stronger and more earnest attention, which enforces by its aid the several ideas of the poem and gives them to his imagination with unusual strength and grandeur.[95]

---

93 Ibid., iii.
94 Ibid., i.
95 Ibid., ii.

12 RESTORATION THEATRE

JOHN HAWKINS, LOOKING BACK FROM 1776, provides an overview of the nature of Restoration drama, which he finds had become a medium focused on low entertainment. We also find interesting his comments on the relationship of the theater with the development of popular music.

> The Restoration was followed by a total change in the national manners; that disgust which the rigor of the preceding times had excited, drove the people into the opposite extreme of licentiousness; so that in their recreations and divertissements they were hardly to be kept within the bounds of moderation …
>
> The [Reformation theaters] were truly and emphatically styled theaters, as being constructed with great art, adorned with painting and sculpture, and in all respects adapted to the purposes of scenic representation. In the entertainments there exhibited music was required as a necessary relief, as well to the actors as the audience, between the acts: compositions for this purpose were called Act-tunes, and were performed in concert; instruments were also required for the dances and the accompaniment of songs. Hence it was that, upon the revival of stage-entertainments, music became attached to the theaters, which from this time, no less than formerly the church had been, became the nurseries of musicians; insomuch, that to say of a performer on any instrument that he was a playhouse musician, or of a song, that it was a playhouse song, or a playhouse tune, was to speak of each respectively in terms of the highest commendation.[1]

However successful the theater had become as an entertainment form for the public, for the playwrights it was a time to lament the decay of drama as an art. Nathaniel Lee, in the prologue to his *Nero*, reflects on the state of theater in London in the late seventeenth century.

> Good Plays, and perfect sense as scarce are grown,
> As civil Women in this damned lewd town.[2]

And in the dedication of his *Rival Queens*, he observes,

> If poetry be a virtue, she is a ragged one; and never, in any age, went barer than now. It may be objected, she never deserved less.

---

[1] John Hawkins, *A General History of the Science and Practice of Music* (1776) (New York: Dover Reprint, 1963), II, 684ff. He also points out that this was the period when women were first allowed to appear on the stage. [Ibid., II, 658]

[2] Nathaniel Lee (ca. 1648–1692) was educated at Cambridge and had an unsuccessful career in acting before turning to writing for the stage. He became insane by 1684 and was committed to Bedlam but was released in 1688.

Sir Charles Sedley found some relationship for the decline in the long period of Puritan influence, as he mentions in the prologue to his *Bellamira*.

> Is it not strange to see in such an age
> The Pulpit get the better of the Stage?
> Not through rebellion as in former days,
> But zeal for sermons and neglect for plays.

The most famous actor of the seventeenth century, Thomas Betterton, in conversation with Charles Gildon, assigns part of the failure of contemporary theater to the discipline and training of the actors themselves.

> Though I am of opinion that the decay of the stage is in great measure owing to the long continuance of the war; yet, I confess, I am afraid, that too much is derived from the defects of the stage itself. When I was a young actor under Sir William Davenant, we were under a much better discipline, we were obliged to make our study our business, which our young men do not think it their duty now to do; for they now scarce ever mind a word of their parts but only at rehearsals, and come thither too often scarce recovered from their last night's debauch; when the mind is not very capable of considering so calmly and judiciously on what they have to study, as to enter thoroughly into the nature of the part, or to consider the variation of the voice, looks, and gestures, which should give them their true beauty, many of them thinking the making a Noise renders them agreeable to the audience, because a few of the upper gallery clap the loud efforts of their lungs, in which their understanding has no share. They think it a superfluous trouble to study real excellence, which might rob them of what they fancy more, midnight, or indeed whole night's debauches, and a lazy remissness in their business.
>
> Another obstacle to the improvement of our young players, is, that when they have not been admitted above a month or two into the company, though their education and former business were never so foreign to acting, they vainly imagine themselves masters of that art, which perfectly to attain, requires a studious application of a man's whole life.[3]

It is interesting that Betterton was one of several theater people in the seventeenth century who failed to appreciate Shakespeare, finding only his *Merry Wives of Windsor* a worthy comedy. One of the contributors to the decline of drama was the popularity of opera, but Betterton believed that if there was just,

> as much encouragement from our dignified audience, as from the vulgar; or if our [critics] could distinguish between good and bad so far as to encourage the former, and explode the latter, they would soon have plays more worthy of the English genius, and opera would retire beyond the Alps.[4]

---

3   Gildon, *The Life of Mr. Thomas Betterton* [1710], 14ff.

4   Ibid., 173ff.

The critics, of course, were very active and we see them in the prologue to Farquhar's *The Twin-Rivals*, attributed to a 'Mr. Motteux,' portrayed as participants in a battle against any new play.

> With Drums and Trumpets in the Warring Age,
> A Martial Prologue should alarm the stage.
> New plays—before acted; A full audience near,
> Seem towns invested, when a siege they fear.
> Prologues are like a Forlorn Hope sent out
> Before the play, to skirmish, and to scout:
> Our dreadful foes the critics, when they spy
> They cock, they charge, they fire—then back they fly.

Nearly all playwrights during the seventeenth century had written angry responses to the critics. One worried about the influence of the critics on the audience during the play and proposed to replace them with female critics. In the prologue, attributed to a 'Mr. Duke,' to Lee's *Lucius Junius Brutus*, we find,

> But oh! you leading Voters of the Pit,
> That infect others with your too much Wit,
> That well affected Members do seduce,
> And with your malice poison half the house,
> Know your ill managed Arbitrary sway,
> Shall be no more indured but ends this day.
> Rulers of abler conduct we will choose,
> And more indulgent to a trembling Muse;
> Women for ends of Government more fit,
> Women shall rule the Boxes and Pit.[5]

In spite of this atmosphere, there are some interesting comments by these playwrights relative to the definition of drama. William Congreve, in an essay, 'Concerning Humor in Comedy,' is primarily concerned with the definition of genuine humor. He observes,

> Wit is often mistaken for humor.
> Folly, is sometimes mistaken for humor.
> Personal defects are misrepresented for humor.
> External habit of body is often mistaken for humor.
> Affectation is generally mistaken for humor.

---

5   Gildon [Ibid., 21] had a different view, pointing out that Harrington, in his *Oceana*, suggests that all women who have 'suffered any blemish to their reputation' should be excluded from the audience of plays, so as to deter them from further lewdness.

Rather, he says, 'Humor shows us as we *are*.' Expanding this to a formal definition, he offers,

> Humor is a singular and unavoidable manner of doing, or saying anything, peculiar and natural to one man only; by which his speech and actions are distinguished from those of other men.[6]

George Farquhar, in a treatise called 'A Discourse upon Comedy,' suggests that drama, more than the other arts, is prone to criticism due to its universality.

> Most of our other Arts and Sciences bear an awful distance in their prospect, or with a bold and glittering varnish dazzle the eyes of the weak-sighted vulgar. The *Divine* stands wrapt up in his Cloud of Mysteries, and the amused laity must pay tithes and veneration to be kept in obscurity.

Drama, on the other hand, suffers from being *too* close to the human experience.

> *Poetry* alone, and chiefly the *Drama*, lies open to the insults of all pretenders; she was one of Nature's eldest offsprings, whence by her birthright and plain simplicity she pleads a genuine likeness to her mother; born in the innocence of Time, she provided not against the assaults of succeeding ages; and, depending altogether on the generous end of her invention, neglected those secret Supports and serpentine Devices used by other Arts that wind themselves into Practice for more subtle and politic designs.[7]

On the Purpose of Drama

For the audience, no doubt, the purpose of the theater was mere entertainment. Lee seems to recognize this in the epilogue of his *Oedipus*, which concludes,

> Charm! Song! and Show! a Murder and a Ghost!
> We know not what you can desire or hope,
> To please you more, but burning of a Pope.

As for the more serious playwrights, the purpose of drama remained an educational one, to raise the moral values of the viewer. Betterton contends that even the 'most formidable enemy' admits,

> that the wit of man cannot invent any more efficacious means of encouraging virtue, and depressing vice.

---

6 *The Complete Works of William Congreve* (New York: Russell & Russell, 1964), III, 161. William Congreve (1670–1729) is considered the best of the Restoration writers of comedy and was particularly admired by Voltaire. He studied at Trinity College, Dublin, and worked in various government offices in London.

7 *The Complete Works of George Farquhar* (New York: Gordian Press, 1967), II, 326ff. George Farquhar (1677–1707) studied at Trinity College in Dublin and was an actor and a soldier.

> Hence I believe it is evident, that they suppose the moral lessons, which the stage presents, may make the greatest impressions on the minds of the audience; because the instruction is conveyed with pleasure, and by the ministration of the passions, which always have a stronger remembrance, than the calmer precepts of reason.[8]

Although, Betterton observes, the pulpit is the more sacred place for 'dispensing the most holy mysteries of the Christian religion,'

> the practice is so forcibly recommended from the stage by a purifying our passions, and the conveyance of delight, the stage may properly be esteemed the handmaid of the pulpit.

A necessary component, if drama is to educate the audience in a positive way, he contends, is the character of the actor himself.

> I think there is no manner of doubt but that the lives and characters of those persons, who are the vehicles ... of these instructions, must contribute very much to the impression the fable or moral will make. For to hear virtue, religion, honor recommended by a prostitute, an atheist, or a rake, makes them a jest to many people, who would hear the same done with awe by persons of known reputation in those particulars. Look but into religion itself, and see how little the words and sermons of a known drunkard, or debauchee affect his parishioners; and what an influence a divine of pious and regular life has on his congregation.

Congreve also emphasizes the educational purpose of drama and in so doing offers an explanation of the epilogue customarily spoken at the end.

> After the action of the play is over, and the delight of the representation at an end; there is generally care taken, that the Moral of the whole shall be summed up, and delivered to the audience, in the very last and concluding lines of the poem. The intention of this is, that the delight of the representation may not so strongly possess the minds of the audience, as to make them forget or oversee the Instruction.[9]

Congreve in a discussion of the use of language in oratory, poetry and prose, also speaks of the importance of the communication of passion in drama.

> If figures and epithets are natural to passion, and if they compose the diction of poetry, certainly tragedy, which is the sublime and first-rate poetry, and which ought every where to abound in Passion, may very well be allowed to use epithets and figures, more especially in a scene consisting entirely of passion, and still more particularly in the most violent parts of that scene.[10]

---

8   Ibid., 18ff.

9   'Amendments of Mr. Collier's' in *The Complete Works of William Congreve*, III, 174.

10 Ibid., III, 180.

ON THE AESTHETICS OF MUSIC

Congreve, in an essay, 'Amendments of Mr. Collier's,' was writing of the association of 'inspiration' with the 'Divine,' when he adds a remarkable contemporary definition.

> The word *inspiration* when it has *divine* prefixed to it, bears a particular and known signification. But otherwise, to *inspire* is no more than to *Breathe into*; and a man without profaneness may truly say, that a trumpet, a fife, or a flute deliver a musical sound, by the help of Inspiration.[11]

One wonders if the origin of this is found in some medieval philosophers who incorrectly believed it was the flute which made music, not the player.

As we have mentioned above, many observers during the seventeenth century blamed the popularity of opera for the decline of drama in both Italy and England. It is no surprise, therefore to find some of these playwrights making rather negative comments about opera. In Richard Steele's *The Conscious Lovers* (II, iii), Indiana suggests the 'entertainment' of opera does not compare with drama.

> Though in the main, all the pleasure the best opera gives us, is but mere Sensation. Methinks it's pity the mind can't have a little more share in the Entertainment. The Musick's certainly fine; but, in my thoughts, there's none of your composers come up to old Shakespeare and Otway.

In Vanburgh's *A Journey to London* (II, i), Arabella suggests that dice make better music than a 'sleepy Opera!' Opera is mentioned again in his *The Provoked Husband* (V, iii), where Lord Townly infers that the high price of tickets in the theater keeps the poor people out. Then, the subject of opera is introduced.

> MASQUERADER. Right, my Lord. I suppose you are under the same astonishment, that an Opera should draw so much good company.
> LADY GRACE. Not at all, Madam; it is an easier matter sure to gratify the ear, than the understanding.[12]

We might also mention that Congreve, in the introduction to his *Opera of Semele*, explains that since his work is intended to be set to music, he has not felt obligated to observe the 'equality of measure' in his lines which were intended to be used in Recitative. He adds,

> For as that style in Musick is not confined to the strict observation of time and measure, which is required in the composition of Airs and Sonatas, so neither is it necessary that the same exactness in numbers, rhymes, or measure, should be observed in words designed to be set in that manner, which must ever be observed in the formation of Odes and Sonnets. For what they call Recitative in Musick, is only a more tuneable speaking, it is a kind of Prose in Musick; its

---

11 Ibid., III, 184.

12 *The Complete Works of John Vanbrugh* (London: Nonesuch Press, 1927), III, 264, 266 contains the music for two songs of Act IV, one with an optional version for flute.

Beauty consists in coming near Nature, and in improving the natural accents of words by more Pathetick or Emphatical Tones.

It should be added that Congreve has written the words for a brief masque, *The Judgment of Paris*, with music by 'Mr. John Eccles, Mr. Finger, Mr. Purcel, and Mr. Weldon.' It appears, on the basis of its publication, that this entire work was sung, with the exception of a number of 'symphonies.'

On the Purposes of Music

The most common purpose of music found in early literature is to soothe the listener or player. A typical example is found in Otway's *Alcibiades* (V, lines 108ff),[13] where the king (just before he is murdered!) calls for his page,

> Boy take thy Lute, and with a pleasing Air
> Appease my sorrows, and delude my care.

A similar instance is found in Nathaniel Lee's *Gloriana*, a play covering the life of Augustus Caesar, which begins with a banquet scene. After a stage direction,

> [Ovid enters followed by Musick, and sings
> while the Emperor sits melancholy.]

A song begins,

> Let Business no longer usurp your High mind,
> But to dalliance give way, and to pleasure be kind.

Perhaps a strange twist on this purpose is found in Nathaniel Lee's *Rival Queens* (IV, ii), where we find this curious dialogue,

> ALEXANDER. Ha! let me hear a song.
> CLYTUS. Musick for Boys—Clytus would hear the groans
>   Of dying persons, and the Horses neighings;
>   Or if I must be tortured with shrill voices,
>   Give me the cries of Matrons in sacked towns.

Beginning with the Renaissance one finds mention of the value of music for use in courtship. In George Etherege's Comedy of Manners, *The Man of Mode* (V, ii), Busy, a waiting

---

13 Thomas Otway (1652–1685) was highly esteemed by his contemporaries as a playwright.

woman, volunteers to sing a song, 'As Amoret with Phillis sat.' Harriet observes 'She has a voice that will grate your ears worse than a cat-call.' After she sings, two listeners observe,

> Mr. Dorimant. Musick so softens and disarms the mind.
> Harriet. That not one arrow does resistance find.[14]

A humorous comment on this purpose is found in Congreve's *The Old Batchelour* (III, ii), where, after the lyrics of a love song is given, Silvia tells her suitor, the old bachelor, 'If you could sing and dance so, I should love to look upon you too.' The bachelor, Heartwell, answers,

> Why it was I sung and danced; I gave Musick to the voice, and life to their measures—Look you here, Silvia, [*Pulling out a Purse and chinking it*] here are Songs and Dances, Poetry and Musick—hark! how sweetly one Guinea rhymes to another—And how they dance to the Musick of their own Chink. This buys all together …

The most important purpose of music, of course, is to communicate emotions. In an atmosphere where drama was focused on entertainment, this purpose is not mentioned. We do find in Congreve a brief hint into the contemporary perception of the power of music to incite the emotions, when he cites a Mr. Collier, who used the expression 'Gun-Powder-Treason Plot upon Musick and Plays.' Congreve adds that he concluded, 'Musick is as dangerous as Gun-Powder.'[15]

On Performance Practice

In Richard Steele's *The Tender Husband* (III, i) we get an interesting characterization of a French singer, and the implication that an English singer is lacking the characteristics of the former. After listening to a lady sing, her music teacher, a 'Spinet-Master,' responds,

> You sing it very well; but, I confess, I wish you'd give more into the French Manner. Observe me, Hum it *A-la-Françoise.*
> *With Studied Airs, etc.*
> The whole person, every limb, every nerve sings—The *English* way is only being for that time a mere musical instrument, just sending forth a sound without knowing they do so—Now, I'll give you a little of it, like an *English* woman—You are to suppose I've denied you 20 times, looked silly, and all that—Then with hands and face insensible—I have a mighty cold.
> *With Studied Airs, etc.*[16]

---

14 Sir George Etherege (1633–1691) is known for his emphasis on manners. Regarding this song, the original publication carried a note reading 'Song by Sir C. S.'

15 'Amendments of Mr. Collier,' in *The Complete Works of William Congreve*, III, 206.

16 Richard Steele (1672–1729) attended Oxford, but left before graduating. He entered the army under an assumed name, for which he was disinherited. He became a very influential writer, especially in his collaboration with Joseph Addison.

A similar comment on French singing suggests that the French songs are all skill and passion, but without thought. In George Etherege's *The Man of Mode* (IV, ii), Sir Fopling is urged to sing and he admits he studied in Paris with 'Lambert, the greatest master in the world, but I have his own fault, a weak voice.' He finally sings the song, which he believes was composed by 'Baptist,' an illusion to Lully. The heart of this passage is found in the reaction by the listeners.

> MR. DORIMANT. I shall not flatter you, Sir Fopling, there is not much thought in it. But it is passionate and well turned.
> MR. MEDLEY. After the French way.

Regarding instrumental practice, we might add that in William Wycherley's *The Gentleman Dancing-Master* (III, i)[17] violinists are associated with dancing-masters and barbers. Don Diego adds the reflection, 'indeed all that deal with Fiddles are given to impertinency.'

During the seventeenth century in France the small bagpipe, called a musette, became a favorite instrument among aristocratic players who enjoyed pretending they were poor peasants. The royal oboists, who also played this instrument sometimes took off the canter, playing it as a small oboe—which, of course, it is. We know some professional oboists in Europe who therefore consider the musette as part of the oboe family. With this perspective, our attention was attracted to a point in John Vanbrugh's *The Relapse* (V, v), where the stage direction reads, 'To the *Hautboys*,' but the next dialogue, by Sir Tunbelly Clumsy, begins, '*Bag-pipes*, make ready there.'[18]

ON MUSIC IN THE PLAYS

During the Jacobean period there was almost no music used in Tragedy, but in the works of Nathaniel Lee we find music again employed. His stage directions call for an interesting variety of music to open scenes, including 'soft Musick'[19]; a 'lofty March,' played by trumpets[20]; two child singers[21] and a 'plaintive Tune, representing the present condition of Thebes.'[22] But what is meant at the beginning of *Mithridates* by the stage direction, 'A noise of Musick

---

17 William Wycherley (1641–1715) studied at Oxford, joined the court in exile in France and on his return to London was imprisoned for his debts.

18 In Congreve's *Squire Trelooby* (I, xi) there is a comic scene with two musicians playing on 'Glyster-pipes.'

19 *Sophonisba* (I, ii) and *Caesar Borgia* (IV, i), followed by a wedding song.

20 *Sophonisba* (III, iii).

21 *Theodosius* (IV, ii).

22 *Oedipus* (I, i).

and *tuning* Voices is heard?' Sometimes a play begins with a stage direction reading simply 'fiddles playing.'[23]

James Thomson wrote a masque, *Alfred*, for which the music was composed by Thomas Arne.[24] Thomson's stage direction for the beginning of Act I, scene iii, is unusually complex for the period.

> [Solemn music is heard at a distance.
> It comes nearer in a full symphony: after which
> a single trumpet sounds a high and awakening air.
> Then the following stanzas are sung by two aerial spirits unseen.]

Act II, scene iv, begins with a stage direction calling for a 'Symphony of martial music.'

In Congreve's *Semele*, a libretto intended to be used for an opera, Act III, scene one, begins with a stage direction which indicates prelude music in the character of a more modern overture. Congreve uses 'movement' here in the French style, meaning a change in character.

> [The God of Sleep lying on his Bed.
> A soft Symphony is heard.
> Then the Musick changes to a different Movement.]

A program direction at the beginning of III, vii, calls for 'a mournful Symphony.'

In Aphra Behn's *The Forced Marriage*, Act II begins with a stage direction which indicates that music 'softly plays,' until a curtain is lowered, and then 'the Musick plays aloud till the Act begins.'[25]

In some cases the music is used to establish a specific mood for the action which follows. In George Villiers *The Rehearsal* (V, i), for example, a stage direction reads 'Soft Music,' which is followed by this dialogue.

> KING USHER. What sound is this invades our ears?
> KING PHYSICIAN. Sure 'tis the Musick of the moving Spheres.[26]

A particularly interesting instance is found in John Vanbrugh's *Aesop* (V, i),[27] where we find the unusual stage direction,

---

23 *The Princess of Cleve* (I, i). The opening dialogue includes 'prithe leave off playing fine in Consort, and stick to Time and Tune.'

24 James Thomson (1700–1748) was highly respected by both Voltaire and Lessing, but has never been esteemed by his own countrymen.

25 Mrs. Aphra Behn (1640–1689) was the first English woman to earn a living by writing. After the death of her merchant husband, her experiences included service as a spy in the Netherlands and a period of time in prison for debts.

26 George Villiers, duke of Buckingham (1628–1687), intended this work as a satire on the current heroic drama style.

27 Sir John Vanbrugh (1664–1726) was not only a playwright but a celebrated architect, whose work included Blenheim Palace and the Haymarket Opera—which he also managed.

> *[The Trumpets sound a Melancholy Air until Aesop appears;*
> *and then the violins and hautbois strike up a Lanchashire Hornpipe.]*

Vanburgh's *The Pilgrim* (V, iii) contains 'strange Musick' off stage, which one character supposes has its origin with fairies.

In Aphra Behn's *The Forced Marriage* (V, ii) we find a very rare instance where a stage direction indicates the music is to 'continue all this scene.' Sometimes instrumental music is used for functional stage purposes, as in 'A Symphony playing all the while,' as a god descends from the ceiling in Behn's *The Emperor of the Moon* (III, iii).

Music, usually trumpets, is often used to introduce high ranking character onto the stage. A typical example is found in Nathaniel Lee's *Rival Queens* (II, i), where the arrival of Alexander the Great is announced by the 'Noise of Trumpets sounding far off.'[28] Most unusual is a place in *Theodosius* (I, i) where the leading noble is announced by 'Recorders flourish.' On the other hand, a grandiose instance is found in Congreve's *The Mourning Bride* (I, i), where a stage direction, before the entrance of the king, calls for a 'Symphony of Warlike Musick.'

The reader will recall the ancient Roman cult festival of the Moon, in which trumpets and percussion played a central role. This provides the occasion of a humorous moment in Behn's *The Emperor of the Moon* (III, ii), when Harlequin perceives the arrival of the emperor,

> But hark, the sound of Timbrels, Kettle-Drums and Trumpets—The Emperor, Sir, is on his way, prepare for his reception.

But the stage direction which follows reads,

> *[A strange Noise is heard of Brass Kettles,*
> *and Pans, and Bells, and many tinkling things.]*

In contrast, in Act III, scene iii, of this play, the emperor's arrival in a procession accompanied by 'the Flutes playing a Symphony.'

---

28 Other instances in *Oedipus* (I, i) and in *Constantine the Great*. Trumpets announce arrival of Sulpitius, in Otway's *History and Fall of Caius Marius* (II, line 414).

ART MUSIC

The Restoration plays are filled with the lyrics for songs, sometimes with an indication of the composer who 'set' the words.[29] Curiously, these songs often have no relationship with the plot, rather they seem to be simply interpolated as if it were felt there was some need for musical entertainment. This can clearly only be taken as a feeble attempt to compete with the much more popular Italian opera.

Some songs carry a stage direction indicating a specific song is to be *notated*. A stage direction in Nathaniel Lee's *Oedipus* (III, i), for example, reads, 'Musick first. Then Sing.' To this stage direction is appended a further note, 'This to be set through.'[30] Such a specific indication invites one to wonder about the rest of the songs. It is our belief that some of these were sung with the music improvised. In fact, there is a specific request for an improvised song in Sir Charles Sedley's *The Mulberry Garden* (III, ii), where we find the following dialogue,

> VICTORIA. Are not these Verses somewhat too weak to stand alone?
> JACK WILDISH. Faith, Madam, I am of your mind, put a Tune to them, it is an easy Stanza.
> *[Victoria sings.]*

Perhaps this is also what is meant by a song in Richard Steele's *The Tender Husband*, which was published with a note reading, 'Designed for the Fourth Act, but not Set.'[31]

Some references to songs in these plays indicate a well-known song, as in Congreve's *Love for Love* (V, i), when Valentine requests, 'I would have Musick—Sing me the Song that I like.' After the song, he reflects, 'No more, for I am melancholy.' We suspect that such references are to the popular repertoire of broadside ballads, as seems likely in Farquhar's *The Beaux Stratagem* (III, iii), which contains the lyrics of a love song, which the stage direction indicates is to be sung to the tune of 'Sir Simon the King.' This is a rare instance where, before the action resumes, the singer is paid.

The availability of these ballads, which were published in considerable numbers, may also be the explanation for the numerous instances in these plays in which there is a specific request for a *new* song. In Congreve's *The Old Batchelour* (II, ii), for example, Araminita requests, 'O I am glad we shall have a Song to divert the discourse—Pray oblige us with the latest new Song.' In his *The Double-Dealer* (II, i), before a song is sung, Mellefont not only request a new song, but asks to hear it in a rehearsal.

---

29 In Congreve's *Love for Love* we are given the lyrics for two songs, together with the information that the music was written by John Eccles and another by Mr. Finger. Congreve's *The Way of the World* (III, i) tells us the composer was Eccles and names the singer as 'Mrs. Hodgson.' Farquhar's *Love and a Bottle* (III, i) includes a song for which the stage direction tells us the composer was 'Mr. Richardson' and his *The Inconstant* includes a song composed by Daniel Purcell. Daniel Purcell is named as composer again in Richard Steele's *The Funeral* (V, iv). Aphra Behn's *The Lucky Chance* (III, i) includes a song with the indication, 'made by Mr. Cheek.'

30 His tragedy, *Theodosius* was published with art songs composed by Henry Purcell which were sung after each act. The music is reproduced in *The Works of Nathaniel Lee* (Metuchen: Scarecrow Reprints, 1968), II, 305ff. This volume also includes a song sung in Act V of *The Duke of Guise*, the play co-authered with Dryden [Ibid., 473].

31 The lyrics are given in *The Plays of Richard Steele* (Oxford: Clarendon Press, 1971), 213.

What's here, the Musick? Oh, my Lord has promised the Company a New Song ... [*Musicians crossing the Stage*] Pray let us have the favor of you to practice the Song before the Company hear it.

In William Wycherley's *Love in a Wood* (I, ii) a lady, Flippant, announces she will sing a new song, and the lyrics are given. After this song she observes that it is 'the fashion for women of quality to sing any Song whatever, because the words are not distinguished.' In his *The Gentleman Dancing-Master* (II, i) a lady has sung 'a new Song' the previous evening and another character reflects 'Madam, I dreamed all night of the Song you sung last.'

In Vanbrugh's *The Provoked Wife* (II, ii) Lady Fancyfull asks her private singing teacher, 'Is the town so dull, Mr. Treble, that it affords us never another New Song?' He gives her a new song which he acquired the day before and makes the comment, 'Make what Musique you can of this Song, here.' A reference to a song 'a newly married Lady made within this week' concludes Vanbrugh's *The Provoked Wife*.

Finally, in Otway's *The Orphan* (III, lines 452ff), a page offers to sing the 'last new song' he has learned, one about 'my Lord and Lady, who were caught together, you know where.' Lord Castalio is shocked.

> CASTALIO. You must be whipped Youngster, if you get such songs as these ...
> PAGE. Why, what must I sing, pray, my dear Lord?
> CASTALIO. Psalms, Child, Psalms.
> PAGE. Oh dear me! Boys that go to school learn Psalms, but Pages that are better bred sing Lampoons.

In the plays of Aphra Behn there are some curious and rare examples of music which has a negative impact on the listener. Her *Abdelazer* begins with 'still Musick' followed by a love song. The Moor Abdelazer reacts 'On me this Musick lost?—this sound on me, that hates all Softness?' The Queen of Spain wants to make love, the music continues playing softly, but again Abdelazer complains, 'Cease that ungrateful Noise.'[32] In *The Young King* (II, i), Orsames's philosophy teacher, Geron, plays an instrumental piece on the lute, but Orsames responds,

> I do not like this Musick;
> It pleases me at first,
> But every touch thou giv'st that is soft and low
> Makes such impressions here,
> As puzzles me beyond Philosophy
> To find the meaning of;
> Begets strange notions of I know not what,
> And leaves a new and unknown thought behind it,
> That does disturb my quietness within.

---

32 A similar instance of music which is not appreciated is found at the beginning of Behn's *The Emperor of the Moon*.

There is one instance where we find a description of the private singing of a lady. In Vanbrugh's Comedy, *The Provoked Wife* (II, ii), we find this dialogue between a lady and her private singing teacher.

> MR. TREBLE. I know no body sings so near a Cherubin as your Ladyship.
> LADY FANCYFULL. What I do I owe chiefly to your skill and care, Mr. Treble. People do flatter me indeed, that I have a voice, and a *je-ne-scai quoy* in the conduct of it, that will make Musick of anything. And truly I begin to believe so, since what happened the other night: would you think if, Mr. Treble; walking pretty late in the park, a whim took me to sing *Chevy-Chase*, and would you believe it? Next morning I had three copies of Verses ...
> MR. TREBLE. Are there any further commands for your Ladyship's humble servant?
> LADY FANCYFULL. Nothing more at this time, Mr. Treble. But I shall expect you here every morning for this month.

Finally, there are a few references to serenades in these plays and they are generally uncomplimentary with respect to the music. In Aphra Behn's *Sir Patient Fancy* (I, i) there is a discussion of a potential serenade.

> SIR CREDULOUS EASY. What think you then of the Bagpipe, Tongs, and Gridiron, Cat-calls, and loud-sounding Cymbals?
> LODWICK KNOWELL. Naught, naught, and of known use; you might as well treat her with viols and flute-doux, which are enough to disoblige her forever.

Next, there is a discussion of perhaps hiring the King's Musick. When Lodwick reminds Sir Credulous that he must obtain a song, the latter responds,

> A Song! hang it, it is but rummaging the Play-books, stealing thence is lawful Prize.

This serenade, when it occurs, is only mentioned in a stage direction reading, 'A confused Noise of the Serenade.'

Later in this same play (III, ix) there is another serenade, preceded by a procession in the street for which the stage direction calls for an elephant (!) and 'others playing on strange confused instruments.' When the first song is ineffective, Sir Credulous calls out 'you Ballad-singers, have you no good songs of another fashion?' A musician ironically recommends a ballad called 'Ill-wedded Joys, how quickly do you fade.'[33]

---

[33] In *The Amorous Prince* (II, iii) a serenade is sung by the drunk Lorenzo, who tells his musicians, 'Let them be soft low notes, do you hear?'

FUNCTIONAL MUSIC

One cannot help noticing that the references to church music in these plays tend to be descriptions of rather unorthodox music. It is possible that this was the only safe way, in the Puritan English environment, to mention church music at all.

Nathaniel Lee, in *Oedipus* (II, i), refers to military music to participate in a Greek cult ceremony, although in historical practice this was actually a Roman tradition. Oedipus calls out,

> A vast Eclipse darkens the laboring Planet:
> Sound there, sound all our instruments of war;
> Clarions, and Trumpets, Silver, Brass, and Iron,
> And beat a thousand drums to help her labor.

In George Villiers *The Rehearsal* (V, i) this same ancient cult ceremony is satirized in a scene where, instead of the war-like instruments, the moon is serenaded by a series of popular songs, including 'Robin Hood', 'Trenchmore', and 'Dance the Hey'.

In Behn's *Sir Patient Fancy* (III, vii) there is a reference to spirits which haunt a house, allowing the playwright an opportunity for anti-Catholic sentiment.

> SIR PATIENT. Ah, the house is beset, surrounded and confounded with profane tinkling, with Popish Horn-pipes, and Jesuitical Cymbals, more Antichristian and Abominable than organs, or anthems.
> NURSE. Yea verily, and surely it is the spawn of Cathedral Instruments played on by Babylonish Minstrels, only to disturb the Brethren.

In this same playwright's *The Widow Ranter* (IV, i), which is set in Virginia, there is an Indian religious ceremony, for which there are extensive stage directions. It begins with,

> [The Musick playing louder, the Priests and Priestesses
> dance about the Idol with ridiculous Postures, and crying.]

Then 'soft musick' is called for, followed by,

> [The Musick changes to confused Tunes,
> to which the Priests and Priestesses dance.]

Military music references in these plays sometimes carry the sense of dread so familiar with such references in earlier literature, as for example in Sedley's *Antony and Cleopatra* (II, i), after a stage direction 'A noise of Drums,' we find,

> You hear how Drums and Trumpets fill the Air,
> And for a scene of blood our minds prepare.

A specific example of repertoire, 'Trumpets sound a dead March,' is found in Lee's *Lucius Junius Brutus* (II, i).

For military musical signals to work, they must be recognized by the soldiers. It is from this perspective that, in Otway's *The Souldiers Fortune* (I, lines 300ff), a character compares whores who ply their trade on 'automatic pilot' to 'an old soldier that understands all his exercise by beat of Drum.' An apparently well-known military signal is mentioned in George Farquhar's *The Recruiting Officer* (I, i) a stage direction calls for, 'Drum beating the Granadeer-March.' While it is rare for the specific music played by drums on the stage to be named, even more extraordinary is the epilogue of this play, which is devoted to a humorous exposition on this march.

> All ladies and gentlemen, that are willing to see the Comedy called the *Recruiting Officer*, let them repair tomorrow night by six a clock to the sign of the Theater Royal in Drury Lane and they shall be kindly entertained—
> *We scorn the vulgar Ways to bid you come,*
> *Whole Europe now obeys the Call of Drum.*
> *The Soldier, not the Poet, here appears,*
> *And beats up for a Corps of Volunteers:*
> *He finds that Musick chiefly does delight ye,*
> *And therefore chooses Musick to invite ye.*
>
> Beat the Granadeer March—Row, row, tow—Gentlemen, this piece of Musick, called an *Overture to a Battel*, was composed by a famous *Italian* Master, and was performed with wonderful success, at the great Operas of *Vigo*, *Schellenberg*, and *Blenheim*; it came off with the applause of all Europe, excepting *France*; the *French* found it a little too rough for their *Delicatesse*.
> *Some that have acted on those glorious stages,*
> *Are here to witness to succeeding Ages,*
> *That no Musick like the Granadeer's engages.*
>
> Ladies, we must admit that this Musick of ours is not altogether so soft as *Bonancini's*, yet we dare affirm, that it has laid more people asleep than all the *Camilla's* in the world; and you'll condescend to own, that it keeps one awake, better than any *Opera* that ever was acted.
>
> The Granadeer March seems to be a composure excellently adapted to the genius of the *English*; for no Musick was ever followed so far by us, nor with so much alacrity; and with all deference to the present subscription, we must say that the Granadeer March has been subscribed for by the whole Grand Alliance; and we presume to inform the ladies that it always has the pre-eminence abroad, and is constantly heard by the tallest, handsomest men in the whole army.

Finally, in Nathaniel Lee's *Sophonisba* (IV, i), there is a very rare song which imitates the sound of the military drum,

> *Hark, hark, the Drums rattle,*
> *Dub a dub to the Battle.*
> *Tararara, Tararara the Trumpets too tattle,*
> *Now, now they come on, and pell mell they mingle.*

ENTERTAINMENT MUSIC

As we have mentioned above, music itself in these plays tends to be used for the entertainment of the audience. A typical example is found in Nathaniel Lee's *Rival Queens* (IV, ii) where there is a break for entertainment, described in the stage directions as,

> *[Here follow an Entertainment of Indian Singers and Dancers: the Musick flourishes.]*

Second-hand references to entertainment music tends to be rather disrespectful. In Otway's *The Cheats of Scapin* (III, lines 340ff), for example, an order is given to hire casual musicians for a dinner.

> Then did you hear, send out and muster up all the Fidlers, (Blind or not Blind, Drunk or Sober) in the Town; let not so much as the Roaster of Tunes, with his cracked Cymbal in a Case, escape ye.

In Congreve's *Squire Trelooby* (II, xi) a song is sung by two musicians disguised as lawyers.

There are many references to drinking songs in these plays and indeed the observation is made in Otway's *Friendship in Fashion* (II, line 266), that 'Musick is as great an encouragement to drinking, as fighting.'[34]

A familiar term in the literature of this period is the 'music-meeting,' which is taken to be a private chamber music session, if not an actual concert. One may wonder if these were sometimes meetings of somewhat lower aspirations. In Congreve's *The Way of the World* (V, i) an associations made with 'singing and dancing, and such debaucheries; going to filthy plays,' etc., which includes,

> and profane Musick-meetings, where the lewd Trebles squeak nothing but Bawdy, and the Basses roar Blasphemy.

Dance music in this theater repertoire is almost invariably associated with violins. It is because this is so common that humor is found in Wycherley's *The Gentleman Dancing-master* (IV, i), where a dancing-master winds the strings so tightly they break, so it won't be discovered that he cannot play the violin.

The only real exceptions to violin dance music are found in the plays of Behn. *The Widow Ranter* (II, ii), which is set in Virginia, calls for a dance for which only a bagpipe player is available. In *The Emperor of the Moon* (I, iii) there is a dance to a 'Flute Doux.'

In Farquhar's Comedy, *Love and a Bottle* (II, ii), Mockmode, a young man newly graduated from the university brags of the music he can play on his violin, even though he knows nothing about his repertoire, the titles of which are expressed in the old academic manner

---

34 Additional drinking songs can be found in Vanbrugh's *The Provoked Wife* (III, ii); George Etherege's *The Man of Mode* (IV, i); and his *She Would if she could* (IV, ii), where the two singers are both drunk.

of the solfege abbreviations used to identify early music. The reference to the Music of the Spheres here suggests this was still a topic known to the public.[35]

> MOCKMODE. I can play the *Bells* and *Maiden Fair* already. *Alamire, Bifabemi, Cesolfa, Delasol, Ela, Effaut, Gesolrent*. I have them all by heart already. But I have been plaguily puzzled about the etymology of these notes; and certainly a man cannot arrive at any perfection, unless he understands the derivation of the terms.
> RIGADOON. [a dancing master] O Lord, Sir! That's easy. *Effaut* and *Gesolrent* were two famous *German* musicians, and the rest were *Italians*.
> MOCKMODE. But why are they only seven?
> RIGADOON. From a prodigious great bass-viol with seven strings, that played a Jig called the *Musick of the Spheres*: The seven Planets were nothing but fiddle-strings.

In Behn's *The Emperor of the Moon* (II, v) a character maintains she danced to the 'Musick of the Spheres.'

---

35 Farquhar mentions the Music of the Spheres again in *The Inconstant* (IV, iii).

13 DRYDEN

John Dryden (1631–1700), who has been called the greatest literary man of his age,[1] was born to a Puritan family with Republican conviction and completed his university work at Cambridge. Some question his personal ethics, for eagerness to write in praise of whoever happened to be head of the government and for his conversion to Catholicism after the accession of a Catholic King. As a poet his chief activity was in dramatic poetry, although it is the essays he attached to these plays when they were published which are valued today. He was buried next to Chaucer in Westminster Abbey.

ON THE PHYSIOLOGY OF AESTHETICS

The great issue among the English philosophers of the seventeenth century was the recognition of Reason over the Church's long emphasis on Faith. Dryden, in his only important statement on this question, sides with the older view, in pointing to the limits of Reason.

> Dim, as the borrowed beams of Moon and Stars
> To lonely, weary, wandering travelers,
> Is Reason to the Soul: and as on high,
> Those rowling fires discover but the sky
> Not light us here; So Reason's glimmering ray
> Was lent, not to assure our doubtful way,
> But guide us upward to a better day.
> And as those nightly tapers disappear
> When day's bright Lord ascends our hemisphere;
> So pale grows Reason at Religions sight …
>
> Revealed Religion first informed thy sight,
> And Reason saw not, till Faith sprung the light.[2]

---

1 Bernard Grebanier, *English Literature* (Great Neck: Barron, 1959), 249.

2 'Leligio Laici,' in *The Works of John Dryden*, ed. Edward Hooker (Berkeley: University of California Press, 1956), II, 109, 111.

On Education

Dryden occasionally makes some passing references to professors which reflect a certain disrespect for the academic world. In one of these, where he is commenting on the public who reads the young poets, he adds,

> The young Gentlemen themselves are commonly misled by their Pedagogue at school, their Tutor at the University, or their Governor in their travels. And among of those three sorts are the most positive Blockheads in the world.[3]

Perhaps we find a similar unflattering reference to professors and philosophers in an essay on Heroic plays, attached to his *The Conquest of Granada*. Here Dryden raises the subject of dealing with spirits and magic on stage, which he defends as something which had been believed by all previous ages and as a topic perfectly suited to poets.

> For [poets] speculations on this subject are wholly poetical; they have only their fancy for their guide; and that, being sharper in an excellent poet, than it is likely it should be in a phlegmatic, heavy gownman.[4]

He must have been criticized for such statements, for in the dedication to *Love in a Nunnery*, he takes the opportunity to defend himself.

> I am, ridiculously enough, accused to be a condemner of universities; that is, in other words, an enemy of learning; without the foundation of which, I am sure, no man can pretend to be a poet.[5]

ON THE PSYCHOLOGY OF AESTHETICS

In the only observation on the emotions in general which we should like to quote, Dryden reveals great insight. In the introduction of his translation of Ovid's *Epistles*, he emphasizes the universality and genetic nature of the emotions.

> If the imitation of Nature be the business of a poet, I know no author who can justly be compared [to Ovid], especially in the description of the passions. And to prove this, I shall need no other judges than the generality of his readers: for all passions being inborn with us, we are almost equally judges when we are concerned in the representation of them.[6]

---

3   Dedication of the *Aeneis*, in Ibid., V, 327.
4   *The Works of John Dryden*, ed. Walter Scott (London: William Miller, 1808), IV, 21ff.
5   Ibid., IV, 353.
6   *The Works of John Dryden*, ed. Edward Hooker, I, 111.

Another observation on the emotions seems to reflect his Puritan background.

> Wherever inordinate emotions are, it is Hell. Such only can enjoy the country, who are capable of thinking when they are there, and have left their passions behind them in the town.[7]

ON THE PHILOSOPHY OF AESTHETICS

Of the general philosophical topics on aesthetics which had been argued for centuries, the only one which Dryden seemed to be personally interested in was the question of whether art should imitate nature, and to what degree. In general it appears to have been his view that this was the proper aim of art, as he makes clear in the essay which precedes *The State of Innocence*,

> This undeniably follows, that those things which delight all Ages, must have been an imitation of Nature.[8]

He praises this quality in a poem in honor of Sir Godfrey Kneller, finding that this artist so approached Nature that his paintings seemed about to speak.

> Such thy skill,
> That Nature seems obedient to thy will:
> Comes out, and meets thy pencil in the draught:
> Lives there and lacks but words to speak her thought.
> At least thy Pictures look a Voice; and we
> Imagine sounds, deceived to that degree,
> We think it is somewhat more than just to see.[9]

On the other hand, in some places Dryden seems hesitant to recommend that art should attempt to be an exact portrayal of nature. In his preface to *The Indian Emperour*, Dryden addresses this while explaining why prose should not be used in a serious play.

> The one great reason why prose is not to be used in serious plays, is because it is too near the nature of conversation: there may be too great a likeness; and the most skillful painters affirm, that there may be too near a resemblance in a picture: to take every lineament and feature is not to make an excellent piece, but to take so much only as will make a beautiful resemblance

---

7 'Dedication to the Georgics,' in Ibid., V, 144.
8 Ibid., XII, 91.
9 Ibid., IV, 461. Kneller, born in Germany, was court painter to Charles II.

of the whole; and, with an ingenious flattery of Nature, to heighten the beauties of some parts, and hide the deformities of the rest.[10]

And in his dedication of *The Rival Ladies*, Dryden wonders if such a goal is even possible.

> For the stage being the representation of the world, and the actions in it, how can it be imagined, that the picture of human life can be more exact than life itself is?[11]

Regarding the process of the artist, at the end of his preface to *Troilus and Cressida*, Dryden observes,

> If the rules be well considered, we shall find them to be made only to reduce Nature into Method, to trace her step by step, and not to suffer the least mark of her to escape us.[12]

And in his poem, 'To the Earl of Roscomon,' Dryden offers the advice that Nature only appears when Art is well disguised.[13]

In conclusion, we might mention an example of Dryden's humor in his *The Indian Emperour* (II, iii), when the native lady, Cydaria, observes,

> Strange ways you practice there to win a heart,
> Here love is Nature, but with you it is Art.

On Poetry

In an essay called 'Notes and Observations on *The Empress of Morocco*,' Dryden lists his requirements for a successful poet.

> A man should be learned in several sciences, and should have a reasonable philosophical, and in some measure a mathematical head; to be a complete and excellent poet. And beside this should have experience in all sorts of humors and manners of men, should be thoroughly skilled in conversation, and should have a great knowledge of mankind in general.[14]

One of the qualities of the fine poet which was often mentioned by the ancient Greek philosophers was a certain enthusiasm, a 'divine fury' they called it, which fills and inspires

---

10 Ibid., IX, 6.
11 Ibid., VIII, 95.
12 Ibid., XIII, 248.
13 'To the Earl of Roscomon,' in Ibid., II, 173, line 34.
14 Ibid., XVII, 182.

the poet. Dryden mentions this in his introduction to 'Eleonora,' a poem in honor of the Countess of Abingdon.

> We, who are Priests of Apollo, have not the Inspiration when we please; but must wait till the God comes rushing on us, and invades us with a fury, which we are not able to resist: which gives us double strength while the Fit continues, and leaves us languishing and spent, at its departure.[15]

But, in contemporary England, Dryden was aware of a great industry of commercial poets who wrote for the lower classes. He mentions these in 'An Essay of Dramatick Poesie.'

> Those eternal Rhymers, who watch battle with more diligence than the ravens and birds of prey; and the worst of them surest to be first in upon the quarry …[16]

In a preface to a new play by his own son, Dryden comments on the impact of this kind of poetry on public taste.

> This I dare venture to maintain, that the Taste of the Age is wretchedly depraved, in all sorts of poetry, nothing almost but what is abominably bad can please. The young Hounds who ought to come behind, now lead the pack, but they miserably mistake the scent. Their poets, worthy of such an audience, know not how to distinguish their characters; the manners are all alike, inconsistent and interfering with each other. There is scarce a man or woman of God's making in all their Farces; yet they raise an unnatural sort of laughter, the common effect of Buffoonry; and the Rabble which takes this for wit, will endure no better, because it is above their understanding.[17]

While Dryden also wrote his share of poetry addressed to the masses, he was aware of higher aesthetic principles.

> A poet indeed, must live by the many, but a good poet will make it his business to please the few.[18]

Dryden's only discussion on the purpose of poetry is centered in his thoughts on epic poetry, which he called 'Heroick' poetry. In his dedication of his translation of Virgil's *Aeneis*, he contends that its purpose must be both entertaining and educational.

> A heroick poem is undoubtedly the greatest work which the soul of man is capable to perform. The design of it, is to form the mind to heroick virtue by example; it is conveyed in verse, that it may delight, while it instructs.[19]

---

15 Ibid., III, 231.
16 Ibid., XVII, 9.
17 'Preface to *The Husband His own Cuckold*,' in Ibid., IV, 471ff.
18 'Preface to *The Husband His own Cuckold*,' in Ibid., IV, 472.
19 Dedication of the *Aeneis*, in Ibid., V, 267ff.

Dryden's great preference for epic poetry can be seen in his conclusion that 'Heroique Poetry is certainly the greatest Work of Human Nature.'[20] He adds that the difficulty of this form is confirmed by how few attempt it, as compared to the number of poets who write plays. What Dryden apparently could not see, and from our perspective is clear, was that it was the development of the dramatic theater in the sixteenth and seventeenth centuries which replaced the need for epic poetry.

On Drama

As a poet, it was dramatic poetry, his activity as a playwright, which consumed most of Dryden's professional life. In his 'An Essay of Dramatick Poesie,' Dryden offers a concise definition of drama.

> A play ought to be a just and lively image of human nature, representing its passions and humors, and the changes of fortune to which it is subject; for the delight and instruction of mankind.[21]

An additional purpose for drama is given in a poem written for the opening of a theater at Oxford, in 1681, where Dryden suggests that the purpose of drama is to entertain and in so doing offer solace from the work day.

> This place the seat of peace, the quiet cell
> Where Arts removed from noisy business dwell,
> Should calm your wills, unite the jarring parts,
> And with a kind Contagion seize your hearts ...
> ......
>
> Some vacant hours allow to your delight,
> Mirth is the pleasing business of the night,
> The Kings prerogative, the peoples right.[22]

Dryden amplifies on these purposes in the preface of his *Tyrannick Love*, where he mentions that the purposes generally assigned to dramatic plays are for the pleasure of the audience and instruction in *moral* principles. He then considers its effectiveness in the precepts of religion.

> For to leave that employment altogether to the clergy, were to forget that religion was first taught in verse (which the laziness or dullness of succeeding priesthood, turned afterwards into prose). And it were also to grant, which I never shall, that representations of this kind may not as well

---

20 'Discourse of Satire,' in Ibid., IV, 26ff.
21 Ibid., XVII, 15.
22 Ibid., II, 180.

be conducing to Holiness, as to good manners. Yet far be it from me, to compare the use of dramatic poetry with that of Divinity. I only maintain, against the enemies of the stage, that patterns of piety, decently represented, and equally removed from the extremes of superstition and profaneness, may be of excellent use to second the precepts of our religion.[23]

It was perhaps something of this nature that Dryden had in mind in the dedication to *The Spanish Fryar*, where he observes that while a good plot and fine acting may help the success of a play, only if it contains Truth will it survive long and 'Time is the surest Judge of Truth.'[24]

Dryden identifies another purpose of drama, to affect the emotions of the audience, at the end of a discussion of one of the famous 'Unities' of plot construction.

There is no such absolute necessity that the time of a stage action should so strictly be confined to twenty-four hours, as never to exceed them, for which Aristotle contends, and the Grecian stage has practiced. Some longer space, on some occasion, I think may be allowed, especially for the English theater, which requires more variety of incidents than the French ... And better a mechanical rule were stretched or broken, than a great Beauty were omitted. To raise, and afterwards to calm the passions, to purge the soul from pride, by the examples of humane miseries, which befall the greatest; in few words, to expel arrogance, and introduce compassion, are the great effects of Tragedy.[25]

In another place Dryden emphasizes how important this is from the perspective of the playwright.

The work of Tragedy is on the passions ... A poet cannot speak too plainly on the stage ... the sense is lost if it be not taken flying: but what we read alone we have leisure to digest. There an author may beautify his sense by the boldness of his expression, which if we understand not fully at the first, we may dwell upon it, until we find the secret force and excellence ... We must beat the Iron while it is hot, but we may polish it at leisure.[26]

In addition to achieving these objectives, Dryden emphasized the importance of the poet's imagination. We read in the Prologue to *Tyrannick Love*,

Poets, like lovers, should be bold and dare.
They spoil their business with an over-care.
And he who servilely creeps after sense,
Is safe, but never will reach an excellence.
Hence 'tis, our poet in his conjuring,
Allowed his Fancy the full scope and swing.[27]

---

23 Ibid., X, 109.
24 Ibid., XIV, 102ff.
25 Dedication of the *Aeneis*, in Ibid., V, 269ff.
26 Ibid., 276.
27 Ibid., X, 114.

In his preface to *Secret Love*, Dryden mentions that his play follows all the 'strictest of dramatic laws,' but adds that most playwrights now despise these rules and that they represent a form of 'beauty which our common audiences do not easily discern.'[28] After Dryden wonders if the playwright himself is capable of judging his own work, his most interesting comment follows. Dryden concludes that in terms of the 'official rules,' yes; but as for the choice of language itself, it is 'the Child of Fancy,' and cannot be subjected to 'measure.'

Dryden makes a few interesting comments about the English theater before his era. In discussing the plays of William D'Avenant, Dryden refers to the closing of the theaters, as a result of Puritan influence, during the Cromwell period.

> It being forbidden him in the rebellious times to act tragedies and comedies, because they contained some matter of scandal to those good people, who could more easily dispossess their lawful sovereign, than endure a wanton jest, he was forced to turn his thoughts another way, and to introduce the examples of moral virtue, writ in verse, and performed in recitative music. The original of this music, and of the scenes which adorned his work, he had from Italian operas.[29]

It is particularly surprising, for the modern reader, to find rather blatant criticism of Shakespeare by Dryden. One of the passages is is found in the preface to *Troilus and Cressida*, where Dryden explains that the English language is one in progress of development and lacks as yet perfect grammar.

> Yet it must be allowed to the present age, that the tongue in general is so much refined since Shakespeare's time, that many of his words, and more of his phrases, are scarce intelligible. And of those which we understand some are ungrammatical, others coarse; and his whole style is so pestered with figurative expressions, that it is as affected as it is obscure.[30]

In another place,[31] Dryden observes that people often think that during the period of Shakespeare the English language was in its highest point of development. He argues to the contrary, finding in the works of Shakespeare 'in every page either some solecism of speech, or some notorious flaw in sense.' In particular, he points to *Winter's Tale*, *Love's Labour Lost* and *Measure for Measure* as being 'so meanly written, that the comedy neither caused your mirth, nor the serious part your concern.' With regard to wit, Dryden arrives at a conclusion which seems extraordinary to the modern reader.

---

28 Ibid., IX, 115.

29 'Of Heroic Plays,' a preface to *The Conquest of Granada* in *The Works of John Dryden*, ed. Scott, IV, 16.

30 *The Works of John Dryden,* ed. Hooker, XIII, 225.

31 'An Essay on the Dramatic Poetry of the Last Age,' in *The Works of John Dryden*, ed. Scott, IV, 211ff. Dryden associates the improvement of language after Shakespeare with the restoration of the king, and the sophistication of the French manners which he brought with him.

Shakespeare, who many times has written better than any poet, in any language, is yet so far from writing wit always, or expressing that wit according to the dignity of the subject, that he writes, in many places, below the dullest writers of ours, or any precedent age.

Regarding the state of contemporary theater in England, Dryden makes a wry observation,

Both the best and worst of the modern poets will equally instruct you to admire the ancients.[32]

He finds the playwrights, like many of the poets, interested in money, not art.

So Poetry, which is in *Oxford* made
An Art, in *London* only is a trade.[33]

In view of such comments, it is no surprise to find that Dryden had a generally poor appreciation for the capability of the general public. In the preface to *An Evening's Love*, he explains that he was not inclined to low comedy, in part because writing the dialogue required one to be 'much of conversation with the vulgar.'

I am sometimes ready to imagine that my disgust of low comedy proceeds not so much from my judgment as from my temper; which is the reason why I so seldom write it; and that when I succeed in it, (I mean so far as to please the audience) yet I am nothing satisfied with what I have done; but am often vexed to hear the people laugh, and clap, as they perpetually do, where I intended them no jest; while they let pass the better things without taking notice of them. Yet even this confirms me in my opinion of slighting popular applause, and of condemning that approbation which those very people give, equally with me, to the Zany of a Montebank ...
To entertain an audience perpetually with humor, is to carry them from the conversation of Gentlemen, and treat them with the follies and extravagances of Bedlam.[34]

On the other hand, Dryden admits he writes for this very public. In the preface to his *The Indian Emperour*, he confesses,

The humor of the people is now for Comedy, therefore in hope to please them, I write Comedies rather than serious play.[35]

Moreover, in the dedication of *The Vindication*, Dryden defends the public, whatever their reaction might be.

---

32 *The Works of John Dryden,* ed. Hooker, XVII, 21.
33 'Prologue to the University of Oxon' (1673), in Ibid., I, 136ff.
34 Ibid., X, 202ff.
35 Ibid., IX, 12.

> To clap and hiss are the privileges of a freeborn subject in a play-house: they buy them with their money, and their hands and mouths are their own property.[36]

And he is true to his word, when, in the preface to his *The Wild Gallant*, Dryden indicates that he accepts even a negative judgment by the public.

> It would be a great impudence in me to say much of a Comedy, which has had but indifference success in the action. I made the town my judges; and the greater part condemned it: after which I do not think it my concernment to defend it.[37]

When Dryden compares the English theater with the French, he can be quite sarcastic. In the Epilogue to *Aureng-Zebe*, he makes a comment he makes in several places, that the French dislike the action of English theater, while the English felt uncomfortable with the complicated civility of the French.

> The French, abhors our Target-fight:
> But those damned Dogs can never be in the right.
> True English hate your Monsieur's paltry Arts;
> For you are all Silk-weavers, in your hearts.
> Bold Brittons, at a brave Bear-garden fray,
> Are roused: and, clattering Sticks, cry, Play, play, play.
> Meantime, your filthy Foreigner will stare,
> And mutter to himself, Ha! *gens Barbare!*

Cutting, but not quite so blatant is this passage in the preface to *The Tempest or the Enchanted Island*,

> The writing of prefaces to plays was probably invented by some very ambitious poet, who never thought he had done enough. Perhaps by some Ape of the French Eloquence, who used to make a business of a letter of gallantry, a [critical study] of a Farce; and in short, a great pomp and ostentation of words on every trifle. This is certainly the talent of that nation, and ought not to be invaded by any other. They do that out of gaiety which would be an imposition upon us.[38]

In two places Dryden is more specific in his objections to the French, and therefore more informative. In the preface to *All for Love*,

> Yet, in this nicety of manners does the excellency of French poetry consist: their heroes are the most civil people breathing; but their good breeding seldom extends to a word of sense. All their wit is in their ceremony; they lack the genius which animates our stage; and therefore it is but necessary when they cannot please, that they should take care not to offend. But, as the

---

36 Ibid., XIV, 325.
37 Ibid., VIII, 3.
38 Ibid., X, 3.

civilest man in the company is commonly the dullest, so these authors, while they are afraid to make you laugh or cry, out of pure good manners, make you sleep. They are so careful not to exasperate a critic, that they never leave him any work; so busy with the broom, and make so clean a riddance, that there is little left either for censure or for praise. For no part of a poem is worth our discommending, where the whole is insipid; as when we have once tasted of soured wine, we stay not to examine it glass by glass.[39]

In another passage which has its focus on the drama, we find,

Neither can we accept of those Lay-Bishops, as some call them, who under pretense of reforming the Stage, would intrude themselves upon us, as our superiors, being indeed incompetent judges of what is Manners, what Religion, and most of all, what is Poetry and Good Sense … As little can I grant, that the French dramatic writers, excel the English. Our authors as far surpass them in genius, as our soldiers excel theirs in courage. It is true, in conduct they surpass us either way. Yet that proceeds not so much from their greater knowledge, as from the difference of Taste in the two nations. They content themselves with a thin design, without episodes, and managed by few persons. Our audience will not be pleased, but with variety of accidents, an underplot, and many actors … However it be, I dare establish it for a Rule of Practice on the Stage, that we are bound to please those, whom we pretend to Entertain. And that at any price, Religion and Good Manners only excepted … There is a sort of Merit in delighting the spectators.[40]

Finally, as a working playwright, Dryden often is critical of the critics. He seemed to generally characterize them as he does in his Prologue to *All for Love*, an adaption of Shakespeare's *Antony and Cleopatra*.

> What flocks of critics hover here today,
> As vultures wait on armies for their prey,
> All gaping for the carcass of a play!

In several prefaces to his plays, Dryden attacks critics for being only interested in finding minor mistakes in the works of playwrights. A typical complaint is found in the Prologue to *Tyrannick Love*.

> And malice in all critics reigns so high,
> That for small errors, they whole plays decry;
> So that to see this fondness, and that spite,
> You'd think that none but Madmen judge or write.[41]

In the second prologue of *Secret Love*, Dryden announces he will ignore the critics—which of course he never did.

---

39 Ibid., XIII, 12.

40 Preface to 'Examen Poeticum,' in Ibid., IV, 367ff.

41 Ibid., X, 114.

> Our poet's sturdy, and will not submit.
> He'll be before-hand with them, and not stay
> To see each peevish Critick stab his play:
> Each puny censor, who his skill to boast,
> Is cheaply witty on the poets cost.[42]

Finally, Dryden did not write extensively on the subject of painting, but in his poem, 'Sir Godfrey Kneller,' he provides his perspective on the history of painting, beginning with early man.[43]

> From hence the rudiments of art began;
> A coal, or chalk, first imitated man:
> Perhaps, the shadow taken on a wall …
>
> By slow degrees, the Godlike Art advanced;
> As man grew polished, Picture was enhanced;
> Greece added posture, shade, and perspective.

With the Romans the advance of Art stopped until the arrival of the Renaissance.

> Thus in a stupid Military State,
> The pen and pencil find an equal fate …
>
> Long time the sister arts, in Iron sleep,
> A heavy Sabbath did supinely keep;
> At length, in Raphael's Age, at once they rise;
> Stretch all their limbs, and open all their eyes.

ON THE AESTHETICS OF MUSIC

The thoughts which Dryden had relative to the definition of music are all expressed in context with the comparison of music with other arts. The most extensive of these is a dedication of Purcell's *The Vocal and Instrumental Musick of The Prophetess*, published in 1691, which was actually written by Dryden. Evidence that this is Dryden's work includes the fact that Henry Purcell's signature at the end is in Dryden's hand.

> Music and Poetry have ever been acknowledged sisters, which walking hand in hand, support each other; as poetry is the harmony of words, so music is that of notes; and as poetry is a rise above prose and oratory, so is music the exaltation of poetry. Both of them may excel apart, but sure they are most excellent when they are joined, because nothing is then wanting to either

---

42 Ibid., IX, 120.

43 Ibid., IV, 462ff.

of their perfections; for thus they appear like wit and beauty in the same person. Poetry and painting have arrived to their perfection in our country: music is yet but in its nonage, a forward child, which gives hope of what it may be hereafter in England, when the masters of it shall find more encouragement. [Music is] now learning Italian, which is its best master, and studying a little of the French Air to give it somewhat more of gayety and fashion. Thus being farther from the Sun, we are of later growth than our neighbor countries, and must be content to shake off our barbarity by degrees.

Painting is, indeed, another sister, being like them, an imitation of Nature. But I may venture to say she is a dumb Lady, whose charms are only to the eye: a mute actor upon the stage, who can neither be heard there nor read afterwards. Besides, that she is a single piece; to be seen only in one place, at once: but the other two, can propagate their species; and as many printed or written copies as there are of a poem or a composition of Musick, in so many several places, at the same time the poem and the Musick, may be read, and practiced and admired. Thus painting is a confined and solitary art, the other two are as it were in consort, and diffused through the world; partaking somewhat of the Nature of the Deity, which at once is in all places. This is not said in disparagement of that noble Art; but only to give the due precedence to the others, which are more noble and which are of nearer kindred to the soul.[44]

We might also mention a lovely reference to a topic still very much discussed in the seventeenth century, the Music of the Spheres, found in a poem written after the death of a young lady, who was highly talented in poetry and painting.

> That all the people of the sky
> Might know a Poetess was born on Earth.
> And then if ever, Mortal Ears
> Had heard the Musick of the Spheres![45]

On the Purpose of Music

In *The Indian Emperour* (II, iii), Cortez speaks of the purpose of both feasts and music being to bring delight. The purpose of music most frequently mentioned in early literature is to soothe the player or listener, so in *The Duke of Guise* (V, ii) Malicorne cries out, 'I want a Song to rouse me, my blood freezes: Musick there!' And in a poem written for the opening of a theater in Oxford, in 1681, we find,

> Oh! may its genius, like soft Musick move,
> And tune you all to concord and to love.[46]

---

44 Ibid., XVII, 324ff.
45 Ibid., III, 110.
46 Ibid., II, 180.

In *The Tempest* (II, ii), off-stage music in two-parts is heard, with instrumental accompaniment. Ferdinand responds,

> Where should this Musick be? in the air, or the Earth?
> It wounds no more, and sure it waits upon some God
> On the Island, sitting on a bank weeping against the Duke
> My father's wreck. This musick hovered over me
> On the waters, allaying both their fury and my passion
> With charming Airs.

Another song (III, ii) for the purpose of soothing includes dialogue ending with humor.

> GONZALO. 'Tis cheerful Musick, this, unlike the first;
>   And seems as 'twere meant to unbend our cares,
>   And calm your troubled thoughts.
>   [Ariel invisible Sings.]
>   *Dry those eyes which are overflowing,*
>   *All your storms are over-blowing …*
> ALONZO. This voice speaks comfort to us.
> ANTONIO. Would 'twere come; there is no Musick in a Song
>   To me, my stomach being empty.

The most important purpose of music is to express emotions and we have an extraordinary testimonial to this purpose in one of Dryden's most famous odes, his 'A Song for St. Cecilia's Day, 1687,'[47] a work which was set to music by Giovanni Draghi. He begins by suggesting that the earth and man were created in harmony[48] by God.

> From Harmony, from heavenly Harmony
> This universal frame began:
> From Harmony to Harmony
> Through all the compass of the notes it ran,
> The Diapason closing full in Man.

But he quickly turns to the emotional essence of music, in a burst of enthusiasm, 'What Passion cannot Musick raise and quell!' Now he presents a remarkable survey of the emotional qualities which he associates with various musical instruments, expressed in his most vivid choice of words.

---

[47] The best known ode which Dryden wrote for the celebration of St. Cecilia's Day (in 1697) carries the title 'Alexander's Feast or The Power of Music.' It is more celebrated as poetry, but is less valuable for our purposes as it is an allegorical work which brings to life several ancient Greek gods. We read of 'flying fingers' on the lyre addressed to Jove and of trumpets, drums and hautboys in praise of Bacchus.

[48] It is interesting that modern research is discovering relationships between music and a variety of elements of Nature and that the most recent research in physics has found that each organ of the body produces a specific pitch.

The TRUMPETS loud clangor
Excites us to arms
With shrill notes of anger …
   ……

The double double double beat
Of the thundering DRUM …
   ……

The soft complaining FLUTE
In dying Notes discovers
The woes of hopeless lovers,
Whose dirge is whispered by the warbling LUTE.
   ……

Sharp VIOLINS proclaim
Their jealous pangs, and desperation,
Fury, frantick indignation,
Depth of pains, and height of passion …
   ……

But oh! what Art can teach
What human voice can reach
The sacred ORGANS praise?
Notes inspiring holy love,
Notes that wing their heavenly ways
To mend the choirs above.

Dryden concludes with a reference to the music of the spheres and the trumpet of the Day of Judgment, whose 'Musick shall untune the sky.'[49]

A frequently mentioned purpose of music during the Renaissance was relative to its help in courting the ladies. Thus we notice in Dryden's comedy, *Secret Love* (III, i), the character, Celadon, who walks around with a string ensemble, 'a whole noise of Fiddles,' to be ready to court the ladies. In Act V, scene i, this ensemble is referred to as the 'Queens Musick.'

Genuine music therapy is called for in *The Indian Queen* (III, ii), when Ismeron calls for music for the purpose of helping Zempoalla.

You Spirits that inhabit in the Air,
With all your powerful Charms of Musick try
To bring her Soul back to its harmony.

---

49 Ibid., III, 201ff. The editorial comment [Ibid., 459] emphasizes at length the editors' view that this poem represents a hallmark of the late arrival of humanism in the music of England. We regard this opinion to be based on a very narrow view of English music during the sixteenth and seventeenth centuries.

This is followed by a stage direction reading, 'Song is supposedly sung by Aerial-Spirits.' The lyrics appear for a song,[50] but the intended therapy is not effective.

> ZEMPOALLA. Death on these trifles: Cannot your Art find
>   Some means to ease the passions of the mind?
>   Or if you cannot give a lover rest,
>   Can you force love into a scornful breast?
> ISMERON. It is Reason only can make passions less;
>   Art gives not new, but may the old increase;
>   Nor can it alter love in any breast
>   That is with other flames before possessed.

On Opera

The play, *The State of Innocence*, was intended to be a libretto for an opera, but as Dryden admits in the preface to its publication, the work never made it to the stage. In the play, nevertheless, one finds a few clues to the prospective music which Dryden envisioned. In Act I, scene one, a stage direction calls for a song of rather epic nature,

> and a Song expressing the change of their condition; what they enjoyed before; and how they fell bravely in Battel, having deserved Victory by their Valor; and what they would have done if they had conquered.

At the end of II, ii, a stage direction reads 'soft Musick and a Song is sung,' and 'soft Music' is called for again in V, iv, together with 'a Song and Chorus.'

Dryden called his play *King Arthur* a 'dramatic opera,' and in fact it was set to music by Purcell. In the dedication, Dryden compliments Purcell and then appears compelled to explain that he has had to alter his poetry in some places to fit the requirements of the music.

> There is nothing better than what I intended, but the music; which has since arrived to a greater perfection in England than ever formerly; especially passing through the artful hands of Mr. Purcell, who has composed it with so great a genius, that he has nothing to fear but an ignorant, ill-judging audience. But the numbers of poetry and vocal music are sometimes so contrary, that, in many places, I have been obliged to cramp my verses, and make them rugged to the reader, that they may be harmonious to the hearer; of which I have no reason to repent me, because these sorts of entertainments are principally designed for the ear and eye; and therefore, in reason, my art, on this occasion, ought to be subservient to his. And, besides, I flatter myself

---

50 The lyrics for another song appear in V, i. Lyrics for songs can be found in most of Dryden's plays. Among the more unusual are a sailor's drinking song, among several others, in *The Tempest*; *Amboyna*, which includes a wedding song (which a character notes was sprightly sung) and a song describing a sea battle; and in *Love in a Nunnery* (II, iii), where the musician-servant sings a song in French.

with an imagination, that a judicious audience will easily distinguish betwixt the songs wherein I have complied with him, and those in which I have followed the rules of poetry, in the sound and cadence of the words.[51]

As for this libretto itself, there are much greater numbers of musicians mentioned in the stage directions and they are much more specific. For example, one stage direction (IV, i) reads 'A Bass and two Trebles sing the following Song to a Minuet.' There are also unusual references in the stage directions to instrumental music, such as in V, i, 'A concert of Trumpets within,' and later 'a Warlike Concert.'

Dryden's most extensive discussion of opera is found in the preface to his libretto for the opera, *Albion and Albanius*.[52] The music for this opera was composed by Louis Grabu, a Frenchman who became Composer-in-ordinary to Charles II. Dryden, who had worked with Purcell, saw no less ability in Grabu, pointing in particular to,

> his extraordinary talent, in diversifying the Recitative, the lyrical part, and the Chorus. In all which ... the best judges, and those too of the best quality, who have honored his rehearsals with their presence, have no less commended the happiness of his genius than his skill. And let me have the liberty to add one thing; that he has so exactly expressed my sense, in all places, where I intended to move the passions, that he seems to have entered into my thoughts, and to have been the poet as well as the composer. This I say, not to flatter him, but to do him right; because amongst some English musicians, and their scholars ... the imputation of being a French-man, is enough to make a [political] Party [against him], who maliciously endeavor to decry him. But the knowledge of Latin and Italian poets, both which he possesses, besides his skill in Musick, and his being acquainted with all the performances of the French operas, adding to these the good sense to which he is born, have raised him to a degree above any man, who shall pretend to be his rival on our stage. When any of our countrymen excel him, I shall be glad, for the sake of old England, to be shown my error.

Next, Dryden offers this definition of opera.

> An Opera is a poetical tale or fiction, represented by vocal and instrumental Musick, adorned with scenes, machines and dancing. The supposed persons of this musical Drama, are generally supernatural, as Gods and Goddesses, and Heroes, which at least are descended from them, and are in due time, to be adopted into their number. The subject therefore being extended beyond the limits of human nature, admits of that sort of marvelous and surprising conduct, which is rejected in other plays.

The essential problem in opera is one of right (music) versus left (story) hemispheres of the brain, for they are not particularly well adapted to work equally in a simultaneous

---

51 *The Works of John Dryden*, ed. Scott, VIII, 119.
52 *The Works of John Dryden*, ed. Hooker, XV, 3ff.

mode. Dryden is quite correct, therefore, when he observes that while beauty of expression is important,

> the Songish part [musical accompaniment] must abound in the softness and variety of numbers: its principal intention, being to please the hearing, rather than to gratify the understanding.

Dryden admits he has been unable to determine the origin of opera, which he now several times calls 'Dramatique Musical Entertainment,'[53] and his best guess is incorrect, that its origin was among the entertainment music of the Spanish Moors. Nevertheless, he suggests that anyone interested today in writing opera should study the Italians who have brought this form into perfection.

> But however it began (for the above is only conjectural), we know that for some centuries, the knowledge of Musick has flourished principally in Italy, the Mother of learning and the arts; that poetry and painting have been restored there, and so cultivated by Italian masters, that all Europe has been enriched out of their treasury: and the other parts of it in relation to those delightful arts, are still as much provincial to Italy, as they were in the time of the Roman Empire.

Although, as he has indicated above, the principal roles are given to gods and heroes, he adds that it is still appropriate to admit shepherds,

> by reason of the spare time they had, in their almost idle employment, had most leisure to make verses, and to be in love; without somewhat of which passion, no opera can possible subsist.

He finds the Italians have a distinct advantage in opera due to the very nature of their language.

> It is the softest, the sweetest, the most harmonious, not only of any modern tongue, but even beyond any of the learned [Greek and Latin]. It seems indeed to have been invented for the sake of poetry and Musick: the vowels are so abounding in all words, especially in the termination of them, that excepting some few monosyllables, the whole language ends in them. Then the pronunciation is so manly and so sonorous, that their very speaking has more of Musick in it, than [German] poetry and song.

The French, he maintains, 'who now cast a longing eye to [Italy], are not less ambitious to achieve elegance in poetry and Musick.' However, he finds them restricted by nature.

> But after all, as nothing can be improved beyond its own species, or farther than its original nature will allow (as an ill voice, though never so thoroughly instructed in the rules of Musick, can ever be brought to sing harmoniously ...), so neither can the natural harshness of the French, or their perpetual ill accent, be ever refined into perfect harmony like the Italian.

---

53 Ibid., 5.

The English, he finds, are hampered by 'effeminacy of our pronunciation,' which he suggests was inherited from the Danes, and by a scarcity of female rhymes.

Dryden now offers several rules for the poet who would write for an opera. The first necessity, he says, is 'double rhythms, and ordering of the words and numbers for the sweetness of the voice.' These, he says, are,

> the main hinges, on which an opera must move; and both of these are without the compass of any Art to teach another to perform; unless Nature in the first place has done her part, by enduing the poet with that nicety of hearing, that the discord of sounds in words shall as much offend him, as a seventh in Musick would a good composer.

Next in importance for Dryden, is choice of vocabulary.

> The chief secret is in the choice of words; and by this choice I do not here mean elegancy of expression, but propriety of sound to be varied according to the Nature of the subject.

Under this subject, Dryden again turns to the inherent problems of the English language. He says that in writing for song he has had to actually invent new words and it is in this context that he mentions the objections which all earlier poets had expressed, that they had to alter their words for the sake of the composer and his music. Dryden adamantly promises he will never do this again.

> I am often forced to coin new words, revive some that are antiquated, and botch others; as if I had not served out my time in poetry, but was bound an apprentice to some doggerel Rhymer, who makes songs to tunes, and sings them for a lively-hood. It is true, I have not been often put to this drudgery; but where I have, the words will sufficiently show, that I was then a slave to the composition, which I will never be again. It is my part to invent, and the musicians to humor that invention.

Dryden makes an extraordinary observation later, when he returns to his concern that the efforts of the composer, Grabu, will be accepted by the English composers and critics. Of the public he is not concerned, because he seems aware of the fact that music is both universally and genetically understood by all men.

> For the greatest part of an audience is always unimpressed, though seldom knowing; and if the Musick be well composed, and well performed, they who find themselves pleased, will be so wise as not to be imposed upon and fooled out of their satisfaction.

Dryden offers an observation on the French versus the English with respect to opera.

> When operas were first set up in France, they were not followed over eagerly; but they gained daily upon their hearers, till they grew to that height of reputation, which they now enjoy. The English I confess, are not altogether so musical as the French.

Later, in the prologue, he attributes the development of musical sophistication by the French to the former court of Louis XIV.

> In France, the oldest man is always young,
> Sees opera's daily, learns the tunes so long,
> Till foot, hand, head, keep time with every song.
> Each sings his part, echoing from pit and box
> With his hoarse voice, half harmony, half pox.
> Le plus grand Roy du Monde is always ringing;
> They show themselves good subjects by their singing.[54]

We might add that in the stage directions for this libretto, Dryden mentions a much broader range of instruments than are found in his plays. He mentions by name such instruments as 'Base Voil,' trumpet, harp and 'Ho-boys.' He also includes a number of 'symphonies,' which appear to mean a brief instrumental work, often for the purpose of allowing the appearance or movement of stage machinery. One of these precedes a song (III, i), another is a 'Sinphony of Fluts-Doux.'

Finally, in his poem in honor of the painter, Sir Godfrey Kneller, Dryden speaks of the fact that the taste of the present age discourages the artist from striving for the highest, most exalted, in art. In this context, he briefly reflects in passing a lower artistic level for opera, as compared to the theater.

> For what a Song, or senseless Opera
> Is to the Living Labor of a Play …[55]

The most important English musician in history is honored in a Dryden poem called, 'An Ode, on the Death of Mr. Henry Purcell,' which was later set to music by John Blow. Dryden begins by mentioning the singing of birds, an inevitable topic for poets, but contends their music is no challenge to Purcell.

> So ceased the rival Crew when Purcell came,
> They sung no more, or only sung his fame,
> Struck dumb they all admired the God-like Man.

Dryden concludes by crediting Heaven for Purcell's music.

> The Heavenly Choir, who heard his notes from high,
> Let down the Scale of Musick from the sky:
> They handed him along,
> And all the way He taught, and all the way they sung.[56]

---

54 Ibid., 15.

55 Ibid., IV, 465ff.

56 Ibid., IV, 468ff.

ART MUSIC

Of all the music mentioned in the plays by Dryden, our attention was drawn to his use of music to establish the emotional atmosphere. We find this, for example, in instances of prelude music such as *The Indian-Queen*. At the beginning the stage direction indicates, 'as the Musick plays a soft Air,' which is soon followed by 'when the curtain is almost up, the Musick turns into a tune expressing an alarm.' *Oedipus* also begins with instrumental music intended to set an emotional tone for the beginning of the action. The stage direction reads, 'The curtain rises to a plaintive tune, representing the present condition of Thebes.'[57]

In other instances the music seems intended to be associated with the emotions of the characters. Ill-suited lovers in *Marriage A-La-Mode* (III, i) are directed in the stage direction to traverse the stage, he whistling and she 'singing a dull melancholy tune,' the lyrics for which are not given in the text. Perhaps a similar intent is implied in *Cleomenes* (III, ii), where the stage direction reads, 'Soft Musick all the while Ptolemy and Cassandra are adoring and speaking.'

All for Love (III, i) begins with a stage direction which calls for music to introduce the characters, and, while using ancient instruments, seems to associate a strong and weak character of the music with the characters.

> The entrance on both sides is prepared by Musick; the Trumpets first sounding on Antony's part: then answered by Timbrels, etc., on Cleopatra's.

One also finds in Dryden's plays examples of art song. First, however, we should remind the reader that the sixteenth-century humanists were adamant that the poetry should be written first and the music composed second, to fit the words. The Baroque saw this process reverse itself, as we can see evidenced in the *Kind Keeper* (III, i) where Brainsick[58] recalls,

> I rose immediately in my night-gown and slippers, down I put the notes slap-dash, made words to them like lightning …

The lyric poets of ancient Greece were fond of including contests in music in their pastoral works. Such musical contests can still be found in seventeenth-century pastoral poetry and it is therefore no surprise to find a humorous example in Dryden's play, *An Evening's Love* (V, i). In this case two rather combative lovers about to be married are challenged to a musical contest to decide who should 'wear the breeches' in the marriage. The gentleman, Wildblood, is hesitant,

---

57 One example of instrumental music at the beginning of a play seems intended to allow the audience time to reflect. At the beginning of *Secret Love*, an actor reads a prologue which deals with the rules of playwriting and then leaves the stage. Now a stage direction reads, 'The Prologue goes out, and stays while a Tune is played, after which he returns again.'

58 This work was written shortly after the publication of Bunyan's *Pilgrim's Progress* and the name 'Brainsick' seems clearly a humorous reference to the many such names in Bunyan.

I never sung in all my life; nor ever durst try when I was alone, for fear of braying.

The lady observes, 'if we cannot sing now, we shall never have cause when we are married.' They warm up with solfege, they tune and they sing a song, for which the lyrics are given. When the song is finished, we read,

> WILDBLOOD. Your judgment Gentlemen: a Man or a Maid?
> BELLAMY. If you make no better harmony after you are married then you have before, you are the miserablest couple in Christendom.

A particularly interesting incidence of an on-stage song is found in *Oedipus* (III, i). The stage is completely darkened, followed by Tiresias's lines,

> Must you have Musick too? then tune your voices,
> And let them have such sounds as Hell never heard
> Since Orpheus bribed the shades.

The song which follows is preceded by a very interesting stage direction. First, we are told 'Musick first. Then Sing.' A bracket, which appears to be associated with the word 'sing,' adds, 'This is to be set through.' Since in the literature of this period in England, the word 'set,' when associated with music, refers to music which is *notated*, one is forced to wonder if some of the songs in these plays, which exist on paper only in the form of the lyrics, were improvised.

In Dryden's allegorical play, *Amphitryon* (III, i) Phaedra provides a rare example of a character who does not appreciate a song accompanied by strings.

> What, with Cats-guts and Rosin! This *Sol-la* is but a lamentable, empty sound.

In *King Arthur* (II, ii) there is a song by shepherds after the style of the pastoral poetry of the ancient Greeks. In the charming lyrics of this song the shepherds observe that while the city folks are off getting killed in war, the shepherds are in their lovers' arms and playing flutes.

In Dryden's comedy, *Sir Martin Mar-all* (V, i) there is a satire on the traditional serenade. Warner explains that he will retrieve his lute from the barbers shop and play and sing in a room, in the dark, while Sir Martin pretends to play a lute under the window while making grimaces with his mouth, as if singing. A maid tells the lady, 'We shall have rare Musick,' while the lady herself mentions that she hears the tuning of a lute. At the conclusion of the serenade, we find this dialogue,

> SIR MARTIN. Ha! what do you say, Madam? how does your Ladyship like my Musick?
> MILLISENT. O most heavenly! just like the Harmony of the Spheres that is to be admired, and never heard.

In sixteenth- and seventeenth-century literature, the reader is surprised to find instances of violence associated with serenades. Sometimes this takes the form of people throwing objects at the musicians or people physically attacking the musicians. Dryden, in *An Evening's Love* (II, i), includes a serenade after which the musicians fall into fighting with other servants.

Finally, in *The Assignation; or, Love in a Nunnery*, there is a servant, Benito, who is an amateur musician. We first see him (in I, i) standing before a large dressing mirror, playing guitar and singing to himself. Another character, Aurelian, comments of him,

> He courts himself every morning in that glass at least an hour; there admires his own person ... and studies postures and grimaces ... Then the rogue has the impudence to make sonnets, as he calls them; and, which is greater impudence, he sings them too; there's not a street in all Rome which he does not nightly disquiet with this villainous serenade: with that guitar there, the younger brother of a cittern, he frights away the watch; and as for his violin, it squeaks so lewdly ... It is a mere cat-call.

When Benito begins to sing for others in this scene, Aurelian begins to kick him. The stage direction adds, 'As Aurelain kicks harder, Benito sings faster....'

FUNCTIONAL MUSIC

There is little reference to church music in Dryden, however in the preface to his *Tyrannick Love*, while discussing the potential of dramatic poetry in influencing the audience in matters of religion, he digresses to comment on church music.

> By the harmony of words we elevate the mind to a sense of devotion, as our solemn musick, which is inarticulate poetry, does in churches; and by the lively images of piety, adorned by action, through the senses allure the soul: which while it is charmed in a silent joy of what it sees and hears, is struck at the same time with a secret veneration of things Celestial, and is wound up insensibly into the practice of that which it admires.[59]

In *Love in a Nunnery* (IV, iii) a scene set in a chapel begins with a stage direction reading 'Instrumental and vocal music.' Dryden gives us some idea of the music he had in mind when he has the duke reflect,

> You have treated me with harmony so excellent, that I believed myself among a choir of angels.

We might also mention a reference to a pagan religious ritual of the ancient Romans, in *Aureng-Zebe* (V, i),

> Trumpets and Drums shall fright her from the Throne,
> As sounding Cymbals aid the laboring Moon.

---
59 *The Works of John Dryden*, ed. Hooker, X, 109.

There are numerous examples of trumpet playing, used for a variety of functional purposes familiar to life at this time. In *King Arthur* (II, ii) a trumpet behind one side of the stage signals for a parley and is answered by an opposing trumpet on the other side.[60] A trumpet introduces Haemon in *Oedipus* (I, i) and in Act IV, scene i, a trumpet sounds for the purpose of identifying the native country of a character. In *The Spanish Fryar* (I, i) an interesting instance of a trumpet signal for recognition of a noble.

I hear the General's Trumpets: Stand, and mark
How he will be received; I fear, but coldly.

As one might expect there are many stage directions which refer to the military use of the trumpet. One of these is unusually interesting. In *King Arthur* (III, ii), Emmeline, when she thinks the battle is over, makes a rather dark reference to the trumpet's association with the military.

Are all those trumpets dead themselves, at last,
That used to kill men with their thundering sounds?

Dryden, in his essay on Heroic plays, addresses the use of trumpet signals in the play which follows, *The Conquest of Granada*. His suggestion that this only reflects real life illustrates why we include the music of the drama in these volumes.

To those who object to my frequent use of drums and trumpets … I answer [it is a long tradition on the English stage] … But, I add further, that these warlike instruments, and even their presentation of fighting on the stage, are no more than necessary to produce the effects of an heroic play; that is, to raise the imagination of the audience, and to persuade them, for the time, that what they behold in the theater is really performed. The poet is then to endeavor an absolute dominion over the minds of the spectators.[61]

In the play which follows, there are no more appearances of trumpet signals than one would ordinarily find in these plays, although there are some unusual references. In (III, i) there is a dance song, the lyrics for which are given, which is followed by the stage direction,

After the dance, a tumultuous noise of drums and trumpets.

Ordinarily, in early literature, the sound of a trumpet signal was unnerving to the listener, for it was associated with the horrors of war. In this play, following a stage direction indicating the sounding of an alarm (III, i) we find contrasting reactions.

---

60 A similar exchange is found in *The Spanish Fryar* (V, i).
61 *The Works of John Dryden*, ed. Scott, IV, 22ff.

ALMAHIDE. The noise my soul does through my senses wound.
LYNDARAXA. Methinks it is a noble, sprightly sound,
   The trumpet's clangor, and the clash of arm!
   This noise may chill your blood, but mine it warms.

Still different is Emmeline's comment, in *King Arthur* (I, ii), as the men leave for battle,

   But lead me nearer to the trumpet's face;
   For that brave sound upholds my fainting heart.

14 RESTORATION POETRY

FOR TWO THOUSAND YEARS ALL POETRY WAS SUNG. Now, while most poetry was no longer sung, it is interesting to find poets still speaking as if it were. Not only do the English Restoration poets speak of the 'harmony' of their verses and begin by writing rhetorically 'I sing of …,' but they actually *call* their poetry *music*. Mark Akenside, for example, writes,

> Attend, ye gentle powers
> Of musical delight! and, while I sing …[1]

And James Thomson similarly reflects,

> Tutored by Thee, hence Poetry exalts
> Her voice to ages; and informs the page
> With music, image, sentiment, and thought,
> Never to die.[2]

On the other hand, much poetry at this time was merely functional, usually in praise of one or another noble. A typical example which mentions music, is William Congreve's 'Ode to the Duke of Malborough.' Among its lines we find,

> Nor there they Song should end; tho' all the Nine [Muses]
> Might well their Harps and Heavenly Voices join
> To Sing that Glorious Day,
> When bold *Bavaria* fled the Field,
> And Veteran *Gauls* unused to yield,
> On *Blenheim's* Plain imploring Mercy lay!

Perhaps because of the large amount of this kind of poetry, it is apparent that poetry itself lost some prestige as an art in the view of the public. We can see this, for example, in William Congreve's play, *Love for Love* (I, i), where Scandal observes,

---

[1] 'The Pleasures of Imagination,' I, lines 6ff, in *The Poetical Works of Mark Akenside*, ed. Alexander Dyce (London: Bell and Daldy, 1845). Mark Akenside (1721–1770) was born of humble origins and eventually became a physician and activist in Scottish affairs.

[2] 'Summer,' in 'The Seasons,' in *The Poetical Works of James Thomson* (London: Bell and Daldy, c. 1860), I, 98. James Thomson (1700–1748) was highly respected by both Voltaire and Lessing, but has never been esteemed by his own countrymen.

No, turn Pimp, Flatterer, Quack, Lawyer, Parson, be Chaplain to an Atheist, or Stallion to an Old Woman, anything but a Poet; a Modern Poet is worse, more servile, timorous and fawning, than any I have named.[3]

The poet, Edward Young, also acknowledges the poor reputation which poets had gained.

To our having, or not having, this idea of perfection in the poem we undertake, is chiefly owing the merit or demerit of our performances, as also the modesty or vanity of our opinions concerning them. And in speaking of it I shall show how it unavoidable comes to pass, that bad poets, that is, poets in general, are esteemed, and really are, the most vain, the most irritable, and most ridiculous set of men upon earth …

He that has an idea of perfection in the work he undertakes *may* fail in it; he that has not, *must* …

Now this idea of perfection is, in poetry, more refined than in other kinds of writing; and, because more refined, therefore more difficult; and, because more difficult, therefore more rarely attained: and the non-attainment of it is the source of our vanity. Hence the poetic clan are more obnoxious to vanity than others …

Good writers have the lowest, and bad writers the highest, opinion of their own performances.[4]

Because of the large quantity of Restoration poetry, we intend to focus in this chapter only on that poetry which offers insight on the performance of music. However, because of the intellectual brilliance and wisdom of the greatest of these poets, Alexander Pope, we must not omit some of his observations on subjects which are fundamental to the creation of the arts in general. First, we were impressed by some of his insights on the separate functions of Reason and the emotions. In his 'An Essay on Man,' one finds,

On life's vast ocean diversely we sail,
Reason is the [compass], but passion is the gale.
......

Love, hope, and joy, fair pleasure's smiling train,
Hate, fear, and grief, the family of pain,
These mixed with art, and to due bounds confined,
Make and maintain the balance of the mind:
The lights and shades, whose well-accorded strife
Gives all the strength and color of our life.
......

On different senses different objects strike;
Hence different passions more or less inflame,

---

3   William Congreve (1670–1729) is considered the best of the Restoration writers of comedy and was particularly admired by Voltaire. He studied at Trinity College, Dublin, and worked in various government offices in London.

4   Edward Young, 'A Discourse on Lyric Poetry,' in *Edward Young: The Complete Works* (Hildesheim: Olms, 1968), I, 414ff.

> As strong or weak the organs of the frame;
> And hence one master passion in the breast,
> Like Aaron's serpent, swallows up the rest.
>
> ……
>
> Whatever warms the heart, or fills the head,
> As the mind opens, and its functions spread,
> Imagination plies her dangerous art,
> And pours it all upon the peccant part.
> Nature its mother, habit is its nurse;
> Wit, spirit, faculties, but make it worse;
> Reason itself but gives it edge and power;
> As heaven's blessed beam turns vinegar more sour.
>
> ……
>
> Yes, nature's road must ever be preferred;
> Reason is here no guide, but still a guard.[5]

We were also interested to read, in this same poem, Pope's comments on the relationship of instinct and Reason.

> Say, where full instinct is the unerring guide,
> What pope or council can they need beside?
> Reason, however able, cool at best,
> Cares not for service, or but serves when pressed,
> Stays till we call, and then not often near,
> But honest instinct comes a volunteer,
> Sure never to overshoot, but just to hit.[6]

All writers of this era complain about being ill-used by critics. Perhaps the most famous response by a poet to the critics, and *not* one intended as a comment on education in general, was penned by Alexander Pope.

> A little learning is a dangerous thing;
> Drink deep, or taste not the Pierian spring:
> There shallow draughts intoxicate the brain,
> And drinking largely sobers us again.[7]

---

5. 'An Essay on Man,' Epistle II, lines 107ff, in *The Works of Alexander Pope* (New York: Gordian Press, 1967), II, 384ff. Alexander Pope (1688–1744) was born to the family of a prosperous merchant, but as he was also born Catholic he was denied an education at any of the great universities. Thus, the greatest English poet of the eighteenth century was the product of his own education through reading. An illness as a child left him a four foot high hump-back.

6. Ibid., Epistle III, lines 83ff.

7. 'An Essay on Criticism,' lines 215ff, in *The Works of Alexander Pope*, II, 47.

ON THE AESTHETICS OF MUSIC

In these volumes we have cited numerous examples of philosophers who, on purely an intuitive or deductive basis, seemed to perceive the basic bicameral nature of our brain and its function. A poem by Thomas Sheridan (1687–1738), a priest and schoolmaster friend of Swift, is a remarkable example. He is absolutely, and astonishingly, correct in his assigning of right or left eye and ear functions vis-a-vis their actual relationship with the brain hemispheres.

> With my left eye, I see you sit snug in your stall,
> With my right I'm attending the lawyers that scrawl.
> With my left I behold your bellower a cur chase;
> With my right I'm reading my deeds for a purchase.
> My left ear's attending the hymns of the choir,
> My right ear is stunned with the noise of the crier.[8]

James Thomson also makes a reference to these separate faculties, but finding understanding in the head and music in the heart

> To show us artless reason's moral reign,
> What boastful science arrogates in vain;
> The obedient passions knowing each their part;
> Calm light the head, and harmony the heart![9]

Alexander Pope, in a poem which he called 'An Essay on Criticism,' reflects on the similarities between music and poetry and suggests the highest art is that which goes to the heart.

> Music resembles poetry; in each
> Are nameless graces which no methods teach,
> And which a master hand alone can reach.
>   ......
> Great wits sometimes may gloriously offend,
> And rise to faults true critics dare not mend;
> From vulgar bonds with brave disorder part,
> And snatch a grace beyond the reach of art,
> Which, without passing through the judgment, gains
> The heart, and all its end at once attains.[10]

---

8   Quoted in *The Poetical Works of Jonathan Swift* (London: Bell and Daldy, n.d.), III, 245.
9   'Epitaph on Miss Stanley,' in *The Poetical Works of James Thomson*, II, 225.
10 'An Essay on Criticism,' lines 143ff, in *The Works of Alexander Pope*, II, 42ff.

In a poem of Mark Akenside we can see how firmly accepted was the dogma which still pervades our Western world today: that the subjects of the left hemisphere of the brain are valued considerably above those of the right hemisphere.

> For man loves knowledge, and the beams of Truth
> More welcome touch his understanding's eye,
> Than all the blandishments of sound his ear …[11]

And in Gay's 'Daphnis and Chloe,' the lady is interested in speech above music.

> 'Tis true, thy tuneful reed I blamed,
> That swelled thy lip and rosy cheek;
> Think not thy skill in song defamed,
> That lip should other pleasures seek:
> Much, much thy musick I approve;
> Yet break thy pipe, for more I love,
> Much more to hear thee speak.[12]

On Music and Society

Among the Restoration poets we find some interesting commentary on the historical development of music and poetry. The poet Mark Akenside makes the interesting suggestion that it was because early poetry was sung, that it was able to enter the world of philosophy.

> Armed with the lyre, already have we dared
> To pierce divine Philosophy's retreats,
> And teach the Muse her lore; already strove
> Their long divided honors to unite,
> While, tempering this deep argument, we sang
> Of Truth and Beauty.[13]

James Thomson, in his poem 'Liberty,' discusses the progress of music after the Dark Ages as it revived and the culture moved north.

> Music again
> Her universal language of the heart
> Renewed; and, rising from the plaintive vale,
> To the full concert spread, and solemn choir.

---
11 'The Pleasures of Imagination, II, lines 100ff,' in *The Poetical Works of Mark Akenside*.
12 In *The Works of John Gay* (London: Edward Jeffery, 1745), III, 145.
13 'The Pleasures of Imagination, II, lines 62ff,' in *The Poetical Works of Mark Akenside*.

> Even bigots smiled; to their protection took
> Arts not their own, and from them borrowed pomp:
> For in a tyrant's garden these awhile
> May bloom, though freedom be their parent soil.
> And now confessed, with gently growing gleam
> The morning shone, and westward streamed its light.
> The Muse awoke. Not sooner on the wing
> Is the gay bird of dawn. Artless her voice,
> Untaught and wild, yet warbled through the woods
> Romantic lays. But as her northern course
> She, with her tutor Science, in my train,
> Ardent pursued, her strains more noble grew:
> While Reason drew the plan, the Heart informed
> The moral page, and Fancy lent it grace.[14]

Alexander Pope includes in his poetry several references to the poor musical taste of nobles. In the Epistle III of his 'Moral Essays,'

> Who starves by Nobles, or with Nobles eats?
> The wretch that trusts them, and the rogue that cheats.
> Is there a Lord, who knows a cheerful noon
> Without a fiddler, flatterer, or buffoon?
> Whose table, wit or modest merit share,
> Unelbowed by a gamester, pimp, or player?[15]

A similar criticism of the taste of the noble is found in Epistle IV,

> Light quirks of music, broken and uneven,
> Make the soul dance upon a jig to Heaven.[16]

Quite a different view of the enlightened noble's taste is found in Patrick Delany,

> A soul ennobled and refined
> Reproaches every baser mind:
> As strains exalted and melodious
> Make every meaner music odious.[17]

---

14 'Liberty,' IV, in *The Poetical Works of James Thomson*, II, 73ff.

15 'Moral Essays,' Epistle III, lines 237ff, in *The Works of Alexander Pope*, III, 149.

16 Ibid., Epistle IV, lines 143ff.

17 Patrick Delany (ca. 1685–1768), Chancellor of St. Patrick's, 'The Pheasant and the Lark' (1730), quoted in *The Poetical Works of Jonathan Swift*, II, 182.

John Gay wonders why England is not so devoted to music as other countries.

> Why must we climb the Alpine mountain's sides
> To find the seat where Harmony resides?
> Why touch we not so soft the silver lute,
> The cheerful haut-boy, and the mellow flute?
> 'Tis not the Italian clime improves the sound,
> But there the Patrons of her sons are found.[18]

Music was a frequent vehicle for figures of speech during the English Baroque. One example we like is by Jonathan Swift and it is addressed to the Prince of Wales, who would become King George II. The final line refers to the unhappy fates of Charles I, Cromwell and James II during the seventeenth century.

> Now take your harp into your hand,
> The joyful strings, at your command,
>   In doleful sounds no more shall mourn.
> We, with sincerity of heart,
> To all your tunes shall bear a part,
>   Unless we see the tables turn.[19]

We also find it interesting that one still finds reference to the fabled Music of the Spheres in Restoration poetry. James Thomson, as had occasional writers over a long period before him, suggests that composers may find their inspiration in this celestial music.

> O yon high harmonious spheres,
> Your powerful Mover sing;
> To Him your circling course that steers,
> Your tuneful praises bring.
>
> Ungrateful mortals, catch the sound,
> And in your numerous lays,
> To all the listening world around,
> The God of nature praise.[20]

Pope, in his poem, 'An Essay on Man,' argues that God was wise in not making man's senses more sensitive than they are, as he would likely be miserable. Of music, he says,

---

18 'Epistle IV,' in *The Works of John Gay*, III, 34. John Gay (1685–1732) was born of humble stock and worked for a while as a silk merchant. He became one of the most beloved of English literary figures.

19 'Parody on the Speech of Dr. Benjamin Pratt.' Jonathan Swift (1667–1745) is the best known prose writer at the end of the English Baroque and shared a grandfather with Dryden. He rarely deals with artistic matters, preferring to satirize manners. Reared in Ireland, he became active in English politics until he returned to Dublin as dean of St. Patrick's.

20 'Hymn to God's Power,' in *The Poetical Works of James Thomson*, II, 141.

> If nature thundered in his opening ears,
> And stunned him with the music of the spheres,
> How would he wish that heaven had left him still
> The whispering zephyr, and the purling rill?[21]

Poems in Honor of St. Cecilia

Among the Restoration poems are several dedicated to the honor of St. Cecilia's Day, a traditional day to honor music. Joseph Addison has written two such poems.[22] In his 'A Song for St. Cecilia's Day,' he begins in praise of the patron saint.

> Let all Cecilia's praise proclaim,
> Employ the echo in her name,
> Hark how the flutes and trumpets raise,
> At bright Cecilia's name, their lays;
> The organ labors in her praise.
> Cecilia's name does all our numbers grace,
> From every voice the tuneful accents fly,
> In soaring trebles now it rises high,
> And now it sinks, and dwells upon the base.
> Cecilia's name through all the notes we sing,
> The work of every skillful tongue,
> The sound of every trembling string,
> The sound and triumph of our song.

Now he turns to the purposes of music, treating in turn emotions, character development and religion.

> For ever consecrate the day,
> To music and Cecilia;
> Music, the greatest good that mortals know,
> And all of heaven we have below.
> Music can noble hints impart,
> Engender fury, kindle love;
> With unsuspected eloquence can move,
> And manage all the man with secret art …
>
> Music religious heats inspires,
> It wakes the soul, and lifts it high,

---

21 'An Essay on Man,' lines 201ff, in *The Works of Alexander Pope*, II, 363.

22 Joseph Addison (1672–1719) was a fellow at Magdalen College, Oxford, and was very active in politics, eventually becoming Secretary of State.

And winds it with sublime desires,
And fits it to bespeak the Deity.
The Almighty listens to a tuneful tongue,
And seems well-pleased and courted with a song.
Soft moving sounds and heavenly airs
Give force to every word, and recommend our prayers.

He concludes with a poetic reference to the Day of Judgment.

When time itself shall be no more,
And all things in confusion hurled,
Music shall then exert its power,
And sound survive the ruins of the world.

The second poem on this subject by Addison is called 'Ode for St. Cecilia's Day,' written in 1699 and set to music by Daniel Purcell. In this work he concentrates on aesthetic characterizations of the violin, flute, organ and trumpet.

First let the sprightly violin
The joyful melody begin,
And none of all her strings be mute;
While the sharp sound and shriller lay
In sweet harmonious notes decay,
Softened and mellowed by the flute.

Next, let the solemn organ join
Religious airs, and strains divine,
Such as may lift us to the skies,
And set all Heaven before our eyes.

Let then the trumpet's piercing sound
Our ravished ears with pleasure wound.
The soul overpowering with delight,
As, with a quick uncommon ray,
A streak of lightening clears the day,
And flashes on the sight.
Let Echo too perform her part,
Prolonging every note with art,
And in a low expiring strain
Play all the concert over again …

And now the choir complete rejoices,
With trembling strings and melting voices.
The tuneful ferment rises high,
And works with mingled melody.

Quick divisions run their rounds,
A thousand trills and quivering sounds
In airy circles over us fly,
Till, wafted by a gentle breeze,
They faint and languish by degrees,
And at a distance die.

As in the above case, most of these St. Cecilia Odes were set to music. William Congreve wrote a poem, 'A Hymn to Harmony,' in honor of St. Cecilia's Day of 1701, which was set to music of 'John Eccles, Master of Her Majesties Musick.' John Oldham's 'Ode for an Anniversary of Musick on St. Cecilia's Day,' was set to music by 'Dr. Blow.'

Begin the song, your instruments advance
Tune the voice, and tune the flute,
Touch the silent, sleeping lute,
And make the strings to their own measures dance.
Being gentlest thoughts, that into language glide,
Bring softest words, that into numbers slide.
Let every hand, and every tongue,
To make the noble consort, throng.
Let all in one harmonious note agree
To frame the mighty song,
For this is musick's sacred Jubilee.

Hark, how the wakened strings resound,
And break the yielding air,
The ravished sense, how pleasingly they wound,
And call the listening soul into the ear;
Each pulse beats time, and every heart,
With tongue, and fingers, bears a part.
By harmony's entrancing power,
When we are thus wound up to ecstasy;
Methinks we mount, methinks we tower,
And seem to antedate our future bliss on high.

How dull were life, how hardly worth our care,
But for the charms that musick lends!
How faint its pleasures would appear,
But for the pleasure which our art attends!
Without the sweets of melody,
To tune our vital breath,
Who would not give it up to death,
And in the silent grave contented lie?

Musick's the cordial of a troubled breast,

The softest remedy that grief can find;
The gentle spell, that charms our care to rest,
And calms the ruffled passions of the mind.
Musick does all our joys refine,
It gives the relish to our wine,
'Tis that gives rapture to our love,
And wings devotion to a pitch divine;
'Tis our chief bliss on earth, and half our heaven above.

Come then, with tuneful throat and string,
The praises of our art let's sing;
Let's sing to blest Cecilia's fame,
That graced this art, and gave this day its name;
With musick, wind and mirth conspire
To bear a consort, and make up the choir.[23]

Alexander Pope also contributed an Ode to St. Cecilia's Day, one which begins with a call to the Muses,

Descend, ye Nine! descend and sing;
The breathing instruments inspire,
Wake into voice each silent string,
And sweep the sounding lyre!
In a sadly-pleasing strain
Let the warbling lute complain:
Let the loud trumpet sound,
Till the roofs all around
The shrill echoes rebound:
While in more lengthened notes and slow,
The deep, majestic, solemn organs blow.
Hark! the numbers soft and clear,
Gently steal upon the ear;
Now louder, and yet louder rise,
And fill with spreading sounds the skies;
Exulting in triumph now swell the bold notes,
In broken air, trembling, the wild music floats;
Till, by degrees, remote and small,
The strains decay,
And melt away,
In a dying, dying fall.[24]

---

[23] In *The Works of John Oldham* (London: Bettenham, 1722), II, 254. John Oldham (1653–1683) was a satirist best remembered for his 'Satyrs Upon the Jesuits,' of 1681.

[24] 'Ode on St. Cecilia's Day,' in *The Works of Alexander Pope*, IV, 397ff.

Next Pope offers a catalog of the purposes and virtues of music.

> By Music, minds an equal temper know,
> Nor swell too high, nor sink too low.
> If in the breast tumultuous joys arise,
> Music her soft, assuasive voice applies;
> Or when the soul is pressed with cares,
> Exalts her in enlivening airs.
> Warriors she fires with animated sounds;
> Pours balm into the bleeding lover's wounds:
> Melancholy lifts her head,
> Morpheus rouses from his bed,
> Sloth unfolds her arms and wakes,
> Listening Envy drops her snakes;
> Intestine war no more our Passions wage,
> And giddy Factions hear away their rage.
> ......
> Music the fiercest grief can charm,
> And fate's severest rage disarm:
> Music can soften pain to ease,
> And make despair and madness please.

Jonathan Swift offers a strange addition to the repertoire of Odes to St. Cecilia.

> Grave Dean of St. Patrick's, how comes it to pass,
> That you, who know music no more than an ass,
> That you who so lately were writing of drapiers,
> Should lend your cathedral to players and scrapers [violinists]?
> To act such an opera once in a year,
> So offensive to every true Protestant ear,
> With trumpets, and fiddles, and organs, and singing,
> Will sure the Pretender and Popery bring in,
> No Protestant Prelate, his lordship or grace,
> Durst there show his right, or most reverend face:
> How would it pollute their crosiers and rochets,
> To listen to minims, and quavers, and crotchets![25]

---

25 'Dr. Swift to Himself on St. Cecilia's Day.'

On Purposes of Music

Among the purposes of music mentioned in this repertoire of poetry, the purpose of pleasure is infrequently mentioned. In a poem called 'Song,' Sir Charles Sedley finds some practicality in this purpose.

> Let us indulge the joys we know
> Of Musick, Wine and Love;
> Were sure of what we find below,
> Uncertain what's above.[26]

James Thomson, in his 'The Castle of Indolence,' wonders of God,

> Yet the fine arts were what he finished least.
> For why? They are the quintessence of all.[27]

Later in this poem he observes of musicians themselves,

> And where they nothing have to do but please:
> Ah! gracious God! thou knowest they ask no other fees.

The purpose of music most frequently mentioned in early literature is to soothe the listener or player. James Thomson's 'The Castle of Indolence,' mentions this purpose among other virtues of music.

> A certain music, never known before,
> Here lulled the pensive, melancholy mind;
> Full easily obtained. Behoves no more,
> But sidelong, to the gently waving wind,
> To lay the well-tuned instrument reclined;
> From which, with airy flying fingers light,
> Beyond each mortal touch the most refined,
> The gods of winds drew sounds of deep delight:
> Whence, with just cause, the harps of Aeolus it heights.

> Ah me! what hand can touch the string so fine?
> Who up the lofty diapason roll
> Such sweet, such sad, such solemn airs divine,
> Then let them down again into the soul:
> Now rising love they fanned; now pleasing dole
> They breathed, in tender musings, through the heart;
> And now a graver sacred strain they stole,

---

26 *The Poetical and Dramatic Works of Sir Charles Sedley* (New York: AMS Press, 1969), II, 196.

27 In *The Poetical Works of James Thomson*, II, 293ff.

> As when seraphic hands a hymn impart:
> Wild warbling nature all; above the reach of art![28]

Sometimes we find this purpose contained in references to the Greek gods, as in Matthew Prior,

> If Wine and Musick have the power,
> To ease the sickness of the soul;
> Let Phoebus every string explore;
> And Bacchus fill the sprightly bowl.[29]

Similarly, in Joseph Addison,

> When Orpheus tuned his lyre with pleasing woe,
> Rivers forgot to run, and winds to blow,
> While listening forest covered as he played,
> The soft musician in a moving shade.[30]

On the other hand, some poems refer to this purpose as directed to specific contemporaries. Gay, in a poem to the Dutchess of Marlborough, on the death of her famous husband, observes,

> Numbers [verse], like musick, can even grief control,
> And lull to peace the tumults of the soul.[31]

Epistle X of Pope's 'Moral Essays' concludes,

> Vexed to be still in town, I knit my brow,
> Look sour, and hum a tune, as you may now.[32]

In Congreve's hymn to St. Cecilia, the poet comments on the immediacy of music's impact in achieving his purpose.

> While Reason stilled by Hopes or Fears betrayed,
> Too late advances, or too soon retreats.
> Musick alone with sudden charms can bind
> The wandering sense, and calm the troubled mind.

---

28 In *The Poetical Works of James Thomson*, II, 274. The 'harp of Aeolus' was in instrument devised to be placed in the window and played by the wind.

29 'A Song,' *The Literary Works of Matthew Prior* (Oxford: Clarendon, 1959), I, 196. Matthew Prior (1664–1721) was a friend of Gay and Swift and liked to call himself 'only a poet by accident.'

30 'Epilogue to the British Enchanters,' lines 1ff.

31 'Epistle V,' in *The Works of John Gay*, III, 39.

32 'Moral Essays,' Epistle X, lines 49ff, in *The Works of Alexander Pope*, III, 227.

The most fundamental purpose of music is to communicate feelings, a purpose which is curiously infrequently mentioned among these poems. One would expect to find more examples such as Shenstone's poem, 'Love and Music,' which begins,

> Shall Love alone for ever claim
> An universal right to fame,
> An undisputed sway?
> Or has not Music equal charms,
> To fill the breast with strange alarms,
> And make the world obey?[33]

James Thomson, in his 'The Seasons,' suggests that the purpose of music to express love is so universal that it serves the same purpose even among the animal kingdom.

> 'Tis love creates their melody, and all
> This waste of music is the voice of love;
> That even to birds, and beasts, the tender arts
> Of pleasing teaches.[34]

In another poem, 'An Ode on Aeolus's Harp,' his focus is the woe of love.

> Those tender notes, how kindly they upbraid,
> With what soft woe they thrill the lover's heart![35]

Finally, there is an occasional reference which touches on music therapy. A poem by William Wycherley contains the interestingly specific observation in this regard.

> Your verse, like your prescriptions, is so mean,
> That, like bad Musick, it provokes the Spleen.[36]

In another poem, we are closer to the Greek concept of the affect of music on character, as Edward Young refers to music as the parent of good actions.

---

33 William Shenstone, 'Love and Music,' in *The Poetical Works of William Shenstone* (Edinburgh: James Nichol, 1854), 144. William Shenstone (1714–1763) was one of the minor figures in English literature of the early eighteenth century, but was possessed of a perceptive intelligence.

34 'Spring,' in 'The Seasons,' *The Poetical Works of James Thomson*, I, 22.

35 In Ibid., II, 227.

36 'To a Doctor of Physick, on his Writing a Satyr against Wit,' in *The Complete Works of William Wycherley* (New York: Russell & Russell, 1964), IV, 177. William Wycherley (1641–1715) studied at Oxford, joined the court in exile in France and on his return to London was imprisoned for his debts.

How Music charms! How Meter warms!
Parent of actions good and brave!
How Vice it tames, and worth inflames,
And hold proud empire over the grave![37]

ART MUSIC

Among the references to art music in Restoration poetry there are two which include mention of Handel. Shenstone's 'Ode' which was intended to be performed by a chorus of citizens, with an instrumental part for viol d'amour, includes the lines,

Hear but this strain—'twas made by Handel,
A wight of skill and judgment deep![38]

Alexander Pope was critical of the ever larger forces of musicians used in performance and, it seems to us, suspicious of the impact the music had on the audience.

Joy to great Chaos! let division reign:
Chromatic tortures soon shall drive them hence,
Break all their nerves, and fritter all their sense:
One Trill shall harmonize joy, grief, and rage,
Wake the dull Church, and lull the ranting Stage;
To the same notes thy sons shall hum, or snore,
And all thy yawning daughters cry, *encore*.
Another Phoebus, thy own Phoebus, reigns,
Joys in my jigs, and dances in my chains.
But soon, ah soon, Rebellion will commence,
If Music meanly borrows aid from Sense.
Strong in new Arms, lo! Giant Handel stands,
Like bold Briareus, with a hundred hands;
To stir, to rouse, to shake the soul he comes,
And Jove's own Thunders follow Mar's Drums.
Arrest him, Empress; or you sleep no more—[39]

In other countries one finds among the repertoire of art songs a number of love songs. The representatives of such repertoire in England are rather curious. Samuel Butler portrays a rather dark side of love.

---

37 Edward Young, 'Ode to the King,' in *Edward Young: The Complete Works* (Hildesheim: Olms, 1968), I, 412. Edward Young (1683–1765), best known for his poetry, was born in his father's rectory and later became dean of Salisbury.

38 William Shenstone, 'Ode,' in *The Poetical Works of William Shenstone*, 142.

39 'The Dunciad,' Book IV, lines 54ff, in *The Works of Alexander Pope*, IV, 193ff.

All writers, though of different fancies,
Do make all people in romances,
That are distressed and discontent,
Make songs and sing to an instrument.[40]

An unusual love poem by Richard Steele is addressed to his lover's spinet.

Thou soft Machine that do'st her Hand obey,
Tell her my Grief in thy harmonious lay.[41]

Pope safely depersonalizes the subject by placing it in the context of a pastoral setting.

Where Thames reflects the visionary scene:
Thither, the silver-sounding lyres
Shall call the smiling loves, and young desires;
There, every Grace and Muse shall throng,
Exalt the dance, or animate the song;
There youths and nymphs, in consort gay,
Shall hail the rising, close the parting day.[42]

On Opera

The most interesting commentary on music in the works of these Restoration poets is on the subject of opera, a subject on which they are invariably hostile. Among the more tame examples, Shenstone was probably thinking of Italian opera when he wrote of the songs of birds,

My doubt subsides—'tis no Italian song,
Nor senseless ditty, cheers the vernal tree...[43]

After Dryden converted to Catholicism in 1686, Charles Sackville wrote an anti-Catholic commentary, recommending that Dryden use the Catholic fables as material for new operas.

---

40 Unnamed poem in *The Poetical Works of Samuel Butler* (New York: Appleton, 1854), II, 256.

41 Richard Steele, 'The Lying Lover.' This work was published in 1704 with music by William Crofts. It was advertised as 'with figured bass. Symphony at the end for the flute.' The actual music for another of Steele's poems, 'The Conscious Lovers,' with music by Johann Ernst Galliard, is reproduced in *The Occasional Verse of Richard Steele* (Oxford: Clarendon, 1952), 27. It is interesting that this particular song was intended for the premiere of a play, but no singer could be found. [Ibid., 86]

42 'Imitations of Horace,' Book IV, Ode I, lines 24ff, in *The Works of Alexander Pope*, III, 416.

43 William Shenstone, 'Elegy VI,' in *The Poetical Works of William Shenstone*, 10.

> Thy mind, disused to truth, must entertain
> With tales more monstrous, fanciful, and vain
> Than even thy poetry could ever feign.
> Or sing the lives of thy own fellow saints—
> 'Tis a large field and thy assistance wants.
> Thence copy out new operas for the stage
> And with their miracles divert the age.[44]

Turning to the more outspoken poets, Richard Steele was one who was adamantly opposed to Italian opera. We can see this in the Epilogue he wrote for the play, *The Tender Husband*, whose lines include,

> Britons, who constant war, with factious rage,
> For liberty against each other wage,
> From foreign insult save this English stage.
> No more the Italian squalling Tribe admit,
> In tongues unknown; it is Popery in wit.
> The songs (their selves confess) from Rome they bring;
> And 'tis High Mass, for ought you know, they sing.
> Husbands take care, the danger may come nigher,
> The women say their eunuch is a Friar.

Steele has also written an intentionally insipid little poem called 'Lyric for Italian Music,' of which he sarcastically comments that his poem will not 'disturb the head, but merely serves to be added to sounds proper for the syllables.' He even wrote a poem to celebrate the departure of the famous Italian singer, Nicolino Grimaldi, who left England to return to Italy in 1712. Among other insults, he reminds the reader that the singer was a castrato.

> Begone, our nation's pleasure and reproach!
> *Britain* no more with idle trills debauch;
> Back to thy own unmanly *Venice* sail,
> Where luxury and loose desires prevail;
> There thy emasculating voice employ,
> And raise the triumphs of the wanton boy.[45]

Joseph Addison laments the decline in British drama caused by the popularity of Italian opera.

> Long has a race of heroes filled the stage,
> That rant by note, and through the gamut rage;

---

44 *The Poems of Charles Sackville* (New York: Garland, 1979), 19. Charles Sackville, earl of Dorset (1638–1706), was the recipient of the dedication of Dryden's 'Essay of Dramatic Poesie.'

45 'On Nicolini's leaving the Stage.'

In songs and airs express their martial fire,
Combat in trills, and in a fugue expire.
While, lulled by sound, and undisturbed by wit,
Calm and serene you indolently sit,
And, from the dull fatigue of thinking free,
Hear the facetious fiddle's repartee.
Our home-spun authors must forsake the field,
And Shakespeare to the soft Scarlatti yield.[46]

In his 'Epistle III,' John Gay satirizes French opera through a character who has returned to tell of life in Paris.[47] He finds there that 'Opera claims the foremost place' and in a discussion of the *Toilette* mentions 'Madame today puts on her Opera face.' Eventually, we get an interesting view of French opera, seen through English eyes, followed by a stated preference for Italian music. The extraordinary thing for the modern reader here, customs described in French sources as well, is the participation of the audience, including crowding onto the stage itself!

Adieu, Monsieur—The Opera hour draws near,
Not see the Opera! all the world is there;
Where on the stage the embroidered youth of France
In bright array attract the female glance:
This languishes, this struts, to show his mien,
And not a gold-clocked stocking moves unseen.
But hark! the full Orchestra strike the strings;
The Hero struts, and the whole audience sings.

My jarring ear harsh grating murmurs wound,
Hoarse and confused, like *Babel's* mingled sound.
Hard chance had placed me near a noisy throat,
That in rough quavers bellowed every note.
Pray, Sir, says I, suspend awhile your song,
The Opera's drowned; your lungs are wondrous strong;
I wish to hear your *Roland's* ranting strain,
While he with rooted forfeits strows the plain.
Sudden he shrugs surprise, and answers quick,
Monsieur apparemment n'aime pas la musique.
Then turning round, he joined the ungrateful noise;
And the loud Chorus thundered with his voice.

O soothe me with some soft Italian air,
Let harmony compose my tortured ear!
When Anastatia's voice commands the strain,

---

46 'Prologue to Smith's Phaedra and Hippolitus,' lines 1ff.
47 'Epistle III,' in *The Works of John Gay*, III, 20ff.

> The melting warble thrills through every vain;
> Thought stands suspense, and silence pleased attends,
> While in her notes the heavenly Choir descends.
>
> But you'll imagine I'm a *Frenchman* grown,
> Pleased and content with nothing but my own,
> So strongly with this prejudice possessed,
> He thinks *French* musick and *French* painting best.
> Mention the force of learned *Corelli's* notes,
> Some scraping fiddler of their Ball he quotes;
> Talk of the spirit *Raphael's* pencil gives,
> Yet warm with life whose speaking picture lives;
> Yes, Sir, says he, in color and design,
> *Rigaut* and *Raphael* are extremely fine!

Gay makes his personal prejudice quite clear in the final lines of this poem.

> Should I let Satire loose on English ground,
> There fools of various character abound;
> But here my verse is to one race confined,
> All Frenchmen are of *Petit-maitre* kind.

Finally, we might mention an elegy by Gay on the death of a performer.

> But bear me faintly through the lonely grove;
> No more these hands shall over the spinnet bound,
> And from the sleeping strings call forth the sound;
> Musick adieu, farewell Italian airs![48]

Among the anti-Italian opera reflections by Swift is a rather nasty poem of 1731 called 'Apollo.' Someone had apparently become obsessed with the observation that, among the Greek gods, Apollo never married a female god. Swift offers to solve this 'problem' by contending that Apollo, like the famous Italian singer known in London as 'Nicolini,' was a castrato.

> Yet, with his beauty, wealth, and parts,
> Enough to win ten thousand hearts,
> No vulgar deity above
> Was so unfortunate in love.
> Three weighty causes were assigned,
> That moved the nymphs to be unkind.
> Nine Muses always waiting round him,
> He left them virgins as he found them.

---

48 'Araminta,' in Ibid., III, 124.

> His singing was another fault;
> For he could reach to B in *alt*:
> And, by the sentiments of Pliny,
> Such singers are like Nicolini.
> At last, the point was fully cleared;
> In short, Apollo had no beard.

Alexander Pope was also inevitably critical of opera, as in this reference to the court's preference to Italian opera,

> Get place and wealth—if possible with grace;
> If not, by any means, get wealth and place.
> For what? to have a box where eunuchs sing,
> And foremost in the circle eye a king.[49]

In the same work, Pope makes a similar comment and in a footnote he indicates he was thinking of *The Siege of Rhodes*, by William Davenant, the first opera sung in England.

> No wonder then, when all was love and sport,
> The willing Muses were debauched at Court:
> On each enervate string they taught the note
> To pant, or tremble through an eunuch's throat.[50]

In his curious attack on literary charlatanism, 'The Dunciad,' Pope finds,

> Already Opera prepares the way,
> The sure fore-runner of her gentle sway:
> Let her thy heart, next Drabs and Dice, engage,
> The third mad passion of thy doting age.
> Teach thou the warbling Polypheme to roar,
> And scream thyself as none ever screamed before![51]

Pope intends his most famous 'Epigram on the Feuds about Handel and Bononcini,' as an expression of his boredom with the discussion of opera in the press.

> Strange! all this difference should be
> 'Twixt Tweedle-*dum* and Tweedle-*dee*![52]

---

49 'Imitations of Horace,' Book I, Epistle I, in *The Works of Alexander Pope*, III, 338.
50 Ibid., Book II, Epistle I, lines 151ff.
51 'The Dunciad,' Book III, lines 301ff, in Ibid., IV, 182.
52 Quoted in Ibid., IV, 445.

FUNCTIONAL MUSIC

As the poets were critical of opera, some are also brave enough to satirize the church. Samuel Butler wrote a long epic poem, 'Hudibras,' inspired by *Don Quixote*, which was extremely popular and enjoyed many editions. It is a strange work, with little plot, which found its popularity in its coarse and bigoted satire of the Puritans. One of the characters is, Crowdero, an itinerant fiddler. We first meet him as a metaphor for the Puritan's distaste for instrumental music. Here we see the fiddler [Music] blamed for its ill-effect on society.

> But to that purpose first surrender
> The Fiddler, as the prime offender,
> The incendiary vile, that is chief
> Author and engineer of mischief;
> That makes division between friends,
> For profane and malignant ends.
> He and that engine of vile noise,
> On which illegally he plays,
> Shall (*dictum factum*) both be brought
> To condign punishment, as they ought.[53]

Later, when Butler is discussing this fiddler, he takes the opportunity to satirize the predilection of the Catholic Church princes for entertainment.

> … they hold their luxuries,
> Their dogs, their horses, whores, and dice,
> Their riots, revels, masks, delights,
> Pimps, buffoons, fiddlers, parasites;
> All which the Saints have title to.[54]

A more conventional view is found in a line in Alexander Pope's 'Eloisa to Abelard,' which finds the 'swelling organs lift the rising soul.'[55]

A more typical subject for poets is description of the music of the angels, or Heaven. We especially enjoy Edward Young's refusal to sing in the Heavenly choir unless it is conduced by the artist, Raphael!

> But sing no more—no more I sing,
> Or reassume the lyre,
> Unless vouchsafed an humble part
> Where Raphael leads the choir.[56]

---

[53] Samuel Butler (1612–1680), 'Hudibras,' Part I, Canto ii, lines 667ff. The reader will notice the pun on 'division,' a standard element of improvisation at this time.

[54] Ibid., I, ii, lines 1013ff.

[55] 'Eloisa to Abelard,' line 272.

[56] Edward Young, 'Resignation,' in *Edward Young: The Complete Works*, II, 123.

James Thomson writes of the music of the angels in two of his poems.

> Whose flaming love their tuneful harps employ
> In solemn hymns Jehovah's praise to sing,
> And make all heaven with hallelujahs ring.[57]
>
> ......
>
> Methinks I hear the full celestial choir,
> Through Heaven's high dome their awful anthem raise;
> Now chanting clear, and now they all conspire
> To swell the lofty hymn from praise to praise.[58]

Alexander Pope, in his poem, 'The Dying Christian,' hears the music of heaven and pens one of his most famous lines.

> The world recedes; it disappears!
> Heaven opens on my eyes! my ears
> With sounds seraphim ring:
> Lend, lend your winds! I mount! I fly!
> O Grave! where is thy Victory?
> O Death! where is thy Sting?[59]

Finally, Swift refers to the legend of the ancient Roman religious cult which tells of using cymbals and drums in a worship service of the moon.

> Wise people, who believed with reason
> That this eclipse was out of season,
> Affirmed the moon was sick, and fell
> To cure her by a counter spell.
> Ten thousand cymbals now begin,
> To rend the skies with brazen din;
> The cymbals rattling sounds dispel
> The cloud, and drive the hag to hell.
> The moon, delivered from her pain,
> Displays her silver face again.[60]

---

57 'Upon Happiness,' in *The Poetical Works of James Thomson*, II, 171.
58 'An Ode on Aeolus's Harp,' in Ibid., II, 228.
59 'The Dying Christian to his Soul' (1712), in *The Works of Alexander Pope*, IV, 409.
60 'A Simile on our Want of Silver.'

Much functional music of the Restoration was directed toward the praise of the English nobles. Pope, in his 'The Dunciad,' addresses this practice as part of his satire of writers who seek to flatter the great.

> With horns and trumpets now to madness swell,
> Now sink in sorrows with a tolling bell;
> Such happy arts attention can command,
> When fancy flags, and sense is at a stand.
> Improve we these. Three Cat-calls be the bribe
> Of him, whose chattering shames the monkey-tribe;
> And his this Drum, whose hoarse heroic bass
> Drowns the loud clarion of the braying Ass …
> So swells each wind-pipe; Ass intones to Ass;
> Harmonic twang! of leather, horn, and brass;
> Such as from laboring lungs the Enthusiast blows,
> High Sound, attempered to the vocal noise;
> Or such as bellow from the deep Divine …
> All hail him victor in both gifts of song,
> Who sings so loudly, and who sings so long.[61]

Swift writes of a duke who has come under depressed circumstances.

> His wings are clipped: he tries no more in vain
> With bands of fiddlers to extend his train.[62]

In another poem, Swift makes a reference to the medieval tradition of musicians processing the actors though a village to the place where the play would be given.

> In every town we wait on Mr. Mayor,
> First get a license, then produce our ware;
> We sound a trumpet, or we beat a drum:
> Huzza! (the schoolboys roar) the players are come.[63]

References to military music among these poems are frequent and usually emphasize the shrill or brazen quality of the sounds. Consider, for example, how similar in style the following poets are.

> Congreve:
> Loud Trumpets with shrill Fifes are heard;
> And hoarse resounding Drums.

---
61 'The Dunciad,' Book II, lines 227ff, in *The Works of Alexander Pope*, IV, 147ff.
62 'The Dean and Duke' (1734).
63 'A Prologue. Billet to a Company of Players.'

War, with discordant notes and jarring noise,
The Harmony of Peace destroys.[64]

Addison:
But now the trumpet, terrible from far,
In shriller clangors animates the war,
Confederate drums in fuller consort beat,
And echoing hills the loud alarm repeat.[65]

James Thomson:
Who bids the trumpet hush his horrid clang,
Nor blow the giddy nations into rage.[66]

Swift:
Carteret was welcomed to the shore
First with the brazen cannon's roar;
To meet him next the soldier comes,
With brazen trumps and brazen drums …[67]
......
So by the brazen trumpet's bluster
Troops of all tongues and nations muster.[68]

Pope:
Rend with tremendous sound your ears asunder,
With gun, drum, trumpet, blunderbuss, and thunder.[69]

Only a few of the poems refer to the aspect of military music so often mentioned by the ancient Greeks, the ability of music to give courage to the soldier. Edward Young writes of this with respect to the percussion.

How the drums all around
Soul-rousing resound![70]

---

64 Hymn in Honor of St. Cecilia's day.
65 'The Campaign,' lines 239ff.
66 'Britannia,' in *The Poetical Works of James Thomson*, II, 187.
67 'Epigram on Wood's Brass Money.'
68 'Prometheus' (1724).
69 'Imitations of Horace,' Satire I, lines 25ff, in *The Works of Alexander Pope*, III, 291.
70 Edward Young, 'The Best Argument for Peace,' in *Edward Young: The Complete Works*, II, 57.

A similar reference to percussion is found in the works of Matthew Prior.

> While then your Hero drowns his rising fear
> With Drums Alarms and Trumpets Sounds …[71]
>
> By sounding Trumpets, Hear, and rattling Drums,
> When William to the open Vengeance comes.[72]

A very popular kind of functional music in England was the music of the hunt, in particular the fox hunt. Typical references are found by Samuel Butler,

> … the shrill horn,
> Resounded from the hills,[73]

and Alexander Pope, in his 'Windsor Forest,'

> Now range the hills, the gameful woods beset,
> Wind the shrill horn, or spread the waving net.[74]

William Somerville wrote a long poem called 'The Chase,' which covers the entire subject of hunting.[75] He begins by inviting the reader to abandon the theaters and its music for the more manly pursuit of hunting.

> While crowded theaters, too fondly proud
> Of their exotic minstrels, and shrill pipes,
> The price of manhood, hail thee with a song,
> And airs soft-warbling; my hoarse-sounding horn
> Invites thee to the Chase, the sport of kings;
> Image of war, without its guilt.[76]

The hunting day begins with a musical wakeup call, which also serves to excite the hunting dogs, who in turn excite the horses.

> Thy early meal, or thy officious maids,
> The toilet placed, shall urge thee to perform
> The important work. Me other joys invite,
> The horn sonorous calls, the pack awaked

---

71 'An Ode in Imitation of Horace,' in *The Literary Works of Matthew Prior*, I, 117.
72 'Presented to the King, 1696,) in Ibid., I, 157.
73 'Autumn,' in 'The Seasons,' in *The Poetical Works of James Thomson*, I, 116.
74 'Windsor Forest,' lines 95ff, in *The Works of Alexander Pope*, I, 346.
75 William Somerville (1682–1742) was born a wealthy nobleman in Warwickshire.
76 'The Chase,' I, lines 1-ff.

Their matins chant, nor brook my long delay.
My courser hears their voice; see there with ears
And tail erect, neighing he paws the ground;
Fierce rapture kindles in his reddening eyes,
And boils in every vein.[77]

The hunting horns play as the company rides through the fields,

What gay heart-cheering sounds
Urge through the breathing brass their mazy way![78]

and for the death of the animals.

Bid the loud horns, in gaily warbling strains,
Proclaim the felon's fate; he dies, he dies.[79]

ENTERTAINMENT MUSIC

Alexander Pope, writes of court entertainment music in his 'The Dunciad,'

Much to the mindful Queen the feast recalls
What City Swans once sung within the walls.[80]

In the poetry of Pope we also find rare mention of actual popular tunes. In his 'Imitations of Horace,' he writes of the public interrupting plays by crying for popular tunes, in this case 'The Coal-black Joke,' an indecent song in a ballad opera, *The Beggar's Wedding*.

The many-headed monster of the pit;
A senseless, worthless, and unhonored crowd;
Who, to disturb their betters mighty proud,
Clattering their sticks before ten lines are spoke,
Call for the farce, the bear, or the black-joke.[81]

Pope mentions popular tunes again in Book II, Epistle II, of this work, where a visiting young Frenchman reflects,

---

77 Ibid., II, 86ff.
78 Ibid., IV, 410ff.
79 Ibid., IV, 461ff.
80 'The Dunciad,' Book I, lines 95ff, in *The Works of Alexander Pope*, IV, 107.
81 'Imitations of Horace,' Book II, Epistle I, lines 305ff, in Ibid., III, 367.

> And here, while town, and court, and city roars,
> With mobs, and duns, and soldiers, at their doors;
> Shall I, in London, act this idle part?
> Composing songs, for fools to get by heart?[82]

John Gay has written a poem describing an itinerant musician named Bowzybeus,[83] whom we first find asleep from drink.

> When fast asleep they Bowzybeus spied,
> His hat and oaken staff lay close beside.
> That Bowzybeus who could sweetly sing,
> Or with the rosined bow torment the string:
> That Bowzybeus who with fingers speed
> Could call soft warblings from the breathing reed;
> That Bowzybeus who with jocund tongue,
> Ballads and roundelays and catches sung.

Folks passing by awaken him and plea for some songs,

> No sooner began he raise his tuneful song,
> But lads and lasses round about him throng.
> No ballad-singer placed above the crown
> Sings with a note so shrilling sweet and loud,
> No parish-clerk who calls the psalm so clear,
> Like Bowzybeus soothes the attentive ear.

Bowzybeus sings a very wide variety of songs, beginning with songs about nature, followed by songs describing 'fairs and shows.' Among these songs are 'Jack Pudding,' 'Rare shews' and songs about Punch, but one is quite different,

> Then sad he sung *The Children in the Wood*.
> Ah barbarous uncle, stained with infant blood!

Next he turns to songs of war.

> To louder strains he raised his voice, to tell
> What woeful wars in *Chevy-chase* befell,
> When *Piercy* drove the deer with hound and horn,
> Wars to be wept by children yet unborn!

---

82 Ibid., Book II, Epistle II, lines 123ff.
83 'Saturday; or, the Flights,' in *The Works of John Gay*, II, 116ff.

Now he sings more songs of England, and then,

> Then he was seized with a religious qualm,
> And of a sudden sung the hundredth psalm.

He finally finished singing and 'as he reels along,' goes on his way, still drunk!

15 RESTORATION NON-FICTION

SOME OF THE MOST IMPORTANT REPRESENTATIVES of Restoration non-fiction prose will be found in the chapters dealing with philosophy and the journals. Here will be found material taken primarily from treatises and essays.

ON THE PHYSIOLOGY OF AESTHETICS

Today philologists agree that some form of emotional communication through music existed before the development of speech in early man. Strong elements of music remain in our speech, particularly in the right hemisphere of the brain's input of emotional coloring to give meaning to the left hemisphere vocabulary and in the melodic contour of our every sentence. It should be no surprise then, that Jonathan Swift, in a treatise on 'Genteel Conversation,' includes the knowledge of music as necessary for the development of elegant speech.

> It may be objected, that the publication of my book, may, in the long course of time, prostitute this noble art to mean and vulgar people. But, I answer; that it is not so easily acquired, as a few ignorant pretenders may imagine. A Footman can swear, but he cannot swear like a Lord. He can swear as often: but, can he swear with equal delicacy, propriety, and judgment? No certainly; unless he be a lad of superior parts, of good memory, a diligent observer, one who has a skillful ear, some knowledge in music, and an exact Taste; which hardly falls to the share of one in a thousand.[1]

In another treatise, Swift writes of the affect of the emotions on Reason.

> Workmen often fling in a small quantity of fresh coals, which seems to disturb the fire, but very much enlivens it. This seems to allude to a gentle stirring of the passions, that the mind may not languish.[2]

---

[1] Jonathan Swift, 'An Introduction to A Complete Collection of Genteel and Ingenious Conversation,' in *The Prose Works of Jonathan Swift* (Oxford: Blackwell, 1957), IV, 112. Jonathan Swift (1667–1745) is the best known prose writer at the end of the English Baroque and shared a grandfather with Dryden. He rarely deals with artistic matters, preferring to satirize manners. Reared in Ireland, he became active in English politics until he returned to Dublin as dean of St. Patrick's.

[2] 'Thoughts on Various Subjects,' in Ibid., I, 242.

With regard to the relationship of Reason and the emotions, William Wycherley offers this conclusion:

> It is very rare that Reason cures our passions, but one passion is cured by another. Reason generally places itself on the strongest side, and therefore there can be no violent passion, but has its Reason to authorize it.[3]

On Education

Matthew Prior wrote a brief treatise on education in which his point of view was entirely functional, as we can see in his first words:

> What we commonly call school learning is so necessary that he who has it not in some degree can hardly be accounted a man. The several parts of it are to the mind what our different limbs are to the body, as we cannot see without eyes, or walk without feet, so neither can we judge rightly of what we have seen, or tell exactly how or were we have walked without the assistance of arithmetic and geometry.[4]

Even as a poet himself, he fails to see any literary value to language, only a purpose of manners in the most functional sense.

> It has been truly said that he who is master of three or four languages may be reckoned three or four men, understanding and being understood in as many countries. But if he utters impertinences, he is only the same fool so many times multiplied, if he had been bred by his friends at home, to what an honest farmer would call reading and writing, he could have been ridiculous only from the Isles of Orkney to the Cliff of Dover. But, being sent to one of our universities first, and thence to a foreign academy, his sphere of activity is enlarged and he has the privilege to be laughed at in Paris or Madrid, at Rome or Constantinople. Languages in the mouth of a fool are like weapons in the hand of a madman, the more he has of them, the more harm he may do to himself as well as to every body within his reach.

Even in the study of the arts, Prior finds only functional value, as for example to improve conversation. In discussing the arts worthy of study, he makes a specific exception of music.

> To these I add Music, but with these cautions that it takes up too much of our time and does not furnish us with the best company. Those who are obliged to get their livelihood by it have addicted so much of their life to the study of it that they have very little knowledge in any other

---

3 *The Complete Works of William Wycherley*, IV, 130. William Wycherley (1641–1715) studied at Oxford, joined the court in exile in France and on his return to London was imprisoned for his debts.

4 'Heads for a Treatise upon Learning,' in *The Literary Works of Matthew Prior*, I, 578ff. Matthew Prior (1664–1721) was a friend of Gay and Swift and liked to call himself 'only a poet by accident.'

science. I wish the art were more encouraged, and that musicians were not forced even to practice so much that they have not time to study their own science, much less any other; but so it is—now a Gentleman musically given cannot blow his flute or strike his violin alone; and as to conversation he is insensibly in a Chorus instead of a Company, and although when he came into the Opera he thought he took his place in a box or in the pit before the Entertainment is half done he finds himself in the middle of the Orchestra.

Jonathan Swift, in some manuscript notes for a projected treatise on the 'Education of Ladies,' finds music one of the essential elements.

The Lady was a considerable heiress used too fondly, lives in town, had that kind of education which is called the best: learning Italian, French, musick and singing, all which she forgot [and] fell into plays, visits, assemblies, etc.[5]

Alexander Pope offers two observations on education which we find interesting.

Learning is like mercury, one of the most powerful and excellent things in the world in skillful hands; in unskillful, the most mischievous.

......

Fine sense and exalted sense are not half so useful as common sense. There are forty men of wit for one man of sense; and he that will carry nothing about him but gold, will be every day at a loss for want of readier change.[6]

ON THE PSYCHOLOGY OF AESTHETICS

Matthew Prior discusses the 'passions' in a treatise he calls simply 'Opinion.' His first contention is that our emotional involvements change according to our age. He paraphrases a Spanish maxim he had heard, as follows:

When we are born our mind comes in at our toes, so goes upward through our legs, to our middle, thence to our heart and breast, lodges at last in our head and from thence flies away. The meaning of which is that childish sorts and youthful wrestlings, and trials of strength, amorous desires, courageous and manly designs, council and policy succeed each other in the course of our lives till the whole terminates in death. The consequence of it is obvious, our passions change with our ages, and our opinion with our passions.[7]

---

5   Swift, 'Education of Ladyes,' in *The Prose Works of Jonathan Swift*, XII, 307.

6   'Thoughts on Various Subjects,' in *The Works of Alexander Pope*, X, 550. Alexander Pope (1688–1744) was born to the family of a prosperous merchant, but as he was also born Catholic he was denied an education at any of the great universities. Thus, the greatest English poet of the eighteenth century was the product of his own education through reading. An illness as a child left him a four foot high hump-back.

7   'Opinion,' in *The Literary Works of Matthew Prior*, I, 578ff.

Turning to the arts, Edward Young speculates on why men are so interested in the passions and offers, among other reasons,

> Because they are such powerful and universal springs, that almost all the pleasures, pains, designs and actions of life are owing to them, and therefore it is in our interest to know them well; or, because every man carrying them in his own breast, he thinks he knows them well already, and is therefore an able judge of such compositions, and thus his pride has a fondness for them.[8]

Jonathan Swift takes a more practical view in a treatise, 'A Letter to a Young Gentleman,' which deals primarily with advice for the young clergymen. He briefly raises the subject of the 'passions,' since historically it was inseparable from oratory, and hence relevant to preaching. He concludes this discussion with a curious decision that perhaps emotions are not a significant factor in preaching to Englishmen.

> But I do not see how this talent of moving the passions, can be of any great use towards directing Christian men in the conduct of their lives, at least in these Northern climates; where, I am confident, the strongest eloquence of that kind will leave few impressions upon any of our spirits, deep enough to last till the next Morning, or rather to the next meal.[9]

Finally, Pope offers two maxims on the emotions.

> Our passions are like convulsion-fits, which, though they make us stronger for the time, leave us the weaker ever after.[10]
>
> ......
>
> The world is a thing we must of necessity either laugh at or be angry at; if we laugh at it, they say we are proud; if we are angry at it, they say we are ill-natured.[11]

On the traditional philosophical subject of Pleasure and Pain, there is one writer who reminds us of the particularly narrow perspective of the Puritans. The Reverend Edward Young, in his 'Letters on Pleasure,' paints a dark view of Pleasure.

> What an extravagant dominion does pleasure exercise over us! It is not only the pestilence that walks in darkness, but an arrow that destroys at noon-day. The moon hides her face at our midnight enormities, and the morning blushes on our unfinished debauch ... Our luxury is beyond example, and beyond bounds; it stops not at the poor; even they that live on alms are infected with it.

---

8   Edward Young, 'A Vindication of Providence,' Preface, in *Edward Young: The Complete Works*, II, 325. Edward Young (1683–1765), best known for his poetry, was born in his father's rectory and later became dean of Salisbury.
9   'A Letter to a Young Gentleman,' in *The Prose Works of Jonathan Swift*, IX, 69.
10 'Thoughts on Various Subjects,' in *The Works of Alexander Pope*, X, 551.
11 Ibid., X, 553.

Pleasure, under the color of being harmless, has an opiate in it; it stupefies and besots. In the soft lap of pleasure conscience falls asleep. Vice, losing its horror, becomes familiar.[12]

Rev. Young continues by contending there are three kinds of happiness:

There is a happiness from the exertion of reason, where reason is given: this is the happiness of a man. There is an inferior happiness from the gratification of sense, where reason is denied: this is the happiness of a brute. And there is a calamitous happiness where reason is suppressed or abused: and this is the happiness of a wretch.

ON THE PHILOSOPHY OF AESTHETICS

Mark Akenside defines imagination as a 'power of human nature which seems to hold a middle place between the organs of bodily sense and the faculties of moral perception.'[13] The powers of imagination with regard to the arts, he finds are,

the inlets of some of the most exquisite pleasures we are acquainted with, men of warm and sensible tempers have sought means to recall the delightful perceptions they afford, independent of the objects which originally produced them. This gave rise to the imitative or designing arts; some of which, like painting and sculpture, directly copy the external appearances which were admired in nature; others, like music and poetry, bring them back to remembrance by signs universally established and understood.

'The passions,' he contends are 'supreme in the noblest works of human genius.' In this regard, he maintains that ridicule is at the root of all comic matter in the arts. Later, he returns to the importance of the passions, and Truth, as elements of music and the other 'elegant arts.'

The pleasures which we receive from the elegant arts, from music, sculpture, painting, and poetry, are much more various and complicated. In them, besides greatness and beauty, or forms proper to the imagination, we find interwoven frequent representations of truth, of virtue and vice, of circumstances proper to move us with laughter, or to excite in us pity, fear, and the other passions.[14]

The question of taste is addressed by Jonathan Swift, in a treatise on the education of ladies, and he equates high taste with 'men and women of fashion.' To develop the highest taste requires considerable time, in Swift's judgment, therefore he sets aside a number of professions which keep their members too busy to acquire taste. Among those he excludes

---

12   Edward Young, 'Letters on Pleasure,' in *Edward Young: The Complete Works*, II, 439ff.
13   'The Pleasures of Imagination,' in *The Poetical Works of Mark Akenside*, 1ff. Mark Akenside (1721–1770) was born of humble origins and eventually became a physician and activist in Scottish affairs.
14   Ibid., 83.

from the possibility of developing the highest taste are all merchants, tradesmen and similar occupations, as well, all politicians, lawyers, physicians, mathematicians and 'gentlemen lovers of music,' who have all 'amusements enough of their own.'[15]

With regard to the artist, Wycherley was concerned that he spend too much time on his craft.

> Too much pains or art, in setting off Wit or Beauty, are often more the lessening of either, than an addition to them.[16]

On Poetry

Alexander Pope has left some interesting comments on poetry. Much ink had been invested during the seventeenth century on a debate over the artistic principles of the 'ancient versus modern' philosophers. Pope objected in particular to those who criticized the imitation of ancient poetry.

> They who say our thoughts are not our own, because they resemble the ancients, may as well say our faces are not our own, because they are like our fathers: and, indeed, it is very unreasonable that people should expect us to be scholars, and yet be angry to find us so.[17]

Pope contended that poetry itself had its origin with the most ancient shepherds who occupied themselves while tending their flocks.[18] Pastoral poetry of his age he defines as follows:

> A pastoral is an imitation of the action of a shepherd, or one considered under that character. The form of this imitation is dramatic, or narrative, or mixed or both; the fable simple; the manners not too polite nor too rustic: the thoughts are plain, yet admit a little quickness and passion, but that short and flowing: the expression humble, yet as pure as the language will afford; neat, but not florid; easy, and yet lively. In short, the fable, manners, thoughts, and expressions are full of the greatest simplicity in nature.

After warning that the poet must give up 'all the reasonable aims of life,' Pope adds,

> There are indeed some advantages accruing from a genius to poetry, and they are all I can think of,—the agreeable power of self-amusement when a man is idle or alone; the privilege of being admitted into the best company; and the freedom of saying as many careless things as other people, without being so severely remarked upon.[19]

---

15 'Of the Education of Ladies,' in *The Prose Works of Jonathan Swift*, IV, 225.
16 *The Complete Works of William Wycherley*, IV, 114.
17 Quoted in *The Works of Alexander Pope*, I, 9.
18 'A Discourse on Pastoral Poetry,' in Ibid., I, 257ff.
19 Quoted in Ibid., I, 6.

On Drama

Edward Young, writing on the distinction between poetry and drama, makes the interesting point that Tragedy must center in the emotions. It is also interesting that he has a lack of appreciation for Dryden.

> Dryden, destitute of Shakespeare's genius, had almost as much learning as Jonson, and, for the buskin, quite as little taste. He was a stranger to the pathos; and, by numbers, expression, sentiment, and every other dramatic cheat, strove to make amends for it; as if a saint could make amends for the lack of conscience … The noble nature of tragedy disclaims an equivalent: like virtue, it demands the heart; and Dryden had none to give. Let epic poets think: the tragedian's point is rather to feel.[20]

Swift, in an essay which precedes his 'A Tale of a Tub,' finds a humorous correspondence between the design of a theater and the characters of the patrons.

> I confess, there is something yet more refined in the contrivance and structure of our modern theaters. For, first, the pit is sunk below the stage with due regard … that whatever weighty matter shall be delivered thence (whether it be lead or gold) may fall plum into the jaws of certain critics which stand ready open to devour them. Then, the boxes are built round, and raised to a level with the scene, in deference to the ladies, because, that large portion of wit laid out in raising pruriences and protuberances, is observed to run much upon a line, and ever in a circle. The whining passions and little starved conceits, are gently wafted up by their own extreme levity, to the middle region, and there fix and are frozen by the frigid understanding of the inhabitants. Bombast and buffoonery, by nature lofty and light, soar highest of all … [to the] twelve-penny gallery, and there is planted a suitable colony, who greedily intercept them in their passage.[21]

Pope also offers a humorous maxim on the theater.

> It is observable that the ladies frequent tragedies more than comedies; the reason may be, that in tragedy their sex is deified and adored, in comedy exposed and ridiculed.[22]

On the Critics and Public

In most writers of this period in England one finds highly personal complaints over the negative influence of the critics. Swift, representing such objections, reflects,

---

20 Edward Young, 'Conjectures on Original Composition,' in *Edward Young: The Complete Works*, II, 574.
21 'A Tale of a Tub,' Introduction, in *The Prose Works of Jonathan Swift*, I, 36ff.
22 'Thoughts on Various Subjects,' in *The Works of Alexander Pope*, X, 560.

> When a true genius appears in the world, you may know him by this infallible sign; that the dunces are all in confederacy against him.[23]

Alexander Pope, on the other hand, in a preface to the publication of his poems, finds both sides over enthusiastic.

> I am afraid this extreme zeal on both sides is ill-placed; poetry and criticism being by no means the universal concern of the world, but only the affair of idle men who write in their closets, and of idle men who read there. Yet sure, upon the whole, a bad author deserves better usage than a bad critic.[24]

He has similar concerns with respect to the undue expectations of the general readers.

> I am inclined to think that both the writers of books, and the readers of them, are generally not a little unreasonable in their expectations. The first seem to fancy that the world must approve whatever they produce, and the latter to imagine that authors are obliged to please them at any rate. Methinks, as on the one hand, no single man is born with a right of controlling the opinions of all the rest; so on the other, the world has no title to demand that the whole care and time of any particular person should be sacrificed to its entertainment.[25]

Pope cautions the writer to have the good sense to ignore praise which is only flattery and warns that one cannot please all readers.

> Were he sure to be commended by the best and most knowing, he is as sure of being envied by the worst and most ignorant, which are the majority.

Finally, he contends that his respect for the public is demonstrated in his willingness to destroy material which he concluded not worthy.

> For what I have published I can only hope to be pardoned; but for what I have burned I deserve to be praised.

---

23 'Thoughts on Various Subjects,' in *The Prose Works of Jonathan Swift*, I, 242.
24 Quoted in *The Works of Alexander Pope*, I, 4.
25 Quoted in Ibid., I, 3ff.

ON THE AESTHETICS OF MUSIC

Jonathan Swift, in a fragment of a treatise on the spirit, makes some interesting comments which touch on the separate brain hemispheres and their relative attention to speech and music.

> It is to be understood, that in the language of the spirit, *cant* and *droning* supply the place of *sense* and *reason*, in the language of men Because, in spiritual harangues, the disposition of the words according to the art of grammar, has not the least use, but the skill and influence wholly lie in the choice and cadence of the syllables. Even as a discreet composer, who in setting a song, changes the words and order so often, that he is forced to make it nonsense, before he can make it music …
>
> Now, the art of *Canting* consists in skillfully adapting the voice, to whatever words the spirit delivers, that each may strike the ears of the audience, with its most significant cadence. The force, or energy of this eloquence, is not to be found, as among ancient orators, in the disposition of words to a sentence … but agreeable to the modern refinements in music, is taken up wholly in dwelling, and dilating upon syllables and letters. Thus it is frequent for a single vowel to draw sighs from a multitude; and for a whole assembly of saints to sob to the music of one solitary liquid.[26]

In a more humorous vein, Sir Charles Sedley, in 'An Essay on Entertainments,' discusses how to plan a supper. Don't invite just old men, he advises, they talk only of the past; and don't invite just young men, for they talk only of their 'debauches.'

> The conversation should not dwell upon state affairs, private business, or matters of interest, which men are apt to dispute with more heat, concern and animosity, than is consistent with the good humor and mirth principally intended at such meetings; in which we should rather talk of pleasant, cheerful and delightful subjects, such as Beauty, Painting, Musick, Poetry, and the Writers of the past and present Age; whereby we may at once improve and refresh our Wits.[27]

In the opening remarks of a proposal to create a music academy in London, Defoe speaks of the purposes of music, its meaning to him and his rather old-fashioned academic association of it with mathematics.

> I have been a lover of [music] from my infancy, and in my younger days was accounted no despicable performer on the viol and lute, then much in vogue. I esteem it the most innocent amusement in life; it generally relaxes, after too great a hurry of spirits, and composes the mind into a sedateness prone to everything that is generous and good; and when the more necessary parts of education are finished, it is a most genteel and commendable accomplishment; it saves a great deal of drinking and debauchery in our sex, and helps the ladies off with many an idle hour, which sometimes might probably be worse employed otherwise.

---

26 'A Discourse Concerning the Mechanical Operation of the Spirit,' in *The Prose Works of Jonathan Swift*, I, 182ff.
27 *The Poetical and Dramatic Works of Sir Charles Sedley*, II, 99.

> Our quality, gentry, and better sort of traders must have diversions; and if those that are commendable be denied, they will take to worse; now what can be more commendable than music, one of the seven liberal sciences, and no mean branch of mathematics?[28]

Matthew Prior, in writing of the purpose of music, reaches back to the ancient Greek belief regarding the influence of music on the character.

> If six bells, as John Keil tells me, can make more than a thousand millions of changes, what must be the result of the jangling of ten or twelve passions sustained by an infinite variety of objects in minds upon which every thing can operate. The dawning of light excites us into cheerfulness, the approach of night depresses us into melancholy; a different weight of air raises or depresses our spirits, a trumpet alarms us to an ardor and action of war, and a flute softens us again into thoughts of love and delight.[29]

EDUCATIONAL MUSIC

In an essay entitled, 'The Way to make London the Most Flourishing City of the Universe,' Defoe wonders why London has no university of its own. This eventually led him to propose the creation of an academy of music, 'to prevent the expensive importation of foreign musicians.' One cannot help but notice that this interesting discussion bears much in common with the principles advanced a few years later for the first European school of music, the national school of music in Paris formed during the French Revolution.

> An academy, rightly understood, is a place for the propagation of science, by training up persons thereto from younger to riper years, under the instruction and inspection of proper artists; how can the Italian opera properly be called an academy, when none are admitted but such as are, at least are thought, or ought to be, adepts in music? If that be an academy, so are the theaters of Drury Lane, and Lincolns-inn Fields; nay, Punch's opera may pass for a lower kind of academy. Would it not be a glorious thing to have an opera of our own, in our own most noble tongue, in which the composer, singers, and orchestra should be of our own growth? Not that we ought to disclaim all obligations to Italy, the mother of music, the nurse of Corelli, Handel, Bononcini, Geminiani; but then we ought not to be so stupidly partial to imagine ourselves too brutal a part of mankind to make any progress in the science. By the same reason that we love it, we may excel in it; love begets application, and application perfection. We have already had a Purcell, and no doubt there are now many latent geniuses, who only lack proper instruction, application, and encouragement, to become great ornaments of the science, and make England emulate even Rome itself.

---

28   Daniel Defoe, 'Augusta Triumphans: or, the Way to make London the Most Flourishing City in the Universe.'
29   'Opinion,' in *The Literary Works of Matthew Prior*, I, 592.

What a number of excellent performers on all instruments have sprung up in England within these few years? That this is owing to the opera I will not deny, and so far the opera is an academy, as it refines the taste and inspires emulation.

But though we are happy in instrumental performers, we frequently send to Italy for singers, and that at no small expense; to remedy which I humbly propose that the governors of Christ's Hospital will show their public spirit, by forming an academy of music on their foundation, after this or the like manner.

That out of their great number of children, thirty boys be selected of good ears and propensity to music.

That these boys be divided into three classes, viz., six for wind instruments, such as the hautboy, bassoon, and German flute.

That sixteen others be selected for string instruments, or at least the most useful, viz., the violin and bass violin.

That the remaining eight be particularly chosen for voice, and organ, or harpsichord. That all in due time be taught composition. The boys thus chosen, three masters should be elected, each most excellent in his way; that is to say, one for the wind instrument, another for the stringed, and a third for the voice and organ, etc.

Handsome salaries should be allowed these masters, to engage their constant attendance every day from eight till twelve in the morning … The multiplicity of holidays should be abridged, and only a few kept; there cannot be too few, considering what a hindrance they are to juvenile studies. It is a vulgar error that has too long prevailed all over England to the great detriment of learning, and many boys have been made blockheads in complaisance to kings and saints dead for many ages past.

The morning employed in music, the boys should go in the afternoon, or so many hours, to the reading and writing school, and in the evening should practice, at least two hours before bed-time, and two before the master comes in the morning. This course held for seven or eight years, will make them fine proficients; but that they should not go too raw or young out of the academy, it is proper, that at the stated age of apprenticeship, they be bound to the hospital, to engage their greater application, and make them thorough masters, before they launch out into the world; for one great hindrance to many performers is, that they begin to teach too soon, and obstruct their genius.

What will not such a design produce in a few years? Will they not be able to perform a concert, choir, or opera, or all three, among themselves, and overpay the charge, as shall hereafter be specified?

For example, we will suppose such a design to be continued for ten years, we shall find an orchestra of forty hands, and a choir or opera of twenty voices, or admitting that of those twenty only five prove capital singers, it will answer the intent.

For the greater variety they may, if they think fit, take in two or more of their girls, where they find a promising genius, but this may be further considered of.

Now, when they are enabled to exhibit an opera, will they not gain considerably when their voices and hands cost them only a college subsistence? and it is but reasonable the profits accruing from operas, concerts, or otherwise, should go to the hospital, to make good all former and future expenses, and enable them to extend the design to a greater length and grandeur; so that instead of £1,500 per annum, the price of one Italian singer, we shall for £300 once in ten years, have sixty English musicians regularly educated, and enabled to live by their science.

There ought, moreover, to be annual probations, and proper prizes or premiums allotted, to excite emulation in the youths, and give life to their studies.

As an afterthought, on the subject of repaying the public for the cost of such an academy, Defoe suggests taking the students out to play spiritual music for the lower classes. Curiously, he values this as a form of entertainment and not for any ethical or cultural role in the music itself.

That such an entertainment would be much preferable to drinking, gaming, or profane discourse, none can deny; and till it is proved to be prejudicial, I shall always imagine it necessary.

FUNCTIONAL MUSIC

There is an interesting document signed by Jonathan Swift, as Dean of St. Patrick's in Dublin, in which he attempts to forbid any musicians who work for the cathedral from appearing in civic performances.

I do hereby require and request the Very Reverend Sub-Dean, not to permit any of the Vicars-Choral, choristers, or organists, to attend or assist at any public musical performances, without my consent, or his consent, with the consent of the Chapter first obtained.

And whereas it has been reported, that I have a license to certain vicars to assist at a club of fiddlers in Fishamble Street, I do hereby declare that I remember no such license to have been ever signed or sealed by me; and that if ever such pretended license should be produced, I do hereby annul and vacate the said license; entreating my said Sub-Dean and Chapter to punish such vicars as shall ever appear there, as songsters, fiddlers, pipers, trumpeters, drummers, drum-majors, ... according to the flagitious aggravations of their respective disobedience, rebellion, perfidy, and ingratitude.[30]

Swift was objecting here to his musicians participating the previous day in the first concert which Handel conducted in Dublin. In spite of this ban by Swift, it was in his cathedral a few weeks later that the premiere performance of the *Messiah* was given.

---

30 'Exhortation to the Chapter of St. Patrick's, Dublin, January 28, 1742, in *The Prose Works of Jonathan Swift*, XIII, 196ff.

ENTERTAINMENT MUSIC

We notice the activities with which ballad singing and the theater are associated in Defoe's 'Journal of the Plague Year,' [1664–1665], where he quotes a civic order relative to keeping the citizens indoors.

> All plays, bear-baitings, games, singing of ballads, buckler-play, or such-like causes of assemblies of people be utterly prohibited.[31]

William Wycherley makes a serious judgment on entertainment and its effect on the general taste.

> The slight and frivolous amusements, in vogue, do not less hurt our taste and discernment of what is really good, than our most criminal passions.[32]

---

31 Daniel Defoe, 'A Journal of the Plague Year,' (Garden City: Doubleday, n.d.), 51. Daniel Defoe (1660–1731), a staunch Presbyterian, was the son of a London butcher and spent some years in that trade himself. Eventually he produced hundreds of literary works, while on the side serving as a spy.

32 *The Complete Works of William Wycherley*, IV, 129.

16 RESTORATION FICTION

IT IS ONLY AT THE END OF THE ENGLISH BAROQUE that the full-length novel first appears. Earlier efforts tended to be prose-romances, by such writers as Sidney, Greene and Nashe. These later novels, reflecting as they do real life in English society, offer interesting insights regarding musical practice. Indeed, Samuel Richardson, in the preface to his novel, *Clarissa Harlowe*, states that an important purpose in his novel is that it is 'addressed to the public as a history of *life* and *manners*.'[1] At the end of this novel, Richardson again reminds the reader that the various letters and conversations he has created 'are presumed to be *characteristic*.'[2]

From the rather large body of Restoration fiction, we will confine ourselves to the subject of music.

ON THE AESTHETICS OF MUSIC

Henry Fielding mentions opera as he pauses in the narrative of his novel, *The Adventures of Joseph Andrews*, to make some comments on the distinction between 'high' and 'low' people in English society.

> High people signify no other than people of fashion, and low people those of no fashion ... Now the world being thus divided into people of fashion and people of no fashion, a fierce contention arose between them; nor would those of one party, to avoid suspicion, be seen publicly to speak to those of the other, though they often held a very good correspondence in private. In this contention it is difficult to say which party succeeded; for whilst the people of fashion seized several places to their own use, such as courts, assemblies, operas, balls, etc.; the people of no fashion, besides one royal place, called his Majesty's Bear-garden, have been in constant possession of all hops, fairs, revels, etc. Two places have been agreed to be divided between them, namely, the church and the playhouse.[3]

---

1   Samuel Richardson, *Clarissa Harlowe* (New York: AMS Press Reprint, 1972), V, xliii. Samuel Richardson (1689-1761) was reared in the company of spinsters and his novels are considered to reflect unusual knowledge of female psychology.

2   Ibid., XII, 360.

3   Henry Fielding, *The Adventures of Joseph Andrews*, II, xiii. Henry Fielding (1707-1754) became a successful novelist after an unsuccessful period of writing farces and comedies.

Later in this same novel, Fielding provides an insight to the definition of a gentleman in English society at this time.

> The character I was ambitious of attaining was that of a fine gentleman; the first requisites to which, I apprehended, were to be supplied by a tailor, a perriwig-maker, and some few more tradesmen, who deal in furnishing out the human body …
>
> The next qualifications, namely, dancing, fencing, riding the great horse, and music, came into my head: but, as they required expense and time, I comforted myself, with regard to dancing, that I had learned a little in my youth, and could walk a minuet genteelly enough … as to the horse, I hoped it would not be thought of; and for music, I imagined I could easily acquire the reputation of it; for I had heard some of my school-fellows pretend to knowledge in operas, without being able to sing or play on the fiddle.[4]

A gentleman is described in Samuel Richardson's novel, *Sir Charles Grandison*, as being,

> generally engaged four months [of Winter] in the diversions of this great town; and was the common patron of all the performers, whether at plays, operas, or concerts.[5]

Responding to the growing popularity of concerts and opera, Alexander Pope, in his 'The Art of Sinking in Poetry,' attributed to the fictitious 'Martinus Scriblerus,' presents a variety of humorous proposals relative to the building of an ideal theater to hold ten thousand spectators. In a reflection about the behavior of the audience, he makes a comment in passing about composers for which we wish he had supplied more information.

> It may be convenient to place the Council of Six in some conspicuous situation in the theater, where, after the manner usually practiced by composers in musick, they may give signs (before settled and agreed upon) of dislike or approbation. In consequence of these signs the whole audience shall be required to clap or hiss, that the town may learn certainly when and how far they ought to be pleased.[6]

---

4   Ibid., III, iii.

5   Samuel Richardson, *Sir Charles Grandison*, XIV, 128.

6   'The Art of Sinking in Poetry,' in *The Works of Alexander Pope*, X, 407. Alexander Pope (1688–1744) was born to the family of a prosperous merchant, but as he was also born Catholic he was denied an education at any of the great universities. Thus, the greatest English poet of the eighteenth century was the product of his own education through reading. An illness as a child left him a four foot high hump-back.

On the Purpose of Music

The most commonly given purpose of music in early literature is to soothe the listener or performer. A typical example is found in Samuel Richardson's novel, *Sir Charles Grandison*, where he relates of a lady, 'One lesson upon her harpsichord sets everything right with her.'[7] In his novel, *Clarissa Harlowe*, we find a young lady attempting to calm her emotions by expressing them through music.

> I have been forced to try to compose my angry passions at my harpsichord; having first shut close my doors and windows that I might not be heard below.[8]

The young lady goes on to compose an 'Ode to Wisdom,' which she sets to music. The original publication includes this music.

In his novel, *The Life of Mr. Jonathan Wild*, Henry Fielding presents even the lowest criminal as being in need of the soothing quality of music.

> He spent his time in contemplation, that is to say, in blaspheming, cursing, and sometimes singing and whistling.[9]

The most important purpose of music is the communication of emotions. We find a particularly vivid illustration in the brief novel, *Adventures of Covent-Garden*, by George Farquhar, as a song is being performed.

> He found her in an undress sitting on her beds-feet in a very melancholy posture; her nightgown carelessly loose discovered her snowy breasts, which agitated by the violence of her sighs, heaved and fell with a most languishing motion; her eyes were fixed on the ground, and without regarding Peregrine, she raised her voice in a mournful and moving sweetness, singing, 'Fool, Fool, that considered not when I was well,' concluding which with a deep sigh, she cast a complaining look on Peregrine, intimating that he alone had occasioned her sorrows.

Farquhar also gives us the reaction of the listener, Peregrine,

> He heard that tuneful start of grief which made his ravished soul strike unison with the complaining harmony.[10]

---

7   Samuel Richardson, *Sir Charles Grandison*, XV, 41.

8   Samuel Richardson, *Clarissa Harlowe*, VI, 64. The music is found on page 67. In Ibid., XII, 189, the will is given for Clarissa Harlowe and she wills another young lady 'my harpsichord, my chamber-organ, and all my music-books.'

9   Henry Fielding, *The Life of Mr. Jonathan Wild*, II, xiii.

10 *The Complete Works of George Farquhar*, II, 212. George Farquhar (1677–1707) studied at Trinity College in Dublin and was an actor and a soldier.

There are also, in this literature, some examples of performers who are not emotionally in the mood to perform. Samuel Richardson, in his novel *Pamela*, describes a young lady not in the emotional mood to play, even for herself.

> And, indeed, these and my writing will be all my amusement: for I have no work given me to do; and the spinnet, if in tune, will not find my mind, I am sure, in tune to play upon it.[11]

And, similarly, we find later,

> When I was at my devotion, Mrs. Jewkes came up, and wanted me sadly to sing her a psalm, as she had often on common days importuned me for a song upon the spinnet: but I declined it, because my spirits were so low I could hardly speak, nor cared to be spoken to.[12]

Henry Fielding, in his novel, *Tom Jones*, pauses to comment on the practice by playwrights to use music to emotionally prepare the audience for the scene to be presented. His comments suggest that there was a much greater use of such music in the plays of this period than is reflected in the printed texts.

> This is an art well known to, and much practiced by our tragic poets; who seldom fail to prepare their audience for the reception of their principal characters.
> Thus the hero is always introduced with a flourish of drums and trumpets, in order to rouse a martial spirit in the audience, and accommodate their ears to bombast and fustian … Again, when lovers are coming forth, soft music often conducts them on the stage, either to soothe the audience with the softness of the tender passion, or to lull and prepare them for that gentle slumber in which they will most probably be composed by the ensuing scene.[13]

The purpose of music emphasized by the ancient Greeks, to affect character, is satirized by Jonathan Swift in his contribution to the fictional 'Memoirs of Scriblerus'.

> The bare mention of music threw Cornelius into a passion. How can you dignify (quoth he) this modern fiddling with the name of Music? Will any of your best Hautboys encounter a wolf now days with no other arms but their instruments, as did that ancient piper Pythocaris? … Does not Aelian tell us how the Libyan mares were excited to [mating] by Music? (which ought in truth to be a caution to modest women against frequenting Operas; and consider, brother, you are brought to this dilemma, either to give up the virtue of the ladies, or the power of your Music). Whence proceeds the degeneracy of our morals? Is it not from the loss of ancient music, by which (says Aristotle) they taught all the virtues? Else might we turn Newgate [prison] into a college of Dorian musicians, who should teach moral virtues to those people.

---

11   Samuel Richardson, *Pamela*, I, 117.
12   Ibid., I, 150.
13   Henry Fielding, *The History of a Foundling*, IV, i.

After citing a number of familiar testimonials found in ancient literature to the power of music, Swift continues his satire by having a character attempt a trial by playing his Lyra from his balcony.

> The uncouth instrument, the strangeness of the man and of the music, drew the ears and eyes of the whole mob that were got about the two female champions, and at last of the combatants themselves. They approached the balcony, in as close attention as Orpheus's first audience of cattle, or that of an Italian Opera, when some favorite Air is just awakened … The mob laughed, sung, jumped, danced, and used many odd gestures, all which he judged to be caused by the various strains and modulations. 'Mark (quoth he) in this the power of the Ionian, in that you see the effect of the Aeolian.' But in a little time they began to grow riotous, and throw stones. Cornelius then withdrew, but with the greatest air of triumph in the world.[14]

It is related to this subject, or perhaps music therapy, that we find in Dafoe's 'Memoirs of a Cavalier,' a Cavalier commenting on his mother's dream at the time of his birth.

> The very evening before I was born, she dreamed she was brought to bed of a son, and that all the while she was in labor a man stood under her window beating on a kettle-drum, which very much discomposed her.[15]

ART MUSIC

Samuel Richardson, in his novel, *Sir Charles Grandison*, provides an unusually detailed picture of domestic music in a gentleman's home in Restoration England.[16] A room, the 'music-parlour,' is devoted to music and it is described as 'adorned with a variety of fine carvings, on subjects that do honor to poetry and music.' The company retreats to this room after a 'sumptuous and well-ordered' dinner. Several of the guests participate in the music-making, which begins with the request of Sir Charles,

> 'May I ask you, my Harriet?' pointing to the harpsichord. I instantly sat down to it. It is a fine instrument. Lord G_____ took up a violin; my uncle, a bass-viol; Mr. Deane, a German flute; and we had a little concert of about half an hour.

Next a gentleman performed a work on an organ, while he sang. The reaction of one listener is remarkable.

---

14 'Memoirs of Scriblerus,' in *Satires and Personal Writings of Jonathan Swift* (London: Oxford University Press, 1956),126ff.

15 Daniel Defoe, 'Memoirs of a Cavalier,' in *The Works of Daniel Defoe* (New York: Henson, 1905), V, 1. Daniel Dafoe (1660–1731), a staunch Presbyterian, was the son of a London butcher and spent some years in that trade himself. Eventually he produced hundreds of literary works, while on the side serving as a spy.

16 Samuel Richardson, *Sir Charles Grandison*, XIX, 45ff.

How did our friends look upon one another as the excellent man proceeded!—I was astonished. It was happy I sat between my aunt and Lucy!—They each took one of my hands. Tears of joy ran down my cheeks. Every one's eyes congratulated me. Every tongue, but mine, encored him. I was speechless. Again he obliged us. I thought at the time, I had a foretaste of the joys of heaven!—How sweet is the incense of praise from a husband; that husband a good man; my surrounding friends enjoying it!

In these novels, such domestic music-making usually entails the performance by a young lady, as we find in Henry Fielding's novel, *Tom Jones*,

It was Mr. Western's custom every afternoon, as soon as he was drunk, to hear his daughter play on the harpsichord; for he was a great lover of music, and perhaps, had he lived in town, might have passed for a connoisseur; for he always excepted against the finest compositions of Mr. Handel. He never relished any music but what was light and airy; and indeed his most favorite tunes were 'Old Sir Simon the King,' 'St. George he was for England,' 'Bobbing Joan,' and some others.

His daughter, though she was a perfect mistress of music, and would never willingly have played any but Handel's was so devoted to her father's pleasure, that she learnt all those tunes to oblige him. However, she would now and then endeavor to lead him into her own taste; and when he required the repetition of his ballads, would answer with a 'nay, dear Sir'; and would often beg him to suffer her to play something else.[17]

In Fielding's novel, *Amelia*, a young lady admits that she 'never had any delight in music' and had experienced little success in her attempts to study the harpsichord. But, when a man challenged her to exceed the ability of her sister, she began to practice with great diligence.

You have often, I believe, heard my sister Betty play on the harpsichord; she was, indeed, reputed the best performer in the whole country.

I was the farthest in the world from regarding this perfection of hers with envy. In reality, perhaps, I despised all perfection of this kind; at least, as I had neither skill nor ambition to excel this way, I looked upon it as a matter of mere indifference.

Hebbers first put this emulation in my head. He took great pains to persuade me, that I had much greater abilities of the musical kind than my sister; and that I might with the greatest ease, if I please, excel her; offering me, at the same time, his assistance, if I would resolve to undertake it.

When he had sufficiently inflamed my ambition, in which, perhaps, he found too little difficulty, the continual praises of my sister, which before I had disregarded, became more and more nauseous in my ears; and the rather, as music being the favorite passion of my father, I became apprehensive (not without frequent hints from Hebbers of that nature) that she might gain too great a preference in his favor.

To my harpsichord then I applied myself night and day, with such industry and attention, that I soon began to perform in a tolerable manner. I do not absolutely say I excelled my sister, for many were of a different opinion; but, indeed, there might be some partiality in all that.

---

17   Henry Fielding, *The History of a Foundling*, IV, v.

Hebbers, at least, declared himself on my side, and nobody could doubt his judgment. He asserted openly, that I played in the better manner of the two; and one day, when I was playing to him alone, he affected to burst into a rapture of admiration, and squeezing me gently by the hand, said, 'There, Madam, I now declare you excel your sister as much in music, as,' added he, in a whispering sigh, 'you do her, and all the world, in every other charm.'[18]

In the novels of Samuel Richardson there are a number of portraits of the young lady being asked to perform in the home. In his novel *Pamela*, for example,

Dinner not being ready, the young ladies proposed a tune upon the spinnet. I said, I believed it was not in tune. They said, they knew it was but a few months ago. If it is, said I, I wish I had known it; though indeed, ladies, added I, since you know my story, I must own, that my mind has not been long in tune, to make use of it. So they would make me play upon it, and sing to it; which I did, a song my dear good lady made me learn, and used to be pleased with, and which she brought with her from Bath: and the ladies were much taken with the song, and were so kind as to approve my performance. And Miss Darnford was pleased to compliment me, that I had all the accomplishments of my sex.[19]

Later in this same novel we find another instance of this kind of private domestic music.

I will only add that Miss L_____, the dean's daughter, is a very modest and agreeable young lady, and a perfect mistress of music; in which the dean takes great delight also, and is a fine judge of it. The gentlemen coming in, to partake of our coffee and conversation, as they said, obtained of Miss to play several tunes on the harpsichord; and would have me play too. But really Miss L_____ so very much surpassed me, that had I regarded my reputation for playing, above the desire I had (as I said, and truly said) to satisfy the good company, I ought not to have pretended to touch a key after such a mistress of it. Miss has no voice, which is a great pity; and at the request of every one, I sung to her accompaniment, twice or thrice; as did Lady Towers, whose voice exceeds her taste.[20]

A final reference to domestic performance in *Pamela* occurs after the company has had their afternoon tea service.

Mr. B_____, after tea, at which I was far from being talkative (for I could not tell what to say, though I tried as much as I could not to appear sullen), desired the countess to play one tune upon the harpsichord. She did; and sung, at his request, an Italian song to it very prettily; too prettily, I thought. I wanted to find some faults, some great faults in her: but, O madam! she has too many outward excellences! Pity she lacks a good heart!

He could ask nothing that she was not ready to oblige him in! Indeed he could not!

---

18   Henry Fielding, *Amelia*, Chapter I, vii.

19   Samuel Richardson, *Pamela*, II, 40. The author provides the lyrics for this song.

20   Ibid., III, 143.

> She desired me to touch the keys. I would have been excused: but could not. And the ladies commended my performance. But neither my heart to play, nor my fingers in playing, deserved their praises. Mr. B_____ said, indeed, You play better sometimes, my dear.—Do I, sir? was all the answer I made.[21]

In Richardson's novel, *Clarissa Harlowe*, we are provided an interesting discussion of the *social* expectations of the young lady singing before private gatherings of society in early eighteenth-century England.[22] A Miss Howe first describes the singing of Miss Harlowe, after commenting on her melodious voice when she read poetry.

> But if her voice was melodious when she *read*, it was all harmony when she *sung*. And the delight she gave by that, and by her skill and great compass, was heightened by the ease and gracefulness of her air and manner, and by the alacrity with which she obliged. Nevertheless, she generally chose rather to hear others sing or play, than either to play or sing herself.

Miss Howe now recalls the advice given her by Miss Harlowe on the etiquette of being asked to sing.

> We form the truest judgment of persons by their behavior on the *most familiar* occasions. I will give an instance or two of the corrections she favored me with on such a one. When *very young*, I was guilty of the fault of those who want to be courted to sing. She cured me of it, at the first of our happy intimacy, by her own *example*; and by the following correctives, occasionally, yet privately enforced:
> 'Well, my dear, shall we take you at your word? Shall we suppose that you sing but indifferently? Is not, however, the *act of obliging* (the company so worthy!) preferable to the *talent of singing*? And shall not young ladies endeavor to make up for their defects in *one part* of education, by their excellence in *another*?'
> Again, 'You must convince us, by attempting to sing, that you *cannot* sing; and then we will rid you, not only of *present* but of *future* importunity.' An indulgence, however, let me add, that but *tolerable* singers do not always wish to meet with.
> Again, 'I know you will favor us by and by; and what do you by your excuses but raise our expectations, and enhance your own difficulties?'
> At another time, 'Has not this accomplishment been a part of your *education*, my Nancy? How, then, for *your own* honor, can we allow of your excuses?'
> And I once pleading a cold, the usual pretense of those who love to be entreated—'Sing, however, my dear, *as well as you can*. The greater the difficulty to you, the higher the compliment to the company. Do you think you are among those who know not how to make allowances? You *should* sing, my love, lest there should be anybody present who may think your excuses owing to affectation.'
> At another time when I had truly observed that a young lady present sung better than I; and that therefore I chose not to sing before that lady—'Fie, said she (drawing me on one side), is

---

21 Ibid., IV, 110ff.
22 Samuel Richardson, *Clarissa Harlowe*, XII, 282ff.

not this pride, my Nancy? Does it not look as if your principal motive to oblige was to obtain applause? A generous mind will not scruple to give advantage to a *person of merit*, though not always to *her own* advantage. And yet she will have a high merit in *doing that*. Supposing this excellent person absent, who, my dear, if your example spread, shall sing after you? You knew every one *else* must be but as a foil to you. Indeed I must have you as much superior to other ladies in these *smaller* points as you are in greater.'

Often, as the above suggests, when we read of the young lady singing in the private home, she seems expected to resist. In Richardson's novel, *Sir Charles Grandison*, however, one young lady is always eager to sing.

They, as we do, admire her voice and her playing. They ask her for a song, for a lesson on her harpsichord. She plays, she sings, at the very first word.[23]

In this same novel there is also a domestic music scene which touches on music education. A Miss Byron describes a scene with her cousin, James.

You know and admire my grandmamma's cheerful compliances with the innocent diversions of youth. She made Lucy give us a lesson on the harpsichord, on purpose, I saw, to draw me in. We both obeyed.

    I was once a little out in an Italian song. In what a sweet manner did he put me in! touching the keys himself, for a minute or two. Every one wished him to proceed; but he gave up to me, in so polite a manner, that we all were satisfied with his excuses.[24]

And finally in this novel, a 'Lady G_____' relates how the relationship of a married couple is reflected in their music.

He has been long careless, and now he is, at times *imperious* as well as careless. Very true! Nay, it was but yesterday that he attempted to hum a tune of contempt, upon my warbling an Italian air. An opera couple, we! Is it not charming to sing *at* (I cannot say *to*) each other, when we have a mind to be spiteful? But he has a miserable voice. He cannot sing so fine a song as I can. He should not attempt it. Besides, I can play to my song; that cannot he. Such a foe to melody, that he hates the very sight of my harpsichord. He flies out of the room, if I but move towards it.[25]

In William Congreve's novel, *Incognita*, we find a satire of the Italian's love of serenades. He refers to the serenade, by the way, a 'ridiculous entertainment.'

Not a window in the streets but echoed the tuning of a lute or thrumming of a Gitarr: for, by the way, the inhabitants of Florence are strangely addicted to to the love of Musick, insomuch that scarce their children can go, before they can scratch some instrument or other. It was no

---

23 Samuel Richardson, *Sir Charles Grandison*, XVII, 104.

24 Ibid., XVIII, 60.

25 Ibid., XVII, 81.

unpleasing spectacle to our cavaliers to behold the diversity of figures and postures of many of these musicians. Here you should have an affected valet, who mimicked the behavior of his masters, leaning carelessly against the window, with his head on one side, in a languishing posture, whining, in a low, mournful voice, some dismal complaint; while, from his sympathizing Theorbo, issued a bass no less doleful to the hearers. In opposition to him was set up perhaps a cobbler, with the wretched skeleton of a Gitarr, battered and waxed together by his own industry, and who with three strings out of tune, and his own tearing hoarse voice, would rack attention from the neighborhood, to the great affliction of many more moderate practitioners, who, no doubt, were full as desirous to be heard.[26]

A rather extraordinary account of instrumental music is given by Swift, in his *Gulliver's Travels*, in his description to 'Brobdingnag,' a land of giants.

I had learned in my youth to play a little upon the spinet; Glumdalclitch kept one in her chamber, and a master attended twice a week to teach her. I call it a spinet, because it somewhat resembled that instrument, and was played upon in the same manner. A fancy came into my head, that I would entertain the king and queen with an English tune upon this instrument. But this appeared extremely difficult, for, the spinet was nearly sixty feet long, each key being almost a foot wide; so that, with my arms extended, I could not reach to above five keys; and to press them down required a good smart stroke with my fist, which would be too great a labor, and to no purpose. The method I contrived was this. I prepared two round sticks about the bigness of common cudgels; they were thicker at one end than the other; and I covered the thicker end with a piece of a mouse skin, that by rapping on them, I might neither damage the tops of the keys, nor interrupt the sound. Before the spinet, a bench was placed about four feet below the keys, and I was put upon the bench. I ran sideling upon it that way and this, as fast as I could, banging the proper keys with my two sticks; and made a shift to play a Jig to the great satisfaction of both their majesties. But, it was the most violent exercises I ever underwent, and yet I could not strike above sixteen keys, nor, consequently, play the bass and treble together, as other artists do; which was a great disadvantage to my performance.[27]

When Gulliver traveled to 'Laputa,' he found a people who could hear the Music of the Spheres.

On the second morning, about eleven o'clock, the king himself in person, attended by his nobility, courtiers, and officers, having prepared all their musical instruments, played on them for three hours without intermission; so that I was quite stunned with the noise; neither could I possible guess the meaning, till my tutor informed me. He said, that the people of their island had their

---

26 William Congreve, *Incognita*, in *The Complete Works of William Congreve*, 115. William Congreve (1670–1729) is considered the best of the Restoration writers of comedy and was particularly admired by Voltaire. He studied at Trinity College, Dublin, and worked in various government offices in London.

27 Jonathan Swift, *Gulliver's Travels*, in *The Prose Works of Jonathan Swift*, XI, 126ff. Jonathan Swift (1667–1745) is the best known prose writer at the end of the English Baroque and shared a grandfather with Dryden. He rarely deals with artistic matters, preferring to satirize manners. Reared in Ireland, he became active in English politics until he returned to Dublin as Dean of St. Patrick's.

ears adapted to hear the music of the spheres, which always played at certain periods; and the court was now prepared to bear their part in whatever instruments they most excelled.[28]

In these volumes we have argued that an indispensable element of art music is the presence of the contemplative listener, such as we find in William Congreve's novel, *Incognita*. Before the lyrics are given for a song sung by Leonora, we read 'Having tuned her lute, with a voice soft as the breath of angels, she sung to it this following Air.' After the song, we read of the listener's reaction.

> The song ended grieved Hippolito that it was so soon ended; and in the ecstasy he was then rapt, I believe he would have been satisfied to have expired with it.[29]

Another example is found in Fielding's novel, *Tom Jones*, when Jones is transfixed by the harpsichord playing of Sophia. Mrs. Honour relates,

> La! says I, Mr. Jones, what's the matter? a penny for your thoughts, says I. Why, hussy, says he, starting up from a dream, what can I be thinking of, when that angel your mistress is playing?[30]

A clear illustration of a non-listener is found in Fielding's novel, *The Adventures of Joseph Andrews*. A song is heard, sung from another room, but the listener, Adams,

> had been ruminating all this time on a passage in Aeschylus, without attending in the least to the voice, though one of the most melodious that ever was heard.[31]

On Opera

As in the other English literature of this period, one often finds rather derogatory remarks about opera. Defoe, in discussing the entertainments of the coliseum of ancient Rome, comments in passing,

> the cutting in pieces forty or fifty slaves, and the seeing twenty or thirty miserable creatures thrown to the lions and tigers, was no less pleasant to them than the going to see an opera, a masquerade, or a puppet-show is to us.[32]

---

28 Ibid., XI, 162ff.
29 William Congreve, *Incognita*, in *The Complete Works of William Congreve*, 15. 148.
30 Henry Fielding, *The History of a Foundling*, IV, xiv.
31 Henry Fielding, *The Adventures of Joseph Andrews*, II, xii.
32 Daniel Defoe, 'Robinson Crusoe,' (Garden City: Doubleday, n.d.), III, 120.

In Henry Fielding's novel, *The Adventures of Joseph Andrews*, a Frenchman commenting on the poor dress at English opera, observes, 'I positively assure you, at the first opera I saw since I came over, I mistook the English ladies for chambermaids!'[33] In Richardson's novel, *Clarissa Harlowe*, a line mentions in passing that a young lady and her mother never missed being present at the opera, which is referred to as a 'diversion.'[34]

In his novel, *Pamela*, Richardson devotes a lengthy passage to opera, which is rich in its insights to the English gentleman's perspective of Italian opera at this time.[35] This passage is contained in a fictional letter written by a Mrs. B____ to Lady Davers. Mrs. B_____ begins by writing that she will relate her opinion of an opera she attended the previous evening. At the beginning she recites arguments that had been used in ancient literature against music, in particular that it is transitory, exists in the air and does not last and therefore is, in itself, insignificant and also that it is effeminate. Next she mentions an argument frequently used against opera, that it inappropriate for great characters to sing, rather than speak.

> But what can I say when I have mentioned what you so well know, the fine scenes, the genteel and splendid company, the charming voices, and delightful music!
>
> If, madam, one were all ear, and lost to every sense but that of harmony, surely the Italian opera would be a transporting thing!—But when one finds good sense, and instruction, and propriety, sacrificed to the charms of sound, what an unedifying, what a mere temporary delight does it afford! For what does one carry home, but the remembrance of having been pleased so many hours by the mere vibration of air, which being but sound, you cannot bring away with you: and must therefore enter the time passed in such a diversion, into the account of those blank hours from which one has not reaped so much as one improving lesson?
>
> I speak this with regard to myself, who know nothing of the Italian language: But yet I may not be very unhappy that I do not, if I may form my opinion of the sentiments by the enervating softness of the sound, and the unmanly attitudes and gestures made use of to express the passions of the men performers, and from the amorous complainings of the women; as visible in the soft, too-soft, action of each.
>
> Then, though I cannot but say that the music is most melodious, yet to see a hero, as an Alexander, or a Julius Caesar, warbling out his achievements in war, his military conquests, as well as his love, in a song, it seems to be to be making a jest of both.

Another point she makes is very curious. She argues for national isolationism and condemns music for the fact that it is *universal*.

> Every nation, Mr. B_____ says, has its peculiar excellence: The French taste is comedy and harlequinery; the Italian, music and opera; the English, masculine and nervous sense, whether in tragedy or comedy — why can't one, methinks, keep to one's own particular national excellence, and let others retain theirs? For Mr. B_____ observes, that when once sound is preferred to

---

33 Henry Fielding, *The Adventures of Joseph Andrews*, II, iv.

34 Samuel Richardson, *Clarissa Harlowe*, XII, 335.

35 Samuel Richardson, *Pamela*, IV, 48ff.

> sense, we shall depart from all our own worthiness, and at best, be but the apes, yea, the dupes, of those whom we may strive to imitate; but never can reach, much less excel.

At the end of her letter, she returns to the idea that music is merely air. One must point out that she reflects here the long, and misdirected university concept of 'speculative' music, in which music is defined only as physical sound. It not only misses the point, but misleads, for the real essence of music is the communication of *feeling*.

> But what have I said, what can I say, of an Italian opera? Only, little to the purpose as it is, I wonder how I have been able to say so much: for who can describe sound? Or what words shall be found to embody air?—And when we return, and are asked our opinion of what we have seen or heard, we are only able to answer, as I hinted above, the scenery is fine; the company splendid and genteel; the music charming for the time; the action not extraordinary; the language unintelligible; and for all these reasons—the instruction none at all.

Mr. B_____ himself now enters the room. Mrs. B_____ shows him her comments on opera, asks his opinion and quotes his observations. His first remarks center on the problem of doing opera in translation, all of which, of course, is only a reflection of the attitude advanced by the early humanists, that the words are more important than the music.

> Operas, said he, are very sad things in England, to what they are in Italy; and the translations given of them abominable: and indeed our language will not do them justice.
> Every nation, as you take notice, has its excellencies; and you say well, that ours should not quit the manly nervous sense, which is the distinction of the English drama. One play of our celebrated Shakespeare will give infinitely more pleasure to a sensible mind, than a dozen English-Italian operas. But, my dear in Italy they are quite another thing: and the sense is not, as here, sacrificed so much to the sound, but that they are both very compatible.

Mrs. B_____ now asks Mr. B_____ to add a sheet himself to this letter and he does so. His portion concentrates on the humanists' emphasis of words above music, claiming in fact that in Italy the story was always more important than the music. We have questioned in another volume this misconception of the original Italian opera, that it was literally sung *speech*, rather than musical in intent. Surely any rational person today would conclude that if this were intended by the late sixteenth-century persons involved in the first opera, there would have been no need or purpose achieved in creating opera. They would have been far more effective in producing another Italian play. Now, Mr. B____'s letter is quoted.

> In Italy, judges of operas are so far from thinking the drama, or poetical part of their operas, nonsense, as the unskilled in Italian rashly conclude in England, that if the Libretto, as they call it, is not approved, the opera, notwithstanding the excellence of the music, will be condemned. For the Italians justly determine, that the very music of an opera cannot be complete and pleasing, if the drama be incongruous, as I may call it, in its composition; because, in order to please, it must have the necessary contrast of the grave and the light; that is, the diverting, equally

blended through the whole. If there be too much of the first, let the music be composed ever so masterly in that style, it will become heavy and tiresome; if the latter prevail, it will surfeit with its levity: Wherefore, it is the poet's business to adapt the words for this agreeable mixture: for the music is but secondary, and subservient to the words; and if there be an artful contrast in the drama, there will be the same in the music, supposing the composer to be a skillful master.

Now, since in England the practice has been to mutilate, curtail and patch up a drama in Italian, in order to introduce favorite airs, selected from different authors, the contrast has always been broken thereby, and the opera damned, without every one's knowing the reason: And since ignorant, mercenary prompters, though Italians, have been employed in the hotch-potch, and in translating our dramas from Italian into English, how could such operas appear any other than incongruous nonsense?

Mr. B_____ concludes by defining 'Recitativos.'

To avoid the natural dissonance and irregularity in common speech, recitativos in music, and dramatical performances were invented; and although the time in pronouncing the words contained in them, is scarce longer than in common conversation; yet the harmony of the chords of the thorough-bass, which then accompanies the voice, delights the ears of discerning judges: Wherefore recitative is a regular way of speaking musically, as I may say, in order to avoid and correct the irregularities of speech often found in nature, and to express the variety of the passions, without offense to the ear.

FUNCTIONAL MUSIC

Alexander Pope, in his fictional 'Memoirs of P. P.,' writes the following satire of the Puritan goal of eliminating complicated and artistic church music in favor of music more like that described in the Old Testament.

Now was the long expected time arrived, when the Psalms of King David should be hymned unto the same tunes to which he played them upon his harp; (so was I informed by my singing-master, a man right cunning in psalmody:) now was our over-abundant quaver and trilling done away, and in lieu thereof was instituted the Sol-fa, in such guise as is sung in his Majesty's Chapel. We had London singing masters sent into every parish, like unto excisemen; and I also was ordained to adjoin myself unto them, though an unworthy disciple, in order to instruct my fellow parishioners in this new manner of worship. What though they accused me of humming through the nostril, as a sackbut; yet would I not forego that harmony, it having been agreed by the worthy parish-clerks of London still to preserve the same. I tutored the young men and maidens to tune their voices as it were a psaltery; and the church on the Sunday was filled with these new hallelujahs.[36]

---

36 'Memoirs of P. P., Clerk of this Parish,' in *The Works of Alexander Pope*, X, 440.

Another curious description of church music is found in Defoe's 'Robinson Crusoe,' when he recalls attending a special religious service celebrating the victory of the English over the French at Ramillies.

> When I came there it was my fate to be placed between the seats where the men of God performed the service of His praise, and sung out the anthems and the *Te Deum*, which celebrated the religious triumph of the day.
>
> As to the men themselves, I liked their office, their vestments, and their appearance: all looked awful and grave enough, suitable in some respects to the solemnity of a religious triumph; and I expected they would be as solemn in their performances as the Levites that blew the trumpets at Solomon's feast, when all the people shouted and praised God.
>
> But I observed these grave people, in the intervals of their worshiping God, when it was not their turn to sing, or read, or pray, bestowed some of the rest of their time in taking snuff, adjusting their perukes, looking about at the fair ladies, whispering, and that not very softly neither, to one another, about this fine lady, that pretty woman, this fine duchess, and that great fortune, and not without some indecencies, as well as words as of gestures ...
>
> Immediately the organ struck up for the *Te Deum*, up starts all my gentlemen, as if inspired from above, and from their talking together, not over-modestly, fall to praising God with the utmost precipitation, singing the heavenly anthems with all the grace and music imaginable.
>
> In the middle of all this music and these exalted things, when I thought my soul elevated with Divine melody, and began to be reconciled to all the rest, I saw a little rustling motion among the people, as if they had been disturbed or frighted. Some said it thundered, some said the church shook; the true business was, the *Te Deum* within was answered without by the thunder of a hundred pieces of cannon and the noise of drums, with the huzzas and shouts of great crowds of people in the streets ...
>
> When the anthem was sung, and the other services succeeded them, I, that had been a little disturbed with the lucid intervals of the choristers and the gentlemen that sat crowded in with them, turned by eyes to other places, in hopes I should find some saints among the crowd, whose souls were taken up with the exalted raptures of the day.
>
> But, alas! it was all one, the ladies were busy singling out the men and the men the ladies.[37]

One of the duties of the military trumpeter was to serve as an ambassador when needed, as it was an internationally recognized custom that a trumpeter could safely cross enemy lines. Thus, in Dafoe's 'Memoirs of a Cavalier,' a fictional account of the wars in Germany, there is a line, 'The duke being pressed by Tilly's trumpeter for an immediate answer.'[38]

Finally, we find in Fielding's novel, *The Adventures of Joseph Andrews*, mention of a dance about to begin and reference to 'the fiddler preparing his fiddle.'[39]

---

37 Daniel Defoe, 'Robinson Crusoe,' III, 151ff.
38 Daniel Defoe, 'Memoirs of a Cavalier,' in *The Works of Daniel Defoe*, V, 55.
39 Henry Fielding, *The Adventures of Joseph Andrews*, III, vii.

17 RESTORATION MANNERS

IN THIS CHAPTER WE CONSIDER not only those literary works specifically addressed to manners, but also observations in individual diaries and correspondence which reflect privately on the manners of Restoration England.

ON THE PHYSIOLOGY OF AESTHETICS

We find in this literature several interesting comments on the physiological conflict between Reason and the emotions, which has its physical origin in the separate, but equal hemispheres of the brain. William Shenstone found most people lacked sensitivity in both brains,

> There seem near as many people that lack passion as lack reason.[1]

He correctly finds a form of expression indigenous to each hemisphere of the brain.

> The French use the word 'naïve' in such a sense as to be explained by no English word; unless we will submit to restrain ourselves in the application of the word 'sentimental.' It means the language of passion or the heart, in opposition to the language of reflection and the head.[2]

The Earl of Chesterfield, in a letter to his son, cautions on addressing the wrong hemisphere in this regard.

> He who addresses himself singly to another man's reason, without endeavoring to engage his heart in his interest also, is no more likely to succeed, than a man who should apply only to a king's nominal minister and neglect his favorite.[3]

---

[1] William Shenstone, *Men and Manners* (Boston: Houghton Mifflin, 1927), 66. William Shenstone (1714–1763) attended Oxford, but did not finish. He was one of the minor figures in English literature of the early eighteenth century, but was possessed of a perceptive intelligence.

[2] William Shenstone, Ibid., 76.

[3] Earl of Chesterfield, letter to his son, September 5, 1748. In this same letter he suggests that women should be approached toward their passions, for 'Women are only children of a larger growth.' The Earl of Chesterfield, Philip Stanhope (1694–1773), was an orator and statesman of some distinction. His enduring fame rests in his correspondence, especially that addressed to his son.

Shenstone found he could read these two sides of the personality in the face.

> The soul appears to me to discover herself most in the mouth and eyes; with this difference, that the mouth seems the more expressive of the temper, and the eye of the understanding.[4]

Chesterfield makes a similar observation,

> I have often guessed, by people's faces, what they were saying, though I could not hear one word they said.[5]

Finally, Thomas Otway, speaking of the disappointed lover in his fictional 'Love-Letters,' refers to one of the oldest expressions of the dominance of the left hemisphere—the place of honor at the *right* hand.

> It is like seating me at your *Side-table*, when I have the best Pretense to your *Right Hand* at the Feast.[6]

Shenstone finds education and environment to be the determining influences on character.

> People's characters are to be collected from their education and place in life. Birth itself does but little. Kings, in general are born with the same propensities as other men; but yet it is probably, from the license and flattery that attends their education, that they will be more haughty, more luxurious, and more subjected to their passions, than any men beside. I question not but there are many attorneys born with open and honest hearts, but I know not one, that has had the least practice, who is not selfish, trickish, and disingenuous.[7]

With regard to the purely academic side of education, however, Shenstone was quite critical.

> The vacant skull of a pedant generally furnishes out a throne and a temple for vanity.[8]

ON THE PSYCHOLOGY OF AESTHETICS

The most frequently discussed subject regarding the emotions during the English Baroque was that emotion known as melancholy. Shenstone offers an interesting observation on this subject, regarding some elegies he has written.

---

4 William Shenstone, *Men and Manners*, 95.
5 Earl of Chesterfield, letter to his son, March 10, 1746.
6 Thomas Otway, 'Love-Letters,' II. Otway (1652–1685) was highly esteemed by his contemporaries as a playwright.
7 William Shenstone, *Men and Manners*, 36ff.
8 Ibid., 72.

They are written rather with the spirit of *Melancholy* than that of Poetry; if Melancholy may be said to be fraught with any spirit at all as I believe it *may*; for I believe a pretty *Spirit* may be distilled from *Tears*.[9]

In his discussion of the emotions in general, Shenstone reflects, and rejects, the Puritan attitude toward the subduing of the emotions.

While we labor to subdue our passions, we should take care not to extinguish them. Subduing our passions, is disengaging ourselves from the world; to which, however, whilst we reside in it, we must always bear relation; and we may detach ourselves to such a degree as to pass an useless and insipid life, which we were not meant to do. Our existence here is at least one part of a system.[10]

In addition, on the subject of the control of the emotions, he observes,

Mankind suffers more by the conflict of contrary passions, than that of passion and reason. Yet, perhaps, the truest way to quench one passion is to kindle up another.[11]

Putting aside the question of the struggle between Reason and the emotions, and the control of the latter, Shenstone nevertheless found a strong relationship between the emotions and the most sensitive and talented persons.

People of real genius have strong passions; people of strong passions have great partialities.[12]

......

People of the finest and most lively genius have the greatest sensibility, of consequence the most lively passion.[13]

Shenstone returns here to his observation on the importance of the face for revealing the feelings of the person.

How important is the eye to the appearance of an human face! the chief index of temper, understanding, health, & love![14]

Shenstone's most curious conclusion with regard to the emotions was that they are not universal, a conclusion which is considered incorrect in the modern perspective. He arrived at his belief primarily through observation that not all men laugh at the same things.

---

9   Letter to Lady Luxborough, June 1, 1748, in *Letters of William Shenstone* (Minneapolis: University of Minnesota Press, 1939), 106.
10 Shenstone, *Men and Manners*, 53.
11 Ibid., 79.
12 Ibid., 79.
13 Ibid., 60.
14 Ibid., 69.

> Trifles will burst one man's sides, which will not disturb the features of another; and a laugh one cannot join, is almost as irksome as a lamentation …
>
> When therefore my mind is not in tune with another's, what strikes his, will not vibrate on mine.[15]

This contention notwithstanding, Shenstone offers judgment of an instance of universality:

> There is no word in the Latin language, that signifies a female friend. 'Amica,' means a mistress; and perhaps there is no friendship between the sexes wholly disunited from a degree of love.[16]

Two other writers focused on the role of the emotions in communication. Margaret Cavendish points to their power in oratory.

> There is a strange hidden mystery in eloquence, it has a magical power over mankind, for it charms the senses, and enchants the mind, and is of such a commanding power, as it forces the will to command the actions of the body and soul … makes the souls of men the tongue's slaves … binds the judgment, blindfolds the understanding, and deludes the Reason; also it softens the obdurate hearts, and causes dry eyes to weep … it refines the drossy humors, polishes the rough passions … On the other side, it can enrage the thoughts of madness, and cause the soul to despair.[17]

And Chesterfield writes his son,

> Wherever you would persuade or prevail, address yourself to the passions; it is by them that mankind is to be taken.[18]

Shenstone also wrote extensively on the nature of Pleasure and Pain. He introduces his discussion with a conclusion which one finds expressed more and more during the late Baroque in England,

> It seems obvious that God, who created the world, intends the happiness and perfection of the system he created.[19]

---

15 Ibid., 21.

16 Ibid., 41.

17 Margaret Cavendish, *Sociable Letters* [1664] (Menston: The Scolar Press, 1969), Letter XXVIII. Margaret Cavendish (1624–1673), Duchess of Newcastle, wrote plays, essays, poetry and philosophy. Contemporary reaction to the present work was mixed. Charles Lamb thought it a jewel of a book; Pepys thought she was insane and conceited.

18 Earl of Chesterfield, letter to his son, February 9, 1746.

19 Shenstone, *Men and Manners*, 63.

But, Shenstone sees even this idea as a relative one, and warns,

> Were a man of pleasure to arrive at the full extent of his several wishes, he must immediately feel himself miserable. It is one species of despair to have no room to hope for any addition to one's happiness.[20]

All early philosophers had discussed the fact that there seemed to be an inevitable link between Pleasure and Pain. Shenstone offers several observations touching on the origins of this association.

> Extreme volatile and sprightly tempers seem inconsistent with any great enjoyment. There is too much time wasted in the mere transition from one object to another. No room for those deep impressions, which are made alone by the duration of an idea; and are quite requisite to any strong sensation, either of pleasure or of pain.[21]
>
> ......
>
> Our passions are permitted to sip a little pleasure; but are extinguished by indulgence, like a lamp overwhelmed with oil.[22]
>
> ......
>
> Surprise quickens enjoyment and expectation banishes surprise. This is the simple reason why few pleasures that have engrossed our attention previously, ever answer our ideas of them. Add to this, that imagination is a great magnifier, and causes the hopes we conceive to grow too large for their object—thus expectation does not only destroy the advantage of surprise, and so flattens pleasure, but makes us hope for an imaginary addition, which gives the pain of disappointment.[23]

Finally, Shenstone, in several places, appears to weary of the conflict between Pleasure and Pain.

> Pleasure and Pain continue to interfere! & I could be well enough content if they would come separate: for I would have my Pleasures untainted; & then when Pain was to arrive, would prepare myself for it by giving myself up to no other Expectation.[24]

Similarly, to a lady friend,

> There is Room for much Debate upon the Pains or Pleasures of melancholy, *afterwards*.[25]

---

20   Ibid., 53.
21   Ibid., 80.
22   Ibid., 27.
23   Ibid., 84ff.
24   Letter to Lady Luxborough, August 24, 1748, in *Letters of William Shenstone*, 118ff.
25   Ibid., 168.

ON THE PHILOSOPHY OF AESTHETICS

We begin with a few observations which touch on the artist's mental state in general. First, Alexander Pope, in a letter of 19 December 1734 to Jonathan Swift, addresses the topic of the artist's imagination.

> Imagination has no limits, and that is a sphere in which you may move on to eternity; but where one is confined to truth, or, to speak more like a human creature, to the appearances of truth, we soon find the shortness of our tether.[26]

William Shenstone briefly discusses inspiration, suggesting that if it does not at once come, the artist should be patient.

> Ask to borrow sixpence of the Muses, and they tell you at present they are out of cash, but hereafter they will furnish you with five thousand pounds.[27]

> ......

> Second thoughts oftentimes are the very worst of all thoughts. First and third very often coincide. Indeed second thoughts are too frequently formed by the love of novelty, of showing penetration, of distinguishing ourselves from the mob, and have consequently less of simplicity, and more of affectation.[28]

Shenstone also proposes that it is appropriate that an artist seek to be popular.

> I cannot see why people are ashamed to acknowledge their passion for popularity. The love of popularity is the love of being beloved ...
> I am afraid humility to genius is as an extinguisher to a candle.[29]

On Taste

Shenstone was the only writer of this period in England to write extensively on the subject of Taste. In his *Men and Manners*,[30] as an illustration of the difficulties of making final definitions of taste, he imagines a discussion between a citizen, a courtier and a professor. The

---

[26] Quoted in *The Works of Alexander Pope*, VII, 330. Alexander Pope (1688–1744) was born to the family of a prosperous merchant, but as he was also born Catholic he was denied an education at any of the great universities. Thus, the greatest English poet of the eighteenth century was the product of his own education through reading. An illness as a child left him a four foot high hump-back.

[27] Shenstone, *Men and Manners*, 52.

[28] Ibid., 70.

[29] Ibid., 51.

[30] Ibid., 2ff.

citizen maintains that the basic principles of art are universal, only the technicalities are left to the 'experts.'

> I am told continually of taste, refinement, and politeness; but I think the vulgar and illiterate generally approve the same productions with the connoisseurs. One rarely finds a landscape, a building, or a play, that has charms for the critic exclusive of the mechanic. But, on the other hand, one readily remarks students who labor to be dull, depraving their native relish by the very means they use to refine it. The vulgar may not indeed be capable of giving the reasons why a composition pleases them. That mechanical distinction they leave to the connoisseur.

The courtier says no this is not true, pointing out that poetry, for example, depends on such things as metaphor and allusion, the subtleties of which are beyond the citizen. The professor, of course, points out that while the citizen can understand art on some level, with instruction can appreciate it even more.

> All ranks and stations have their different spheres of judging. That a clown of native taste enough to relish Handel's Messiah, might unquestionably be so instructed as to relish it yet more.

The professor adds that the artist must never actually aim his work at the level of the common citizen.

> Let a writer then in his first performances neglect the idea of profit, and the vulgar's applause entirely. Let him address them to the judicious few, and then profit and the mob will follow. His first appearance on the stage of letters will engross the politer compliments; and his latter will partake of the irrational huzza.

Shenstone offers several other interesting generalizations on the subject of taste.

> We say, he is a man of sense who acknowledges the same truths that we do; that he is a man of taste who allows the same beauties. We consider him as a person of better sense and finer taste, who discerns more truths and more beauties in conjunction with ourselves. But we allow neither appellation to the man who differs from us.[31]
>
> ......
>
> Virtue should be considered as a part of taste (and perhaps it is so more in this age, than in any preceding one) and should as much avoid deceit or sinister meanings in discourse, as they would do puns, bad language or false grammar.[32]
>
> ......
>
> Wherever there is a lack of taste, we generally observe a love of money, and cunning: and wherever taste prevails, a want of prudence, and an utter disregard to money ...

---

31 Ibid., 59.
32 Ibid., 60.

> The person of a good taste requires real beauty in the object of his passion; and the person of bad taste requires something which he substitutes in the place of beauty ...
> Persons of fine taste are men of the strongest sensual appetites.[33]

We find particularly interesting a little summary of Shenstone's conclusions resulting from his contemplation on the subject of taste as found in the general population. He proposes that out of one hundred persons one might expect to find taste in the following proportions:[34]

Pedants	15
Persons of common sense	40
Wits	15
Fools	15
Persons of a wild uncultivated taste	10
Persons of original taste, improved by art	5

After all this, Shenstone concludes,

> I am sick of the word *taste*; but I think the *thing* itself the only proper *ambition*, and the *specific pleasure* of all who have any share in the faculty of imagination.[35]

On Beauty

Shenstone is also one of few Restoration English writers who attempts to offer original thinking on the subject of Beauty. First, he suggests the understanding of Beauty is a conditioned one, and not universal.

> Our taste of beauty is, perhaps, compounded of all the ideas that have entered the imagination from our birth. This seems to occasion the different opinions that prevail concerning it. For instance, a foreign eye esteems those features and dresses handsome, which we think deformed.[36]

He appears to have been most interested in this question with regard to individual peculiarities.

> I know not, if one reason of the different opinions concerning beauty be not owing to self-love. People are apt to form some criterion from their own persons, or possession. A tall person approves the look of a folio or octavo: a square thick-set man is more delighted with a quarto.

---

33   Ibid., 92.
34   Ibid., 90.
35   Letter to Richard Graves, February 16, 1751, in *Letters of William Shenstone*, 215.
36   Shenstone, *Men and Manners*, 97.

Taste produces different effects upon different complexions. It consists, as I have often observed, in the appetite and the discernment; then most properly so called, when they are united in equal proportions.

Where the discernment is predominant, a person is pleased with fewer objects, and requires perfection in what he sees. Where the appetite prevails, he is so much attached to beauty, that he feels a gratification in every degree in which it is manifested. I frankly own myself to be of this latter class. I love painting and statuary so well, as to be not undelighted with moderate performances.[37]

With regard to the traditional question whether Art should imitate Nature, Shenstone seemed concerned only with the art of formal gardens.

Art should never be allowed to set a foot in the province of nature, otherwise than clandestinely and by night.[38]

Regarding some of the individual arts, it would appear that for Shenstone the purpose of poetry was for the expression of the emotions.

I think [there is] nothing truly poetic, at least no poetry worth composing, that does not strongly affect one's passions.[39]

Something like this may have been in the mind of Jonathan Swift when, in a letter to Alexander Pope of 9 February 1736, he observed,

What I gain on the side of philosophy, I lose on the side of poetry; the flowers are gone, when the fruits begin to ripen.[40]

Shenstone expressed dismay at the fall in popularity of the drama at the end of the English Baroque.

Their profession is, like that of a painter, one of the imitative arts, whose means are pleasure, and whose end is virtue. They both alike, for a subsistence, submit themselves to public opinion: and the dishonor that has attended [drama], seems not easily accountable.[41]

Shenstone, like all writers at this time, complained about the critics.

A poet that fails in writing, becomes often a morose critic. The weak and insipid white wine makes at length excellent vinegar.[42]

---

37 Ibid., 90ff.
38 Ibid., 26.
39 Ibid., 43.
40 Quoted in *The Works of Alexander Pope*, VII, 342.
41 Shenstone, *Men and Manners*, 73.
42 Ibid., 46.

His advice to young writers was simply to ignore that which cannot be changed.

> It is impossible for a man of sense to guard against the mortification that may be given him by fools, or heteroclite characters, because he cannot foresee them.[43]

ON THE AESTHETICS OF MUSIC

In our volume on the aesthetics of musical performance in sixteenth-century England we drew the reader's attention to, and explained the cause for, the revolution in manners through which musical performance became no longer appropriate to the gentleman and became the province of the 'slave.' In Margaret Cavendish's *Sociable Letters*, dating from the mid-seventeenth century, we find music still listed as an important study for the gentleman.

> For proper and fit sciences for noble persons to be learned and known, as fortification, navigation, astronomy, cosmography, architecture, Musick, and history; and for Wit, as scenes, songs, poems, and the like.[44]

Curiously, however, for women, she finds music not appreciated for its own sake, but merely for its use in dance.

> Neither does our sex take much pleasure in harmonious Musick, only in violins to tread a measure.[45]

We might also add that Cavendish also complains that everyone is obsessed with following the 'Mode.' But the just and wise will disapprove of an activity if the only purpose is to thus follow the fashion. Among a large number of examples, she includes music.

> Neither do they affect Mode-Songs or Sounds, because they are in the fashion to be sung or played, but because they are well-set tunes, or well-composed Musick, or witty songs, and well sung by good voices, or well played on instruments.[46]

Nearly a century later, in the letters of Chesterfield, we find a dramatic revolution in manners has occurred. Now, as he writes to his son in Venice, he argues that the gentleman is not to actually perform music himself.

---

43   Ibid., 69.
44   Margaret Cavendish, *Sociable Letters*, Letter XVIII.
45   Ibid., Letter XXI.
46   Ibid., Letter LXIII.

> There are liberal and illiberal pleasures as well as liberal and illiberal arts ... As you are now in the musical country, where singing, fiddling and piping are not only the common topics of conversation, but almost the principal objects of attention; I cannot help cautioning against giving into those (I will call them illiberal) pleasures (though music is commonly reckoned one of the liberal arts), to the degree that most of your countrymen do when they travel in Italy. If you love music, hear it; go to operas, concerts, and pay fiddlers to play to you; but I insist upon your neither piping nor fiddling yourself. It puts a gentleman in a very frivolous, contemptible light; brings him into a great deal of bad company; and takes up a great deal of time, which might be better employed. Few things would mortify me more, than to see you bearing a part in a concert, with a fiddle under your chin, or [an instrument] in your mouth.[47]

In a letter of 22 June 1749, Chesterfield adds that inasmuch as the Italian now value music above painting and sculpture, he regards it as 'a proof of the decline of that country.'

On the Perception of Music

William Shenstone devotes attention to several aspects regarding the perception of music. One comment reminds us of Aristotle's curiosity over why we prefer music which is familiar to us, rather than new music. Shenstone's observation is somewhat different and we wish he had supplied more information with respect to his conclusion.

> There seems a pretty exact analogy between the objects and the senses. Some tunes, some tastes, some visible objects, please at first, and that only; others only by degrees, and then long.[48]

Another interesting observation deals with the universality of musical materials, apart from any personal preferences.

> It is evident enough to me, that persons often occur, who may be said to have an ear to music, and an eye for proportions in visible objects, who nevertheless can hardly be said to have a relish or taste for either. I mean, that a person may distinguish notes and tones to a nicety, and yet not give a discerning choice to what is preferable in music. The same, in objects of sight.
> On the other hand, they cannot have a proper feeling of beauty or harmony, without a power of discrimination for those notes and proportions on which harmony and beauty so fully depend.[49]

In one very interesting discussion, Shenstone touches on the fact we know today that non-musicians listen to music with the left ear (right hemisphere of the brain), while musicians who listen to conceptual detail in music listen with the right ear (left hemisphere, where

---

47 Earl of Chesterfield, letter to his son, April 19, 1749.
48 Shenstone, *Men and Manners*, 91.
49 Ibid., 95.

the notation and grammar of music dwell). This has led to some suggesting that one result of modern music school training is to ruin their students as listeners! Shenstone discusses this as follows,

> I have heard it claimed by adepts in music, that the pleasure it imparts to a natural ear, which owes little or nothing to cultivation, is by no means to be compared to what they feel themselves from the most perfect composition—The state of the question may be best explained by a recourse to objects that are analogous—Is a country fellow less struck with beauty than a philosopher or an anatomist, who knows how that beauty is produced? Surely no. On the other hand, an attention to the cause may somewhat interfere with the attention to the effect—They may, indeed, feel a pleasure of another sort—The faculty of reason may obtain some kind of balance, for what the more sensible faculty of the imagination loses.[50]

All philologists today believe that music preceded speech and that speech began as a development of simple emotional utterances, varying only in pitch and melodic pattern, in early man. We carry much of this in our genes yet today, as the right hemisphere of the brain adds emotional color to give meaning to our speech and in the melodic contour found in each sentence we speak. William Shenstone provides an interesting discussion of the importance of a writer having a musical ear. His comments, which are also very relevant to the issue of the separate hemispheres of the brain, make us wonder if, instead of saying speech developed after music, we should perhaps say speech is a form of music.

> It may in some measure account for the difference of taste in the reading of books, to consider the difference of our ears for music. One is not pleased without a perfect melody of style, be the sense what it will. Another, of no ear for music, gives to sense its full weight without any deduction on account of harshness.
>
> Harmony of period and melody of style have greater weight than is generally imagined in the judgment we pass upon writing and writers. As proof of this, let us reflect, what texts of scripture, what lines in poetry, or what periods we most remember and quote, either in verse or prose, and we shall find them to be only musical ones.[51]

In this regard he adds later,

> I have sometimes thought Virgil so remarkably musical, that were his lines read to a musician, wholly ignorant of the language, by a person of capacity to give each word its proper accent, he would not fail to distinguish in it all the graces of harmony.[52]

---

50   Ibid., 96.
51   Ibid., 49.
52   Ibid., 73.

Finally, Shenstone contributes this curious thought,

> One reason why the sound is sometimes an echo to the sense, is that the pleasantest objects have often the most harmonious names annexed to them.[53]

On the Purposes of Music

Shenstone emphasizes the purpose of pleasure in music, as he advises a friend,

> I would recommend some musical instrument that is most agreeable to you. I have often looked upon music as my dernier resort, if I should ever discard the world, and turn eremite entirely. Consider what other amusement can make an equal impression in old age.[54]

Chesterfield points to the purpose of the communication of emotions, but conditions this on the premise of accuracy in performance.

> The best compositions of Corelli, if ill executed and played out of tune, instead of touching, as they do when well performed, would only excite the indignation of the hearers, when murdered by an unskilled performer.[55]

A curious, and very rare, view of the problem of the emotions versus Reason is offered by Samuel Butler. In his characterization of a musician, he suggests that the emotions of music are a kind of treason, are not real, and evaporate.

> Is his own Siren, that turns himself into a beast with musick of his own making. His perpetual study to raise *passion* has utterly debased his *reason*; and as music is wont to set false values upon things, the constant use of it has rendered him a stranger to all true ones … This puts him into the condition of a traitor, whom men hate but love the treason; so they delight in music, but have no kindness for a musician. The scale of music is like the ladder that Jacob saw in a dream, reaching to heaven with angels ascending and descending; for there is no art in the world that can raise the man higher, but it is but in a dream, and when the music is done, the mind wakes and comes to itself again. And therefore a musician, that makes it his constant employment, is like one that does nothing but make love, that is half mad, fantastic and ridiculous to those that are unconcerned. Cupid strings his bow with the strings of an instrument, and wounds hearts through the ear.[56]

---

53 Ibid.
54 Letter to Richard Graves, September 23, 1741, in *Letters of William Shenstone*, 27.
55 Earl of Chesterfield, letter to his son, July 9, 1750.
56 Samuel Butler, *Characters*, 'A Musitian.'

ART MUSIC

Margaret Cavendish offers a curious reflection after hearing Art Songs performed in a private home.

> The other day, at Mrs. D. U's house, I heard harmonious and melodious musick, both instruments and voices, but in my opinion, there is no musick so sweet, and powerful as oratory, for sweet words are better than a sweet sound, and when they are joined together, it ravishes the soul; wherefore lyric poetry has advantage of all other poetry, because both sound and sense are harmonious, wherefore the ancients had both their epic poems, and comedies, and tragedies, in verse, and tunes set to them, and sung, both in their theaters of war and peace, as in the fields and stages.[57]

She also offers (in a very long sentence!) her perception of the distinctions between art song and the popular ballads. It is interesting that she associates improvisation with art song rather than with popular song.

> The last week your sister Katherine and your sister Frances were to visit me, and so well pleased I was with their neighborly and friendly visit, as their good company put me into a frolic humor, and for a pastime I sung to them some pieces of old Ballads; whereupon they desired me to sing one of the songs my Lord made, your brother set [to music], and you were pleased to sing; I told them first, I could not sing any of those songs, but if I could, I prayed them to pardon me, for neither my voice, nor my skill, was proper or fit for them, and neither having skill nor voice, if I should offer to sing any of them, I should so much disadvantage my Lord's poetical wit, and your brother's musical composition, as the fancy would be obscured in the one, and the art in the other, nay, instead of Musick, I should make discord, and instead of wit, sing nonsense, knowing not how to humor the words, nor relish the notes, whereas your harmonious voice give their works both grace and pleasure, and invites and draws the soul from all other parts of the body, with all the loving and amorous passions, to sit in the hollow cavern of the ear, as in a vaulted room, wherein it listens with delight, and is ravished with admiration; wherefore their works and your voice are only fit for the notice of souls, and not to be sung to dull, unlistening ears, whereas my voice and those songs, would be as disagreeing to your voice and old Ballads, for the vulgar and plainer a voice is, the better it is for an old Ballad; for a sweet voice, with quavers, and Trilloes, and the like, would be as improper for an old Ballad, as… diamond buckles on clouted or cobled shoes, or a feather on a monk's hood; neither should old Ballads be sung so much in a tune as in a tone, which tone is between speaking and singing, for the sound is more than plain speaking, and less than clear singing, and the rumming or humming of a wheel should be the Musick to that tone, for the hummings is the noise the wheel makes in the turning round, which is not like the Musick of the Spheres; and Ballads are only proper to be sung by spinsters, and that only in cold Winter nights, when a company of good housewives are drawing a thread of flax; but as they draw threads of flax, so time draws their threads of life, as their web makes them smocks, so times web makes them death's shirts, to which, as to death,

---

57 Cavendish, *Sociable Letters*, Letter CXVII.

afterwards those good housewives are married, and lie in the bed of earth, their house being the grave, and their dwelling in the region of oblivion; and this is the fate of poor spinners, and ballad-singers, whereas such a singer as you, such a composer as your brother, such a poet as my Lord, are clothed with renown, marry fame, and live in eternity …[58]

The Diary of John Evelyn records a number of artists he heard perform in London, among them a locally famous freak, 'the hairy woman,' whom he met in 1657 and whom he reports 'played well on the harpsichord.'[59] Two diary entries for 1674 are quite interesting.

> [November 19] I heard that stupendous violin, Signor Nicholao (with other rare musicians), whom I never heard mortal man exceed on that instrument. He had a stroke so sweet, and made it speak like the voice of a man, and, when he pleased, like a concert of several instruments. He did wonders upon a note, and was an excellent composer. Here was also that rare lutanist, Dr. Wallgrave; but nothing approached the violin in Nicholao's hand. He played such ravishing things as astonished us all.
>
> [December 2] At Mr. Slingsby's, Master of the Mint, my worthy friend, a great lover of music. Heard Signor Francisco on the harpsichord, esteemed one of the most excellent masters in Europe on that instrument; then, came Nicholao with his violin, and struck all mute, but Mrs. Knight, who sung incomparably, and doubtless has the greatest reach of any English woman; she had been lately roaming in Italy, and was much improved in that quality.

Evelyn also reflects on the singing of his own daughter, on the day of her death,

> She had an excellent voice, to which she played a thorough-bass on the harpsichord, in both which she arrived to that perfection, that of the scholars of those two famous masters, Signors Pietro and Bartholomeo, she was esteemed the best; for the sweetness of her voice and management of it added such an agreeableness to her countenance, without any constraint or concern, that when she sung, it was as charming to the eye as to the ear.[60]

Of particular interest, among the entries in Evelyn's diary, are descriptions of concerts performed in private homes. He mentions, for example, having dinner at a gentleman's home, in 1672, which was followed by 'a concert of music.'[61] A similar entry for 23 September 1680, describes hearing in his own home a recital by Signor Pietro,

> a famous musician, who had been long in Sweden in Queen Christina's court; he sung admirably to a guitar, and had a perfect good tenor and bass.[62]

---

58 Cavendish, *Sociable Letters*, Letter CCII.
59 *The Diary of John Evelyn*, for September 15, 1657. John Evelyn (1620–1706) began his famous diary in 1640.
60 *The Diary of John Evelyn*, for March 10, 1685.
61 *The Diary of John Evelyn*, for December 23, 1672.
62 In this entry, Evelyn briefly alludes to a murder committed by Queen Christina, something we have not read elsewhere.

An entry for 25 July 1684, describes a dinner at the home of Lord Falkland, Treasurer of the Navy, after which,

> we had rare music, there being amongst others, Signor Pietro Reggio, and Signor John Baptist, both famous, one for his voice, the other for playing on the harpsichord, few if any in Europe exceeding him. There was also a Frenchman who sung an admirable bass.

In 1685 Evelyn had dinner at Lord Sunderland's,

> being invited to hear that celebrated voice of Mr. Pordage, newly come from Rome; his singing was after the Venetian recitative [manner], as masterly as could be, and with an excellent voice both treble and bass; Dr. Walgrave accompanied it with this theorbo lute, on which he performed beyond imagination, and is doubtless one of the greatest masters in Europe on that charming instrument.[63]

Evelyn heard the singer Pordage the following day at a dinner at the home of Lord Arundel, who had just been released from the Tower. On this occasion he also heard 'that excellent and stupendous artist,' Signor John Baptist, on the harpsichord.

In the correspondence of this period one finds additional references to personal music making. In several letters, the poet Thomas Gray speaks of his activity as a musician. On 3 July 1735, for example, he writes,

> I have composed a hymn about it mighty moving and [play] it perpetually, for I have changed my harp into a harpsichord and am as melodious, as the day is long.[64]

Alexander Pope, in a letter of 15 August 1731 to Lord Oxford, relates,

> The said Faustina, alias Mrs. Hasse, has sent to Lady Cobham divers notes of music and new airs, which those that can play and sing shall communicate to the less deserving who are mere auditors and auditoresses.[65]

On Opera

The earliest Restoration references to opera, especially Italian opera, in the correspondence and diaries of the period seem to reflect a sense of perplexity at the sudden popularity of the medium. In John Evelyn's report of attending the opera in 1659, for example, we read,

---

63 *The Diary of John Evelyn*, for January 27, 1685.

64 Letter to Walpole, July 3, 1735, in *Correspondence of Thomas Gray* (Oxford, Clarendon Press, 1971). Thomas Gray (1716–1771) spent the greater part of his adult life in academic seclusion in Cambridge.

65 Quoted in *The Works of Alexander Pope*, VIII, 288. Faustina Bordoni, a famous opera singer, married the composer Hasse in 1730.

I went to visit my brother in London; and, the next day, to see a new opera, after the Italian way, in recitative music and scenes, much inferior to the Italian composure and magnificence; but it was prodigious that in a time of such public consternation such a vanity should be kept up, or permitted. I, being engaged with company, could not decently resist the going to see it, though my heart smote me for it.[66]

William Wycherley, in a letter to Alexander Pope, thanks him for his help in polishing his verses, which he calls 'putting my Rhymes in Tune,' and adds the observation,

since good sounds set off often ill sense, as the Italian songs, whose good [melodies], with the worst words, or meaning, make the best musick.[67]

In a letter of 22 March 1709, to Colonel Hunter, Jonathan Swift writes relative to the founding of the paper known as the *Tatler*.

The vogue of operas holds up wonderfully, though we have had them a year; but I design to set up a party among the wits to run them down by next winter, if true English caprice does not interpose to save us the labor.[68]

Toward the end of this period one finds specific complaints regarding the influence of Italian opera. Jonathan Swift, in a letter of 10 January 1721, to Alexander Pope, blames politics and the introduction of opera and masquerades for the decline in the 'taste for wit and sense' in the world.[69] John Gay in a letter to Jonathan Swift, of 15 February 1728, on the success of his *Beggar's Opera*, remarks on the decline of English opera.

Lord Cobham says that I should have printed it in Italian over against the English, that the ladies might have understood what they read. The outlandish (as the call it) [normal] opera has been so thin of late that some have called that the Beggar's Opera, and if the run continues I fear I shall have remonstrances drawn up against me by the royal academy of music.[70]

Some writers are much more outspoken in their hostility towards opera in general. William Shenstone, in answer to a lady who wrote of her friends 'refined taste of operas & oratorios,'

---

66 *The Diary of John Evelyn*, for May 5, 1659. The opera was probably one by William Davenant.

67 Letter of April 11, 1710, in *The Complete Works of William Wycherley*, 239. William Wycherley (1641–1715) studied at Oxford, joined the court in exile in France and on his return to London was imprisoned for his debts.

68 Quoted in *The Prose Works of Jonathan Swift*, II, xxv. Jonathan Swift (1667–1745) is the best known prose writer at the end of the English Baroque and shared a grandfather with Dryden. He rarely deals with artistic matters, preferring to satirize manners. Reared in Ireland, he became active in English politics until he returned to Dublin as Dean of St. Patrick's.

69 Quoted in Ibid., IX, 27.

70 Quoted in *The Works of Alexander Pope*, VII, 115.

> May Heaven preserve his hearing, that he may not only hear what the *Multitude*, but what your *Ladyship* says & then I believe he need not *regret* so much as *despise* what the *Opera-Folk* sing.[71]

Chesterfield advises his son to see everything, 'from opera and plays down to the Savoyards' raree-shows.' 'Everything,' he says, 'is worth seeing once.'[72] In another letter, he tells his son he does not need to write down his expenses of things unworthy of the time, such as 'chair-hire, operas, etc.'[73]

At the beginning of the eighteenth century, the popularity of opera has clearly begun to fade. John Vanbrugh, a playwright but better known as an architect, built an opera house in Haymarket. In a letter of 1708, he speaks of losing much money on his opera house but believes opera will yet thrive in London, especially when a period of peace comes. He indicates that the taste for opera is not yet universal in all classes.

> That though the pit and boxes did very near as well as usual, the gallery people (who hitherto had only thronged out of curiosity, not taste) were weary of the Entertainment.[74]

In a letter of 1719 he mentions that the receipts at the opera only cover approximately one-half the costs.[75]

Thomas Gray, in June 1736, reports that the audience for the opera had fallen considerably due to competition from the newly opened Vauxhall Gardens, called initially Spring-garden.[76] In his early letters, Gray occasionally mentions attending the opera, but gives few details. Ironically, the most information is found in an outline for a proposed, but never written, book, the fourth chapter of which would have been devoted to opera. Following are the subjects he apparently intended to discuss.

> Goes to the Opera; grand Orchestra of Humstrums, Bagpipes, Salt-boxes, Tabours, & Pipes. Anatomy of a French Ear, showing the formation of it to be entirely different from that of an English one, & that sounds have a directly contrary effect upon one & the other. Farinelli at Paris said to have a fine manner, but no voice. Grand Ballet, in which there is no seeing the dance for Petticoats. Old Women with flowers & jewels stuck in the curls of their gray hair; red-heeled shoes & roll-ups innumerable, hoops & Paniers immeasurable, paint unspeakable. Tables, wherein is calculated with the utmost exactness, the several degrees of red, now in use …[77]

---

71 Letter to Lady Luxborough, May 5, 1748, in *Letters of William Shenstone*, 104.

72 Earl of Chesterfield, letter to his son, April 15, 1745.

73 Earl of Chesterfield, letter to his son, January 10, 1749.

74 Letter to tearl of Manchester, July 27, 1708, quoted in *The Complete Works of John Vanbrugh*, IV, 24. Sir John Vanbrugh (1664–1726) was not only a playwright but a celebrated architect, whose work included Blenheim Palace and the Haymarket Opera—which he also managed and which failed.

75 Letter to Jacob Tonson, December 31, 1719, quoted in Ibid., IV, 124.

76 Letter to Walpole, June 11, 1736, in *Correspondence of Thomas Gray*.

77 Quoted in Ibid., I, 139.

We also read of the extreme measures taken in an attempt to make opera once again popular. In London, in May 1742, Gray reports attending Pergolesi's opera, *Olimpiade*, which turned out to be a pasticcio, with some of Pergolesi's music being replaced by that of other composers.

Finally, we have among the correspondence and diaries of this period some interesting accounts of the performance of art music in foreign lands. The *Diary* of John Evelyn reports his hearing an opera in Venice in 1645.

> This night, having with my Lord Bruce taken our places before, we went to the Opera, where comedies and other plays are represented in recitative music, by the most excellent musicians, vocal and instrumental, with variety of scenes painted and contrived with no less art of perspective, and machines for flying in the air, and other wonderful notions; taken together, it is one of the most magnificent and expensive diversions the wit of man can invent. The history was, Hercules in Lydia; the scenes changed thirteen times. The famous voices, Anna Rencia, a Roman, and reputed the best treble of women; but there was an eunuch who, in my opinion, surpassed her; also a Genoese that sung an incomparable bass. This held us by the eyes and ears till two in the morning.[78]

Thomas Gray reports hearing a 'fine concert of music' in Venice, which included,

> among the rest two eunuchs' voices, that were a perfect feast to ears that had heard nothing but French operas for a year.[79]

In Rome he reports hearing 'a fine concert,' in which,

> La Diamantina, a famous virtuosa, played on the violin divinely, and sung angelically; Giovannino and Pasqualini (great names in musical story) also performed miraculously.[80]

The playwright, James Thomson, in a letter written in Paris in 1732, offers his impressions of Italian music and of French opera.

> The language and music in Italy are enchanting. Being but an infant in the language I ought not to pretend to judge of it, yet cannot I help thinking it not only very harmonious, and expressive, but even not at all incapable of manly graces. As for their music, it is a sort of charming malady that quite dissolves them in softness, and greatly heightens in them that universal indolence men naturally fall into when they can receive little or no advantage from their industry. They talk of the Tarantula in Italy, for whose bite music is a cure. That Tarantula must, I fancy, mean the bad government, for whose oppression music if not a cure is at least some relief, by gently lulling them into a sweet forgetfulness of misery. Now that I mention music, one cannot, I

---

78 *The Diary of John Evelyn*, in a long entry for May 21, 1645.

79 Letter to Richard West, November 21, 1739, in *Correspondence of Thomas Gray*. In December 1739, while in Vienna, Gray observes that everyone is hoping for a safe delivery by Maria Theresa of a child, for then there will be balls and operas, which otherwise would not be given until Carnival.

80 Letter of May 21, 1740, in Ibid.

believe, have a stronger instance of the power of custom with regard to taste than one meets with here [in Paris] in the French opera. While they themselves die away in rapture at what they call their beaux morceaux, others whose taste is formed by the Italian music would rather hear the Screech-owl than their screaming heroines. Their excessive vanity has led them into this difference of taste of their own, although to have it they must forsake Nature.[81]

FUNCTIONAL MUSIC

The *Diary* of John Evelyn, in a famous entry of 1662, records the first use of strings in English church music, the previous tradition being the use of wind instruments.

> One of his Majesty's chaplains preached; after which, instead of the ancient, grave, and solemn wind music accompanying the organ, was introduced a concert of twenty-four violins between every pause, after the French fantastical light way, better suiting a tavern, or a playhouse, than a church. This was the first time of change, and now we no more heard the cornett which gave life to the organ; that instrument quite left of in which the English were so skillful.[82]

A curious instance of church related music is mentioned by Thomas Gray, who reports being awakened one morning by 'the Noise of a Bagpipe at the door,' which turned out to be a group wearing strange masks and celebrating Plough-Monday, the first Monday after Epiphany.[83]

The *Diary* of John Evelyn, when he records his dining with the king, also describes the music to accompany the meal, as part of an entertainment given for the Venetian ambassadors.

> The dinner was most magnificent and plentiful, at four tables, with music, kettle-drums, and trumpets, which sounded upon a whistle at every [toast].[84]

In 1687, visiting Christ's Hospital, Evelyn heard quite different music during dinner.

> They sung a psalm before they sat down to supper in the great Hall, to an organ which played all the time, with such cheerful harmony, that it seemed to me a vision of angels.[85]

---

81 Letter to Lady Hertford, October 10, 1732, in *James Thomson, Letters and Documents* (Lawrence: University of Kansas Press, 1958), 82. James Thomson (1700–1748) was highly respected by both Voltaire and Lessing, but has never been esteemed by his own countrymen.

82 *The Diary of John Evelyn*, for December 21, 1662.

83 Letter to Walpole, January 14, 1735, in *Correspondence of Thomas Gray*.

84 *The Diary of John Evelyn*, for December 18, 1685.

85 *The Diary of John Evelyn*, for March 10, 267.

A rather unusual reference to functional music is found in the *Diary* of John Evelyn, where he mentions the use of 'drums to direct the watermen to make the shore,' on the Thames River during periods of fog.[86]

A humorous reference to hunting music is found in Samuel Butler's Characters.

> [The hunter] believes no music in the world is comparable to a chorus of [dogs] voices, and that when they are well matched they will hunt their parts as true at first scent, as the best singers of catches, that ever opened in a tavern, that they understand the scale as well as the best scholar, that ever learned to compose by the mathematics; and that when he winds his horn to them, it is the very same thing with a cornet in a Choir; that they will run down the hare with a fugue, and a double D-fol-re-Dog hunt a thorough-bass ...[87]

Finally, we might mention that among Chesterfield's letters to his son are references to dance, which he again finds demeaning and of value only for posture development.

> Dancing is in itself a very trifling, silly thing; but it is one of those established follies to which people of sense are sometimes obliged to conform.[88]
>
> ......
>
> You must dance well, in order to sit, stand, and walk well; and you must do all these well, in order to please.[89]

ENTERTAINMENT MUSIC

We find in this literature two rather interesting descriptions of the lowly entertainment musician. In the first, Butler portrays the fiddler in the typical low English humor of this period.

> A fidler commits a rape upon the ear ... He ... sets men together by the ears, enchants them with his magical rod, his fidlestic, out of themselves, and makes them skip as if they were bit with a tarantula ... He tickles their ears ... while he picks their pockets ... The roughness of his bow makes his strings speak, which otherwise would be silent and unuseful, and when he grows humorous himself, (which is not seldom) and will not play, he is used as niggedly till he does. He is an earwig, that creeps into a mans ear and torments him, until he is got out again. The scrapings of his fiddle and horse-tail (like horse-radish) with white wine and sugar, or brandy make excellent sauce for a whore. He scratches and rubs the itch of lovers upon his fiddle, to the wonderful delight of those that have catched it, till it turns to a worse disease: for his fiddlestic is but a rubber made of a horses tail to carry sinners with, and he scrubs and firks them till they

---

86 *The Diary of John Evelyn*, for November 15, 1699.
87 Samuel Butler, *Characters*, 'A Hunter.' Samuel Butler (1612–1680) was one of the lesser poets of the Dryden period.
88 Earl of Chesterfield, letter to his son, November 19, 1745.
89 Earl of Chesterfield, letter to his son, January 3, 1751.

kick and sling, as if the Devil were in them. The noise of cats-guts sets them a caterwauling, as those, that are bitten with a mad dog, are said to foam at the mouth and bark … He is [welcome in] all taverns, as being as useful to relish a glass of wine as anchovies of caviar, serves like stum to help of bad wine, and conduces wonderfully to over reckoning. He is as great a provocative, as a Romance, to love, and at weddings is a prime ingredient … He does not live but rub out, spends time while he keeps it, is very expert in his way, and has his trade at his fingers ends.[90]

William Shenstone, in a discussion of Vanity, has left a curious portrait of a humble bagpipe player.

I remember a bagpiper, whose physiognomy was so remarkable and familiar to a club he attended, that it was agreed to have his picture placed over their chimney-piece. There was this remarkable in the fellow, that he chose always to go bare-foot, though he was daily offered a pair of shoes. However, when the painter had been so exact as to omit this little piece of dress, the fellow offered all he had in the world, the whole produce of three nights harmony, to have those feet covered in the effigy, which he so much scorned to cover in the original. Perhaps he thought it a disgrace to his instrument to be eternalized in the hands of so much apparent poverty.[91]

Finally, we should acknowledge the large body of broadside ballads which are extant from the seventeenth century. These were published in the form of poetry, without the music, and the universal understanding today is that they were all sung to known popular tunes. Scholars do not want to think of these ballads as *real* poetry, for they were written by professional rhyme-makers to serve as a kind of journalism. And they seem to us more a kind of public information form of journalism, than music. Who, we wonder, would stand around and *sing* a ballad with the title, 'Strange and Dreadful News from Holland or The Sad Account of a Fearful Storm' (November 1686), or 'The Manifestation of Joy upon the Publication of His Majesty's Declaration Allowing Liberty of Conscience' (4 April 1687).

Whatever we call them, they are certainly mirrors of ordinary life and it is for this reason that we regret that the lyrics of these ballads so rarely offer insights on musical practice. Generally one only finds an occasional familiar metaphor, such as the trumpet of the Day of Judgment, or a reference to the trumpets and drums of war. Nevertheless, we will quote a few lines to indicate the general level. In 'A Warning for all Good Fellow to Take Heed of Punks Enticements,' we find musicians enticing persons to the tavern.

Bagpipers and Fidlers,
With Phife playing Drummers:
With Musicke will merry be,
To welcome all commers:
That unto such places lewd,
Often repair:

---

90 Butler, *Characters*, 'A Fidler.'
91 Shenstone, *Men and Manners*, 13.

Yet hath them and sing with me,
Come no more there.⁹²

While Butler associated these ballad singers with 'Cat-purse' and 'Orange-Women,'⁹³ it must be acknowledged that some writers highly valued this form of folk music. William Shenstone writes,

> There is nothing give me greater pleasure than the simplicity of style & sentiment that is observable in old English ballads.⁹⁴

......

> The ways of ballad-singers, and the cries of halfpenny pamphlets, appeared so extremely humorous, from my lodgings in Fleet-street, that it gave me pain to observe them without a companion to partake.⁹⁵

The poet Thomas Gray was sent some ballads by a friend and his response is particularly interesting.

> I have got the old Ballad … it is in my eyes a miracle not only of ancient simplicity, but of ancient art. The great rules of Aristotle & Horace are observed in it by a writer, who perhaps had never heard their names.⁹⁶

---

92 *The Pepys Ballads* (Cambridge: Harvard University Press, 1929), I, 263.
93 Butler, *Characters*, 'A Jugler.' He refers to pick-pockets and venders at plays.
94 Letter to Thomas Percy, January 4, 1758, in *Letters of William Shenstone*, 345.
95 Shenstone, *Men and Manners*, 35.
96 Letter to Edward Bedingfield, October 31, 1757, in *Correspondence of Thomas Gray*.

18 PEPYS

SAMUEL PEPYS (1633–1703) was a notable exception to the trend which began in sixteenth-century England, in which gentlemen disassociated themselves with the performance of music. His famous diary, covering the years 1660–1669, is a testimonial to his own love of music, his close attention to the musical scene and his private performance and attempts at composition. The diary is particularly valuable because it was never intended to be published, even being written in a private code, and therefore is much more candid than the publication of a gentleman could have been at this time.

He served as a kind of minister of the Navy under James II, during which time he introduced important economies into the Navy—and managed to improve his own economy immensely. Later he served in the House of Commons and was elected President of the Royal Society.

As mentioned above, this man's diary reflects not only a love, but almost an obsession for music. In 1663 Pepys comments that he is fearful 'of being too much taken with musique, for fear of returning to my old dotage thereon and so neglect my business as I used to.'[1] In his diary entry for 9 March 1666, he again fears he will neglect business for his love of music, concluding,

> However, music and women I cannot but give way to, whatever my business is.

Indeed, on 30 July 1666, he reports his wife is angry because he has been spending too much time with a young singer, but he apologizes again that 'music is the thing of the world that I love most.' The following 12 February 1667, Pepys, eager to compare an Italian choir with one under Cooke, again reveals how much music means to him.

> I do consider that [music] is all the pleasure I live for in the world, and the greatest I can ever expect in the best of my life.

For 16 November 1667, Pepys describes going to Whitehall to hear a performance under Pelham Humfrey,[2] but apparently Humfrey and his musicians did not show up. Instead Pepys goes to another room where,

---

1 Pepys Diary, February 17, 1663.
2 Humfrey (1647–1674) from childhood was associated with court music in England.

> I did hear the best and the smallest organ that ever I saw in my life, and such a one as, by the grace of God, I will have the next year if I continue in this condition, whatever it cost me. I never was so pleased in my life.

Pepys' most philosophical comments on music come in a letter of 5 November 1700, after the period covered by the famous diary. A correspondent had sent Pepys a proposal for a new method of teaching mathematics, written by Dr. David Gregory, the Savilian Professor of Astronomy at Oxford. It is evident that Pepys was still thinking of music as a branch of mathematics, for he wrote to the professor pointing out that his proposal had omitted music. In the course of his offering his views on the nature and purpose of music, we also see a reflection of his long experienced frustration that none of his composer friends would offer him a simple, effective set of rules for composition. It is quite nice to read that nothing has changed: the composers point to the official rules and then ignore them in the interest of art.

> I would now recommend to your giving the same regard to ... Musick, a science peculiarly productive of a pleasure that no state of life, public or private, secular or sacred; no difference of age or season; no temper of mind or condition of health exempt from present anguish; nor, lastly, distinction of quality, renders either improper, untimely, or unentertaining. Witness the universal gusto we see it followed with, wherever to be found, by all whose leisure and purse can bear it. While the same might to much better effect, both for variety and delight to themselves and friends, be ever to be had within their own walls, and of their own composures too as well as others, were the doctrine of it brought within the simplicity, perspicuity, and certainty common to all other parts of mathematical knowledge, and of which I take this to be equally capable with any of them, in lieu of that fruitless jargon of obsolete terms and other unnecessary perplexities and obscurities wherewith it has been ever hitherto delivered, and from which, as I know of nothing eminent, or even tolerable, left us by the Ancients, so neither have I met with one modern Master (foreign or domestic) owning the least obligation to it for any their now nobler compositions; but on the contrary charging all (and justly too) upon the happiness of their own genius only, joined with the drudgery of a long and unassisted practice. A condition not to be looked for from the more generous and elevated spirits of those we are here concerned for; and therefore most deserving, as well as most needing, the abilities and application of our present most learned Professor to remedy.[3]

Far from being absorbed with the conceptual nature of music, Pepys' great love of music was expressed more directly through his own performance. He owned his own instruments and performed on flute, lute, theorbo, violin and viol and on one occasion even considered taking lessons in whistling.[4] He had an insatiable curiosity about everything regarding music and his diary is filled with references to various instruments, individual musicians and an extensive number of actual compositions. In many of his observations on music, one can see his views were shaped by his own experience. For example, Pepys enjoyed private, amateur

---

3   *Private Correspondence of Samuel Pepys*, ed. J. Tanner (London: Bell and Sons, 1926), II, 109.
4   Pepys Diary, May 17, 1661.

music making, but apparently felt uncomfortable if a professional musician was present on such an occasion. He describes a performance of music in a home on 29 July 1664, adding,

> But I begin to be weary of having a master with us, for it spoils methinks the ingenuity of our practice.

As a private listener Pepys preferred simple compositions which communicated directly without the complexities enjoyed by the 'experts.' An entry of 22 July 1664, describes hearing,

> the best piece of musique, counted of all hands in the world, made by Seignor Carissimi, the famous master in Rome. Fine it was indeed, and too fine for me to judge of.

For the same reason he found little enjoyment in contrapuntal music. On 15 September 1667, he observes in his diary,

> I am more and more confirmed that singing with many voices is not singing, but a sort of instrumental music, the sense of the words being lost by not being heard, and especially as they set them with fugues of words, one after another; whereas singing properly, I think, should be but with one or two voices at most, and that counterpoint.

It is this view which is reflected in an entry of December 1666. Here Pepys refers to a visit to the court organist, John Hingston,[5] to get him to either write, or rewrite, one of Pepys' songs.

> I took him to the Dogg tavern and got him to set me a bass to my 'It is decreed,' which I think will go well; but he commends the song, not knowing the words, but says the ayre [melody] is good, and believes the words are plainly expressed. He is of my mind, against having [many] eighth-notes necessarily in composition. This did all please me mightily.[6]

On 10 December 1667, Pepys again mentions that he runs into Hingston and attempts to question him about composition, but is disappointed with the response.

> I do find that he can no more give an intelligible answer to a man that is not a great master in his art than another man—and this confirms me that it is only want of an ingenious man that is master in Musique, to bring music to a certainty and ease in composition.

Pepys becomes obsessed with discovering a simpler process of composition. In his diary he writes on 20 March 1668,

> At my chamber all the evening, writing down some things and trying some conclusions upon my viol, in order to the inventing a better theory of Musique than has yet been abroad; and I think verily I shall do it.

---

5 John Hingston (1612–1683) was also in charge of tuning and repairing the court keyboards.

6 Pepys Diary, December 19, 1666.

Three days later he writes he is thinking of acquiring a harpsichord,

> to confirm and help me in my music notions, which my head is nowadays full of, and I do believe will come to something that is very good.

On 29 March 1668, he reports that he had the opportunity to discuss composition with John Banister.[7]

> I had very good discourse with him about music, so confirming some of my new notions about music that it puts me upon a resolution to go on and make a Scheme and Theory of music, not yet ever made in the world.

Other than the fact that the surviving compositions of Pepys are in the nature of elementary songs, we are inclined, on the basis of the following, to think his new method of composition must also have been a simple one. He reports attempting to have a discussion with Hooke, who evidently brushed him off,

> so the reason of Concords and Discords in music—which they say is from the aequality of the vibrations; but I am not satisfied in it, but will at my leisure think of it more and see how far that does go to explain it.[8]

Apparently nothing ever came of this new system of composition and the last we read of it is on 11 January 1669.

> So home; and there at home all the evening, and made Tom to write down some little conceits and notions of mine in Musique, which does mightily encourage me to spend some more thoughts about it; for I fancy, upon good reason, that I am in the right way of unfolding the mystery of this matter better than ever yet.

On Music of the Court

The early diary references to the music of the court are often centered on the presence of French influence, beginning with this curious notice of 1660.

> The king did put a great affront upon Singleton's Musique, he bidding them to stop and bade the French Musique play—which my Lord says does much out-do ours.[9]

---

7   John Banister (1625–1679), born the son of a member of the London Waits, became proficient on numerous instruments. It was he who was displaced by the Frenchman, Grabu, as head of court music. He went on to organize concerts in the private sector.

8   Pepys Diary, April 2, 1668.

9   Pepys Diary, November 20, 1660.

In 1665 a French musician, Louis Grabu,[10] was appointed 'composer to his Majesty's musique.' The resentment among the English did not die quickly, for we read in an entry of 1667,

> Here they talk also how the king's violin, Bannister, is mad that the king has a Frenchman [Louis Grabu] come to be chief of some part of the king's music—at which the duke of York made great mirth.[11]

Pepys himself heard a large scale work for chorus and orchestra conducted by Grabu, in this same year, and was not impressed.

> To White-hall and there ... to hear the music which the king is presented this night by Monsieur Grebus, the master of his music—both instrumental (I think 24 violins) and vocal, an English song upon peace; but God forgive me, I was never so little pleased with a consort of music in my life—the manner of setting of words and repeating them out of order, and that with a number of voices, makes me sick, the whole design of vocal music being lost by it ... I did not see many pleased with it; only, the instrumental music he had brought by practice to play very just.[12]

The following year, however, he attends a rehearsal and reports,

> to the fiddling concert and heard a practice mighty good of Grebus.[13]

To give some credit to Grabu, he worked during a difficult time for court music. Pepys reports a conversation with the court organist, Hingston, when the latter informed him that the king's musicians were on the verge of starvation, being five years behind in their wages.

> Nay, Evens, the famous man upon the harp, having not his equal in the world, did the other day die for mere want, and was fain to be buried at the alms of the parish—and carried to his grave in the dark at night.[14]

The tone of Pepys' comments on court music change with the return of Humprey from France. A musician Pepys evidently did not like, he finds him upon his return much affected with French manners, 'an absolute Monsieur, full of form and confidence and vanity.' Pepys also objects that Humphrys is criticizing everyone's skill but his own.

> The truth is, everyone says he is very able; but to hear how he laughs at all the king's music here ... that they cannot keep time nor tune nor understand anything, and that Grebus the Frenchman, the king's Master of the Musique, how he understands nothing nor can play on any

---

10 Grabu (d. 1694) was a French composer, however of Spanish origin. Dismissed from the court in 1674, he remained active in London.
11 Pepys Diary, February 20, 1667.
12 Pepys Diary, October 1, 1667.
13 Pepys Diary, April 15, 1668.
14 Pepys Diary, December 19, 1666.

instrument and so cannot compose, and that he will give him a lift out of his place, and that he and the king are mighty great, and that he has already spoke to the king about Grebus, would make a man piss.[15]

In a similar mood, Pepys finds no particular enjoyment in the music of Humfrey.

I to White-hall and there got into the Theater-room and there heard both the vocal and instrumental music, where the little fellow [Pelham Humfrey] stood keeping time; but for my part, I see no great matter, but quite the contrary, in both sorts of music. The composition I believe is very good, but no more of delightfulness to the ear or understanding but what is very ordinary.[16]

On Opera

The diary entry for 2 August 1664, reveals the plans of Thomas Killigrew, manager of the King's Company and of the Theater Royal, for bringing opera to London. He tells Pepys,

We shall have the best scenes and machines, the best Musique, and everything as magnificent as is in Christendome; and to that end he has sent for voices and painters and other persons from Italy.

In a lengthy account for 12 February 1667, Pepys discusses the problems in establishing opera in London. He first describes meeting with Tom Killigrew, manager of the King's Drury Lane theater, and Robert Murray, a courtier and amateur musician, and 'the Italian Seignor Baptista—who has composed a play in Italian for the opera which T. Killigrew does intend to have up.' The Italian composer, having only a copy of the libretto, sat at a harpsichord and played and sang a complete act of the opera.

My great wonder is how this man does to keep in memory so perfectly the music of that whole Act, both for the voice and for the instrument too—I confess I do admire it.

Pepys was much impressed by this display of talent, but makes the argument he would often make, that no one can make any sense out of vocal music in a language they do not speak. But he says, 'I was mightily pleased with the music.'
Killigrew now details the improvements in the new theater, built after the fire. The stage, he says, 'is now a thousand times better and more glorious than ever before.' They have better candles now, for light, and everything is more civil, no longer like a 'bear-garden.' Instead of two or three violins, now they have nine or ten of the best. He speaks of making a number of trips to Italy to find quality music, but the London public would have none of it.

---

15 Pepys Diary, November 15, 1667.
16 Pepys Diary, November 16, 1667.

He has ever endeavored, in the last king's time and in this, to introduce good Musique; but he never could do it, there never having been any music here better than ballads. 'No,' he says 'Hermit poore and Chevy Chase was all the music we had—and yet no ordinary Fidlers get so much money as ours do here, which speaks of our rudeness still.'

On Music of the Theater

The diary entries by Pepys on the music he heard used in the theater are among the few eyewitness account of the music which is otherwise known to us only in the form of lyrics in published plays. Pepys, always interested primarily in the music, complains in his diary entry for 6 February 1668, that the theater was so crowded that he could 'see but little and hear not at all.' Therefore, when he attended a performance of *The Faithful Shepherdess* on 26 February 1669, which was poorly attended, he observed,

> The emptiness of the house took away our pleasure a great deal, though I liked it the better; for that I plainly discern the music is the better, by how much the House is the emptier.

He had first discussed theater acoustics in his diary entry of 8 May 1663, speaking of the Theater Royal and its early example of an orchestral pit.

> The house is made with extraordinary good contrivance; and yet has some faults, as the narrowness of the passages in and out of the pit, and the distance from the stage to the boxes, which I am confident cannot hear. But for all other things it is well. Only, above all, the Musique being below, and most of it sounding under the very stage, there is no hearing of the basses at all, nor very well of the trebles, which sure must be mended.

In general, Pepys liked what he heard and one finds such entries as that for 19 April 1667, where he reports hearing a musical adaptation of *Macbeth* by Davenant and finds the 'variety of dancing and music the best I ever saw.' Most of his diary entries, however, are simple comments on one or another singer which he either did or did not like. A typical example follows his attending a performance of *The Faithful Shepherdess* on 14 October 1668, when he mentions that the singing of a French eunuch was beyond all he had ever heard.

Judging by one entry in the diary of Pepys, it would appear that some of the music heard in the plays was produced at the last moment. In the entry for 7 May 1668, Pepys comments on his enjoyment in seeing several actors all dressed in their costumes, and privately complains that these mere actors become so confident in their talk when they come off the stage. Then he adds a note about a song which would be used in *The Mulberry Garden*, which premiered the following day.

> Here took up Knepp into our coach and all of us with her to her lodging, and hither comes Bannester with a song of hers that he has set in Sir Charles [Sedley]'s play for her, which is I think but very meanly set; but this he did before us, teach her; and it being but a slight, silly, short song, she learnt it presently. But I did here get him to prick me down [notate] the notes of the Echo Song in *The Tempest*, which pleases me mightily.

In so far as the quality of the music Pepys heard in these dramatic plays, he was by far his most enthusiastic over a composition for wind ensemble in the *Virgin Martyr* by Dekker, which he describes on 27 February 1668.

> What did please me beyond anything in the whole world was the wind-musique when the Angel comes down, which is so sweet that it ravished me; and indeed, in a word, did wrap up my soul so that it make me really sick, just as I have formerly been when in love with my wife; that neither then, nor all the evening going home and at home, I was able to think of anything, but remained all night transported, so as I could not believe that ever any music has that real command over the soul of a man as this did upon me; and makes me resolve to practice wind-music and to make my wife do the same.

He attends this play again on 2 March 1668, and this music has the same effect.

> Above all the Musique at the coming down of the Angel which at this hearing the second time does so still command me as nothing ever did, and the other music is nothing [compared] to it.

Two months later he sees the play again and mentions that he 'heard the music that I like so well.'[17]

We may assume the individual songs from these plays were made available for the public for amateur performance. Indeed in Pepys' diary for 23 August 1667, he tells of a visitor bringing two 'flagelettes' and some music used at the king's playhouse, which they played together and which Pepys looks forward to playing later with his wife.

On Civic Music

Pepys reports hearing civic music in several towns and his reaction varies considerably. On 9 October 1667, he hears the Cambridge 'town musique' and makes the curious comment, 'Lord, what sad music they made—however, I was pleased with them.' On 11 October 1667, he hears the Huntington civic music and finds them better than that of Cambridge. On 13 June 1668, he hears some civic musicians at the spa at Bath and finds them as good as anything he had ever heard in London. At Marlborough, however, he hears music of which he

---

17 Pepys Diary, May 6, 1668.

only comments that their 'innocence pleases me.'[18] In Reading, on 17 June 1668, he hears the 'worst music we have had.'

Perhaps the comment which most clearly reflects the long decline in the honorable civic musical organizations since the Renaissance comes in an diary entry for 23 October 1668. He is in Thetford and reports,

> How the king and these gentlemen did make the fiddlers of Thetford to sing them all the bawdy songs they could think of.

ART MUSIC

The sixteenth-century humanists in Italy and France argued extensively for the principle that in sung poetry, it is the words which carry meaning and emotion. It is the very nature of music itself, however, which made their position untenable. Pepys, for reasons of his rather simple approach to music, was of the 'old school.' He found hearing an art song in a language he did not speak failed to move him. In the following, he is speaking not only of the meaning of the words, in order to judge the composer's choice of music to go with them, but even such subtleties as accents peculiar to that language. On one occasion in 1667, he was invited to the home of Lord Brouncker to hear a private concert by visiting musicians from Italy.

> By and by [came] the music, that is to say, Seignor Vincentio, who is the master composer, and six more [musicians], of which two were eunuchs and one woman, very well dressed and handsome enough but would not be kissed, as Mr. Killigrew, who brought the company in, did acquaint us. They sent two harpsichords before; and by and by, after tuning them, they began; and I confess, very good music they made; that is, the composition exceeding good, but yet not at all more pleasing to me than what I have heard in English by Mrs. Knipp, Captain Cooke and others. Nor do I dote on the eunuchs; they sing indeed pretty high and have a mellow kind of sound, but yet I have been as well satisfied with several women's voices, and men also ... The woman sung well, but that which distinguishes all is this: that in singing, the words are to be considered and how they are fitted with notes, and then the common accent of the country is to be known and understood by the listener, or he will never be a good judge of the vocal music of another country. So that I was not taken with this at all, neither understanding the first nor by practice reconciled to the latter, so that their motions and risings and fallings, though it may be pleasing to an Italian or one that understands that tongue, yet to me it did not. [I] do from my heart believe that I could set words in English, and make music of the, more agreeable to any Englishman's ear (even the most judicious) than any Italian music set for the voice and performed before the same man, unless he be acquainted with the Italian accent of speech. The composition

---

18 Pepys Diary, June 15, 1668.

as to the instrumental part [the Musique part] was exceeding good, and their justness in keeping time by practice much before any that we have, unless it be a good band of practiced fiddlers.[19]

An interesting insight to a rather practical form of this question, the struggle between poet and composer, we find in a diary entry for 13 February 1667. In addition, we find here interesting references to improvisation, both in the 'humoring' of individual notes and in the cadences.

> Discourse most about plays and the opera; where among other vanities, Captain Cooke had the arrogance to say that he was fain to direct Sir W. Davenant in the breaking of his verses into such and such lengths, according as would be fit for music, and how he used to swear at Davenant and command him that way when W. Davenant would be angry, and find fault with this or that note; but a vain coxcomb I perceive he is, though he sings and composes so well … After dinner, Captain Cooke and two of his boys to sing; but it was indeed, both in performance and composition, most plainly below what I heard last night, which I could not have believed. Besides, overlooking the words when he sung, I find them not at all humored as they ought to be, and as I believed he had done all [as] he had notated—though he himself does indeed sing in a manner, as to voice and manner, the best I ever hard yet; and a strange mastery he has in the making of extraordinary surprising cadences, that are mighty pretty; but his bragging that he does understand tones and sounds as well as any man in the world, and better than Devenant or anybody else, I do not like by no means.

Although Pepys himself played a variety of instruments, as a listener he generally preferred vocal music. A typical diary entry describes his going to a public building to hear a private instrumental concert.

> I must confess, whether it be that I hear it but seldom, or that really voices is better, but so it is, that I found no pleasure at all in it, and methought two voices were worth twenty of it.[20]

FUNCTIONAL MUSIC

In his diary Pepys makes numerous observations on the music of the church. Sometimes he primarily comments on the quality of the choir, as in 1664 when he calls the choir at the famous St. Pauls 'the worst that ever I heard.'[21] On the other hand, after hearing the service at Windsor, St. George's Chapel in 1666, he writes,

---

19 Pepys Diary, February 16, 1667.
20 Pepys Diary, August 10, 1664.
21 Pepys Diary, February 28, 1664.

And here, for our sakes, had this anthem and the great service sung extraordinary, only to entertain us ... A good Choir of voices.[22]

In the early years covered by the diary there are some unusual descriptions. In September 1660, he reports hearing 'a dull Anthem,'[23] and the following month, at Whitehall, an anthem 'ill sung, which made the king laugh.'[24] Three months later he reports 'a long Psalm was set that lasted an hour while the Sexton gathered his year's contribution through the whole church.'[25]

With regard to the court church music, his comments would seem to indicate that the music of the Queen's Chapel was the more progressive. In 1666 he writes that he does not like the music at the Queen's Chapel,[26] but two weeks later he makes the first of several references to what must have been some form of unusual instrumental accompaniment (the 'Musique').

[I] heard a good deal of their mass and some of their Musique, which is not so contemptible, I think, as our people would make it, it pleasing me very well.[27]

One wonders if by 'contemptible' there was some form of movement by the instrumentalists. Otherwise, what could he possibly mean when he writes,

but that they do jump most excellently with themselves and their instrument—which is wonderful pleasant.'[28]

An entry a few months later also possibly refers to unusual instrumental accompaniment. On this occasion he liked the composition but found the voices harsh and suspected it was their choice of instruments that caused it[29]

It is in the Queen's Chapel as well, where he also heard Italian singers. In 1667 he mentions the Italian music, 'whose composition is fine, but yet the voices of the Eunuchs I do not like.' He goes on to make one of his favorite contentions that vocal music can only really be understood by the people who speak the language of the text.[30] The following year, however, he seems quite delighted.

---

22 Pepys Diary, February 26, 1666.
23 Pepys Diary, Sept 2, 1660.
24 Pepys Diary, Oct. 14, 1660.
25 Pepys Diary, January 6, 1661.
26 Pepys Diary, April 1, 1666.
27 Pepys Diary, April 15, 1666.
28 Pepys Diary, April 7, 1667.
29 Pepys Diary, Sept 8, 1667.
30 Pepys Diary, April 7, 1667.

> To the Queen's chapel and there did hear the Italians sing; and indeed, their music did appear most admirable to me, beyond anything of ours—I was never so well satisfied in my life with it.[31]

With regard to the King's Chapel, during the early years Pepys appears most complimentary. He frequently praises the anthems of Henry Cooke[32] and one such reference describes a rehearsal.

> After dinner to White-hall chappell with Mr. Childe; and there did hear Captain Cooke and his boy make a trial of an anthem against tomorrow, which was rare Musique.[33]

An entry of September 1662 may refer to the use of wind instruments, 'a most excellent Anthem (with Symphony's between) sung by Captain Cooke.'[34] In an entry for September 14, the following week, he appears to document the first use of strings.

> I heard Captain Cookes new Musique; this the first day of having Vialls and other Instruments to play a Symphony between every verse of the Anthem; but the Musique more full then it was the last Sunday, and very fine it is.[35]

Later entries in the diary, following the return of Humpfrey and the introduction of more complex contrapuntal styles, find Pepys not so pleased.

> [To White-hall] and heard a fine Anthem, made by Pelham [Humfrey] who is come over in France, of which there was great expectation; and indeed is a very good piece of Musique, but still I cannot call the Anthem anything but Instrumental music with the Voice, for nothing is made of the words at all.[36]

A similar entry the following year reads,

> To the Chapel and did hear an Anthem of Silas Taylors making—a dull old-fashion thing of six and seven parts that nobody could understand.[37]

Finally, we might cite a reference of September 1667, to performance practice in church music.

---

31 Pepys Diary, March 22, 1668.

32 Captain Henry Cooke (1615–1672) composed in all styles, including opera. He must have been an exceptional teacher, for his students included Blow, Humfrey and Purcell.

33 Pepys Diary, Feb. 23, 1661.

34 Pepys Diary, Sept 7, 1662.

35 Pepys Diary, Sept 14, 1662. Some historians date the appearance of the first strings two months later, with a December 1662 entry in the diary of John Evelyn.

36 Pepys Diary, November 1, 1667.

37 Pepys Diary, June 28, 1668.

> I went to the King's Chapel ... and there I hear Cresset sing a Tenor part along with the Church music; very handsomely, but so loud that people did laugh at him—as a thing done for ostentation.[38]

The King's '24 violins' took over the burden of functional music during the second half of the seventeenth century. They were an idea copied from Paris and first appear in the coronation of 1661.[39] But the violins also supplied the dinner music for the king,[40] as well as dance music—'after supper some fiddles and so to dance.'[41]

Regarding military music, Pepys' most widely quoted comment is found in his diary for 3 February 1661:

> So to White-hall, where I stayed to hear the trumpets and kettle-drums—and then the other drums; which is much cried up, though I think it dull, vulgar music.

Some authorities regard this entry as a reference to the new 'Turkish' percussion instruments which were becoming popular in military music.

Military drums and trumpets were still a fundamental form of communication with the public. Sometimes, for example, it was necessary to call militia in cases of public disorder, as in the case of a public protest over some citizens put in a pillory for beating their master.

> ... drums all up and down the city was beat to raise the train-bands for to quiet the town.[42]

Or to alert the citizens to a fire,

> Drums beat and trumpets, and the guards everywhere spread—running up and down in the street.[43]

Pepys' diary documents that he was always the keen observer, noticing, for example, when a drum cadence seemed inappropriate.

> Here in the streets I did hear the Scotch march beat by the drums before the soldiers, which is very odd.[44]

---

38 Pepys Diary, Sept 8, 1667.
39 Pepys Diary, April 23, 1661.
40 Pepys Diary, August 28, 1667, for example.
41 Pepys Diary, February 23, 1669.
42 Pepys Diary, March 26, 1664.
43 Pepys Diary, November 9, 1666.
44 Pepys Diary, June 30, 1667.

When he sees the King accompanied by his 'Kettledrums and Trumpets,' going to the Exchange to lay the corner-stone for a new building in 1667,[45] he may have recalled a conversation the previous year with a French visitor on the subject of Louis XIV.[46] He is told that when the King goes to see his mistress, Madame La Valiere, he goes with his trumpets and timpani, who 'stay before the house while he is with her.'

Only one reference is found for military music of a non-functional nature. Pepys reports a conversation of 2 November 1666, with the court 'Serjeant Trumpet' [Gervase Price], in which he is told that one of the Italian composers is writing a piece for three trumpets which he will teach them to play and he 'believes they will be admirable Musique.'

ENTERTAINMENT MUSIC

In the diary of Pepys there are a number of references to a variety of popular entertainment forms, heard in the taverns and in the streets. Of these, the only ones of interest to us are the descriptions of casual multi-part popular singing. His diary records on 9 November 1663, for example, his hearing impromptu singing in a tavern 'in three parts very finely.' On 27 July 1663, while out for a walk, he reports coming across, under some trees,

> some Citizens, met by chance, that sing four or five parts excellently. I have not been more pleased with a snapp of Musique, considering the circumstances of the time and place, in all my life anything so pleasant.

An entry for 17 April 1668, describes popular singing in the grotto of a tavern, in which Pepys found 'admirable pleasure,' may also have been part-songs.

---

45 Pepys Diary, October 23, 1667.
46 Pepys Diary, June 19, 1663.

19 RESTORATION JOURNALS

JOURNALS AND NEWSPAPERS WERE NOT NEW TO THIS PERIOD, but the extensive coverage of music and manners was. Richard Steele began the *Tatler* on 12 April 1709, writing primarily under the name Isaac Bickerstaff, as a paper designed for the conversation of the coffee house crowd. These journals are valuable in part for their presentation of this class, much of it middle-class, which is virtually absent in traditional political biographies and histories. Some have also pointed to these issues as the birthplace of modern short stories.

Steele and Joseph Addison created the *Spectator* with the issue of 1 March 1711. For the first year its actual circulation was small, rarely more than four thousand issues, but its influence became much larger as bound volumes were sold at the rate of nine thousand each year.

These journals are filled with references to music, musical humor and musical instruments, however, we present below only those passages which offer the modern reader insight into aesthetics, manners or taste relative to music of this period.

ON THE AESTHETICS OF MUSIC

In the *Tatler* for 15 August 1710, Addison lists 'Eloquence, Musick, and Poetry,' as 'those things which refine our lives.' In the *Spectator* for 16 June 1711, in discussing the 'Diversions of Life,' Addison observes,

> A man that has a taste of Musick, Painting, or Architecture, is like one that has another sense, when compared with such as have no relish in those arts.

Several issues of these journals suggest that music was an important hallmark of the cultured lady, as we see, for example, in the *Spectator* for 17 March 1712, where Steele publishes a fictitious letter by a man praising his 'virtuous lovely woman,' and mentions as part of her 'good breeding and polite education,' that she 'sings, dances, plays on the lute and harpsichord.' Ladies with similar accomplishments are mentioned in the issues for 5 August and 1 November 1712.

On the other hand, some contributors cast doubt on the general appreciation of music by the English society at this time. Jonathan Swift, writing in Irish journal, the *Intelligencer* [Number III, 1728], in an essay in which he defends and praises Gay's 'Beggars Opera,' quotes the Addison definition given above, but doubts whether the average man has any independent basis for judgment of those arts.

> As to Poetry, Eloquence and Musick, which are said to have most power over the minds of men, it is certain that very few have a taste or judgment of the excellencies of the two former; and if a man succeeds in either, it is upon the authority of those few judges, that lend their taste to the bulk of readers, who have none of their own. I am told there are as few good judges in Musick, and that among those who crowd in operas, nine in ten to hither merely out of curiosity, fashion or affectation.

On the Perception of Music

Looking at this literature as a whole, one has clear reason to doubt whether either Steele or Addison themselves had much depth in their understanding of music. Steele, for example, writing on the supremacy of sight among the senses, in the *Spectator* of 1 September 1712, suggests that it is the addition of *sight* to hearing which gives significance to music, by which he means the addition of Reason to hearing, or as we would say today, the left hemisphere of the brain giving meaning to the right. In any case, this is only new language for the old misinformed conclusion that music has no meaning unless it is a rational concept, which in earlier times in the university meant mathematics.

> The *sight* informs the statuary's chisel with power to give breath to lifeless brass and marble, and the painter's pencil to swell the flat canvas with moving figures actuated by imaginary souls. Musick indeed may plead another original, since Jubal by the different falls of his hammer on the anvil, discovered by the ear the first rude Musick that pleased the Antediluvian fathers; but then the *sight* has not only reduced those wilder sounds into artful Order and Harmony, but [through notation] conveys that Harmony to the most distant parts of the world without the help of sound.

Among other journals which deal with the perception of music, Addison, in the *Tatler* for 14 February 1710, writes an essay on Silence. In commenting on the power of silence, he uses music as an illustration.

> I have my self been wonderfully delighted with a Master-Piece of Musick, when in the very tumult and ferment of their harmony, all the voices and instruments have stopped short on a sudden, and after a little pause recovered themselves again as it were, and renewed the concert in all its parts. Methoughts this short interval of silence has had more Musick in it than any the same Space of Time before or after it.

In the *Tatler* for 1 April 1710, Addison mentions a painting, 'The Consort of Musick,' by Zampieri, which pictured famous painters, each holding an instrument which corresponded to their character. Addison then speculates how the various instruments might also serve as metaphors for styles of conversation, in the process offering his view of the individual character of the various instruments. The percussion, for example, he finds are like 'Blusterers in Conversation,' with lots of noise but 'seldom any wit, humor, or good breeding.' Nevertheless they are appropriate to the ignorant and to ladies of little taste. The lute he considers the opposite to the percussion, having a soft sound, 'exquisitely sweet, and very low, easily drowned in a multitude of instruments.' The lute, then, corresponds to 'men of fine genius, uncommon reflection, great affability … and good taste.'

The trumpet, an instrument he finds of 'no compass of Musick, or variety of sound,' having only four or five notes, although it is pleasing enough, he equates with the gentleman of fashionable education and breeding, yet who are shallow, with weak judgment and little understanding.

Regarding the violin, it is interesting that Addison first thinks of its use in improvisation.

> Violins are the lively, forward, importunate wits, that distinguish themselves by the flourishes of imagination, sharpness of repartee, glances of satyr, and bear away the upper part in every consort. I cannot however but observe, That when a man is not disposed to hear Musick, there is not a more disagreeable sound in harmony than that of a violin.

Addison associates every sensible, 'true-born Britain' with the Bass-Viol, as 'Men of rough sense, and unpolished parts … but who sometimes break out with an agreeable bluntness, unexpected wit, and surly pleasantry.' Musically, he finds this instrument one which 'grumbles in the bottom of the consort, with a surly masculine sound, strengthens the harmony, and tempers the sweetness of the several instruments that play along with it.'

The 'Rural Wits,' which he associates with horns, he is not quite sure should be permitted in polite society. The bagpipe, with its perpetual repetition of a few notes over a drone, he associates with the 'dull, heavy, tedious story-tellers.'

These comments, Addison admits, are concerned only with 'male instruments,' the female ones he promises to discuss in a later issue. In the meantime, however, he warns the reader to,

> make a narrow search into his life and conversation, and upon his leaving any company, to examine himself seriously, whether he has behaved himself in it like a drum or trumpet, a violin or a Bass-Viol; and accordingly endeavor to mend his Musick for the future.

As he promised, Addison discusses the 'female' instruments in his issue of 11 April 1710. The flute he finds an instrument with small compass, sweet and soft, which lulls and soothes the ear and raises 'a most agreeable passion between transport and indolence.' This reminds him of the conversation of a 'mild and amiable woman, that has nothing in it very elevated, or at the same time any thing mean or trivial.' The flageolet, on the other hand, is like a young lady 'entertaining the company with tart ill-natured observations, pert fancies, and little turns which she imagined to be full of life and spirit.' Curiously, Addison also considers the oboe to be part of the flute family.

> I must here observe that the Hautboy is the most perfect of the flute-species, which, with all the sweetness of the sound, has a greater strength and variety of notes; though at the same time I must observe, that the hautboy in one sex is as scarce as the harpsichord in the other.

The 'Prude,' characterized by 'the gravity of her censures and composure of her voice,' he associates with the 'ancient serious matron-like instrument the Virginal.' The 'Romantic instrument called a Dulcimer,' he finds a pleasant rural instrument, as is also the hornpipe, while the Welsh harp is a 'Female Historian.' It is interesting that he includes among the female instruments, the timpani.

> But the most sonorous part of our consort was a She-Drum, or (as the vulgar call it) a Kettle-Drum, who accompanied her discourse with motions of the body, tosses of the head, and brandishes of the fan. Her Musick was loud, bold and masculine. Every thump she gave alarmed the company, and very often set somebody or other in it a blushing.

Some interesting remarks on the nature of program music are made by Addison in the *Spectator* for 27 June 1712.

> It is certain there may be confused, imperfect notions of this nature raised in the imagination by an artificial composition of notes; and we find that great masters in the art are able, sometimes, to set their hearers in the heat and hurry of a battle, to overcast their minds with melancholy scenes and apprehensions of deaths and funerals, or to lull them into pleasing dreams of groves and Elisiums.
>   In all these instances, this secondary pleasure of the imagination proceeds from that action of the mind, which compares the ideas arising from the original objects, with the ideas we receive from the statue, picture, description, or sound that represents them. It is impossible for us to give the necessary reason why this operation of the mind is attended with so much pleasure, as I have before observed[1]; but we find a great variety of entertainments derived from this single principle.

On Emotions in Music

Addison, in a discussion of opera in the *Spectator* of 3 April 1711, makes a fundamental error regarding the perception of music, in view of which the reader must question his basic understanding of music and many of his subsequent comments on it. He did not understand that what music *really* communicates is emotion and that this emotional understanding is

---
[1] He refers here to a discussion in the issue of 24 June 1712, in which he had quoted Locke as contending that light and colors are creations of the imagination and have no material basis.

universal and genetic. Because of the close affinity of emotions and music in the right hemisphere of the brain, and especially the genetic musical information which modern clinical research suggests is carried into birth, it appears the old saying that 'music is the international language' is in fact true.[2] But this expression relates to the emotions expressed through music and has nothing to do with words or any other rational concepts.

It is most curious that Addison seems unaware of his own fundamental contradiction, in this regard. On one hand, in the *Spectator* for 21 March 1711, he objects strongly that the English people are listening to opera in a language they do not understand. Yet, in this issue of 3 April, he builds his case that the source of the emotions are the words. The physiological truth is that words may be sung, but the emotions are in the music!

In this April issue, he understands the music of opera to be something which expressed the *words*, thus his great concern here with the inevitable problems in translating libretti. It follows that since each language has a different form of tone and accent, Addison thought music should be therefore fundamentally different in each country. Addison's conclusion which follows is incorrect and cannot be supported by either common practice or medical research.

> For this reason the Italian artists cannot agree with our English musicians, in admiring Purcell's compositions, and thinking his tunes so wonderfully adapted to his words, because both nations do not always express the same passions by the same sounds ...
>
> A composer should fit his Musick to the genius of the people, and consider that the delicacy of hearing, and taste of harmony, has been formed upon those sounds which every country abounds with: In short, that Musick is of a relative nature, and what is harmony to one ear, may be dissonance to another.

Addison apparently based his concept that music should be fundamentally different in each country in part on the basis of his perceived distinction between French and Italian opera. In his discussion of this we find the curious information that the audience in Paris participated, and, according to some sources, even went upon the stage.

> Signor Baptist Lully acted like a man of sense in this particular. He found the French Musick extremely defective, and very often barbarous. However, knowing the genius of the people, the humor of their language, and the prejudiced ears he had to deal with, he did not pretend to extirpate the French musick, and plant the Italian in its stead; but only to cultivate and civilize it with innumerable graces and modulations which he borrowed from the Italian. By this means the French Musick is now perfect in its kind; and when you say it is not so good as the Italian, you only mean that it does not please you so well, for there is scarce a Frenchman who would not wonder to hear you give the Italian such a preference. The Musick of the French is indeed very properly adapted to their pronunciation and accent, as their whole opera wonderfully favors the genius of such a gay airy people. The Chorus in which that opera abounds, gives the Parterre frequent opportunities of joining in consort with the stage. This inclination of the audience to

---

2   Addison later associates music in this regard with architecture, painting, poetry and oratory, but he is again incorrect. There is nothing universal or genetic in painting, architecture, poetry or oratory.

sing along with the actors, so prevail with them, that I have sometimes known the performer on the stage do no more in a celebrated song, than the clerk of a parish church, who serves only to raise the psalm, and is afterwards drowned in the Musick of the congregation.

In all fairness to Addison, we must acknowledge that there were others at this time who apparently misunderstood the true role of music in opera. The *Spectator* for 26 December 1711, for example, carries a letter to the editor signed by Thomas Clayton, Nicolino Haym and Charles Dieupart, three men who figured in the development of opera in England in the early years of the eighteenth century, in which the argument is again made that emotion is found in the words, not in the music.

We conceive hopes of your favor from the speculations on the mistakes which the town run into with regard to their pleasure of this kind; and believing your method of judging is, that you consider Musick only valuable as it is agreeable to and heightens the purpose of poetry, we consent that That is not only the true way of relishing that pleasure, but also that without it a composition of Musick is the same thing as a poem where all the rules of poetical numbers are observed, but the words of no sense or meaning; to say it shortly, mere musical sounds are in our Art no other than nonsense verses are in poetry. Musick therefore is to aggravate what is intended by poetry; it must always have some passion or sentiment to express, or else violins, voices, or any other organs of sound, afford an entertainment very little above the rattles of children.

Curiously, Addison discovered in common ballads the universality of emotion in music which he failed to notice in Italian opera. In his first discussion of this, in the *Spectator* issue for 21 May 1711, he begins with an anecdote about Moliere which argues for the universality of emotions.

Moliere, as we are told by Monsieur Boileau,[3] used to read all his comedies to an old woman who was his house-keeper, as she sat with him at her work by the chimney-corner; and could foretell the success of his play in the theater, from the reception it met at her fire-side …
So … an ordinary song or ballad that is the delight of the common people cannot fail to please all such readers as are not unqualified for the entertainment by their affectation or ignorance; and the reason is plain, because the same paintings of nature which recommend it to the most ordinary reader, will appear beautiful to the most refined.

In this passage, Addison again appears to be thinking of emotion only in terms of the words, even though he is discussing ballads set to music. In the issue of 25 May 1711, he discusses

---

[3] The original, in the *Works of Boileau* (1711–1712), II, 89,

Moliere has often shown me an old maid of his, to whom, he told me, he read his Comedies; assuring me, that when any part of the pleasantry did not strike her, he corrected it; because he frequently found at his theater, that those very places did not succeed.

In our own days as a member of a touring concert organization, we knew a conductor who, not being impressed with the acclamation of audiences of thousands of persons, would invariably request the opinion of a local stage hand at the end of the concert.

the most popular of all ballads, 'Chevy Chase,' and here he comes closer to associating the emotions with the music.

> Had this old song been filled with epigrammatical turns and points of wit, it might perhaps have pleased the wrong taste of some readers; but it would never have become the delight of the common people, nor have warmed the heart of Sir Philip Sidney 'like the sound of a trumpet'; it is only Nature that can have this effect, and please those tastes which are the most unprejudiced or the most refined.

In discussing another often mentioned ballad, 'Children of the Wood,' Addison, in the issue of 7 June 1711, once again seems to place his understanding of the emotions on the words. We believe modern clinical research would suggest that he is asking more of language, in this regard, than is possible.

> This song is a plain simple Copy of Nature, destitute of all the helps and ornaments of Art. The tale of it is a pretty tragic story, and pleases for no other reason, but because it is a Copy of Nature. There is even a despicable simplicity in the verse; and yet, because the sentiments appear genuine and unaffected, they are able to move the mind of the most polite reader with inward meltings of humanity and compassion.

The problem is, when he says 'the sentiments … move the mind,' he is thinking of language, being unaware that the 'sentiments' are in a different hemisphere of the brain [together with music] than those of language.

More accurate is Steele, in the *Spectator* for 24 September 1712, who notes in a fictitious letter, 'A loose trivial song gains the affections, when a wise Homily is not attended to.' That is, it is the music, not the words, which carry emotion.

On Performance Practice

A complaint in the *Spectator* for 25 October 1711, which is about a visiting woman from the city who improvises during village church music, reflects some of the kinds of ornamentation improvised in opera at this time.

> But what gives us the most offense is her theatrical manner of singing the psalms. She introduces above fifty Italian Airs into the Hunderdth Psalm, and whilst we begin 'All People' in the old solemn tune of our fore-fathers, she in quite a different key runs divisions on the vowels, and adorns them with the graces of Nicolini … we are certain to hear her quavering them half a minute after us to some sprightly airs of the opera.
>
> I am very far from being an enemy to church musick; but fear this abuse of it may make my parish ridiculous, who already look on the singing psalms as an entertainment, and not part of their devotion.

In a comment very similar to an objection of Michael Preatorius in 1619, who could not understand why performers did not tune their instruments at home before presenting themselves at the church for performance, the *Tatler* for 2 May 1710, observes,

> When I granted his request, I made one to him, which was, that the performers should put their instruments in tune before the audience came in; for that I thought the resentment of the Eastern Prince, who, according to the old story, mistook *tuning* for *playing*, to be very just and natural.

One does not read much about the conductor in England at this time, but his existence is documented in the *Spectator* for 29 November 1711. Addison mentions a noise maker in the upper gallery of the opera and suggests that in the future he might be used to preside over the audience, 'like the Director of a Consort, in order to awaken their attention, and beat time to their applauses.'

ART MUSIC

In the *Tatler* for 9 September 1710, Addison,[4] having been unable to sleep the previous night due to a serenade, devotes himself to this topic. He notes that in London the civic musicians are often hired by young men to sing their serenades for them.

> For as the custom prevails at present, there is scarce a young man of any fashion in a Corporation who does not make Love with the Town-Musick. The Waits often help him through his courtship.

Addison states that 'authors of all countries are unanimous' in believing that the tradition of the evening serenade began in Italy, adding in an indirect jab at Italian opera, that it was the castrati who began this tradition. That it was Italy in which this custom began, seems evident to Addison because of the mild climate there. To sing outdoors at night in colder England—well, one might as well serenade in Greenland! Indeed, he maintains that the trills he has heard in London serenades were caused by the cold weather.

Secondly, he points to the fact that everyone in Italy is so musical by nature, a fact which he regards as another clue to the origin of the serenade.

> Nothing is more frequent in that country, than to hear a cobbler working to an opera tune … There is not a laborer, or handicraftsman, that in the cool of the evening does not relieve himself with solos and sonatas.
>
> The Italian soothes his Mistress with a plaintive voice, and bewails himself in such melting Musick, that the whole neighborhood sympathizes with him in his sorrow …
>
> On the contrary, our honest countrymen have so little an inclination to Musick, that they seldom begin to sing till they are drunk, which also is usually the time when they are most disposed to serenade.

---

[4] The paper is ascribed to Steele, but scholars believe it to be by Addison.

A fictional letter, written by Steele, in the *Spectator* of 28 April 1712, reports the objection of a bridegroom to an intended humorous tradition of serenading newly married couples on the following morning with percussion.

> To my surprise I was awakened the next morning by the thunder of a set of drums. These warlike sounds are very improper in a marriage consort, and give great offense; they seem to insinuate, that the joys of this state are short, and that jars and discord soon ensue. I fear they have been ominous in many matches, and sometimes proved a prelude to a battle in the Honeymoon.

These journals are also valuable for their inclusion of announcements of private concerts in and around London, which add to our understanding of the concert life in that city at this time. The *Spectator* for 1 May 1711, for example, carries mention of a forthcoming 'Consort of Musick' to be held in the Haberdashers-hall. The *Spectator* for 18 January 1712 carries an advertisement for a series of concerts organized by three men previously associated with opera, Thomas Clayton, Nicolino Haym and Charles Dieupart. Curiously, it was these same three writers who had earlier argued that emotion is found only in the words, who now apparently find emotion elsewhere.

> We think it a groundless imputation that we should set up against the Opera in it self. What we pretend to assert is, that the songs of different authors injudiciously put together, and a foreign tone and manner which are expected in every thing now performed amongst us, has put Musick it self to a stand; insomuch that the ears of the people cannot now be entertained with any thing but what has an impertinent gaiety, without any just Spirit; or a Languishment of Notes, without any Passion or common sense.

Some announcements are rather unusual. The *Spectator* for 7 April 1712 carries the announcement of a vocal and instrumental concert for the benefit of one, 'Mr. Edward Keen, the father of twenty children.' This must have been a regular *raison d'être* for Keen's concerts for a similar advertisement can be found in 1707, and in fact another as early as 1699.[5] The *Spectator* for 21 July 1714 reports music made by the master of a tavern on a variety of kitchen objects, in a repertoire that included arias from Italian operas.

On Opera

In the very first issue of the *Tatler*, for 12 April 1709, Richard Steele mentions a complaint frequently made during this period, that the popularity of Italian opera had caused the decline of theater in England.[6]

---

[5] See *The Spectator*, ed. Donald Bond (Oxford: Clarendon Press, 1965), III, 291, fn. 3.

[6] Regarding the popularity of Italian opera, the *Tatler* for 27 April 1710, carries a fictional advertisement for an opera in which the composer 'hopes he has pretensions to the favor of all Lovers of Musick, who can get over the prejudice of his being their Countryman.'

> It is not now doubted but plays will revive, and take their usual place in the opinion of persons of wit and merit, notwithstanding their late apostacy in favor of dress and sound.

In an issue the same month, for 19 April 1709, Steele is somewhat more outspoken in his attack on opera.

> Letters from the Hay-market inform us, that on Saturday night last the opera of *Pyrrhus and Demetrius* was performed with great applause. This intelligence is not very acceptable to us friends of the theater; for the stage being an entertainment of the Reason and all our faculties, this way of being pleased with the suspense of them for three hours together, and being given up to the shallow satisfaction of the eyes and ears only, seems to arise rather from the degeneracy of our understanding, than an improvement of our diversion. That the understanding has no part in the pleasure is evident, from what these letters very positively assert, to wit, that a great part of the performance was done in Italian.

The issue of 7 May 1709, continues arguments of this kind and attacks for the first time the Italian singers who were castrati.

> When the seat of wit was thus mortgaged, without equity of redemption, an architect arose, who has built the Muse a new palace, but secured her no retinue; so that instead of action there, we have been put off by song and dance. This latter help of sound has also began to fail for want of voices; therefore the palace has since been put into the hands of a surgeon, who cuts any foreign fellow into an Eunuch, and passes him upon us for a singer of Italy.

The burial of the most famous English actor of the seventeenth century, Thomas Betterton, inspired the *Tatler* to once again attack opera. An argument used against it here is a very ancient one, that music is of only brief duration and then disappears.

> I extremely lament the little relish the Gentry of this nation have at present for the just and noble representations in some of our Tragedies. The Operas, which are of late introduced, can leave no trace behind them that can be of service beyond the present moment. To sing and to dance are accomplishments very few have any thoughts of practicing.[7]

The *Tatler* for 3 January 1710, reports a small audience at the opera, which it attributes to the fact that the tumbler was not scheduled to appear. This issue does comment, however, on the acting ability of the famous singer, Nicolini.

> Every limb, and every finger, contributes to the part he acts, insomuch that a deaf man might go along with him in the sense of it. There is scarce a beautiful posture in an old statue which he does not plant himself in, as the different circumstances of the story give occasion for it.

---

7 *Tatler*, May 4, 1710. An earlier issue, for 10 January 1710, had also mentioned in passing 'the Gentry's immoderate frequenting the Operas.' The issue of 14 March 1710 complains that the Gentry at the opera is occupied in looking around at the people in the audience 'without any manner of regard to the stage.'

The most famous article in the early eighteenth-century journals on the subject of opera was written by Addison for the *Spectator* issue of 21 March 1711.

> It is my design in this paper to deliver down to posterity a faithful account of the *Italian* Opera, and of the gradual progress which it has made upon the *English* stage: for there is no question but our great grand-children will be very curious to know the reason why their forefathers used to sit together like an audience of foreigners in their own country, and to hear whole plays acted before them in a tongue which they did not understand.
>
> *Arsinoe* was the first opera that gave us a taste of *Italian* musick. The great success this opera met with, produced some attempts of forming pieces upon *Italian* plans, which should give a more natural and reasonable entertainment than what can be met with in the elaborate trifles of that nation. This alarmed the poetasters and fidlers of the town, who were used to deal in a more ordinary kind of ware; and therefore laid down an established rule, which is received as such to this day, *That nothing is capable of being well set to Musick, that is not Nonsense.*

Addison next discusses the frequent errors he has heard in attempting to translate the Italian into English, resulting in the placement of words against music which is consequently inappropriate. This proving unsuccessful, he describes the next alternative.

> The next step to our refinement, was the introducing of Italian actors into our opera; who sung their parts in their own language, at the same time that our countrymen performed theirs in our native tongue. The king or hero of the play generally spoke in Italian, and his slaves answered him in English. The lover frequently made his court and gained the heart of his princess in a language which she did not understand ...
>
> At length the audience grew tired of understanding half the opera, and therefore to ease themselves entirely of the fatigue of thinking, have so ordered it at present that the whole opera is performed in an unknown tongue. We no longer understand the language of our own stage ...
>
> One scarce knows how to be serious in the confutation of an absurdity that shows itself at the first sight. It does not want any great measure of sense to see the ridicule of this monstrous practice; but what makes it the more astonishing, it is not the taste of the rabble, but of persons of the greatest politeness, which has established it.

He concludes by suggesting, as others had done, that even if 'the Italians have a genius for Musick above the English,' it is nevertheless to be regretted that opera had caused the public to lose interest in English theater. As he continues, he questions even the importance of music itself.

> Musick is certainly a very agreeable entertainment, but if it would take the entire possession of our ears, if it would make us incapable of hearing sense, it would exclude Arts that have a much greater tendency to the refinement of human nature ...
>
> At present, our notions of Musick are so very uncertain, that we do not know what it is we like; only, in general, we are transported with anything that is not English. So it be of a foreign

growth, let it be Italian, French, or [German], it is the same thing. In short, our English Musick is quite rooted out, and nothing yet planted in its stead.

Addison, in the *Spectator* for 3 April 1711, comments on the general absurdity of sung plays.

> There is nothing that has more startled our *English* audience, that the *Italian Recitativo* at its first entrance upon the stage. People were wonderfully surprised to hear generals singing the word of command, and ladies delivering messages in Musick. Our countrymen could not forbear laughing when they heard a lover chanting out a Billet-doux, and even the superscription of a letter set to a tune.

In a satire on singing in Italian, Addison, in the 5 April 1711, issue of *Spectator*, writes of a fictitious plan for an opera in Greek.

> The only difficulty that remained, was, how to get performers, unless we could persuade some gentlemen of the universities to learn to sing, in order to qualify themselves for the stage.

Further issues of the *Spectator* contain continual demeaning characterizations of opera by Addison. In the issue for 15 March 1711, he refers to the 'forced thoughts, cold conceits and unnatural expressions of Italian opera,' and in the issue for 11 December 1711, he calls attending the opera 'throwing away your time.'

In the *Spectator* for 6 March 1711, Addison even criticizes opera stage sets, which he generally finds designed only 'to gratify the senses and keep up an indolent attention in the audience.' Among the interesting examples he provides is the release of sparrows on stage, with a consort of 'flagellet' players off-stage to supply the birds' song. Addison also mentions that opera, such as Handel's *Rinaldo*, had brought indoors 'thunder, lightning, illuminations and fireworks,' which people could now enjoy without catching cold outdoors. Also regarding sets, a fictitious advertisement appeared in the *Spectator* for 16 March 1711, which read,

> On the first of April will be performed at the Play-house in the Hay-market an opera called *The Cruelty of Arteus*. N.B. The scene wherein Thyestes eats his own children, is to be performed by the famous Mr. Psalmanazar, lately arrived from Formosa: The whole Supper being set to Kettle-drums.

Of these writers, it was Steele who described the audiences who attend opera. When he first addresses this topic, he seems to blame the stage itself for the subsequent behavior of the audience. He writes in the *Spectator* for 26 March 1711,

> The word *Spectator* being most usually understood as one of the audience at public representations in our theaters, I seldom fail of many letters relating to plays and operas. But indeed there are such monstrous things done in both, that if one had not been an eye-witness of them, one could not believe that such matters had really been exhibited. There is very little which concerns human life, or is a picture of nature, that is regarded by the greater part of the company. The

understanding is dismissed from our entertainments. Our mirth is the laughter of fools, and our admiration the wonder of idiots; else such improbable, monstrous, and incoherent dreams could not go off as they do, not only without the utmost scorn and contempt, but even with the loudest applause and approbation.

A fictitious letter to the editor of the *Spectator* for 12 September 1711 addresses the 'Impertinencies' which occur when individuals become part of a crowd, such as at an opera.

Sometimes you have a set of whisperers, who lay their heads together in order to sacrifice every body within their observation; sometimes a set of laughers, that keep up an insipid mirth in their own corner, and by their noise and gestures show they have no respect for the rest of the company. You frequently meet with these sets at the opera.[8]

Steele, in his *Spectator* issue for 29 July 1712, again turns his attention to the uncultured nature of English audiences at the opera. He publishes a fictitious letter supposedly written by an English opera singer now performing in Italy.

I little thought in the green years of my life, that I should ever call it an happiness to be out of dear England; but as I grew to woman, I found myself less acceptable in proportion to the increase of my merit. Their ears in Italy are so differently formed from the make of yours in England, that I never come upon the stage, but a general satisfaction appears in every countenance of the whole people. When I dwell upon a note, I behold all the men accompanying me with heads inclining, and falling of their persons on one side, as dying away with me. The women too do justice to my merit, and no ill-natured worthless creature cries, 'the vain thing,' when I am wrapped up in the performance of my part, and sensibly touched with the effect my voice has upon all who hear me. I live here distinguished, as one whom Nature has been liberal to in a graceful person, an exalted mien, and heavenly voice. These particularities in this strange country, are arguments for respect and generosity to her who is possessed of them. The Italians see a thousand beauties I am sensible I have no pretense to, and abundantly make up to me the injustice I received in my own country, of disallowing me what I really had. The humor of hissing, which you have among you, I do not know anything of; and their applauses are uttered in sighs, and bearing a part at the cadences of voice with the persons who are performing …

The whole city of Venice is as still when I am singing, as this polite hearer was to Mrs. Hunt. But when they break that silence, did you know the pleasure I am in, when every man utters applause, by calling me aloud the 'Dear Creature,' the 'Angel,' the 'Venus'; 'What Attitude she moves with!—Hush, she sings again!' We have no boisterous wits who dare disturb an audience, and break the public peace merely to show they dare. Mr. Spectator, I write this to you…to tell you I am very much at ease here, that I know nothing but joy; and I will not return, but leave you in England to hiss all merit of your own growth off the stage.

Regarding the influence of opera on individual patrons, Steele reveals how familiar some members of the audience had become with some Italian operas in his recalling, in the

---

8   In the issue of 20 June 1711, Steele mentions one listener who sat in the gallery, beating time with a cudgel.

Spectator of 20 August 1711, of a citizen who entered a tavern, with an opera score under his arm and 'practiced his Airs to the full house who were turned upon him.' In his issue of 8 February 1712 he complains that women have been so taken by Italian opera that they have taken on a new interest in Latin, thinking of it as an earlier Italian language. Budgell, in the *Spectator* for 29 April 1712, was so concerned for the influence of opera on women that he recommends 'the Puppet-show much safer for them than the Opera.'

A decade later, the journals seem more light-hearted on the subject of opera, or perhaps they had found humor to be the best vehicle for criticism. Jonathan Swift, writing in Irish journal, the *Intelligencer* [Number III, 1728], in an essay in which he defends and praises Gay's 'Beggars Opera,' reflects back over the first controversial period of Italian opera in London and offers this summary.

> This comedy likewise exposes with great justice that unnatural taste for Italian Musick among us, which is wholly unsuitable to our Northern Climate, and the genius of the people, whereby we are overrun with Italian-Effeminacy, and Italian Nonsense. An old Gentleman said to me, that many years ago, when the practice of an unnatural vice grew so frequent in London that many were prosecuted for it, he was sure it would be the Fore-runner of Italian Operas and Singers; and then we should lack nothing but stabbing or poisoning, to make us perfect Italians.

Mary Wortley Montagu contributed a letter to the editor of the journal *The Nonsense of Common-Sense*[9] [Number III, for January 3, 1738], under the fictitious name of 'Balducci.' The writer claimed to be an authority in 'the business of statuary and machinery,' and, having noticed the great sums of money spent by the English on singers from his country, Italy, he proposes to invent mechanical singers which could make possible financial savings.

> By my Art, I have found out a method of making a statue imitate so exactly the voice of any *Singer* that ever did, or ever can appear upon the stage, that I'll defy the ravished listener to distinguish the one from the other. Nay, what is more, this statue shall sing any *Opera* Air the audience pleases to call for, and shall chant it over again and again, as long as they please to cry, *Ancora*, which is an honor, I presume, they will as often confer upon my artificial machines, as ever they did upon any of the natural machines of Italy; and to add to the astonishment of all persons of polite taste, it shall perform at first sight any of the most difficult pieces of Musick the learned Mr. H[ande]l can compose. Then, Sir, by the help of my wonderful art in machinery, I can make my statue walk about, and tread the stage with as good a grace, and look upon the pit with as much contempt, as ever did the famous *Senesino*;[10] by which means it will be able to perform its part in the *Recitativo*, and shall rage with fury, die away in raptures, or stare with amazement and surprise, in as natural a manner, and with as true a taste, as any actor that ever trod the stage.

Balducci offers additional advantages for such a mechanical singer: it could immediately absorb all instructions from the music critics, it would rescue the Academy of Musick from

---

9   Only nine issues, from 16 December 1737 to 14 March 1738, of this weekly newspaper are extant.

10   Francesco Bernardi (1680–1750), known as Senesino, was a famous castrato.

spending all its time trying to pacify fighting singers and it would make composers such as Handel happy, as their music would be sung as written and not be subject to improvisation by live singers. He recommends that as English nobles tour Italy and hear 'some new singer just blazed out at Venice, Naples or Rome,' he will immediately go there and bring the singer back in effigy, charging the noble only for his trip and expenses. Since, he observes, England has already assembled great collections of Italian pictures, statues, busts and antiques, his mechanical singers will make it possible to add famous singers to its collections as well.

> However, I do not propose to diminish the price of an *Opera ticket*, or that any of my singers shall perform in private for a *less mighty Purse* than the proudest of our late performers; for this, I know, would spoil all; nothing can be fit for persons of an elegant taste that can be had at a small price. Yet I am not so avaricious as to propose to take all the profits to myself. On the contrary, I shall be satisfied with my net charges, and a very moderate salary. As for the residue of the profits, which will certainly amount to a large sum yearly, the disposal of it shall be left to the great wisdom of the directors of the *Academy of Musick*; in which case I would humbly propose, it should be distributed yearly by way of charity, for the subsistence of those antiquated *Beaus* and *Belles*, who in their younger years had ruined themselves by attending *Operas, Masquerades*, etc.

By the 1730s there were two opera companies in London, but by 1738 one of them, the 'Opera of the Nobility,' had apparently closed. It was in reference to this that Lord Chesterfield contributed an article, 'Close of the Opera,' to the 14 October 1738, issue of *Common Sense*.

> Such is the uncertainty and unstability of the things of this world, that there is scarce any event which ought to surprise us, or anything new to be said upon it ...
> I confess this happened to me lately, when I heard that Operas were no more, and that too at a time when the vigor and success, with which a subscription was carried on, both by the great and the fair, seemed to promise them in their fullest luster.

In attempting to decide if the closing of the opera represents a national loss or a national advantage, Chesterfield first reviews the role of music reflected in ancient Greek literature. He mentions in particular the stories of the aulos performing the Pyrrhic melodies which so inspired the Greek armies.

> This tune, by the way, must have infinitely exceeded our best modern marches, which, by what I have been able to observe in Hyde Park, rather sets our army a-dancing than a-fighting. I ascribe this difference wholly to the unskillfulness of our modern composers; for I will never believe that my countrymen have not as much potential courage in them as the Greeks, if properly excited.

After retelling the tale about Pythagoras causing a lust-filled youth to cool down by playing a certain kind of music, he observes,

> Our Operas have not been known to occasion any attempts of this violent nature; which I likewise impute to the effects of the composition, and not to any degree of insensibility or modesty

in our youth, who, it must be owned, give a fair hearing to music, and whose short bobs seem admirably contrived for the better reception of sounds.

Lord Chesterfield, after citing the incident in which music caused an apparent change in personality in Alexander the Great, provides some interesting contemporary anecdotes involving music.

> I am apt to believe that in music, as in many other arts and sciences, we fall infinitely short of the ancients. For I take it for granted, that we should be open to the same impressions, if our composers had but the skill to make them. However, though music does not now cause those surprising effects which it did formerly, it still retains power enough over men's passions to make it worth our care: and I heard some persons, equally skilled in music and politics, assert that King James was sung and fiddled out of this kingdom by the Protestant tune of Lillybullero; and that somebody else would have been fiddled into it again, if a certain treasonable Jacobite tune had not been timely silenced by the unwearied pains and diligence of the administration …
>
> The Swiss, who are not a people of the quickest sensations, have at this time a tune, which, when played upon their fifes, inspires them with such a love of their country, that they run home as fast as they can: which tune is therefore, under severe penalties, forbidden to be played, when their regiments are on service, because they would instantly desert.

Regarding this last anecdote, Chesterfield suggests that he can think of some situations in London, such as court or legislative functions, when it would be valuable to have such a tune played which would cause everyone to immediately run home.

> I would therefore most earnestly recommend it to the learned Dr. Green, to turn his thoughts that way. It is not from the least distrust of Mr. Handel's ability, that I address myself preferably to Dr. Green: but Mr. Handel, having the advantage to be by birth a German, might probably, even without intending it, mix some modulations in his composition, which might give a German tendency to the mind, and therefore greatly lessen the national benefit I propose by it.

Finally, Chesterfield returns to his original question, regarding the significance of the closing of the opera.

> How far the polite part of the world is affected by the cessation of Operas, I am no judge myself; but I asked a young gentleman of wit and pleasure about town, whether he did not apprehend that he should be a sufferer by it in his way of business, for that I presumed those soft and tender sounds soothed and melted the fairest breasts, and fitted them to receive impressions? He answered me very frankly, that, as far as he could judge, the loss would be but inconsiderable to their profession; that some years ago, indeed, the taste of music, being expressive and pathetic, had inspired tender sentiments, and softened stubborn virtue; but the fashion being of late for both the composers and the performers only to show what tricks they could play, had rather taught the ladies to play tricks too, than made the proper impressions upon them, and that he oftener found them tired than softened at the end of an Opera. But he confessed that they

might happen to miss the Opera books a little, because, as most of his profession could make a shift to read the English version at least, they found, in those incomparable dramas, sentiments proper for all situations, which might not otherwise have occurred to them, and which, by emphatical signs and looks, they could apply to the proper objects; insomuch that he had often known very pretty sentimental conversations carried on through a whole opera by these references to the book.

Having thus shown the power and effects of music both among the ancients and the moderns, and the good and ill uses which may be made of it, I shall submit it to persons wiser than myself, what is to be done in this important crisis. I look upon Operas to have been the great national establishment of music, and I am persuaded that innumerable sects will rise from their ruins, and break into various conventicles of vocal and instrumental, which, if not attended to, may prove of ill consequence.

Several years later, after Italian opera had been restored in London, Lord Chesterfield contributed a humorous article to the 14 November 1754 issue of *The World*.

I am sensible that Italian Operas have frequently been the objects of the ridicule of many of our greatest wits, and viewed in one light only, perhaps not without some reason. But as I consider all public diversions singly with regard to the effects which they may have upon the morals and manners of the public, I confess I respect the Italian Operas as the most innocent of any.

For one thing, he suggests, humorously bringing up the old objection which was seriously argued forty years earlier, no one understands the words anyway.

Were what is called the poetry of it intelligible in itself, it would not be understood by one in fifty of a British audience; but I believe that even an Italian of common candor will confess, that he does not understand one word of it. It is not the intention of the thing, for should the ingenious author of the words, by mistake, put any meaning into them, he would, to a certain degree, check and cramp the genius of the composer of the music, who perhaps might think himself obliged to adapt his sounds to the sense: whereas now he is at liberty to scatter indiscriminately, among the Kings, Queens, heroes, and heroines, his Adagios, his Allegros, his Pathetics, his Chromatics, and his Jigs. It would also have been a restraint upon the actors and actresses, who might possibly have attempted to form their action upon the meaning of their parts; but as it is, if they do but seem, by turns to be angry and sorry in the two first acts, and very merry in the last scene of the last, they are sure to meet with the deserved applause.

Signor Metastasio attempted some time ago a very dangerous innovation. He tried gently to throw some sense into his Operas, but it did not take: the consequences were obvious, and nobody knew where they would stop.

Another virtue of Italian opera which Chesterfield advances, is that by the time it is over everyone is so tired, they go home to bed and avoid getting into trouble.

The most delightful portion of Chesterfield's article is his discussion of the Italian singers, their manners and their impositions on English society.

Having thus rescued these excellent musical dramas from the unjust ridicule which some people of vulgar and illiberal tastes have endeavored to throw upon them, I must proceed, and do justice to the Virtuosos and Virtuosas who perform them. But I believe it will be necessary for me to premise, for the sake of many of my English readers, that VIRTU among the modern Italians signifies nothing less than what VIRTUS did among the ancient ones, or what VIRTUE signifies among us; on the contrary, I might say that it signifies almost everything else. Consequently those respectable titles of Virtuoso and Virtuosa have not the least relation to the moral characters of the parties. They mean only that those persons, endowed some by nature, and some by art, with good voices, have from their infancy devoted their time and labor to the various combinations of seven notes, a study that must unquestionably have formed their minds, enlarged their notions, and have rendered them most agreeable and instructive companions, and as such, I observe that they are justly solicited, received, and cherished by people of the first distinction.

As these illustrious personages come over here with no sordid view of profit, but merely *per far piacer a la nobilita Inglese*, that is, to oblige the English nobility, they are exceedingly good and condescending to such of the said English nobility, and even gentry, as are desirous to contract an intimacy with them. They will, for a word's speaking, dine, sup, or pass the whole day with people of a certain condition, and perhaps sing or play, if civilly requested. Nay, I have known many of them so good as to pass two or three months of the summer at the country-seats of some of their noble friends, and thereby mitigate the horrors of the country and mansion-house, to my lady and her daughters. I have been assured by many of their chief patrons and patronesses, that they are all the best creatures in the world; and from the time of Signor Nicolini down to this day, I have constantly heard the several great performers, such as Farinelli, Carestini, Monticelli, Gaffarielli, as well as the Signore Cuzzoni, Faustina, etc., much more praised for their affability, the gentleness of their manners, and all the good qualities of the head and heart, than for either their musical skill or execution.[11] I have even known these, their social virtues, lay their protectors and protectresses under great difficulties, how to reward such distinguished merit. But benefit-nights luckily came in to their assistance, and gave them an opportunity of insinuating, with all due regard, into the hands of the performer, in lieu of a ticket, a considerable bank-bill, a gold snuff-box, a diamond-ring, or some such trifle. It is to be hoped, that the illustrious Signor Farinelli has not yet forgot the many instances he experienced of British munificence, for it is certain that many private families *still remember them.*

He closes with a common objection that the Italian singers take all this money home to Italy.

Some of them, when they have got ten or fifteen thousand pounds here, unkindly withdraw themselves, and purchase estates in land in their own countries.

---

11 On the contrary, of course, these two ladies were infamous for their fights on stage before the audience.

EDUCATIONAL MUSIC

We have seen in the novels of this period, testimony that music was considered a necessary part of the education of young ladies. A similar reflection is found in the *Tatler* for 23 May 1710, which compares the cultural education of a young lady and her brother.

> This state of her life is infinitely more delightful than that of her brother at the same age. While she is entertained with learning melodious airs at her spinet, is led round a room in the most complaisant manner to a Fiddle, or is entertained with applauses of her beauty and perfection …

It is in this regard that a fictional letter to the editor of the *Tatler*, for 18 November 1710, carries the question by a father whether it is necessary to his daughter's education that he pay for lessons on the spinet, even though 'I know she has no ear.' This also carries an implication, of course, of how common this practice must have been.

The *Spectator* for 11 April 1711, carries a fictitious advertisement for a school for young women, promising among other things that 'those that have good voices may be taught to sing the newest opera Airs.' The *Tatler* for 8 October 1709, carries a fictional announcement of music instruction for gentlemen.

> This is to give notice to all ingenious Gentlemen in and about the Cities of London and Westminster, who have a mind to be instructed in the noble Sciences of Musick, Poetry, and Politicks, That they repair to the Smyrna Coffee-house in Pall-mall, betwixt the hours of eight and ten at night, where they may be instructed gratis, with elaborate Essays by word of mouth on all or any of the above mentioned Arts. The Disciples are to prepare their bodies with three dishes of Bohea, and purge their brains with two pinches of snuff.

Finally, the *Spectator* for 9 July 1711, mentions an 'itinerant Singing-Master' who apparently went from village to village teaching the melodies used for the Psalms.

FUNCTIONAL MUSIC

A correspondent to the *Spectator* issue of 28 March 1712, complains about the introduction of lighter music in the church.

> For a great many of our Church Musicians being related to the theater, they have, in imitation of these epilogues, introduced in their farewell Voluntaries a sort of Musick quite foreign to the design of church services, to the great prejudice of well-disposed people. Those fingering gentlemen should be informed, that they ought to suit their Airs to the place and business; and that the musician is obliged to keep to the text as much as the preacher … For when the preacher has often, with great piety and art enough handled his subject … I have found in my self, and in the

> rest of the pew, good thoughts and dispositions, they have been all in a moment dissipated by a merry Jig from the organ loft … Pray Sir do what you can to put a stop to these growing evils.

Addison, writing in the *Spectator* for 14 June 1712, wishes as much attention could be given to the improvement of church music as has been devoted to the music of the stage in recent years. He wonders why the excellent texts, in both Hebrew and English, available to composers do not inspire them to greater efforts. As we have seen before, Addison is thinking of the purpose of music being to support language and finds its virtue there, rather than from any inherent qualities.

> Since we have such a treasury of words, so beautiful in themselves, and so proper for the Airs of Musick, I cannot but wonder that persons of distinction should give so little attention and encouragement to that kind of Musick, which would have its foundation in Reason, and which would improve our virtue in proportion as it raised our delight. The passions that are excited by ordinary compositions, generally flow from such silly and absurd occasions, that a man is ashamed to reflect upon them seriously; but the fear, the love, the sorrow, the indignation that are awakened in the mind by hymns and anthems, make the heart better, and proceed from such causes as are altogether reasonable and praise-worthy. Pleasure and duty go hand in hand, and the greater our satisfaction is, the greater is our religion.

Addison then briefly reviews the use of music in the Old Testament and in the religious rites of the ancient Greeks, after which he wishes,

> Had we frequent entertainments of this nature among us, they would not a little purify and exalt our passions, give our thoughts a proper turn, and cherish those divine impulses in the soul, which every one feels that has not stifled them by sensual and immoderate pleasures.
>
> Musick, when thus applied, raises noble hints in the mind of the hearer, and fills it with great conceptions. It strengthens devotion, and advances praise into rapture.

Steele published a fictional letter to the editor of the *Spectator* of 7 October 1712, which describes a gentleman attending a church service in London in which he reports on 'a young lady in the very bloom of youth and beauty, dressed in the most elegant manner imaginable.' Except for the fact that she chose to stand during the entire service, everyone noticed that she was the very picture of modesty, goodness, sweetness and 'ardent devotion.'

> Well, now the organ was to play a voluntary, and she was so skillful in Musick, and so touched with it, that she kept time, not only with some motion of her head, but also with a different air in her countenance. When the Musick was strong and bold, she looked exalted, but serious; when lively and airy, she was smiling and gracious; when the notes were more soft and languishing, she was kind and full of pity. When she had now made it visible to the whole congregation, by her motion and ear, that she could dance, and she wanted now only to inform us that she could sing too, when the Psalm was given out, her voice was distinguished above all the rest, or rather people did not exert their own in order to hear her. Never was any heard so sweet and so strong.

The organist observed it, and he thought fit to play to her only, and she swelled every note; when she found she had thrown us all out, and had the last verse to herself in such a manner, as the whole congregation was intent upon her, in the same manner as you see in cathedrals they are on the person who sings alone the anthem.

Nothing is more familiar in Europe still today than to find street entertainers employing a drum to draw a crowd. Thus, it is no surprise to find in the *Spectator* for 8 November 1714,

The celebration of this night's solemnity was opened by the obstreperous joy of drummers, who, with their parchment thunder, gave a signal for the appearance of the mob under their several classes and denominations.

ENTERTAINMENT MUSIC

Judging by these journals, the most conspicuous amateur musicians were lawyers. An anonymous letter to the editor of the *Tatler*, for 4 March 1710, complains that lawyers drink all morning and engage in singing to the dulcimer and violin late at night. Addison adds that he knew two law students who had studied the oboe and concludes by recommending a civic law ordering that 'no Retainers to the Law, with Dulcimer, Violin, or any other Instrument, in any Tavern within a Furlong of the Inns of Court, shall sing any Tune, or pretended Tune whatsoever.' Another complaint is made about lawyers who study the oboe and are 'proficients in Wind-Musick,' in the *Spectator* for 16 August 1711. Steele, in the *Spectator* for 16 January 1712, presents a fictitious letter by a mistress to a lawyer:

This man makes on the violin a certain jiggish noise to which I dance, and when that is over I sing to him some loose Air that has more wantonness than Musick in it.

In earlier times, barbers were frequently mentioned as amateur musicians, but now we find only one reference, in the *Spectator* for 30 July 1712, which mentions a barber whose fiddle was broken.

There are frequent references in these journals to the public places where the middle and lower classes enjoyed entertainment music. Typical among these are the *Spectator* for 23 May 1711, which mentions the singing of Catches 'at all Hours' alternating with drinking and smoking in a tavern and the issue for 21 July 1712, in which Steele mentions visiting an entertainment of 'the lower Order of Britons' at the Bear-Garden, where he heard, among other things, a performance by two disabled drummers.[12]

The common fiddler was still associated with the last of the wandering minstrels and was the subject of much derision. In the *Tatler* for 18 August 1709, for example, the fiddler

---

12 The *Spectator* for 30 April 1712, discusses Lapland and mentions, unfortunately without detail, 'the famous stories of their drums.'

is listed together with 'Pimps, Footmen and Lackeys.' The *Spectator* for 17 May 1711, refers to 'Fidlers' playing for a dance, and the issue for 26 February 1712, mentions 'some Fiddles heard in the Street.'

In the *Spectator* for 26 November 1711, we find mention of beggars singing a song called, 'The Merry Beggars.'

BIBLIOGRAPHY

Adams, Robert. *Ben Jonson's Plays and Masques*. New York: Norton, 1979.
Addison, Joseph and Richard Steele. *The Spectator*. London: Dent; New York, Dutton, 1945.
Akenside, Mark. *The Poetical Works of Mark Akenside*. Edited by Alexander Dyce. London: Bell and Daldy, 1845.
Ashmole, Elias. *The Autobiographical Notes of Elias Ashmole*. Edited by Conrad Hermann Josten. Oxford: Clarendon Press, 1966.
Ashton, John. *Social Life in the Reign of Queen Anne*. London: Chatto & Windus, 1911.
Ashton, Robert. *James I*. London: Hutchinson, 1969.
Aubrey, John. *Brief Lives*. Edited by O. Dick. Ann Arbor: University of Michigan Press, 1957
Avison, Charles. *An Essay on Musical Expression* [London, 1753]. New York: Broude Reprint, 1967.
Bacon, Francis. *The Works of Francis Bacon*. Edited by James Spedding. Cambridge: Cambridge University Press, 1869.
Barry, Great. *A Discourse of Military Discipline*. Brussels: Mommart, 1634.
Beaumont and Fletcher. *Complete Plays*. Cambridge: University Press, 1912.
Bentley, Richard. *The Works of Richard Bentley, D. D.* Edited by Alexander Dyce. London: MacPherson, 1838.
Berkeley, George. *The Works of George Berkeley, Bishop of Cloyne*. Edited by A. Luce. London: Nelson, 1964.
Bridge, Joseph, 'Town Waits and their tunes.' *Proceedings of the Musical Association* (London, 1927–1928).
Browne, Thomas. *Sir Thomas Browne's Works*. Edited by Simon Wilkin. London: Pickering, 1836.
Bryant, Arthur. *King Charles II*. London: Collins, 1955.
Bunyan, John. *The Works of John Bunyan*. Edited by George Offor. London: Blackie and Son, 1853.
Burney, Charles. *General History of Music*. New York: Dover, 1957.
Burrows, Donald, 'London: Commercial Wealth and Cultural Expansion,' in *The Late Baroque Era*. Englewood Cliffs: Prentice Hall, 1994.
Burton, Robert. *The Anatomy of Melancholy*. Edited by Floyd Dell. New York: Tudor Publishing Company, 1938.
Butler, Charles. *The Principles of Musik in Singing and Setting* [1636]. New York: Da Capo Press, 1970.
Butler, Samuel. *Characters*. Edited by Charles W. Daves. Cleveland, Press of Case Western Reserve University, 1970.
Butler, Samuel. *The Poetical Works of Samuel Butler*. New York: Appleton, 1854.
Cavendish, Margaret. *Sociable Letters* [1664]. Menston: The Scolar Press, 1969.
Cleland, James. *The Institution of a Young Nobleman*. Oxford, 1607.
Congreve, William. *The Complete Works of William Congreve*. New York: Russell & Russell, 1964.
Cowley, Abraham. *The Complete Works of Abraham Cowley*. Edited by Alexander Grosart. New York: AMS Press, 1967.
Crashaw, Richard. *The Complete Poetry of Richard Crashaw*. Edited by George Williams. New York: New York University Press, 1972.
Crewdson, Henry Alastair Ferguson. *The Worshipful Company of Musicians*. London: Charles Knight, 1971.
Croft-Murray, Edward, 'The Wind-Band in England.' in *Music & Civilisation* (London, 1980).

Dart, Thurston, 'The Repertory of the Royal Wind Music.' *The Galpin Society Journal* 11 (May, 1958): 70–77, http://www.jstor.org/stable/842105.

Dauney, William. *Ancient Scottish Melodies*. Edinburgh: Edinburgh Print. & Pub. Co, 1838.

Davey, H. *History of English Music*. London, 1921.

Defoe, Daniel. *A Journal of the Plague Year*. Garden City, New York: Doubleday, Doran, 1940.

_____, *The Works of Daniel Defoe*. New York: Henson, 1905.

Dekker, Thomas. *The Dramatic Works of Thomas Dekker*. Edited by Fredson Bowers. Cambridge: University Press, 1955.

_____, *The Non-Dramatic Works of Thomas Dekker*. Edited by Alexander Grosart. New York: Russell & Russell, 1963.

Digges, Thomas. *An Arithmetical Warlike Treatise*. London: Richard Field, 1590.

Donne, John. 'A Sermon preached at Pauls Crosse,' in *Five Sermons*. Menston: Scolar Press, 1970.

_____, 'Paradoxes and Problems,' in *Selected Prose*. Edited by Helen Gardner. Oxford: Clarendon Press, 1967.

_____, *Devotions Upon Emergent Occasion*. Edited by Anthony Raspa. Montreal: McGill-Queen's University Press, 1975.

_____, *The Complete Poetry of John Donne*. Edited by John T. Shawcross. New York: New York University Press, 1968.

Donnington, Robert. *The Interpretation of Early Music*. New York: Faber and Faber, 1964.

Dryden, John. *The Works of John Dryden*. Edited by Edward Hooker. Berkeley: University of California Press, 1956.

_____, *The Works of John Dryden*. Edited by Walter Scott. London: William Miller, 1808.

Du Praissac. *The Art of Warre*. Cambridge: Roger Daniel, printer to that famous Uniuersitie, 1639.

Dunlap, Rhodes. *The Poems of Thomas Carew*. Oxford: Clarendon Press, 1964.

Durant, Will and Ariel. *The Age of Louis XIV*. New York: Simon and Schuster, 1963.

Durant, Will. *The Age of Reason Begins*. New York: Simon and Schuster, 1961.

Earle, John. *Microcosmography* [1628]. St. Clair Shores: Scholarly Press, 1971.

Elton, Richard. *The Compleat Body of the Art Military*. London; Robert Leybourne, 1650.

Evelyn, John. *The Diary of John Evelyn*. Oxford: Clarendon Press, 1955.

Farmer, Henry. *Handel's Kettledrums*. London: Hinrichsen, 1965.

_____, *Military Music*. London: William Reeves, 1912.

Farquhar, George. *The Complete Works of George Farquhar*. New York: Gorian Press, 1967.

Fielding, Henry. *The Works of Henry Fielding*. London: J.M. Dent & Co., 1893–99.

Fletcher, Giles and Fletcher, Phineas. *Giles and Phineas Fletcher Poetical Works*. Edited by Frederick Boas. Cambridge: University Press, 1909.

Freeman, Rosemary. *English Emblem Books*. Menston, Yorkshire: Scolar Press, 1968.

Fuller, Thomas. *The Holy State and the Profance State* [1642]. Edited by Maximilian Walten. New York: AMS Press, 1966.

Gay, John. *The Works of John Gay*. London: Edward Jeffery, 1745.

Gildon, Charles. *The Life of Mr. Thomas Betterton, the Late Eminent Tragedian* [1710]. London: Frank Cass Reprint, 1970.

Gray, Thomas. *Correspondence of Thomas Gray*. Oxford: Clarendon Press, 1971.

Grebanier, Bernard. *English Literature*. Great Neck: Barron, 1959.

Grove, George. *The New Grove Dictionary of Music and Musicians*. Edited by Stanley Sadie. London: Macmillan, 1980.
Hall, Joseph. *The Works of Joseph Hall, D. D.* Edited by Philip Wynter. New York: AMS Press, 1969.
Harris, James. *Three Treatises*. London: H. Woodfall, Jun., 1744.
Harvey, William. *Lectures on the Whole of Anatomy*. Translated by C. D. O'Malley. Berkeley: University of California Press, 1961.
_____. *The Works of William Harvey*. Edited by Robert Willis. New York: Johnson Reprint Corp., 1965.
Hawkins, John. *A General History of the Science and Practice of Music* [1776]. New York: Dover Reprint, 1963.
Herbert, Edward. *Occasional Verses*. Menston: The Scolar Press, 1969.
Herbert, George. *The Poems of George Herbert*. Edited by Ernest Rhys. London: Walter Scott, 1885.
Herrick, Robert. *The Poetical Works of Robert Herrick*. Edited by L. C. Martin. Oxford: Clarendon Press, 1963.
Heywood, Thomas. *The Dramatic Works of Thomas Heywood*. New York: Russell & Russell, 1964.
Hibbert, Christopher. *Charles I*. New York: Harper, 1968.
Hobbes, Thomas. *The English Works of Thomas Hobbes*. Edited by William Molesworth. London: Bohn, 1839.
Holaday, Allan. *The Plays of George Chapman: the Comedies*. Urbana: University of Illinois Press, 1970.
Holman, Peter, 'London: Commonwealth and Restoration,' in *The Early Baroque Era*. Englewood Cliffs: Prentice Hall, 1994.
Hume, David. *David Hume, The Philosophical Works*. Aalen: Scientia Verlag, 1964.
_____. *The Letters of David Hume*. Edited by J. Grieg. Oxford: Clarendon, 1932.
Hutcheson, Francis. *An Essay on the Nature and Conduct of the Passions*. London: A. Ward, 1742.
_____. *An Inquiry Into the Original of our Ideas of Beauty and Virtue*. London: Thomas Gent, 1726.
_____. *Francis Hutcheson On Human Nature*. Edited by Thomas Mautner. Cambridge: University Press, 1993.
James I, King of England. *Basilicon Doron* [1599]. Menston: Scolar Press, 1969.
_____. *New Poems of James I*. Edited by Allan Westcott. New York: AMS Press, 1966.
Jones, Paul. *The Household of a Tudor Nobleman*. Urbana: University of Illinois, 1918.
Jonson, Ben. *The Complete Poetry of Ben Jonson*. Edited by William Hunter. New York: Norton, 1963.
Lafontaine, Henry. *The King's Music*. New York: Da Capo Press, 1973.
Lee, Nathaniel. *The Works of Nathaniel Lee*. Metuchen: Scarecrow Reprints, 1968.
Locke, John. *The Correspondance of John Locke*. Edited by E. S. De Beer. Oxford: Clarendon, 1976.
_____. *The Works of John Locke*. London: 1823; Reprinted in Aalen: Scientia Verlag, 1963.
Lovelace, Richard. *The Poems of Richard Lovelace*. Edited by C. H. Wilkinson. Oxford: Clarendon Press, 1930.
Mace, Thomas. *Musick's Monument* [1676]. Paris: Éditions du Centre National de la Recherche Scientifique, 1966.
Magalotti, Lorenzo. *Relazione d'Inghilterra* [1668]. Waterloo, Ont.: Wilfrid Laurier University Press, 1980.
Marston, John. *The Works of John Marston*. Edited by A. H. Bullen. London: Nimmo, 1887.
Marvell, Andrew. *The Complete Works of Andrew Marvell*. New York: AMS Press, 1966.
McGrady, Richard, 'The Court Trumpeters of Charles I and Charles II.' *The Music Review* 35 (1974): 223-30.
Middleton, Thomas. *The Works of Thomas Middleton*. New York: AMS Press, 1964.
Milton, John. *The Works of John Milton*. Edited by Frank Patterson. New York: Columbia University Press, 1931-1938.
Morgenstern, Sam. *Composers on Music*. New York: Pantheon, 1956.
Morley, Henry. *Ideal Commonwealths*. Port Washington: Kennikat Press, 1968.
Nichols, John. *The Progresses of King James the First*. London: J. B. Nichols, 1828.

Newton, Isaac. *The Correspondence of Isaac Newton*. Edited by H. W. Turnbull. Cambridge: University Press, 1959.
____. *Unpublished Scientific Papers of Isaac Newton*. Edited by Rupert Hall. Cambridge: University Press, 1962.
Nichols, John. *The Progresses of Queen Elizabeth*. London, 1805.
North, Roger. *Memoirs of Music*. Edited by Edward Rimbault. London: Bell, 1846.
____. *The Musicall Gramarian*. Oxford: Oxford University Press, 1925.
Oldham, John. *The Works of John Oldham*. London: Bettenham, 1722.
Ornsby, G., ed., 'The Correspondence of John Cosdin, D. D.' *Surtee Society* (London, 1869).
Overbury, Thomas. *The 'Conceited Newes' of Sir Thomas Overbury and His Friends*. Edited by James Savage. Gainesville: Scholars' Facsimiles, 1968.
Panoff, Peter. *Militärmusik*. Berlin: K. Siegismund, 1944.
Parker, Willis, L. *Samuel Pepys' Diary*. New York: Illustrated Editions Co., 1932.
Parrott, Andrew, 'Grett and Solompne Singing.' *Early Music* 6 no. 2 (April, 1978): 182–187, doi: 10.1093/earlyj/6.2.182.
Penn, William. *The Select Works of William Penn*. London: William Phillips, 1825.
Pepys, Samuel *Private Correspondence of Samuel Pepys*. Edited by J. Tanner. London: Bell and Sons, 1926.
____. *The Pepys Ballads*. Cambridge: Harvard University Press, 1929.
____. *The Samuel Pepys Diary*. Berkeley: Unviersity of California Press, 1970–1983.
Playford, John. *An Introduction to the Skill of Music* [1674]. Ridgewood: Gregg Press, 1966.
Pope, Alexander. *The Works of Alexander Pope*. New York: Gordian Press, 1967.
Prior, Matthew. *The Literary Works of Matthew Prior*. Oxford: Clarendon, 1959.
Reese, Gustave. *Music in the Renaissance*. New York: Norton, 1959.
Richardson, Samuel. *The Novels of Samuel Richardson*. London: Chapman & Hall, 1902.
Royce, Josiah. *The Spirit of Modern Philosophy*. Boston: Houghton, Mifflin, 1892.
Rymer, Thomas. *The Critical Works of Thomas Rymer*. Edited by Curt Zimansky. New Haven: Yale University Press, 1956.
Sackville, Charles. *The Poems of Charles Sackville*. New York: Garland, 1979.
Savile, George. *The Complete Works of George Savile*. Edited by Walter Raleigh. Oxford: Clarendon, 1912.
Sedley, Charles. *The Poetical and Dramatic Works of Sir Charles Sedley*. New York: AMS Press, 1969.
Sévigné, Françoise Marguerite. *Letters of Madame de Sévigné*. Edited by Richard Aldington. London: Routledge, 1937.
Shaftesbury, Anathony Ashley Cooper. *Characteristics of Men, Manners, Opinions and Times*. London: Purser, 1737–1738.
Shenstone, William. *Letters of William Shenstone*. Minneapolis: University of Minnesota Press, 1939.
____. *Men and Manners*. Boston: Houghton Mifflin, 1927.
____. *The Poetical Works of William Shenstone*. Edinburgh: James Nichol, 1854.
Simpson, Christopher. *A Compendium of Practical Music* [1667]. Oxford: Blackwell, 1970.
____. *Division-Violist* [1654]. London: Curwen, 1965, facsimile.
Smart, Peter. *A Catalogue of Superstitious Innovations*. London: Hunscott, 1642.
____. *A Sermon Preached in the Cathedrall Church of Durham, July 7, 1628*. London: Bernard Alsop and Thomas Fawcet, 1640.
Spectator, The. Edited by Donald Bond. Oxford: Clarendon Press, 1965.

Springell, Francis. *Connoisseur & Diplomat*. London: Maggs Bros., 1963.
Standford, Francis. *The History of the Coronation of…James II*. London, 1687.
Steele, Richard and Joseph Addison. *The Tatler*. London: Dent; New York, Dutton, 1953.
Steele, Richard. *The Occasional Verse of Richard Steele*. Oxford: Clarendon, 1952.
_____. *The Plays of Richard Steele*. Oxford: Clarendon Press, 1971.
Suckling, John. *The Works of Sir John Suckling*. Edited by Hamilton Thompson. New York: Russell & Russell, 1964.
Swift, Jonathan. *Satires and Personal Writings of Jonathan Swift*. London: Oxford University Press, 1956.
_____. *The Poetical Works of Jonathan Swift*. London: Bell and Daldy, n.d.
_____. *The Prose Works of Jonathan Swift*. Oxford: Blackwell, 1957.
Temple, William. *Five Miscellaneous Essays by Sir William Temple*. Edited by Samuel Monk. Ann Arbor: University of Michigan Press, 1963.
Thomson, James. *The Poetical Works of James Thomson*. London: Bell and Daldy, c. 1860.
_____. *James Thomson, Letters and Documents*. Lawrence: University of Kansas Press, 1958.
Traherne, Thomas. *Thomas Traherne, Centuries, Poems and Thanksgivings*. Oxford: Clarendon Press, 1958.
Turner, James. *Pallas Armata*. London: M.W. for Richard Chiswell, 1683
Vanbrugh, John. *The Complete Works of John Vanbrugh*. London: Nonesuch Press, 1927.
Vaughan, Henry. *The Works of Henry Vaughan*. Edited by L. C. Martin. Oxford: Clarendon Press, 1957.
Waller, Edmund. *Edmund Waller, Poems*. Menston: Scolar Press, 1971.
Walls, Peter, 'London, 1603–49,' in *The Early Baroque Era*. Englewood Cliffs: Prentice Hall, 1994.
Walton, Izaak. *The Compleat Angler*. London: Oxford University Press, 1935.
Ward, Ned. *The London Spy*. Edited by Arthur Hayward. New York: Doran, 1927.
Weiss, Piero. *Letters of Composers Through Six Centuries*. Philadelphia: Chilton, 1967.
Wilson, John. *Roger North on Music*. London: Novello, 1959.
Wither, George. *Works of George Wither*. New York: B. Franklin, 1967.
Woodfill, Walter. *Musicians in English Society*. Princeton: Princeton Univeristy Press, 1953.
Wycherley, William. *The Complete Works of William Wycherley*. Edited by Montague Summers. New York: Russell & Russell, 1964.
Young, Edward. *Edward Young: The Complete Works*. Hildesheim: Olms, 1968.

INDEX

A

Adam, first man, 215
Addison, Joseph, 1672–1719, English poet and writer, 10, 261 310 fn. 16, 354ff, 360, 364, 371, 445ff
Akenside, Mark, 1721–1770, English poet, 347, 351, 381
Alfred the Great, Anglo-Saxon king, and musician, 849–899 AD, 139
Allegre, Lorenzo, 17th century London composer, 95
Anne, Queen of England, 9
Aristotle, 32, 42, 65, 134ff, 141, 266, 327, 417
Aristoxenus, ancient writer on music, 271
Arundel, Earl of, in 1636, 5
Aston, Anthony, late Baroque writer, 35
Avison, Charles, 1709–1770, English organist, philosopher, 21ff, 23, 26ff, 29ff, 31, 37ff

B

Baberini, Cardinal, 139
Bacon, Francis, 1561–1626, English philosopher, 77, 223
Banister, John, 1625–1679, 9, 434
Baptist, John, harpsichordist, 422
Baptista, Seignor, Italian composer, 436
Beaumont, Francis, 1584–1616 and John Fletcher, 1579–1625, Eng. playwrights, 159, 160ff, 163ff, 165, 168ff, 170ff, 173ff, 175ff, 180, 181, 182, 183ff, 185, 186ff, 188ff, 193ff, 198ff, 201, 206ff
Begabredus, ancient Anglo minstrel, 139
Behn, Aphra, 1640–1689 English playwright, 312ff, 315ff, 317, 319ff
Bentley, Richard, 1662–1742, English writer, 246, fn. 85
Berkeley, George, 1685–1753, English philosopher, 258ff
Betterton, Thomas, 1635–1710, English actor, 304, 306, 454
Blow, John, 340, 356
Bononcini, Italian singer, 26 fn. 16, 367, 386
Brathwaite, Richard, 1588–1673, English writer on manners, 3
Britton, Thomas, organizer of concerts, 9
Browne, Edward, son to Thomas Browne, 220
Browne, Thomas, 1605–1682, English physician and writer, 209, 210, 211, 214, 217ff
Browne, William, 1591–1643, English poet, 96
Bunyan, John, 1628–1688, Puritan preacher, writer, 57ff, 62ff, 65, 69, 73ff, 279
Burney, Charles, 1726–1814, English music historian, 35ff
Burton, Robert, 1577–1640, Vicar at St. Thomas, Oxford, 57ff, 63ff, 66, 70ff
Busino, Horatio, Venetian ambassador in London, 1618, 2
Butler, Charles, d. 1747, English philosopher on music, 22, 27, 32, 35
Butler, Samuel, 1612–1680. English poet, 362ff, 368, 372, 419, 427ff
Byrd, William, 1540–1623, great English composer, 28, 32ff

C

Caldara, 26, fn 16
Caporale, cellist in London, 11
Carew, Thomas, 1594–1639, English Cabalier poet, 107, 109
Carissimi, composer from Rome, 433
Castelvetro, Spanish playwright, 136
Castiglione, Baldassare, 1478–1529, Italian author of *The Courtier*, 3
Cavendish, Margaret, 1624–1673, English writer, 410, 416, 420
Cavendish, William, Duke of Newcastle, 3
Chapman, George, 1559–1634, English playwright, 164ff, 166ff, 167, 172, 180ff, 182ff, 201ff, 203
Charles I, 1600–1649, King of England, 4ff, 138, 353
Charles II, 1630–1685, King of England, 6ff, 11, 18, 223, 337
Charles, Thomas, 17th century English composer, 95
Chaucer, early English poet, 321

Cheek, Mr., composer, 314, fn. 29
Chesterfield, Earl of (Philip Stanhope), 1694–1773, English writer, 407ff, 410, 416, 424, 427, 459ff
Christian IV, 1577–1648, King of Denmark, 1
Christmas, Mr., best trumpeter in England, 220
Clayton, Thomas, 1673–1725, early English opera composer, 10
Cleland, James, 17th century English writer on manners, 4
Collins, John, 17th century English physicist on music, 239
Congreve, William, 1670–1729, English playwright, 305, 307ff, 310, 312, 314ff, 319ff, 347, 356, 360, 370, 399, 401
Constantine V, 139
Cooke, Henry, 1615–1672, English composer, 439ff, 442
Corelli, Italian composer, 26 fn. 16, 45, 279, 386, 419
Cowley, Abraham, 1618–1667, English poet, philosopher, 64ff, 94, 96, 99, 111, 114ff
Crashaw, Richard, 1613–1649, English Metaphysical School poet, 99, 106, 108, 114, 116ff, 123ff, 126
Cromwell, Oliver, 1599–1658, English civilian leader, 5ff, 223, 353
Cumberland, Earl of, 3
Curtes, Mr., 17th century English composer, 95

D

Dato, Carolo, Florentine noble, 133
Davenant, William, 1606–1668, English poet and playwright, 10, 328, 367, 437, 440
David, of the Old Testament, 34
Defoe, Daniel, 1659–1731, 385ff, 389, 401, 405
Dekker, Thomas, 1572–1632, English playwright and poet, 100, 155ff, 159, 161, 163, 165 167ff, 171, 174ff, 178ff, 181, 182, 184, 185, 188, 190, 195, 197, 200, 201, 204ff, 207, 210, 212, 213, 215, 217, 218ff, 220ff, 438
Delany, Patrick, poet, 352
Diamantina, violinist, 425
Donne, John, 1573–1631, English philosopher, Dean of St. Paul's, 58ff, 66, 72, 74, 93, 95, 100, 102, 105, 112
Dowland, Robert, 1591–1641, lutenist, son of John Dowland, 4
Draghi, Giovanni, composer, 334
Dryden, John, 1631–1700, English poet, 270, 321, 363

E

Earle, John, 1600–1665, English writer, Chaplain to Charles II in exile, 212, 216, 218, 219, 221
Eccles, John, composer, 314 fn. 29, 356
Edward VI, 17
Elizabeth I, 17
Etherege, George, 1633–1691, English playwright, 309, 311
Evelyn, John, 1620–1706, English diarist, 18, 421ff

F

Farquhar, George, 1678–1707, English playwright, 305ff, 314, 318, 319, 393
Faustina, famous soprano and wife of Hasse, 422
Ferrabosco, Alfonso, the younger, 1575–1628, English composer, 10, 109, 202
Fielding, Henry, 1707–1754, English novelist, 391ff
Finger, Mr., composer, 314, fn. 29
Fletcher, Phineas, 1582–1650, English poet, 95ff, 96ff, 123, 286
Flud, Robert, 1574–1637, English scientist, 24
Ford, John, 1586–c. 1639, English lawyer and playwright, 158
Francisco, Signor, harpsichordist, 421
Fuller, Thomas, 1608–1661, Chaplain to Charles II, and writer, 210ff, 213, 216

G

Galen, 2nd century physician, 59
Galileo, 129, 230
Gay, John, 1685–1732, English pjoet and playwright, 351ff, 360ff, 365, 374, 423, 445, 458
Geminiani, Italian composer in London, 386
George I, 9
George II, 353
Gibbons, Orlando, 1583–1625, English composer, 34
Gildon, Charles, 1665–1724, English biographer and critic, 274ff
Grabu, Louis, d. 1694 Spanish-French composer in London, 337, 339, 435
Gray, Thomas, 1716–1771, English poet and writer, 422, 424ff, 429
Gregory, David, 17th century English professor at Oxford, 432

Grimaldi, Nicolino, Italian singer, 364, 367
Guido, medieval writer on music, 272
Gwynn, Nell, 1650–1687, English actress, 6

H

Hadly, best flageolet player in England, 220
Hall, Joseph, 1574–1656, Bishop, Church of England, 60, 63, 65ff, 69ff
Handel, Georg, 1685–1759, great German composer, 9, 26 fn. 16, 32, 36, 362, 367, 386, 388, 396, 413, 456, 459, 460
Harington, Sir John, 1561–1612, English noble, writer, 2
Harrington, James, 1611–1677, English politician, writer, 61, 75
Harris, James, 1709–1780, English philosopher, 300ff
Harvey, William, 1578–1657, English physician, 59, 62, 66, 68
Hasse, 26, fn. 16
Hawkins, John, 1719–1789, English writer, 9, 303
Herbert, Edward, Lord of Cherbery, d. 1648, English poet, 95, 98
Herbert, George, 1593–1633, English Rector near Salisbury and poet, 101ff, 107ff, 110, 119, 126
Herrick, Robert, 1591–1674, English Cavalier poet, 95ff, 97ff, 100, 102ff, 105, 111, 114, 116ff, 121, 123, 126,
Heywood, Thomas, 1575–1648, English playwright, 156, 160, 167, 174, 179, 181, 184ff, 187ff, 190, 196, 197, 202
Hingston, John, 1612–1683, court organist, 433, 435

Hobbes, Thomas, 1588–1679, English Restoration philosopher, 223, 263ff
Hodgson, Mrs., singer, 314, fn. 29
Homer, 141
Hook, English composer, 434
Hooke, Robert, 17th century English physicist on music, 241
Horace, ancient Roman pjoet, 136, 266, 269, 272, 374
Hume, David, 1711–1776, English philosopher, 245ff
Humfrey, Pelham, organist, 431, 435ff, 442
Hutcheson, Francis, 1694–1746, Irish philosopher, 263, 290ff

I

Ignatius, third bishop of Antioch after Peter, 139

J

James I, King of England, 1603–1625, 1, 68 (as writer), 107, 204
James II, 8, 353, 431
Johnson, Samuel, 258
Jonson, Ben, 1572–1637, English playwright, poet, 2, 94, 98ff, 103ff, 105ff, 109, 112, 156ff, 159ff, 163ff, 165ff, 169, 171, 183ff, 190, 192ff, 196, 198ff, 202, 206ff, 286

K

Kercherus, Athan., German philosopher, 116
Killigrew, Thomas, 17th century producer of opera in London, 436, 439
Kneller, Godfrey, 1646–1723, English painter, 323, 332, 340
Knight, Mrs., soprano, 421

L

Lanier, Nicholas, leader of the king's music in the 17th century, 7
Laniere, John, 17th century English composer, 95
Lawes, Henry, 1595–1662, English composer, 95, 123, 137, 222 fn. 55
Lawes, William, 1602–1645, English composer, 95, 123
Lee, Nathaniel, 1648–1692, English playwright, 303ff, 305ff, 309, 311ff, 317ff
Lessius, Leonard, 1554–1623, Dutch philosopher, 114
Locke, John, 1632–1704, English Restoration philosopher, 231ff, 246, 279
Locke, Matthew, 1621–1677, English composer, 7
Louis XIV, 340, 444
Lovelace, Richard, 1618–1657, English Cavalier poet, 95, 104, 106 fn. 54, 111, 120

M

Mace, Thomas, 1613–1709, English music theorist, 23, 31, 33ff, 35, 37ff
Markham, Gervase, 1568–1637, English poet, writer, 70
Marston, John, 1575–1634, English playwright, 157, 159, 162, 164, 166, 169, 173, 175ff, 178, 180, 182ff, 184ff, 189ff, 193ff, 196, 200, 203ff, 205ff
Marvell, Andrew, 1621–1678, English poet, secretary to Milton, 102, 104, 120ff, 122, 223
Mattheson, Johann, 1681–1764, German composer and philosopher, 36
Mersenne, French philosopher, 224

Middleton, Thomas, 1570–1627, English playwright, 155ff, 164, 166, 168ff, 174ff, 176, 180, 185, 187, 195ff, 197, 200, 204, 206
Milton, John, 1608–1674, English poet, 93, 129, 279, 286
Moliere, 450
Montagu, Mary Wortley, 17th century English writer, 458

N

Newton, Isaac, 1642–1727, English Restoration philosopher, scientist, 237ff
Nicholao, Signor, violinist, 421
Nicolini, singer, 454
North, Francis, c. 1677 treatise on music, 240
North, Roger, 1651–1734, English lawyer, writer on music, 4ff, 8, 34, 41ff

O

Oldenburg, Henry, 17th century secretary of the Royal Society, 241
Oldham, John, 1653–1683, English writer, 356ff
Otway, Thomas, 1652–1685, English playwright, 308ff, 315, 318ff, 408
Overbury, Thomas, 1581–1613, English poet and writer, 211, 213ff, 216, 217, 219
Ovid, 322

P

Peerson, Martin, 1572–1650, English organist and composer, 23
Penn, William, 1633–1718, English philosopher, moved to America, 241fff
Pepin the Short, King, 714–768 AD, 139

Pepys, Samuel, 1633–1703, English diarist, 11ff, 14, 431
Pergolesi, composer, 425
Pietro, Signor, tenor, 421
Plato, 50, 141, 214
Playford, John, 1623–1686, English music theorist, 5, 23ff, 25, 28, 31, 33, 37
Pope, Alexander, 1688–1744, English poet, 348ff, 350ff, 357, 360, 363, 367ff, 369ff, 371ff, 373, 379ff, 382ff, 384, 392, 412, 422ff
Pordage, Mr., Roman singer, 422
Praetorius, Michael, 452
Price, Gervase, court "Serjeant Trumpet," 444
Prior, Matthew, 1664–1721, English writer, 360, 372, 378ff, 386
Ptolemy, ancient mathematician, 271
Purcell, Daniel, composer, 314 fn. 29, 355
Purcell, Henry, 1659–1695, the greatest English composer, 8, 11, 26, 35, 277ff, 309, 332, 336, 340, 386
Pythagoras, ancient Greek philosopher, 141, 217

Q

Quantomio of Pesarino, 17th century London composer, 95

R

Rameau, Jean-Philippe, 1683–176426, fn. 16
Raphael, Renaissance painter, 273, 368
Reggio, Pietro, singer, 422
Richardson, Samuel, 1689–1761, English novelist, 391ff
Rymer Thomas, 1641–1713, English philosopher, 267ff

S

Sackville, Charles, 1638–1706, English writer, 363
Saul, of the Old Testament, 34
Sedley, Charles, 1639–1701, English writer, 34, 304, 314, 317, 359, 385, 438
Senesino (Francesco Bernardi, 1680–1750, famous castrato in England, 458
Sévigné, Marie, marquise de, 1626–1696, French author, 6
Shaftesbury (Anthony Cooper), Earl of, 1671–1713, English philosopher, 279ff, 290
Shakespeare, 16th century English playwright, 97, 103, 268, 286, 304, 308, 328, 331
Shenstone, William, 1714–1763, English writer, 361ff, 363, 408ff, 423, 428
Sheridan, Thomas, 1687–1738, English poet, 350
Shirley, James, 1596–1666, English playwright, 181, 191
Simpson, Christopher, d. 1669, English composer, 22, 24, 29, 34
Smart, Peter, 17th century Puritan preacher, 17
Socrates, ancient Greek philosophr, 243
Somerville, William, 1682–1742, English poet, 372
Steele, Richard, 1672–1729, Irish writer, 308, 310, 314, 363ff, 445
Suckling, John, 1609–1642, English Cavalier poet, 103, 107
Swift, Jonathan, 1667–1745, Irish writer, 264, 353, 366, 369ff, 371, 377, 379ff, 381, 383ff, 385, 388, 394ff, 412, 423ff, 445ff

T

Talbot, James, professor of Hebrew, 1689–1704, at Cambridge, music critic, 32
Taylor, Silas, composer, 442
Temple, William, 1628–1699, English philosopher, 264ff, 269, 271, 272
Thomson, James, 1700–1748, English playwright, 312, 347, 350ff, 359ff, 361, 369, 371 425
Tomkins, Thomas, 1572–1656, English composer, 123
Tourneur, Cyril, 1575–1626, English playwright, 167, 173, 198
Traherne, Thomas, 1634–1674, English poet, 100
Tubal, inventor of brass instruments in Genesis 4:22, 190
Turner, James, early writer on military music, 19

V

Vanbrugh, John, 1664–1726, English writer, 308, 311ff, 315ff, 424
Vaughan, Henry, 1621–1695, Welsh physician and Metaphysical poet, 106 fn. 54, 113
Villiers, George, 1628–1687, Engllish playwright, 312, 317
Virgil, ancient Roman poet, 325, 418

W

Waller, Edmund, 1606–1687, English Puritan poet, 95ff, 113, 122
Wallgrave, Dr., lutanist, 421
Walton, Izaak, 1593–1683, English biographer, 110, 211, 215
Webster, John, 1580–1625, English playwright, 157, 182, 189, 199
William III, 1650–1702, King of England, 8
Wilson, John, 17th century English composer, 95
Wither, George, 1588–1667, Jacobean poet, 93ff, 97ff, 100ff, 102, 105ff, 108ff, 112ff, 121ff, 124ff, 126ff
Wotton, William, 1666–1727, English philosopher, 269ff
Wycherley, William, 1641–1715, English playwright, 37, 311, 315, 319, 361, 378, 382, 389, 423
Young, Edward, 1681–1765, English poet, 348, 361, 368, 371, 380ff, 383

Z

Zampieri, painter, 447

ABOUT THE AUTHOR

Dr. David Whitwell is a graduate ('with distinction') of the University of Michigan and the Catholic University of America, Washington DC (PhD, Musicology, Distinguished Alumni Award, 2000) and has studied conducting with Eugene Ormandy and at the Akademie fur Musik, Vienna. Prior to coming to Northridge, Dr. Whitwell participated in concerts throughout the United States and Asia as Associate First Horn in the USAF Band and Orchestra in Washington DC, and in recitals throughout South America in cooperation with the United States State Department.

At the California State University, Northridge, which is in Los Angeles, Dr. Whitwell developed the CSUN Wind Ensemble into an ensemble of international reputation, with international tours to Europe in 1981 and 1989 and to Japan in 1984. The CSUN Wind Ensemble has made professional studio recordings for BBC (London), the Koln Westdeutscher Rundfunk (Germany), NOS National Radio (The Netherlands), Zurich Radio (Switzerland), the Television Broadcasting System (Japan) as well as for the United States State Department for broadcast on its 'Voice of America' program. The CSUN Wind Ensemble's recording with the Mirecourt Trio in 1982 was named the 'Record of the Year' by The Village Voice. Composers who have guest conducted Whitwell's ensembles include Aaron Copland, Ernest Krenek, Alan Hovhaness, Morton Gould, Karel Husa, Frank Erickson and Vaclav Nelhybel.

Dr. Whitwell has been a guest professor in 100 different universities and conservatories throughout the United States and in 23 foreign countries (most recently in China, in an elite school housed in the Forbidden City). Guest conducting experiences have included the Philadelphia Orchestra, Seattle Symphony Orchestra, the Czech Radio Orchestras of Brno and Bratislava, The National Youth Orchestra of Israel, as well as resident wind ensembles in Russia, Israel, Austria, Switzerland, Germany, England, Wales, The Netherlands, Portugal, Peru, Korea, Japan, Taiwan, Canada and the United States.

He is a past president of the College Band Directors National Association, a member of the Prasidium of the International Society for the Promotion of Band Music, and was a member of the founding board of directors of the World Association for Symphonic Bands and Ensembles (WASBE). In 1964 he was made an honorary life member of Kappa Kappa Psi, a national professional music fraternity. In September, 2001, he was a delegate to the UNESCO Conference on Global Music in Tokyo. He has been knighted by sovereign organizations in France, Portugal and Scotland and has been awarded the gold medal of Kerkrade, The Netherlands, and the silver medal of Wangen, Germany, the highest honor given wind conductors in the United States, the medal of the Academy of Wind and Percussion Arts (National Band Association) and the highest honor given wind conductors in Austria, the gold medal of the Austrian Band Association. He is a member of the Hall of Fame of the California Music Educators Association.

Dr. Whitwell's publications include more than 127 articles on wind literature including publications in Music and Letters (London), the London Musical Times, the Mozart-Jahrbuch (Salzburg), and 52 books, among which is his 13-volume *History and Literature of the Wind Band and Wind Ensemble* and an 8-volume series on *Aesthetics in Music*. In addition to numerous modern editions of early wind band music his original compositions include 5 symphonies.

David Whitwell was named as one of six men who have determined the course of American bands during the second half of the 20th century, in the definitive history, *The Twentieth Century American Wind Band* (Meredith Music).

A doctoral dissertation by German Gonzales (2007, Arizona State University) is dedicated to the life and conducting career of David Whitwell through the year 1977. David Whitwell is one of nine men described by Paula A. Crider in *The Conductor's Legacy* (Chicago: GIA, 2010) as 'the legendary conductors' of the 20th century.

> 'I can't imagine the 2nd half of the 20th century—without David Whitwell and what he has given to all of the rest of us.' Frederick Fennell (1993)

ABOUT THE EDITOR

CRAIG DABELSTEIN began studying the piano at age seven and took up the saxophone at age twelve. Mr Dabelstein has Bachelor of Arts (Music) and Bachelor of Music degrees from the Queensland Conservatorium of Music, where he majored in the performance of classical saxophone repertoire. He also has a Graduate Diploma of Learning and Teaching and a Graduate Certificate in Editing and Publishing from the University of Southern Queensland.

He has held the principal alto and tenor saxophone chairs in the Australian Wind Orchestra and has been an augmenting member of the Queensland Philharmonic Orchestra, the Queensland Symphony Orchestra, and the Queensland Pops Orchestra. For many years he was also a member of the Queensland Saxophone Quartet.

He has been a casual conductor of the Young Conservatorium Symphonic Winds, and has previously been a saxophone teacher at the Queensland Conservatorium of Music. He is a regular conductor of the Queensland Wind Orchestra, having served as their artistic director and chief conductor from 2004 to 2009.

Craig Dabelstein is a research associate for the *Teaching Music Through Performance in Band* series of books, contributing analyses to volumes 7, 8, 1 (rev. edn), and the *Solos with Wind Band Accompaniment* volume. He served as the copyeditor and layout designer of the *Australian Clarinet and Saxophone Magazine* from 2007 to 2009 and he has written many CD and book reviews for *Music Forum* magazine. He is the editor of the second editions of the books by Dr. David Whitwell including *A Concise History of the Wind Band*, *Foundations of Music Education*, *Music Education of the Future*, *The Sousa Oral History Project*, *Wagner on Bands*, *Berlioz on Bands*, *The Art of Musical Conducting*, and the *Aesthetics of Music* series (8 volumes) and *The History and Literature of the Wind Band and Wind Ensemble* series (13 volumes). From 1994 to 2012 he was a staff member at Brisbane Girls Grammar School. He now teaches woodwinds and conducts bands at St. Joseph's College, Gregory Terrace, Brisbane, Australia.

www.ingramcontent.com/pod-product-compliance
Lightning Source LLC
Chambersburg PA
CBHW080721300426

44114CB00019B/2445